The Mind in Therapy

Cognitive Science for Practice

The Mind in Therapy
Cognitive Science for Practice

Katherine D. Arbuthnott
Campion College, University of Regina
Regina, Saskatchewan, Canada

Dennis W. Arbuthnott
Arbuthnott & Associates
Regina, Saskatchewan, Canada

&

Valerie A. Thompson
University of Saskatchewan
Saskatoon, Saskatchewan, Canada

LEA LAWRENCE ERLBAUM ASSOCIATES, PUBLISHERS
2006 Mahwah, New Jersey   London

Lawrence Erlbaum Associates, Inc., Publishers
10 Industrial Avenue
Mahwah, New Jersey 07430

Cover design by Tomai Maridou

Library of Congress Cataloging-in-Publication Data

The mind in therapy : cognitive science for practice / Katherine D. Arbuthnott, Dennis W. Arbuthnott,
and Valerie A. Thompson.

ISBN 0-8058-5367-7 (cloth : alk. paper).
ISBN 0-8058-5675-7 (pbk. : alk. paper).

Includes bibliographical references and index.

Copyright information for this volume can be obtained by contacting the Library of Congress.

Books published by Lawrence Erlbaum Associates are printed on acid-free paper,
and their bindings are chosen for strength and durability.

Printed in the United States of America
10 9 8 7 6 5 4 3 2 1

For Chris, Shane, and Devin,
whose minds always impress and inspire us
and
For Jamie, whose encouragement and support make it possible,
and whose love and laughter make it worthwhile.

Contents

Acknowledgments

This work was supported in part by a Social Science and Humanities Research Council (SSHRC) grant to K. Arbuthnott and D. Arbuthnott, and Natural Science and Engineering Research Council (NSERC) grants to K. Arbuthnott and V. Thompson. We are grateful for the helpful feedback received on earlier drafts of the chapters from the following: Laura Taylor, Elizabeth Brass, Kinda Kealy, Gladys Behnsen, Walter Leckett, Morgan Traquair, Judy Young, Marilee Allerdings, Stephen Wernikowski, P. L. Bastian, Marlene Harper, and Veronica Hutchings.

1

Introduction

Human mental capacities and processes are the raw materials with which psychotherapists work. Thus cognitive science research, which examines processes of thought, memory, and emotion, is potentially of tremendous value for psychotherapeutic practice (D'Zurillo & Nezu, 2001; Ingram & Kendall, 1986). As many clinicians have noted, knowledge about cognitive abilities, tendencies, and limitations could benefit both assessment and treatment by providing therapists with a clearer focus for intervention (e.g., Ingram & Kendall, 1986; Nasby & Kihlstrom, 1986; Winfrey & Goldfried, 1986). Furthermore, the cognitive processes of therapists themselves can lead to potential biases of interpretation that may influence their effectiveness, and it is important to understand them (Turk & Salovey, 1986). However, most recent syntheses of our rapidly expanding body of knowledge about cognition are not readily accessible to therapists, in either language or methodology, so the findings are not fully utilized by the psychotherapeutic community. The cognitive literature, describing, as it does, detailed experiments that don't match their interests and training, tends to be difficult for most therapists to read. Conversely, most cognitive researchers are not familiar enough with the practice of psychotherapy to present their results to therapists in a way that clarifies their usefulness. The purpose of this book is to bridge the gap between empirical findings of cognitive science and psychotherapeutic practice. We review research focusing on a range from complex mental activities such as problem solving and decision making to basic functions such as attention and memory, and highlight the findings that are most relevant to therapeutic practice.

Research indicates that, although therapy is effective for mental health difficulties, clients' outcome does not differ according to the orientation of their therapist (Chambliss & Ollendick, 2001; Elkind, 1994; S. D. Miller, Duncan, & Hubble, 1997; Saunders, 2004; Wampold, 2001). This is surprising, given the large theoretical and methodological differences between therapeutic orientations such as psychoanalysis, cognitive behavioral therapy, humanistic therapy, experiential therapy, and family therapy. The absence of clinically relevant differences across therapeutic orientation has led to a consideration of factors that are common to all modalities, such as the therapeutic relationship (S. D. Miller et al., 1997; Norcross, 2002; Wampold, 2001), and to integrative approaches to psychotherapy (e.g., Norcross, 1997; Norcross & Goldfried, 1992; Saltzman & Norcross, 1990; Stricker & Gold, 2003). However, one of the most fundamental commonalities in all therapeutic endeavors, and indeed in all human activity, is cognition. Thus, both therapists' and clients' cognitive processes are likely among the common factors that influence therapeutic outcome. As in the case of other common factors, a better grasp of their operation can greatly improve the use of cognitive resources for clients' benefit.

The operation of cognitive processes imposes constraints and opens avenues for therapeutic change. The constraints include both operational limits such as attentional capacity (see chapter 7), and habitual limits such as confirmation bias in decision making and reasoning (see chapters 9 & 10). Avenues for change include precise assessment of client difficulties and limitations (Nasby & Kihlstrom, 1986), and interventions aimed at altering cognitive contents and processes (e.g., A. Wells, 2000; Winfrey & Goldfried, 1986). For centuries, philosophers have taken for granted that the world is mediated through our minds. We have no direct access to reality, and know the world only as it is filtered through cognitive processes such as perception and memory. Understanding how the "filter" works will simultaneously protect therapists from incorrect interpretations of the filtered reality (e.g., mistaking priming effects for importance in memory; see chapter 3) and provide opportunities to shift comprehension to benefit their clients. For example, realizing that our mood influences our cognitive style such that we think more creatively in good moods and more analytically in bad moods (chapter 13) can prevent us from interpreting a problem as unsolvable whichever mood we are in and suggests that we can use mood alteration as one means to influence problem solving.

It is sometimes argued that cognitive scientists' formulations of mental processes such as attention, memory, and reasoning are too mechanistic and reductionistic to contribute much to the complex, interwoven realities that are the target of psychotherapy. We disagree. Knowledge of how these processes operate, and of the constraints imposed by their habitual use, can deepen our understanding of how psychotherapeutic techniques function to improve clients' lives and of why some techniques don't work for some clients. For example, the application of techniques such as reframing and restructuring of belief systems can only be improved by knowledge of how mental frames and structures operate in the first place. Approaches such as cognitive behavioral therapy include techniques to consider the content structures of memory (e.g., R. E. McMullin, 2000), but cognitive psychology can enable therapists to consider the processes by which these structures are formed and changed.

Of all the information available to us, some types influence our thoughts and actions to a much greater degree than others (e.g., see chapters 7, 9, & 10). Certain interpretation biases are used to simplify input, facilitating rapid thinking and decision making with a reasonable, but not perfect, degree of accuracy. Since many schools of psychotherapy promote self awareness for both therapist and client in order to minimize bias, it is particularly helpful for therapists to be aware of the cognitive processes underlying such biases. The chapters in this book outline what we know about such information use and biases in attention (chapter 7), memory (chapters 3–6), categorization (chapter 8), decision making and reasoning (chapters 9 & 10), and problem solving (chapter 2). Psychotherapy already makes use of these design features of the human mind, usually without awareness, and therefore not always to the best effect, and sometimes even to clients' and therapists' detriment. Explicit recognition will allow therapists to maximize their use of interpretation biases in the service of their clients' goals.

During the past few decades, cognitive scientists have developed detailed models of mental processes, building from the components of perception and thought (e.g., attention, memory) to complex mental activities (e.g., problem solving, decision making). As it is precisely these mental processes that they target in their work, an up-to-date cognitive model is of enormous value to therapists. Each chapter in this book reviews an area of cognitive research, targeting findings that are particularly relevant to psychotherapeutic practice and theory, and highlighting therapeutic implications and applications. The book is directed widely to all therapeutic orientations, not only those employing cognitive behavioral techniques, because all therapies use the basic processes of the human mind to effect change. The aim of this book is to increase therapists' understanding of their own and their clients' mental processing, thereby increasing the effective therapeutic use of the capabilities and idiosyncrasies of human cognition.

Such an understanding is potentially of great benefit to both experienced and developing therapists. The former will explore new ways to conceptualize techniques that they have found effective or new tools to add to their therapeutic armamentarium. The latter will be given a framework of cognitive functions that can serve as a foundation for more applied knowledge. Regardless of their level of experience, some therapists will find that the ideas in these chapters do not greatly change their practice, whereas others will find that they substantively alter therapeutic encounters. All will find that knowledge of cognitive processes improves their comprehension of their clients' interpretation of their world and the possibilities for change via the many noninvasive therapeutic techniques.

The book is intended to ground psychotherapy in science, but not in the way that manualized or empirically based treatment does (Chambliss & Ollendick, 2001; Henry, 1998; Silverman, 1996). The chapters have more in common with knowledge- or technology-transfer than with outcome-based therapy research. Knowledge transfer involves applying empirically supported findings and theories from basic science to a specific practical area or problem. That is the strategy of this book. Our approach is also consistent with the ideas of technical eclecticism as a form of psychotherapeutic integration (e.g., Beutler, Alomohamed, Moleiro, & Romanelli, 2002; A. A. Lazarus, 1992; Norcross & Newman, 1992). We describe selected findings and theories of cognitive science that are relevant to both the thinking of the therapist and that of the client, outline the implications of these findings and theories for therapeutic practice, and provide concrete examples of how a therapist might alter or strengthen her or his practice based on them. Therapy techniques based on these extensions of cognitive science have not often been empirically tested. However, we hope that the ideas in this book will both assist therapists immediately and prompt more applied research to test the speculative extensions.

Some caveats before we proceed: This book will not emphasize neuropsychology. Although knowledge of the anatomy and neural pathways underlying such processes as attentional control, language, and facial processing is useful for psychotherapists, other writers have provided excellent summaries (e.g., Cozolino, 2002). We contend that knowledge of *what* occurs in each of these anatomical locations, the metaphorical software, is likely to be of greater use to the theory and practice of individual change that is the goal of psychotherapy. As a rule, the book also will not compare the cognitive performance of special populations with that of normal populations, discussing instead human processes in general. Evidence suggests that individuals differ in the range of performance, but not in the way that cognitive performance is accomplished, so understanding the overall process is primary to assessing the minor variations evident across individuals and groups.

To maximize the usefulness of this information for psychotherapists, each chapter is structured in a similar manner. In each we begin with general definitions of key terms, and then explain why findings in the area are important for therapists. We follow with a more detailed presentation of the findings. To make the clinical implications as clear as possible, in most chapters we also include a hypothetical case illustration, which is used to demonstrate the extension of key cognitive points to a therapeutic context. These hypothetical cases are based on actual therapy cases but have been combined, reformatted, or both to highlight the relevant concepts and to protect the anonymity of our clients. The introduction to the case illustration for each chapter generally appears midway through the chapter, following the presentation of definitions and basic concepts. Continuations of the case then follow at various points throughout the chapter, to illustrate how cognitive information might be used to improve treatment. And finally, because each chapter contains a considerable amount of material, each ends with a brief summary of the key points addressed in the chapter, in order to facilitate learning.

The next eleven chapters (chapters 2–12) review both "higher mental processes" such as problem solving (chapter 2), categorization (chapter 8), reasoning and decision making (chapters 9–11), metacognition (chapter 12), and more basic processes such as attention (chapter 7) and memory (chapters 3–6). Higher processes are obviously key in psychotherapy, both for clients and for therapists. For example, therapists must assess their client's issues and resources, whether or not they employ formal assessment, and this is essentially a process of categorization (chapter 8). Difficulties with processes such as problem solving or decision making often bring clients to psychotherapy, and therapists must engage in both of these processes in designing their treatment and choosing the techniques they will use with each client. The basic processes of attention and memory, however, set the stage for these larger-scale acts of thinking, in that we can only consider thoughts and feelings that have entered our attention or memory. These basic processes are thus central to psychotherapy (and all human functioning), and provide unique opportunities for therapeutic intervention, as discussed in each of these chapters.

The three chapters before the conclusion deviate somewhat from the mainstream cognitive literature. Chapter 13 describes the interplay between emotion and cognition. Emotion is also a mental process, and therefore theoretically falls within the domain of cognitive science. Although cognitive researchers have turned their attention to this important process only recently, findings about the ways in which thinking and feeling interact are vital to therapeutic work, and thus are reviewed in some detail. Chapter 14 discusses recent studies of inhibition by both cognitive and clinical researchers; it examines the conditions under which inhibition both harms and benefits mental health and functioning. Chapter 15 considers how cognitive theory is being used to test some of the basic principles and methods of psychodynamic therapy. These chapters do not contain case illustrations, but rather address therapeutic issues throughout.

The final chapter integrates and summarizes the main points. Although the challenges of studying an invisible phenomenon such as human cognition require researchers to look at mental components separately (Juola, 1986), we think holistically, with all processes operating simultaneously. Furthermore, psychotherapy also requires attention to entire persons, not just to various aspects of their thinking. Thus it is important that readers be left with an awareness of how these processes might interact over the course of therapy. The chapter discusses which cognitive processes are relevant at various points in therapy, from the initial session to termination, putting together the many pieces that have been laid out throughout the book. In sum, the book will enable therapists to understand cognitive processes and use their understanding to benefit their clients and enhance the effectiveness of their practice.

2

Problem Solving:
The Structure of Psychotherapy

> *A person is confronted with a problem when he wants something and*
> *does not know immediately what series of actions he can perform to*
> *get it.*
>
> —Newell and Simon (1972, p. 72)

Much that happens in psychotherapy is a process of problem solving. Clients entering therapy develop, with the assistance of the therapist, a variety of change goals, including internal, external, and behavioral changes. Internal goals typically involve feeling differently or changing self-defeating thought patterns. External goals involve, for example, improving relationships, employment, or living conditions or specific behavior goals, such as changing addictive or abusive behaviors. Of course, individuals solve many such problems independently over the course of their lives, but problems that cannot be solved using a person's usual repertoire of resources and strategies are the basis for psychotherapy. The client and psychotherapist engage in a collaborative process designed to solve the presenting or underlying problem. Thus, knowledge of processes that facilitate and hinder problem solving can be extremely useful for psychotherapists. Although we are not the first to make this assertion (e.g., Carkhuff, 1987; D'Zurilla & Nezu, 2001; Egan, 1994; Ingram & Kendall, 1986; Ivey & Ivey, 1999), previous authors discussed only a limited range of problem-solving research.

There are two qualitatively different approaches to solving problems, depending on the solver's familiarity with the specific type of problem. If one has experience with a problem type (i.e., expertise), solutions can be formulated based on knowledge and experience. This describes much of the problem solving in therapy,[1] since psychotherapists have expertise in the types of problems that they treat. In unfamiliar or unique situations, solutions must either be created from scratch or adapted from prior experience, processes known as *heuristic* and *analogical* reasoning. Psychotherapists of many different schools and approaches attempt to transfer to their clients the expertise they have in general problem solving or the knowledge they have relevant to solving a particular kind of problem. However, because all clients and their life circumstances contain unique elements, therapists also help their clients to "custom build" solutions. Thus, some of the problem solving that occurs in psychotherapy falls into the domain of heuristic or analogical problem solving, as therapist and client collaborate to find new solutions to a client's problems, or to extrapolate solutions from past successes.

Since Newell and Simon's groundbreaking work in the 1970s, cognitive psychology has yielded much information about how people solve problems. Although early research focused on simple logic or physical problems, the field has expanded to include problem solving in a wide variety of domains, including medical diagnoses and decision making, textbook learning, sports problems, and many others (e.g., Adelson, 1981; Lesgold et al., 1988). These studies reveal a remarkable degree of consistency in their findings, regardless of whether the topic of study is college students learning to solve physics problems or medical residents learning to read x-rays. Thus, the findings can be readily generalized to personal problem solving, as practiced in psychotherapy.

Case Illustration:

A man in his early 40s was referred for therapy. He had recently been transferred from another city to assume a high level position in a midsized corporation. He had been divorced for four years and his 2 children (ages twelve and fourteen) remained with their mother. He entered therapy describing a general malaise and some symptoms of minor depression. He reported feeling lonely and was interested in developing a relationship and a support system in his life. He had not been in any relationships since his divorce. He described himself as shy, committed to work, and nervous about "starting all over away from my kids and family." He returned to his previous location every second weekend to visit with his children in his parents' home. During divorce proceedings, he had been prescribed a low dose of an antidepressant but had reacted poorly to it and so was reluctant to consider medication.

For clarity, we will use Newell and Simon's (1972) terminology for the elements of problem solving. The *goal* is the end point or solution to the problem, which, in psychotherapeutic terms, is known as the desired change or contract. Problem solving consists of goal-directed activity, beginning at an *initial state*, and moving through a series of intermediate steps to the final *goal state*. At each point, people expand their knowledge of the problem situation using inferences developed from the given information and retrieval of relevant information from their own long-term memory. Psychotherapists speak of these same elements as the presenting problem, current behavior, and change goal. The essence of the process is to determine which intermediate steps should be taken and how to take them to ensure success in solving the problem.

In addition to the initial and goal states, Newell and Simon (1972) labeled two other basic components of a problem solving task: operators and constraints. *Operators* refer to the types of actions that are available to move one from the initial state to the goal state, and the *constraints* refer to any limitations that the person must deal with in their use of the possible actions. The resources the client has available to attain the desired outcome, including skills, knowledge, familial and social assets, medical assistance, and community resources, are operators with respect to life problems. Constraints include all limiting elements, whether they are external (such as limited financial resources or problematic relationships) or internal limitations imposed by a client's preferences, styles, or psychological/emotional patterns (e.g., desire not to move residence, take medication, etc.).

Typically, people start by organizing the information at their disposal, including information about all four components of a problem (initial state, goal, operators, constraints, known all together as the *problem space*), forming a mental representation of the situation. This organization or representation is a key process in the search for an effective solution (Nickerson, 1994). Several influential theories of counseling and therapy focus on the explication, clarification, and utilization of aspects of problem space. For example, some skills-based approaches from the client-centered humanistic schools describe therapy largely as the application of an array of therapist skills to the problems experienced by the client in a respectful and collaborative working relationship (Carkhuff, 1987; Egan, 1994; Ivey & Ivey, 1999). Similarly, cognitive behavioral therapies (CBT) elaborate and apply problem space clarification and problem-solving strategies as their primary treatment strategy (D'Zurilla & Nezu, 2001).

Problems can be well- or ill-defined, according to the information one has about the four components. Well-defined problems fully specify all four, whereas ill-defined problems lack clear information about one or more components. The types of problems encountered in academic classes and in some problem-solving research tend to be well-defined. However, life problems and those encountered in the course of personal, work, and social environments are more likely to be ill-defined (Nickerson, 1994). For example, if a client has the goal of improving his marital relationship, the initial state is usually the best defined (e.g., my partner is controlling and unsupportive, constantly criticizing me; when I attempt to confront my partner I am criticized even more), but the other three components are either unknown or only vaguely described. For a typical client, the goal state is not clear, as many situations could represent an improved relationship, and it is likely that neither the efficacious actions (operators) or limitations (constraints) are obvious, particularly when another person is involved. The client may be embedded in and overwhelmed by the current state, and one task for the therapist is to assist the client in defining the remaining elements. For ill-defined problems, clients must provide the missing information themselves (Kahney, 1986), often by making assumptions, making decisions, and learning from previous solution attempts. This is where the expertise of a therapist is very helpful.

Case Illustration:

Problem Space Organization: Using Newell and Simon's (1972) descriptors and assuming skillful application of exploration and rapport-building skills, the therapist assists the client in clarifying the problem space. An expanded and clarified version of the referral information becomes the initial state or presenting problem. In exploring and developing the client's change goals, the therapist begins to give form to the goal state. Although Daniel was aware of his current unhappiness and a desire to feel less lonely, his change goal or desired state had not been articulated. By asking what a happy or "not lonely" life might look like, the therapist already begins to expand the problem space and introduce possibilities for actions using operators and identifying constraints or blocks that may need attention. It became clear early in therapy that Daniel had already demonstrated many problem-solving skills (operators) in his job. For example, in his new workplace environment, he was able to introduce himself to other employees and develop a good working relationship with them. He was also rated as an effective and considerate supervisor. Similarly, his social and relationship maintenance skills with his children and extended family were strong. He had many interests including athletics and music. In summary, he had many strengths or operators, but for some reason he had trouble transferring these skills into his personal life. Part of Daniel's envisioning of the goal state included a physically and socially active life in his new location, including friendships and a relationship. He wanted to do this while maintaining a high level of commitment to his work and maintaining a good relationship with his children and parents.

Exploring and developing these latter goals revealed some constraints. Specifically, it would be very difficult to satisfy all aspects of his goal state or desired changes given his need for perfection, which he articulated as, "If you can't do something right, then don't even start." He had experienced multiple changes and losses since his affair, had a tendency toward self-blame (e.g., "I'll always feel guilty for wrecking my family"), and had a clearly stated reluctance to developing a new life (e.g., "I just don't feel right having fun when I know the kids need me back home"; "I feel like I'm doing something wrong even when I notice an attractive woman"). These and other constraints stopped Daniel from making any steps or taking small actions toward achieving his goals.

EXPERT PROBLEM SOLVING

One of the central findings of problem-solving research is that experts and novices represent and approach problems differently.[2] We are using the terms *expert* and *novice* as they are defined in the problem-solving literature and do not mean to imply that the actual helping relationship reflects power dynamics such as are implied by these terms. Indeed, this may sometimes be the case but certainly would not describe the majority of therapist–client relationships. Rather, the therapist is hopefully more of an expert in solving human problems such as those experienced by the client, as therapists are both educated and experienced in considering solutions to typical human difficulties. For example, although humanistic therapists consider themselves more as companions accompanying the client on a problem-solving journey, such therapists can be characterized as experienced guides, like those accompanying hikers through unfamiliar territory. In such cases, clients may come to appreciate their own expertise in a problem area through the intervention of a humanistic or solution-focused therapist.

Psychotherapists are experts in the domain of human functioning and satisfaction, whereas clients are relative novices. Of course, everyone has considerable knowledge in the domain of human life, especially one's own, but therapists have specifically studied a wider range of issues than any single individual will encounter and have gained considerable practical experience by working with numerous others over the course of their careers. This is why experience in psychotherapy often makes as much difference as initial training (e.g., Berman & Norton, 1985; Dawes, 1994; M. L. Smith & Glass, 1977; Stein & Lambert, 1984; Strupp & Hadley, 1979). This differentiation can partially explain why therapists are so often helpful to clients in resolving life issues.

Expertise particularly influences the solution of ill-defined problems. With ill-defined problems, an individual's knowledge about that type of problem can help to structure the problem representation so that the unspecified information does not impede resolution. In other words, with sufficient knowledge, ill-defined problems can be treated as well-defined ones, filling in missing information with details about that type of problem from the individual's memory. In the case illustration, for instance, Daniel was unaware of many of the current operators and constraints relevant to his issue, and simply bringing them out through exploring and explicating his life experience was helpful. Many therapists and their clients would confirm that systematically exploring and mapping clients' experiences is often helpful on its own. Increased expertise thus facilitates solution to a wider range of problems. Psychotherapists who have gained expertise through experience and practice can often assist in reformulating problems in terms that make potential solutions more obvious. For example, goals such as an improved relationship can be clarified and specified more precisely by therapeutic exploration, and with knowledge of family system dynamics, a therapist can often predict the types of actions that are most useful in attaining that goal, as well as those that would be contraindicated. To be more specific, a therapist with the knowledge that relationships with a high ratio of positive to negative interactions (Gottman, 1994) are more likely to last, may discourage a couple from fighting intensely until a healthier ratio has been established.

How do experts approach problems differently than novices? Not only do experts know more about their area than novices, but their knowledge is also better organized. This difference has been characterized as one in which experts classify a problem in terms of deeper features, such as the relations between problem elements or solution requirements, whereas novices classify a problem based on the elements themselves, such as the people or objects described in the problem (Adelson, 1981; Chan, 1997; Chi, Glaser, & Rees, 1982).[3] For example, physics students tend to represent problems in terms of the objects that are mentioned in them, such as pulleys and inclined planes, rather than in terms of principles, such as force dynamics or acceleration. Thus, when asked to solve a problem that features an inclined plane, they are likely to base their solution on previous successful attempts at solving inclined plane problems. Experts, in contrast, are more likely to represent situations in terms of the relevant principles in the situation (e.g., force dynamics) and to consider solutions based on underlying principles. The therapeutic equivalent to this is that clients represent their problems more often in terms of the symptoms, whereas therapists describe issues in terms of psychological dynamics. For example, an adolescent describing a breakup with her boyfriend describes the pain of the experience and her actions, whereas the therapist represents the issue in terms of the client's attachment style or the developmental stage of the relationship.

The main advantage of such knowledge is the ability to recall a solution to a problem type, rather than having to work one out from scratch. We've all experienced frustration in trying to solve a problem, only to have someone with expertise provide a solution within seconds. Even when a solution can't be directly recalled, experts can often rely on their knowledge to "narrow the field." For example, a psychotherapist who specializes in the treatment of depressive disorders will consider a limited number of mood-modifying strategies with their depressed client (e.g., referral for medication, self-talk exercises), whereas suggestions given by family and friends seem unlimited and are less targeted to the specific issue (e.g., "You have to get out more"; "You need a hobby"). In some cases, the nonexperts' ideas have a place in a thoughtfully developed treatment plan, but therapists with expertise are helpful in sorting "the wheat from the chaff" and spend their time considering relevant, rather than irrelevant, solutions (and thus save their clients time and effort).

When confronted with a problem in their domain, experts frequently spend *more* time than novices initially encoding a problem (Chi, Feltovich, & Glasser, 1981; Larkin, McDermott, Simon, & Simon, 1980), but then proceed to solve the problem much more rapidly and effectively. One way to characterize the difference is that experts form more sophisticated mental representations of problems than novices, classifying problems in ways similar to "problem schema" contained in their long-term memory (Zeitz, 1997). This initial problem classification may require more thought and time for experts, as they seek to match a current problem with the types of problems in their memory, but once a problem is classified in this manner, the actions needed to reach a solution become much easier to identify. Novices, conversely, must make use of much less useful general-purpose strategies that often require considerably more trial and error before a solution is reached.

The ability to focus on relevant aspects of the problem is also helpful in another way. Discrimination of irrelevant information is important for human problem solvers because we have limited attentional and working memory capacity[4] (see chapter 7), so limiting the "clutter" in working memory increases our ability to concentrate on productive angles, thereby enhancing our efficiency and the likelihood of finding an acceptable solution. In other words, given that we can only keep a finite amount of information in mind at once, the more space that is taken up by irrelevant details of the problem, the less capacity there will be available to work toward a solution.

In the context of psychotherapy, every therapist has some strategies for isolating the relevant features of an issue, typically using those elements considered basic to healthy human functioning by their guiding therapeutic model. Different schools of therapy specify somewhat different essential elements, but each approaches life problems by focusing attention on a few elements, rather than attempting to consider the full multidimensional spectrum of a client's context. For example, psychodynamic and systems theories focus on relationship roles and dynamics, especially those that match a client's early experience, considering behavior patterns secondary to emotional and relational meaning. Behavioral theories and their descendant, cognitive behavioral theories, tend to do the opposite, with behavior or thought and its consequences central, and previous histories of secondary importance. From a problem-solving perspective, the valuable process is having some reasonable means by which to isolate one or two features of a multidimensional situation around which to structure the problem space description. This will simplify the selection of operators and provide a more structured environment in which to plan change from the current unsatisfactory state to the desired goal state.

This discussion highlights the expert process used by psychotherapists in defining a client's problem. The therapist, like experts in other domains, invests considerable effort in representing the problem, including the initial state, the goal, the available operators, and the constraints. Although there is no taxonomy of life problems analogous to types of physics or logic problems (Nickerson, 1994), therapists' training does involve study of classes of human problems as specified by their central model, whether classes are defined medically (e.g., *DSM-IV-TR* diagnoses), interpersonally (e.g., object relations or family systems theories), or socially (e.g., feminist therapy theories). Furthermore, experienced therapists have engaged in previous problem-solving activities with other clients, and thus also have knowledge of previous successful resolutions to guide them.

To reiterate, there are two important processes in successful problem solving: (a) defining and representing a problem and (b) planning appropriate actions to move from the current state to the goal state. Both of these processes are improved with greater experience, and both are well represented in psychotherapeutic methodology (e.g., D'Zurillo & Nezu, 2001; Egan, 1994). The key initial task in psychotherapy is to develop a model of the client's issue, including the presenting problem, any underlying problems, and the desired outcome. An important aspect of this process is to isolate the relevant from the irrelevant elements of the problem so that effort is not wasted on irrelevant aspects. This skill is one of the keys in a therapist's arsenal, that is, reframing the client's experiential and usually incomplete description of the problem within the context of issues that are solvable, given the therapist's model. All theories of therapy incorporate models of which elements in an individual's internal and external worlds are central and which should therefore be highlighted in considering the client's difficulty. Every therapist has strategies for discriminating the relevant and irrelevant features of client issues, relying either on a single therapeutic theory or eclectically combining several theories. This serves to limit the elements that need to be considered in the search for a solution, and it also restricts the number of potential alternative solutions to those that include the specified elements. For example, in a family therapy session in which a fifteen-year-old tearfully rages at his parents that they have invaded his privacy and destroyed trust by searching his room, a behavioral- or systems-oriented therapist might encourage the parents to avoid reacting to their son's emotion as it distracts from the main issue or because it is a power tactic to avoid responsibility. Instead, they are directed to focus on the behavioral and communication dynamics between them. An experiential or emotion-focused therapist may do the opposite and focus both the boy and the parents on their respective experiences, having them describe those to each other. Either strategy could be useful in that the therapist skillfully isolates certain elements to provide a focus and designs interventions to produce change from that perspective. The common element across these therapists is the attempt to define and focus on relevant aspects of the problem, reducing attention to the rest.

This limiting and simplifying aspect of successful problem solving is necessary, given the constraints of humans' attentional and working memory abilities, as discussed in chapter 7. For now, it is sufficient to note that one of the main tasks of problem solving is to formulate the problem in a simplified manner, isolating a few key elements on which to focus our problem-solving efforts. Psychotherapy practice has developed methods to accomplish this, even in a domain as complex and multidimensional as human life.

Experts' mental representations of problems are not completely abstract, based as they are on previous learning and experience. However, problem type representations and models can be used flexibly, so they can be applied to a wide range of situations within the field of expertise. In addition to representing problems and solutions themselves, experts also have more detailed knowledge of the conditions under which a certain solution would be effective, and are thus more able to assist their clients to selectively target problem-solving actions. Furthermore, the range and richness of experts' schema (Chi et al., 1982) allows them to be more flexible, both in dealing with inconsistencies between a current problem and previous examples (Feltovich, Johnson, Moller, & Swanson, 1984) and in adapting their thinking when new information becomes available (Feltovich, Spiro, & Coulson, 1997; Lesgold et al., 1988). In addition, they are better able to monitor their own performance during problem solving (Glaser, 1996), using their knowledge to assess success with their selected plan and using feedback to choose a different option, should the initial one fail. The expertise of the therapist in assisting the client in targeted problem solving and developing expertise in their areas of difficulty is an important part of therapy.

Case Illustration:

Expert Problem Solving: The therapist spent considerable time clarifying the problem space. This in itself was helpful to Daniel, as a feeling of dissatisfaction and having some idea of what he "should do" but not doing it blocked him. (E.g., he would often say to himself as he watched the news, "I know I'd feel better if I turned off the television and did some exercise." Unfortunately he didn't and then would add self-criticism to his burden.) Having the therapist assist in defining the problem space helped him to think about goals, operators, constraints, and the relationship among them rather than simply replaying his current state.

At this point in therapy, many psychotherapists begin to focus on what they consider to be the more relevant features of a problem. This focus is usually based on the theoretical stance(s) from which they work and is of course dependent on training and experience. Isolating relevant features will assist Daniel in developing some structure to the problem space and then generating potential steps and actions that will help him reach the goal state. For example, a dynamic therapist with a developmental approach to therapy may have Daniel focus on the process of change, loss, grief, and his historical pattern of learning and reacting to major life events. A therapist with a cognitive behavioral approach may intervene by focusing on some of the constraints he imposes on himself by his ineffective thinking and self-talk, developing action plans to approach the goal state. In either case, a psychoeducational approach in applying a theoretical framework to Daniel's issues would be experienced as helpful in understanding his experience and in seeing some possible solutions. In particular, one comment he made in the course of therapy ("I never realized just how much I lost and how incredibly heavy I feel now. I've never expressed grief, never thought I could since it was my fault the family is not together") would seem to indicate using a developmental approach would be helpful. Other quotes above lend themselves to a cognitive restructuring approach. In either case, limiting the number of key or relevant factors important to the problem space definition and defining goals help the client avoid overloading his working memory and becoming overwhelmed.

NOVICES: SOLVING UNFAMILIAR PROBLEMS

Although psychotherapists are usually able to use their expertise to solve or simplify clients' problems, clients do present problems with which clinicians are unfamiliar. Almost every client's situation has unique aspects that require more general problem-solving strategies. This is especially true for therapists in training or newly graduated therapists. When faced with unfamiliar problems, people tend to rely on general-purpose heuristic approaches (Hunt, 1994; Newell & Simon, 1972). Heuristics are rules of thumb that are often but not always useful, such as the strategy to act only to increase pleasure and decrease pain. In addition, many of the heuristic rule-of-thumb strategies present contradictory action possibilities (e.g., "If it feels good, do it" and "No pain, no gain" or "He who hesitates is lost" and "Haste makes waste"). Many clients begin therapy with already developed but ineffective heuristic problem-solving strategies. The advantage of heuristics is that they can be adapted to almost all situations. In addition, they represent a strategic, purposeful approach and thus are a vast improvement over trial and error. The drawback of heuristics is that they are relatively weak approaches, often requiring a large investment of effort with little guarantee of success. In this section, we discuss the effectiveness of various heuristic methods, as well as factors that can facilitate or inhibit successful solutions.

Hill Climbing

This strategy involves choosing actions that only lead to particular outcomes that are more similar to the goal than to the current state. The analogy is to a hiker who is lost in a thick fog and is trying to get to the top of a hill, in hopes of finding her way above the fog. As she has few clues to tell her which direction is likely to be useful, she sets out in a random direction and then determines whether she is heading uphill or downhill. If uphill, she continues; if downhill, she reverses direction. Although simple, hill climbing is one of the least powerful heuristic approaches, because it is basically a systematic version of trial and error (Robertson, 2001). For example, the aforementioned strategy of judging actions on the basis of pleasure or pain, and choosing only those that increase pleasure, is an example of hill climbing.

Although this approach is generally not powerful, there are situations in which it may be useful, such as when there are few options to try, or where there is little evidence to suggest that one option is better than another. However, successful use of hill climbing requires that there be a clear means to evaluate the outcome of each option. Our lost traveler, for example, would be lost for a long time if the slope were too gentle to allow her to diagnose uphill versus downhill travel. Also, there is a danger in becoming stuck in a less-than-optimal solution if problem solving requires temporarily selecting the opposite action, such as when working through a problem requires one to tolerate feeling worse for a period of time. For example, an alcoholic client who stops drinking will experience withdrawal symptoms as a consequence of his or her behavior change. If the client were using the pleasure/pain heuristic, he or she might decide that drinking small amounts of alcohol was a better solution than abstinence, thus increasing the risk of returning to more harmful behavior.

Working Backward

Often, it is useful to begin at the desired end point and trace a route backward to the starting point. Working backward involves mentally moving from the goal state to the initial state, noticing what actions need to be taken at each step. This is often easier than working forward, as there may be only a few ways to reach the goal, but many more choices from one's current situation, only a few of which will ultimately lead to the goal. Thus, planning from the goal back to one's current position would involve fewer decisions than first making a decision from among the many currently available. For example, the technique of having clients imagine their lives in twenty years' time and then considering current actions that would lead to a desired future is an example of working backward (e.g., "Imagine it is twenty years from now, and you are describing your satisfactory life to a friend. What have you done in the last twenty years?"). Similarly, some therapists ask the "miracle question," that is, they have clients imagine that therapy has been successful beyond their wildest dreams and then ask them to describe what has changed (e.g., de Shazer, 1988; O'Hanlon & Weiner-Davis, 1989). As a specific example, with a client who expressed a wish to stop being depressed, clarifying the goal state of "not depressed" as happy led to assisting the client to describe her personal version of happiness. The question, "What happens just prior to the feeling of happiness?" led to the reply, "I am calling friends and have someone to do things with." Thus, working backward for this client helped her and the therapist realize that rather than the multiple choices available to make any human happy, this client had unique elements in her vision of happiness. This further assisted the client and therapist to isolate the most relevant aspects of the problem space (i.e., her social life). Working backward can clarify clients' often implicit theories; in contrast, expert problem solving uses the theoretical orientation of the therapist. Brief therapies (see Hoyt, 2003) have particularly popularized the use of the strategy of working backward in psychotherapy.

Means-End Analysis

A more powerful strategy is means-end analysis (see Robertson, 2001), in which a person assesses the difference between the initial and goal states, and develops a plan to reduce that difference. This plan requires an individual to identify a series of subgoals, often by working both backward from the goal state (What is only a few steps away from the end state?) and forward from the initial state (Given where I am now, what can I do to move a few steps forward?). Operators then need to be identified that can achieve each subgoal. This process is repeated until the goal has been obtained. For example, if a client's goal is to establish a better relationship with his child, he could note that the goal state includes pleasant conversations between them, whereas their current state does not. One subgoal would then be to initiate conversations with his child. However, as primarily pleasant conversations are desired, a second subgoal might be to identify times when both the client and the child are present and relaxed. This decomposition process can result in a "goal stack," which is a prioritized list of the subgoals and operators necessary to achieve a solution and an ordered plan for their execution. Problem decomposition—dividing a problem into subgoals that can be solved independently—is one of the main components of planning. It is often used by experts as well as novices, and may be one type of assistance a psychotherapist provides to their clients.

Although means-end analysis is a relatively powerful problem-solving strategy, it also has potential drawbacks. Specifically, it requires the person to keep a lot of information available in working memory which, as mentioned, has a limited capacity. The person must represent a number of different subgoals, their operators, and the sequence of events that must be followed, and the person must keep track of which subgoals have been achieved and which are yet to be completed. All told, this places quite a burden on working memory, with the result that errors can be expected (M. D. Byrne & Bovair, 1997). For instance, in the aforementioned example of initiating conversations with his child after identifying when both are present and relaxed, the client may forget to assess his own and the child's state and initiate a conversation only to have it become a familiar argument, because both were in a state of stress.

Case Illustration:

Solving unfamiliar problems: After fully defining the problem space and putting some of the therapist's expertise into structuring and explicating the most relevant features of Daniel's issue, there were still unique aspects that required individually developed problem-solving strategies. For example, Daniel often used the heuristic hill-climbing strategy. He was often aware of actions he needed to take, but when he felt badly he experienced this as a signal to avoid the task ("It just feels too hard"). Using the working backward and means-end strategies were more successful for Daniel as he found he could carry out smaller tasks when he kept his goal state in mind and was less overwhelmed when he did not try to do too much at once, as his perfectionistic tendencies dictated. For example, actively disputing his thoughts just prior to exercising was an effective strategy. The counter for "If you can't do it right, don't even start" was "Starting small is the way to reach my goals."

IMPASSE, INSIGHT, AND RESTRUCTURING

Problem solvers often reach an impasse: a point in the process where they become stuck and stop advancing toward the goal (Jones, 2003), an experience that is frequently encountered in psychotherapy (e.g., Goulding & Goulding, 1979). Moving beyond this impasse is often accompanied by an "aha" experience, in which one has a sudden insight about the solution to the problem (Goulding & Goulding, 1979; Ohlsson, 1992; Perls, 1969; Polster & Polster, 1973). Insight involves a sudden restructuring of the problem space (the collective set of the four problem-solving components) in such a way that the solution becomes obvious. These moments of insight are a characteristic feature of some types of therapy, including gestalt and psychodynamic approaches, and could even be identified as a goal for these therapeutic models. Solving insight problems has some of the same characteristics as normal problem solving (C. A. Kaplan & Simon, 1990; Keane, 1989), such as the benefit of considering several moves in advance (MacGregor, Ormerod, & Chronicle, 2001), but it also has some unique features (Metcalfe, 1986), such as including constraints that must be overcome to solve the problem (Kershaw & Ohlsson, 2004). In this section, we identify some of the conditions that tend to produce an impasse in problem solving, and we discuss means by which successful restructuring can take place.

Impasse

Impasse occurs when the person forms a model of the problem situation that diverts attention from solution-relevant details (Knoblich, Ohlsson, & Rainey, 2001; Robertson, 2001). Often, this model misrepresents crucial details, fails to represent critical information, or includes unnecessary constraints. Although impasses do not always lead to insight, when they do, it is because an individual uses this difficulty to restructure their representation of the problem and the operators available to them (Jones, 2003; Kershaw & Ohlsson, 2004). In psychotherapy, impasses more often reflect recognition that two goals are mutually exclusive, at least as the client has represented them. Solutions to a therapeutic impasse frequently involve either changing the goals themselves, or changing the client's representation or understanding of one or both of the goals, such that the operators necessary to reach each goal do not prevent his reaching the other. For example, a client who was struggling to make a relationship choice between his wife and his affair partner kept attempting to explain to both how difficult this was for him, in the hopes that they would stop pressuring him. He needed to change his goal from reducing his distress to developing the ability to act in the face of his distress.

One tendency that can impede a change of representation is *functional fixedness*. Functional fixedness refers to the tendency to use resources in only a habitual way. Thus, the person may fail to identify a useful property of a tool or operator because she is fixed on a single function of the object in question. Functional fixedness occurs because memory tends to operate in a context-dependent manner (Barsalou, 1989; Keane, 1989; see chapter 4), and thus highlights elements of an object that are most likely to be useful in a particular context. Other, less usual elements may not come readily to mind. For example, in the context of an orchestra, the musical qualities of a piano are highlighted; in the context of attempting to move a piano up the stairs, the quality "heavy" is more dominant. Thus, people may fail to take advantage of the operators that are available to them, because they are fixed on a single dimension of that operator. A classic demonstration of functional fixedness is Maier's (1931) two string problem, in which two strings attached to the ceiling must be tied together. The problem is that the strings are too far apart for the person to reach both at once. The test room contained several other objects including a chair, some paper, and a pair of pliers, and the problem can only be solved by tying the pliers to the end of one string, getting it swinging in a wide arc, and then catching it while holding onto the end of the other string. Functional fixedness describes people's tendency to use the pliers only for their usual purpose, as a grasping and squeezing tool, rather than employing their properties as a weight. Similar therapeutic impasses may be maintained when clients do not consider resources that are available in culturally atypical ways. For example, if a client is unhappy in her work environment, but only considers changes proposed by work colleagues, she may overlook a solution or career opportunity that arises in a conversation with her spouse. A more typical clinical example would be a client who shouts to make her point and continues to do so even though there is overwhelming evidence that this does not lead to success. A coaching strategy which assisted this client to shift from the use of a resource (her voice) in a habitual way (loud when making a point) to a use of the same resource in a new way (softer, quieter voice with questioning inflection) led to quick success and positive feedback from others in her social and work environments.

Therapeutic impasses may arise or be maintained because the client is fixed on his habitual idea about how to accomplish one goal, and this contradicts another goal. For example, a client may aspire to attain great success in his career, and also to please his partner. If his ideas about how to accomplish these goals are to work long hours in his job (career goal), and to accommodate to his partner's wishes (relationship goal), when the partner demands more of the client's time and attention, an impasse arises because the client cannot do both of these at once. However, it is possible that career success could be attained without working long hours, or that the partner could be pleased even when some requests were denied. To consider such options, though, the client would have to consider operators for both career and relationship that are different from their usual behaviors.

A second problematic tendency is known as *negative set*. Negative set results from behavioral persistence, in that the person continues to apply a habitual strategy when a more efficient solution is available. A more colloquial way to describe this is the rather amazing capacity of human beings to do more of the same, often with increased vigor and intensity, even when a little does not work. If a particular type of problem has been successfully solved using one approach, people have a tendency to continue using that approach even when it proves unsuccessful with a subsequent problem. Examples of negative set are endemic to mathematics students, who attempt to follow the steps of a well-known procedure to solve all problems, including those for which it is unsuited (e.g., Luchins & Luchins, 1959; B. H. Ross, 1987). This tendency is also often observed in relation to personal problems. For example, a man who typically defused marital tension by taking his wife out to dinner or buying her flowers continued to attempt this solution even when the situation changed (e.g., with the birth of children) and his actions ceased to improve the climate between them.

A similar tendency is noted when individuals continue to commit resources to a losing course of action in order to justify an original investment. This is known as the sunk costs fallacy (i.e., I've invested so much already and if I quit, I'll lose it all). This tendency has been observed in situations as diverse as gambling and military strategy (e.g., committing more troops to a conflict because to withdraw would dishonor the memory of those who have died). This tendency can be seen in therapy when clients continue to invest their energy in poor relationships, jobs, or even in therapy itself despite much evidence that their efforts will not improve the situation.

Both functional fixedness and negative set impede problem solving by emphasizing an irrelevant aspect of the problem space for the current problem, leading to an inadequate problem representation. As discussed earlier, solution to these difficulties comes from the insight that is gained by restructuring the problem representation, either by emphasizing aspects more relevant to the solution or by removing unnecessary constraints on operators. These impediments to problem solving are frequently encountered by psychotherapists. Therapeutic techniques that encourage a different representation of problems, such as reframing or challenging habitual thought processes, and much of solution-focused psychotherapy are designed specifically to provide creative consideration of the relationship between a problem and a client's existing resources. Many therapists assign homework designed specifically to alter habitual patterns of behavior or thinking (e.g., Dattilio, 2002; Hudson & Kendall, 2002; Kazantzis & Deane, 1999; Kazantzis, Deane, & Ronan, 2000; Neimeyer & Feixas, 1990). Conversely, Milton Erickson deliberately evoked negative set in therapy, by inducing a "yes set" in clients before asking them whether they would consider his treatment suggestion (e.g., "Can I call you by your first name?" "Are you comfortable?" "Are you willing to follow my instructions to solve this problem?"; O'Hanlon, 1987). In this case, the set that was induced by early examples and then used for later examples was to respond "yes" to the therapist's questions.

However, psychotherapists themselves are subject to these same tendencies, and they sometimes rigidly adhere to a single structure of steps or a theoretical bias in treatment rather than more sensitively or creatively responding to a client's circumstances. For example, if a particular technique such as exploring a worst case scenario works very well for a client or two in a given week, we may find ourselves using this technique with many clients, even those for whom the technique is not especially relevant; this is an example of the therapist's negative set. This tendency may be further exacerbated by adhering too rigidly to the prescriptions of specific therapeutic models or manualized treatment protocols. In addition to the benefits for problem simplification provided by a therapeutic model, some models also restrict the consideration of relevant actions (i.e., operators). For example, feminist therapy recommends analysis of a client's political and socioeconomic context and designs interventions to improve such conditions. In contrast, many cognitive behavioral approaches do not consider the social context of their clients, but focus instead on thoughts and behavior patterns. Although often very helpful, limiting interventions to either of these actions could unnecessarily restrict a client's problem-solving efforts by restricting the range of operators considered to reach the client's change goal. Every therapeutic approach restricts operators in some way, but it is important that therapists do this consciously so that they can expand the field of operators to include other treatment modalities when necessary. Theoretical developments in many therapeutic systems indicate recognition of this point. For example, rational emotive therapy has become rational emotive behavioral therapy, and the behaviorism of the mid 20th century developed into cognitive behavioral therapy.

Restructuring

Moving beyond a problem-solving impasse requires the person to re-represent or restructure the problem. This restructuring can be achieved in a number of ways:

1. Focus on a different aspect of the problem (Robertson, 2001). This involves rethinking assumptions about the available operators and elaborating the initial representation in an attempt to discover new, potentially relevant details. This is often the purpose of therapeutic methods such as the gestalt two-chair technique, psychodrama reenactments, narrative therapy externalization, and psychodynamic interpretation, to name just a few. It may also be useful to think about the constraints that are present, and indeed, to question whether or not those constraints actually present a barrier (Ohlsson, 1992). Therapists often accomplish the latter, using skills such as confrontation, where discrepancies between two aspects of the client's experience are pointed out and each explored in detail. Finally, the therapist might attempt to recontextualize the problem in order to highlight different functions and properties of the available resources. For example, having the client assume the therapist's role (e.g., "What would you say to me if our roles were reversed?") or providing advice for a hypothetical other (e.g., "What advice would you give to your child if he or she approached you with this problem?") can often help clients to restructure their problem. Many therapeutic modalities (e.g., redecision therapy, psychodrama) make this technique of taking on another's role in present day or early scene reenactment a major focus of solving their clients' stated and underlying problems.

2. Simplify the load on working memory by considering a scaled-down version of the problem, or relaxing the constraints (C. A. Kaplan & Simon, 1990). This type of thinking is facilitated by counterfactual questions (see chapter 11) such as "What would happen if. . . ." Alternatively, one might try thinking of extreme or ideal cases in order to identify potentially relevant solution principles (Robertson, 2001). Techniques such as exploring a client's worst case scenario, catastrophic fears, or miraculous fantasies represent this strategy.

3. Find a useful analogy (Robertson, 2001). This allows the person to take advantage of a known situation, and can be a very powerful solution strategy (see section on reasoning by analogy). Unfortunately, discovery of an appropriate analogue, even one from one's own prior experience, is unlikely to occur spontaneously and may require a lot of support and guidance. Once identified, however, a good analogy can be a powerful problem-solving tool.

Case Illustration:

Impasse, insight, and restructuring: Daniel had already made substantial progress toward his goals and was participating mainly in solitary activities, going to movies, and was feeling much better. However, he had also reached an impasse in his therapy. His unease in engaging socially and sense of disloyalty toward his children, ex-wife, and parents blocked him from establishing a social life in his new location. It seems his explicitly stated change goal to establish new friendships and a relationship was in conflict with an unstated constraint to avoid any sense of disloyalty and lack of perfection in relation to his children, parents, or ex-wife. His avoidance of the discomfort that any such actions may produce is an example of a negative set.

The therapist could choose from many techniques and approaches to help Daniel break through this impasse. A dynamic, developmental, or emotionally focused therapist may attempt to restructure the problem space by attending to issues of grief and loss, focusing on unfinished business from prior relationships, and introducing strategies for letting go. Alternatively, a cognitive behavioral therapist may restructure the problem space by continuing the self-disputing technique with beliefs about loyalty and add a broader perspective through identifying schematic themes and patterns (e.g., identifying that Daniel's reluctance to act protects him from a sense of vulnerability and potential hurt).

REASONING BY ANALOGY

Considerable research has investigated the use of a previous experience (or analogy) to solve a current problem (e.g., Gick & Holyoak, 1980; Holyoak & Thagard, 1997; Spellman & Holyoak, 1996). The use of analogy in problem solving is simply the useful application of knowledge from one situation (the source example, known as the analogue) to a related problem (the current problem). Despite the widespread practice of teaching problem solving in disciplines such as mathematics or physics by providing an example to use in reasoning about subsequent problems, evidence indicates that analogies are used infrequently, even when a relevant analogue is readily available (Gick & Holyoak, 1980).

Some psychotherapeutic schools explicitly use analogies as a therapeutic method. The many examples of the use of narrative or metaphor in Ericksonian hypnotherapy exploit analogical problem solving (e.g., Battino, 2002; Close, 1998; O'Hanlon, 1987; O'Hanlon & Hexum, 1990). Findings of the difficulty in using analogous problems thus has serious implications for the use of narrative and metaphorical techniques to assist clients. Fortunately, this literature also indicates some means to optimize the use of analogies.

There are three basic steps for deriving a solution from analogy (Holyoak, 1995). First, one must create or identify an appropriate source problem (analogue). For example, suppose a narrative therapist and a client contracted to change the client's self-criticism, but the client responds to interventions by arguing for his faults more vehemently. The therapist might devise a story in which an anxious, self-critical protagonist encounters an emergency situation in which he must act to save a child, in spite of vocal criticisms of his risk-taking actions from some bystanders (e.g., "What do you think you're doing?" "You can't do that," "You'll only make things worse," and the like). However, because the protagonist pays attention to the critical bystanders, he hesitates at a key point, and the child, although rescued, receives an injury that would otherwise have been avoided. This story is the source analogue for the client's problem.

Second, one needs to map the elements of the current situation onto the corresponding elements of the source analogue. This involves mapping not only the objects in question, but their roles and relationships as well (Gentner, Rattermann, & Forbus, 1993). In the analogue created by the therapist, the protagonist corresponds to the client, the critical bystanders correspond to the client's self-criticism, and the rescued child and the preventable injury represent the proposed solution strategy. The relationship between the protagonist and the bystanders is that of actor:critic, the same as that between the client and his internal self-doubts. Finally, one needs to adapt the solution principle from the analogue and apply it to the current problem. In the example, the therapist hopes that the client will consider acting despite the criticism (rescuing the child). The preventable injury is included as a cautionary note about paying too much attention to criticism during action, and the therapist could have the client reconstruct the story so that the ending is compatible with a reduction in self-criticism.

The extent to which a source analogue can be useful depends on the degree of similarity between the source situation and the current one. Researchers have identified two types of similarity that determine whether an analogy will be used successfully (Holyoak, 1995; Holyoak & Thagard, 1997): structural and surface similarity. *Structural similarity* refers to the degree to which the underlying causal principles in the source and the current problem overlap. In the previous example, the causal principle involves criticism that impedes necessary action, making the source and current problem structurally similar. Similar relationships between the elements, similar constraints in the two situations, and whether the operators that produced the desired outcome in the analogue will achieve a similar end in the current situation are all examples of structural similarity. *Surface similarity* refers to the degree to which the element in the source and current situation are physically and semantically similar. For example, similarity in the roles (e.g., authority or dependent) and the individuals (e.g., similar physical or personality characteristics) in the two situations reflect surface similarity. The previous example has relatively little surface similarity between the analogue and the client's issue because the client is not in a position to rescue anyone, his critics are not external, and no physical similarities between himself and the protagonist have been described except the anxious, self-critical nature of both the client and the protagonist.

Identifying and Retrieving Source Analogues

Ironically, although the utility of an analogy is determined by the degree of structural overlap, it is the lack of surface similarity that can prevent a therapist or client from retrieving a relevant analogue. Given the cue-dependent nature of long-term memory retrieval (discussed in chapter 4), something in the current problem must serve as a retrieval cue for the source problem. Thus, the greater the surface similarity between the situations, the more likely the earlier problem is to come to mind or be recognized as useful to the current situation (Holyoak & Koh, 1987). Unfortunately, good analogues often bear little surface resemblance to the current situation, so the probability of spontaneously generating an appropriate source analogue is very small and often requires very explicit instructions to do so (Gick & Holyoak, 1980). Thus, the discovery of a suitable analogue may require considerable support and guidance from the therapist. Questions such as those used in solution-focused therapy (Has this happened before? How did you solve it then?) often help (O'Hanlon & Weiner-Davis, 1989), as do the techniques that focus on finding an exception to the problem and using that as the analogue on which to base potential solutions.

The cue-dependent nature of long-term memory has another potentially negative implication for analogical reasoning. Specifically, the greater the surface similarity between the current situation and a previous one, the more likely it is that the latter will be retrieved as a potential analogue, even though it may not be appropriate (B. H. Ross, 1987). That is, the principles involved in the current situation may be quite different from those in the source situation, even though the surface characteristics are similar. In that case, people may be misled into using an inappropriate analogue, simply because of a perceived similarity of surface features. For example, a client may recall how she solved a relationship problem with an ex-spouse when a problem arises with her current partner. However, if the personalities of the two partners and their relationship agreements with the client differ, the previous situation may not be helpful in solving the current problem. Another previous situation that is much less similar to the current one in surface characteristics, such as a difficulty with a coworker, could be useful but it is much less likely to be recalled.

Case Illustration:

Use of analogy: Daniel had provided much historical material that had some of the previously described properties of source analogues. For example, several of his stories from childhood indicated that one does not recover from loss and consequently, doing things perfectly is the only way to succeed. When he was 10, a loved family pet died and although he wanted another one, his mother stated, "We can never get another pet because nothing can replace Rex," or after quitting a baseball team his father said, "You'll be sorry. Once this opportunity is gone, you'll never get another chance to be as good as you can be." He also remembered wanting to respond to his mother with, "You can so get over it mom, and I want a new dog." He immediately connected this with his present situation saying, "But I'm in charge now and I can start again." The solution to the source problem (although unspoken in the original story) became the analogue for a solution in the present, whether he was addressing issues of loss or inaccurate beliefs.

Family of origin and Bowenian models of family therapy are examples of therapies based on finding analogues to present situations, usually in early life experiences. For example, an unassertive client who becomes silent when asking for a raise could be encouraged to remember becoming silent when facing resistance from authority figures earlier in life (e.g., asking parents for a new bike, asking a school principal's permission to be absent for a family holiday). These remembrances can become analogues of the current state if they were unsuccessful in the earlier episodes or potential analogues from which to adapt solution strategies if they were successful. The benefit of using analogues from the client's own experience is that such examples are readily available in memory. However, analogies such as those presented in generic stories (e.g., J. C. Mills & Crowley, 1986) or those specifically designed to address the client's issues (e.g., Lankton & Lankton, 1986) can also be effective.

Mapping Elements From Source to Current Problem

The second challenge, once an appropriate analogue is identified, is to map the elements of the two problems, to use the previous problem solution to find a solution to the current problem. There are a number of reasons why a person may fail in mapping the elements from the source to the current problem, even after a relevant analogue has been found (Robertson, 2001):

1. Lack of factual knowledge. The person may be missing a key bit of information or may have misconceptions and misunderstandings about the elements in a problem or in the principle that defines its solution. For instance, a client may not understand that the nature of relationship dynamics is the important element in a family difficulty, and thus the mapping should be between individuals who share relationship characteristics, rather than physical or role similarities. For example, a young man may have learned to respond unassertively to criticism from his mother, because his mother refused to let an issue go until her son complied. If that young man then marries a woman who desires argument and discussion, rather than agreement, this will be a marital issue if he maps his mother to his wife because they are both women with significant relationships with him (role similarity). However, if he recognizes that the dynamics with his wife are more similar to those with friends who are more democratic in their social relations, no such issue will arise.

2. The imperfect correspondence between target and analogue. It may be that some elements play the same role in the source and target situations, whereas others play different roles or are irrelevant. Successful mapping is facilitated when the elements of the source analogue, and the relationships among them, map in a straightforward manner onto the current situation (Gentner et al., 1993; Markman & Gentner, 1997). For example, analogical therapy failed for this reason in the following case: A therapist developed a metaphor of an angry bear to represent a 10-year-old child who was referred for acting out by hitting other children. In developing the analogy into an intervention, the therapist suggested that the child speak gently to the bear to calm it down, but the child responded, "That's stupid. Everyone knows that bears can't talk!" In addition, the goals in the source example and current problem must be very similar for people to make use of the source in a productive manner (Spellman & Holyoak, 1996).

3. Negative set. The person may believe that elements in the source analogue impose unnecessary constraints on the situation and may have difficulty in changing or modifying those roles. For example, if the young man with issues in assertiveness with the significant women in his life uses successful memories of his encounters with coworkers as his analogy, he may erroneously believe that a more

distant relationship is necessary for him to behave assertively with women, simply because that is the case in his analogy.

Considerable attention is usually paid to mapping when constructing therapeutic metaphors or narratives (e.g., Battino, 2002; Close, 1998; Lankton & Lankton, 1986; J. C. Mills & Crowley, 1986; M. White & Epstein, 1990). Ericksonian therapists often aim to create metaphors similar in structure and solution to the current problem, but not so close as to elicit the client's blocks with respect to their issue. This is also essentially the strategy of psychodynamic therapy, to create relationship mappings between a current dynamic and a historical relationship (i.e., interpretation or reframing), although the hope here usually is to facilitate a different resolution than in the earlier relationship. As stated earlier, the correspondence between elements in the sample and current problems is a key factor. For example, if a client is struggling with issues of assertiveness with her employer, a narrative therapist might create a story about a child who needed to solve a problem with her parent by forthrightly expressing her preferences. The elements in the problem and story situations match quite closely (client:child, employer:parent) with respect to relationship dynamics, and the solution used to solve the problem in the story (forthright expression) is thus suggested as the solution for the current problem.

Adapting Solution Principles

In most situations, the analogue solution must be adapted to apply to the current problem. For example, forthright expression appropriate for a parent cannot be used directly for a conversation with an employer. There are a number of ways to increase the probability of successfully applying a solution principle from the source analogue to the current problem. First, the solution must be clearly understood and at a level of abstraction that allows it to be transferred to conceptually similar, but physically dissimilar, situations. To this end, the person needs to abstract and articulate the solution principle from the source analogue. Research indicates that it is important for the solution principle to be explicitly articulated (Chi, Bassok, Lewis, Reinman, & Glaser, 1989; Chi, de Leeuw, Chiu, & LaVancher, 1994; Novick & Holyoak, 1991). Also, it is better if a solution principle is generated by the person himself, rather than provided by a third party. This has implications for the use of analogy in some paradoxical and Ericksonian therapies. In these models, it is assumed that learning can occur unconsciously and that drawing explicit attention to the parallels between an analogue and current problem dilutes the effectiveness of the intervention. However, research in this context suggests that using educational approaches (e.g., cognitive behavioral therapy, psychodynamic therapy), to explicitly draw parallels and review learnings may be more effective for this particular technique.

Second, research clearly indicates that people are much better at learning and using sample problems or developing principles for a particular problem type when they are presented with two or more example problems (e.g., Gick & Holyoak, 1983). Therapists, however, often present a single metaphorical intervention, trusting that clients will use that to facilitate solution of their own problem, either consciously or unconsciously. This research suggests that multiple metaphorical tales would be more efficacious.

Expert Use of Analogy

With increased knowledge of problem types and their underlying principles, experts are better placed than novices to make use of appropriate analogues. As discussed earlier in this chapter, novice problem solvers are more likely to retrieve analogues when they share surface features with the current situations, but the utility of an analogue is based on the degree of structural similarity between the source and target. Thus, the fact that experts tend to represent their knowledge in terms of general principles means that they are better able to retrieve analogues based on structural, rather than surface, similarity. When faced with a novel problem in their domain, experts are more likely to retrieve and apply an appropriate analogue.

This is why having the therapist directly provide the client with an appropriate analogy is sometimes more efficacious than having the client identify an analogue. As previously mentioned, the therapeutic technique of crafting stories or metaphors that match the client's problem and a proposed solution strategy (e.g., Battino, 2002; Close, 1998; Erickson, Rossi, & Rossi, 1976; Lankton & Lankton, 1986; J. C. Mills & Crowley, 1986; O'Hanlon & Hexum, 1990) is an example of this. The differences between expert and novice problem representation, however, suggest a possible complication in using this technique. Success in the use of analogies is increased when the similarities between the problems are greater, but experts classify problems according to the relations between elements (i.e., the actors, actions, and goals), whereas novices are more likely to use similarities between the elements themselves (Chi, Feltovich, & Glaser, 1981). Thus, therapists may develop metaphors that seem like obvious analogues to them and to other professionals (i.e., structurally similar), but which clients are less likely to identify as relevant to their problems (i.e., little surface similarity). Creating metaphors with a greater degree of surface similarity then, rather than evoking the client's blocks, may increase the efficacy of therapeutic metaphors.

In many respects, manualized treatments represent a reasoning-by-analogy approach to therapeutic treatment, requiring the therapist to map and adapt the manualized approach to the individual case of each client. This is useful, not only because research evidence of the efficacy of the approach has been obtained, but also because it capitalizes on the expertise of the therapist to adapt the source analogue to the client's issue. This may be particularly beneficial to clients when therapists also use their expertise to increase clients' skills in solving their particular type of problem (e.g., D'Zurilla & Nezu, 1999). However, focus on managed care or very brief therapies can push therapists toward telling their clients what to do rather than working with them to thoroughly define all four problem components (current state, goal state, operators, constraints). When this occurs, even if the specific problem that initiated therapy may be solved, the benefit to the client may be substantially reduced.

CONCLUSIONS

The previous discussion illustrates that psychotherapy and its methods can readily be characterized in the context of problem solving. But what advantage does this provide? What is the benefit to psychotherapy to characterize the activity in this way? The advantages are those described by problem representation: Considering psychotherapy as an example of problem solving provides an overall framework to approach problems, such as the define-plan-act-learn structure (e.g., Bransford & Stein, 1984; Hayes, 1981, as cited in Nickerson, 1994) or Mahoney's (1979) SCI-ENCE[5] sequence. Furthermore, considering therapeutic work in this framework highlights the important role for the psychotherapist: that of contributing expertise in classifying and solving a particular class of problems. Making use of the research on effective problem solving enables psychotherapy to isolate the most relevant activities in the process and to use the evidence about successful problem solving strategies and blocks to maximize the efficiency of interventions.

Problem solving is a natural activity, one that develops over the course of childhood. Three specific abilities are necessary for optimal problem solving: the formation of goal-attaining strategies, mental representation of problems, and planning (S. Ellis & Siegler, 1994). The first of these abilities, strategy formation, is present at birth (Rovee-Collier, 1987; Tronick, 1989; Willats, 1990). Mental representation of goals and problems develops slightly later, in toddlerhood (DeLoach, Cassidy, & Brown, 1985; Hannah & Meltzoff, 1993), but the ability to plan an entire problem-solving sequence requires considerable self-regulation and is thus not fully developed until middle childhood (Klahr, Fay, & Dunbar, 1993). Even the latter, however, begins to develop relatively early in life, as children three to four years of age are able to plan how to solve a problem with the assistance of adults and use self-directed speech to guide their actions toward goals (Berk & Landau, 1993). Development over later years of childhood involves expansion of situations in which problem solving is used successfully and an increase in the range of strategies children are able to use (S. Ellis & Siegler, 1994). In addition to providing support for the contention that problem solving is an inherent human ability, this evidence suggests that problem solving can be a useful guiding framework even for child therapists. Although very young children are clearly constrained in the types of problem solving actions (operators) available to them, they are capable of conceptualizing and working toward goals, especially with the help of an adult.

In summary, we have argued that psychotherapy is a process of problem solving and can thus benefit from knowledge of problem solving processes obtained through cognitive research. As experts in human functioning, psychotherapists assist clients by representing multidimensional problems in more readily solvable ways, usually with the assistance of the simplifying assumptions of their guiding therapeutic model. Once a problem is thus conceptualized, possible solutions become evident, and successful accomplishment of various subgoals can more easily be attained. The advantage of considering psychotherapy in the context of a problem-solving framework is that the benefits of all therapeutic models can be appreciated, independent of the content of any one model. All schools of psychotherapy provide their practitioners with heuristics for distinguishing relevant from irrelevant issues, and most also suggest considering particular resources for solving problems defined in that manner. Specific findings, such as the use of analogous problems, development of problem-solving abilities, and typical impediments to flexible problem solving, highlight the potential benefits of this literature to psychotherapeutic efficacy.

KEY POINTS

- Psychotherapy can be viewed as a problem-solving process.
- Problem-solving can be characterized by four elements: current state, goal state, operators and constraints.
- Problems are most efficiently solved when all four elements are clearly described.
- With expertise, problems can most efficiently be solved by categorizing the problem type, and relying on remembered solution strategies for that type of problem.
- With unfamiliar problems, several heuristics can be used: hill climbing, working backward, means-end analysis, or analogy.
- Problem impasses are most easily and successfully dealt with by restructuring the problem representation.

NOTES

1. In this chapter, we are not specifically discussing the manualized cognitive behavioral treatment known as problem-solving therapy (D'Zurilla & Nezu, 2001). Such treatment is an obvious example of the use of problem-solving knowledge in psychotherapy, but it is our contention that all types of therapy involve solving clients' problems, with problems defined widely, as in the Newell and Simon (1972) quotation that opens the chapter.

2. Expertise, of course, is defined in relation to a particular problem domain. There are various ways to define expertise. In some fields, there is an accepted standard of practice or level of achievement, beyond which one is deemed to be an expert. This is generally the case in psychotherapeutic disciplines such as psychology, psychiatry, and social work. In other fields, expertise is a matter of peer recognition. Although it is hard to generalize across domains, as a general rule, an expert usually has about 10 years of experience in a domain (H. A. Simon & Chase, 1973) or has spent upward of 10,000 hours engaged in deliberate, focused practice (Ericsson & Charness, 1994). One outcome of this experience is a qualitative change in problem-solving skill, regardless of the domain in question: Experts and novices represent and approach problems differently.

3. With respect to the classification of problems according to deep (i.e., relational) versus surface (i.e., descriptive) elements, it should be noted that, in life problems, surface

features are often relevant, whereas they can usually be treated as irrelevant elements in academic problems. For instance, a work relationship is different from a family relationship, and one's father is different from one's neighbor, in ways that are likely more relevant to a problem formulation or solution than whether an inclined plane or a fulcrum is present in a physics problem. This is not to say that abstracting the structure of a problem such as relationship dynamics is not valuable for life problems in the same way that abstracting force dynamics is for physics. Rather, the point is that surface features in life problems cannot usually be ignored when considering the more structural elements, because important possibilities and constraints are usually associated with different surface elements such as specific individuals.

4. Working memory is the seat of current thought, plans, and memories; in other words, it is the place in which we store, represent, and reason with information "on line." Unfortunately, unlike other types of memory, working memory has a very limited capacity, and the attempt to hold or manipulate too much information at one time inevitably results in errors and omissions.

5. *S*pecify the problem, *C*ollect information, *I*dentify possible causes, *E*xamine possible solutions, *N*arrow solutions and experiment, *C*ompare your progress, *E*xtend, revise, or replace your solution.

3

Memory Retrieval Cues and Priming

Psychotherapy, as all human endeavor, is fundamentally dependent on memory. In an initial session, therapists usually take a client's history, which involves a systematic search of memory related to a specific issue, or to psychological health in general. When conducting assessments either through a structured interview or in written or computerized form, the assessor/therapist also systematically searches the client's distant and recent memories. Similarly, a contracting or goal-setting session involves questioning the client about the current complaint and context, which involves memory for recent events, as well as the client's vision of the desired outcome. As these conversations occur, therapists use their memory to both recall the types of information needed and store information about this case. Throughout treatment, therapists of all theoretical persuasions routinely rely on clients' reports of their experiences, including successes and difficulties associated with the treatment itself. Therapists also rely on clients to recall the content of therapeutic suggestions and comments, integrating them into their lives in a manner that moves them toward their desired goal. This reliance on memory usually goes unnoticed, because it is the normal everyday state of humans—we constantly base our current thoughts and actions on the foundation of our previous experience. However, knowledge of the processes by which memory functions can improve performance in many situations, including psychotherapy.

We tend to experience ourselves and others in our lives in an absolute way: We think of ourselves as having a stable personality with specific

characteristics and a consistent and immutable history. But cognitive research suggests that we should consider ourselves more relatively: Our
personality, characteristics, and the features of our historical recollections
are always influenced by our current context. The phenomenon that explains this relativity most clearly is priming. The basic idea of priming is
simple: The mental contents of our minds are continuous because one
thought influences the likelihood of similar ones. Mental contents are influenced by external events (conversations, movies, books, news events,
etc.) and by internal events (ruminations, dreams, planning, etc.). Thus,
thoughts do not represent absolutes about an individual, but rather are
evoked in large part by contextual factors and thus should be considered in
relation to the recent environment (physical and mental). This also has implications for memory. The specific memories we recall, and what elements of those remembered events we focus on, are also influenced by
contextual factors. Thus, memory researchers consider a memory to be a
constructed event, composed of selected elements stored from the original
experience and retrieved in response to the current retrieval cue and mental, physical, and social context. As with thoughts, memories should be
considered contextual, rather than as absolute representations of the past.
This chapter will review the evidence of this contextual influence on
memory, present models of memory that explain such interactivity, and
suggestions for how this knowledge might be used by therapists.

THE ASSOCIATIVE STRUCTURE OF MEMORY

Memory is fundamentally associative (Bransford & Stein, 1984; Mandler,
1967; Tulving, 1962). This means that items stored in our memory are
linked or associated with other items in some manner. The associative
links can be semantic (i.e., related to meaning), contextual (i.e., items that
were experienced in the same location or at the same time), or perceptual
(e.g., items that look or sound alike). Although memory theorists have discussed memory as an interconnected network of information for centuries,
Collins and Quillian (1969) were the first to formalize this as a model of
memory. In their model, semantic memory (general knowledge) was represented as an associative network, with every concept related to every
other concept through links between them. For example, the concept
"bird" is associated with feathers, nest, eggs, specific types of birds such
as robins and ducks, animals, and so forth. These memory connections,
which vary in strength, provide the basic building blocks by which knowl-

edge is represented in memory (Reisberg, 1997). The strength of the association between any two concepts is influenced by how frequently they've been thought of in connection to each other. Retrieving information from such an associative network involves a search beginning at one concept (the retrieval cue) and traveling from one concept to another via the interconnecting links until the target information is reached. In psychotherapy, early retrieval cues usually include a description of the presenting problem which then leads to an exploration and expansion of the problem space, as described in chapter 2. This expansion into the associated concepts of the client is facilitated by the therapist, who provides additional retrieval cues through the application of therapeutic skills (e.g., empathy) and knowledge (e.g., the typical age of onset for schizophrenia).

This associative organization of memory is evident, for example, in semantic fluency tasks such as the FAS (name as many words as you can that begin with F, A, and S) or category naming (name as many birds as you can) tests. Responses to these and other tasks tend to be clustered in subgroups of related examples, such as robin, bluejay, sparrow or chicken, duck, goose (Bousfield, 1953; Bousfield & Sedgewick, 1944). These associations form the basis of most mnemonic systems designed to improve memory for specific types of information, such as the method of loci (e.g., associating items on a list with various locations in one's house) or peg word (e.g., associating to-be-learned items with rhymed objects such as "one a bun, two a shoe") systems (Ashcraft, 2002). For example, advice often given to help one recall names is to associate the person's name with some visual or personal characteristic they have, so that noticing that characteristic will help one recall the name. Similarly, acronyms make use of linguistic associates by connecting the acronym to a question, and then "unpacking" the acronym to retrieve the specific information needed. For instance, the acronym HOMES can be used for the names of the Great Lakes between Canada and the United States: Huron, Ontario, Michigan, Erie, and Superior. There are many examples of therapeutic acronyms used by therapists to assist both themselves and their clients in a variety of situations, for example, A. Ellis' (1970) activating event-belief-consequence (ABC) model, attention deficit hyperactivity disorder (ADHD), and the like.

The process by which this network operates is known as *activation*, which can be thought of as a process of energizing a concept in memory. When a concept, idea, or memory is activated to a certain level, it is brought to mind, or "retrieved," from the memory network. A concept becomes activated when it receives an input signal, such as perceptual input related to that concept. For example, seeing a robin on the lawn activates the concept "robin" or "bird," or looking at an old photograph activates a memory of that event and those people. Due to the interconnections between concepts, when one concept is activated, that activation spreads to other concepts connected to the initial idea. In other words, activation spreads through the memory network along the associative links (Collins & Quillian, 1969). Anecdotally, most of us have experienced this as we traced trains of thought back through associated links to determine how we arrived at an unusual or novel topic of thought. For example, while walking to the office, one of us noticed that he was thinking about a particular musician. Curious about this, as he had been unaware of any direct cue, he began to trace his observations and memory. He quickly realized that as he had just walked through a mall, there was not only an advertisement for the musician's new CD in a music store but also an instrumental version of one of this musician's songs playing in the mall. In addition, he also remembered that he had begun to hum the song and was wondering whether the musician would be coming to town this season.

Activation spreads from a concept in all directions at once, but stronger or better-established links carry activation more efficiently. The activation level of a particular concept depends on how much activation it has received from either perceptual input or spreading activation from associated concepts. Activation of concepts thus occurs through the effects of context, which includes both the physical environment (perceptual input such as the poster of the musician) and one's current mental environment (associated concepts such as previous memories of seeing that musician; D. G. Payne & Wenger, 1998). This spread of activation occurs very rapidly and without conscious awareness, and can even occur when one is unaware of the initial stimulus (Hirshman & Durante, 1992; Marcell, 1980; McRae & Boisvert, 1998). Activation of a concept does not persist beyond several seconds, unless additional input is received. Thus, the recency of activation of a concept also influences its current level of activation. In the previous example, the recent activation of ideas and memories of the musician resulted in current thoughts about him. However, unless one continued to review ideas about that musician, it is unlikely that the musician would continue to occupy the person's thoughts beyond several minutes.

The activation of a concept via spreading activation is known as priming. The metaphor "priming" harkens back to the days when we obtained our water from wells using hand pumps. When a pump had been unused for a time, one could lessen the work required to get water running by pouring a small amount of water down the pump head. Thus, the metaphor refers to the effect something similar has on later production. In terms of memory, this metaphor refers to the effect of previous thoughts, conversations, and memory retrieval on the subsequent mental contents and memory. A cue (external or internal context) primes related and expected concepts in memory, facilitating retrieval of the primed concepts (Neely, 1977). A primed concept may not be retrieved if the activation it receives does not exceed a certain threshold level but, because activation accumulates, priming increases the ease with which that concept can be retrieved if it receives activation from some other source. Thus, primed concepts are more likely to be subsequently retrieved than other concepts that have not been primed by their associates. For example, passing the poster of the musician may not have activated memories of the musician enough to bring him to mind, but the combination of seeing the poster and hearing one of the musician's songs did promote thoughts of the musician. Throughout the day, the person may find himself using that musician as a topic of conversation or an example illustrating some point, rather than thinking of other examples that were thought of less recently.

Activation of memories by environmental cues can also influence behavior, as goals are also stored in memory and situational cues can activate relevant goals, within or outside of awareness (Fitzsimons & Bargh, 2004). For example, social goals such as achievement or cooperation can be primed by cues such as particular locations (such as a library; Aarts & Dijksterhuis, 2003) that influence our behavior in goal-relevant ways, even when we are not aware of the activation of the goal.

In therapy, many clients (and often therapists) assume that if a client recalls a particular memory vividly and frequently, it is because that memory is centrally important. However, it may just be that the memory is simply being cued more frequently. For example, a client who often remembered past slights assumed these were strong memories that needed attention rather than that she was cued to these memories by current slights, such as feeling ignored by waiters or store clerks, having family members be late for commitments to her, and the like. The potential confusion here is that the therapist or client could assume there is unfinished business from the past rather than a current pattern to shift. Of course, a skilled therapist could address this issue either by addressing the past or the present, but it is important for therapists to be aware of the nature of priming so they can assist clients to manage their issues in the most efficient manner.

THE CUE-DEPENDENT NATURE
OF MEMORY RETRIEVAL

The previously mentioned mnemonic strategies of associating to-be-learned material with well-known or easily recalled information highlights the most important element of this associative model: the cue-dependent nature of memory retrieval. To recall any item from memory, we must first cue the search for that item. This is why hints, which cue the network near the desired memory, are so helpful in memory retrieval (Reisberg, 1997). For example, asking a client about her relationship with family members can cue memories of family events, such as dinner conversations or holiday gatherings. As any student knows, a good method to develop ideas for an essay is to read other authors' thoughts on the subject, priming the student's own related knowledge. The stronger the association between the cue and the target memory (the event or information you are trying to remember), the easier the retrieval search is. Thus, it is not the strength of a memory itself that determines its recall, but rather the strength of the connection between the memory and whatever cue is currently available. Advertisers attempt to use this aspect of memory to their advantage by displaying their advertisements frequently in an attempt to strengthen the associations between their product and a desired state (e.g., happiness, satisfaction). Important personal memories are strongly associated with many different types of cues, which is why they are often easily recalled. However, even for those memories, if we were prompted with a poor cue, retrieval would be difficult.

Case Illustration:

Sara was thirty-two, single, and worked as an administrator. She was referred by her family physician who described her as shy, lacking in self-confidence, and having low self-esteem. Her self-description was stated rather angrily and tearfully: "I am weak. . . . Everyone walks all over me . . . and I let them. . . . I'm sick and tired of it." Her stated goal was to develop strength and courage, and a partial description of the goal space (chapter 2) was that she wanted to state her needs, wants, and preferences clearly and take action to attain them even when discouraged or resisted by others.

In beginning therapy, the therapist clarified Sara's problem space using numerous retrieval cues based on the referral description (e.g., "I'm told you are shy. Can you comment on that?") and helping Sara build on her own cues presented as she told her story (e.g., vague referrals to being shy in school were used to elicit more specific memories of events). She presented informa-

tion about her emotional state clearly but did not provide much information about the nature of the situations that led to her statement that she was weak. Consequently, questions that elicited and clarified examples of "Everyone walks all over me" were used as cues to assist her in exploration, and a consistent pattern became evident. She provided stories about a coworker who "stole" a promotion and a boss who had her do things she didn't want to do ("You don't mind making the coffee, do you? I really appreciate it.").

In clarifying her feelings through the use of empathy and questioning (which cued descriptions of particular aspects of Sara's experience), she revealed that she wanted to stand up for herself but couldn't. She experienced intense anger and terror at the thought of taking action. The therapist used this description of her feeling state as a further cue to gather history related to the issue. "So you are feeling very angry and terrified at the same time. . . . That sounds painful. . . . Is that a familiar feeling? . . . Can you tell me about other times you have felt this way?" Sara responded to these cues by telling many stories involving males, in particular her father and three older brothers, who had frequently teased and embarrassed her when she was growing up. The stories included episodes ranging from the distant past (e.g., brothers embarrassing her as she developed breasts) to last week (her dad telling her it was stupid to buy a house when she wasn't married). At the same time, there was clearly a lot of affection and love in her relationship with the men in her family, as evidenced by the fact that her brothers and father frequently contacted her to discuss feelings, thoughts, and plans with her. There were multiple and frequent links among these associated experiences, so Sara frequently revisited them all when a new event cued or activated them.

This model of associative memory was initially developed to explain semantic memory (i.e., general knowledge, the basis we use to understand our world), and most of the empirical evidence supporting the model has involved semantic knowledge. But psychotherapy involves autobiographical memory, that is, memory for the events of our lives. How does this associative network model apply to these memories? The most elaborate model of autobiographical memory, developed by Conway (1997a), also builds on this associative base of interconnected memories. Conway posits three separate but interconnected networks of autobiographical knowledge representing lifetime periods, general events, and event-specific details. *Lifetime period knowledge* involves information about significant others, locations, actions, and goals associated with distinct thematic periods of our lives (e.g., when my children were babies, when I worked at a university counseling center). *General event knowledge* involves repeated events (e.g., walks to work through the park), single events composed of several more minor incidents (e.g., our trip to the Channel Islands), and sets of events associated with a given goal-related theme (e.g., learning to drive a car). *Knowledge of event-specific details* involves the micro-details of events; it is the memory for the sensory and reflective details of unique events. Knowledge at this level is essentially a record of perceptual and cognitive processing that occurred during the experience of an event. Each of these types of knowledge is interconnected with respect to specific events, but access to the different types of knowledge varies within each type of network (see chapter 4 for more details of Conway's model).

Case Illustration:

> *The pattern of therapy that developed was that Sara could describe her emotional state even though she was overwhelmed by it, but needed substantial prompting to broaden her description of an event to include a narrative of the events preceding and consequent to her feelings. As she expanded her descriptions to include her own and others' behaviors and statements, her overwhelming feeling of terror began to recede, although her sense of anger toward her experienced injustice remained very strong. In addition to using her emotional state as a cue to further exploration, the therapist also asked for single events ("What was the most embarrassing thing you remember?"), general events ("What happened over and over in your house?") and event-specific details ("What was most difficult about these events?"), priming multiple points of access to her autobiographical knowledge base. In answering these questions, Sara realized over a few sessions that her pattern was to feel humiliated by males and to suppress her response as she feared the loss of their caring if she expressed her anger. The therapist and Sara chose three or four of her memories that seemed to be prototypes of the problematic feeling / thinking / behavior pattern to work through in detail.*

As with semantic memory, autobiographical memory retrieval is also cue dependent, and in addition to external retrieval cues, cues can also be created internally by elaborating an initial cue with information that has been associatively activated. For example, an external cue, such as the poster of a musician, can activate a memory of seeing the musician. If one wishes to recall this event in more depth, the initial recalled details, such as the sight of the musician on stage or a recalled story the musician told while performing, can be elaborated to cue other associated memories, such as who one's companions were at this event. As Conway (1997a) states, a cue provides initial access to the knowledge base and begins a search that operates via spreading activation. A cue can "get us in the room," but we still have to search to find what we need. The output of this search is evaluated against some criterion, and the process is recycled, using an elaborated cue from the previous stage, until the target memory is reached. For example, when given the cue "truth" and told to retrieve a specific childhood memory, a participant in one of our studies reported the following train of thought: *"Truth. . . . Probably something with friends because when we were little, you always have little fights. Something with next-door neighbors maybe. Well, we played that one game . . . but I don't remember any specific time. . . . OK, I've got one."* (Arbuthnott, Ylioja, & Topp, 2004). This participant used the initial cue (truth) to access a lifetime period (when we were little), which led to a general event (playing a game with neighbors), which then led to a memory of a specific event that included event-specific details (*"I remember her mom sitting on the floor in the kitchen."*). Similarly, another participant was given the cue "tree" and reported: *"When I think of tree I think of my cottage. And when I think of my cottage I think of the time it burnt."* This participant used the initial cue to access a general setting (her cottage), which then led to a general event (the time the cottage burned), which then evoked event-specific details (*"I remember looking through and . . . like basically it burned to the ground. . . . we had had a purple toilet. And there was just great purple porcelain chunks. Some of the silverware you could still make out, piles of stretched forks and stuff like that."*).

Given the cue-dependent nature of memory retrieval, the nature of recall cues used in psychotherapy are important. If one's goal is to recall a specific memory (e.g., your nineteenth birthday), the best cues for that event will be distinctive (e.g., the first time you were taken out for alcoholic drinks by your parents). That is, the retrieval cue will be associated only with that memory and not with any others (i.e., one-to-one mapping between the cue and the memory). In that case, consideration of the cue will lead to activation of only the target event. Although such cues are optimal for retrieval of a specific event, it is unlikely that therapists would have knowledge of such cues, except in the case of unique cultural milestone events, such as that in the example. Rather, the cues typically used to trigger memory retrieval in therapy are cues that would be familiar to most clients (e.g., your grade two classroom, family mealtimes). Such cues are usually associated with many previous events (i.e., one-to-many mapping between the cue and memories) and are efficacious if the recall of any relevant memory is the goal, but they are not efficient for the recall of a particular memory. For example, the technique of using an emotional state as a memory retrieval cue ("When have you felt this before?"; e.g., Goulding & Goulding, 1979) will result in retrieval of some memories that feature that emotion, but it is likely a particular memory will not be reliably re-trieved using such a cue. Although there is considerable debate about the exact number of human emotions (e.g., Ekman, 1994; Scherer, 1994), most emotion researchers agree that the number is finite. Furthermore, emotions are automatic responses to personally meaningful and relevant events (external or internal) and are thus evoked by particular types of en-vironmental and mental events. Thus, it is unlikely that any given emotion will have been experienced only once in a person's life, as would be neces-sary for this to be a distinctive cue. If our goal is to evoke a single memory, such as the first occasion in which we felt particular emotion, this tech-nique is a poor one. It is very likely that a memory will be retrieved, but it is unlikely that this memory will match any specific criterion, such as be-ing the first experience of that emotion. (There is increased likelihood that the event recalled will be the most recent occurrence, or the most fre-quently retrieved event, given the mechanism of spreading activation.) However, if our therapeutic goal is to find a concrete example of a prob-lematic thought/feeling/behavior pattern, an emotional retrieval cue would be very efficacious because retrieval of any of the associated memories would suffice.

The latter objective is probably the most valuable for therapeutic pur-poses in any case, as the goal of most therapeutic models is to identify and alter problematic patterns of thought, feeling, and/or action. For this pur-pose, any vivid example can serve as the template for increasing under-standing and the client's response choices. However, therapists who sub-scribe to a psychodynamic perspective may mistakenly assume that a single causal event must be identified before therapeutic change can oc-cur. This assumption is problematic for two reasons. First, for any habitual emotion/thought pattern, it is unlikely that a single source exists. Rather, most automatic patterns develop over several repetitions of similar events, with slight variations on each occasion due to the complexity of interper-sonal encounters. Thus, the search for a prototypical source for the devel-opment of pathology is doomed to failure on this count. Second, as the psychodynamic goal is to bring to awareness a repressed pattern of as-sumptions, any instance of the pattern in question will serve as a template for insight or corrective experience (M. M. Goulding & R. L. Goulding, personal communication, July, 1984; see also Bucci, 1997, with respect to psychoanalysis). Thus, the technique of using present emotional experi-ence as a memory cue is appropriate, provided the therapist does not ex-pect the client to retrieve a memory of *the* seminal event (which likely does not exist except in unusual circumstances such as trauma).

Search for an autobiographical memory is not as simple as search for semantic information because autobiographical memories are also considered and modified in the light of changing self-concepts and goals (e.g., shifts in mood from one day to the next, starting a new relationship). According to Conway (1997b) and others, autobiographical memory "accessibility and accuracy are properties determined as much by the present as the past" (pp. 150–151). Control processes that select the cues with which to probe memory and incorporate the individual's current goals and self-concept into the search and the termination criteria are therefore involved in autobiographical memory search. For example, the specific cues (e.g., "Who walks all over you?") and techniques (e.g., "Tell them what you wanted") that a therapist utilizes to activate a set of memories influence the aspects of those memories that are retrieved. The combined influence of the cue-dependent nature of retrieval and the control processes ensure that autobiographical memories are not simply stored records of previous events, but rather constructions created from the information stored in long-term memory as accessed in a given context for a specific purpose. The construction occurs through spreading activation mechanisms, but the content of the resulting memory is strongly influenced by the current retrieval context. In the previous example, the retrieved memory of a previous injustice would include considerable detail about the client's feelings and wants, whereas previous retrievals of that same memory may not have included such details.

The ease of retrieval is strongly influenced by which level of the autobiographical knowledge hierarchy is first accessed by the cue. If a cue first accesses lifetime period knowledge, as in the example of retrieval to the "truth" cue, activation spreads to several general events, and retrieval of event-specific knowledge for only one of the events is more difficult (i.e., one-to-many mapping of cue to events and many-to-many mapping of events to details). For example, an instruction such as "Tell me about your childhood" may lead to a response such as "I don't remember anything from my childhood," because the cue doesn't prime any specific memories. Conversely, if a cue first accesses a general event, as in the memory retrieved in response to the "tree" cue, activation spreads to both the associated lifetime period and event-specific details (both one-to-one mappings), and retrieval is much easier. The same client who reports having no memories of his childhood, may be able to answer a question such as "What was your grade six teacher's name?" as the question cues a much more specific aspect of autobiographical knowledge. Thus, memories are constructions, created when retrieval cues interact with our deliberate control efforts, leading to the activation of knowledge in our long-term memory (Conway, 1997b). This is the reason for the instability of memory content observed when the same memory is recalled on different occasions: Different contexts, cues, and retrieval processes necessarily result in the retrieval of different aspects of a memory (or the construction of different memories). "Remembering is not the re-excitation of innumerable fixed, lifeless and fragmentary traces. It is an imaginative reconstruction, or construction, built out of . . . a whole active mass of organised past reactions or experience . . ." (Bartlett, 1932, pp. 204, 213). This view of constructing or reconstructing memory in a meaningful and useful way to facilitate client change is an integral part of many postmodern approaches to psychotherapy (see Neimeyer & Bridges, 2003, pp. 272–313), including constructivist (e.g., Mahoney, 2003) and narrative (M. White & Epston, 1990) therapies. However, it is useful for therapists of all orientations to keep in mind that clients' memory reports are always constructions based on their current goals and the interaction with the therapist.

IMPLICATIONS FOR THERAPISTS

Why is knowledge of memory processes important for therapists to understand? First, as humans, therapists are also strongly influenced by their context. Thus, their current reading, workshop, or training experiences will highlight certain issues in their minds, and they are much more likely to notice such elements in their clients' presentations. This is likely one of the mechanisms behind the phenomenon of "hit parade" issues whereby more cases of a particular problem seem to arise in a given time period (e.g., assertiveness in the 1970s, childhood trauma in the 1990s). The nature and wording of therapists' inquiries, teachings, and suggestions are influenced by their own current concerns through the mechanism of priming. This, in turn, influences what occurs to the client, including the particular features of memories they recall and notice because those therapeutic inquiries serve as the client's retrieval cues. Thus, the therapists' current interests and beliefs bias the thoughts and answers of the client. While this process is a natural one and is potentially beneficial for problem solving (see chapter 2), if neither party understands the nature of this contextual influence, misinterpretation of a client or the client's situation could result. Priming suggests that the process between a therapist and client creates a mutually defined reality in the sense that attention is drawn toward certain (primed) elements of memory and thought and away from others, both in a current session and across sessions.

Case Illustration:

In the past week, the therapist had learned that his own parents were separating after his mother had discovered that his father had been having a long-term affair and had chosen to move in with the affair partner. The therapist had a good relationship with both parents who live in the same city but was feeling angry with his father and more sympathetic toward his mother. This issue was, understandably, much on the therapist's mind, priming his attention to family discord, deception, and feelings of hurt and anger. This was the backdrop to therapy with Sara, and he was aware that he needed to avoid bringing his own feelings into his sessions.

In one session, Sara's issue and the therapist's current state of mind were problematic. He had had a major confrontation with his father the previous night and later described to his clinical supervisor that he had been accusing his dad of "not really caring about me as you were living a lie with me and mom all these years." Thus, the current mental state that was primed in the therapist was that males in families can't be trusted, and he had an undercurrent of anger toward his own father. The focus of the session was for the client to demonstrate her strength and courage and improve her sense of self confidence by role re-enacting old scenes in which she wanted to make her needs known (two of the three scenes involved her father and brothers and the other her boss). Sara was quite successful at this, describing a sense of strength rather than terror at her anger and as the session was winding down, she stated that she was ready to practice this in "real life." The therapist supported this and coached her about being forthright with her anger. The therapist was automatically attentive to this focus on anger and expression, given the issues that were primed in his own life. This was partially consistent with Sara's contract, but it neglected the issue of balance between expression and affection that Sara desired. Sara's consistent description of liking many of the males around her was less evident to the therapist, because it was inconsistent with the thoughts that were currently primed in his mind. As she was leaving the therapy room, Sara expressed some distress that she would be seeing her father for his sixtieth birthday later that day and she was worried that her anger would spill out indiscriminately ("I don't know what I'll do when I see him"). The therapist asked her to remain and was able to help her distinguish between the purpose of the role play (personal change), bringing this change into her day-to-day life (what to say to dad or any other man when I want to express my needs) and the genuine love and affection she wanted to maintain in her relationship with her father. In this case, the therapist's current state had been primed and he unconsciously pushed the client to focus on anger even though she had set a goal that included a positive balance of affection with the men in her life. It is often important that therapists are aware of what is primed in themselves as they prompt their clients. This is where having good clinical supervision that attends to the "self of the therapist" is important (American Association for Marriage and Family Therapy, 2000).

Interpretation of a life issue or of a person that arises from the collaboration between therapist and client should not be considered to define the person or her life absolutely. Rather, the selective interpretation can be used effectively to attain the client's desired change, without resulting in either the client's or the therapist's total commitment to the particular interpretation that evolves in the context. For example, family of origin, gestalt, or Jungian therapists often refer to "parts" of the person. The family of origin therapist may frame this in terms of the "inner child," the gestalt therapist as "the frightened part of you sitting in the other chair," and a Jungian analyst as an "archetype." Although therapists prime clients to frame their issues in terms of these theories, they do not literally believe that there is a separate entity within a client. The risk is that if we do not teach our clients to make a similar distinction, problems can arise as clients (and indeed some therapists) confuse metaphor and reality (or the map and the territory). Therapists often note that the issue a client is diagnosed with depends on the theoretical inclination of the therapist and whatever self-help framework the client has been exposed to. Similarly, clients' actions and personalities are different at home than they are in social settings or in the therapist's office.

Any time clients' memories are probed, priming influences their responses. This has implications for responses to self-report questionnaires and for the selection of memories, thoughts, and concerns reported in a therapy session. This is why the wording of questions is a central concern for the development of reliable questionnaires and should also be considered in therapeutic conversations. In this respect all questions are leading, in that the wording of a question necessarily primes certain aspects of the semantic and autobiographical memory networks and does not prime others. The classic study of Loftus and Palmer (1974) illustrates this: Participants estimated higher speeds prior to a car accident when the questions used a verb associated with higher speeds (e.g., *smashed*) than when lower impact verbs (e.g., *bumped*) were used. This illustrates perhaps the most subtle effect of priming: to bias memory search to match the implications of words contained in the retrieval cue. The mechanism of this effect is that, when more than one concept is activated, activation spreads from both concepts simultaneously, so that concepts common to both will be activated fastest (Reisberg, 1997). In this case, activation spreads from the words in the question as well as the content of the query, and associates of both are activated above threshold first (whether those associates are episodic or based on general knowledge). This is especially important for psychotherapists, who can inadvertently cause such biased memory search by their use of words. For example, a therapist who asks a client to recall the times they were "neglected" in their childhood is likely to receive different reports than one who asks the client to recall the times they were "ignored." Or a therapist who follows a description of a recent distressing assault with either "What happened next?" or "How did you feel?" is priming different aspects of the client's memory of her experience. In the interests of helping clients accept and deal with their emotional reactions to life events, therapists may have a tendency to use the more dramatic and intense labels, but they should be aware when they make this choice, the events they learn about may be recalled differently than they would have been with other retrieval cues. Similarly, therapeutic practices (mainly cognitive behavioral) that include filling out mood and progress questionnaires before and after each session need to be considered with an understanding of priming. Indeed, issues of priming in cognitive behavioral assessment have begun to be addressed (e.g., Blankstein & Segal, 2001).

The rich possibilities of identifying and utilizing retrieval cues offer much to a therapist. For example, if as therapists we prime a client's negative feelings toward a family member by mirroring only the family member's faults, we may inadvertently and needlessly damage that relationship. A client who spends a great deal of time complaining about his son's disrespectful and contemptuous attitude toward him will still be going home to interact with that child. However, at times such focus on negative aspects of relationships can be necessary to achieve a client's goals. Conversely, drawing attention to the positive aspects of individuals with whom the client has troubled relationships may assist the client in achieving goals related to improving those relationships. Such use of priming needs to be carefully tailored to serve the therapeutic goals of individual clients and situations.

It is not just the wording of questions that primes retrieval of memories. Therapists are taught to guide and direct the therapeutic processes of exploration, goal setting, and action planning through the use of skills of increasing influence (e.g., Ivey & Ivey, 1999). In addition, many therapies and therapists encourage a psychoeducational approach in which concepts are presented to clients and a variety of skills are taught to them. These will also prime our clients' memories and reactions. There is considerable debate among therapists as to the degree of influence we should exercise in our clients' lives, but the bottom line is that no matter how careful we are, we cannot avoid priming and other kinds of influence. As this is the case, we need to be aware of influencing by priming and use it thoughtfully and in the best interests of our clients.

Although the specific language of associative memory models has not been used, this knowledge about the processes of memory is already integrated into therapeutic practice. Many therapeutic techniques make explicit use of the associative and constructive nature of memory. For example, the technique of reframing involves associating a client's issues with themes that differ from those that the client has habitually used, themes that are themselves associated with more potential solutions to a current problem. This important and widely applied technique deliberately seeks to establish new interconnections in a client's memory, so that the cues that have triggered distress can now lead to new thoughts and actions. For example, many therapists reframe problems or issues in terms of normal human growth and development. A problem of teenage rebelliousness can be reframed as an unskilled attempt to establish independence, an action that necessitates both the appreciation and assistance of the parents. This technique is often augmented by interventions that will bias the new associates over the older, more problematic ones, either by repetition, recency, or somehow making the association distinctive through introducing it in a dramatic or intensely emotional event. Similarly, a client with intrusive memories of early childhood trauma and assault is taught to visualize a dramatic rescue when his distress level reaches a previously agreed-on threshold with the purpose of cuing different thoughts and reactions and helping him to regulate his own emotional state. Similarly, hypnotherapists have long emphasized the importance of language choice (Erickson et al., 1976; Lankton & Lankton, 1986), realizing that every word is associated with certain attitudes or values that can either assist or hinder the client in accessing resources important to his change task.

Case Illustration:

In addition to all the examples that demonstrated Sara's problem pattern, the therapist also attempted to cue other experiences by asking about exceptions and times when she did express her needs and wants. Unfortunately, there were no examples with men in which she felt she had expressed herself in the face of their resistance. There were many examples with female family members and friends and even with men who asked her to express her views. In order to build alternative cues and anchoring, there was one lighter session in which the client was to imagine her father and brothers in dresses to remind herself that expressing her wants and needs should be okay with both sexes. This image cued her laughter and considerably lightened the feeling she had at times around the men in her family. This distinctive image in her imagination could also serve to prime her changed behavior and feelings at relevant times in the future.

The contextual effect of priming can also provide another direct means of intervention. This phenomenon means that the material we expose ourselves to will influence our thoughts, memories, beliefs, and impressions. Therefore the movies, novels, TV programs, theatre, and music clients regularly consume will influence their thinking and mental contents, especially if this is a frequent activity for them. If this is similar to the issues they are dealing with (e.g., someone dealing with issues of violence or fear reading only murder mysteries), one useful intervention may be to change the content of these entertainments (bibliotherapy techniques; Lankton & Lankton, 1986).

CONCLUSION

The process by which memories of past events are brought forward to influence current thinking is of great interest to psychotherapists. This chapter described the associative nature of memory, which operates by activating associates of current thoughts and memories. The implication of this structure and process for therapists is that the choice of words, questions, and experiences that a therapist provides to a client will influence the memories and thoughts that the client reports. Armed with this knowledge, therapists can use this process to facilitate change for their clients, while avoiding the pitfalls that are associated with assuming that memories are absolute and unchanging objects.

KEY POINTS

- Memory is organized in associative networks, with events and concepts associated via previous perceptual, conceptual, or contextual connections.

- Memories are retrieved using cues, and the choice of cues will influence which memories and knowledge are activated and retrieved.
- Techniques such as reframing and indirect suggestion make use of these features of memory by establishing new associations to troublesome memories.

4

Autobiographical Memory:
The Stories and Scenes of Our Lives

Autobiographical memory, or memory for one's life, is the lifeblood of psychotherapy. Memory of our experiences is central to our identity and our sense of self (e.g., G. Cohen, 1989), and people who suffer injury to their long-term memory through stroke or brain injury often lose their sense of personal coherence. But what is memory? It is such a fundamental part of our everyday thinking that we seldom consider what this ability is. Metaphors for memory often include the sense that it is a store of past experiences, similar to a library or a video recording. However, research indicates that such metaphors are inadequate to explain the complexity of our memory, and often lead to incorrect assumptions (Conway, 1997b). Memories for specific events or people in our lives are experienced as "mental objects" in that we can often assume an objective stance toward them, as if we were observing the memory from the outside and can easily make judgments such as how clear the memory is.[1] However, it appears that such mental objects are not simply located in whole from a vast store of past experiences, but rather are constructed to satisfy the needs of current goals and contexts (see chapter 3). In therapy, even theoretical modalities that concentrate on the present, such as cognitive behavioral therapy, rely on clients' recollections about therapeutically targeted behaviors or complaints. Thus, knowing how such memory operates is vital for psychotherapists.[2] This chapter will elaborate on the model of autobiographical memory introduced in chapter 3. There is also some evidence that difficulties such as affective disorders influence the normal operation of memory processes to some degree, and these findings will be noted throughout the chapter and discussed in greater depth in chapter 13.

ORGANIZATION OF AUTOBIOGRAPHICAL MEMORIES

One common description of autobiographical memory is that it is a record of events organized according to their relationship to one's self. In the developmental literature, there is evidence that a sense of identity is essential for autobiographical memory. One theory suggests that a child's autobiographical memory emerges once they have attained a self-concept or can recognize themselves as a person that exists across various times and places (Howe, Courage, & Edison, 2003; K. Nelson, 2003). One marker for self-concept is the child's ability to recognize herself in a mirror or photograph, an accomplishment that occurs around two years of age. Howe et al. (2003) claim that objective self-representation allows the child a way to organize memories for events that were personally experienced. This theory provides a novel explanation for childhood amnesia that accounts for the demonstrated effectiveness of infants' long-term memory as well as our inability to recall autobiographical events from our earliest years. Childhood amnesia is the inability to remember events that occurred in our infancy and is puzzling because research clearly indicates that infants and young children have considerable memory for events they experience well before the age of two (Meltzoff, 1995; Rovee-Collier & Shyi, 1992). Infants are shown to imitate distinctive actions across delays of months (Bauer, 1996), and we all learn many important things during the amnesic period, including language. Howe et al. claim that this amnesia is attributable to the absence of the "self" as an organizing concept for personal memories (but see K. Nelson, 2003). Evidence for this claim is that self-recognition, as demonstrated through mirror recognition, is related to toddlers' recollection of personally experienced events (Harley & Reese, 1999; Howe et al., 2003).

So our representation of self appears to be the central organizing principle for autobiographical memories. What else do we know about how our personal memories are organized? Because autobiographical memory is so important for our sense of self, all of us have an intuitive theory of such memory, but autobiographical memory is apparently a more complex system than our intuitive theories, such as the previously described video storage metaphor, suggest. In the previous chapter, memory was described as an associative network of information. Autobiographical memory, however, is not simply a collection of episodes. Rather, autobiographical knowledge refers to several different types of memory ranging from large-scale themes or goals, such as those evident in a biography, to detailed reliving of previous moments that occur with some types of recollection. Moreover, autobiographical memory relies on two primary sources of information: general autobiographical knowledge and phenomenology, or the sense of reliving the event (Mazzoni & Kirsch, 2002; Rubin, Burt, & Fifield, 2003). Both of these sources of information are integral to all clients and therapists no matter what therapeutic approach is used. For example, when a client re-experiences the phenomenological characteristics of an event or relives an experience, such as the horror of a traffic accident, he may either be presenting his primary issue (distressing and intrusive images and memories), or he may be providing information that expands and clarifies the problem space (re-experiencing is one constraint that prevents him from driving). Autobiographical memory researchers posit that the organization of such diverse information is hierarchical as well as associative (Conway & Pleydell-Pearce, 2000).

One of the most prominent and complete hierarchical models of autobiographical memory structure and process is that developed by Conway (Conway, 1997a; Conway & Bekerian, 1987; Conway & Pleydell-Pearce, 2000). As discussed in chapter 3, this model distinguishes three types of autobiographical information—lifetime periods, general events, and event-specific knowledge—which represent a hierarchy from the most abstract to the most concrete autobiographical knowledge.

Lifetime period knowledge organizes personal memories according to major segments or transitions in one's life, such as residence in particular areas, major relationships, or career stages. These segments can partially overlap with the same time periods, such as "when I first lived away from home" and "when I went to university." Lifetime period knowledge is also thematic and reflects our main life goals during each period. Such periods extend over years in one's life, bounded by developmental and life transitions; these are the memories that are the least vulnerable to loss through brain injury (Barsalou, 1988; Eysenck & Keane, 1995).

General event knowledge, on the other hand, is knowledge of personal events and categories of events that are of shorter duration and narrower focus than lifetime periods. These event categories may be the most typical level at which we organize our experiences. For example, when Burt, Kemp, and Conway (2003) had experimental participants sort diary entries and photographs, participants most often organized events into general episodes that spanned several days and were associated by their content (i.e., relationships, goals, or projects). These memories are organized in terms of distinctive details that specify the context of the events and distinguish them from other general events. For example, when carrying out a kitchen renovation all memories related to this are placed together even though they may be quite different actions, such as arranging for a loan and removing linoleum. Although we can usually determine when these events occurred, and may store in our memories the temporal organization or order in which they occurred, our autobiographical memories contain relatively little direct information that specifically locates particular events in time (S. A. Anderson & Conway, 1993; W. F. Brewer, 1996; Conway & Rubin, 1993).

We "know" the information about lifetime periods and general events, and can readily express this knowledge in language, but we do not have a sense of re-experiencing the original event. Event-specific knowledge, on the other hand, is more experiential and includes a re-evoking of sensory and affective experiences that occurred during the original event. Event-specific knowledge is our recollection of the phenomenological details that accompany personal events, that is, the sights, sounds, smells, and emotions associated with each episode. Such phenomenological knowledge is close to a record of our previous sensory experiences. Recollection of such details, what Rubin (e.g., Rubin, Burt, et al., 2003) calls "reliving," is often what we consider the mark of autobiographical memory. In this context, visual imagery is especially important for our sense of memory vividness (Rubin & Greenberg, 2003). When we can clearly see a scene in our mind's eye, we experience this as a vivid memory, even when other details, such as sounds or exact sequences of actions, are not as clear.

One other feature of autobiographical knowledge, especially of lifetime period and general event knowledge, is its narrative structure. We tend to organize events into stories in both thinking and memory (Fivush & Haden, 2003; Freeman, 1993; Habermas & Bluck, 2000; Rubin, 1995). Narrative structure is an important aspect of our thinking, a conclusion that is supported by the fact that narrative reasoning—as measured by an individual's ability to comprehend, identify the important elements in, and recall a story—is very resistant to brain injury (Rubin & Greenberg, 2003). Habermas and Bluck (2000) define four aspects of narrative reasoning: temporal coherence, causal coherence, thematic coherence, and the cultural concept of biography. Specifically, when we recount our autobiographical memories, our recollections generally involve a series of events ordered in a time line (*temporal coherence*), presented in a logical sequence according to known causal mechanisms (*causal coherence*), and organized around one or more central themes (*thematic coherence*). The final component, the *cultural biography* concept, indicates that our autobiographical memories generally include the types of events that our culture considers important in a life story. Although narrative structure may not be essential for some types of autobiographical recall (Rubin & Greenberg, 2003), our organization of memories into narratives may influence our ability to retrieve records of those events from different cues. Narrative may be especially important for our understanding of emotional events, as our prototypes for emotions (see chapter 13) seem to be framed according to a narrative structure (Hogan, 2003; Oatley, 1992). This narrative structure may be disrupted for our memories of traumatic events, leading to dissociation and disrupted memory for such events (e.g., Nijenhuis & van der Hart, 1999; van der Kolk & Fisler, 1995). However, this narrative disruption with traumatic memories may be related to such memories becoming more important to one's life story, influencing the organization and interpretation of other personal memories, rather than being isolated from the rest of autobiographical memory (Berntsen, Willert, & Rubin, 2003). For example, Berntsen et al. observed that young adults who had developed posttraumatic stress disorder (PTSD) symptoms as a result of their traumatic experience reported that the traumatic event had become a stronger part of their self-concept and had more negative influence on their current life than was the case for non-PTSD trauma sufferers. An important component of many therapeutic approaches to recovery from symptoms of PTSD includes the integration of the traumatic memories, so that they can be accessed and considered without overwhelming distress or dissociation. Part of this process is developing a narrative of the traumatic events which can be integrated into, instead of split off and separated from, our autobiographical life story (e.g., J. G. Allen, 2001; Foa, 1997; J. L. Herman, 1992; Schiraldi, 2000); a narrative that won't unduly influence our interpretation of other nontraumatic life experiences (Berntsen et al., 2003).

Case Illustration:

    Ray was in his mid forties, worked at a security firm after a career in law enforcement, and had been in a stable common-law marriage for over ten years. His wife (Dawn) accompanied him to his first therapy session. He was self-referred and stated that he needed to stop using pornography as it upset Dawn. He agreed that he shouldn't use pornography but did not think it was as "big a deal as she thinks." She said she had noticed a gradual increase in his accessing pornography and while she had always been uncomfortable with him doing this, it was the increasing access along with a decrease in their own intimacy (both emotional and sexual) that precipitated her demanding he address this issue. She also disclosed (after asking his permission) that he was sexually assaulted as a child and wondered if there was a connection. At this point, he disagreed with her for the first time saying he was "over that" and there was no relationship between his past and pornography use. As the therapist quizzed him about the assault, he became quite agitated. By the end of the assessment and goal-setting phase of therapy, Ray, Dawn, and the therapist agreed that Ray and the therapist would begin individual therapy to address the first stated issue, that is, Ray's somewhat ambivalently stated goal to eliminate pornography for the good of his relationship and a mild belief that it was the right thing to do. In addition to the issue that precipitated his seeking therapy, Ray also described intermittent bouts of a mild to moderate depression since adolescence. This had been treated relatively successfully with antidepressant medication. There may also have been a need for concurrent or subsequent couples therapy, which all agreed would be with another therapist.

As individual therapy began, the therapist gathered information about Ray's pattern and history of pornography use; his attitudes and beliefs about pornography, women, and relationships; and all information relevant to describing a problem space (chapter 2). In gathering and exploring this information, a clear pattern emerged: Whereas Ray could relatively easily talk about his adult history of sexuality and accessing pornography, he could not do the same with his earlier sexual history. At that point, and after some discussion and education about trauma, Ray agreed that he needed to consider his early trauma history. He had never told anyone (other than his brief disclosure to Dawn) that he had been repeatedly and extensively abused by an older male cousin who was his babysitter. He was experiencing all of the major symptoms of PTSD, including intrusive memories and flashbacks, hypervigilance, and avoidance (which was the symptom that Dawn had noticed as he increasingly avoided her attempts to be sexually intimate). Simply talking about the history had a destabilizing effect on Ray, who was becoming depressed again and spending days at a time in bed. The therapist began a modified course of exposure therapy for PTSD (e.g., J. G. Allen, 2001) within the context of stabilization. Ray's memory for the abuse (which occurred when he was age seven to ten and ended when his cousin moved) was very disjointed. He could present brief descriptions of aspects of scenes either without emotion or with overwhelming event-specific details. While there were aspects of all types of autobiographical memory present, including lifetime periods ("while we were living in the grey house on the corner"), general events ("I dreaded Saturday nights"), and event-specific details ("I felt sick when he kissed me"), there certainly was not any narrative or sense of coherence to the memories of these events in his life. He described a consistent avoidance of remembering and aborting any thinking about what had happened to him as a way to manage his distress. At this point he revealed that in some ways he actually felt better when he was depressed as he was not overwhelmed with distress from flashbacks.

As part of therapy, the therapist assisted him in developing a narrative of the set of events, which covered all aspects of narrative reasoning, to help Ray make some sense of this part of his life. Developing a sense of narrative and coherence is common among virtually all theoretical approaches to treating trauma. As Ray was encouraged to systematically attend to all his available memories and learn to manage and ease any accompanying pain and discomfort, he also developed a sense of meaning and narrative of these difficult life events. These included all the characteristics of narrative reasoning, including temporal coherence (an escalating pattern of assault over the 4 years, culminating in an attempt at intercourse which Ray resisted), causal coherence ("I didn't stop him because he punched me in the stomach and told me my mom and dad would give me away if I told"), thematic coherence ("Why didn't someone protect me?" "My parents didn't know; they weren't in the house." "I was too scared to tell and covered my feelings."), and cultural biography ("This is not a story to share, especially with my parents; it would kill them.") and how the event had influenced his self-concept ("I'd look like a pathetic wimp and I don't want anyone to feel sorry for me.").

Autobiographical memories are thus stored in categories that are organized in a hierarchical fashion. As mentioned, one categorical feature that is common to all autobiographical memories is the self: Our self-schema is a feature in all autobiographical memories. A *schema* is a set of associated memories that are organized around a particular familiar concept or event. For example, we could describe our knowledge of a client as our schema for that client, which would contain our memories for how they look and sound, their habitual emotional and conversational responses to certain types of situations, and their therapeutic contract and history with us. As we work with them, we would come to use this schematic knowledge to make predictions about them and treatment plans for them. However, as well as organizing our experiences, our schematic knowledge, including our self-schema, also shapes what we experience and therefore what we remember. For example, if my self-schema includes the belief that I am shy, not only my memories but my actions (e.g., avoiding others) will contribute to new memories that will reinforce the schema.

AUTOBIOGRAPHICAL MEMORY RETRIEVAL

Autobiographical memory is apparently not the video record that we intuitively experience it to be; rather, it is a combination of retrieval from associative cues, integration of the resulting information, and inference using general autobiographical knowledge. Retrieval of autobiographical memories usually accesses all of the three levels of knowledge described by Conway (i.e., lifetime periods, general event knowledge, and event-specific knowledge), but the sense of reliving an event requires event-specific knowledge. As with any retrieval, the process begins with a cue that accesses the memory network (see chapter 3). Although the process of retrieving autobiographical memories involves retrieval from records stored in long-term memory, it is also a constructive process, involving selection of records and their integration into a form that serves the rememberer's current goal. As discussed in chapter 3, autobiographical memories are dynamic mental constructions created in response to a particular context and goal. The autobiographical knowledge base, composed of information at various levels of abstraction, provides the basis for the construction of specific memories. Autobiographical knowledge is activated by cues in the present situation, and this activation is monitored, evaluated, and elaborated by control processes (see chapter 12) relevant to the current retrieval goal. Control processes include monitoring of retrieved memories, withdrawal of attention from details that do not match current goals, and elaboration of retrieval cues that are relevant to a current goal. The stability of a pattern of activation across all three levels of autobiographical knowledge, as influenced by the control processes, determines the success of a memory retrieval attempt. The resulting autobiographical memory is a compilation of knowledge from all three levels, selected and constructed to effectively serve the rememberer's current goal and situation. For example, when reminiscing over drinks with old friends, we may integrate old memories into a form that suits a humorous rather than serious mood because that is the tone of the current conversation. We can do this even though the remembered experience also contains event-specific knowledge that is painful.

For this reason, two recollections of the same event are seldom identical, as different occasions usually involve different goals and different cues with which to probe long-term memory (Conway, 1997a). The importance of construction processes to autobiographical memory retrieval are illustrated by the behavior of patients who have brain injury to their frontal lobes. These patients frequently describe confabulated memories, based on actual people and locations from their past, but integrated in a way that describes a false experience (Stuss & Benson, 1986). Thus, it appears that in these patients, the activation of stored autobiographical knowledge is retained, but the ability to organize these activated records into an accurate and coherent narrative consistent with the person's life has been impaired. Furthermore, neuropsychological evidence indicates that the loss of several types of abilities through brain damage, including language and visual abilities, result in difficulties in autobiographical memory (i.e., amnesia; Rubin & Greenberg, 2003). Furthermore, memory construction is impaired when participants are asked to recall an event while they perform a secondary task, indicating the important contribution of central control processes (Conway, 1997b).

Within this architecture, Conway posits two types of autobiographical retrieval process, direct and intentional retrieval, distinguished by their effort and the order in which these three types of knowledge are accessed. With direct retrieval, the cue is a current sensory experience that accesses a similar phenomenal sensation in the event-specific knowledge base. For example, when we encounter a distinctive odor, we often rapidly recall our previous experience of that odor and the events surrounding it (Chu & Downes, 2002; Proust, 1922/1960). This type of retrieval is automatic and rapid, requiring little cognitive effort. Individuals who have experienced a traumatic event often report this type of retrieval of the traumatic event (termed *flashback*): A particular sight or sound will suddenly evoke the traumatic scene (or a part of it). Therapists also sometimes use this process to have a client rapidly access a previous event, such as when Bob Goulding encouraged a client to experience a current emotion deeply and then asked them when they had experienced that emotion previously (e.g., Goulding & Goulding, 1979, p. 137). Direct retrieval, however, is a relatively rare form of autobiographical recollection, dependent as it is on the reinstatement of specific sensory or affective details. Although direct retrieval is relatively rare, when it occurs, the resulting memory is very stable (i.e., consistent across several retrievals). This is because the activation in the autobiographical memory network spreads from the most specific knowledge (event-specific detail) to more general knowledge (placing the experience within a general event and lifetime period). Because there are relatively few pathways from this specific knowledge back to the general events in which they were experienced, the memory that is constructed will be more stable than memories that are constructed from more general to more specific knowledge because there are many connections to specific knowledge from a general event. For example, one of the authors often remembers a specific event when he smells fish. It is a memory of dragging his first catch proudly through sawdust and gravel from a lake by a sawmill. When this memory is primed, it is remembered in much the same way each time. On the other hand, when asked to remember "positive childhood events," this memory will be one of several that are accessed but will not appear with the same intensity of sensory or event-specific detail.

Involuntary memory retrieval, the appearance of a spontaneous autobiographical memory in one's mind without intentional retrieval effort (Berntsen, 1996, 1998) is another example of direct retrieval. Such memories are quite common in everyday life. Most diary studies of such memories suggest that they occur a few times per week. Such experiences usually occur when people are alone or when they are engaged in routine activities that don't demand their full concentration (Berntsen, 1998). Although involuntary, such memories are almost always triggered by easily identifiable cues, frequently visual or auditory cues that refer to a central feature of the involuntary memory (Berntsen, 1996, 1998).

However, intentional retrieval is used more often to access personal memories, especially in a context such as psychotherapy. This type of retrieval involves an effortful cue-following and constructive process. A rememberer will first access general event or lifetime period knowledge, and use the retrieved information to generate more specific cues to the target event. This retrieval process thus proceeds in a more cyclic and incremental fashion than direct retrieval, sampling knowledge contained in both lifetime periods and general events before accessing event-specific knowledge. This process is necessarily reconstructive: A retrieval cue is used to activate the autobiographical knowledge base at the level of lifetime periods or general events, and the accessed knowledge is used to make inferences and create further cues, activating additional knowledge, until event-specific details are accessed. For example, a client makes a statement that she is often in conflict and it causes her distress. A therapist may probe by asking, "Could you give me an example?" or "Could you give an example when conflict was not distressing or you were not in conflict?" This leads the client to activate general events that may broaden to lifetime periods depending on the orientation of the therapist. A psychodynamically oriented therapist will be interested in early lifetime periods, a cognitive behavioral therapist will be interested in current examples, and a solution-focused or strengths-based therapist will be looking for exceptions from more current lifetime periods. During this process, the retrieved knowledge is integrated with the current memory goals, essentially tailoring a memory relevant to the needs of the current situation (e.g., the needs of the therapy itself in the previous examples; Conway, 1997a). The effortful nature of this process of constructing an autobiographical memory is demonstrated by the length of time autobiographical memory retrieval takes: It often takes research participants about ten seconds to produce a memory from a cue in laboratory studies (see examples in chapter 3), whereas other types of retrieval such as the generation of an example in response to a category cue takes about one second (Rubin & Greenberg, 2003).

As is clear from the aforementioned description, we can access our memories beginning at any of the three levels of autobiographical knowledge, but general events are usually the preferred starting point (Burt et al., 2003). For example, in laboratory studies of autobiographical memories, when individuals are asked to retrieve a specific memory in response to a cue (e.g., Sheen, Kemp, & Rubin, 2001; J. M. G. Williams, 1995), they most often start with retrieval of a general event and then proceed to a more specific incident within that category (Arbuthnott et al., 2004).

Case Illustration:

As Ray, with the help of the therapist, developed a fairly comprehensive narrative of the events surrounding his abuse, his symptoms of intrusive memories receded almost totally as did his vigilance and constant state of high arousal and anxiety. Most of the memories were explored and developed using intentional methods of retrieval, although there were examples of direct retrieval. For example, during one session in which he described a recent experience ("When Dawn kisses me in a certain way, I feel nauseous like when my cousin did it"), he had a spontaneous connection between this feeling and the first time his cousin persuaded him to kiss him. It was also during one of these narrative development sessions regarding his sexual experiences that Ray discovered the connection between the abuse and pornography. In priming memory regarding his pornography use, the therapist had Ray describe his feeling state when accessing pornography. The feelings included both sexual arousal and a sense of safety. In answering the question, "Can you remember other times when you felt this way?" Ray recalled finding a pornographic magazine at 12. He was quite aroused and felt "so relieved" that he was normal that he began regularly finding pornography (magazines first, then movies when in his mid twenties, and finally Internet pornography about 5 years ago). This connection was concurrently primed in a couple's therapy session in which his pornography use was reframed as a way to feel like a man and experience sexual interest without the vulnerability that intimacy can bring (like revealing to his partner the ongoing symptoms he had experienced for years).

With clients accessing autobiographical memory, therapists can use the differences between direct and intentional retrieval strategically, to either "cool down" or "heat up" a session. If a client accesses many event-specific details that are overwhelming, then more intentional retrieval could help to make emotions more objective. On the other hand, if a client has difficulty accessing emotion, then promoting or setting the scene for direct accessing is a way to alter the emotional tone of a session. Most therapists intuitively use techniques to help clients manage their state, but knowing that each technique relies on a different form of memory retrieval can improve the use of such processes.

EMOTIONAL AND DISTINCTIVE MEMORIES

Laboratory studies of cued autobiographical recall (in which a participant retrieves a personal memory in response to a cue word such as "tree") reveal an interesting pattern: Individuals over thirty years old are likely to recall more memories from their late teens and early twenties than from any other time of their life, a phenomenon known as the "reminiscence bump" (Rubin, Rahhal, & Poon, 1998). This pattern is also observed in the recall of public knowledge, such as news events or popular culture, with participants more accurately recalling such events from their early adulthood and rating them as more important (Schuman & Rieger, 1992). One reason for this pattern is that our memory for unique or first-time experiences is particularly sharp (G. Cohen & Faulkner, 1988), and more such events occur during our early adulthood than later in our lives. However, recent research indicates that for emotionally charged memories, the reminiscence bump is observed for pleasant memories but not for unpleasant memories (Berntsen & Rubin, 2002). For unpleasant events, memory seems to follow a forgetting function that is similar to that for general information—recollection fades with the passage of time (Berntsen & Rubin, 2002; Rubin & Berntsen, 2003). In part, this difference between pleasant and unpleasant memories is attributable to our normative cultural expectations about the timing of major events in a person's life, or "life scripts"[3] (Rubin & Berntsen, 2003). Such expectations generally include age ranges only for positive life events such as graduation, marriage, or childbirth, and more such transitional events are expected to occur in early adulthood than at other times of life (Rubin & Berntsen, 2003; Bluck & Habermas, 2000; Shum, 1998). These life scripts provide useful retrieval cues when a person is asked to recall positive emotional events such as their happiest memory, but they are less useful for negative emotional events such as their saddest memory. For psychotherapists, this means that when clients are asked to recall positive autobiographical events to provide a contrast to a current negative emotional state (e.g., solution-focused therapy), they are more likely to remember a time during their early adulthood. This may give the false impression that this was the best time of the client's life and that aging is inevitably associated with less positive emotions. However, this would be a false conclusion, as this pattern is due to human memory processes, rather than the absolute distribution of emotionally positive or negative events over the course of a lifetime. In fact, studies of affective experience over the life span indicate that older adults experience more positive and less negative emotion using both self-report (Mroczek & Kolarz, 1998) and linguistic analysis methods of research (Pennebaker & Stone, 2003).

The reminiscence bump phenomenon and the influence of life scripts on retrieval of emotionally charged memories highlight the role of schematic knowledge in memory retrieval. Schemas, which represent very familiar information, can serve as powerful memory cues, making information associated with such schemas easier to retrieve. In terms of autobiographical memory, lifetime period knowledge is essentially schematic, organized around self-schema that change with lifetime transitions. Thus, recollection of particular autobiographical memories will be strongly influenced by a client's schematic knowledge, potentially giving both the client and therapist a biased view of their actual life experience.

For psychotherapists, the emotional content of autobiographical memory is particularly important. What do we know about the organization and retrieval of emotionally charged memories, other than that positive events are subject to a reminiscence bump? As reviewed in chapter 13, emotional intensity makes events more memorable, likely due to the importance of emotion as an event-specific detail. Thus, emotional events are not forgotten as quickly as more neutral events (e.g., Bohannon & Symons, 1992), and such events are thus more likely to be featured in our life narratives, including those which result in seeking psychotherapy.

There is research evidence that we sometimes use our autobiographical memory as a means to regulate our mood. Specifically, when we are in a negative mood, we can use recall of pleasant memories as a means to improve our mood (M. S. Clark & Isen, 1982). This strategy seems to be particularly useful for those who have high self-esteem, as they seem to spontaneously retrieve more positive memories than those with lower self-esteem (S. M. Smith & Petty, 1995). Furthermore, the recollection of pleasant memories seems to improve the mood of those with high self-esteem more than it does for those with lower self-esteem (Setliff & Marmurek, 2002). This finding is of particular relevance to therapists; whereas review of positive autobiographical memories would be a good technique to use with clients who show good self-esteem, it may be less effective with clients with self-esteem difficulties.

Another phenomenon related to the influence of autobiographical memory on mood regulation is the "overgeneral memory effect" (J. M. G. Williams, 1995). When participants in laboratory studies are given a cue word such as "tree" and asked to recall a specific event associated with that cue, some individuals seem unable to do this, reporting only general event memories instead. Specific events are described as ones that occur on a specific day at a specific location, and thus do not always include event-specific details, although they often do. Memories for general events in this context cannot be localized to a specific time and place. Most participants have no difficulty with this task, but depressed individuals tend to report general event memories as opposed to specific ones. For example, a participant might report, "We used to go to the lake on hot summer days" rather than "One day at the lake, we found a whole bunch of tiny frogs." As described earlier, it is likely that most participants will respond to this task by beginning their retrieval with general event or lifetime period knowledge, gradually isolating a specific event (Arbuthnott et al., 2004). However, depressed individuals appear to abort their retrieval prior to accessing a specific event (e.g., recollection of the general activity of going to the lake, but not the specific day the frogs were found; J. M. G. Williams, 1995), and thus report weaker phenomenological experience (Rubin, Schrauf, & Greenberg, 2003). Furthermore, the less a depressed person shows this pattern, the better their prognosis, and interventions that enable depressed individuals to engage in more specific recall are associated with amelioration of their symptoms (Segal, Williams, & Teasdale, 2002; Serrano, Latorre, Gatz, & Montanes, 2004; J. M. G. Williams, Teasdale, Segal, & Soulsby, 2000).

Williams hypothesizes that this overgeneral memory tendency serves a mood-regulation function for depressed individuals, but there is some controversy about how this regulation results in overgeneral memories for these individuals. One possibility is that consideration of specific memories leads to stronger emotional experience than reviewing general events. Consistent with this possibility, students who report specific memories are more frustrated by a difficult laboratory task (tanagrams) than those who report general memories (Raes, Hermans, de Decker, Eclen, & Williams, 2003).

Another possibility is that depressed individuals in general have difficulty regulating their emotions, and this difficulty creates interference in a memory retrieval task. Specific memories are more effortful to retrieve than general memories, and thus emotion-regulation difficulties will selectively interfere with specific memories more than general memories. In other words, a depressed individual may not be able to control their emotions enough to focus on retrieving specific memories. Although complicated, research examining this latter possibility has important consequences for psychotherapists, and thus will be described in some detail. Philippot, Schaefer, and Herbette (2003) hypothesize that emotion distracts attention from other tasks, and therefore emotional experience must be inhibited when we are engaged in effortful activities or tasks that require concentration. Thus, they argue, successful retrieval of specific memories, being effortful, requires the inhibition of emotions associated with the activated memories. The retrieval of general memories is neither as effortful, nor are such memories as strongly associated with emotion, as is the retrieval of specific memories (see earlier discussion of event-specific details). Depressed individuals, who are less able to inhibit ongoing emotional experience, thus often abort their retrieval attempts at the level of general events because they are unable to inhibit emotion strongly enough to allow them to concentrate on the effortful retrieval of specific memories. Philippot et al. (2003) tested this hypothesis by examining whether participants would show stronger emotion in a mood-induction procedure following general or specific memory retrieval. If their hypothesis of emotion inhibition to facilitate retrieval of specific memories were correct, mood induction would have greater influence following retrieval of general events because emotions would not be inhibited in that condition. The results of two studies supported their hypothesis: Participants reported stronger emotion following general event retrieval than retrieval of specific memories. Ironically, these results suggest that overgeneral memory retrieval shown by depressed individuals may actually work against mood-regulation goals. Given the strategic inhibition of emotion with retrieval of specific memories, depressed individuals might be better served to recall specific memories, consistent with the evidence that encouraging specific recall reduces depression (J. M. G. Williams et al., 2000). More generally, this also fits the therapeutic technique of working through issues, evident in psychodynamic and humanistic therapies (e.g., L. S. Greenberg & Safran, 1987). These therapies require detailed consideration and re-experiencing of difficult past events. The speculation that detailed consideration of difficult events improves mood is also supported by evidence that clients suffering traumatic symptoms show improved mental and physical health as a result of writing about their disturbing memories in a diary (Pennebaker & Seagal, 1999).

In addition to its relationship to depression, overgeneral memory is associated with other negative consequences. For example, overgeneral memory retrieval is associated with deficits in problem solving (Goddard,

Dritschel, & Burton, 1996) and in imagining or planning for the future (J. M. G. Williams et al., 1996). Thus, the ability to retrieve specific auto-biographical memories, including event-specific details, appears to be important for well-being and effective cognitive functioning. This evidence supports the long-established psychotherapeutic practice of concretely discussing events in a patient's life and provides some explanation for how such techniques assist in a client's return to mental health.

When we experience emotion during an event, the intensity of that emotion is usually reduced when we recollect it (e.g., Holmes, 1970). However, the decrease in emotional intensity associated with an event is not equivalent for positive and negative emotions. The decrease is more rapid for negative emotions, a phenomenon known as the "fading affect bias" (Suedfeld & Eich, 1995; Walker, Vogl, & Thompson, 1997). This may be because people take steps to deal with the situation that is causing the negative emotion and to reduce the intensity of the felt emotion (S. E. Taylor, 1991); no such effort is applied when experiencing positive emotions. Whatever the reason for the effect, dysphoric individuals (mild to moderate depression scores on the Beck Depression Inventory) show a different pattern in that emotional intensity associated with recalled events fades equally for positive and negative emotions (Walker, Skowronski, Gibbons, Vogl, & Thompson, 2003), due to both slower fading of negative emotions and faster fading of positive emotions. Thus, when mentally healthy, our memories selectively bias the recalled affect associated with our memories to be felt at a greater intensity for positive emotions than for negative emotions. However, this process is disrupted by depression. Consequently, depressed individuals are less able to regulate their mood using autobiographical memories, because when such recollections are associated with emotions, negative emotions are just as likely to be felt as strongly as positive emotions. Coupled with the evidence that individuals with low self-esteem (which often accompanies depression) are more likely to retrieve negative memories, this renders reminiscence a generally poor strategy of mood regulation for depressed individuals, except under psychotherapeutic conditions, in which both positive and negative event-specific details can be encouraged and worked through. (See chapter 13 for other memory biases associated with depression.)

Case Illustration:

Ray clearly demonstrated some of the characteristics of emotional and dis-tinctive memories. For example, his memories reflected the reminiscence bump, as early adulthood was the time of his life when he not only experienced many things for the first time but also did not experience the PTSD symptoms. This issue had been raised in couple's therapy, as Ray would often go out with younger members of the police force as a way of recapturing these times. This led to hurt feelings and guilt at home when Dawn would react, feeling that he did not care as much about her as his old life. In addition, he described an experience akin to the overgeneral memory effect when he felt depressed. At these times, he would know that he had been abused and by whom, but there were no event-specific distressing emotions and physical sensations to manage. He fairly frequently stated that he felt some relief along with the depressive symptoms.

Source Monitoring

Once we have retrieved or constructed an autobiographical memory, we often consider the source of our recollection. For example, if we retrieve a memory from a considerable time ago, we often consider whether we correctly recall the details or not. For example, one of us retrieved a memory of one of her children's second birthday, but then noted that the details of her memory could not have corresponded with the birthday of that child because the event took place in a house they did not own until that child was six years old. Thus, the source of the memory was either two different events or part memory and part imagination. As Conway notes, a memory is not a memory if it is not identified as such. We consistently use our minds to consider alternative courses of action, mentally rehearse planned actions, and imagine events associated with stories recounted by our friends and families (Arbuthnott et al., 2003). All of these events also become memory traces, and thus there are a great number of sources for a particular recalled event in addition to autobiographical experience. Furthermore, even if our recalled memories are identified as memory, we must often identify what the specific source for the recalled details was. For example, the process of accurate citation requires us to remember whether we learned information from one person or another, and inadvertent plagiarism can result when we do not recall that a particular idea was expressed recently by someone else (Marsh, Landau, & Hicks, 1997). Thus, one of the processes associated with memory recall is source monitoring (M. K. Johnson, Hashtroudi, & Lindsay, 1993; Mitchell & Johnson, 2000), in which a person attempts to recall the sources associated with particular memories. This aspect of memory is more prone to error than other aspects, as most of us experience when trying to recall where we learned a particular piece of information.

The source monitoring framework postulates that characteristics of a memory (such as its sensory and contextual details) and reasoning are used in attributing memory source (M. K. Johnson et al., 1993). Qualitative phenomenal differences between memories for actual events and imagined events are reliably observed: Memories of actual events contain more event-specific details including perceptual, contextual, and semantic information than memories for imagined events (Arbuthnott et al., 2002; Henkel & Franklin, 1998; M. K. Johnson, Foley, Suengas, & Raye, 1988; Lindsay, Johnson, & Kwon, 1991; Mather, Henkel, & Johnson, 1997; McGinnis & Roberts, 1996; Suengas & Johnson, 1988). There is also evidence that increased affect is shown for actual memories (M. K. Johnson et al., 1988; Mather et al., 1997). Conversely, memories for imagined events sometimes have more reflective or cognitive details related to the process of imagination or planning (M. K. Johnson et al., 1988; but see Arbuthnott et al., 2002; Kealy & Arbuthnott, 2003; Suengas & Johnson, 1988, for exceptions). For example, when we imagine an upcoming trip in order to review our travel arrangements, we need to invent details such as how many people are in the airport when we check in. Subsequently, we may recall how we decided whether to include a scenario with many fellow-travelers, or only a few in our imagined scenario, unlike the case for an actual experience where we simply arrive at the airport and notice how many people there are.

Source monitoring decisions, especially those seeking to discriminate between actual and imagined experiences, use these phenomenological differences to determine the source of a memory. Judgments about the source of a memory (e.g., whether it is an actual event or a fantasy) are hypothesized to involve comparison of the quantity and quality of a memory's characteristics with what we expect memories from different sources to include. If a memory meets the criterion level of a certain source, it is assumed to have originated from that source. As described, true memories have stronger phenomenology related to event-specific details, whereas imagined events may have stronger memories of the cognitive processes involved in their creation, such as thoughts or planning. This type of source monitoring—based on matching our memories to the average characteristics expected from imagined or real events—is usually quick and involves little conscious effort. For example, differentiating between a past event such as winning a local championship is quite easily distinguished from a past fantasy of moving beyond that to an Olympic gold medal. Although the imagined event has positive feelings attached, it either includes little event-specific detail or else a memory for how we decided on such details, such as imagining that the Olympics occurred in Switzerland because we have always wanted to visit there. In contrast, the actual event includes unusual event-specific details, such as a specific friend hurting your wrist while hugging you in congratulations. We can also use deliberate source decision processes, which involve retrieving supporting memories, considering relations with other autobiographical events, and reasoning (M. K. Johnson et al., 1993; Mitchell & Johnson, 2000). This process is influenced both by information stored as general event or lifetime period knowledge and by our beliefs about memory and how it works.

CONCLUSION

So what are the important things for therapists to know about autobiographical memory? In addition to its associative, cue-dependent nature (as discussed in chapter 3), the fact that autobiographical memory is a constructive process is important to consider. This construction is based on beliefs and general knowledge of our life histories and recalled phenomenological details. Memory for the events of our lives also show several interesting patterns, including better recall for events that occur in our early adulthood (the reminiscence bump) and better recall of pleasant as opposed to unpleasant events. The latter likely influences our use of autobiographical memories to regulate mood, recalling positive events as a way to pull ourselves out of negative moods. However, depressed individuals exhibit several variations in autobiographical memory processes. First, they are inclined to retrieve overgeneral memories when asked to recall specific events. Second, the pattern of intensity for pleasant and unpleasant events is different than that for most people, in that negative events are recalled just as vividly as positive events. Each of these differences can serve as a focus in psychotherapy, as research indicates that a return to more typical patterns of retrieval is associated with less depression.

KEY POINTS

- Autobiographical memory is organized according to our self-schema.
- Autobiographical memory is organized both associatively and hierarchically, with knowledge of the events of our lives stored as lifetime period knowledge, general event knowledge, and event-specific detail knowledge.

- Retrieval of autobiographical memories can occur both directly, through associative matches between current perceptual experience and previous event-specific details, and intentionally, through effortful elaboration of retrieval cues.
- Intentional retrieval of autobiographical memories can begin with any level of knowledge, but the most efficient method seems to begin with general event knowledge.
- Autobiographical memories show a "reminiscence bump," whereby we recall events that occurred in late adolescence and early adulthood much more frequently than events that occur at other times in our lives. This is also observed for pleasant emotional memories, but not for negative emotional memories.
- Autobiographical recall of positive memories can be used to regulate our moods, especially for those with high self-esteem. Healthy people have a positivity bias in their recall. Depressed individuals, while more negative, are actually more accurate about the balance of positive and negative emotion in their historical recall.
- Depressed individuals show a phenomenon known as overgeneral memory, in which they are less able to retrieve specific event details than are mentally healthy individuals. This may be due to mood-regulation difficulties that accompany depression, in that retrieval of specific memories is both more effortful and more arousing than retrieval of general event memories.
- Source monitoring refers to recollection of the specific source of a remembered event and is less reliable than memory for events themselves.

NOTES

1. Describing memories as objects does not imply that they are devoid of emotional or experiential components.
2. There are several book-length treatments of autobiographical memory that are quite accessible, including Conway (1997a), Korte (1995), Rubin (1995), and Schacter (1996).
3. This term sometimes has a different connotation for psychotherapists (e.g., Berne, 1972). In the cognitive literature, life script refers to the culturally expected events that are present in the lives of most members of the culture. For example, in Western culture, we expect most individuals to graduate from school, marry, have children, and so forth.

5

Autobiographical Memory Errors

Considerable debate has arisen in the past decade over autobiographical memory errors that can occur in psychotherapy (e.g., Read & Lindsay, 1997). In the context of therapeutic discussion of a client's life memory, assessments of memory accuracy usually are not relevant. If a client describes a particular historic event (childhood or more recent), the description itself and the client's reactions to the described event are usually the target of therapeutic interest and discussion. Moreover, therapists' underlying theoretical stance about memory accuracy varies considerably across modalities. Psychodynamic theorists assume a considerable degree of inaccuracy in all memories, based on the client's character structure; cognitive behavioral therapists assume some degree of inaccurate interpretation (and therefore memory), based on dysfunctional beliefs; and family therapists assume a self-biased perspective from all family members. Therapists more focused on a client's social situation, such as social workers or feminist therapists, may be more inclined to assume veridicality in clients' memory reports, as they are more likely to adopt an advocacy role in clients' lives. However, most therapists do not assume complete consistency between a client's recollection and the details of the historical event, but rather take historical recollection to be a combination of historical fact and perception and retrieval processes that are distorted by the client's particular personality and issues. In working through therapeutic issues, the interplay between internal sources of bias in perception and memory, and external events, is an important aspect of treatment for therapists of all modalities. For example, an adolescent from a family with four younger siblings described his problem as being in a family in which the parents loved the other children more than him. There were many loud shouting matches about this issue, and the client regularly expressed deep grief, despair, and suicidal intentions as a response to this problem. In doing a thorough assessment, which included home visits, the therapist noticed that the client was regularly treated with love and respect by his parents and admiration by his siblings. The contradiction between the biased memory of his prior experiences and his current state thus became a major focus of therapy. This emphasizes how important it is for practitioners of all therapeutic models to understand the processes of memory and how they can be distorted. Because cognitive science research indicates that most types of memory errors occur independent of personality or psychopathology, therapists should be aware of these generic human memory biases so as to better interpret normal memory errors as well as the role of particular psychological disorders in memory.

For decades, researchers have demonstrated that memory is subject to consistent errors (Bartlett, 1932; Schacter, Norman, & Koutstaal, 1997) in ways that are of central importance to forensic psychologists. More recently, this research has overlapped with psychotherapy, especially with respect to trauma treatment and childhood sexual abuse (D. Brown, Scheflin, & Hammond, 1998; Read & Lindsay, 1997). The concern is that the practices of therapists increase the incidence of faulty memory, leading to false allegations of abuse and trauma. The way our autobiographical memory is organized and operates leads to particular types of errors (e.g., Reisberg, 1997) in the same way that we are susceptible to perceptual illusions because of the way our sensory organs operate.

OVERCONFIDENCE

One type of error that we all show is overconfidence in our memory abilities. Specifically, when asked to rate our likelihood of recall for particular events or information, our ratings are usually higher than our subsequent recall accuracy (e.g., Chandler, 1994; Neisser & Harsch, 1992; G. L. Wells, Luus, & Windschitl, 1994). For example, when we are asked to recall and then rate our confidence in the answer to a general information question such as "What is the capital of Brazil?" our confidence is typically higher than our accuracy. This effect is most commonly studied using general information (semantic memory), but it has also been observed in studies of face recognition (Perfect, 2002) and thus is likely also true for autobiographical memory. We are not completely inaccurate; confidence judgments and accuracy do correlate, especially when they are measured within individuals (i.e., we are more confident in the accuracy of correct items than we are of incorrect ones). However, when correlations are examined between people, the correlations are more uncertain, especially for unfamiliar types of recollection, such as recognition of unfamiliar faces (Lindsay, Read, & Sharma, 1998; Perfect, 2002; Read, Lindsay, & Nicholls, 1998). In other words, when confidence is examined between individuals, those reporting great confidence in their memories are no more accurate than those who show little confidence. This between-person difference is not explained by personality variables, but rather by beliefs about one's memory ability, which is likely influenced by one's previous test-taking experience in school (Perfect, 2002) and other types of feedback.

Most relevant to psychotherapists, researchers have examined whether confidence judgments distinguish correct (true) from incorrect (false) memories. Under some conditions, confidence ratings differ between correct and incorrect memories (Heaps & Nash, 2001; Henkel, Franklin, & Johnson, 2000; Mather et al., 1997; Zaragoza & Mitchell, 1996) or between memories for experienced and imagined events (Kealy & Arbuthnott, 2003), with correct and experienced memories rated more confidently than incorrect or imagined events. Similarly, in eyewitness identification contexts, strong confidence-accuracy correlations are observed when a range of witnessing conditions are tested (Lindsay, Nilsen, & Read, 2000; Read et al., 1998). Other results, however, show equivalent confidence ratings for actual and imagined experiences (e.g., M. K. Johnson et al., 1988), or show weak relationships between confidence and accurate memory judgments (Barclay, 1988; Kelley & Lindsay, 1993; Lindsay et al., 1998; Takahashi, 1998). For example, Lindsay et al. (1998) observed that conditions that resulted in higher confidence ratings for correct memory also resulted in higher confidence in false identifications. Thus, although the research evidence is not totally consistent, it is likely that confidence could be high for some incorrect memories. If the accuracy of a memory is relevant to the therapy, then knowledge of possible reasons for errors can be important. In this case, therapists will want to both clarify the sources of error (e.g., subsequent retelling of the event in a social context, imagined review of the event, etc.) and make accurate recollection of the event less relevant to treatment. For instance, many marital therapists with clients who hold tightly to their version of an event may have to explain, "Since we don't have the video, perhaps we can work to establish a shared future perception of events rather than attempting to determine whose perception of the past is most accurate." This may include educating clients about memory. If the client's goals involve assessing the accuracy of their memories, as is sometimes the case with individuals who suspect they were abused in their childhood, the therapist can still query whether determining memory accuracy per se is the most appropriate strategy to achieve the client's ultimate goal (e.g., peace of mind, better self-understanding and acceptance), or whether some other strategy can be devised that circumvents the assessment of memory accuracy (e.g., self-acceptance without assigning historical blame).

As social beings, we are strongly influenced by a person's confidence, despite this uncertain correlation between confidence and accuracy. This has been demonstrated for jurors assessing the testimony of eyewitnesses (G. L. Wells, Lindsay, & Ferguson, 1979) and is likely true for therapists responding to their clients. Given the discrepancy between accuracy and confidence that has been observed experimentally, therapists should be aware of the influence of a person's expressed confidence in the accuracy of their recollections and should counteract this tendency in themselves (see chapter 12). Therapists working with couples and families have to deal with these effects due to confidence in most sessions, as they attempt to rebalance a system so that all have influence, whether or not they state their cases with confidence.

SCHEMATIC KNOWLEDGE ERRORS

Other types of errors are more directly related to the structure and operation of our memory. Specifically, we are successful learners because we perceive and understand our world by relating new information to known information. One important example of this is understanding: Much of what we understand about a new situation is based on its relation to our previous knowledge. For example, when a colleague says, "My students are very good at the details of their research, but they struggle with the big picture," I understand her statement based on my previous knowledge of her situation: She is working with graduate students who are testing students in an elementary school in an effort to understand the development of academic skills. The details thus involve interaction with children, and the big picture involves theories of skill learning. This contribution of memory to comprehension is necessary for effective communication (Grice, 1975) and is the mechanism underlying the value of learning to everyday action. Without this memory contribution, my colleague would need to fill in all the details of her situation each time she and I speak. However, despite its necessity and great functionality, this interaction of perception and memory can lead to memory errors. Specifically, perception and understanding are biased by our previous knowledge (Reisberg, 1997), especially familiar and schematic knowledge. Such knowledge makes us more efficient in our interactions with the world, helping us to locate relevant information in memory or fill in the gaps for things we don't recall. However, this process simultaneously creates the possibility of error because we perceive and remember the world as we expect it to be, based on our previous knowledge. The use of schematic knowledge to fill in the gap to fit expectations and to promote understanding by using previous experience also fits with the cybernetic and family therapy concept of homeostasis, whereby a system such as a couple or a family attempts to maintain stability or the status quo and a therapist often intervenes to induce change, thus challenging their schematic expectations.

Many training programs for psychotherapists and clinicians recognize this and include communication theory and skill training as a way to assist new therapists to be aware of, and avoid when necessary, communicating biases that are ineffective in particular therapeutic sessions. The general view of this type of training is that although we cannot avoid having biases from past experience, if we are aware of them we can then make a choice as to whether to communicate them, avoid them, or even refer the client elsewhere if the biases are interfering in therapy (e.g., Gudykunst, Ting-Toomy, Sudweeks, & Stewart, 1995).

One example of the influence of previous knowledge on current thought is stereotypes. Stereotypes are category prototypes (see chapter 8) that have been previously learned, such as the gender stereotypes that women are usually smaller and weaker than men or that men can't express their feelings as well as women. Although this is not always true (leading to the negative consequences associated with stereotypes), it is true more often than not, leading to the formation of the relative prototypes for women and men. Such stereotypes have been shown to greatly influence our memory judgments (see chapter 12). Although we are not aware of it, new information tends to be influenced by stereotypes; they contribute to our efforts to understand and learn new information (B. K. Payne, Jacoby, & Lambert, 2004). For example, if we see a small individual among a group of peers, we may unconsciously assume that the individual is female due to body size. Similarly, our expectations, which are based on previous knowledge, influence both the ways we interpret new information and the associative links established between the new information and existing memory. For example, if I see my son speaking animatedly with another person (current perception), and notice that his conversation partner looks similar to his description of a new friend (previous memory), I may interpret the situation as my son speaking with his new friend, without necessarily being aware of this inference process. Later, I will then recall the scene as my son and his new friend talking, rather than segregating my perception of the scene from the inference that I made based on my previous memory. Similarly, if a woman sees her fiancé talking to an attractive woman with his hand on her arm and smiling (current perception) and the woman notices that her fiancé's conversation partner looks like his ex-wife (previous memory), she may not be able to separate her perception from her inference, later recalling the scene as indicating her fiancé was not finished with his previous relationship. An argument then ensues in which she accuses him of not loving her enough and he accuses her of being unreasonably jealous. Of course, it could turn out that someone's inference is accurate, but the confusion of perception (actual event) with an inference usually leads to misunderstanding and distress in a relationship. Many theoretical approaches to couple therapy, including behavioral (e.g., Atkins, Dimidjan, & Christensen, 2003), cognitive behavioral (e.g., Baucom, Epstein, & LaTaillade, 2002), and relationship-enhancement training programs (e.g., Gordon & Durana, 1999; S. D. Miller & Sherrard, 1999), specifically use communication skills training as a way to avoid these biases although they are not usually presented as a way to avoid memory errors.

One consequence of this interweaving of new information and prior knowledge is biased selection, both at encoding and retrieval. Events and details that fit with our understanding and expectation are more likely to be remembered than events that seem out of place. For example, research indicates that we are much more likely to falsely recall expected details in a scene, such as books in a teacher's office, than other types of details (such as sports equipment in a teacher's office; Pezdek, Whetstone, Reynolds, Askari, & Dougherty, 1989). Such memory errors serve to put our memory of past events more in line with our knowledge and beliefs, even though the world is often not quite as orderly. One purpose our cognitive processes serve is to simplify the world for us, allowing us to operate functionally even though our impressions are not necessarily accurate.

Schema can also have the opposite effect on memory, in that we are more likely to notice details that differ from the typical schema, details that make a particular event distinctive. And, as we have better memory for things that we have noticed, unusual details can be recalled better than expected ones. For example, many restaurants attempt to make their establishment more memorable than others by having distinctive features like singing waiters or a distinctive decoration theme. Thus, in addition to using their schema of important people in their lives to interpret their behavior, clients will also sometimes recall when those people acted in ways that violated their expectations. For example, if their mother is usually even-tempered and patient, children will recall as particularly salient times when their mother erupted in anger. Thus, we are more likely to directly recall distinctive information associated with an event but, if we can't recall a specific detail, we will use our schematic knowledge to fill in the gap, resulting in memory errors that fit with our expectations.

Case Illustration:

Sam was fifteen and had been referred by his father and stepmother after a suicide attempt and a history of parent–child conflict. His father (Joe) was diagnosed with multiple sclerosis four years earlier. The illness was quite aggressive and the father was currently an invalid. Sam was the child of Joe and his former wife who left when Sam was two (Sam had no contact with his biological mother since then). Four years later, Joe married Susan and they have two young boys (eight & six years old). Sam was a marginal student and had received no prior counseling. He was, however, diagnosed with ADHD two years earlier and was prescribed Ritalin. He stopped taking the medication about one year later.

Susan, Joe, and Sam all attended the first session. Both parents described the issue as Sam feeling like he was not part of the family. Sam confirmed this but framed it as both parents loving the younger children more than him and favoring them with privileges he never had when he was their age. This issue often escalated into intense screaming matches and recriminations. One month earlier, Sam had overdosed on painkillers, was hospitalized briefly, and referred for therapy. Sam was relatively engaged in this part of the assessment, providing his own opinion including that not only were his brothers favored but he was expected to help out more since his father became ill and received no appreciation for his efforts. The parents acknowledged their need for more assistance and that Sam carried more of this load than the younger boys. They described Sam as a "sweet and loving boy" until shortly after the birth of his first brother when he became somewhat moody and withdrawn. Since his father's diagnosis, Sam was frequently angry, screaming at all family members, throwing things, and a few times hitting his brothers and stepmom. Intense sadness and expressions of despair ("No one loves me. No one understands how I feel. I might as well be dead.") followed these outbursts. Interestingly there were no incidents of angry outbursts in any area of his life except at home.

Among the family dynamics that emerged during the initial assessment was that both Joe and Susan were oldest children and had been very responsible at an early age. In addition, both believed that children should be protected from the world by keeping distressing information from them (e.g., Joe had never talked to Sam about his biological mother or why she left; Susan and Joe had not provided any education regarding multiple sclerosis; although Sam liked Susan he had not been consulted by them around their marriage or living together).

The family and therapist decided that Sam would receive individual therapy with periodic family sessions. Sam was actually quite enthusiastic about attending counseling, as he saw it as a way to tell his side of the story. As the therapist completed his assessment, he made several home visits made necessary by Joe's medical condition. In observing the family, the therapist noticed many instances in which Sam was treated with respect by his parents and with admiration by his younger brothers.

A cognitive behavioral approach to Sam and his problem may attempt to reveal the thoughts and beliefs underlying his current attitudes and actions, whereas a more psychodynamic approach would explore Sam's life experiences to determine the development and etiology of his relationships and self-concept. It was clear that Sam truly believed that his brothers were loved more than he was and that he experienced deep distress as a result of it. When asked to describe the reasons for his sense of being unloved, Sam launched into descriptions of many stories during the last several years in which his brothers were favored. In a family session, however, his parents gave a very different perspective in which they described differential treatment of their kids as age appropriate. At this point, whether using an intergenerational or a cognitive behavioral family approach, it was obvious that the beliefs and family memories of Mom, Dad, and Sam were different. This indicated that at least one of the individuals had incorrect memories.

MEMORY JUDGMENTS

Once we have retrieved a memory, we judge whether we have recalled the event accurately or not; this process is known as memory judgment. Such judgments can occur automatically, such as when we assume that a memory is correct, or more effortfully, such as when we deliberately search for evidence about the accuracy of our memories. Errors in judging memory accuracy are related to two different types of information: phenomenological detail and belief. As described in previous chapters, autobiographical recollections contain both rich phenomenological information, such as sensations or emotions experienced during the original events (event-specific knowledge), and general knowledge about the events of one's life (general event and lifetime period knowledge). For example, when recalling a child-hood event such as a family gathering, a client could re-experience the sights and sounds of that day or could know where, when, and with whom they gathered without having any accompanying mental imagery. The former memory includes event-specific details, whereas the latter describes a general event. Mazzoni and Kirsch (2002) explicitly distinguish between these re-trieval and inference processes involved in assessing autobiographical memo-ries. Evidence suggests that specific memories retrieved with either direct or intentional retrieval processes are associated with phenomenological experi-ences such as vividness and intensity. In contrast, memory beliefs (such as knowing that something occurred when one was a child through other sources that are a part of general event and lifetime period knowledge) have no such phenomenological aspects (see also Rubin & Berntsen, 2003). In many treat-ments for trauma and other memories that are accompanied by distress and emotional pain, therapists are actually hoping to convert specific event mem-ories into memory beliefs without reinstituting a dissociative state. Both types of knowledge are essential to our autobiographical memories, and both can be the source of errors in memory judgment. Cognitive research indicates that sources of memory bias and inaccuracy are somewhat different for general knowledge (general event and lifetime period) and phenomenological aspects of memory (event-specific knowledge), although the two frequently combine as we judge the accuracy of our memories.

False memory judgments typically result from errors in source monitor-ing. As described in the previous chapter, when a memory is recalled, a judgment process must be engaged to determine the original source of the recalled event. Mistaking an imagined event as one that actually occurred accounts for most experimentally demonstrated false memories. As de-scribed in chapter 4, source monitoring decisions make use of phenome-nological differences between experienced and imagined events to iden-tify the source of a memory, as actual events are associated with more vivid phenomenological details.

Phenomenological Characteristics

Research indicates that we use the recalled phenomenology of a previous experience as an important indicator of the memory's accuracy. Autobio-graphical memory can contain resonance of all the sensory experiences that were originally experienced, and internal reinstatement of these sen-sory experiences often convinces us that a memory is accurate. For example, in one study we asked participants to specify why they were confident in the accuracy of memories that they generated in response to cue words (Arbuthnott et al., 2004). Participants all reported believing that memories with phenomenological characteristics such as clear and intense emotions, visual details, and other sensory details were very likely to be true. These reports particularly specified emotions and sensory details as reasons to believe the accuracy of memories. Participants believed that strong emotion could only be associated with actual experience and that very clear visual details or other sensations such as smell, temperature, or tactile feelings could only come from direct experience. Visual imagery associated with an original event is considered particularly important (Rubin, Schrauf, & Greenberg, 2003) in that the vividness and intensity of recalled events is one factor that strongly convinces us of a memory's consistency with our previous experiences. Many clients report vivid visual images accompanied by intense emotion (including images of sexual abuse) and think they may be true because of the intensity of the experience. This factor is so important to autobiographical memory that brain-injured individuals who are unable to visualize also have greatly disrupted autobiographical memory (i.e., they are amnesic; Rubin & Greenberg, 1998).

However, imagined experience can be a source of mental phenomenology that is similar to that experienced in memories, because we remember imaginary events such as fantasies and dreams the same way we remember actual life experiences. Imagery is perceptual experience in the absence of external sensory stimulation or input (Richardson, 1994). Imagery techniques are effective in many contexts and thus are used in many psychotherapy modalities, including cognitive behavioral therapy (D. Edwards, 1990), transpersonal therapy (Foote, 1996), emotionally focused therapy (M. Martin & Williams, 1990), and health psychology (see Arbuthnott, Arbuthnott, & Rossiter, 2001, for a review). Therapy uses imagery and imagination in numerous ways, from directly instructing clients to imagine certain events to asking them to elaborate on, or introduce, fictitious or fantastical elements into perceptual or emotional elements of historical events, for example, imagining a positive ending to a previously painful memory. Indeed this is not surprising, as human imagination gives one much greater scope than limiting oneself to only the sensory stimulation that is immediately present in any situation (or memory), which not many of us can do without extensive practice. Imagery techniques have become a particular target of memory researchers as a practice increasing the risk of false memories (e.g., Hyman & Pentland, 1996), but there is necessarily an integrative relationship between imagery and memory, both in therapy and in everyday thought. Mental imagery is a fundamental component of thinking and memory review.

Nevertheless, imagery does seem to be central to errors we make about previous experiences (Conway, 1997b; Lampinen, Odegard, & Bullington, 2003). Memory and imagery are intimately connected, and our thoughts are a constant interaction of imagery (or imagination) and memory. For example, most of us use imagery to comprehend the conversation and stories of people in our lives (Arbuthnott et al., 2003). In psychotherapeutic conversation, there is a fluid interchange between memory, imagery, and current experience. For example, a client entering therapy to deal more effectively with change might easily move from describing current experience (feeling terrified to accept a foreign post even though she wishes to do so) to past events (being forced to move with her family many times with disastrous results) to imagery and metaphor ("Every time I have to change, I feel like I'm walking a tightrope high above the ground with no safety net"). As discussed in Conway's (1997a) model of autobiographical memory, cues bring associated memories to mind, and those memories are then integrated with beliefs and other inferences and organized to fit the current context. For example, when we listen to a client's story of dissatisfaction with his home life, we bring to mind memories of what "home life" means, the feeling of dissatisfaction, elements we consider important to domestic satisfaction, and so forth. We then reorganize those remembered items into the new context being described by the client. Thus, as well as being constructive, the process of memory retrieval necessarily involves imagery. It seems impossible to entirely divorce imagery from therapy or indeed from the normal day-to-day operation of the human mind. However, specific therapeutic imagery techniques need to be applied judiciously and skillfully in most therapy situations and are contraindicated in some.

Therefore, although characteristic differences between perceived and imagined events are well established, this does not necessarily mean that the identified differences are routinely used when we are considering whether a recalled event was experienced or imagined (e.g., Henkel et al., 2000). Studies of personal memories indicate better recall for vivid events associated with visual and affective detail (W. F. Brewer, 1988a, 1988b; Galton, 1880; R. T. White, 1982; Wagenaar, 1986), but these characteristics may not influence explicit judgments of memory source. Moreover, phenomenology can be influenced by factors other than memory, making beliefs that such characteristics ensure memory accuracy problematic. For example, cognitive researchers have shown that several manipulations increase our sense of vividness, including guided imagery (Heaps & Nash, 2001; Hyman & Pentland, 1996; Rubin et al., 2003). Contextual factors such as conversational imagery encoding (Kealy & Arbuthnott, 2003) or repeatedly imagining the same scene (Arbuthnott, in press; Toglia, 1995) can increase the sensory and emotional phenomenology of imagined events. Consistent with the increase in phenomenological experience, research indicates that suggested childhood events that were never experienced are endorsed as true more when they have been imagined (Hyman, Husband, & Billings, 1995; Porter, Yuille, & Lehman, 1999). Furthermore, emotional and sensory stimulation is the explicit goal of many media events such as movies or novels, so it is likely that memory of such media-induced experiences would also be associated with vivid phenomenology.

Neuroimaging data indicates that similar brain regions are involved in remembering and imaging events (Gonsalves & Paller, 2000), possibly accounting for the strong influence of imagery on memory judgment. For example, the processes of bringing a memory to mind and creating an imagined event using familiar people and settings involve the same left frontal regions of the brain (Conway et al., 2002). However, regions involved in holding the event in mind differ for memories and imagined events: Holding a memory in mind activates occipito-temporal regions, presumably reflecting sensory memories, whereas holding an imagined event in mind continues to require the left frontal area (Conway et al., 2002). These researchers speculate that both retrieving and imaging memories involve similar control processes, but that, once retrieved, experienced events involve more sensory–perceptual episodic knowledge stored in occipital regions, whereas imagined events contain generic imagery generated from frontal networks. However, recalling a previously imagined event could, potentially, involve the same processes as recalling a previously experienced event. This would account for the evidence that repeatedly imagining the same scene increases the imagined event's phenomenological similarity to memory (Arbuthnott, in press; Lampinen et al., 2003).

Thus, in the case of imagery or media exposure, if an individual does not explicitly recall the source of such experiences, the risk of memory misattribution based on sensory and affective strength would be high, given the evidence of people's beliefs about the source of vivid phenomenology. Despite the systematic phenomenological differences observed for true and false memories (Henkel et al., 2000; Henkel, Johnson, & De Leonardis, 1998; M. K. Johnson, Nolde, & De Leonardis, 1996; Mather et al., 1997; K. Norman & Schacter, 1998), memory errors are frequently made. Similarly, although we usually have relatively little difficulty distinguishing narratives of events that we ourselves have experienced (auto-biographical memory) and those that we have created or heard described by others, as the narratives associated with ourselves and others become more similar, it would seem likely that some confusion would occur. This seems to be the case (Arbuthnott et al., 2003; Sheen et al., 2001). For example, Sheen et al. observed that twins experience a particular type of false memory in which both twins recall themselves as the protagonist in an event, even though only one of them could have been. Consistent with the role of phenomenological characteristics in such errors, these disputed memories had more visual imagery than the twins' other memories.

Our beliefs about the role of emotion and sensory detail in memory accuracy may be a primary reason that we are more confident in the accuracy of our memories than we should be (Barclay, 1988). Furthermore, if psychotherapists also hold such beliefs, they could contribute to clients' false judgments of their memories for experiences that have been encountered in therapeutic imagery. On the other hand, such beliefs might also be amenable to educational efforts to correct such erroneous assumptions, and psychotherapists could serve a valuable teaching role in this regard.

General Knowledge and Beliefs

Considerable evidence indicates that some autobiographical memory errors are caused by phenomenological characteristics of a memory in question. However, David Rubin has also observed that individuals judge the accuracy of their memories based on their knowledge of the context of the event (Rubin, Schrauf, & Greenberg, 2003). Rubin finds that participants' rating of belief in the accuracy of their recollection correlates most strongly with their knowledge of the event's setting. This suggests that, when judging whether we have experienced or imagined a remembered event, we are likely to consider general event or lifetime period knowledge even more strongly than event-specific details. Thus, memory errors also result from our general autobiographical knowledge and beliefs. For example, a family member observed a client with obsessive-compulsive disorder lock the door and walk away without checking. When the family member presented this observation to the client, the family member was met with disbelief ("I don't believe you, I always check, I do it the same way every time") even though their goal was to stop checking.

As described in Conway's (1997a) model, part of our autobiographical knowledge consists of simply knowing that something happened, rather than re-experiencing the phenomenological sensations of the event. For example, although we cannot recall the sensory details associated with our birthplace, most of us know the location where we were born. For such knowledge, our judgments of accuracy are more strongly related to our intuitive theories of memory and our beliefs about our world in general (Mazzoni & Kirsch, 2002). For example, we are much more likely to judge an event that is plausible within our life narrative as more likely to have been experienced than one that is unlikely or inconsistent with our knowledge of ourselves (Arbuthnott et al., 2003; Pezdek, Finger, & Hodge, 1997; Pezdek & Hodge, 1999). For example, Pezdek and Hodge (1999) observed that 44% of children aged five to twelve mistakenly recalled having experienced a suggested plausible event (getting lost in a shopping mall), but only 10% of the children reported recalling a suggested implausible event (receiving a rectal enema). Thus, in the absence of event-specific details, experimental manipulations that increase individuals' beliefs about the plausibility or frequency of a certain type of experience increase the rate of false memory judgments (Mazzoni, Loftus, & Kirsch, 2001).

In therapeutic terms, manipulations of what a client believes to be true (or likely) can thus also influence her memory judgments. Therapist statements about the likely meaning of certain clusters of symptoms (see chapter 8), or statements about the prevalence of certain types of experience during the client's lifetime, can thus result in mistaken judgments about memory knowledge. For example, Mazzoni and Kirsch (2002) told experimental participants that playing certain types of music in neonatal nurseries was a common practice over the years of their birth. As a result, participants' beliefs that they had experienced such music when they were infants increased. This example also highlights the important contribution of our intuitive theories of memory. Most people realize that we do not usually have recollective experience of events from our very early childhood (childhood amnesia), so the absence of phenomenological experiences of early childhood memories is not interpreted as diagnostic of whether an event occurred or not (Strack & Bless, 1994). For these events, changing our beliefs about the likelihood of an occurrence during our early childhood likely directly influences our autobiographical judgments.

Case Illustration:

> *In one session, Sam described a series of events that had led to an incorrect and damaging memory judgment. He recalled a dream he had "when I was in grade two" and after his first brother was born. He dreamed that his biological mom had been standing over his bed with a knife and was going to kill him.*

He knew it was her because he had seen a picture of her (which Joe and Susan didn't know). The dream was very intense, and the emotional and physical sensations lingered for several days. In fact, even as he related the dream eight years later, Sam demonstrated a high degree of distress and reported experiencing many event-specific details that were still painful. Sam then began to wonder if his dream was really what happened when he was two and his mother left. Since his dad wouldn't talk to him about his mom, he thought something awful must have happened. As he played this story over in his mind, he eventually came to believe it could be true and had even told friends, "I think my mom might have tried to kill me." He also reported that after this dream, he didn't feel right about Susan. Sam's sharing of this dream triggered a horrified response from his dad and also led to sharing much more about Sam's mother and Susan sharing her sense of losing him since her first biological child was born.

SOCIAL INFLUENCES

Another potent source of memory errors seems to be social interaction with others, especially those who also experienced an event. In addition to the effects of others' expectation that one would recall a particular event (e.g., Orne, 1962), Hyman and Pentland (1996) postulated that when people have related information in their own autobiographical knowledge base, they incorporate suggested information from others into their memories and then believe that a described experience was their own. Niedzwienska (2003) tested this hypothesis by having Polish students recall their memories of two events that are shared by all students in their culture, a final secondary school exam and a formal ball preceding their graduation. Participants recalled these events twice, approximately four months apart. Midway between the initial and final recollections, half of the participants watched a film of these two events, which included decorations not mentioned by participants, and another film in which a young woman (an experimental confederate) gave a detailed description of what was apparently her own recollection of these events, which the participants then imagined using a guided imagery procedure. The confederate incorporated several fictitious details that were not mentioned by participants in their original recollections, such as fruit placed on exam desks and dancing a particular dance at the ball. The intervening films were designed to approximate the effect of reminiscing about a common event with peers. The results showed that the details provided by reminiscence partners can influence our own memory for an event. In the context of generally consistent accounts across the two sessions, those who had viewed the intervening films sometimes incorporated the fictitious details given in the filmed account into their second recollection. In fact, all but one of the students who had viewed the intervening films incorporated at least one of the fictitious details into their recollection. Niedzwienska concluded that learning about some else's experience had altered participants' reports of their own experiences because the remembered details associated with the events included both their own memories and those they had watched and imagined in the intervening session. During the final recollection, participants then failed to distinguish between these two sources of memory, resulting in the false reports including the imagined details as autobiographical. Similarly, in their retrospective survey of memory errors, Arbuthnott et al. (2003) noted that several participants described confusion about whether a recalled experience was their own or was recounted by a friend. We also observed that imagery routinely occurred when participants listened to descriptions of events recounted by others. This increases the difficulty in source discrimination by associating imagined sensory and contextual records with the heard event. Moreover, social communication is one of our primary sources of learning, leading to cultural transmission from adults to children of knowledge such as language, cultural history, commonly accepted scientific knowledge, and the like. Thus, we have considerable practice in using the reports of others as sources of learning for our own memories, greatly increasing our success in learning about our environment. Anecdotally, most of us can attest to this social source of memory in the following common experience. When we are unfamiliar with a topic in a current conversation but do not want to ask for information, we simply listen to others until we can confidently speak about the topic as if we knew about it all along.

This process can perhaps account for memory errors associated with misleading information or leading questions. Research across several decades has demonstrated that participants can be induced to make errors by interspersing inconsistent information between encoding and retrieval, or by framing a question that includes inconsistent information (e.g., Ayers & Reder, 1998; Loftus & Palmer, 1974). We may differ in our vulnerability to this social influence on our memory reports, with individuals who are more socially acquiescent and those who report more dissociative experience showing higher levels of suggestibility in a misinformation paradigm (Eisen, Morgan, & Mickes, 2002). However, even individuals who are most susceptible to suggestion will only show errors when they are uncertain, such as when someone else has introduced information that is inconsistent with their own recollections of an event (Eisen et al., 2002).

Case Illustration:

Sam reported that his sense of not being loved came from noticing that his brothers received a lot more hugging and physical attention than he did. He frequently reviewed memories of them receiving such affection. Since his parents wouldn't talk to him about the past or his father's illness, he began to talk to friends. Most of his friends encouraged his sense of mistreatment with stories of their own about bad stepmothers and stepfathers and abandonment in a time of need. These stories primed Sam's memory for similar events and created sources for memory confusions resulting from the integration of his friends' stories with his own. In summary, it seemed that in the absence of input from his parents, Sam developed his memories and beliefs from other sources. His parents perpetuated this system by treating him as a responsible adult and "protecting" him by keeping information from him. This resulted in several memory errors, including the stereotyping of parents and children, building expectations based on biased selection of remembrances, and confusing his dream (of his mother trying to kill him) with reality.

At this point in therapy, a modified narrative approach to developing a coherent family history was chosen as the method of intervention for Sam and his family. With the assistance of the therapist, Susan, Joe, and Sam simply shared memories of their own history filling in missing information for each other (e.g., from Joe, "Your mother left with another man and I don't know where she is. I wish she would contact you." From Susan and Joe, "We were expected to work hard and I guess we expect the same from you." From Sam, "That time I ran away and you didn't stop me, I really thought you didn't want me back"). As much as possible, the therapist helped them share specific memories with event-specific details as well as sharing general event and lifetime period memories. As each member shared memories, the therapist also helped them recall positive memories and reinforced those as important. The parents recalled their sadness about their lack of attention and began to develop a plan to change their beliefs and schema of how a family should operate. Sam was able to realize that he had received a lot of incorrect information and indeed had invented some of his history, likely by integrating material he had imagined as he listened to his friends' stories.

Of course, there were many issues to attend to in this family in addition to developing a set of more consistent, jointly held memories (anger management, stress due to illness and uncertainty, developing action plans to demonstrate love and caring for everyone); however, this development of historical narrative for the family was probably the most significant intervention of this relatively long-term therapy.

MINIMIZING MEMORY ERRORS

Despite the clear evidence that many features of our memory lead to possible errors, our autobiographical knowledge is generally accurate in its outlines. Autobiographical memory is basically accurate in the sense that recollected experiences correspond with the central classes and details of actual events. Memory errors, including those associated with mental imagery and media experience, distort the details of events but do not apparently create completely fictional histories in one's mind. Most of the memory errors observed in research involve inaccuracy or confusion regarding details, such as sources and time of occurrence, but not of the essential events themselves. As Conway (1997a) put it, "Volatility of access, errors, incompleteness, and even wholly false memories in the context of basic accuracy are the hallmarks of autobiographical memory" (p. 150).

It is our memory for detail, then, that is especially prone to mistake, particularly when we encounter many events that are similar (Arbuthnott et al., 2003; Jobe, Tourangeau, & Smith, 1993). For example, Conway (1997a) theorized that "minor source monitoring errors, in which an automatic inference is retained in memory as a detail of an event, are probably highly frequent. More gross errors in which whole fantasies become entangled in autobiographical memory knowledge are probably less frequent" (pp. 176–177). Furthermore, such errors can frequently be reduced when people are encouraged to use more stringent source monitoring criteria (Stangor & McMillan, 1992). As discussed earlier in this chapter, an autobiographical memory is composed of several types of information, including information about large-scale lifetime periods and phenomenological details associated with specific events. If we consider a wider range of this information when judging a memory as accurate, the quality of our judgments should improve accordingly. As Conway (1997a) notes, if an event is not consistent with lifetime period or general event knowledge, it will be rejected either on the basis of empirical evidence (i.e., recollection of knowledge inconsistent with the target event) or because the cue does not trigger sufficient recollections (Conway, Collins, Gathercole, & Anderson, 1996). Thus, an imagined or fictional experience that is not consistent with other records in the autobiographical database is unlikely to be endorsed as autobiographical.

There are a number of techniques that therapists can use to encourage clients to make more accurate memory judgments, including educating them about the characteristics of memories (see chapter 12) and encouraging them to use strict source monitoring criteria when the accuracy of their recollection is important. These strategies are effective in reducing memory errors, since informing people about the likelihood of memory errors reduces their incidence (Gallo, Roberts, & Seamon, 1997), as does explicitly drawing their attention to the source of their memories (e.g., Lindsay & Johnson, 1989).

A client's autobiographical memory is central to the process in psychotherapy, and thus knowledge of how autobiographical memory is organized and operates is vital for psychotherapists. This knowledge, including the knowledge of errors that are common in autobiographical memory retrieval, can armor therapists against faulty judgments about their clients' lives, thus facilitating more effective diagnosis and treatment.

With respect to the worry that therapeutic imagery can increase a client's false memories, several precautions can be taken to minimize such difficulties. For example, therapists can encourage the use of rigorous source monitoring for events that have been discussed in therapy or, when using therapeutic imagery, they can use metaphorical imagery that does not involve familiar events or people in a client's life (see Arbuthnott et al., 2001). In any event, therapists' knowledge of the routine sources of error in autobiographical memory will increase the accuracy of their own interpretations of a client's life events, potentially eliminating errors that rest on the therapist's conclusions and comments. Furthermore, as therapists and clients discuss the events of a client's life, the therapist can remain alert to problematic beliefs that clients hold about how memory works and re-educate them accordingly.

Our purposes for eliciting memory recollection are also important to consider. For therapeutic purposes, our interest is often in the client's view of her life events rather than on the details of her recollections. For this purpose, strict attention to the accuracy of memory is not necessary because there is considerable evidence that our large-scale autobiographical memory is accurate (Conway, 1997a). So, for instance, when our interest is in a client's schematic knowledge or basic assumptions, rather than in her recollection, per se, we might encourage rather lax source monitoring because this better suits our purposes. For example, a client who wishes to become more assertive describes a set of memories in which his siblings bully him and then says, "I'm probably making this up to justify feeling sorry for myself." He could be encouraged to worry less about accuracy (along with a little education about memory errors) as long as the description of the event provides knowledge of his thoughts and behavior. Of course, if there are real-life implications indicating that accuracy is important, therapists need to proceed cautiously.

CONCLUSION

As discussed in the previous chapter, autobiographical memory is a constructive process, based on beliefs and general knowledge of one's life history and recalled phenomenological details. Each of these components is vulnerable to errors, including errors related to social factors such as information that a certain type of event is plausible. Errors associated with phenomenological details are also associated with beliefs, in that people seem to believe that memory is the only source of vivid phenomenology, although research clearly demonstrates that other mental processes can involve such phenomenology. Therapists should remain alert to these possible sources of error in their clients' reports, and refrain from adding to such errors by making unsubstantiated pronouncements about the likely sources of clients' difficulties. With these cautions in mind, our clients' autobiographical memories can be a rich source of material in therapy, for both diagnosis and treatment planning, and for treatment itself in the case of mood regulation.

KEY POINTS

- We are regularly overconfident in our memory ability and accuracy.
- We are prone to make errors consistent with our expectations, beliefs, and existing knowledge.
- Autobiographical memory is generally accurate, but is prone to several types of errors in detail.
- Erroneous judgment of a memory as a previous experience can be based on phenomenological characteristics or beliefs, both of which are prone to errors.
- Judgment errors can be minimized by engaging in strict source monitoring, requiring retrieval of more information from lifetime periods, general knowledge, and event-specific details as a means to determine the accuracy of a memory.
- Whenever possible, mental experiences such as imagery should make use of distinctive cues, such as bizarre details, to distinguish them from actual memories.

6

Prospective Memory and Psychotherapeutic Homework

Prospective memory is our ability to remember to do future actions: We often form plans to accomplish something that we are unable to perform immediately, such as passing on a message to a friend who is not present or making an appointment when we have access to a telephone or our date book. So we make mental notes to ourselves to do the action in the future, when the conditions are right for their completion. For successful completion of the intention, we must recall our intended action at the appropriate moment without a specific reminder to check our memory (McDaniel, Guynn, Einstein, & Breneiser, 2004). Both research and anecdotal experience indicate that we do not accomplish this perfectly, resulting in head slapping/Homer Simpson moments when we remember that we were supposed to do something that we have forgotten to do. Usually this is simply annoying, but there can also be serious consequences for prospective memory failure, such as the father who forgot to take his infant child to daycare, resulting in the infant dying of exposure when left in the car all day. Although research in the area of prospective memory is in its infancy relative to research on retrospective memory, we have discovered some things about both personal and contextual factors that make prospective memory more successful. This chapter reviews recent research on prospective remembering, highlighting the factors that influence prospective memory success, especially for those situations most relevant to psychotherapy.

THERAPEUTIC IMPORTANCE

Many psychotherapeutic practices and techniques require clients to act on goals that are formulated during a therapy session, but enacted in the client's everyday life—in other words, prospective memory tasks. Techniques that involve establishing new reactions to difficult situations, such as cognitive behavioral imagery (Foote, 1996) or the neurolinguistic programming and Ericksonian concept of anchoring (Battino, 2002; Lankton, 1980) involve prospective memory. For example, therapists establishing an imaginary "safe place" for a traumatized client or strengthening positive self-talk by classically conditioning the task to a physical sensation hope that their clients can access these resources developed in the therapy session when they need them in the future. Similarly, therapists of virtually all schools of therapy often design homework activities or intersession assignments (ISAs) to help clients extend the changes made in a therapy session to their daily lives (e.g., L. S. Greenberg & Paivio, 1997; Lankton & Lankton, 1986; Mahoney, 2003; Neimeyer & Feixus, 1990). In particular, the manualized approaches of cognitive behavioral therapists and workbook-assisted protocols of treatment include many homework assignments (e.g., Bourne, 2000; Emery, 2000; Olsen & Stephens, 2001). However, as therapists know, such assignments are not always completed (e.g., Leahy, 2002; Tomkins, 2002).

Therapists typically assume that such failure reflects lack of motivation or resistance to therapeutic change (Dattilio, 2002; Leung & Heimberg, 1996; Openshaw, 1998; Worthington, 1986), but because homework involves prospective memory it is likely that at least some failures to complete homework are attributable to prospective memory lapses (Arbuthnott & Arbuthnott, 1999). Unpublished research from our lab (Arbuthnott & Arbuthnott, 2004) indicates that homework completion involves prospective memory at least as much as it does motivational factors. In a naturalistic study of therapeutic homework, 37% of homework assignments that clients did not complete were attributed to reasons typically considered noncompliance, such as failing to do the assigned task because it was too difficult or caused too much discomfort. For example, one client was to have a conversation with his wife about his discomfort with her way of disciplining their children, but he reported deciding not to bring the issue up because it would cause too much conflict between them. However, 63% of the assignments that were not done were forgotten: Some clients remembered that they were supposed to do something but forgot what it was, and others completely forgot that they were to do anything at all. Although this study relied on clients' self-reported reasons for their homework failure, the specific cases that were reported as forgotten were consistent with factors that we know influence memory, such as poorer recall when a client's situation demanded unusual amounts of attention (e.g., "My mother suddenly became ill, so I didn't even think of my own issues this week"; "We had a crisis at work, so I completely forgot"). Thus, our suggestion that a considerable portion of homework noncompletions can be attributed to prospective memory factors has some support, and it is useful for therapists who use homework assignments as part of their treatment to understand prospective memory processes.

Case Illustration:

Melinda was 38 years old, married, and had a two-year-old son with a chronic but not life-threatening health condition. She practiced law until her son was born, and then she and her husband decided that she would remain at home until their child entered school. She also considered this as an opportunity to consider a career change although she had been quite successful in her practice. She was diagnosed with a generalized anxiety disorder in her mid twenties and was referred to a cognitive behavioral group treatment program. This treatment was moderately successful. Since that time, she also received four to six sessions of individual therapy each year, which helped her maintain the gains she had made in earlier treatment.

Unfortunately, her symptoms returned after the birth of her child. She experienced many of her original symptoms as well as some that reflected her current life circumstances, including high levels of anxiety, lack of sleep due to a "racing mind," inability to concentrate on tasks because disturbing thoughts of danger to all members of her family intruded, catastrophic thinking, overprotection of her child, and daily panic attacks. She had been referred to another group treatment program and then to individual therapy but neither were effective at this time. She had been prescribed an antianxiety medication and although it helped ease her symptoms, the effects did not last. When she attended individual psychotherapy, she was quite sleep deprived. She had lost twenty-five pounds in the last six weeks and was terrified that in her state she would do something that would be harmful to her child. When questioned about her observations of the failure of a previously successful treatment, she replied, "My mind is so scattered, I just can't do all the things they ask, and there is so much to do with the baby and the house. I'm so confused." She stated that her husband was very supportive of her, and their relationship was a source of strength in her life.

In further defining the problem space, she set her goals as reducing anxiety and enjoying being a stay-at-home mother. The major constraint in reaching the goal was that she seemed so captured by her distressing experience that she could not complete any of the therapeutic assignments and she rarely felt at peace. Since in most treatments for anxiety, carrying out intersession assignments and breaking old patterns by doing new things in response to old symptoms are very important, it was clear that prospective memory factors would be important in this case. In fact, she specifically stated that unless her husband reminded her, she would not even think about the workbook assignments set in her psychoeducational group treatment. This had unfortunately developed into a relationship issue with her husband accusing her of "not trying" as he attributed her noncompletion to motivational factors and her countering with "You don't understand how hard it is."

PROSPECTIVE MEMORY PROCESSES

Consider for a moment how difficult it is to perform an action in the future: When we cannot accomplish one of our goals immediately, we form an intention to act at some later time, and we store that resolution in memory. At that later time, while we are engaged in other activities, we must recall the earlier goal, usually without any reminder to do so, and then execute the intended action either instead of or simultaneously with the activity we are currently doing (Brandimonte, Einstein, & McDaniel, 1996). For example, a client who has a marital difficulty may decide to have an important conversation with her spouse, and she planned to do so at the end of the day. To accomplish this intention, when both the client and her spouse arrive home after the work day, the client must recall that plan in the midst of her usual postwork routine and then interrupt both her own and her husband's routine in order to initiate the conversation. In such situations, there are seldom specific directions from the environment to trigger the recall (e.g., no one reminds the client when she arrives home that she planned to do something now). So the intention must be recalled in the appropriate situation, without much environmental support.

As a result of the difficulty of such tasks, most of us can readily list examples of prospective memory failures (e.g., Einstein & McDaniel, 1996; Wilkins & Baddeley, 1988). However, research indicates that prospective memory performance is usually quite good, especially for young adults (Einstein, Holland, McDaniel, & Guynn, 1992). For example, studies in which university students record their plans for the upcoming week, and then return at the end of the week to report how many of these plans had been successfully completed show that approximately 75% of the plans are completed (Marsh, Hicks, & Landau, 1998). Marsh et al. found that completion rates were highest (83%) for plans with specific dates and times (e.g., appointments and assignments) and lowest (64%) for informal plans such as those to communicate with others (e.g., writing letters, phone calls), to complete transactions with friends (e.g., to borrow or return items), or to set up appointments.

The completion rate of therapeutic plans is likely more similar to that for informal plans as observed in Marsh, Hicks, and Landau (1998), because such plans are seldom associated with specific dates and times. For example, in the aforementioned study in our lab, only 49% of therapeutic assignments were completed.

Prospective/Retrospective Components

The successful completion of prospective plans involves both prospective and retrospective aspects of memory (A.-L. Cohen, Dixon, Lindsay, & Masson, 2003; Kvavilashvili, 1987). Specifically, researchers distinguish between memory that we intended to do something (the prospective component) and recall of the specific action that we planned to do (the retrospective component). For example, if I plan to buy milk on my way home from work, my intention to do something after work is the prospective component, and the specific plan to buy milk is the retrospective component. In most cases, when we resolve to do something in the future, we have in mind a specific situation in which that action can be accomplished. That situation can then serve as a *cue* to remind us of the earlier intention (i.e., the prospective component). In the buying milk example, both the time (after work) and the context (passing the grocery store) can serve to cue my memory for the intention. Thus, there is usually some cue to trigger the prospective component of memory, and once we become aware of this cue, we can search our retrospective memory for the content of our intention (e.g., recalling what I meant to buy at the grocery store). Einstein and McDaniel (1996) call this the "notice-and-search" model of prospective memory: Once we notice a prospective cue, we then search our memory for the content of our plan. Some researchers restrict the term *prospective memory* to the prospective component (e.g., Graf & Uttl, 2001), but both aspects are vital for successful completion of future plans, including therapeutic homework and other intentions arising from therapy sessions.

Experientially, this distinction between the intention and the content of the plan is familiar in that we can experience forgetting either the intention cue or the content of our future plans independently. For example, when a client forgets to complete her homework assignment, she may remember what that assignment was when the therapist asks her, indicating recall of the retrospective component of the plan, such as the client who exclaimed on entering the office, "I totally forgot that I was going to write three positive things every day until I walked into the waiting room and saw the poster" (a list of positive parenting techniques). The therapist sent home a copy of the poster that the client put on her bathroom door as a reminder to complete the assignment. Unfortunately, examples such as this may reinforce a sense that the client is resistant rather than simply forgetting unless the therapist understands prospective memory processes. Conversely, we may also recall that we meant to do something in a particular context, but not remember what it was. For example, when we meet a friend we might remember that we meant to give him a message but not recall what that message was.

Consistent with our subjective experience, research indicates that these two components of prospective memories are distinct. There is clear evidence that different brain activity is associated with prospective and retrospective aspects of a prospective memory task (Leynes, Marsh, Hicks, Allen, & Mayhorn, 2002; West, Herndon, & Crewdson, 2001). Furthermore, prospective and retrospective aspects are influenced by different contextual factors (A.-L. Cohen, West, & Craik, 2001). Response to prospective cues (prospective component) is enhanced by the distinctiveness of the cues, whereas the accuracy of prospective action (retrospective component) is enhanced when the cue and action are semantically related (e.g., see "car"—say "truck" vs. see "car"—say "tree"; Cohen et al., 2001; Marsh et al., 2003). As explained next, cue distinctiveness attracts our attention, facilitating recollection of a prospective plan. The relationship between a cue and the intended action influences how easily the intended action is retrieved, but does not influence whether or not we notice the cue.

Our memory for the content of intended plans (retrospective component) is usually better than our success at noticing the presence of the intention cue (prospective component; Guynn, McDaniel, & Einstein, 1998; Schaefer, Kozak, & Sagness, 1998). For example, Schaefer et al., (1998) asked participants to complete five simple tasks (e.g., sharpen a pencil, place an envelope on the desk, etc.) after they had finished 30 minutes of a visual search task (like "Where's Waldo?" activities). Following completion (or noncompletion) of the prospective memory tasks, participants were given a questionnaire asking about the prospective tasks. Participants remembered more about the tasks on the questionnaire than their performance (i.e., actually doing the tasks) had indicated. Similarly, when a psychotherapist asks clients to report on their homework plan of the previous week, clients often remember what that plan was even if they have forgotten to act on it. This superior performance for the retrospective component is not surprising because we must perform the prospective component of a task without specific instruction to search our memory, whereas memory searches generally involve such a direction. In prospective memory situations, something must alert us to the significance of the occasion (i.e., that conditions are now right to complete our earlier intention), before we are even aware that we should look for something in our memory. To make this even harder, we must do this while engaging in some other activity or thought.

Intention Superiority

Despite the evidence that prospective and retrospective aspects of remembering to do future actions are distinct, it appears that an intention places information about the planned action in a special status in memory. Specifically, when we have a particular intention (a plan to do something in the future), memory for material related to that planned action is more easily activated in memory (see chapter 3), an effect known as "intention superiority" (Goschke & Kuhl, 1993; Marsh, Hicks, & Bink, 1998; Marsh, Hicks, & Bryan, 1999). This memory benefit for planned actions thus improves the success of our subsequent recall of these actions. That is, we are more likely to notice and respond to environmental cues related to those actions. This is likely related to the benefits of goal setting as outlined in chapter 2. The initial studies showing intention superiority had participants memorize simple action scripts, such as procedures for making coffee or setting a table. They were then told which one of the scripts they would be asked to perform later. Participants made memory judgments (recognition or lexical decision) for words that were included in all of the memorized scripts plus other nonstudied words (Goschke & Kuhl, 1993; Marsh, Hicks, & Bink, 1998). Results consistently showed that decision times were faster for words used in the scripts participants intended to perform than for words used in the scripts which they had no intention to perform. Similarly, when memory was tested midway through performing one of the action scripts (i.e., a partially completed intention), decision times were faster for words describing that script. Conversely, when memory was tested after the action script had been completed, decision times were slower for words describing the completed script than for words describing the other memorized script. When the action intention was canceled prior to completion (e.g., "I forgot to bring the props, so you won't be doing the action"), reaction times were also slowed, similar to the effect of action completion (Marsh et al., 1999). The intention superiority effect has now also been replicated in several other task contexts, with material such as simple words or phrases rather than action scripts describing the intention (Leynes et al., 2002; Marsh, Hicks, & Watson, 2002; Maylor, Darby, & Della Sala, 2000). These studies suggest that setting ourselves a goal to complete in the future increases the accessibility of that action in our memories, but that once the goal is completed or canceled, the memory for that action temporarily becomes less accessible. Thus, if we design cues that are related to the action in some way, we take advantage of this intention superiority because our memory for the related material (i.e., the cue) will have privileged access in memory. For example, intention superiority is likely partly responsible for the benefits of forming "implementation intentions" (Gollwitzer, 1999; Gollwitzer, Fujita, & Oettingen, 2004). This involves planning specific actions in specific situations, such as a dieter planning to say, "no thanks" when a hostess offers him a rich dessert, rather than leaving an intention more general (e.g., to eat less). The specific situation can provide a prospective cue, increasing the likelihood of successfully following intentions. In therapy, a father who lacked assertiveness with his children decided to consistently confront his daughter when she did not do her assigned household tasks (perhaps also a prospective memory failure). He used the intention superiority effect by developing an intention to check that his daughter did her chores. He provided himself a cue by putting a colorful sticky note on his mirror so he would notice it when he changed after work. The writing on the note ("Check Zoe's chores") provided the cue to the content or the retrospective component of the homework.

INFLUENCES ON PROSPECTIVE
MEMORY SUCCESS

Several factors are observed to influence prospective memory performance, including how much self-initiated processing is necessary to recall the intended task, the nature of the activity that is occurring when the prospective intention should be recalled, the importance of the intention, and age. Some of these factors are personal, such as age and motivation (importance), and some are contextual, such as the cue to signal the prospective intention and the nature of the ongoing activity (Brandimonte &

Passolunghi, 1994). Attending to these factors in psychotherapy sessions will increase both the success of change goals and the client's self-confidence and self-efficacy beliefs.

Cues

One of the factors that distinguishes prospective memory from retrospective memory is the absence of specific directions to search memory (Graf & Uttl, 2001). Instead, some aspect of the external or internal environment must jog a person's memory about the intention. This aspect of the environment is known as the *cue*, and the nature of the prospective cue distinguishes different types of prospective memory tasks, such as event-based, time-based, or activity-based tasks (e.g., Einstein & McDaniel, 1996; Maylor, 1996). The difference between these tasks is the nature of the prospective cue (events, time, or activity). Cues vary in their attentional demands and in how much self-initiated processing is necessary. Tasks that require more self-initiated cuing, such as those that are time-based (e.g., take medication at 9 o'clock; take eggs off stove in 6 minutes) or habitual (e.g., take medication every day at 9), are harder than tasks with some type of environmental cuing, such as event-based tasks (Maylor, 1996). The least demanding cues are external, such as concrete objects (e.g., the grocery store as a cue to remind you to buy milk on the way home from work, a telephone to remind you to make a doctor's appointment; known as event-based cuing), situations (e.g., arriving home from work as a cue to remind you to exercise), or activities (e.g., arguing with your spouse as a cue to remind you to paraphrase his statements). Distinctive events can capture attention (Cockburn, 1996; McDaniel, Robinson-Riegler, & Einstein, 1998), and the more likely a cue is to capture attention, the more successful it is at triggering successful prospective recall (Einstein, McDaniel, Manzi, Cochran, & Baker, 2000; Marsh, Hicks, & Hancock, 2000; McDaniel & Einstein, 2000). McDaniel and his colleagues (e.g., McDaniel et al., 2004) call this noticing the significance of the prospective cue (or situation), which then alerts us to search our memory for the content of the intention.

A common strategy used to improve prospective remembering is to provide oneself with an external aid to facilitate recall at the appropriate time. Typical external aids, such as notes and calendars, are effective concrete cues that are meant to trigger recall of prospective intentions better than internally generated cues. For example, interviews of university students indicate that most of them (97%) routinely use external reminders such as notes, diaries, or placing objects in noticeable places in order to remember their future plans (J. E. Harris, 1982; Marsh, Hicks, & Landau, 1998). Even elementary school-aged children frequently think of using external reminders when they are asked how they remember to do something in the future (Kreutzer, Leonard, & Flavell, 1982). Research also indicates that older adults, who show prospective memory impairment in some circumstances, are able to use external memory aids just as effectively as younger adults (Einstein & McDaniel, 1990). This use of external reminders takes advantage of the relative ease of event-based prospective tasks versus other kinds: When we have an external cue to the prospective situation (i.e., the event), prospective memory performance is better than when we must initiate the activity on our own (e.g., time-based tasks). Providing ourselves with an external reminder, such as writing appointments on a calendar, thus shifts time-based tasks into event-based ones.

The improvement in prospective memory with external cues is greatest when the cue is distinctive in some way, thereby capturing our attention in the midst of ongoing activity (Uttl & Graf, 2000). For example, the invention of the brightly colored sticky note has greatly assisted psychotherapists who regularly assign homework. This distinction can be perceptual intensity, such as color, loudness, or strong odor, or it can be conceptual, such as surprising or bizarre ideas. Having a couple place a tape recorder on the table can become a cue to initiate a communication homework assignment. Turning it on can further cue them to use the skills taught in sessions rather than regressing into old fight patterns. (Of course, remembering to get the recorder out, getting tapes, and putting it on the table are also all prospective tasks and may need to be addressed when giving ISAs.) The Ericksonian strategy of assigning bizarre rituals, such as a couple rehanging all the paintings and pictures in their home, is not only a joint task, but the changes due to altered pictures in each room become environmental cues to use newly developed skills. Similarly, the paradoxical strategy of assigning more of the symptom connects the cue (the symptom) and the prospective task (do the symptom more), educating the client about their control over the symptom. Perceptually distinctive cues are helpful in most situations (West & Craik, 2001), but conceptual distinctiveness depends on the relationship between the cue and the activity that is occurring when the cue appears. Similarly, a better perceptual match between prospective cues at encoding (when the plan is formulated) and retrieval (when the plan is enacted) improves prospective noticing (A.-L. Cohen et al., 2001). For example, if instructions are given in verbal form (e.g., "tree"), and cues are then given in pictorial form (e.g., a line drawing of a tree), performance is worse than if both the instructions and the cues are given in the same format (verbal or pictoral). Early research indicated that conceptual cues (e.g., press the button if a word names a plant) were more effective than perceptual cues (e.g., press the button if a word appears in green; McDaniel et al., 1998), but more recent research contradicts this impression (West & Craik, 2001). Rather, the relationship of a prospective cue and the ongoing activity (i.e., what you are doing when you need to re-call the future intention) are relevant to conceptual, but not perceptual, cues. Distinctive perceptual cues, such as vividly colored words or notes, seem to be effective regardless of current activity, likely because they cap-ture a person's attention long enough for them to realize the significance of the cue (i.e., that it signals they are to do something; McDaniel & Ein-stein, 2000). Conceptual cues, on the other hand, show better prospective performance when they occur in the context of a conceptual task. For ex-ample, people are more likely to notice that a word is a plant (conceptual cue) if they are rating how pleasant words are (a conceptual task), than if they are indicating whether words begin with a vowel or a consonant (a perceptual task).

How the cue is related to the intention itself can also influence prospec-tive remembering. If the association between the cue and the planned ac-tion is especially strong (e.g., see spaghetti—select sauce; see chapter 3), noticing the cue may elicit retrieval of the planned action automatically, a process McDaniel, Einstein, and their colleagues (McDaniel et al., 2004) call "reflexive-associative retrieval." For example, a mother wanted to im-prove the level of contact between herself and her recently adopted five-year-old daughter. Together in a play therapy session, they drew three similar pictures of a mom and girl hugging. The pictures were placed in the house and every time one of them looked at a picture, they were to do the action if the other was present. In this case, the cue was a reminder of both the intention and the content of the planned action. These kinds of cues are particularly important with young children, the elderly, and any-one who has difficulty with prospective remembering. Child therapy writ-ings are filled with examples of creatively cuing plans so as to access re-flexive-associative retrieval. When there is little relationship between a prospective cue and planned action, we must consciously notice the cue and then initiate a search of our memory. These two retrieval processes are similar to the distinction between direct and intentional retrieval discussed with respect to autobiographical memory (chapter 4). In the reflexive-associative case, we may accomplish a future intention without much awareness because the cue automatically elicits the planned action. However, in the case of low cue–action association, a person must deliberately and often effortfully notice prospective cues in order to complete prospective intentions. For example, a strong association between cue and action, such as seeing a child's report card, cues a parent to have a conversation with the child about effort. This makes prospective intentions easier to complete than low associations, such as passing a familiar location on the way home from work (the cue) and remembering to go to the grocery store instead of taking the usual route home. Strategies that involve strengthening a learned association between a cue and action can also influence the ease of prospective memory. For instance, Guynn et al. (1998) observed that reminding participants of the association between prospective cues and action (e.g., when you see a green X, press the button) improved prospective memory performance more than reminding them to focus on the cue alone (e.g., remember to look for a green X). Clinicians can assist their clients by consistently providing this cue–action connection.

Case Illustration:

Melinda had already unsuccessfully attempted many of the assignments in a manualized protocol (e.g., relaxation, cognitive self-talk to counter identified dysfunctional thinking, self-soothing imagery). Even when she could remember her homework or was reminded of it by her husband, she felt so overwhelmed by her symptoms that she rarely completed her assignments. Consequently the therapist, with Melinda's assistance, attempted to construct an intervention that would both interrupt the anxiety in session and prompt successful practice between sessions. Given the strength of her kinesthetic experience of anxiety and panic, a brief but distinct body work technique (from bioenergetic therapy), which included both a physical posture and a breathing exercise, was chosen. The hypothesis was that using an exercise that produced kinesthetic sensations would assist with cuing, as it would be a partial match cue. The therapist had the client practice the exercise several times in the session and each time the client practiced, her distress decreased by several subjective units of distress (SUDs). Given her prior inability to remember either the prospective or retrospective components of homework, Melinda spent some time with her therapist developing potential cues. As the exercise was quite unusual for her, Melinda predicted that if she could remember that she was supposed to do something, she would easily remember what it was. She also predicted that because it was a physical assignment, she would be able to carry it out despite her mental confusion. The decision was to use a straightforward time cue that would be signaled by her wrist watch alarm and which would require no additional effort from her. During the next week, she carried out her assignment three out of every four times her alarm sounded. She reported that having something that was "small but strong" was a key to her success.

The next step was to connect this homework to a more personal event, rather than to the time/event cue. The next assignment was to carry out the physical exercise whenever her experience of anxiety reached a certain threshold (in this case, she used the distinct symptom of heart fluttering as a cue). The therapist connected the cue to the action ("When you feel the sensation in your chest which you describe as butterfly wings, I want you to do the exercise"), and had her rehearse the instruction by imagining the cue and then seeing herself do the exercise. A week later, the client reported she had managed to do the exercise approximately 50% of the occasions when she felt the symptom (event). Although this was not a high completion rate, it seemed to make a remarkable difference to her sense of self-regulation and self-efficacy. Concurrent with this homework, Melinda reported a significant reduction in her other symptoms and felt ready to start some of the exercises assigned in her group.

Ongoing Activity

A second contextual influence on prospective memory is the nature of the activity that we are doing at the time when we should do the intended action (referred to in research as the "ongoing activity"). This is the context in which people must become aware of the prospective cue or situation. For example, a shy young musician wanted to make friends and meet young women. He was often in bars and other venues where there were many people of his age; however, he was typically busy playing music in loud and crowded bars, and the people he wished to meet were usually in groups, which raised his fears of embarrassment. In devising a homework assignment, this situation called for a cue that would be strong enough for him to notice and facilitate a new action (contact) rather than the old one (thinking about contact with his eyes on his drum set). In this case, the prospective task was to begin with making eye contact with young women at his band's performances and giving them a smile or nod. The cue was a yellow smiley face, which he discreetly attached to his drum set. Whenever he looked at it, he was to look at the crowd until he made eye contact with someone and smiled or nodded at that person.

Ongoing activities that require attention make prospective memory tasks more difficult, thus impairing their performance. For example, activities that involve planning or monitoring of ongoing thoughts or actions (e.g., solving a problem, making a decision, or playing a musical instrument) interfere with prospective memory, whereas less effortful concurrent tasks such as reciting the alphabet or observing pictures do not interfere with prospective memory (Marsh, Hancock, & Hicks, 2002; Marsh & Hicks, 1998). In the case of strong associations between a cue and action (reflexive-associative retrieval), the attentional demands of an ongoing task may have relatively little effect on the success of prospective intentions (McDaniel et al., 2004), but attentional demands have a large effect on more effortful prospective remembering. For instance, while writing this chapter, the author was cooking eggs, which needed to be monitored for boiling and then removed from the stove a few minutes later. Writing is usually an effortful, attention-demanding activity, and thus, predictably, the eggs were forgotten until well after the time intended. The moral of this example is that time-sensitive activities should not be planned to occur simultaneously with other effortful activities, and therapists must be sensitive to the context in which their clients must remember and carry out ISAs. For example, giving a couple a homework assignment to trade compliments each night after supper in the middle of their children's sport seasons or assigning daily workbook activities to a student at exam time generally is not successful.

For some types of prospective cues, the relationship between the ongoing activity and the prospective cue can also influence prospective performance. Specifically, when the processes necessary for recognizing the prospective cue are similar to the processes we are using in the ongoing task, prospective performance is better (Marsh et al., 2003; Maylor, 1998; Meier & Graf, 2000). This is especially the case for semantic cues (Brunfaut, Vanoverberghe, & d'Ydewalle, 2000; West & Craik, 2001) because the meaning of a cue is not usually processed when our attention is on perceptual features of the environment. For example, when the prospective task is to respond whenever an animal word (e.g., *horse, cat*) appears, our prospective performance is worse when we are indicating the color of words than when we are processing the meaning of words (Marsh, Hancock, & Hicks, 2002). In everyday experiences, this may mean that if our future intention is to take a cake out of the oven at a particular time, we may recall this better if we are preparing dinner than if we are writing a letter at the relevant time. Similarly, if a client's prospective intention is to initiate a particular conversation, he would remember to do so better if his activity at the time he intended this action were social (i.e., meeting with others) than if his activity was physical (e.g., sports). If a father's goal is to improve his relationship with his son, he is more likely to remember when he is in either his son's or other children's presence.

Case Illustration:

Given her prior difficulty in completion, Melinda, together with the therapist, carefully constructed each homework assignment related to the previously effective cognitive behavioral treatment of her anxiety. For example, a cognitive self-disputing exercise to deal with her catastrophic thinking was to be done after her son had gone to sleep and the house was quiet. It was cued by a stylized picture of two people arguing hanging on the door of her son's bedroom where she would see it after putting him to bed. In addition, the therapist had her develop a visual image of intention in the session that included her visualizing two "selves" arguing. While Melinda's attention continued to be periodically captured by her emotional and physical experiences, she gradually increased the completion rate of all assignments. The therapist was careful to keep the number of assignments low and provide repetition of each assignment and of Melinda's intentions in each session.

Once her experience of symptoms had decreased significantly, Melinda decided that she could now return to a group setting and be successful. She had appreciated the support of the other group members and had missed this aspect of the treatment. Earlier she had experienced the stories of other group members as overwhelming and triggering of her symptoms. She reported after returning to the group that she was able to now handle this information.

Rehearsal

As with retrospective memory, how firmly the intention is established in memory also influences prospective memory success. Rehearsal of a prospective intention at the time it is formed more firmly establishes an intention in memory. Similarly, subsequent rehearsal of an intention, such as a self-reminder or a partial-match cue, also improves prospective memory success (McDaniel et al., 1998; R. S. Taylor, Marsh, Hicks, & Hancock, 2004). Rehearsal can also strengthen the association between a prospective cue and the intended action (Guynn et al., 1998). Reminders that stress the association between a cue and intended action result in better performance, whereas reminders of the cue alone do not (Guynn et al., 1998).

Age

Older adults show prospective memory performance that is equal to that of younger people under some conditions (e.g., K. E. Cherry & LeCompte, 1999; Moscovitch, 1982), possibly because they make efficient use of external memory aids (Dixon, de Frias, & Backman, 2001; Einstein &

McDaniel, 1990). However, in the laboratory, elders are consistently worse at prospective memory tasks (Rendell & Thompson, 1999). It can be concluded that the processes that underlie prospective memory—attention and retrospective memory—likely work somewhat less efficiently as we age. The main problem for older adults is the prospective component, that is, noticing the prospective cues when they occur (A.-L. Cohen et al., 2003; A.-L. Cohen et al., 2001). This results in older adults forgetting to complete prospective intentions (West & Craik, 2001), even though when asked, they can recall what that intention was. Thus the distinctiveness of the prospective cue, and the match between ongoing processing and cue, are especially important for older adults (A.-L. Cohen et al., 2001). For example, an elderly veteran from World War II was referred for some intrusive distressing memories of the past which he experienced as he tried to go to sleep, resulting in insomnia. As a part of a treatment plan, he was assigned a night-time distraction exercise that worked when he used it, but he could not seem to remember it until after experiencing the distressing images and by then it was too late. After examining in some depth his night-time routine, the following cue was added to this prospective memory task: He routinely looked at a framed display of his medals just prior to climbing into bed. Because the distraction exercise involved imagining relaxing scenes of water, he framed a photo that reminded him of the exercise and hung it next to his medals. This distinctive cue with direct connection to his assignment resulted in better sleep for the client. Under conditions that encourage reflexive-associative retrieval (i.e., high association between cue and intended action), older adults appear to have equal prospective memory performance as young adults (K. E. Cherry & LeCompte, 1999), further suggesting that the difficulty for older adults is attention. When a prospective intention is such that little attention is required for its completion, older adults have no difficulty with the task.

Importance of the Intention

Another factor that influences prospective remembering is the importance of the intention to the individual. In their study of self-generated plans, Marsh, Hicks, and Landau (1998) noted a significant difference in the importance rating assigned to completed and uncompleted plans: Plans that were subsequently completed had been rated as more important the previous week (see also Andrzejewski, Moore, Corvette, & Herrmann, 1991; Cicogna & Nigro, 1998). However, Kliegel, Martin, McDaniel, and Einstein (2001) found that the importance of an intention influences performance only for time-based tasks, at least in the laboratory. Event-based tasks were unaffected by whether the action was considered important or not. For prospective intentions that require more self-initiation, increased motivation may lead the person to remind himself of the task more frequently (e.g., review their intention), monitor the situation for appropriate conditions (e.g., check the time), or do other things that increase the likelihood of remembering.

Recent data from our laboratory indicate that importance may also be influenced by who initiated the prospective intention. Desjarlais (2002) observed that prospective tasks that students generated themselves were rated as less important than tasks that had been assigned them by someone else. This difference was even observed for relatively trivial tasks that had been assigned by the experimenter, such as studying word lists for a follow-up test in the lab or mailing a completed questionnaire to the experimenter. We speculated that this may be because there are social consequences for failing to complete tasks assigned by someone else, whereas failure in self-generated plans usually affects only the persons themselves. However, this is an important finding for therapists, in that homework assignments are given by someone other than the client himself and thus prospective memory recall may be greater for therapeutic homework assignments than for clients' independent resolutions.

Other evidence suggests that more difficult prospective memory tasks may be accorded more importance. Nigro and Cicogna (2000) observed that participants who had a longer delay between a prospective instruction (two weeks) rated the prospective task as more important than participants who had a shorter delay (two days), even though the intention was the same for the two conditions (to give the experimenter a message when they returned to the lab).

Thus, the importance of a future intention does influence performance, but only when contextual factors such as distinctive cues or recency of memory do not have an effect. As most therapeutic homework assignments are considered important, and have intermediate delays between encoding and retrieval, this factor will be most significant to homework completion when assigned tasks are not cued by external events.

To summarize, research on the influences of prospective memory indicates that prospective remembering is improved by (a) cuing the intended future action with an environmental event that is distinctive enough to be noticed in the future situation, (b) designing cues with strong associations with the intended action to promote reflexive-associative retrieval, (c) planning the future action for times when we are not doing something that is attentionally effortful, and (d) if external cues are not possible, ensuring that the goal is important enough to prompt monitoring or frequent self-reminding. In assigning homework tasks, therapists seldom consider these elements of prospective remembering. Given that the hardest aspect of remembering to complete a future intention is recalling that we had an intention in the first place, designing appropriate prospective cues to signal the intention seems most important. Considering the context in which homework assignments are to be performed would likely significantly improve homework completion, which likely would lead to therapeutic effectiveness.

IMPLICATIONS FOR PSYCHOTHERAPY

Psychotherapeutic homework is observed to be a crucial component of therapeutic treatment (Beyebach, Morejon, Palenzuela, & Rodriguez-Arias, 1996; Burns & Nolen-Hoeksema, 1992; Burns & Spangler, 2000; Carr, 1997; Kazantzis & Lampropoulos, 2002; Openshaw, 1998). Clinical research indicates that both the use of homework (Burns & Auerback, 1992; Burns & Nolen-Hoeksema, 1992; Burns & Spangler, 2000; Kazantzis, 2000; Kazantzis et al., 2000; Neimeyer & Feixas, 1990; Startup & Edmonds, 1994) and completing the assignments (Edelman & Chambless, 1995; Kazantzis & Lampropoulos, 2002; Leung & Heimberg, 1996; Persons, Burns, & Perloff, 1988; S. E. Taylor, 1996) increases the efficacy of psychotherapy. The purpose of homework or ISAs is usually to help clients practice a change they wish to make or to increase their sense of self-efficacy. It is useful if clients are successful in completing these assignments, so that they don't have to deal with therapy-induced failure experience. Furthermore, psychotherapists often assume that there are motivational reasons for failure to complete homework assignments (e.g., Baumeister & Heatherton, 1996; Strean, 1990). Rather than considering how the task was assigned or accepting a client's report that she forgot an assignment, we view our client as "resistant" or "rebellious" and these attributions can affect our therapeutic alliance and work with this client (e.g., Mahoney, 1991; J. H. Wright & Davis, 1994; Yalom & Bugental, 1997). In addition, as many marital and family therapists have experienced, family members can also make motivational attributions for another's noncompletion of an assignment. This can seriously affect the quality of the attachment between partners or among family members. A frequently heard statement that illustrates this is, "If he really cared, he would have done the assignment." Therapists could likely assist their clients and the therapy by first considering issues of prospective memory before assuming issues of motivation and personality when homework assignments are not completed. More importantly, therapists should take prospective memory processes into account when constructing and assigning an ISA, so that issues of forgetting and motivation can be distinguished.

Because homework is a prospective memory task, its success can be improved by considering the factors that have been shown to improve prospective memory performance: cues, ongoing activity, and importance. At least under some conditions, a person's motivation is important because personally important intentions are more likely to be successfully completed, especially when there is no environmental cue to serve as a reminder. Alternatively, careful selection of a meaningful and distinctive cue that will serve as a reminder to perform the planned action can improve the chances of successful completion. Care should also be taken to plan future actions for situations that are not likely to occur concurrently with other attentionally demanding events, although, as in the example of the musician earlier in the chapter, sometimes the goal is to insert a change within the context of events which will capture our attention.

Therapists and clients often spend considerable time formulating an intended action plan and give relatively little attention to considering how this plan will be cued in the future or what the client will be engaged in at that time. Prospective memory research suggests that giving some thought to the prospective memory cue for an intended plan, especially by choosing distinct markers to trigger recall of the intended action, will improve completion rates for homework assignments. Several clinical authors have made similar suggestions (e.g., Coon & Gallagher-Thompson, 2002; Hudson & Kendall, 2002; Kazantzis & Lampropoulos, 2002; Tompkins, 2002). Homework assignments are generally not associated with specific cues except when the assignment is intended as a new response to a specific stimulus, usually the symptom that is the target for change (e.g., a self-depreciating thought or a habitual feeling). For example, 40% of the assignments in our study of therapeutic homework were not associated with any cue (Arbuthnott & Arbuthnott, 2004). Thus, it is likely that homework completion rates could be significantly improved by routinely associating homework tasks with a distinctive cue and then having the client rehearse the cue–action association (Guynn et al., 1998). For example, a specific self-talk task could be assigned to be completed whenever the client sees a bouquet of flowers or some other object. Similarly, homework that is associated with a routine activity (i.e., activity-based prospective tasks; Kvavilashvili & Ellis, 1996), such as a conversation among family members to be carried out after the evening meal, may be remembered more consistently than assignments associated with no cues or generic time cues (e.g., in the evening). Distinctive and salient cues are particularly useful for improving prospective memory. Factors that increase distinctiveness include familiarity and information richness. Less familiar concepts are more distinctive, so reframing techniques may be useful in defining conceptual cues (e.g., O'Hanlon & Weiner-Davis, 1989; M. White & Epston, 1990). Pictures contain more information than words, so imaging the intended situation may be beneficial (e.g., Foote, 1996; Lankton & Lankton, 1986).

Therapists should also consider what activities a client is likely to be engaged in at the time a homework action should be taken. Research clearly indicates that prospective memory is particularly poor when one is engaged in an attention-demanding activity, such as complex family or work situations. Thus, therapists and clients should explicitly consider when a homework assignment is to be completed, avoiding times when the client will be otherwise engaged. For example, if a client plans to discuss an important issue with her spouse, she should be advised to plan to do this activity when she and her spouse are not busy, such as during a relaxing evening rather than during a busy time, such as when they arrive home after work. Prediction of events around the time of an intended action may be difficult, however, so this factor should be kept in mind for debriefing a homework assignment or plan that was not successfully completed.

Finding methods to improve the rates of homework completion is important for psychotherapy efficiency (Burns & Auerback, 1992; Burns & Nolen-Hoeksema, 1992; Burns & Spangler, 2000; Neimeyer & Feixas, 1990; Startup & Edmonds, 1994). Prospective memory research provides an avenue for improvement apart from strategies to improve client motivation and decrease resistance to change.

KEY POINTS

- Prospective memory is memory for future actions and involves both prospective (recalling the intention) and retrospective (recalling the planned action) components.

- Factors that improve prospective memory are distinctive cues, rehearsal of prospective intentions, the attentional demands of ongoing activities, and personal factors such as age and motivation.
- Psychotherapeutic homework involves prospective memory, and thus attention to factors that improve prospective remembering when homework tasks are devised and assigned would improve the rates of homework completion.

7

Attention: The Eye of the Mental Hurricane

> *Everyone knows what attention is. It is the taking possession by the mind, in clear and vivid form, of one out of what seem several simultaneous possible objects or trains of thought. . . . It implies withdrawal from some things in order to deal effectively with others.*
> —William James (1890, pp. 381–382)

Attention is the word used to denote what we are currently aware of. The focus of awareness can be external perception (e.g., the sounds of the morning traffic, the sight of the golden leaves on the lawn), internal sensations (e.g., your body posture, pain), or thoughts and emotions. Perhaps the most important feature of attention is that it is limited: We can only be aware of a small portion of the external and internal information that is present to our senses at any one moment. Attention functions both automatically and voluntarily, and many researchers agree that the focus of attention at any given moment is determined by both automatic and voluntary processes working together (e.g., Banbury & Berry, 1997; Waters, McDonald, & Koresko, 1977). Attention influences most cognitive processes that are of interest to psychotherapists. What we notice influences what we think (e.g., attributions and beliefs), do (e.g., action decisions), and remember (e.g., which details of experienced events we recall).

This chapter reviews the findings of how attention functions. The first section discusses attention as a limited cognitive capacity. The second section reviews factors that influence what we notice, including features of perceptual and mental stimuli (e.g., change, stimulus intensity) and features of the mental context, both long-term (e.g., familiarity) and short-term influences (e.g., recency, expectation). The third section discusses mental control—how we intentionally influence our attentional focus (i.e., concentration, goal priorization) and what limits are set on such control (e.g., multitasking).

LIMITED CAPACITY

Attention can be considered the process of concentrating mental effort on a target (i.e., a verb; "Attend to this") or the energy or "stuff" that is concentrated (i.e., a noun; "She pays attention"). However we look at it, probably the most obvious feature of attention is its limited capacity. We are unable to attend to everything that enters our sense organs and thoughts at any one time. The current controversy over cell phone use while driving is about this limitation. When both driving conditions and the conversation we're having are relatively easy, we have little trouble combining the two activities. However, if the driving becomes effortful, such as with a sudden rainstorm or an accident, or the phone conversation becomes difficult, such as reaching a critical point in an important negotiation or an argument with a loved one, problems arise because we can't adequately attend to both tasks at once (e.g., Strayer & Johnson, 2001). Similarly, carrying on a casual family conversation with the television or radio on can work; however, if the content of the conversation becomes conflictual and intense, those same external sources of stimuli are more likely to interfere. In other words, the two activities interfere with each other because they compete for attentional resources. For therapists, this means that we can't simultaneously plan a dinner party while we work with a client, and we are even limited in how much of what the client presents we can focus on at a time (e.g., body language, word use, and content of conversation). Even with practice at expanding our awareness, such as with meditation, our capacity remains limited. Psychotherapists are often trained to work around this limitation by cycling our observations systematically across a variety of phenomena in the therapy process (e.g., language, nonverbal behavior, potential missing information, introducing a variety of skills to elicit different aspects of the client's experience).

This capacity limitation is evident both in what we are aware of at any given moment and in what we can keep in mind for a second or two. A common mnemonic for the immediate limit is 7 ± 2 items (G. A. Miller, 1956), but a more realistic limit would be 4 ± 1 unrelated items that can be kept in mind at once (Broadbent, 1958; Trick & Pylyshyn, 1993). Limited attentional ability is also sometimes referred to as "working memory capacity." There is considerable controversy over whether attention and working memory are the same resource (Cowan, 1995; Miyake & Shah, 1999), but for our purposes as therapists, the two can be considered synonymous.

Although the limitation that is evident with attention is often discussed using an energy metaphor, the limitation is more likely due to particular cognitive processes such as response selection or planning (Allport, 1989; Baddeley, 1986; Duncan, 1994; McCann & Johnson, 1992; Pashler, 1992). Attention can also be viewed as selective control of which bits of sensory information get encoded into memory, which pieces of information receive further processing, and which motor response is executed (Kintsch, Healy, Regarty, Pennington, & Salthouse, 1999). Whatever its basis, attention is vitally important for most other cognitive processes, including perception and memory. With respect to perception, for example, attention seems to be necessary to bind together various features such as shape and color to form our mental representation of objects (Treisman, 1992; Treisman & Gelade, 1980). Similarly, attention during both initial encoding of material and its retrieval significantly improves memory for the material (Cowan, 1995). Attention results in better encoding of both physical features and *semantic* (meaning) features (Broadbent, 1958; E. C. Cherry, 1953; Cowan, Lichty, & Grove, 1990; Moray, 1959; Treisman, 1964).

For example, when a couple attended therapy to improve their intimacy (both emotional and sexual), it became clear from the first session that the quality of attention was a major factor. The husband frequently complained that he "just wasn't a factor" in spite of his wife's insistence that she loved him. She had recently been elected to political office and often was interrupted by her cellular phone in the midst of family events and had to leave to attend to some crisis. He accused her of not caring, and she would counterattack by accusing him of not understanding or of considering his ambitions above hers. Much of the therapy was centered around the quality with which they attended to one another when they were together (he would expect interruption and so would not initiate anything, and she was overwhelmed by the myriad details required by her office). Simple actions (e.g., shutting off the phone for thirty minutes) and exercises such as looking at each other but not speaking for one minute assisted them in shifting their attention.

Given this limited capacity and the importance of attention for cognitive effectiveness, attention must be focused. Considerable research indicates that we are capable of both single and dual focuses of attention, but the latter is much more difficult. We can improve our ability to divide attention with practice, but such practice must be specific to the tasks being conducted jointly (e.g., W. Schneider & Shiffrin, 1977). The focus of attention can be set both automatically (captured) and voluntarily (controlled); the next two sections review research on each of these mechanisms.

WHAT WE NOTICE: ATTENTIONAL CAPTURE

When we first meet a new client, we notice certain characteristics of the person more than others. Some of what we notice is influenced by what we have learned to assess in our training. Some clinicians note a client's dress and grooming, as these may be the first descriptions to be included in a report. Others note the client's linguistic style, their vocabulary, and the completeness and coherence of their expressions (e.g., Bandler & Grinder, 1975). Still others (e.g., psychodynamic therapists) pay less attention to these characteristics, focusing instead on the details of the client's early life history. Most notice whether the client is friendly, timid, or belligerent because these communication styles impact directly on the comfort of the therapist, as well as on the therapist's transactional choices with the client. Similarly, most notice if the client has a distinct scent, is unusually large or small, or has any unusual characteristic. Each aspect that we are initially aware of strongly influences our diagnosis or thoughts about the client's problem and needs. Moreover, the aspects that we notice will significantly influence both the mental representation we build of the person and the details about them we subsequently remember. These early attentional choices also influence what we subsequently notice about the client, because we are more easily aware of characteristics that are consistent with our early impression than characteristics that contradict that impression, even if both types of characteristics are equally present (e.g., Posner & Snyder, 1975; see also discussion of *confirmation bias* in chapter 9).

Attention operates automatically, or is captured, a good deal of the time, whether we are trying to direct it or not. When attention is captured by external stimuli, this is known as an *orienting response*, and the features that result in such orienting are well known (Sokolov, 1963; Waters et al., 1977). For example, many child therapists will have their play therapy toys and equipment in closed rolling cabinets so their young clients do not orient to these novel stimuli until the therapist is ready to engage them in play (a concept that those who use power point presentations have often not yet developed). Noting features such as the client's size, odor, or dramatic social style represents an orienting response. Attention is also influenced by contextual factors in a manner similar to the priming of memory retrieval (discussed in chapter 3). Noticing characteristics that we are trained to consider reflects this mechanism. Therapists are trained to orient to and comment on observations (e.g., an odor of alcohol, acne) that would be socially inappropriate in other contexts.

Orienting Response: Sensory Factors That Capture Attention

Research indicates that orienting responses are elicited, in humans and other animals, by new stimuli, when the physical properties of repeating stimuli change, or when stimuli significant to an individual are presented (Cowan, 1995; Ohman, 1979; Sokolov, 1963). First, our senses are tuned to detect changes in the environment, as this would most likely have survival implications in the evolutionary context. Thus, any input that either begins or ends abruptly captures our attention, at least momentarily. This is true of all senses. The sudden appearance of a light, or a change in the color of an object, draws our attention to vision (which is why television and movie displays are so hypnotic). Sudden noises such as dogs barking, telephones ringing, or cars skidding similarly draw our attention to audition. And a sudden stab of pain or change in temperature draws our attention to our kinesthetic sense. The corollary to this aspect of our attention is that we *habituate* to any stimulus that is present for a length of time and will thus cease to notice it (Cowan, 1988; Kraut & Smothergill, 1978; Sokolov, 1963; Waters et al., 1977). If we live on a busy street, we will stop "hearing" (i.e., noticing) the sound of cars, despite the continued presence of traffic. This orienting/habituation operation of attention is used in the treatment of pain, tinnitus, or other chronic conditions (e.g., Erickson et al., 1976; O'Hanlon & Hexum, 1990) and in desensitization or exposure-based procedures used to treat phobias (e.g., Wolpe, 1997).

Subtle changes are less likely to attract our attention, and so large changes may occur without our notice, provided the incremental differences from one moment to the next are small. This is the "frog in hot water" effect—the temperature of the water in which a frog is sitting can increase to the boiling point without the frog noticing. Less distressing but common examples are the stories of high school and university students who, on learning about attentional principles, begin to move their instructor's desk one inch every day and can move it several feet before the change is noticed. As Ornstein (1991) notes, this is why we are concerned with some unhealthy changes in our environment, such as infectious epidemics or tainted water scandals, but not others, such as air pollution. In the case of tainted water, people experience becoming sick suddenly, and so they notice the change in their state. However, with air pollution, although the health consequences may be even greater (e.g., asthma and other chronic respiratory diseases), the change from one day to the next is small and thus is not noticed. (Visitors to a polluted area are much more likely to notice the effects of air pollution because for them this is an abrupt change.) In psychotherapy, it is sometimes necessary to draw a client's attention to a specific problem if it has arisen slowly. For example, many victims of domestic abuse seem less aware of the dangerous nature of their situation than is appropriate. Therapists notice the danger for the client because they are not habituated to the client's conditions of abuse and violence. Therapists are thus in a position to alert their clients to the danger by drawing attention to it, perhaps by labeling the situation dramatically (e.g., rape, potential murder), thereby verbally eliciting an orienting response from the client. Of course, this can also have a detrimental effect as the client's attention can then be captured by the dramatic labeling and result in an overreaction. This underscores a theme in this book: Therapists need to be thoughtful and cautious in their choice of language as it influences our clients in major ways.

To summarize, intense, new, and changing stimuli all attract our attention automatically. In the interpersonal context that is usually the focus of psychotherapy issues, the elements of perceptual intensity and change also apply to people. People who speak loudly, gesture largely, or move abruptly all represent intense or frequently changing stimuli, and thus capture the attention of those around them. Similarly, unpredictable individuals who change their presentation from moment to moment are also more likely to be noticed. Many techniques in psychotherapy are new to clients and use both intensity and changing stimuli to take advantage of this orienting response. For example, many of the techniques described in the prospective memory chapter (chapter 6) are designed to attract the client's attention (e.g., brightly colored sticky notes, watch alarms).

Case Illustration:

Angela was twenty-one and living with her father. She had lived with both parents since their separation four years ago. She finished high school at eighteen, was unemployed for two years, and then worked part-time for a security

agency doing night patrols of industrial buildings. She was referred by her fa-
ther, who described her as a bright young woman but who was so "painfully
shy" she could not seem to find any path in her life. She confirmed his descrip-
tion, further revealing that she felt high anxiety and distress whenever in the
presence of anyone she didn't know well. She worried constantly that others
were watching and judging her, and she had been doing so for many years. In
gathering history, she revealed that she had been the target of consistent bully-
ing and humiliation during both elementary and high school years. In her
early years, her shyness and being moderately overweight were the targets of
other students who regularly embarrassed her. In high school, she experienced
a serious acne problem and again, this made her a target for bullying. Her shy-
ness and sensitivity made responding "not an option."

Although obviously nervous at the first session, Angela presented as a
thoughtful and articulate young woman. Her symptoms of self-consciousness
were particularly noticeable. She seemed to think for some time before an-
swering questions and moved awkwardly (e.g., her arms were sometimes out of
synchrony with her legs when she walked; no eye contact, frequent blushing).
She had never had a date although she had been asked out recently and re-
fused. In fact, this was one of the precipitating incidents that led her to accept-
ing her father's suggestion to attend therapy. "I'd like to have a boyfriend but I
knew I was in trouble when I couldn't even go out with someone who I liked."
She described a stable but distant relationship with both parents ("They care
but they were so busy fighting they just didn't pay attention"). Her father had
always been critical of most things (e.g., her schoolwork, appearance, and
performance in music), and her mother had been preoccupied with a chronic
illness. Her older brother was a source of support for her and although he no
longer lived in the same city, they spoke on the phone twice a week.

Angela's goals for therapy were to be able to manage her feelings so she
could initiate some friendships, date, and go to technical school so "I don't
have to face a lifetime of poverty and living at home." Early in therapy it be-
came clear that one of the major constraints to any action was that her think-
ing capacity was overloaded with details. Whenever she considered attending
a social event or going to register at the technical school, she was over-
whelmed with fantasies about others ("What will they think?"), concerns
about her appearance, memories of being humiliated by others, and thoughts
and feelings about being a failure ("All my classmates have jobs or are going
to school"). Due to the intensity of her distress, she oriented to and was cap-
tured by her internal state, leaving no capacity for the relatively simple tasks of
meeting and eliciting information from others and using simple social skills
such as making small talk, smiling, or making eye contact.

Given her history, there were opportunities to use either past- or present-
oriented therapies to help her break the pattern of being so caught in her inter-
nal state of distress that she could neither focus on nor take action in a social

*context. A dynamic therapist may have her do a self-soothing exercise with an
early scene of bullying in order to settle herself. An experiential therapist may
have her develop a deeper awareness by having her attend to the physical sensations of her symptoms of distress without evaluating them. A cognitive behavioral therapist may teach her relaxation skills or have her actively dispute her
beliefs in relation to her distress. The purpose of these techniques is to reduce
some of the symptoms, so that she is not captured by her internal experience and
has more capacity to successfully attend to what is happening outside herself. In
Angela's case, the technique of relaxation training had not been successful ("It
was bad. It simply gave me more time to harass myself"). On the other hand, a
focusing technique in which she simply let herself experience her symptoms and
accept them elicited a sense of calming and increasing confidence.*

Memory Factors That Influence Attention:
Recency, Expectation, and Familiarity

As we discussed in chapter 3, the associative nature of our memories
means that some concepts will be more easily accessible than others at any
moment in time. This priming effect also influences attention, as memory
is central to perceptual interpretation. This influence on attention is not
quite as rapid as perceptual orienting effects, however (Neely, 1977). For
example, once we have learned to read, a string of letters such as CAT is
easier to perceive than CTA, and it would thus capture our attention more
easily. Furthermore, once your ideas about felines have been primed, you
will be more likely to notice any information about cats that appears in
your environment for the next little while. Thus, what you have been
thinking of recently influences your attention. In the context of psychotherapy, this means that if you read a report of a client just prior to meeting
them, you will notice characteristics that are mentioned in the report more
readily than ones that are not. For clients, this is the explanation for the
frequent self-diagnoses of conditions that are the subject of currently popular books or for the usefulness of bibliotherapy (assigning reading to our
clients). The effects of recency are relatively short lived because what is
"recent" will change from moment to moment as thoughts move from one
idea to another. This effect can, however, lead to longer-term consequences by establishing expectations.

The mechanism underlying expectation is also priming of the associative memory network. Recency effects are actually a special case of expectation in that if I mention cats at one moment, there is greater likelihood of my discussing aspects related to cats than to something else such

as mountains. Thus, we unconsciously "expect" to perceive cat-related material for a time and will therefore notice such information more quickly than we will unrelated stimuli. Expectation effects, however, are more typically related to long-term associations. This is the source of the influence our prior training has on what we notice. For example, if I have learned that depression is related to negative thinking, I will expect a depressed client to express negative emotions and thoughts rather than positive ones, and will thus notice the negative examples more readily than the positive ones. This is due to the mechanism of priming. Conversely, if I have learned that depression is a reaction to loss, I will notice examples of losses the client has experienced, whether or not those losses are experienced positively (e.g., a desired move) or negatively (e.g., the loss of a friend). This is why therapists of different theoretical schools can notice completely different aspects of a client. This also accounts in part for Rosenhan's (1973) classic finding that sane people are not noticed by mental health professionals once they have been diagnosed as mentally ill.

Familiarity with or special interest in a particular concept will also increase the likelihood that it is noticed (Corteen & Dunn, 1974; Corteen & Wood, 1972; Hirst, 1986; W. A. Johnson & Dark, 1986; Moray, 1959), partly by influencing the speed of perception (MacLeod & Dunbar, 1988). Frequently used concepts, such as our name or interests, receive memory activation more often than other concepts and are more often in a primed state (or have higher baseline activation in the associative memory network). Thus, ideas such as the central principles of our therapeutic theories are highly likely to attract our attention regardless of other contextual factors, such as the recent reading of a report or the client's conception of a problem. Similarly, the effect of familiarity on attention is often a difficulty for clients, in that their problems can represent a familiar interest, which influences their attention, perception, and interpretation of events. This is particularly noticeable when we use therapeutic techniques designed to shift focus from habitual interpretations, such as thought-countering techniques. Clients often experience these methods as extremely difficult, especially at first, due to the automatic priming of attention to habitual perceptions and thoughts. For example, a couple who were assigned to attend to the positive aspects of each other's actions and then report at the next session could not simply report positives without including several examples that fit their less positive expectations of one another ("He did play with the kids every night, but he was very critical of them").

These influences of memory on attention also explain how our attentional tendencies contribute to biases, such as belief or confirmation

biases (see chapters 9 & 10), and increase the unnecessary conflict between therapists loyal to different theoretical modalities. Human behavior
is so complex that many different types of interventions can be useful in
solving problems or improving situations, as research comparing the relative efficacy of different therapeutic interventions has shown (e.g., Chambliss & Ollendick, 2001; Lafferty, Beutler, & Crago, 1989; Landman &
Dawes, 1982; Saunders, 2004; M. L. Smith & Glass, 1977; Wampold,
2001). Thus, therapists of different schools differ in what they notice (and
diagnose) about a client and the client's situation, but it is highly likely
that no therapist apprehends the complete situation due to their attentional
biases. Despite this, all can be useful to the client because changing any
aspect of a problem often results in reconfiguration of the whole situation
(Erickson et al., 1976; O'Hanlon, 1987; Lankton & Lankton, 1986).

To summarize, what is noticed is also influenced by memory factors,
such as the familiarity and recency of a stimulus, and by our expectations.
Thus, it is often true that we see what we expect to see because that is what
our attention is drawn to.

Case Illustration:

*It was clear in this case that Angela carried a belief/expectation that atten-
tion from others was a "bad thing" and was to be avoided at all costs. This was
further reinforced by her current, almost total isolation from anyone but her
family. Her work assignments were given by telephone, and her only contact
with supervisors or coworkers was once a week. Consequently, there were no
recent experiences she could use to counter her expectation. The next task in
therapy was to assist her in keeping her attention on external tasks in a positive
way. She developed a self-statement to ritually repeat, as she systematically
engaged in social interactions of gradually increasing difficulty (attending a
family dinner, going to get a calendar from postsecondary institutions). The
statement was "Some attention from others is necessary to get information; if I
receive negative attention, I will deal with it in the next session; I am courageous to do this." This shift of attention from a capacity-overwhelming internal state of distress to a ritualized verbal statement worked well enough for her
to complete several easy tasks which were then added to the statement ("and I
just did . . ."). Except for a setback at the hands of a rude family member, she
made steady progress.*

*Another successful technique from this stage of therapy was to engage in a
gestalt awareness technique during times when she was not carrying out tasks.
She was to describe to herself what she noticed perceptually (e.g., the shape
and color of leaves, signs, sounds, etc.). As Angela consciously and consistently shifted her attention from worrying to a neutral or positive element out-*

side herself, her confidence increased further and she began to train herself to orient to an observational stance as a way to notice the world around her. So that therapy did not unintentionally recreate a capacity overload, a rule of therapy was developed that she would not have more than two assignments active at any given time.

Mental Control (Intentional Control of the Focus of Attention; Selective Attention; Vigilance)

Despite the fact that our attention operates automatically and can be captured by environmental stimuli, we are also able to voluntarily allocate attention to stimuli and activities. We are able to decide to pay attention to something, such as a client, and then do that despite other calls on our attention, such as family or health problems. How do we achieve such mental control?

The answers to this question have been the focus of research on *selective attention* for several decades. Findings indicate that we are able to narrow our attentional focus to selected targets based on physical characteristics, such as sensory modality, spatial location, or color (Kahneman & Henik, 1981), and on semantic (meaning) characteristics (W. A. Johnson & Heinz, 1978; Treisman, 1960). Selecting attentional targets based on physical characteristics is easier than selecting those based on meaning, but the latter is also achievable (Broadbent, 1958; W. A. Johnson & Heinz, 1978). For example, one common experimental task is to have participants listen to different narratives in each ear, reporting what is presented in one ear and ignoring what is presented in the other (known as "shadowing"). When the two narratives are presented in different voices (i.e., physically different), it is easier for participants to attend to only the relevant ear than when the two narratives are about different subjects (i.e., different meaning), although participants are able to perform the task under both conditions.

One answer to how we accomplish voluntary selective attending is the facilitating effect of priming. When I decide to pay attention to my client, I have primed the client in my mind, and thus stimuli related to him will be more likely to capture my attention. This process relates to the formation of voluntary goals, which then activate information in memory related to that goal (i.e., priming). This is why the formation of a clear goal is such a vital aspect of therapy (see chapter 2). Once this is accomplished, goal-relevant material will be more likely to attract the client's attention, facilitating successful action. Furthermore, therapists make a useful contribution to a client's process by continually referring to the goal, which serves to refresh the goal representation, thereby prolonging this attentional boost.

Voluntary, goal-driven aspects of attentional control interact with automatic attentional orienting to determine the focus of attention at any given moment (e.g., Cowan, 1988, 1995). The relative strength of each factor also determines the ease of maintaining a voluntary focus: When the desired target of attention has many components that would draw the orienting response, maintaining attention to that target is much less effortful than when other stimuli in the environment present more salient features. For example, paying close attention to a client's verbalizations is easier when her presentation is animated and there are few distractions in the room, than when the client speaks in a monotone and the sound of an emergency vehicle can be heard just outside.

Another cognitive process that enables us to selectively attend to one stimulus among many is inhibition of the distractors. When we focus our attention on one topic or object, we inhibit or suppress our attention to other objects that would distract us from our focus (e.g., Tipper, 1985; Tipper, MacQueen, & Brehaut, 1988). This process of inhibition serves both automatic and voluntary attentional foci, preventing us from becoming overwhelmed by the stimuli in our environment and improving our efficiency in working toward our goals (see chapter 14 for further discussion of inhibitory processes).

Just as there are limits to how much we can attend to at once, there are also limits on our voluntary control of attention. For example, it is impossible to concentrate on a given action indefinitely because our alertness begins to wane, usually after several minutes of intense focused attention (Davies & Parasuraman, 1982). Furthermore, there are limits to how many goals we can pursue at once due to attentional limits, a fact that casts doubt on the efficiency of multitasking. Whenever we switch attention from one goal to another, there is a cost to performance of the second goal (Allport, Styles, & Hsieh, 1994; Meiran, 2000). Furthermore, alternating between two tasks is particularly inefficient because there is a suppression of our mental representation of a goal when we shift attention from it, resulting in particularly poor performance when we then return to that goal within a short period of time (Arbuthnott & Frank, 2000; Mayr & Keele, 2000). We have slightly more success dividing attention between two tasks when the tasks do not use overlapping cognitive resources, such as visual/pictoral and auditory/verbal tasks (Brooks, 1968), although there is always a performance cost associated with combining tasks (Reisberg, 1983). Thus, multitasking, or attempting to accomplish more than one goal at a time, actually interferes with efficiency, despite intuitions to the contrary. This is especially important for those who suffer from stress: The increased effort associated with this practice likely contributes to greater dis-ease associated with work. In therapy, we need to be thoughtful about how many issues we address at any one time. Working in a serial, priorized manner with client issues is likely more effective and efficient than working with several simultaneously. Moreover, some psychiatric disorders such as psychopathy are associated with deficiencies in the ability to shift attention between goals and stimuli (MacCoon, Wallace, & Newman, 2004).

Attentional limitation is also sometimes used to facilitate treatment, by pairing an effortful task with a client's problematic thinking, thereby reducing the focus on the problem. For example, the central technique of eye movement desensitization and reprocessing (EMDR) involves having a client imagine scenarios on their fear hierarchy (the habitual problematic thought/feeling) while keeping their eyes focused on an unpredictably moving object or another task such as therapist or client tapping (the effortful dual task; Shapiro, 1995). Clients usually report lessened intensity of their fear during this process, likely due to the mechanisms associated with alternating attention from one focus to another.

Case Illustration:

At this stage of therapy, Angela was feeling much better, enjoyed time by herself, and had accessed information from several schools (her assignment was to do these face-to-face). However, she had not yet been able to either begin a friendship or have a date. Each time she even thought about these goals, her attention was captured in the manner previously described. At this stage, the therapist and Angela developed a series of imagery exercises in which Angela was to begin by setting an intention (see chapter 6) and then very gradually completing the task in her imagination. For example, she thought the young man who had asked her out was still interested. Her intention was to approach him for coffee. Success was defined as her approach, not his agreement. In her imagination, she made small steps toward writing him a note and mailing it. The first day she got the materials, the second she addressed the letter, the third day she began the content, and so on. She reported that the gradual approach (even in imagination) and repeating the intention assisted her to keep her fears and expectations of embarrassment and rejection at bay. Once the imaginary exercise was completed, it was repeated in "real life" and she sent off the letter with much trepidation but with a sense of true accomplishment. Fortunately the plans made to deal with a "no" were unnecessary in this case and Angela went for coffee with the young man. She used some of the al-

ready learned techniques to intentionally notice things about the young man (e.g., what he said, the clothes he wore, etc.) and to avoid paying attention to her internal state.

Angela also attended to the effects of her early experiences of bullying and the expectations of humiliation and rejection she developed by engaging in some brief narrative therapy. Her therapy was long-term, consisting of about thirty sessions over the course of a one-year treatment.

THERAPEUTIC USES OF ATTENTION

As indicated throughout this chapter, the manipulation of attention is a central process in psychotherapy. First, therapists must control their own thoughts and perceptions to maintain focus on their therapeutic interventions. One of the primary ways we use to select which aspects to focus on is assessment. A good assessment allows a therapist to focus on a few characteristics, narrowing the attended field to a manageable size.

Second, many therapeutic techniques involve changing the client's attentional focus in order to reframe her problems and encourage solution of her issues (e.g., O'Hanlon & Weiner-Davis, 1989). For example, many techniques are designed to shift clients' attentional focus (e.g., reframing, distraction techniques, meditation techniques, Gendlin's focusing) or break attentional habits (e.g., thought-countering, EMDR, thought-field therapy). Experiential and humanistic therapies have especially championed the processes of awareness and attention as primary to understanding and change (e.g., Gendlin, 1996; Korb, Gorrell, & Van De Riet, 1989; also see Bohart, 2003; K. J. Schneider, 2003 for reviews). In addition, many therapeutic approaches, from cognitive behavior therapy (CBT; e.g., Bourne, 2000) to constructive psychotherapy (e.g., Mahoney, 2003) have adapted and developed mindful meditation techniques from a variety of far Eastern teachings as a way to assist clients with developing awareness and shifting attention. Despite the importance of attentional control as a therapeutic tool, however, relatively little direct consideration is given to this element of cognition during training.

Even when attention is directly used in treatment, such as CBT, these strategies are generally based on a simplistic view of attention (A. Wells, 2000). For example, CBT encourages distraction as one means to cope with depression (A. T. Beck, Rush, Shaw, & Emery, 1979; Fennel, Teasdale, Jones, & Damle, 1987) or anxiety (Wise & Hayes, 1983) and yet does not discriminate occasions when the distraction is likely to be helpful or harmful (e.g., Sartory, Rachman, & Grey, 1982). Specifically, distracting ourselves from a negative mood and thoughts in order to accomplish a practical task is likely to be helpful, whereas distracting ourselves during an effortful activity, such as difficult conversation with a family member, is more likely to be harmful. Similarly, CBT theories of threat-focused attention usually examine only external objects of attention that elicit an orienting response rather than including voluntary attention, such as giving oneself a positive attentional target (e.g., "Notice the birds rather than the insects"). More recently, therapeutic strategies based on a more complete understanding of attentional processes are beginning to emerge (A. Wells, 1990; A. Wells, White, & Carter, 1997; see also MacCoon et al., 2004). Similarly, family therapists often use knowledge to change expectations (attentional focus) in order to induce change in a family system. For example, in a family therapy session, the therapist reframes the insistence of a four-year-old to "do it by own self" as a positive developmental step on the path to independence. This helped the parents shift their attention from noticing the inconvenience of their child's obstruction to noticing and appreciating the development of independence. Simple behaviors, such as choosing clothing or putting on his own boots and coat prior to leaving the house, took on a different meaning and the problem solving focused more on parental time management than a needless and painful power struggle with a child. An understanding of human attentional processes based on cognitive findings and extended to psychotherapy is thus extremely valuable knowledge for psychotherapists, both for moment-by-moment interactions in therapy and for treatment techniques designed to influence this important aspect of human functioning.

KEY POINTS

- Attention is a limited resource that is a necessary precursor for most cognitive and behavioral tasks.
- Attention is directed either automatically, as with the orienting response, or voluntarily, as in concentration.
- Automatic attention is captured by sudden environmental change, expectation, and familiarity.
- Voluntary attentional control enables selective attention with selection based on physical characteristics of the stimulus (e.g., sensory modality, spatial location, etc.) or meaning (e.g., stimuli related to a particular topic).

- Establishing clear goals can serve to draw attention to goal-relevant factors through the mechanism of priming, facilitating a client's success with desired changes and actions.
- Switching attention between tasks is effortful, and performance efficiency is reduced immediately after a switch. For this reason, multitasking is often stressful and inefficient and so should be discouraged whenever possible, unless it is used as a therapeutic technique to reduce attention to one of the tasks (e.g., EMDR).

8

Category Judgment

A rose by any other name would smell as sweet. . .

Shakespeare was referring to the idea that what makes something what it is comes from within and has little to do with what lies on the surface. And so, the question is, what makes a rose a rose? And not a daisy or a daffodil? What makes a dog a dog? And how do we distinguish dogs from similar seeming creatures, such as wolves and foxes? Shakespeare's point was that there are deep underlying characteristics of entities that make them what they are and that "surface means nothing."

To see his point, consider how we know that something is a rose. One might say that a rose is something that grows on a thorny bush and has a distinctive, sweet smell. On the other hand, we can now purchase rose plants that have no thorns, and many of the roses sold in flower shops do not have a discernable scent. Are they still roses? Obviously they are (although one might quibble about paying fifty dollars for a dozen of them!). If one took a tulip and attached thorns to the stem and sprayed it with rose scent, would we call it a rose? Clearly not. Whatever it is that makes a rose a rose is something deeper than thorns and scents and petals, such that our concept of rose will stretch to accommodate alterations to what might otherwise be considered to be basic features.

Nonetheless, when it comes time to attach a label to an object or entity, we have only surface features to guide us. Normally, we judge a rose to be a rose because it looks like (or smells like) a rose. We are not privy to its underlying nature or essence, and can only go by what we see and experience. Thus, although we may believe that there is something deep and central about a rose that makes it what it is, our judgments tend to be superficial and based on easily accessed characteristics and properties.

Although this may seem like nothing more than an intellectual exercise, it is anything but that. One of the most profound questions of cognitive psychology is how our conceptual knowledge is organized to enable ready answers to the myriad questions that need to be answered at any given moment: from identifying the objects and people around us (That is a desk; this is my daughter; the thing coming toward me at high speed is a bus), to making predictions about their future states and how that will affect us (I can sit at the desk, it would be better to hug my child than ignore her, the bus will run me over if I don't move), to applying knowledge in novel ways (Can I use a coffee cup to hammer in this nail?). In some cases, one can proceed on the basis of a relatively superficial identification (That is a desk and I may sit behind it); in other cases, our beliefs about the underlying nature of things is what matters (e.g., What is the essence of a good hammer?).

Because the processes of categorization are so fundamental and so central to all cognitive activities, they imbue nearly all aspects of therapy. Consider, for example, that our categorical knowledge is not restricted to physical objects, such as roses and wolves, but also applies to the social world. We thus have access to all kinds of social categories that we use to structure our environment and to make attributions and predictions: kind people, shy people, homosexuals, feminists, liberals, and so on. Here the tension between surface features and underlying essences is crucial, because many stereotypes reflect the belief that the one is a reliable indicator of the other.

Furthermore, it is frequently the way our clients categorize their experiences or each other that is central to the problems they present. For example, a client who categorizes being slapped by her husband as a just desert for bad behavior rather than an act of abuse will need to recategorize before she can take action. A father who categorizes his son's disagreement as disrespect rather than independent thought may need some developmental information to assist him in recategorizing or reframing his son's behavior. All therapists who work cross-culturally must be sensitive to the cultural or religiously defined categories of their clients (e.g., Ivey & Ivey, 1999). If therapists do not attend to these issues sensitively, we can do harm. For example, a client presented for therapy to help her deal with the "abuse I face every day." Her previous therapist had helped her to categorize her young children's normal acts of rebellion and resistance (e.g., re-fusing to get up, rolling their eyes) as abusive, and she had learned to re-spond to these acts with accusations. Systemically, this set up a recursive feedback loop, with her children resisting this labeling and producing more of the behavior that was now defined as abusive.

Categorization also enables therapists to apply their knowledge and experience to the current situation. Although it goes without saying that all individuals are unique, for the purposes of applying our knowledge about depression or bulimia or abusive relationships, we need to be able to categorize the client as being similar in fundamental respects to others who have shared these problems. Thus, as discussed in chapter 2, one of the first tasks in psychotherapy is to assess and diagnose the issue, the situation, or both. Therapists of various schools may diagnose an internal disorder (using the American Psychiatric Association's *Diagnostic and Statistical Manual of Mental Disorders*, fourth edition, text revision [*DSM-IV-TR*]), disordered thinking pattern (cognitive behavioral thera-pists), problematic relationship dynamic (family therapists), or per-son–context difficulty or mismatch (feminist therapists and social work-ers). Regardless of the target of diagnostic activities, all involve the human process of categorization.

WHAT IS A CATEGORY AND WHAT IS IT GOOD FOR?

Definition

Categories are groups of objects that are considered to be the same for some purpose (Markman & Ross, 2003). In cognitive science, categories usually refer to the mental representation of such groupings, rather than the collection of objects themselves. Category representations are used for many important cognitive functions, including classification and predic-tion. People are sensitive to relationships among characteristics within a category (e.g., similarities among dogs) and to information that differenti-ates among categories (e.g., differences between dogs and cats). Different goals or categorization tasks seem to highlight these different feature rela-tionships (Markman & Ross, 2003): When our purpose is to assign a cate-gory to a new instance, our attention is drawn to features that distinguish between categories (diagnostic features; e.g., specific emotions for depression vs. anxiety disorder), whereas when our purpose is to make an inference based on known category membership, our attention is drawn more to relationships among the features of the specific category (within-category structure; e.g., sadness, anhedonia, and lethargy in depression).

Examples

When clients enter therapy, the therapist will make several types of category judgments about them. Some judgments will be similar to those we would make in any social situation, such as assessments of the person's temperament (e.g., volatile vs. easygoing), race, age, and developmental or social status (e.g., child vs. adult, professional vs. blue-collar worker). Similarly, clients will categorize the therapist's temperament, status, and style of interacting. These judgments will be used by both parties to construct interaction with each other and will thus form the initial bases of the therapeutic relationship. Research indicates that such judgments are made automatically and very quickly. For example, Ito and Urland (2003) observed that information about a person's race and gender are registered in the brain within half a second of their perception. Furthermore, there is clear evidence that we use judgments of social category such as race or profession to predict a person's behaviors and motivations (Kunda, 1999; J. W. Sherman, Lee, Bessenoff, & Frost, 1998). We also tend to use a person's membership in different types of social groups, such as intimate groups (family, friends), goal-related groups (work teams or interest clubs), or social categories (ethnicity, religion) as a way to organize our memory of such individuals (S. J. Sherman, Castelli, & Hamilton, 2003).

Some categories are specific to the mental health setting, such as formal assessments (i.e., *DSM-IV-TR* categorization) and the type of issue clients are dealing with (e.g., affective disorder, trouble with emotional regulation, or disordered power relationships in a family). Therapists themselves are members of categories, such as their professional group (e.g., psychologist, social worker, psychiatrist) and their theoretical orientation (e.g., family, cognitive behavioral, or psychodynamic therapist). Typically, our therapeutic specialties are also based on categories of problems (e.g., mood disorder, relationship problems) or categories of people (child, adolescent, elderly). Such categorical basis of specialization speaks to the importance of categorical organization in human thinking and allows therapists to develop a target area of expertise with a limited class of problems or issues that arise at a specific point in the life span. Such category-specific specialization is optimal when category identification and problem solutions (see chapter 2) have a one-to-one relationship, that is, when a particular diagnosis leads to the same treatment for all people with that diagnosis. Although this one-to-one correspondence is rare in psychology, the rationale for diagnosis is to identify a limited number of optimal solution strategies for that class of problems. The practice of specializing in a particular category is to obtain expertise in identifying the most relevant solution strategies (and to limit the number of areas the therapist must be familiar with). The laudable attempt of the American and Canadian Psychological Associations to develop standards for empirically validated treatments is an attempt to move in the direction of this one-to-one matching, although the strategy is not without problems.

Case Illustration:

Jason, a single aboriginal man, aged twenty-three, was referred for therapy by his parole officer. He had recently been released from jail after serving time for several property crimes and one violent assault. He was living with his mother and two younger brothers in a small remote community although he had not lived with her for five years prior to his eighteen months of incarceration. He was alcoholic (sober for two years since being charged) and had become a member of a gang while in jail. Although he identified strongly with the gang, there was no chapter in his hometown. He was referred for assistance with ongoing depression (he had made several suicide attempts when in jail) and was on a moderate dose of antidepressant medication. His grandmother (the family matriarch) accompanied him to his first appointment and expressed great concern that he would harm himself.

Jason understood his depression to be "something wrong in my brain" and did not think there was anything he could do to assist himself. It became clear as the therapist explored the symptoms and history that Jason had been misdiagnosed and had an anxiety disorder rather than depression and that his suicide attempts arose under the conditions of high stress and agitation and were an attempt to end his distress rather than his life. The simple recategorizing of his condition with the introduction of specific manualized anxiety-based interventions was a great relief to this young man. Each step needed to be orally explained and personalized for him, as he had grown up in a different cultural setting and his reading skills were minimal.

One important category for both clients and therapists is their self-conception (Nasby & Kihlstrom, 1986), that is, their judgment about what type of person they are, their abilities, their expectations about how others interact with them, and the like. Much has been written about the importance of the self for both the therapist and the client in psychotherapy, so no further discussion of this topic will be undertaken here, except to note that self-concept is a mental category and thus operates in the same way as other categories discussed here.

What Do Categories Do for Us?

At the most fundamental level, categories organize our knowledge. That is, they are ways of imposing order on what would otherwise be a large, chaotic database. Consider for a minute the number of unrelated facts we know about the world: We have knowledge about word meanings, our life experiences, our interactions with other people. We also have a huge store of knowledge about the physical, social, political, and geographic world. It would not be possible to access this information if it were not ordered and organized in some coherent way.

One of the consequences of categorizations is that disparate instances are treated as similar for some purpose. That is, we likely do not represent information about every single chair that we have encountered in long-term memory; rather, our chair category represents an abstraction or a summary about what constitutes the general category of "chair." This knowledge allows us to identify the objects, entities, and people in the world, even if we have not encountered something exactly like that before.

Categories also organize data and experience in a way that facilitates access to a large amount of information. Thus, having identified something as a member of a category allows us to make appropriate use of it (i.e., to sit on the chair), to interact with it appropriately (i.e., by hugging one's own children but not children who are strangers), and to make predictions about likely future states of the world (i.e., "The speeding bus will kill me if I don't move"). Categorization also enables sophisticated reasoning about novel objects and experiences because we can generalize our knowledge about the category to the new example. Our ability to sort diverse objects and experiences into categories has the function of simplifying our world, allowing us to use previous knowledge to make decisions about current behavior. As Mahoney (2003) puts it, we are categorical creatures that have the tendency to simplify and dichotomize. Much has been written in the developmental literature about the necessity of encountering experiences that can't be categorized using current knowledge in order to promote growth to a new developmental stage (e.g., Kegan, 1994). It is partially the need to develop new categories and ways to categorize which prompts emotional, intellectual, and social maturation.

In social situations, such as a psychotherapy office, we judge the categories of such things as the temperament of other people, the roles they play with us and each other, and the situation in which we find ourselves. We use such social categories to predict the behavior and motivations of new people we meet, based on our categorical assessments. For example, when we encounter a person wearing a uniform who is loudly issuing various commands, we might categorize them as a police officer if we are in a public place, a soldier if we are in a combat zone, or a schizophrenic if we are in a mental hospital. Similarly, that person's relationship to us will be categorized based on our own role assessment (e.g., doctor or tourist) and our current needs (e.g., protection, information, or responsibility). As is clear in these examples, we then use our social category judgments to guide our behavior, approaching a policeman to ask for directions if we are lost, or approaching a patient to offer assistance if we are responsible for their well-being.

With respect to problems associated with clients' categorization, Nasby and Kihlstrom (1986) suggested that individuals who seek psychotherapy likely have difficulty with their social categorization—they may misconstrue particular individuals or themselves, distort their perception of social events and autobiographical recollections, or adopt inappropriate strategies of social interaction. Thus, these authors suggest that therapists assess the specifics of clients' social category representations and plan interventions to change these representations. In other words, most clients seeking therapy have developed unsuccessful or negative systems of categorization, which is often a major constraint in their problem space (chapter 2). Changing or adjusting the way clients categorize aspects of their problems, often by using reframing, redefinition, or educative interventions, is a central requirement of any therapy.

Case Illustration:

Another specific shift in categories arose around Jason's gang membership. As we explored the benefits he experienced as a gang member (the most significant being an easing in his anxiety as he felt a sense of belonging and greater physical safety in the jail setting), the therapist began to redefine his need to belong to "that specific gang" to a need to belong to, and identify with, a group. His tribal council health authority was most helpful as they assisted him in contacting an elder who was teaching traditional ways to a group of young men. As Jason participated in this group over the course of the next six months, the change was remarkable as he felt some security in belonging and

*developed a sense of empathy with the world and others rather than the hostil-
ity and "us versus the world" view of most gangs.*

Stereotypes As Categories

With social categories, such information may involve a stereotype, such as
stereotypes associated with race or gender. The evidence indicates that we
automatically assign category membership to other people based on their
racial and gender characteristics (Ito & Urland, 2003). However, whether
such categorization activates stereotypic associations depends on the
strength of such associations in our memory (Gawronski, Ehrenberg,
Banse, Zukova, & Klauer, 2003) and our current intentions (Olson, Lambert, & Zacks, 2003). The automatic categorization of individuals according to their race does not necessarily mean that we activate racial stereotypes. Rather, if such stereotypic information is strongly associated with
the category of race in our memories, and we are not strongly motivated to
control such socially inappropriate associations, stereotypic thinking will
be activated. As with most categorical knowledge, our experience with a
given category will determine what information is strongly associated
with the category (Shafto & Coley, 2003), so those with considerable experience with people of different races will likely have many nonstereo-
typic associations, whereas those with relatively little experience will have
less specific, more culturally communicated associations.

A common example of categorization leading to stereotyping occurs in
relationship therapy. One member of a couple categorizes the behavior of
the opposite sex partner as being related to his or her gender category (gay
and lesbian couples also categorize, of course, but use categories more related to their situation). If the client's past experience has reinforced this belief, then they will stereotype their partner, leading to such statements as
"Like all men, my husband can't express his feelings" or "Women just want
to talk things to death." Interestingly some therapies and self-help literature
encourage these stereotypes and then attempt to help the members of the
couple learn the skills that counter the stereotype. A cognitive behavioral or
Bowenian intergenerational approach would directly explore the categorizations and challenge the dysfunctional beliefs or rule systems uncovered by
the exploration. Process-oriented relationship therapies (e.g., emotionally
focused couples therapy) attempt to provide countering experiences within
the session that will challenge the categorizations of the partners. Because
all of these approaches can be helpful or harmful, therapists need to be

aware of how they attend to the categorizations of their clients and support or challenge them to achieve positive change. For example, many relationship therapists have experienced the following: One or both members of a couple can interpret a query such as "Why are you together?" or "What are you doing with this man/woman?" as a negative judgment of the relationship. Clients then interpret this to mean that the couple should separate, leading to statements such as "My therapist said we should separate" or "My therapist said I should leave you." Very few therapists will actually give advice about maintaining or leaving a relationship unless there is a physical threat; however, we must be cautious about the ways in which our questions and other interventions can prime particular categorization schemas or even reveal our unstated but present stereotyping.

WHAT INFORMATION DO CONCEPTS REPRESENT?

What information do we access to determine that object is a chair, and not a couch or a table? To know that Sarah is a kind person, and not selfish or aggressive? That someone is depressed, as opposed to grieving or anxious? Why, in other words, are a given set of entities grouped together, instead of with another grouping or set?

Defining Features

A straightforward answer to this question is that members of a category share a set of defining features (E. E. Smith & Medin, 1981). For example, we could define a triangle as a closed geometric form with three sides and interior angles that sum to 180 degrees (Medin, 1989). All triangles have these features, and nontriangles do not have these features.

Unfortunately, there are very few categories in the world that can be so easily defined. Try, for example, to think of the features that define the category "chair" or "kind person." It is rare to find a category that can be defined in terms of a set of unique features. Moreover, this view suggests that category membership should be clear cut: An entity that possesses the key features belongs to the category and everything else is excluded. Instead, however, people's representations appear to have a graded structure, such that some items are more typical of a category than others (e.g., kitchen chair vs. bean bag chair) to the point where some entities are not clearly in or out of the category (e.g., Is a rug furniture?).

Prototypes

One way to deal with this problem is to assume that category representations are inherently fuzzy and graded. Prototype models of categories suggest that items are grouped into categories based on perceptual similarity, with each category having a central exemplar that is constructed from the average characteristics of all category members (Rosch, 1978; J. D. Smith & Minda, 2000). For example, dogs are grouped into a single category on the basis of similar body shape (e.g., four legs, a tail, fur). A slang expression such as "If it walks like a duck and quacks like a duck, then it probably is a duck" reflects an intuitive understanding of prototypes.

In this scheme, entities that share many features with the prototype are the more typical members of the category (Medin, 1989; E. E. Smith & Medin, 1981). Entities that share few features are less typical members. For example, for many city dwellers, a prototypical bird is one that is small, flies, and sings. Robins and sparrows are thus typical members of the category, whereas large, flightless birds such as ostriches and turkeys are less typical. Membership is thus a matter of degree, rather than the all or nothing affair suggested by the defining features model.

Several of the categories suggested by the *DSM-IV-TR* use this probabilistic approach to classification (Medin, 1989). For example, a diagnosis of major depressive episode can be made if a dysphoric mood and/or loss of interest or pleasure, plus four of nine symptoms have been present for a period of two weeks. In the same way that whales and mice share little in the way of surface similarity (but are both members of the category "mammal"), two people can be diagnosed with depression but share only a few of the nine characteristic symptoms.

The typicality of an instance also affects the way we generalize about it. For example, if we learn something new about a typical insect such as ants (e.g., that they communicate using chemicals), we are more likely to generalize this knowledge to all insects than if that same knowledge is acquired about a less typical insect, such as a praying mantis (see Medin, Coley, Storms, & Hayes, 2003, for a review). We expect that the characteristics or attributes of those members of a category that we view as more typical will be shared with other members of the category. For instance, if we hear that flashbacks are a common symptom of posttraumatic stress disorder, we are more likely to generalize this symptom to other forms of anxiety than if we hear that flashbacks are a symptom of stress caused by a blood disorder.

Problems With Prototypes.   The theory that categories are organized around prototypes explains a lot about our conceptual structures. Prototypes explain the variability among category members (i.e., why penguins and robins have different status as birds), how we can assign a novel item to a category even though there is no set of features that defines category membership. Prototypes also explain our reliance on surface features as guides to categorization (e.g., "If it looks like a rose and smells like a rose, then it's a rose"). In sum, there is a lot of truth to the notion of prototypes.

Despite this fact, it has been clear for a long time that prototypes and the notion of similarity are not enough to explain categorization. For one thing, prototypes discard a lot of important information (S. W. Allen & Brooks, 1991; Medin, 1998; Medin & Ross, 1989). A prototype is an abstraction that reflects the sum of one's experience with an entity or category of entities. Although some degree of abstraction takes place, people's conceptual knowledge also reflects specific memories of that experience. Thus, the availability or presence of a single, salient example can bias or anchor our view of an entire category (see Hastie & Dawes, 2001, for a review). Consider, for example, what the name Osama bin Laden has done to change North Americans' category of "Muslim."

In addition, there needs to be a way to identify which features are compared when determining similarity. That is, entities are considered to be similar, and therefore in the same category, because they share features. The more features that are shared, the more similar they are. By this definition, however, any two objects are arbitrarily similar and dissimilar depending on which features one focuses on (G. L. Murphy & Medin, 1985). Plums and lawnmowers, for example, are not usually considered similar, but that is only because we do not have a framework that points out what they have in common: They both weigh less than one thousand pounds, they both are found on earth, they both have an odor, etc. Medin (1989) summed it up succinctly: "It is perhaps only a modest exaggeration to say that similarity gets at the shadow rather than the substance of concepts. Something (else) is needed to give concepts life, coherence, and meaning" (p. 1474).

Categories as Theories

Perhaps the biggest limitation of the prototype view is that, in the end, categories do more than describe the world; they also explain it (Medin, 1989, 1998; G. L. Murphy & Medin, 1985; see also Lakoff, 1987, for related ideas). Our knowledge about birds is not limited to a list of descriptive properties, such as they have wings, fly, and build nests in trees. Specifically, we know that birds fly *because* they have wings, and that flying *enables* them to build nests in trees, which is a survival strategy for keeping away from predators. Thus, our categorical knowledge embodies a complex set of causal dependencies that explain how features are related to each other as well as to the other constructs, such as survival strategies (e.g., Hadjichristidis, Sloman, Stevenson, & Over, 2004; Rehder, 2003; Strevens, 2000).

There is considerable evidence that the human mind seeks explanations that make sense of incoming information about the world (Carey, 1985; Keil, 1989; Gelman, 2000). Thus, it is likely that causal models underlie many of our category representations, especially when we have some experience with a category (Shafto & Coley, 2003). Consistent with this, Kim and Ahn (2002) observed that experienced clinicians and clinical graduate students use causal models of mental disorders as the basis of diagnosis. This is despite the atheoretical nature of the *DSM-IV-TR* and its predecessors, which are organized in a prototypical fashion (Cantor, Smith, French, & Mezzich, 1980). Furthermore, students are instructed to diagnose using these prototypical feature lists, which neither provide an organizing theory for disorders nor preferentially weight or relate symptoms. Although the *DSM-IV-TR* is relatively recent (published in 2000), such atheoretical symptom checklists have been used since 1980. However, with experience, we are inclined to develop causal models of the world and use these as the basis of categorization, rather than maintain a more prototypical basis of diagnosis consistent with the use of feature lists. Categorization on the basis of causal models seems to be as relevant to clinical diagnosis as to categorization in everyday life.

At the beginning of this section, we argued that we need something more than similarity to bind the exemplars of a category together, and this additional "glue" is provided by theories or explanations. Theories highlight the relevance or importance of certain features and explain why we focus on some features and not on others when considering whether two items are similar or not. These theories, therefore, give rise to prototype effects: Typicality and graded categories result from the processes we use to categorize and explain the world (Lakoff, 1987). In Medin's metaphor, prototypes are the shadows cast by our theories, and it is these theories that give concepts life, coherence, and meaning.

Case Illustration:

Jason had several beliefs that needed to change in order for him to manage his anxiety (e.g., "Only cowards feel afraid," "Fear is weak," "Don't let oth-

ers see your fear," etc.). His prototype for strength and courage clearly ex-
cluded any possibility of either experiencing or expressing his fear or anxiety.
However, given his culture, challenging these beliefs in standard cognitive be-
havioral fashion did not work. His strong belief in history and the importance
of ancestors led to the therapist helping him to access memories and telling
him stories that allowed Jason to accept comfort and assistance from others.
Consultation with Jason and the elder also led to the elder relating many
teaching stories to Jason. In these stories the causal categorization was ex-
plored, as both the therapist and the elder related stories that explored the
theme of multiple feelings within a brave and courageous person. Thus, cate-
gorizing the therapy in historical (psychodynamic) terms was more compatible
with Jason's categorization of the world than either a thought-focused strategy
or a brain-focused explanation of his symptoms. Including both prototype and
causal elements in the interventions assisted Jason in redefining the category
of strength to include anxiety and courage as being compatible experiences.
Over the course of this extensive eighteen-month therapy, Jason also devel-
oped a view and image of himself as a warrior who systematically met the
challenges of exposure (in vivo and imagery) of his hierarchy of fears.

THE ESSENCE OF ESSENCES

We return now to the issue of what makes a rose a rose. Shakespeare's observation implied that the essence of a rose lay beyond the surface, and had
to do with inner characteristics and properties that may not be visible. Our
discussion of theories and explanations supports this view; the perceived
superficial similarity that exists among category members is constrained
by our explanations and theories of how things work. This implies a belief
that there are deeper causal relations at work than may be apparent on the
surface, and which give rise to the outward appearance of things.

   Rips (1989) provided an example by way of a hypothetical creature
named a "sorp." The sorp ate seeds and berries, had two wings, lived in a
nest in a tree, and was covered with bluish-grey feathers. The sorp was described as living next to a toxic waste dump, which caused it to undergo a
gradual, but radical transformation. Eventually, the sorp lost its feathers
and instead developed a brittle, iridescent outer shell. It abandoned its
nest, grew two more pairs of legs, and lived off the nectar of flowers. In
other words, the sorp had changed physically from the appearance of a
bird to that of an insect. However, if participants were told that the sorp
was nonetheless successful in attracting a sorp mate and producing sorp
offspring, they indicated that, surface resemblance aside, the sorp was a
bird and not an insect.

Experiments like these demonstrate that people behave as if categories have underlying essences or cores. Psychological essentialism is the belief that entities have a deep, underlying nature that make them what they are, and which constrain and give rise to observable properties and behaviors (e.g., Ahn et al., 2001; Diesendruck & Gelman, 1999; Estes, 2003; Giles, 2003; Medin, 1989; Medin & Ortony, 1989; Rothschild & Haslam, 2003). These essentialist properties are fundamental to the entity and highly resistant to change. According to this view, people may not be able to define these properties or articulate the underlying theory with any precision, but they nonetheless behave as if such properties existed. Thus, despite the traumatic changes undergone by the sorp, it was still perceived to be a bird, rather than an insect, because the surface changes did not affect the inner essence.

Essentialist beliefs are important in the context of psychotherapy because they may affect the attributions and inferences people make about a category. For example, many social categories, such as "homosexuals," "Protestants," "liberals," "wife," "husband," "child," or "old people," may reflect essentialist beliefs (Haslam, Rothschild, & Ernst, 2000, 2002), as may beliefs about mental disorders (Haslam & Ernst, 2002) and personality traits such as aggression (Giles, 2003). Essentialist beliefs are related to motivation helplessness (i.e., the tendency not to engage in problem solving), a desire to diagnose or generalize (e.g., given one instance of aggressive behavior to infer other antisocial characteristics), a tendency to view the characteristic as one that is stable and persists over time and across situations (Giles, 2003), as well as a willingness to make judgments about people based on limited information (Heyman & Gelman, 2000). Such essentialist ideas are reflected in clients' beliefs that change is not possible ("Once an abuser, always an abuser," "Once untrustworthy or unfaithful, never again trustworthy"). Most therapeutic systems attempt to reframe such client views or beliefs or have the clients observe the issue from a variety of perspectives as a way to alter, challenge, or add to the ways our clients typically categorize themselves, others, and the world.

Despite its intuitive appeal, the notion of psychological essentialism is a controversial one (see for e.g., Ahn et al., 2001; Diesendruck & Gelman, 1999; Kalish, 2002; Malt, 1994; Rips, 2000; Strevens, 2000). The problem with this view is the same as that of the defining features view. That is, one of the corollaries to an essentialist belief is a well-defined category: Entities that possess the essence are part of the category; those that do not are not. As we have seen, however, people's behavior seldom reflects this criterion, and some category exemplars fall on the boundaries, resulting in "partial membership" (see Estes, 2003, for an excellent summary of this problem). As we pointed out earlier, even apparently clear-cut categories have fuzzy boundaries, such that, for example, two-dollar bills and IOUs are considered by some to be partial members of the category "U.S. currency." Similarly in therapy most people demonstrate characteristics which both include and exclude them from a category. The rigid adherence to, or overgeneralization of, particular categories by either therapists or clients are limiting factors in change. For example, someone who experiences her partner as both loving and abusive, or loving to one member of the family and not another, has difficulty in deciding which categories to use in making decisions.

There are a number of ways to reconcile the idea of fuzzy boundaries with the belief that categories have essences. These have to do with the assumption that categorical knowledge is applied in contexts that highlight or emphasize some dimensions or properties, and downplay others. That is, the retrieval of category-based knowledge is configured to meet the demands of a particular situation (e.g., Barsalou, 1987; Diesendruck & Gelman, 1999; Rothschild & Haslam, 2003). Items that were clearly in the category when it is applied for one purpose may not fit the demands of another situation equally well. This is similar to the concept in physics that in some contexts we see light as a particle and in others as a wave. Both are useful categorizations in particular contexts.

Categories and Culture

Lakoff (1987) provides a simple example of this situation with the category "bachelor." Membership in this category is well-defined: unmarried, adult, and male. However, this category is interpreted in light of a number of other cultural expectations about marriage and marriageability, and this intersection between a well-defined category and a set of background expectations produces a number of "borderline" cases: homosexuals, the Pope, a Muslim man who is allowed four wives but has only three, and the like.

Complex Category Structures

In other instances, the concept itself might be very complex, such that only small parts of it are relevant in a particular context. Consider, for example, the different shades of meaning for the concept "mother" that are emphasized by each of the following statements (Lakoff, 1987):

> I was adopted and don't know who my real mother is.
>
> I am not a nurturant person, so I don't think I could ever be a real mother to any child.
>
> Necessity is the mother of invention.
>
> He wants his girlfriend to mother him. (pp. 75–76)

Thus, whether or not any particular individual (e.g., a surrogate mother) is considered completely in or out of the category will depend on whether or not we are referring to a childbearing, a nurturing, or a genetic model of motherhood.

Goal-Derived Categories

In other cases, all members of the category will possess the "essence" of the category to a greater or lesser extent. These are categories that are defined with respect to an ideal (Barsalou, 1987). An example would be "things to eat on a diet." This category is defined with respect to the ideal diet food (a highly nutritious, zero-calorie food item) which, of course, does not exist. Thus, although this category clearly has an essence, membership in the category is also graded and fuzzy.

Different Types of Essences

There is evidence to indicate that categories differ as to whether they are defined according to essentialist beliefs. (Ironically, the category of "essentialist categories" is fuzzy.) For example, natural kinds (e.g., animals, plants, and other entities created by the natural environment) are more likely to be defined in terms of essentialist beliefs than humanmade artifacts (furniture, tools, vehicles). That is, there are fewer ambiguous cases of "fruit" than "chairs" (Diesendruck & Gelman, 1999; Estes, 2003). Some social categories, such as gender, race, and ethnicity are similar to natural kinds (Haslam et al., 2000) and are characterized by beliefs that membership in the category is immutable (cannot readily be altered), stable, natural, and having necessary or defining characteristics. Others, such as homosexuality, political groups, and religious groups have a different character. These categories are characterized by the belief that category members are basically "the same" at a fundamental level, that these characteristics of the group can be imputed to individuals (i.e., knowing that someone belongs to the category is sufficient to infer that they share these characteristics), and that membership in the group precludes membership in other categories. Social categories vary among themselves and reflect these clusters of characteristics to varying degrees. We are more likely to hold essentialist beliefs about intelligence than preference for salad dressings (Giles, 2003).

Individual Variability

Finally, the tendency to essentialize varies not only by category, but by context and individual. For example, acts of aggression are most likely to be essentialized when they are perceived as deviant or extreme (see Giles, 2003, for a review). Children who are raised in an abusive environment or who are exposed to globally evaluative judgments (e.g., "You are so smart") are more likely to express beliefs that dispositional characteristics are due to internal, stable factors (again, see Giles, 2003, for a review). Even within a given age range, there is a lot of variability in the tendency to endorse essentialist beliefs about natural kinds, artifacts, and social categories (e.g., Estes, 2003; Heyman & Gelman, 2000; Heyman & Giles, 2004).

Summary

There is evidence to show that people tend to believe that categories are defined with respect to an underlying essence. This essence gives rise to observable surface features, which produce a sense of similarity among category members. For example, members of a religious group might share a number of surface characteristics, such as manner of dress and dietary preference, that result from a shared religious belief. Other characteristics, such as beliefs on moral issues, political affiliations, and so forth, may also arise (or are perceived to arise) from a common set of underlying beliefs, producing a sense of homogeneity and similarity among members.

The belief in essences has implications for therapy, in that essentialist beliefs have implications for conceptual change. If we believe that traits and characteristics such as aggression, shyness, selfishness, and so on are immutable and stable characteristics, then we are not likely to believe that change is possible. We are also likely to make more inferences and generalizations about essentialized categories than nonessentialized ones, and to infer a degree of homogeneity to those categories that is inaccurate. If mental disorders and psychological problems are imbued with essential characteristics, then we might be less inclined to adopt a problem-solving approach to dealing with them. These essentialist beliefs are attended to in a variety of ways by therapists of many different approaches. Clients often enter therapy with beliefs about self, others, and the world that are essentialist (i.e., stable and unchanging). The therapist rarely shares this belief in essentialism and sets out to first make the clients aware of the content of their beliefs and then provide an intervention that assists them in changing the constraining belief(s) in the process of reaching the goal state. These are often referred to as "core beliefs" or schemas in cognitive behavioral (e.g., R. E. McMullin, 2000), and humanistic, integrative therapies (e.g., Hanna, 2002); "core ordering processes" in constructivist therapies (e.g., Mahoney, 2003); and "rules and family beliefs" in family therapies (e.g., Adams, 2003). Some psychodynamic and experiential therapies refer to these essentialist beliefs as "third-degree impasses" indicating the client believes "That's just the way I am, I've always been this way" or as underlying scripts and stories containing essentialist beliefs (e.g., Goulding & Goulding, 1979; Strupp & Binder, 1984). In summary, virtually all therapies acknowledge the importance of essentialist beliefs in the change process and have developed interventions relating to them.

CATEGORIZATION IN REASONING AND DIAGNOSIS

As we discussed throughout this chapter, categorization is an important process in psychotherapy for a number of reasons. First, diagnosis and assessment are categorization tasks, in which the person's symptoms are used to classify his problem (Brooks, Norman, & Allen, 1991; G. R. Norman, Brooks, Coblentz, & Babcock, 1992). Knowledge related to the category (diagnosis) is then used to plan treatment strategies. Even for therapies that do not begin with a formal psychiatric diagnosis, such as humanistic therapies, we classify a client's problems and use our classification to decide on intervention strategies (e.g., Erickson et al., 1976; Perls, 1969). Second, as social creatures, we categorize new people that we meet using social categories (e.g., race, profession), and we predict their behavior and motivations according to our knowledge of such categories. Thus, the process of categorization is vital to the practice of psychotherapy and to the treatment of clients.

As we discussed earlier in this chapter, category designation uses both similarity and causal theory information. We assign a category to a situation based on perceptual similarity with a known category (e.g., recognizing a therapist's office because it is similar to other professional offices such as those of doctors or lawyers) and on the basis of our theories about cause–effect relationships (e.g., each of these offices contains several chairs because such offices are designed for discussion between individuals). Perceptual similarity or prototypical categorization is especially important when we have no causal understanding (A. S. Kaplan & Murphy, 2000; Shafto & Coley, 2003). However, these two organization strategies likely work in concert in most situations, in that causal theories influence our expectations and draw attention to particular features and patterns (i.e., relationships among features) at the expense of other features. For example, if we hold a primarily psychodynamic model of the etiology of mental illnesses, we are particularly attentive to information about clients' family relationships (both family of origin and family of procreation). Conversely, if we hold a cognitive behavioral view of causation, we are attentive to statements about clients' beliefs about the world and themselves. We also make classification decisions by estimating how likely an object is to have been generated by the category's causal model. For instance, if our causal model of depression is that it is initiated by grief or loss, we are unlikely to diagnose a client as depressed if they can report no significant losses in the recent past. However, if our causal model focuses on biochemical imbalances, a diagnosis of depression might be made on evidence that is consistent with such an imbalance, such as changes in appetite or sleeping pattern.

The Role of Prototypes and Similarities
in Diagnosis

In the preceding section, we described evidence that people believe that membership in a category is determined by an underlying essence or core, even if they are not able to articulate what that essence is. However, because we are not privy to this inner state, our categorization decisions must, perforce, be made on the basis of more superficial cues. That is, we must base our decisions on how things look, smell, feel, move, and so on. Whereas people understand that superficial characteristics do not define category membership, it is nonetheless a basic, central cue to determining classification (Medin & Ortony, 1989; Rips, 1989). Thus, we most often decide that something belongs in a category because it resembles the other members of the category that we have met. This is the "looks like a duck" heuristic that we described earlier.

This tendency to rely on similarities and prototypes has profound implications for diagnostic behavior. That is, we might apply a diagnostic label because the person appears to be typical or representative of other related category members. For example, Garb (1996) demonstrated that there is a strong relationship between the perceived similarity of a client to a typical member of a diagnostic category (e.g., antisocial personality disorder, schizophrenia) and the probability that clinicians will make the corresponding diagnosis. Similarity to recently encountered examples can also influence diagnostic behavior. Brooks et al. (1991) found that physicians were more likely to make a correct diagnosis of a skin lesion if the current example bore a high degree of similarity to a situation encountered recently than if the current case differed in its surface features. Similarly, psychotherapists are more likely to notice and apply categories based on the most recent training event they attended.

Because the tendency to rely on similarity and prototype information informs so much of our everyday behavior, it is a very powerful decision-making heuristic. We rely heavily on perceptual information that supports a particular inference and may ignore or downplay other, relevant information. Kahneman and Tversky (1982; see also Kahneman & Frederick, 2002) called this the "representativeness" heuristic. As an example of the power of the representativeness heuristic, consider the following problem. Participants were told that the following personality sketch was written by a panel of psychologists who interviewed and administered personality tests to thirty engineers and seventy lawyers:

> Jack is a forty-five year old man. He is married and has four children. He is generally conservative, careful, and ambitious. He shows no interest in political and social issues and spends most of his free time on his many hobbies, which include home carpentry, sailing, and mathematical puzzles.

Participants were then asked to indicate the probability that Jack is one of the thirty engineers in the sample of one hundred. What do you think? What is the probability that Jack is an engineer, and what information did you base your decision on? Would you change your estimate if you knew that the sample contained seventy engineers and thirty lawyers?

Indeed, our estimate should change dramatically between the two cases. That is, our decision should be moderated by the fact that baseline probability of being an engineer changes from 30% to 70%. This is known as the base-rate (see chapter 9). However, the personality sketch strongly evokes the category "engineer," and Jack is perceived to be much more typical of the "engineer" category than the "lawyer" category. In Kahneman and Tversky's original studies, participants' judgments were swayed by this information to such an extent that they practically ignored the base-rate probability, giving virtually identical estimates regardless of the prior odds.

To illustrate how powerful this representativeness heuristic is, Kahneman and Tversky also provided participants with personality sketches that did not evoke either a lawyer or an engineer prototype (e.g., Dick is quiet, married, highly motivated, and well liked). In this case, participants judged the probability to be 50%, presumably because the sketch could describe either an engineer or a lawyer. Thus, even when the information was worthless, people used it to inform their judgments and equivocated rather than relying on base-rate probabilities.

In chapter 9, we will discuss the importance of base-rates in clinical decision making. In this chapter, however, we want to illustrate the power of similarities and prototypes and demonstrate how easily they can dominate our judgments. Many theories and training material related to communication (e.g., Adler, Towne, & Rolls, 2001) and therapy (e.g., Ivey & Ivey, 1999) skills encourage therapists to suspend or to be aware of their own judgments and categorizations in order to attend appropriately to the client's needs. Consequently, many therapists must balance the encouragement to categorize (e.g., diagnose) with a caution that it may be harmful to the client or their goals (e.g., be aware of sexist or ageist attitudes).

Theories in Diagnosis

The information that is attended to and utilized in a categorization task often depends on the use to which it is put. That is, people rely on different information when they are attempting to categorize new items (such as a new client) into known categories and when that category knowledge is then used to make predictions and decisions about the classified object (or person; Garb, 1996; Markman & Ross, 2003). With classification tasks, participants must discriminate between two or more categories, and thus they learn more about features that discriminate between the categories (e.g., symptoms that discriminate between depression and anxiety disorders). Conversely, when asked to predict a feature of an example of a known category, people learn more about the relationship between features within a category and are more likely to establish a prototypical category representation (e.g., the prototype of depression as low mood, anhe-donia, and lethargy). When participants do a combination of these tasks, such as is the case when therapists first diagnose a client, and then plan a treatment based on their diagnosis, features that are useful for both classi-fication (diagnostic features) and inference (category prototypes) are con-sidered important.

This finding has several implications for psychotherapists. Specifically, when we are performing assessments, this would be analogous to a classifi-cation task, and thus our attention is drawn to characteristics that distinguish among categories. However, if we think of our task as verifying a particular diagnosis, our attention would be aimed more at prototypical than at distin-guishing features. In many assessment situations, the referral includes a hy-pothesized diagnosis, thus setting up the latter situation. As discussed in chapter 9, this can lead to information-present effects or confirmation bias (Nickerson, 1998), in which we notice and weight information that supports rather than disconfirms the hypothesis. This tendency to view assessment as verifying a referral diagnosis may lead to faulty categorization.

G. R. Norman et al. (1992) provided evidence of this tendency: They provided expert radiologists with x-ray films that were difficult to diag-nose. These films were accompanied by a case history indicating either no prior problems or a set of symptoms consistent with a pulmonary disorder. Radiologists were more likely to diagnosis an illness and to spot features in the x-ray consistent with the illness, when they were provided with the symptomatic rather than the normal history, *regardless of whether the x-ray was from a healthy or a sick person.*

They argued that because features or symptoms are not uniquely associ-ated with a particular diagnostic category (e.g., lethargy), the information value of an individual feature increased in the context of other signs (e.g., recent changes in sleep or eating patterns). Thus, if there are several indi-cators that are consistent with a particular diagnosis (e.g., depression), then a feature (e.g., lethargy) might be weighed heavily; in contrast, if the other indicators pointed to a different diagnosis (e.g., anxiety disorder), then the feature (i.e., lethargy) might be deemed irrelevant to the overall pattern. Of course, the danger here is that considering an overall pattern can produce a bias in which disconfirming evidence is overlooked; con-versely, it can also promote a closer look that eliminates irrelevant details.

Clients are often referred for psychotherapy in similar circumstances, such as the following client who was experiencing feelings of low motiva-tion and high lethargy. He had been prescribed an antidepressant in the past. Given this information, it would have been easy to assume a depression and begin treating accordingly without attending to issues of differential diagnoses or categorization. However, the client described an unusually positive life (e.g., good family and community life, recent promotion into a desired position) and so was referred back to a physician where he was eventually diagnosed with a thyroid imbalance. This underscores an even more fundamental level of categorizing; that is, a client referred for therapy does not necessarily have a psychological or emotional problem. We hope that therapists from all theoretical backgrounds will explore the problem space sufficiently before embarking on a treatment protocol based on incomplete information. However, in this era of efficiency and emphasis on brevity, it is sometimes the case that professionals proceed without adequate information. Psychotherapists working as team members with ready access to other professionals are more likely to categorize across fields in addition to within their own.

Case Illustration:

The collaborative, community-based approach to Jason's therapy also led to issues of category for the therapist in relation to cross-cultural therapy and ethical practice. Most aboriginal cultures have strong community values based on interpersonal relationships and connection to the community. The elder involved insisted not only that he must meet with the therapist but that the therapist must participate in some community and family events (e.g., a community feast, a family meal) in order to be considered an appropriate helper for Jason. This cultural difference in defining or categorizing what is helpful led to the therapist having to reconsider the principle of avoiding dual relationships. The health authority, elder, and family members of this aboriginal community clearly saw multiple relationships with preservation of boundaries as a key to helpfulness, whereas the therapist was trained in the tradition of avoiding dual or multiple relationships. This issue was dealt with by extensive consultation and a decision that to participate was in the best interests of the individual client and respect for the culture within which Jason had decided to live. These and other related issues are a constant source of challenge in all cross-cultural therapy.

Once we make an initial assessment in the early stages of therapy, we will be subject to confirmation bias, noticing client behaviors and characteristics that are consistent with our assessment, but overlooking characteristics that are inconsistent with that assessment. Even if we do notice such characteristics, we are likely to consider those consistent with our assessment more important than characteristics that violate our expectations (see chapter 9 for a discussion of confirmation bias in therapy). This is especially true if therapists are convinced that they are right, or if their self-esteem unduly rests on their skill with initial assessment. This situation can lead to the unfortunate consequence of therapists not noticing when their interventions are unsuccessful, leading to clients' discouragement and termination of therapy. Thus, therapy is best served when therapists make diagnoses tentatively, remaining alert to feedback that their categorization of a client or their particular situation may be incorrect.

These problems are likely exacerbated by our current training practices. Considerable effort is devoted to having students learn various psychiatric categories (i.e., *DSM-IV-TR* assessment classes). In these classes, the focus is usually on developing category prototypes (e.g., a typical depressed person, a typical case of obsessive-compulsive disorder), rather than on identifying features that can discriminate between diagnostic categories. Fortunately more training programs are now focusing on differential and dual diagnoses that will mitigate the bias of learning only prototypical diagnostic systems.

Implicit and Explicit Processes in Decision Making

There is a large literature indicating that expert judges in a variety of domains have only a moderate degree of self-insight about their decision-making processes (see Harries, Evans, & Dennis, 2000, for a review). That is, when asked to indicate which cues are important in recommending treatment decisions, physicians reported relying on more cues than they actually did, and overstated the importance of the cues they did use (Harries, Evans, Dennis, & Dean, 1996). A likely explanation for this finding is that people have only partial access to the processes that underlie their judgments and decisions. That is, we can only report on information that is explicitly available to consciousness; much of our decision making, however, may involve the use of implicit knowledge about which we are not able to report (Evans, Clibbens, Cattani, Harris, & Dennis, 2003). These issues are discussed in more detail in the chapters on decision making (chapter 9) and metacognition (chapter 12).

KEY POINTS

- Categories are groups of objects or experiences judged to be the same for some purpose. Social categories include roles, cultural membership, relationships, and the like. This is one of the fundamental and automatic ways that the human mind organizes information, allowing us to make rapid use of previous knowledge.

- Diagnoses are essentially categories of human difficulties.
- One of our most important categories is our self-concept, a category that is often an important target of therapy.
- Categories can be organized according to perceptual similarity (prototype theory) or causal similarity (causal model theory). The categories of the *DSM-IV-TR* are an example of the former (i.e., atheoretical symptom lists), but research indicates that most therapists organize such categories according to their theories about the causes of psychological problems.
- Essentialist beliefs can underlie some category judgments, beliefs that some underlying core element makes a thing what it is. Such beliefs about personality and behavior patterns can underlie therapeutic difficulties, and are often the target of therapeutic intervention.
- Our category decisions are influenced by the judgment context. When we are sorting things into different categories (e.g., anxiety or depression), we attend to characteristics that discriminate between categories (e.g., markers of differential diagnosis such as worrying about the future vs. ruminating about the past). Conversely, when we identify the category of a single example, we attend to the characteristics within the category (e.g., the prototype, such as the cluster of depressive symptoms). Thus, whether we approach assessment blindly or attempt to verify another's diagnosis will influence what aspects of a client and her situation we notice and consider important to her diagnosis, and thus our final conclusion.

9

Decision Making: Gathering and Evaluating Evidence

Whatever may be our wishes, our inclinations, or the dictates of our passions, they cannot alter the state of facts and evidence.
—John Adams (1770)

Therapists are constantly taking in and using information about their clients and their own practice. This information is used to generate reports, guide therapeutic conversation, and to construct and revise intervention strategies and treatment plans. This information is both nonverbal (client's body language, facial expression, voice tone) and verbal (the content of client's communications). For example, therapists must decide the likely cause of clients' symptoms, whether it be dysphoric mood (e.g., anxiety, depression), dysfunctional relationships, or work difficulties. In extreme cases, they also make judgments such as whether clients are a danger to themselves or others, or whether clients can safely return to work following a stress leave. Some of these decisions may be made quickly, based on past experience. Others may require more deliberate thought and may be reached only after considering and weighing the facts and arguments. Clients also take in and use the information from their environments, and therapists are alert to evidence that clients use information from their family, friends, and work colleagues in a biased way that contributes to their difficulties.

Cognitive science has discovered many factors that influence how people take in information, attend to it, and use it to form conclusions and decide actions. This research is directly applicable to psychotherapy practice, both for the ways that therapists consider and use client information, and for the ways that clients may use these human tendencies against themselves, rather than as ways to more successfully navigate life. This chapter and the following one outline what is known about the cognitive processes that underlie these types of decisions: This chapter describes what we know about how we take in information, and chapter 10 examines the evidence about our use of the information we do take in.

There is a broad consensus among researchers in the field that reasoning and decision making are mediated by two broadly defined types of processes (Evans, 2003; Evans & Over, 1996; Sloman, 1996, 2002; Stanovich, 1999, 2002). These processes interact in systematic ways and produce regular characteristics in the decisions people make. The first type of process is *associative*, or *heuristic* (Sloman, 1996, 2002), and is similar to priming or associative memory retrieval as described in chapters 3 and 4. It operates without the necessary involvement of consciousness and underlies many basic cognitive functions, including language comprehension, visual perception, and categorization. As discussed in the previous chapters, associative processes encode and process regularities in the environment, and make use of temporal and similarity relationships to draw inferences. The output of these associative processes produce the sense that an answer has "popped into your head" without having to spend a lot of time searching for the answer. This process is adaptively configured to allow us to take advantage of past experience in making decisions (Evans, 2003) and produce fast intuitive inferences requiring little cognitive effort. For example, a quick decision to avoid conflict in all situations by withdrawing seems automatic, and many clients present such patterns to their psychotherapists as though they were permanent characteristics ("I've always been like that").

Analytic processes, in contrast, entail deliberate reflection. They require conscious processing and are the types of thought processes that most people associate with sound reasoning and judgment. Because such processes require access to attention and working memory, the number of options that can be considered at one time is limited, as is the amount of information about each option that can be considered. Relative to associative processes, deliberate analysis is slow, effortful, and attention demanding. However, despite the capacity limitations, analytic processes permit a type of abstract, hypothetical thinking that is not possible using only heuristic processes (Evans, 2003; Stanovich, 2002). Specifically, they allow decisions to be made by representing models of a situation, considering alternative possibilities, and extrapolating future outcomes (Stanovich, 1999). To use the previous example, conflict-avoidant clients may have realized that this pattern is problematic as they analyze the processes and effects surrounding their avoidance at work and home (e.g., their wishes and opinions do not get implemented), and this awareness may precipitate their seeking therapy.

In some cases, associative and analytic processes may operate independently and simultaneously produce different responses to a situation. This produces what Sloman (2002) calls "simultaneous contradictory beliefs" and is the hallmark of the independent operation of two modes of thought. To understand this, consider the following two lines. Which is longer?

They are in fact of identical length. However, the illusion that the right line is longer than the left one persists, even though you know for certain that they are the same length. Thus, we simultaneously hold two contradictory opinions, one generated by our perceptual system and the other by a system of abstract comprehension. Similarly, many clients enter therapy realizing that their associative or heuristic methods of decision making either do not work or produce distress, or both, but they have been unable to develop an alternative. Many therapeutic systems assist clients to develop alternatives to their "dysfunctional heuristics" or ineffective habitual patterns (thinking, behavioral, and emotional).

In most cases, however, the associative and the analytic processes work in tandem. Many decisions, in fact, reflect an interaction of associative and analytic processes (Sloman, 2002). For example, Evans and Over (1996) argue that preconscious, associative processes may select information from the environment for the analytic system to consider (see the discussion of attentional selection in chapter 7). If this is the case, analytic processes are focused on a highly select subset of representations that appear to be relevant in a given context. In other words, while we may choose some parts of an event to examine more analytically, those chosen parts are not necessarily selected using good analytic reasoning. Thus, it is important to consider ways in which our heuristic or associative processes influence or limit our analytic processes.

For example, a client sought therapy for assistance in deciding which alternatives to surgery for prostate cancer he would pursue, even though his urologist had strongly recommended the surgical option. In exploring alternatives (e.g., radiation, do nothing, etc.), it was clear that his fear of surgery in general and the potential sexual effects of the surgery precluded the surgical option from consideration. An appeal to this client's generally good analytic ability, arguing that all options need the same thorough consideration, led to his agreement to recognize and attend to his fear of surgery and loss of sexual functioning as a necessary precursor to any decision.

Evans (1996) provided a simple experimental demonstration of interaction of heuristic and analytic processes. Participants were given four cards that had a letter on one side and a number on the other. Participants were then asked to verify whether these cards conformed to a simple rule, such as, "If a card has an A on one side, then it must have a 4 on the other." They were asked to indicate which of the cards they would need to turn over to determine whether or not the rule was true. Participants were also asked to indicate which cards they were thinking about prior to making their decision.

The correct answer to this problem is to turn over the cards marked "A" and "7," as these cards would tell you for certain whether the rule was false (i.e., if there was an "A" opposite the "7," or something other than a "4" opposite the "A," the rule has been violated). It doesn't really matter what is opposite the "K" or the "4": The rule would be true regardless of what was on the other side. The most common response, however, was to select the "A" and the "4." These are the items that are mentioned in the rule and therefore draw attention. Moreover, participants spent most of their time thinking about the cards that they ended up selecting and spent relatively little time thinking about the cards that they did not select; their reasoning seemed to be aimed at justifying the cards that were already selected.

This illustrates a theme that recurs throughout decision making and reasoning research, and it is one of the major ways analysis is limited by associative thinking: People's reasoning is dominated by information that is present in the environment, and they tend to neglect consideration of information that is not available (Hearst, 1991). That is, it is easier to make connections between two events than between nonevents, and it is easier to notice the appearance than the removal of something. This is true even when one is primed to consider the absence of an event, as the following paragraph illustrates:

How fast can you spot what is unusual about this paragraph? It looks so ordinary that you might think nothing was wrong with it at all and, in fact, nothing is. But it is atypical. Why? Study its various parts, think about its curious wording, and you may hit upon a solution. But you must do it without our aid; our plan is not to allow any scandalous misconduct in this psychological study. No doubt, if you work hard on this possibly frustrating task, its abnormality will soon dawn upon you. You cannot know until you try. But it is commonly a hard nut to crack. So, good luck!

Is a solution conspicuous now? Was it dramatic and fair, although odd? Authors' hint: Our autographs cannot accompany this communication and maintain its atypicality. (adapted from Hearst, 1991, p. 440)

The solution to this puzzle is that the letter "e" does not appear in the paragraph. Similar failures to attend to the absence of events are also frequent in therapeutic settings. For example, clients may fail to mention an obvious difficulty (e.g., obesity, alcohol use) or their living situation during an initial interview. Therapists are trained to notice such omissions and to elicit missing information in the exploration and assessment processes. On the other hand, therapists may fail to notice their own omissions, such as failure to consider positive aspects of relationships that are the source of difficulty for clients, because the client's conversation focuses only on the problematic factors. Solution-focused therapies have developed a model largely on the basis of such omissions of positive information. For example, asking questions about exceptions where the problem pattern could have occurred but didn't provides important information to use in assisting clients to reach their goals (Hoyt, 2003).

A similar situation occurs when judgments are made about information retrieved from memory: The easy availability of information may block consideration of relevant alternatives. For example, people's beliefs about many issues ranging from welfare mothers to crime rates are influenced by the salient examples presented in the media, such as the fact that people are aware of instances where kidnapping happens, but they may not give sufficient weight to the fact that kidnapping happens only rarely. Most therapists have experienced a parent seeking counseling after news reports of tragic situations involving children (e.g., kidnappings, fatal accidents).

The second way in which associative processes influence analytic processes is to shift analysis in favor of prior beliefs. For instance, the fact that people believe that a particular pattern exists can influence the way that they perceive and remember events, so that a pattern appears to emerge when none exists. For example, L. J. Chapman and Chapman (1967, 1969, 1971) were puzzled by the fact that therapists continued to use projective tests, despite the mountain of evidence suggesting they were unreliable. The answer seemed to be that therapists continued to observe a relationship between their clients' responses to these tests and their diagnosis (J. Baron, 2000), and they did not believe the negative results. To test this, L. J. Chapman and Chapman (1967, 1969, 1971) collected a number of drawings ostensibly produced on the Draw-a-Person Test. Each drawing was labeled with a diagnosis (e.g., suspicious of other people). The labels were added in such a way that there was no relationship at all between the symptoms and features of the drawing. Participants were asked to "discover" which features of the drawings went with which labels. They "discovered" the correlations that clinicians believed to exist (e.g., correlations between suspiciousness and large eyes), even though there was no correlation between the variables (i.e., suspiciousness occurred equally often with large and small eyes).

In many contexts, both feature positive and belief-based processes are highly adaptive. Given the processing limitations imposed by attention and working memory, analysis is possible only if a small amount of information is selected for processing (Evans & Over, 1996). In other words, because analytic reasoning can only be applied to a relatively small amount of information, we would be overwhelmed if required to deal with the massive amounts of information available in the environment. Thus, it is necessary for some sort of mental "triage" to happen and for only a subset of information available in the world to be analyzed. Similarly, with regard to beliefs, it is not realistic to expect people to ignore all of the information and knowledge that they have acquired. The purpose of this knowledge, after all, is to allow people to profit from past experience. However, in psychotherapy we deliberately arrange a situation in which clients can explore and attend to aspects of their lives thoroughly in a secure atmosphere of trust and support. This increases the amount of material that is open to analysis.

In other situations, however, these associative processes can lead us to neglect important considerations. For example, as solution-focused therapists note, therapists are inclined to ignore positive and functional characteristics of our clients, as we attend to their reported difficulties, or, a well-trained cognitive behavioral therapist may pay less attention to emotional processes than to thinking or behavior. This is a potential weakness of almost all therapies, which have therapists attending to some aspects of their clients' experiences but not all. This limiting of information to be considered may have been an intuitive attempt to keep the therapist from being overwhelmed by too much information, but it can result in a therapist missing important pieces of information relevant to assisting their clients. The key to sound decision making is to understand when and how associative processes influence decision making, and to compensate appropriately.

In this and the following chapter, we examine a number of decision-making situations that are relevant to a therapeutic context. In each case, we explore how associative and analytic processes combine to inform reasoning and decision making, and we describe the systematic effects that arise from this interaction. Our goals are to provide tools for good decision making and to enable therapists to efficiently assess problems with clients' and their own decision-making strategies.

Case Illustration:

Janice was referred for therapy through her employee assistance program. She worked for a large corporation (several thousand employees) with whom her therapist had a service provider contract. Her presenting issue was stress related to her workplace. She was intimidated by her supervisor in the human resources department who would "blow up" periodically, shouting at Janice (who was his assistant) and other employees. She described one incident in which he tore up a report that she had written when others were present, leaving her feeling humiliated and embarrassed.

Janice was forty-three when she entered therapy, married, with two adolescent daughters. She described her marital relationship and family life as generally supportive and positive. Her husband had been out of work for a year after his company had eliminated his position, and Janice was now the only wage earner in the family. Consequently, although sympathetic, he was quite anxious when Janice described her interactions with her supervisor, as he worried about their financial viability if she quit or lost her job. This made it difficult for Janice to confide in her husband, as she was nervous it would add to his already high level of stress and anxiety. Relevant history was that Janice had grown up in an alcoholic home in which her father would periodically verbally bully, tease, and embarrass his wife and daughters in front of his drinking friends whom he invited home.

Janice's goals were to manage the job-related stress better and to make a decision about leaving her position. She clearly wanted to quit her job but was afraid to because of the financial consequences. In exploring her history both at work and growing up, it was also clear that Janice had difficulty considering any options other than quitting or learning to tolerate her supervisor's periodic verbal tirades. However, considering either of these possibilities also resulted in high anxiety. She described herself as "frozen in hell, with nowhere to go." The therapist imposed some structure into her situation by describing the importance of considering multiple options before making any decision. He persuaded her to (a) consider a variety of options to her job difficulty, (b) investigate and gather evidence concerning all the options prior to deciding, and (c) consider back-up plans in case things didn't work out as desired with her first choice. Janice was quite relieved with this methodical decision-making process, and it reduced her sense of feeling trapped.

INFORMATION-PRESENT EFFECTS

People's thinking is often grounded by that which is present, neglecting that which is absent. Often, the information that is available in the environment is a strong draw for people's attention (Evans, 1998), leading them to focus on what is present in the environment, and to neglect consideration of relevant, but less contextually salient alternatives. Note that this tendency is essentially the same as the priming effects described in chapter 3.

A concept borrowed and adapted from the developmental literature may assist here (Kegan, 1994). We become "embedded" in what is currently in our lives. This seems to make it difficult to develop and/or use skills that require stepping back and observing. For example, an adolescent tends to be embedded in interpersonal relationships, experiencing such contact intensely. However, this very intensity can impair their ability to think about and observe relationships objectively, considering ideas such as loyalty, commitment, or intimacy from a variety of perspectives. The use of these observation skills is often precipitated by either an internal maturational process and/or an environmental demand, including psychotherapy. The result is that we learn to "dis-embed" and in doing so increase our abilities to experience and influence ever widening spheres of human experience (e.g., self, relationships, institutions). The point is that even though information may be absent from the immediate environment (either physical or cognitive), it doesn't mean it is not relevant. In fact, the missing information can be highly relevant, even necessary, to reaching a balanced decision.

For example, a young adolescent boy who was referred for counseling to assist with his social skill development was part of a group of young boys who acted out in minor ways (smoking, shoplifting, harassing other students). He was deeply embedded in his group membership and refused to notice or consider either the other members' behavior toward him (they actually treated him quite poorly) or the consequences of his actions. He seemed, as many clients do, to "legislate out of existence" relevant aspects of his experience. In this case, after an extended period of relationship development, this young client began observing the abusive treatment he received at the hands of his ostensible support group.

The Constraining Effect of a Salient Example

Our thinking tends to be strongly guided by a current view or example (including the many examples in this book). Many of us use examples to explicate and teach, and we should be aware that providing an example may limit the thinking of those we are teaching. S. M. Smith, Ward, and Schumacher (1993) provided a straightforward demonstration of this. Participants in their study were asked to design and sketch novel items, such as a new type of toy. Half of the participants were provided with an example to get them started, the remainder were not. Participants were told to draw as many new and creative designs as they could, without duplicating existing toys. The results indicated that the participants who started with an example tended to be less creative than those who were not provided with an example. Instead, their drawings were more likely to conform to the drawings provided by the experimenter, even when they were instructed to produce designs that differed from the examples they were given.

Leblanc, Brooks, and Norman (2002; see also Hatala et al., 1999) extended this to a medical setting, in which physicians were provided with case history information that biased them toward or away from a correct diagnosis (of a skin condition). They were then provided with 10 head and shoulder photographs, which were considered to be textbook illustrations of a specific diagnosis. The incorrect suggestions were plausible and based on one feature of the photos, around which an alternate diagnosis could be created. When the correct diagnosis was suggested, participants identified more features relevant to the correct diagnosis and derived the correct diagnosis more often; when the incorrect diagnosis was suggested by the case history, participants decided more often in favor of the alternative and misidentified features of the photos to be consistent with this alternative. The researchers concluded that the influence of a hypothesis diagnosis both focuses the attention of physicians on relevant features and serves to change the interpretation given to physical characteristics. The same is undoubtedly true for psychotherapists, since diagnoses based on the American Psychiatric Association's (2000) *Diagnostic and Statistical Manual of Mental Disorders* (4th ed., text rev. [*DSM-IV-TR*]) and the features that are considered relevant are influenced by practitioners' theories, even though diagnostic material is arranged atheoretically (Kim & Ahn, 2002).

These studies show that how we perceive, interpret, and think about a situation can be strongly influenced by the particular context in which the situation is embedded. In both cases, participants found it difficult to think about that which was not present in the environment (i.e., design aspects that were not in the experimenter's example, or the alternative diagnosis). Indeed, even when it is made obvious that the missing information is highly relevant (e.g., when mock jurors are presented with arguments relevant to only a single side of a legal dispute), people tend not to compensate sufficiently for the missing information (Brenner, Koehler, & Tversky, 1996). Brenner et al. hypothesized that participants who were given one-sided evidence did not spontaneously generate specific arguments for the other side; consistent with their hypothesis, participants who were asked to contrast the potential strength of the unpresented other-side arguments to the presented ones showed less bias than those who evaluated single-sided arguments.

In therapeutic settings, this can mean that beliefs about a new client's difficulties that are created by salient examples and diagnoses provided by referral sources can influence how the client's situation is interpreted (see chapter 8). Similarly, in relationship or family therapy, therapists often have to address beliefs that family members have about each other or themselves. For example, in one session a therapist observed that the step-father gave many verbal and nonverbal signals of approval and affection to his stepson. However, the first time the stepfather corrected his stepson, the boy's mother reacted strongly and protectively saying, "You never liked Shawn from the moment you met him." A wide variety of techniques, including the generic skill of confrontation or the disputing techniques of cognitive behavioral therapy, can assist clients in realizing that there is insufficient evidence for their belief and that they should consider alternatives. Postmodern constructivist approaches to psychotherapy assist clients in realizing that beliefs and opinions are actively maintained structures of meaning, rather than truths set in stone, and can thus be altered when required (e.g., Mahoney, 2003; Neimeyer & Bridges, 2003).

The Constraining Effects of a Prior Hypothesis

A related phenomenon comes up in situations where people gather evidence to test a hypothesis. Hypotheses can be scientific, therapeutic, or personal. For example, therapists may accumulate the evidence they need to decide whether someone is depressed, whether the client's symptoms are caused by a traumatic experience, or whether treatment should be focused on changing the client's self-concept or her significant relationships. In all cases, therapists must identify a key source of the client's difficulties, or at least establish a viable route to a cure. Most clients attending therapy have implicitly or explicitly formed some hypotheses about why they have these problems or why they are the way they are, and they and the therapist collaboratively address whether this is a hypothesis to use or whether to develop alternatives. For example, some clients begin therapy with the hypothesis that some unremembered past trauma will give reason and meaning to their present symptoms. It is one of the therapist's tasks to uncover that hypothesis in the process of exploration and problem space development, and in collaboration with the client, to decide whether that is a useful hypothesis in assisting the client to ease her symptoms and attain her goals. This is further complicated by the therapist's guiding theoretical orientation, which implicitly favors some types of hypotheses over others.

In therapy contexts, evidence is gathered for such questions through therapeutic interviews and conversations, psychometric tests, behavioral observation, or some combination of these. The outcome of these observations can be a formal or informal diagnosis, or a treatment plan based on our model of causes of the client's current situation. In addition, we often wish to teach our clients the skills to make better decisions for themselves, so they will not need to seek therapy each time they are faced with an issue.

In situations where we begin with a tentative hypothesis and proceed to gather evidence bearing on the hypothesis, we tend to be strongly influenced by our focal hypothesis, that is, our current best guess (for reviews, see J. Baron, 2000; Nickerson, 1998). We then proceed to test that hypothesis by thinking of and looking for results that would be obtained if the hypothesis were true, a heuristic known as the positive test strategy.

For example, if we consider that a client is depressed, we might look for evidence that this is the case (e.g., recent changes in sleep and eating habits, depressed mood, lack of energy, etc.). We might not ask about such things as the current state of their intimate relationships or success experiences at work, which would more likely disconfirm the hypothesis of depression and indicate another diagnosis such as adjustment disorder or a relational V-code problem (if the therapist is using the *DSM-IV-TR* diagnostic system). All theories of counseling and therapy have implicitly or explicitly defined criteria for diagnosis, etiology, and treatment application. Practitioners of all schools need to consider ways to potentially disconfirm their hypotheses as well as confirm them. This approach requires time and thoroughness and has become more difficult to apply, as diagnoses and treatments are now expected to be brief and targeted. To use the previous clinical example, if we determine that the change in a person's mood has resulted from environmental or relationship factors, we will not only diagnose differently, but we may also apply differential treatments.

Wason (1960) provided a simple and compelling laboratory demonstration of this situation. Participants were told that the experimenter had in mind a rule that generated sequences of three numbers. Their job was to guess this rule. To help them, they were given a sequence of numbers, 2-4-6, that fit the rule; participants then proposed sequences of numbers and were given feedback about whether their proposals fit the rule. When they were confident, they guessed the rule. The initial sequence clearly suggested hypotheses such as "numbers ascending by 2" or "ascending even numbers," and participants proposed sequences that were congruent with this initial hypothesis (e.g., 8-10-12; 20-22-24; 100-102-104; 3-5-7); for each such sequence, they were told that the example fit the rule. After about half a dozen such trials, the vast majority of participants confidently announced the rule.

However, only about one fifth of the participants correctly identified the experimenter's rule, which was "any three ascending numbers." Of the remainder, most announced a rule that was a subset of the correct rule, such as "numbers ascending by two." To have identified the correct rule, participants either needed to consider alternative hypotheses and propose examples that discriminated between the two possibilities (e.g., 1-5-6, which would be true for the "three ascending numbers" but false for "ascending even numbers") or propose examples that would be false if their guess was correct (e.g., 3-4-5). In the latter case, receiving feedback that the example fit the rule would inform participants that their initial hypothesis could not be correct. Indeed, participants who identified the rule correctly were more likely to test instances that were inconsistent with their initial hypothesis than those who did not.

Wason's initial demonstration illustrates two human tendencies. The first is called *selective testing*, where people tend to focus on a single hypothesis at a time until one is found which meets situational requirements (e.g., Mynatt, Doherty, & Dragan, 1993; Sanbonmatsu, Posavac, Kardes, & Mantel, 1998), including concentrating on a central or *focal* hypothesis at the expense of alternative relevant hypotheses (Sanbonmatsu et al., 1998). For example, a therapist or physician may only consider whether or not a client is depressed, rather than considering multiple possibilities for their difficulties. The second tendency is *positive testing*, a strategy that entails looking for information that would be true if the focal hypothesis were correct (Klayman & Ha, 1987; see Zuckerman, Knee, Hodgins, & Miyake, 1995, for a description of how this strategy can mediate interviewing situations).

Both of these strategies can be adaptive in that they provide adequate results in many ordinary contexts (Sanbonmatsu et al., 1998) but are also implicated in decision-making biases. For example, if my goal is to find an apartment, I may first look at newspaper advertisements. Even if an alternative strategy, such as consulting a real estate agent, may be more efficient, I may not consider any alternatives unless my first strategy is unsuccessful. A more therapeutically relevant example comes from a family therapy session in which a father described his strategy in managing his four-year-old twin girls in public places. "After a couple of attempts to quiet them, I get so flustered with people looking at me and thinking I'm a bad parent—I just lose it and shout at them—and then other people know I'm a bad dad—and I hate doing it—but it works and the girls are quiet for a while." Although this father's selective testing strategy worked in the moment (i.e., managing his children), this family was in therapy to deal with the deteriorating relationship between the father and his daughters and the mother's fear that he would become physically abusive with them.

This "good enough" selective testing strategy is sensitive to the limits of working memory and does not require keeping in mind several possibilities at a time. It is also appropriate in situations where one hypothesis is clearly more important or relevant than the alternatives. This would be the case, for instance, for severe but treatable psychological difficulties such as depression or phobia. Selective testing works best when the results of the investigation provide clear and unambiguous confirmatory or disconfirmatory evidence. When the standards are less clear, or the evidence is ambiguous as is typical in psychotherapy, selective testing is less appropriate. There is evidence that we can overcome this selective testing bias by structuring the testing environment so that evidence for one hypothesis serves as evidence against others (McKenzie, 1998; see diagnosticity of evidence). In fact, simply providing a label for an alternative hypothesis can improve performance (Tweney et al., 1980).

The second tendency revealed by Wason's number sequencing task is *positive testing*, a strategy that entails looking for information that would be true if the focal hypothesis were correct (Klayman & Ha, 1987; see Zuckerman et al., 1995, for a description of how this strategy can mediate interviewing situations). It is important to note that this positive test strategy is most likely a manifestation of "feature positive" thinking, rather than an inability to falsify hypotheses. People do appreciate the implications of contradictory information once that information is presented (e.g., Kareev & Halberstadt, 1993), but our strong tendency is to seek confirming information (see chapter 8 and later in this chapter for discussions of confirmation bias). Indeed, inducing a mindset to seek both confirming and disconfirming information usually requires either explicit instructions (e.g., Gorman & Gorman, 1984) or a significant restructuring of the task (Spellman, Lopez, & Smith, 1999).

As was the case for selective testing, positive testing is adaptive and adequate in some situations, specifically, when the goal is to narrow down a hypothesis that is too broad (Klayman & Ha, 1987). In this case, it is important to sample broadly within the range of the focal hypothesis (the current best guess), in order to pinpoint the correct hypothesis (e.g., the game of 20 questions). Often in therapy, clients are overwhelmed by multiple issues, and the therapist will assist in narrowing the field or problem space until the client can address fewer issues in a prioritized fashion.

In summary, the type of strategy that we use to gather evidence should depend on whether we believe that the initial, focal hypothesis is too narrow or too broad. If we are looking to narrow the hypothesis, sampling evidence that is consistent with the target is necessary. For example, if a client has been identified as depressed, and the therapist needs to decide if he has a depressive or bipolar disorder, asking questions about manic or hypomanic episodes is appropriate. If we are starting from a narrow hypothesis and looking to broaden its scope, we need to test alternative hypotheses (e.g., consider causes other than mood disorder as the source of a client's problems). In cases where we don't know, or where the truth may only partially overlap the target hypothesis, a combination strategy, such as identifying two hypotheses and using a positive test strategy related to both, may produce the best results.

For example, a client presented with symptoms of anxiety and gastrointestinal difficulties. His physician had already considered and tested a variety of medical hypotheses (none of which was validated) and had encouraged the client to consider the alternate hypothesis of a chronic stress reaction. In exploring his current life situation, the client revealed to his therapist that he had recently been promoted from a union to a management position and was having difficulty with the adjustment from frontline worker to supervisor. He also described increasing conflict within his ten-year marriage. As the problem space was further clarified, a common constraint to both stressful situations was his difficulty in stating clearly what he thought or wanted. With the hypothesis that this lack of assertiveness was a cause of distress in both circumstances, the therapist helped him to develop assertiveness skills, predicting that as he more actively engaged in conflicts and disputes at home and work, his anxiety and gastrointestinal symptoms would decrease. Alternatively, if a physical source such as diet was the underlying cause of the anxiety and gastrointestinal difficulties, changes in assertiveness skill would not affect the problem. Selective or positive test strategies would pursue only one of these alternatives at a time, whereas having him actively change his behavior to suit both hypotheses (e.g., act assertively and change diet) may be more efficient.

Case Illustration:

> *After much discussion, Janice wanted to consider the following options: (a) remain in her job but resolve the difficulty, (b) request a transfer to another department, (c) get a new job and then quit, and (d) quit and look for a new job. During this phase of therapy, information-present effects needed attention. The salient and emotionally evocative example of her humiliation when the supervisor tore up her report made it difficult for her to consider options that might require contact with him. This was exacerbated by her belief, present since childhood, that the only solution to bullying was to go away. This was mainly resolved by the therapist's exploration of many situations in which Janice had observed her supervisor's bullying and temper tantrums. She realized that he only did this in the presence of subordinates and behind closed doors (e.g., he tore up her report during a meeting in which he was the only manager present). This simple but important realization (a form of the diagnosticity of evidence) shifted Janice's attitude from one of outright terror for her boss to one of apprehensive curiosity in his presence. This shift helped her to gather more evidence for ways to address the issues while remaining within the corporation. She also embarked on gathering information in relation to all options (e.g., speaking to a union representative about the possibilities of transfer and speaking to an employment counselor about opportunities elsewhere). As the problem space was broadened and alternative options and missing information were included in her considerations, Janice felt more at ease and hopeful that she could eventually make a decision.*

POSITIVE FEATURE BIAS AND THE DIAGNOSTICITY OF EVIDENCE

In the preceding section, we noted that people tend to be influenced by the presence of an example or focal hypothesis when they are gathering evidence. This is a potential problem when it causes one to neglect potentially relevant alternatives. A similar situation arises when interpreting the evidence gathered. For example, suppose that we are with a client who manifests a set of behaviors such as feeling increasingly agitated and anxious. As therapists, we must make one of several decisions. Perhaps we need to construct an assessment and arrive at a formal diagnosis, such as anxiety disorder. Perhaps instead, we need to construct a model of the person's life and lifestyle that would give rise to their current situation, such as a recent illness in a family member or an inability to maintain an exercise program due to a nagging injury. A common strategy used by therapists of many schools is to develop potential hypotheses by asking, "What was happening in your life as the symptom which brought you into therapy appeared?" In any case, we need to develop a treatment plan that will allow the client to move from the current situation to her goal state. The therapist is in the position of reasoning backward from the evidence that has been presented, and making a judgment about how to proceed (Does the issue result from biochemical or social factors? What type of treatment plan would work best?).

Suppose that we develop a working hypothesis based on our observations. For the sake of simplicity, we will focus on the case in which the therapist is making an assessment, although clearly the analysis extends to the other situations as well. In this case, suppose that we decide that the client most probably has an anxiety disorder, given that 70% of those having an anxiety disorder will manifest the behaviors in question. The information about the correlation between the symptom and diagnosis itself may come from a number of sources. It may be based, for example, on the published validity coefficient for a psychometric test, *DSM-IV-TR* guidelines, our experience as therapists, or any combination of these.

Regardless of the source of the information, we must now reason backward from the evidence and make an inference about the focal hypothesis. Given that 70% of the time, someone with an anxiety disorder will show the pattern of behavior (test results, etc.) that we have observed, are there grounds to proceed with the assumption that the client should be treated as if she has an anxiety disorder?

What is the probability that the client has an anxiety disorder? Deciding that we do not have enough information to make a judgment would be correct. There are two other pieces of information that are crucial to the judgment.

The first is the probability that the focal hypothesis (the diagnosis) is true in the general population. This is called the *base-rate*. If the hypothesized condition is rare, then this needs to be factored in to our final conclusions. For example, general anxiety disorders are more frequent than posttraumatic stress disorder (PTSD) but less frequent than situational stress. Or, sadness due to life circumstances such as grief, loss, and disappointment is more common than the sadness due to a depressive episode or disorder. The less probable any diagnosis is, the less likely it is the explanation for the behavior.

The second concerns the degree to which a piece of evidence discriminates between the focal hypothesis (anxiety disorder) and other hypotheses (situational stress or PTSD). This is called the *diagnosticity of the evidence*. If a piece of evidence is equally likely, given both the focal and an alternative hypothesis (such as a general feeling of anxiety and difficulty relaxing), then it does not tell us much about the focal hypothesis. That is, if feeling anxious and agitated is associated with a number of other conditions, it is not a good indicator of anxiety disorder per se.

In sum, making an accurate diagnosis in this instance requires at least three pieces of information. The first we will refer to as *case-specific* information, which is the information that is collected about a particular individual. This probability refers to the ability of the diagnostic tool in question to identify relevant cases. In our example, 70% of those with an anxiety disorder will manifest the particular set of behaviors that we have observed. The second is the *diagnosticity of the evidence*. To determine this, we need to know how likely it is that the behaviors will be observed even when the person does not have an anxiety disorder. In our example, this means how likely it is that someone who is agitated does not have an anxiety disorder (also known as the false positive rate). Finally, one needs to know *base-rate*, which is the probability of someone in the general population having an anxiety disorder.

Overemphasis on Case-Specific Information

Although all three sources of information (case-specific, diagnosticity, base-rate) should contribute to probability judgments, there is ample evidence to indicate that people often overvalue case-specific information at the expense of the other sources. For example, people will often indicate that the probability of anxiety disorder in the above example is close to 70%, regardless of the base-rate.

A familiar example serves to indicate the error entailed in this conclusion. In the news reports, the probability that a suspected terrorist is Muslim is very high—close to 100%. However, even granted that the reports are accurate and representative, this tells us very little about the probability that someone who is Muslim is in fact a terrorist. This is because terrorists comprise a very small portion of the population, so that the base-rate of being a terrorist, regardless of one's faith, is very small. Thus, in order to draw an accurate picture of the relationship between terrorism and religion, we need to anchor our judgment on the base-rate. This is the case in many psychological categories where the diagnosis of a condition will imply the presence of many symptoms but the reverse is less likely to be true; that is, the presence of particular symptoms is less likely to indicate a particular diagnosis (see chapter 8).

In contrast, people tend to undervalue base-rate information, giving it less weight than appropriate (Evans, 2002; Goodie & Fantino, 1995, 1996; J. J. Koehler, 1996), including in cases of expert decision making where it is most important (Evans et al., 2002; for examples relevant to psychological decision making, see Kennedy, Willis, & Faust, 1997; Labarge, McCaffrey, & Brown, 2003). Note that most people tend to *undervalue* base-rates rather than neglect them completely (Koehler, 1996).

One corollary to the overvaluing of case-specific information is that people often give credence to uninformative evidence about a particular case, even when it has little value. That is, a description of a person, even though uninformative in terms of the target hypothesis (i.e., the correct judgment), may be sufficient to draw attention away from the base-rate, and suggest to the person that their best option is to equivocate, giving a 50% probability, rather than relying on the base-rate (Tversky & Kahneman, 1986).

For example, in the Kennedy et al. (1997) study, school psychologists were asked to judge the probability that a young boy had a learning disability based on either (a) the base-rate of that type of learning disability in the population, (b) the base-rate plus clinically useless information (i.e., inter-subset scatter on the Wechsler Intelligence Scale for Children-Revised [WISC-R]), or (c) the base-rate plus clinically relevant information (i.e., the sensitivity and false-positive rates of the test). In the absence of case-specific information, the psychologists correctly gave the base-rate as the probability. However, when given the uninformative information, estimates deviated significantly from the base-rate, suggesting that decisions were influenced by the case-specific information, even though it added no useful information to this specific decision. Finally, in this study, participants were least accurate when given the clinically relevant information, again suggesting that judgments were anchored on the case-specific information, rather than a combination of case-specific and base-rate information.

The Logic Underlying the Use of Base-Rate Information

How do base-rates modify the interpretation of case-specific information? To see, we go back to our original example, in which we observed agitated behavior and drew the tentative conclusion that this was caused by an anxiety disorder. This conclusion was based on the assumption that 70% of people with an anxiety disorder are agitated. Next, we illustrate two cases: one where the base-rate for the hypothesized category is low and the other where it is high. In both cases, we will make the assumption that the observed behavior, agitation, is relatively common, and occurs about 50% of the time in populations where anxiety disorders are not indicated (e.g., most people report feeling anxious or agitated sometime in their lives).

In our first scenario, assume that we are dealing with a population where the base-rate of anxiety disorder is relatively low, say 20% (e.g., the clientele of a general university counseling center). Before we proceed, what is the probability that the individual in question has an anxiety disorder (without doing all of the calculations, come up with a ballpark figure)? To make the illustration easier, let us assume an imaginary sample of one hundred people. Of these, twenty have anxiety disorder (the base-rate figure) and the remaining eighty do not. Of those with anxiety disorder, 70% or fourteen are agitated (case-specific information). Of the eighty people who do not have anxiety disorder, 50% or forty are agitated:

Scenario 1: Low Base-Rate

                                                                Agitated = 14
                          Anxiety Disorder = 20
                                                                Not agitated = 6
100 people
                                                                Agitated = 40
                          Not-Anxiety Disorder = 80
                                                                Not agitated = 40

From the chart, we can see that there are two groups of people who manifest agitated behavior in our sample for a total of fifty-four people (40 + 14). Of those fifty-four, only fourteen have anxiety disorder. Thus, the probability that someone who is agitated should be classified as having an anxiety disorder is only about 25% (14/54). In other words, even though a very large majority (70%) of those who have anxiety disorder are agitated, the reverse probability that someone who is agitated has an anxiety disorder is small (similar to the relationship between Muslims and terrorists).

To see the importance of considering the base-rate, let us see what happens when we change it. That is, let us suppose that we are dealing with a population where anxiety disorder is relatively more common, say 60% (e.g., the clientele of a clinic specializing in anxiety disorders). The other information remains the same, and again, we are interested in knowing the probability that someone who is agitated has an anxiety disorder.

Scenario 2: High Base-Rate

                                                                Agitated = 42
                                Anxiety Disorder = 60
                                                                Not agitated = 18
        100 people
                                                                Agitated = 20
                                Not-Anxiety Disorder = 40
                                                                Not agitated = 20

In this sample, there are sixty-two people who are agitated, of which forty-two, or about three fourths have an anxiety disorder. Thus, the probability that someone who is agitated has an anxiety disorder is close to 75%, as opposed to 25% for the rarer condition shown in Scenario 1.

The situations illustrated in Scenarios 1 and 2 are directly relevant to most therapists. In many cases, the focal hypothesis is a relatively rare category, one whose base-rate in the population is low (e.g., PTSD). Under these circumstances, treating the case-specific evidence at face value can lead to a large distortion—the evidence gives a figure of 70%, whereas the actual value is closer to 25%. Even under the assumption that the base-rate of people who present themselves at a therapist's office is higher than the normal population, as in Scenario 2, failing to factor in the base-rate can still lead to an overestimate (or, in this case, a mistaken diagnosis or "false positive").

Often times, of course, we do not have exact numbers. Although we may not know the exact prevalence of a particular condition in the population, we should have some idea about what it should be. The point is that the prevalence of the condition should inform our judgments about the validity of the case-specific information as a basis for our conclusion. When the focal hypothesis is a rare condition, then we should downgrade the probability of this hypothesis, even when the probability of the symptom given the disorder is very high.

Using Base-Rates in Clinical Settings

There are a number of articles that describe the relevance of base-rates in therapeutic judgment (e.g., Garb, 1998; Kamphuis & Finn, 2002), including the relevance of applying base-rates to subpopulations (Gouvier, Pinkston, Santa-Maria, & Cherry, 2002), so we will not dwell on this at length. The bottom line is that base-rates should normally be incorporated into clinical judgment, except in limited circumstances. One such circumstance is where the base-rate of a particular condition is close to 50%. Another is the rare circumstance in which the test in question is 100% valid (i.e., produces neither false negatives nor false positives).

This will happen when the cluster of behaviors that you have observed is unique under the focal hypothesis, and when the test, procedure, or interview technique that you are using to form your opinion is reliable and gives few false positives. For example, the presence of purging with laxatives and/or vomiting is uniquely connected to bulimia nervosa, so a report of these symptoms can more confidently be used to diagnose this disorder. However, as we know, there are few mental health symptoms that are unique to a single disorder and even fewer psychometric tests that are completely reliable.

Unfortunately, the most prevalent source for diagnostic information, the *DSM-IV-TR*, does not include base-rate information for any mental disorders or the symptoms associated with them, nor is the prevalence of most mental health problems discussed in graduate training. In addition, there is little information available describing the prevalence of any given symptom in those who do not have the disorder with which the symptom is associated.

Information that is available about the prevalence of mental health disorders on government health Web sites (in Canada: www.hc-sc.gc.ca, mental health link; in the United States: www.nimh.nik.gov) indicates that the base-rate of disorders such as depression and anxiety is in the range of the rare occurrence illustrated in Scenario 1, and the rate of psychopathies such as schizophrenia is even lower. In Canada, for example, the prevalence of major depression ranges from 4.1% to 4.6% per year, anxiety disorders occur for 12.2% of the population, and the rate of schizophrenia is 0.3%. Base-rates of certain disorders may be higher for selected populations, such as those who work in dangerous occupations or individuals who present themselves for therapy (who all have some type of mental health difficulty by definition). For example, most people with mood or psychiatric disorders are likely seen by mental health professionals, so base-rates of these disorders among client populations is undoubtedly higher than the national average. Similarly, Stadnyk (2003) found a PTSD rate of 21.8% among corrections workers employed in inpatient facilities for criminal offenders, who routinely witness and are involved in traumatic incidents with inmates.

Using Base-Rates Derived From Experience. Because base-rate information that is so important for our judgment of client issues is not available through therapists' most common information sources, therapists often rely on their accumulating experience to determine how common particular disorders are. Indeed, the available evidence indicates that people are more likely to incorporate base-rate information when it is learned by personal experience (Evans et al., 2002; see also Koehler, 1996, for a review) and may, in some circumstances, even overuse these base-rates (Evans et al., 2002). So, for example, if our experience leads us to believe that the occurrence of a particular category is relatively rare or relatively frequent, this information is likely to be factored into our judgments.

The use of personal experience as our source of information can also be complicated by the fact that it relies on an accurate estimate of the frequency with which the category is observed. As the following sections describe, when making these estimates, we give more weight to the situations in which a positive occurrence (i.e., the diagnosis was made) was obtained than those in which it was absent (i.e., the diagnosis was withheld); our perception of these frequencies is also moderated by our theories and beliefs.

Facilitating the Use of Base-Rates

Cognitive researchers have identified a number of ways to increase the probability that base-rate information is accurately reflected in judgments. These all involve formulating the problem in terms of easy-to-use subsets. One way to do this is to represent the numbers as frequencies, rather than percentages (Cosmides & Tooby, 1996). This allows us to divide the problem space up into sets. The key is to be able to represent the nested relationships among the various elements of a problem (Evans, Handley, Perham, Over, & Thompson, 2000; Girotto & Gonzalez, 2001; Sloman, Over, Slovak, & Stibel, 2003).

For example, Labarge et al. (2003) gave neuropsychologists two versions of a formally identical problem. When given the following version, less than 9% of 131 clinical neuropsychologists (all with PhD or PsyD degrees) provided the correct answer (Labarge et al., 2003), even though the vast majority were correctly able to define each of the statistical terms used:

> The base rate of dementia among patients at an adult neuropsychology clinic is 10%. The dementia screening used in the clinic has a sensitivity of 80% and a specificity of 90%. What is the likelihood that an individual evaluated at this clinic who obtains a positive dementia screening score actually has dementia? (p. 173)

In this sample, the average response was 80%; 35% of the sample gave the sensitivity as the answer, 20% responded with the specificity, and 7% gave the base-rate. The correct answer is 47%. Again, it is important to note that this is a relatively low probability, despite the fact that the test is apparently accurate, with a hit rate of 80% and a false alarm rate of only 10%. It is low because the base-rate of dementia is low. It is also important to note that the respondents' judgments appeared to be anchored in the case-specific information they were provided and did not adequately reflect the low base-rate. Similar findings have been observed with medical practitioners (Cassells, Schoenberger, & Grayboys, 1978) and laypeople, even when the problem is presented using nontechnical language.

Another 135 neuropsychologists were given a problem that was formally equivalent to this one, but written in a way that allowed them to group the information together in a meaningful hierarchy:

> Ten out of every one hundred individuals seen in an adult neuropsychology unit have dementia. Of these ten individuals with dementia, eight will have a positive score on a dementia screening. Of the remaining ninety individuals without dementia, nine will still have a positive dementia screening score. In a sample of one hundred individuals from this clinic, how many of the individuals who have a positive dementia screening score will actually have dementia? (Labarge et al., 2003, p. 173)

This formulation allows one to think about a set of one hundred individuals, who are divided up into sets according to whether or not they have dementia, and according to their test results. Given this version of the question, 63% of the participants gave the correct answer (i.e., 47%), and the overall mean response (42%) was much closer to the correct answer than was the case with the earlier version.

In sum, the neglect of base-rate information can be seen as another example of an information-present effect. Our attention tends to be drawn to individuating information and information that is sensorily present. This information anchors our judgment, focusing our attention on the behaviors that are present or on the sensitivity of a test (i.e., the probability that someone manifests the behaviors, given they belong to a category) and leading us to neglect the important consideration of how likely the hypothesis is to be true in the first place (Tversky & Kahneman, 1986).

The More Is Better Principle and the Diagnosticity of Evidence

Another way that people's judgment is influenced by a focal hypothesis is that they fail to consider the probability that the evidence would be observed if the hypothesis were not true. That is, if the evidence that you have is likely to occur regardless of whether your hypothesis is true, then it is not very informative. This refers to the diagnosticity of the information. Instead, people often seek additional information for their focal hypothesis, even though this information does not discriminate their hypothesis from others (e.g., Doherty, Mynatt, Tweeney, & Schaivio, 1979; Evans, Venn, & Feeney, 2002; Mynatt, Doherty, & Dragan, 1993).

For instance, Chernev (1997) asked participants to evaluate pairs of consumer products (e.g., stair climbers, cordless phones). In each pair, participants expressed a marked preference for one of the products (i.e., because it had a better warranty, was cheaper, etc.). In one condition of the study, participants were given an additional piece of information about the two products that did not discriminate between them because it was common to both (e.g., they came with a six-month subscription to *Sports Illustrated*). Adding this common feature, even though it did not discriminate between the two products, produced a marked increase in participants' evaluation of their preferred product. Thus, this additional information increased confidence in the focal hypothesis, even though it did not discriminate between the focal and alternative hypotheses.

In a therapeutic setting, the diagnosticity of information is relevant because behaviors associated with one disorder will likely be common to other disorders as well. The same is true for decisions such as determining the central focus of treatment. For example, feelings such as sadness or anxiety are common to several issues (e.g., grief, depression, or loneliness for sadness; stress, Type A style, or being in a potentially dangerous situation for anxiety), as are behaviors such as impulsively beginning and ending projects or lying to one's intimates. The similarity of symptoms for a number of different conditions or life circumstances and a dearth of diagnosticity of evidence means that psychotherapists are often faced with choosing a treatment option that would be effective with any of the reasonable hypotheses. For example, therapists who use brief therapies (see, e.g., Hoyt, 2003) generally establish a change contract in collaboration with their clients and work toward the change goal rather than attempting to diagnose a mental health condition, unless there are very clear reasons to do so. Similarly, narrative, humanistic, and constructivist therapists attempt to utilize understanding of life narratives and experiences to further the process of therapeutic change without necessarily diagnosing a client.

The neglect of diagnosticity has a second outcome: Quantity of evidence may be mistaken for quality. The point is that when trying to discriminate between two or more hypotheses, we need evidence that is likely to be observed in one scenario but not in another. This allows us to discriminate between the two explanations. Instead, what sometimes happens is that we gather more evidence that is consistent with our focal hypothesis, even if it does not necessarily discriminate among the alternatives. For example, in a family therapy session, the parents had very different views of their adolescent daughter. The father believed she was "slutty," disrespectful, and out of control. The mother thought of her daughter as spirited and rebellious, but basically a "good kid." Week after week, both continued to cite examples to support their view. Much of the daughter's behavior did not discriminate between the two hypotheses; despite this, the process of collecting such evidence increased both parents' confidence in their own interpretation. To counter this, the therapist began by listing all the examples on a flip chart along with the two hypotheses and then used this information along with input from the daughter to broaden the possible hypotheses about their views of their child (e.g., daughter was experimenting with different roles to determine her identity). The next homework assignment for the parents was to search for examples that supported the other parent's original hypothesis. This resulted in a "normalizing" process in which the father began to see his daughter as experiencing some relatively normal adolescent rebellion and the mother seeing her acting out behaviors as needing to be addressed. Once such alternative interpretations were formulated, negotiating treatment alternatives became much easier.

To make the situation even more concrete, suppose that we see a client who manifests a cluster of behaviors, which we will refer to as B, and comes from a certain familial situation, which we will refer to as F. There are two plausible hypotheses that suggest themselves, which we will call H1 and H2 (these hypotheses can be about any number of things, including a theory about the source of the behavior, a diagnosis, a prognosis, or a useful treatment plan). We tentatively decide on H1, knowing that 70% of those who fit this hypothesis show this cluster of behaviors, B, and want to gather some more evidence to help decide if H1 is true. Which of the following options would be most informative?

1. The probability that B is observed when H2 is true.
2. The probability that F is observed when H1 is true.
3. The probability that F is observed when H2 is true.

Typically, at least half the people who solve this type of problem choose option 2 (Evans et al., 2002). In many cases, this will be useful information, but in terms of deciding between H1 and H2, it is not. Instead, we need to know the probability that we would observe this evidence when the alternative hypothesis is true (option 1). Suppose, for example, we found out that B is observed 80% of the time when H2 is true—the evidence would favor H2. If B were observed only 40% of the time with H2, the evidence instead would favor H1.

Thus, in order to decide which hypothesis is favored by the evidence, we need to gather similar data for the alternative hypothesis. What is the probability that the evidence is consistent with the alternative? Once that is done, option 2 becomes more useful in that it may help to increase confidence in the original hypothesis. Again, however, we should compare options 2 and 3 and determine whether the balance of evidence is more favorable to H1 or H2.

Making Diagnostic Choices

This evidence once again shows an information-present effect. When making judgments about a focal hypothesis, people tend to focus on that hypothesis and to seek confirming evidence for it, rather than attempting to gather evidence to discriminate between alternatives. The hypothesis acts as an anchor that focuses judgments and captures attention. Not surprisingly, therefore, strategies that pull attention away from the focal hypothesis and toward the alternative hypothesis increase the diagnosticity of people's judgments. This is among the reasons that techniques such as reframing or looking for exceptions have become an important part of many therapeutic systems.

For example, Evans et al. (2002) found that by asking participants what evidence they would need to determine whether H1 or H2 is true, rather than asking them what evidence was needed to determine whether H1 is true, they reduced nondiagnostic answers significantly. Specifically, fewer people selected answer 2, and twice as many selected answer 1. For example, if a therapist was trying to decide whether their client had an anxiety disorder, or was actually in some danger of being fired at work, having both hypotheses in mind would increase the likelihood that they would collect evidence that helped to distinguish between the two possibilities. The client's report of feeling anxious at work would likely not determine which hypothesis was true, so more diagnostic evidence would be sought, such as the history of the feeling or reports from the client's union representative. If, however, the therapist considered only the anxiety disorder option, that therapist might consider the anxious feeling sufficient and seek to collect only evidence consistent with this diagnosis, whether or not it helped to discriminate between options.

Summary

In this section, we have reviewed evidence to suggest that our reasoning is often limited to the information that is present in the immediate environment. We have also illustrated how these feature positive effects can lead therapists to neglect important alternative hypotheses and limit our ability to imagine how things might be different than they are.

Case Illustration:

Well into therapy with Janice, the therapist discovered that he was now facing an ethical dilemma. He had been seeing another client from a different department in the same company (Margaret) to deal with relationship issues. Margaret had been dating a company employee for some time and they were considering marriage. Margaret wanted to say "yes" but held back because she thought her potential mate had an anger problem. She had seen him verbally attack waiters or service people and worried that she might become the target. Margaret said that her partner was open to therapy and was willing to seek counseling with her. It was in the course of this discussion that the therapist realized that Margaret's new partner was Janice's supervisor. The therapist also realized that he now had information that could be relevant to both clients. He was well into therapy with both clients, they were expressing high

satisfaction with therapy, and they had both expressed unhappiness with previ-
ous therapists.

Like Janice, the therapist had to consider a variety of options and make a
decision for action. He could simply carry on, making sure to keep very thor-
ough notes so information from one therapy circumstance did not enter the
other (keeping in mind memory and source monitoring implications; see chap-
ter 4). He could terminate therapy with one of the clients and refer the other
(although the high degree of current satisfaction of both clients with therapy
made this difficult). He could find some way to disclose his dilemma to the cli-
ents (if possible without revealing any identities) and let them participate in
the decision making. A further complication was that with the combined infor-
mation from these clients, the therapist's knowledge of the base-rate of the su-
pervisor's bullying behavior had changed, and his concern for the potential ef-
fects for other employees was increasing. He needed to make a decision about
whether and what action to take in regard to this added concern.

Like clients, therapists must consider options, gather information, and seek assistance with these kinds of dilemmas. Fortunately, therapists from all professions have codes of ethics and companion guides to assist them in considering options. Some (e.g., the Canadian code of ethics for psychologists) even include prioritizing principles and a decision-making process that is largely compatible with good principles of gathering and considering evidence prior to making and carrying out a decision. In addition, therapists seek both peer and supervisory consultation in the process of considering and implementing ethical decisions. As well, many of the contracts between employers and employee and family assistance plans include protocols to manage these kinds of situations. This kind of anticipatory or proactive approach to difficult decisions is very helpful to practitioners of all types of therapy.

In summary, both clients and therapists need to follow good information and evidence-gathering skills in considering a variety of options to help clients solve problems in an effective and ethical manner.

PRIOR BELIEFS

In this section, we will describe how therapists' expectations, beliefs, and theories can influence judgments and the evaluation and interpretation of evidence. We have selected three contexts that are particularly relevant to therapists: the role of beliefs in testing hypotheses, in detecting relationships among variables, and in evaluating and weighing evidence. In each case, we present evidence to suggest that prior beliefs predispose people to act in a belief-preserving manner. That is, people tend to seek information that confirms their beliefs, find evidence to suggest relationships among variables that are not correlated, and discredit information that contradicts their beliefs.

Testing Hypotheses

In the preceding section, we reviewed evidence that indicates that selective testing and positive testing of hypotheses can help maintain a focal hypothesis, even when that hypothesis is suboptimal or incorrect. This problem is exacerbated when the hypothesis in question is one which the person is predisposed to believe. There is a great deal of evidence to support the view that once one has taken a position on an issue, the tendency is to engage strategies that preserve this belief.

In an extensive review of the literature, Nickerson (1998) observed that the evidence supporting the existence of confirmation bias is extensive and strong, and that this bias permeates judgments in a vast number of contexts ranging from jury deliberations to policy decisions to science. This tendency produces strong biases in the selection and processing of evidence, and is observed in both lay people as well as expert scientists and therapists (e.g., Fugelsang, Stein, Green, & Dunbar, 2004; D. J. Koehler, 1994; Kuhn, 1989; Nickerson, 1998; Pfeiffer, Whelan, & Martin, 2000). Indeed, even when the foundations for the initial position have been discredited or have been shown to be based on arbitrary criteria (such as random feedback: L. Ross, Lepper, & Hubbard, 1975; L. Ross, Lepper, Strack, & Stienmetz, 1977), the initial position can be hard to overturn. It may also lead to biased memory for events, such that one tends to recall information that is consistent with the preferred hypothesis (Pennington & Hastie, 1993).

Therapeutic Hypotheses.   A number of studies have examined confirmation bias in therapeutic settings. The evidence shows that clinicians are subject to the same types of confirmatory strategies that were described earlier in this chapter: They tend to adopt confirmatory hypothesis-testing strategies (Havercamp, 1993), and they tend to remember and attend to hypothesis-confirming relative to hypothesis-disconfirming evidence (Strohmer, Shivy, & Chiodo, 1990; Pfeiffer et al., 2000). In the latter study, for example, the ratio of confirming to disconfirming information recalled was 3.5 to 1, even when the majority of information presented was disconfirming. Confirmation bias is more likely to be observed when the therapists are testing a self-generated hypothesis than one presented to them by the client or referring professional (Havercamp, 1993), at least when that initial hypothesis is plausible. When the others' hypothesis is implausible, therapists reject it in favor of their own hypothesis and then proceed to test that hypothesis in a confirmatory fashion (Pfeiffer et al., 2000). This effect is observed even when therapists are told they will be held accountable for their decisions (Strohmer & Shivy, 1994; Pfeiffer et al., 2000) and regardless of whether students or experienced practitioners are used as participants. Finally, confirmation bias appears more pronounced when therapists are asked to test negative as opposed to positive hypotheses (Strohmer, Boas, & Abadie, 1996). Specifically, therapists tend to confirm negative hypotheses (e.g., lacks self-control) and disconfirm positive ones (has self-control). It is not clear, however, whether this represents a genuine difference in hypothesis-testing strategy, or alternatively, under the assumption that clients have problems, the therapists substitute the more plausible negative hypothesis for the less plausible positive one and proceed to test in a confirmatory fashion (as was the case in the Pfeiffer et al., 2000 study).

It is important to note that, as was the case with the use of base-rate information, not all people show a confirmation bias all of the time. In the studies described earlier, not all therapists showed a confirmation bias, and among those who did, not all of the information sought was confirmatory. On balance, however, the dominant tendency was to attend to, select, and weight confirmatory information more heavily than disconfirming information.

It is also not realistic to prescribe an atheoretical or hypothesis-free approach to information gathering. Hypotheses are necessary tools for synthesizing, organizing, and interpreting information. The key, rather, is to keep an actively open mind (J. Baron, 2000) and adopt information-gathering strategies that allow hypotheses to be either confirmed or disconfirmed.

Confirmation Bias and the Maintenance of Irrational Beliefs. Nickerson (1998) describes how the tendency to seek out information that is consistent with one's focal hypothesis can help to perpetuate irrational beliefs about gambling, hypochondria, stereotypes, the paranormal, and the like. That is, the presumption that one's beliefs are true predisposes one to seek confirming evidence for those beliefs, discount disconfirming evidence, and interpret ambiguous evidence as supporting the preferred interpretation. This, in turn, can reinforce the strength of the initial (perhaps erroneous) belief.

Illusory Relationships

Personal beliefs and theories can bias the perceptions of relationships. Is social class related to parenting skills? Are men interested in emotional intimacy? Are members of other families or cultures as trustworthy as one's own? Does increased education result in better reasoning? A belief that two variables are related leads one to perceive a stronger correlation than would be the case when making judgments about theory-neutral data (e.g., Alloy & Tabachnick, 1984; L. J. Chapman & Chapman, 1967, 1969, 1971; Freedman & Smith, 1996; Trolier & Hamilton, 1986). Thus, for example, if one believed that parents of a certain social class had better parenting skills than other parents, the correlation that would be observed between these variables would likely be higher than if no such belief were held. The estimate of relationship will be skewed by the belief, but will be not entirely incorrect: In most of the studies cited earlier in this chapter, participants also demonstrated sensitivity to the data; that is, variables that were in fact strongly correlated were more likely to be judged correlated than those that were not.

In other cases, however, researchers have shown that correlations can be perceived, even when the variables are statistically unrelated. This was the case in the L. J. Chapman and Chapman studies described earlier, in which participants "saw" correlations between characteristics of the Draw-a-Person test and clinical diagnoses. Examples in everyday life also abound: People believe that the occurrence of the full moon is accompanied by an increase in erratic behavior, that horoscopes predict one's future, and so forth, regardless of the fact that these variables are not correlated.

Evaluating Belief-Inconsistent Evidence

Finally, there is considerable evidence indicating that beliefs may also determine how much analysis is given to a situation. Situations that accord with our beliefs tend to be analyzed less than situations that are discrepant (e.g., Ditto & Lopez, 1992; K. Edwards & Smith, 1996; Fugelsang et al., 2004; Klaczynski & Robinson, 2000; Koehler, 1994; Kuhn, 1989; Newstead, Pollard, & Evans, 1992). In other words, belief-consistent information can be accepted relatively uncritically, whereas information that contradicts one's belief may be subject to rigorous analysis. Beliefs can also determine how a particular piece of evidence is weighed: Evidence that supports a belief is given more weight than evidence that is belief-inconsistent. Moreover, less evidence is required to decide in favor of a preferred than a nonpreferred alternative (Ditto & Lopez, 1992). For example, a client who believed he was timid and sought therapy in order to develop assertiveness related several stories over the course of the first few sessions which reflected his lack of ability to express his opinion. After the first one or two examples, those stories are likely accepted as "more of the same" or "same-old, same-old." However, a story in which the client successfully expresses his opinion is often skipped over in therapy (by the client) as unimportant unless the therapist specifically queries for more detail and in general makes a big deal out of client successes.

Klaczynski and Robinson (2000) offered an explanation for this phenomenon that is couched in terms of the heuristic and analytic processes described at the beginning of the chapter. Specifically, they proposed that belief-consistent and belief-inconsistent information evokes both qualitatively and quantitatively different analyses. That is, belief-inconsistent information is not only analyzed more than belief-consistent information, but also it is analyzed differently. They proposed that belief-consistent information is analyzed heuristically, accessing gist-based representations (see chapter 8), and justified based on stereotypes, vivid memories, and intuitions. Belief-inconsistent information, in contrast, receives analytic processing and is rejected based on principled, logical reasoning. In both cases, the goal is the same, namely, the preservation of the belief system.

Summary of Belief-Bias Effects

In summary, belief-bias effects are among the most robust and well-documented phenomena in the reasoning literature. In a wide variety of tasks, and across a broad spectrum of participants, it has been repeatedly demonstrated that beliefs affect how one looks for, interprets, and evaluates evidence. It is important to note, however, that the evidence also shows that belief effects operate in tandem with sensitivity to environmental information, demonstrating that peoples' judgments reflect a mixture of belief-based and analytic processing. On the other hand, belief-effects operate even among those who are highly trained (e.g., Fugelsang et al., 2004; Koehler, 1994; Pfeiffer et al., 2000), and unlike many other elements of reasoning competence, they are not systematically related to cognitive ability (e.g., Klaczynski, 1997; Klaczynski & Robinson, 2000; Torrens, Thompson & Cramer, 1999; see also Stanovich & West, 1997). Thus, neither training nor intelligence is sufficient to guarantee objective judgments.

CONCLUSIONS

In this chapter, we have described two heuristic processes—feature positive processes and belief biases—that constrain the operation of analytic processes. These processes work in combination. Thus, heuristic processes may preselect the information that undergoes analytic scrutiny, and thus judgments may reflect a mixture of heuristic and analytic processes.

Although the heuristic processes that we have described here tend to produce suboptimal judgments (i.e., by leading one to neglect important alternative hypotheses, by biasing evaluation of the evidence, etc.), researchers argue that in most instances, heuristic processes are useful and adaptive tools (Gigerenzer, 1998; Evans, 2002; Sanbonmatsu et al., 1998; Sloman, 2002; Stanovich, 2002; Tversky & Kahneman, 1986), producing satisfactory solutions to complex problems. Many of these researchers have argued that these heuristic processes can be attributed to evolutionarily adaptive processes (Evans, 2002; Gigerenzer, 1998; Sloman, 2002; Stanovich, 2002) and that these processes may come in conflict with more recently developed analytic processes. In these models, heuristic processes were designed to provide fast, efficient solutions to problems on the basis of readily available environmental cues. Even belief effects can be seen to be adaptive solutions to many situations. For example, it is sensible to reason on the basis of all available knowledge, including one's belief: Failing to incorporate relevant information into the problem space or downgrading the value of a patently false conclusion would produce disastrous results in many instances.

In contrast, successful solutions to a number of problems in our technological and culturally complex society (see J. Baron, 1998, for an engaging discussion) may not be solvable on the basis of highly contextualized heuristic responses. However, because these evolutionary processes are engaged automatically, they continue to supply input to situations, even when that input may produce counterproductive responses. That is, processes may be engaged that produce contextualized and personalized representations of a problem, even when the person would be better served by a more detached, analytic mode of thought.

One problem is that analytic thinking is effortful and requires both capacity and motivation. Klaczynski and Robinson (2000) point out that engaging analytic thought requires us to represent and analyze the problem appropriately, selectively inhibit irrelevant information, selectively attend to relevant information, and construct appropriate alternative representations. Thus, success on analytic problems is predicted by traditional measures of cognitive capacity (e.g., IQ, working memory) as well as measures of cognitive motivation (e.g., liking for cognitive tasks, need for cognition, preferences for deliberate decision making). These measures contribute independently to performance on a number of tasks (see Stanovich, 1999, for a review; see also Klaczynski, 1997; Klaczynski & Gordon, 1996; Klaczynski & Robinson, 2000).

A further complication is that performance on intellectual tasks, such as decision making and reasoning, requires self-regulatory control, which is depleted by previous self-regulatory efforts (Schmeichel, Vohs, & Baumeister, 2003). Thus, individuals who are controlling themselves in some manner, such as restraining emotional expression or dieting, will do more poorly on decision-making tasks, including considering alternative solutions. Similarly, after making an effortful decision, we will be poorer at other types of control, such as withholding emotional expression or resisting unhealthy food choices (Schmeichel & Baumeister, 2004).

In conclusion, rational thought reflects a mixture of heuristic and analytic processes. These processes are interactive, such that heuristic processes may select the information on which analytic processes are engaged. In this way, reasoning tends to be focused on information present in the environment and influenced by our expectations and beliefs.

KEY POINTS

- Decision making and reasoning use both heuristic and analytic processes. Heuristics are easier and often useful but can be subject to biases based on familiarity and belief. Analytic processes are effortful and require scarce self-regulatory resources, but they facilitate problem solving in a way that heuristic processes cannot.
- Associative and analytic processes may operate independently and simultaneously produce different responses to a situation ("simultaneous contradictory beliefs"), which can contribute to a feeling of "stuckness" in relation to a particular decision.

- Decision making is often biased by information-present or feature positive effects. Such information can include perceived information, a current example, beliefs, or favored hypotheses. The bias occurs due to greater consideration of alternatives related to the present information and leads to confirmation bias, our tendency to overemphasize evidence that confirms our current beliefs and underemphasize disconfirming evidence.

- We are inclined to test a single hypothesis at a time, rather than jointly considering possibilities and determining ways to discriminate among them to find the best solution. Such selective testing also makes us vulnerable to positive test strategies, in which we examine only alternatives that would be true if the current hypothesis were true, rather than being sensitive to the diagnosticity of evidence, evidence that would allow us to discriminate between two different hypotheses.

- We overemphasize case-specific information and neglect base-rate information. This tendency leads us to overemphasize the importance of personal facts and the validity of our assessment instruments, rather than considering how common a particular diagnosis is in the population. Base-rate information that is attained through experience is considered more often than statistical rates, due to associative memory processes.

Reasoning: Evaluating Conclusions and Determining Cause

> *One of psychology's fundamental insights is that judgments are generally the products of nonconscious systems that operate quickly, on the basis of scant evidence, and in routine manner, and then pass their hurried approximations to consciousness, which slowly and deliberately adjusts them.*
>
> —D. T. Gilbert (2002, p. 167)

In the previous chapter, we discussed how gathering and interpreting evidence is subject to two broad classes of cognitive processes: heuristic and analytic. Heuristic processes are fast, efficient means of analyzing information, including attentional processes by which information is selected for further scrutiny and knowledge-based processes by which relevant information is recruited from long-term memory. Analytic processes are those associated with conscious, step-by-step deliberation.

These processes operate in tandem. Sometimes, they produce conflicting responses to a problem, which Sloman (2002) called "simultaneous contradictory beliefs." In clinical settings, this is often the source of the "stuck spot" or the impasse, as described in gestalt therapy (e.g., Korb, Gorrell, & Van DeRiet, 1989). In other cases, heuristic processes select the information from the environment on which analytic processes are engaged. This cognitive triage is necessary, given that we have the cognitive capacity to consider the implications of only one or two options at a time. However, these processes can also produce biased reasoning, because they may lead us to neglect important relevant information. In other words, because the heuristic or "rule of thumb" processes operate before the engagement of rational, analytic processes, the problem space may be missing information that, on further reflection, is necessary to making a sound judgment. Instead, we may be left engaging in a very thorough analysis of partial information.

In this chapter, we extend this analysis to situations in which people generate and evaluate conclusions and arguments. These include situations in which we make an inference based on information retrieved from memory, as well as cases where we are presented with an argument and must evaluate the soundness of a proposed conclusion. As before, we will focus our discussion on two heuristic processes, namely, feature positive and belief effects. Although many of the processes and effects of reasoning discussed in chapters 9 and 10 are similar, they are applicable to the process of counseling and therapy in somewhat different ways. To oversimplify a little, processes related to the gathering and interpretation of evidence are more present in the early stages of therapy (often described as the exploration or assessment stage), in which the problem space is explicated and expanded with emphasis on uncovering and considering evidence (and relationship development). Reasoning processes related to drawing and evaluating conclusions, while covering similar territory, are more relevant to later stages of therapy where, once goals are established, conclusions are drawn and decisions made by both therapist and client for intervention and change. These decisions are then acted on and evaluated for their effectiveness in attaining the goal-state.

Feature positive effects refer to the tendency to be focused on the information that is present in the environment. In the context of making and evaluating arguments, this includes the information that is available in working memory that has been retrieved from long-term memory as well as information that is explicitly available in the current environment. There is much evidence to suggest that the information that is available tends to focus a person's attention, causing him to neglect consideration of relevant alternatives. Thus, analytic processes may be brought to bear on a highly select subset of relevant information. Consequently, success or failure on a reasoning task is mediated by the ability and motivation to generate appropriate alternatives or counterarguments. For example, women in therapy as a result of abusive relationships often make decisions to re-enter the relationship after being persuaded by their partner that he will change and this will never happen again. In addition, most victims of abuse are safer immediately after a violent incident as the "honeymoon phase" of the abusive pattern begins and the sense of danger is less present. Unfortunately, this leads to a lack of analytic reasoning in the face of overwhelmingly emotional feature positive effects.

Prior beliefs also play a big role in making and evaluating arguments. It is easier for people to generate arguments that are consistent with, rather than contrary to, their beliefs (known as "my-side" bias). Furthermore, arguments leading to believable conclusions are judged to be more compelling than arguments leading to unbelievable conclusions, regardless of the strength of the actual arguments (belief bias). As in the preceding chapter, beliefs can determine the conditions under which analytic processes are engaged, so that one is more likely to identify the flaws in an argument when it leads to an unbelievable conclusion.

For example, a cognitive behavioral therapist quickly uncovered his client's belief that he had to be liked by everyone he met. This client more easily thought of arguments that justified the belief (e.g., the golden rule, "You never know when you may need someone's support," "I can't stand it when someone is upset with me") than arguments that contradicted it. In addition, his memories of being liked captured his attention more than when being liked did not matter and led to the rejection of these memories as less relevant. He argued with the therapist that being liked was safer because once he saw his dad argue with a neighbor, and then later the neighbor refused to testify on his father's behalf in a minor court matter. He presented this argument triumphantly and as irrevocable proof that his belief was safest even though it caused a great deal of distress in his life. Whenever the therapist began to introduce disputing techniques, the client would use this and other similar memories to "prove his point."

Our discussion of the literature is presented in three sections. The first section reviews the influence of feature positive effects and discusses two types of processes: (a) situations in which we must generate a conclusion based on information available from memory, and (b) situations in which we must evaluate an argument presented by someone else. The first situation is similar to circumstances in psychotherapy when clients struggle to make a decision that will resolve their issue, whereas the second situation occurs when the therapist actively initiates and evaluates change within the therapeutic context. In addition, participants in relationship and family therapy are frequently managing arguments and positions presented by other family members. Research in this area shows that when we generate our own conclusions, we tend to retrieve only a small subset of the information relevant to making a judgment, so decisions are informed by one or two compelling images. In addition, the fluency with which information is retrieved may influence the confidence that we have in a conclusion, such that our beliefs about a situation are informed not only by the content of memory, but by whether or not it easily came to mind. Conversely, when we evaluate an argument proposed by someone else, reasoning is mediated by the likelihood of generating a compelling alternative conclusion or argument, and often, people have difficulty in generating appropriate alternatives.

The second section reviews the contribution of our prior knowledge and beliefs to the generation and evaluation of conclusions. We describe how people often find it easier to generate arguments for their own position than against it, and argue that part of this difficulty may arise from a preference for one-sided relative to two-sided thinking. We also describe research showing that conclusions that are incompatible with our prior knowledge are critically examined more closely than those we find believable or compatible with our prior knowledge.

In our final section, we tie together all of the processes described in this chapter and the preceding one, and show how they contribute to causal reasoning, that is, how we come to conclude that one thing caused another to occur. As usual, these ideas will be illustrated with a case illustration.

Case Illustration:

Barbara, aged forty-seven, was referred for therapy by her general practitioner. She had been depressed following the death of her father about one year ago. She reported that this puzzled her as her father had been suffering from Alzheimers for many years and Barbara stated, "Really, my dad had been gone for many years . . . I was relieved when he died . . . so why am I so sad and weepy still . . . why am I so afraid that my mom or brother or sister will die?" Barbara was single after ending a disastrous relationship about ten years prior. She had two children with whom she had a good relationship although one was recovering from a near fatal viral infection, and her fear of losing another loved one extended to her children.

Her current life was centered around her work and family. She spent her evenings and free time at home watching television, drinking wine, and talking to a family member on the telephone (no family lived closer than 500 miles). She thought she drank too much but was reluctant to change this as it helped her cope with the overwhelming bouts of sadness she experienced.

Exploration quickly led to a pivotal decision she had made after the ending of her second marriage. She had made a clear decision that she could not trust herself to make a good relationship decision, so she was fated to live alone. In addition, there was an element of self-punishment to her decision, as she felt she had let herself down in both relationships and she was very angry with herself. One salient example of her failure remained very active in her memory. Her relationship had developed in isolation from her family and friends due to distance. Two days prior to the wedding, Barb and her fiancé arrived in her hometown for a community celebration of her wedding. Much to her chagrin and distress her future husband was belligerent and mean to all those close to her. She stated, "At that moment, I knew I should stop everything, but everything was planned, we were business partners, and it just seemed I was committed, so I said to myself 'in for a penny, in for a pound' and thought I could make the best of it. . . . My God, what a mistake, the next five years were awful and I lost everything." As she spoke, she could easily move from this example to many others and compiled a long list of "bad decisions where men are concerned." She even included examples of being mistreated and exploited in friendships. Her conscious decision to avoid other relationships (including friendships) and focus on family resulted in inner turmoil, as she wanted a relationship but believed she would make another bad decision.

FEATURE POSITIVE EFFECTS
IN DECISION MAKING

Estimates of probability inform many of our day-to-day judgments. Our decisions are based on our perceptions of how likely something is to occur, how often it happened in the past, whether or not a venture will be successful, and so on. Such questions are often answered by the availability of relevant information from memory. The information may come in the form of a salient example or concrete memory, or it may be an imagined outcome or an explanation for an event. Salience (those properties that command or attract attention) might be due to news reports, vividness of memory, or ease or fluency with which a piece of information comes to mind (Hastie & Dawes, 2001). In the following sections, we review how judgments can be influenced by irrelevant aspects of the information that is retrieved. For example, repeated exposure to lurid crime reports in the media can lead people to believe that crime is increasing and that they are right to be afraid, regardless of whether there has been an increase in crime or just an increase in the reporting of crime. In psychotherapeutic situations, almost all clients report salient memories and fantasies that are perceived by them as significant constraints in attaining their goals.

Availability of Concrete Examples

The availability of examples informs our judgments of probability in that when examples of a situation come easily to mind, we judge that situation more common than if such examples are lacking. This is called the availability heuristic. Consider these examples: Is someone more likely to die by suicide or murder? When asked, most people respond that murder is more common, although suicide is far more common than murder (Hastie & Dawes, 2001). Are we more or less likely to be a victim of terrorism now than we were ten years ago? Would you be surprised to learn that the risk of terrorist attacks has actually declined in the last ten years? These are classic examples of the availability heuristic: People's frequency estimates of cause of death are correlated with the frequency of reports in the news rather than with the frequency of the events themselves. This is not to say that the correlation is perfect, because people's estimates do reflect actual rates. Nonetheless, vivid, much reported causes of death and injury (plane crashes, tornadoes, etc.) tend to be overestimated, whereas common, less reported causes (strokes, household accidents, etc.) tend to be underestimated (Hastie & Dawes, 2001).

The trouble is that we make estimates based on a biased memory sample, and people are notoriously inaccurate in adjusting for initial inaccuracies (see the section on anchoring and adjustment, later in the chapter). For example, in a family therapy session, the father was being confronted by his seventeen-year-old daughter for having a double standard when rules were presented to her and her sixteen-year-old brother. Dad insisted that the daughter have a much more stringent set of rules for curfew (e.g., reporting when out with friends, coming home earlier, etc.) even though there was clear evidence that the son was participating in much riskier behavior than his daughter, including belonging to a gang. When the father was asked to explain his reasoning, he confidently said that he knew his son was going to be fine because "I had a similar childhood and came through it," whereas he had found his sister after a rape when she was 15 and in his opinion she had never recovered from the assault. In this case, both the multiple examples from his own adolescence and the single, tragic example of his sister influenced his beliefs that boys will survive the rough and tumble of growing up whereas girls need to be protected. He believed he was justified in maintaining this rigid, double standard even though it had precipitated high conflict in the home with both his wife and daughter.

Hastie and Dawes (2001) also described a number of examples where having a biased memory sample can distort therapeutic judgment. For example, they indicated that some of their professional colleagues expressed the opinion that child abusers never stop on their own. However, given that the therapists' sample was heavily weighted toward those seen in therapy (who, by definition, have not stopped on their own), abusers who have stopped on their own were systematically unavailable for sampling. Thus, whereas the therapists' beliefs may have accurately reflected the information that was available, their judgment was skewed by the fact that the information was not a representative sample. Similarly, since many who seek therapy do not feel good about themselves, many professionals believe that low self-esteem is responsible for many undesirable behaviors. As discussed in chapter 9, having base-rate information as well as information from experience would assist in mitigating the development of these kinds of erroneous beliefs in therapists and help therapists challenge similar beliefs in their clients when appropriate. For example, biased sampling occurs in gambling where problem gamblers constantly reinforce and nurture fantasies or actual memories of significant wins in order to justify continuing their behavior. Gambling treatment programs always include base-rate information about the possibilities and mathematics of losing to counter these feature positive effects.

Ease of Retrieval

The ease with which memories are retrieved can also influence judgments of probability. Tversky and Kahneman (1973) provided a simple demonstration of this. They asked participants whether there are more six letter words with *n* in the fifth position, or more six-letter words ending in *ing*. Participants judged the latter to be more common, even though that is logically incorrect (the set of six-letter words ending in *ing* is a subset of the set with *n* in the fifth position). However, it is easier to think of words ending in *ing* than words with *n* in the fifth position, and so the *ing* words are judged to be more common.

Similar processes may be at work in defining attitudes toward social categories. Sia et al. (Sia, Lord, Belssum, Ratcliff, & Lepper, 1997) found that attitudes toward homosexuals, politicians, and other socially defined categories changed as a function of the examples of those categories that came to mind. When the examples changed positively, there was a positive shift in attitude; a negative change produced a decline.

There is also evidence to suggest that the ease with which examples are retrieved affects judgment. That is, examples that come to mind easily are judged more probable than those that do not (Reber & Zupanek, 2002; N. Schwarz & Vaughn, 2002). Indeed, this is often a valid inference. Our memories are organized to make frequently encountered information easily available (see chapter 3), so that things that come easily to mind are likely to be things that occur often in the environment.

In many other instances, however, the ease or difficulty of retrieval is irrelevant to the probability of an event, so that a conclusion based on retrieval fluency may be in error. Schwarz and his colleagues have provided evidence to support this assertion in a number of different domains (e.g., Rothman & Schwarz, 1998; N. Schwarz et al., 1991; N. Schwarz & Vaughn, 2002). Participants in these experiments were asked to list reasons for or against a proposition (e.g., times I have been assertive, behaviors that put me at risk for heart disease, etc.). Generally speaking, perceptions are biased toward the viewpoint being considered. For example, those who listed risk-increasing behaviors perceived themselves to be more vulnerable to heart disease than those who listed behaviors that decreased risk. However, when participants were given a more difficult recall task, such as retrieving many examples (8–12 rather than 3–6), the reverse effect was observed: Participants who generated more evidence were less confident about the original assertion, listing more examples of assertive behavior or more risk-increasing behaviors decreased perceptions of assertiveness and risk! N. Schwarz and Vaughn (2002) proposed that participants were relying on an availability heuristic to guide their assessment of risk. When examples came fluidly and easily to mind, they perceived the probability of risk to be high; when participants had difficulty finding examples, they perceived the probability to be low, presumably because the difficulty of retrieving examples served as evidence that there were few risks available. Recalling more examples is more difficult than recalling a few, and this increase in difficulty is experienced as a decrease in fluency, resulting in the reduced estimates for the many-example conditions.

Consistent with this hypothesis, when participants were likely to adopt a more analytic mode of processing, the pattern reversed. As discussed in chapter 9, motivation is a variable that increases the probability of engaging in analytic rather than heuristic thought. In the Rothman and Schwarz (1998) study, motivation was defined in terms of the personal relevance of the task. Participants whose family had a history of heart disease performed the task quite differently than those who did not. For these participants, listing more reasons had the expected effect on judgments: More risk-increasing behaviors produced higher feelings of vulnerability, and more risk-decreasing behaviors produced lower feelings of vulnerability. Thus, when participants were motivated to engage an analytic mode of processing, they relied on cues other than the ease of retrieval, such as the amount of information available to make their judgments.

In sum, the availability of a memory or set of memories may influence our judgment. Judgments tend to be anchored by the presence of a single salient or strong example, such that examples that come easily to mind are judged more probable than those that do not. Thus, we come to believe that risk of terrorism is high, that crime rates are increasing, that we are all depressed, and that welfare fraud is rampant because examples that support these conclusions are highly accessible.

Fortunately, virtually all established therapies encourage the exploration of already easily accessed examples and heuristics and then also encourage application of analytic thinking by expanding or reframing the problem space in some way. This encourages clients to move beyond easily accessed information to examine other aspects of their experience or to gather additional information available from the environment that is often crucial to finding a solution. Techniques such as the deliberate use of finding resources, strengths, and exceptions in solution-focused therapies (e.g., DeJong & Berg, 1998), the analysis of thought content and process of cognitive behavioral therapy (e.g., McMullin, 2000), or the externalization of problems in narrative therapy (e.g., M. White & Epston, 1990) are prime examples of deliberately moving outside readily accessed and easily presented client information.

It is important to note that the availability of information is often, in fact, a reliable cue. That is, our memories represent frequent events, and the examples that come to mind will reflect natural events (see Gigerenzer, 1998). However, as Hastie and Dawes (2001) point out, problems arise when the events that we have represented in memory are not representative of the environment, as is the case with news reports. Fielder (2000) argues that even when motivations and personal beliefs aren't an issue, biases can arise from a sampling bias. That is, for a variety of reasons, such as proximity, salience, and the focus of attention, the samples drawn are skewed and not representative of the population. Moreover, because most people are not aware of these constraints, they do not adequately compensate for them when making their judgments, a situation that can produce inaccuracies, even when beliefs and motivations are not an issue. Problems can also occur when the context or the mind-set of the person cues an example that is not representative of the population, or when the vividness of an image or example distorts the overall image of the population. Some therapists deal with these and similar constraints by gently nudging their clients to move outside the familiar, whereas others attempt to educate them in the hopes that one therapeutic experience can then be generalized to a wide variety of life concerns.

Availability of Explanations and Imaginings

In the same way that the availability of an example underlies judgments of probability, the availability of an explanation serves as a basis for decision, even when the explanation has been generated in a biased fashion or is inaccurate. This is true of situations in which we are asked to explain hypothetical future events, social theories, or our own preferences and behavior (Koehler, 1991; see also Sloman, 1994). Koehler (1991) reviewed a large number of studies in which participants were asked to generate reasons or arguments supporting one of two or more mutually exclusive alternatives (e.g., reasons why the Yankees will win the World Series this year, reasons why I am good at fundraising, reasons why a particular movie will win an Oscar nomination, etc.). The act of generating reasons increases the perceived probability that the event in question will happen. Similarly, in clinical situations when therapists consider systematically with clients whether something is/was true or not (e.g., Is my relationship abusive? Was I truly mistreated in the past or was this normal?), caution needs to be exercised with the knowledge that simply considering something increases the likelihood that clients will believe the explanation to be true. Although it is the task of therapists to help clients derive meaning (explanation) for events and patterns, we need to cautiously approach those areas in which explanation then becomes a basis for decision.

Again, this is an instance of feature positive thinking. That is, we are anchored by thinking about the current possibility and neglect to consider the evidence that might support an alternative view (Koehler, 1991). Evidence to support this interpretation comes from studies that show that asking participants to produce explanations for the alternative position can reduce their belief in a focal hypothesis (C. A. Anderson & Sechler, 1986), suggesting that the initial confidence in the position was due to one-sided thinking. Therapists who have clients gather evidence for alternative positions rather than for a single idea usually help clients avoid cognitive distortions (e.g., Dryden & Ellis, 2001) and reduce the perceived size, intensity, and urgency of a particular problem so it seems more solvable.

As was the case with the availability of memories, the ease with which explanations can be constructed determines how plausible they seem. As with many metacognitive intuitions, this is likely to be a sound judgment in most instances: Things that are hard to explain are going to be less plausible than those that are easy to explain. Consider, for example, trying to explain how physically training for a race versus mentally rehearsing it will lead to equal improvement. In this case, there is a good reason why one scenario is more difficult to explain than the other. Inferring or concluding that the scenario that is more difficult to explain (mental rehearsal) is less probable is sound reasoning.

In other instances, however, ease of explanation arising from elements of the situation are irrelevant to the plausibility of the explanation and can thus lead to a distorted view of the probabilities (e.g., Pennington & Hastie, 1988, 1992; S. J. Sherman, Cialdini, Schwartzman, & Reynolds, 2002). In the Sherman et al. study, for instance, participants were asked to imagine the probability of contracting an illness called Hyposcenia B. When the symptoms of the disease were easy to imagine (e.g., low energy, muscle aches, and severe headaches), participants judged that they were more likely to contract the disease than when the symptoms were difficult to imagine (e.g., malfunctioning nervous system, inflamed liver). Pennington and Hastie (1988, 1992) studied similar phenomena in the context of jury decisions. They showed that the ease with which a story can be constructed from the evidence plays a large role in determining verdicts. Evidence that was presented in a temporal sequence, and that could be easily formulated into a coherent story, was perceived to be stronger than the same evidence presented in the more usual "witness order." Verdicts likewise reflected the ease of construction, such that the verdicts tended to favor whichever of the prosecution or defense stories were easier to construct.

Clients often enter therapy with an easily imaginable consequence or outcome for something that is not fact but which still is a major constraint or problem in their lives (see chapter 11). Many of the explanations which clients unknowingly use as impediments to change are either developed or maintained by their imagination, so exploring and attending to these explanatory processes is important. For example, clients with specific phobias almost always have explanations in imagination as to why they cannot overcome them. A client who participated well in a standard desensitization cure for a phobia of spiders had an image of a black-widow spider as very large with big teeth, not at all factual but very influential in his avoidance behavior and anxiety. He easily accessed this image, and it consistently interfered with his exposure treatment until the therapist asked him about visual images and imaginary scenarios. Similarly, clients with public speaking anxiety typically carry fantasies of humiliation while speaking, even if that has never happened to them. The point is that explanations that are easily accessed are often imaginary as well as based on memories of actual experiences.

A preference for making decisions based on the ease with which an explanation comes to mind can sometimes lead to bizarre paradoxes, in which the same alternative can be either preferred or rejected, depending on the reasons that can be constructed to support it (Shafir, Simonson, & Tversky, 1993). For example, Shafir (1993) asked participants to suppose that they were one of the jury in a child custody case following a messy divorce. There is only one child involved, and the decision comes down to a few considerations:

Parent A:	Parent B:
Average income	Above-average income
Average health	Very close relationship with the child
Average working hours	Extremely active social life
Reasonable rapport with the child	Lots of work-related travel
Relatively stable social life	Minor health problems

Clearly, there are lots of trade-offs involved. Parent B has some very positive features, but also some very negative ones. The set of features that is accented in decision making depends on how the question is framed. Thus, when asked which parent they would award custody to, the majority indicated Parent B; ironically, however, when asked which parent they would deny custody to, the majority also indicated Parent B! Thus, Parent B was both more likely to be granted and denied custody.

There is a large literature on these sorts of framing effects, in which the preference for one or the other outcome is determined by the way the question is framed (i.e., in terms of gains or losses, survival rates or mortality rates, etc.; see Hawkins & Hastie, 1990, for a review). Shafir et al. (1993) propose that the framing of the issue determines the reasons that people seek to justify their decisions. Thus, it is not simply a matter of judging the overall value of the options available, but of looking for reasons on which to base the decision; the reasons that are constructed can be influenced by the framing of the question. In the child custody problem, for example, when participants were deciding which parent to award custody to, they looked for reasons to prefer one over the other. Thus, they selected the parent with the greatest number of positive features. When they were asked to deny custody, they looked for reasons to dislike one more than the other, and thus chose the parent with the largest number of negative features. Similarly, in the family double standard example given earlier, the father used the evidence from a recent event where his son was cut in a fight to both prove that his son was safe and that his daughter was not.

I Knew It All Along

A similar process has been implicated in hindsight bias, or the "I knew it all along" effect. It is a well-replicated finding that knowing the outcome of an event creates a false belief that one could have predicted the outcome (Hawkins & Hastie, 1990; Hastie & Dawes, 2001). For example, prior to the 2000 presidential election, Sanna, Schwarz, and Stocker (2002) asked participants to predict the percentage of the popular vote each of the candidates would receive. Several weeks later, after the issue had been settled, participants were asked to recall the predictions they had made. Prior to the election, participants predicted that Gore would lead by 4.45%; after the election, participants recalled their predictions (0.58%) to be much closer to the actual outcome (0.32%).

Examples of hindsight bias are common in a variety of settings, especially when we are making a judgment about the outcome of a decision. We see many examples where politicians, doctors, and other decision makers are asked to account for a decision that has gone wrong. There is a tendency to assume the consequences of the event were more predictable and the outcome more inevitable than was clear at the time the decision was taken. Most therapists experience this frequently with clients who say, "I should have known" or "The answer was there if only I had been paying attention." Conversations converging around the theme that hindsight is 20/20 and helping clients stop their self-recriminations are common to all sorts of therapies. Hawkins and Hastie (1990) argue that knowing the outcome of an event focuses attention on that outcome and inhibits consideration of possible alternative outcomes.

Thus, hindsight bias is another example of feature positive thinking, in which our consideration of an issue is anchored on one feature of the environment, in this case, the actual outcome. The outcome appears more likely in retrospect, when it is likely to be the only possibility considered, than in prospect, when many possibilities are presumably considered. This is especially true when there is a causal explanation or reason available to explain the outcome; events that are surprising or seen as due to chance factors are less subject to outcome bias. Moreover, hindsight bias can be reduced by asking people to consider possible alternative outcomes (Slovic & Fischhoff, 1977; see also Koriat, Lichtenstein, & Fischhoff, 1980), again, provided that those outcomes are easy to generate (Sanna et al., 2002). As we discussed earlier, when people have difficulty thinking of alternatives, they may infer from the difficulty of their search that there were not, in fact, many alternatives possible.

For example, a client was having difficulty in recovering from the emotional and psychological effects of a hunting accident. One aspect of the problem was that he kept reviewing the events preceding the accident with the knowledge of the outcome and using his knowledge to hold himself responsible (e.g., he would say, "I was thinking about taking another path, and that path would have kept me far away from my hunting partner"). This statement was made even though at the actual time of the accident neither he nor his hunting companion knew where either path led (see chapter 11). Part of the therapy included a systematic consideration of possible alternatives that introduced chance and unpredictability into the events.

In sum, although many decisions and choices are made in uncertain circumstances, the uncertain nature of the decision process tends to be less salient in hindsight. That is, the fact that an event has happened tends to produce the sense that the observed outcome was, if not inevitable, then at least more likely than it appeared in prospect. According to Hawkins and Hastie (1990), the fact that events turned out in a particular fashion causes us to revise our model of the situation to fit the outcome. In so doing, we elaborate causal explanations for the outcome and downplay information that suggests that things might have turned out differently.

Anchoring

We are often called on to make estimates about uncertain quantities. One way to proceed is to begin with a relevant value and then adjust accordingly. For example, when estimating the rate of return on an investment, we might start with the current rate of return and then adjust up or down depending on the current market situation. Needless to say, the choice of anchor can have a profound effect on the estimate that is made. Regardless of how the anchor value is chosen, people tend to undercorrect: Those who begin with a high anchor value end up with a higher estimate than those who begin with a low anchor value (see G. B. Chapman & Johnson, 2002; Hastie & Dawes, 2001, for reviews). This is true both when the anchoring value is known to be arbitrary and random (Tversky & Kahneman, 1974) and when it is a self-generated estimate (Eply & Gilovich, 2004). For instance, a young client who wanted to take some time to travel estimated that she would need fifty thousand dollars before she could travel. Although this benchmark or anchor came down as she addressed her need for security, it still remained substantially higher than what the therapist believed would be sufficient to quit work and travel for six months.

The number of situations in which anchoring has been shown to affect the outcome of decision processes is enormous. Estimation of risk and uncertainty (Yamagishi, 1994), judgments of self-efficacy (Cervone & Peake, 1986), and predictions of future performance (Czaczkes & Ganzach, 1996) are all affected by the anchor with which we begin the process of estimation. Similarly, negotiations are affected by the anchor values introduced at the beginning (Ritov, 1996). Jury awards are influenced by the amount of compensation requested, even for requests that are implausibly low (one hundred dollars) and impossibly high (one billion dollars; G. B. Chapman & Bornstein, 1996). Evaluation of current performance can be anchored on past performance (Caverni & Pris, 1990); indeed, the status quo serves as a powerful anchor in many contexts (Hastie & Dawes, 2001).

What produces this anchoring effect? G. B. Chapman and Johnson (2002) propose that the anchor serves as a selective retrieval cue: It serves as a prime that makes information that is consistent with it available. For example, suppose you were asked to guess whether the average daily temperature in Toronto in July was higher or lower than 10°C (50°F). Chances are, your thoughts would be primed to think about cool weather, about the fact that Toronto is in Canada, which is known for its cool weather. If you were then asked to provide an estimate of the average July temperature, the primed information is likely to influence your judgment. You may well have revised your estimate upward, based perhaps on the knowledge that Toronto is in a relatively southern part of Canada, but your final estimate is likely to be lower than if you had stared with 40°C (104°F) as your anchor. Thus, the presence of an anchor increases the availability of features that are shared by the target and anchor while reducing the availability of dissimilar cues.

For instance, a fifty-five year old woman sought therapy to deal with depression and loneliness after the death of her husband and her children leaving home. She wished for another relationship but had read that the average male's life expectancy was about ten years less than that of the average female. Using this as an anchor, she then concluded that she could not have another relationship as she would not be able to manage another loss. It was also significant that she never considered she could have a relationship with a younger man. Nor was she able to look at other factors that might help her choose a suitable partner. The anchoring information was so strong that all other factors were ignored.

Incomplete Analysis

This final section on feature positive thinking concerns situations in which we are deciding between one or more alternative courses of action. For example, should I continue the relationship or break it off? Should I change my investment strategy? Is now a good time to retire? Would now be a good time to confront my husband about his drinking? The optimal strategy for reaching a balanced decision would be to outline each of the possible alternatives and consider the probable consequences of each (Hastie & Dawes, 2001). Instead, research shows that when people are making complex decisions of these sorts, they tend to focus on one or two of the alternatives and reason extensively about those alternatives while ignoring the others (Fischhoff, 1996; Pennington & Hastie, 1991). Thus, some alternatives are analyzed in depth, whereas others are relatively neglected.

For example, Fischhoff asked 105 teenaged girls from a variety of social and economic backgrounds to describe in detail recent decisions they had made in a number of domains (school, parents, clothes). Although these were complex situations that afforded several courses of action, in the majority of cases, the participants focused on a single option (e.g., to take up healthier eating habits or whether to start smoking). In only 30% of the cases did the young women describe two or more options, and in even fewer cases, did they describe a problem-solving process of creating new options. Thus, it appears that the girls tended to focus on the implications or consequences of only one option. Indeed, even when they were explicitly asked to consider the alternatives, about 30% of the teenagers were unable to suggest an undesirable consequence that would be certain to accompany their decision, or to suggest what benefits would be foregone by taking a particular decision, as opposed to an alternative one.

Hastie and Dawes (2001) suggest creating an explicit structure, such as a tree diagram, that outlines the alternatives, describes the probable consequences of the alternatives, and evaluates the consequences. For example, an adolescent client had decided to go on a diet. As the therapist explored her reasoning, it was clear that she had only considered the one diet she had just heard about and the positive effects if she was successful. This decision was made even though she was well within the normal weight range for someone her age, height, and body type. This decision was expressed in a session although dietary concerns were not part of the therapy contract or goals. The therapist encouraged the young woman to make a decision tree and follow (with the therapist's coaching) all the possible positive and negative outcomes for several decisions (e.g., what diet to choose, what information she needed to make the decision, how she might handle the potential consequences of each decision). This was a very difficult process for this sixteen-year-old girl and was likely only possible because of the strength of the therapeutic relationship. After developing and considering multiple decisions and outcomes using the decision tree format, the young woman stated, "Wow, I had no idea every decision I make could be so complicated."

Summary of Feature Positive Thinking

Many of the reasoning biases observed are based on excessive attention to features that are available in the environment or memory, rather than an even consideration of all relevant issues. The features that capture our attention can be specific examples, plausible explanations, or knowledge about an actual outcome. In each of these cases, our thinking focuses on these aspects that are easily present in our minds, often to the exclusion of other, equally important, but less easily available, information.

Case Illustration:

As she explored the issues in her life, Barbara realized that her drinking and fear of losing a family member were related to her giving up on relationships. Her drinking helped her tolerate her unfulfilling life, and any deaths in her family reminded her that she was working with a diminishing pool of loved ones with no possibilities for expansion. Barbara clearly wished to re-evaluate her earlier conclusion and make a different decision; however, the myriad examples in her memory and the belief that she could not be trusted to make good decisions (hindsight bias) left her overwhelmed, with no room to establish any alternatives. In fact, she had made a causal attribution that it was her inability look after herself that had caused her unhappiness rather than the behaviors of her two ex-husbands. While there was no doubt that Barb needed to develop her skills of self-care, she also needed to stop taking responsibility for others' behavior. Both feature positive and belief bias effects needed to be addressed in this case.

KNOWLEDGE AND BELIEF EFFECTS
IN THE EVALUATION OF ARGUMENTS

In this section, we discuss how we evaluate arguments, by which we mean a conclusion that is supported by one or more premises. Although this may seem somewhat academic, in fact, we are talking about a wide range of persuasive communications from informal discussions, to television ads, newspaper editorials, and any situation in which one person attempts to persuade another to accept a particular point of view. Our discussion includes situations in which someone generates the conclusion herself, as in when trying to explain her views, opinions, or beliefs to another, as well as situations in which we are trying to evaluate an argument put forward by someone else. These situations are often addressed in therapy where a client is not only attempting to make her own decision, but attempting to do so in the face of another's counterargument. For example, university or high school students often attempt to make a decision about taking a year off, but their parents argue for them to stay in school. Or, one member of a couple may wish to end the relationship, whereas the other desperately wants to mend the relationship. In addition, many of the decisions made within the context of the therapy may include persuasion by the therapist; these and other therapeutic decisions must be evaluated.

Research that examines self-generated conclusions typically asks participants to offer an explanation for their opinions on a variety of current issues, such as why parolees return to crime or what causes children to fail in school (Brem & Rips, 2000; Kuhn, 1989, 1991a, 1991b; Perkins, 1985). Participants are then asked to explain their views, consider alternatives, and provide examples of evidence that supports or refutes their claim. Research that examines how people evaluate others' conclusions presents them with informal arguments such as those found in newspapers (e.g., J. Baron, 1995; K. Edwards & Smith, 1996; Shaw, 1996), formal arguments that have a well-defined structure (e.g., Oaksford, Roberts, & Chater, 2002; Thompson, 1994, 2000), or dialectic, back-and-forth arguments (Rips, 1998), as this example from Stanovich and West (1997) illustrates:

Dale: The welfare system should be drastically reduced in size because welfare recipients take advantage of the system and buy expensive food with their food stamps.

Critic: In fact, 95% of welfare recipients use their food stamps to obtain the
         bare essentials for their families.

Dale: Many people who are on welfare are lazy and don't want to work for a
         living. (p. 345)

Reasoning by Mental Models

We propose that people reason in two stages. First, they form a *situation
model*: a mental representation that provides a meaningful link between
the premises and the conclusion (e.g., Johnson-Laird & Byrne, 1991;
Shaw, 1996). This link may be in the form of a causal explanation (e.g.,
Kuhn, 1991a; Perkins, Farady, & Bushey, 1991), temporal or spatial relationships (Knauff & Johnson-Laird, 2002; Schaeken, Johnson-Laird, &
d'Ydewalle, 1996), verbal relationships (Polk & Newell, 1995), or formal
set relationships (Newstead, Thompson, & Handley, 2002). The second
stage entails a critical examination of the conclusion. This may involve
gathering additional evidence or arguments to support the conclusion (as
in Dale's reply) or alternatively, looking for ways to defeat the conclusion
(as the critic illustrates).

Promoting Logical Analysis

In this section, we are chiefly concerned with processes that either curtail
or facilitate this second step (countering the conclusion). Thus, we are
concerned with processes that undermine or limit our ability to critically
analyze a conclusion, or, alternatively, that promote a thoughtful analysis.
In the preceding chapter, we showed how beliefs can affect the way in
which evidence is analyzed: Evidence that supports a conclusion that is
contrary to our personal beliefs tends to be scrutinized more closely than
evidence supporting belief-consistent conclusions.

A similar process occurs when we are asked to evaluate arguments. Arguments that support a conclusion that is inconsistent with our beliefs tend
to be scrutinized more closely than arguments supporting a belief-consistent
conclusion (see, e.g., K. Edwards & Smith, 1996; Oakhill, Johnson-Laird,
& Garnham, 1989). Ironically, this means that beliefs can actually promote
logical thinking. People are better at discriminating valid from invalid conclusions when the conclusions are less believable to them (e.g., Evans,
Newstead, Allen, & Pollard, 1994; Klauer, Munsch, & Namur, 2000;
Thompson et al., 2003), presumably because they are more inclined to ana-

lyze the arguments more closely in these situations. This may underlie the arguments that clients often put forth to challenge a therapist's suggestions for their treatment (e.g., "I couldn't do that"), or alternative ways to interpret ambiguous situations ("I'm sure she was insulting me").

In other cases, however, conclusions may be accepted or rejected simply on the basis of belief. Shaw (1996), for example, found that participants were more likely to evaluate arguments on the basis of belief than on the basis of overall soundness. Similarly, there is a large body of evidence showing that prior belief determines whether conclusions are accepted or rejected, even when the logic of the argument is transparently simple (Klauer et al., 2000; Newstead et al., 1992; Thompson, 1995, 2000). That is, people accept belief-consistent conclusions and reject belief-inconsistent ones, regardless of the validity of the argument. Consequently, therapy situations in which clients can problem solve without their beliefs being challenged are generally easier to manage than those in which a belief is a constraint or block to reaching the goal state. For example, a client entering therapy with a belief that he is generally competent but has run into a situation with which he is unfamiliar will generally problem solve more easily than a client with a belief that he is not competent. These levels of change are described in a variety of ways, including first or second orders of change, as articulated by Gregory Bateson and the MRI group (e.g., see Watzlawick, Weakland, & Fisch, 1974) and adopted by many theories of family and systemic therapies; a change of schema rather than thought content in cognitive behavioral therapy (e.g., DeRubeis, Tang, & Beck, 2001); or as the change of core ordering processes in constructivist therapies (e.g., Mahoney, 2003). In general terms, this deeper change is often referred to as a paradigm shift with the implication that it is a shift to another level of experiencing the world rather than working within our current one.

The Availability of Concrete Examples

There is a large body of evidence to show that these types of belief effects are mediated by the availability of factual examples or counterexamples (Cummins et al., 1991; De Neys, Schaeken, & d'Ydewalle, 2003; Markovits, 1984, 1986; Quinn & Markovits, 2002; Thompson, 1995, 2000). Judgments about many important issues may be based on the ease with which a concrete image or example comes to mind. A similar effect is observed here, as illustrated below:

Mary: If it froze last night, the tomato plants will die.

John (looking out the window):   It must have frozen, because the plants do not look healthy.

Mary: If it froze last night, the car windows will need to be scraped off.

John (looking out the window):   It must have frozen, because the windows are frosted up.

The logical status of these two arguments is the same: In neither case does the conclusion follow necessarily from the premises. In the first instance, however, there are specific, concrete examples that come to mind and that render the conclusion less likely (e.g., not enough sun, the neighbor's dog, too much water). People are therefore less likely to agree with the conclusion that it froze overnight. In the second instance, few examples come to mind and so we are more inclined to accept the conclusion. Thus, reasoning decisions are mediated by availability of specific counterexamples.

My-Side Bias in the Evaluation of Arguments

A second mediating factor of belief effects concerns the ease with which people can generate confirming and disconfirming arguments. We are typically able to generate more arguments in support of our position than against our position (J. Baron, 1995; Perkins, 1985; Perkins, Farady, & Bushey, 1991; Toplak & Stanovich, 2003; Voss & Means, 1991). This effect is known as the my-side bias and clearly limits our ability to question the validity of arguments and evidence that support our viewpoint.

For example, Kuhn (1991a; see also Kuhn, 1989, 1991b, for an excellent précis) asked 160 participants from diverse educational and economic backgrounds to express their opinions on everyday topics such as "What causes failure in school?" After stating their opinion, participants were asked to provide an argument against their theory and to articulate an alternative to the theory they had provided. The overall success rates on these tasks was only 50% and 60%, respectively. In Perkins' (1985) study using similar scenarios, college undergraduates were able to provide, on average, only one counterargument against their stated position, compared to three arguments in favor. In marital or family therapy, this bias is often addressed by having one member of the family take the other's perspective and then argue from that perspective. This not only assists in evaluating arguments, conclusions, and decisions, but also can bring empathy for the other into the therapy setting. John and Susan were in marital therapy with

Susan providing arguments as to why the relationship should end and John reasons why they should remain together. The quality of the arguments changed markedly after they were each encouraged to role-play a switch in positions.

Case Illustration:

   A solution-focused therapist might look for exceptions and build a model based on applying those exceptions to her current life (Barb had excellent family relationships and was able to give many examples of assertiveness with them). A dynamically oriented therapist may focus on the pattern that Barb could work things out with family members but not relationship partners or friends. This loyalty to family and lack of trust in her abilities with the rest of the world could be traced as far back as elementary school and seemed to keep her from finishing the process of individuation and "growing up." A cognitive behavioral therapist would likely use a variety of disputing techniques to challenge her belief (that she has always failed herself and can't be trusted) while developing exercises and homework assignments to assist with the development of a new belief. An experiential/humanistic therapist might focus on her experience of sadness and helplessness and assist her to self-soothe and develop a sense of efficacy in managing her own emotional state. A constructivist or narrative therapist might help Barb to develop a sense of meaning from her experiences and then develop a new storyline for her life that included looking after herself within potential friendships and a mate relationship. The common elements in these and many other potential interventions is that in every case the therapist would assist Barb in expanding the problem space to include additional elements so that the feature positive and belief bias effects are countered or mitigated in some way. This has the effect of disembedding Barb from the overwhelming experience of grief and sadness and the sense of inevitability that she is trapped with no way out.

   While all of these methods were used in the course of her fifteen sessions of therapy, Barb's intense interest in history led to the therapist most frequently framing issues and solutions in dynamic and narrative terms.

Beliefs About What Makes a Good Argument

Another factor mediating belief effects has to do with people's beliefs about what makes a good argument. In Kuhn's (1991b) study, for example, the inability to generate counterarguments appeared to be due to a profound misunderstanding about the relationship between theories and evidence, such that theories and explanations were confused with genuine evidence (Brem & Rips, 2000; Kuhn, 1991a). Indeed, as discussed in chapter 9, the act of generating an explanation or a theory is often perceived as sufficient grounds on which to accept a conclusion. That is, if we can think of a reason to explain how something occurs, that can constitute sufficient grounds for believing it to be true (Koehler, 1991). Conversely, when asked to provide support or justification for their position, many people are not able to distinguish between the explanation of mechanisms underlying the claims and the evidence that would potentially determine whether or not those claims and explanations really hold (Brem & Rips, 2000; Kuhn, 1991a). For example, in Kuhn's study, after participants stated their position, they were asked what evidence they would give to show that their position was right. Only 40% offered evidence that was clearly differentiated from the theory and which was relevant to the correctness of the theory. Most, instead, offered what Kuhn described as "pseudo-evidence" in which theory and evidence were "fused into a script of how it happens." For example, when offering evidence in favor of why nutrition is the cause of school failure, one participant offered the following: "The points that they get in school. The grades that they get in school to show . . . that they are lacking something in their body. That the kids who were failing lack something in their body."

This substitution of explanation and opinion for evidence is very common in the human experience, including in therapy. However, competent therapists from any theoretical background will want their clients to develop, use, and maintain higher levels of problem-solving and reasoning skills in those important areas that prompted them to seek or be referred for psychotherapy. It is often the case that those in therapy are seeking to make meaning of, or understand, their life experiences (e.g., Carlson, 1988; Kegan, 1994). Therapists of all orientations provide their clients with explicit or implicit explanations concerning their life issues. While this is often one of the keys to successful therapy and provides relief to clients, therapists need to be careful that they or their clients do not confuse a reasonable explanation for evidence concerning the cause of their experience.

In addition to mistaking evidence and theory, there are other metacognitive beliefs (see chapter 12) that contribute to reasoning performance. Many reasoning errors are caused by a failure to consider alternative models of the situation, even when beliefs are not an issue (Evans, Legrenzi, & Girotto, 1999; Johnson-Laird & Byrne, 1991, 2002). Indeed, J. Baron (1995) observed that participants evaluated one-sided arguments to be stronger than arguments considering both sides of an issue, even when the one-sided arguments led to belief-inconsistent conclusions. This appears to be a specific instance of a more general phenomenon, in which the confidence with which an assertion is made is construed as evidence for the accuracy of the assertion (N. Brewer & Burke, 2002; G. L. Wells, Ferguson, & Lindsay, 1981; G. L. Wells & Murray, 1984; G. L. Wells, Olson, & Charman, 2002; Whitely & Greenberg, 1986; see chapter 12). Thus, the preference for (confident) one-sided arguments may contribute to the failure to present or consider alternative views when evaluating and generating arguments.

Kuhn identified a related factor that may underlie our willingness to consider alternative views. Only about 15% of the participants in her study believed that knowledge is an open-ended process of evaluation and judgment. Instead, about 50% of the participants could be described as "absolutists," who regarded knowledge as certain; that is, they believed that the kinds of complex questions that they were asked to consider could be answered with certainty. This kind of belief appears to underlie the response of one participant, who, when asked what evidence a person might give to show that she was wrong, replied, "They couldn't unless they lived in a dream world" (Kuhn, 1991b, p. 166). These sentiments were clearly echoed in additional responses of participants such as the following, who expressed ownership of their viewpoint, rendering it unavailable for scrutiny, "They will never prove me wrong. . . . I've lived it. Absolutely. . . . Don't step on my turf" (Kuhn, 1991b, p. 166). The remaining participants believed that all knowledge is relative: Everyone has a right to his or her own opinion and even experts disagree on important questions; thus, nothing is certain and all opinions are equally valid. This "legislating" of reality or "foreclosing" on any options other than the one present are frequently central in psychotherapy. Therapists of all theoretical inclinations attempt to help clients develop beyond these rigidly held views. Thus, people's beliefs about what makes a good argument may contribute to their willingness to consider alternative views. Indeed, several studies have shown that resistance to belief bias is mediated by willingness to engage in actively open-minded thinking (Klaczynski & Robinson, 2000; Stanovich & West, 1997) and our ability to generate alternative models or representations of the premise information (Thompson et al., 2003; Torrens, Thompson, & Cramer, 1999). In contrast, belief bias appears to be independent of IQ and other similar measures (e.g., Klaczynski & Robinson, 2000; Toplack & Stanovich, 2003; Torrens et al., 1999): Those with greater cognitive ability do better on tests of both formal and informal reasoning, but are equally susceptible to belief bias. For example, Perkins

(1985; Perkins et al., 1991) found a reliable correlation between IQ and a person's ability to generate arguments in favor of his position, but no correlation between IQ and a person's ability to generate other-side arguments (see also Toplak & Stanovich, 2003). These abilities of open-mindedness, seeking alternatives, and taking another's perspective are directly addressed in developmentally based theories (e.g., see Kegan, 1982, 1994) and psychotherapies (e.g., Carlson, 1988; Greenspan, 1997).

Summary of Belief-Based Effects

In sum, when people can rely on their factual knowledge to generate counterexamples, they do so. When they must engage in the more complex task of constructing alternative theories or counterarguments, they often fail. This failure, however, may be only partly attributed to a lack of ability. Recall that when people are provided with unbelievable conclusions, they are able to generate a logical analysis. This implies that the failure to do so when the conclusion is belief-consistent may reflect a lack of motivation, rather than a lack of ability, in that the relevant analytic skills are apparently engaged only when motivation exists. Consistent with this view, overcoming belief bias is linked to a predisposition for active, open-minded thinking rather than to traditional measures of cognitive ability.

So, what can be done to ameliorate belief bias? So far, these effects have proven difficult to reduce in research settings. Even very strong instructions to ignore our beliefs and reason only on the basis of the information provided have little effect (Evans et al., 1994; Newstead et al., 1992). Some success has been found with manipulations that make the structure of the argument clear. For example, Shaw found that asking participants to identify the premises and conclusions of an argument, or to independently rate their belief in the premises and conclusion of an argument, increased the probability that participants evaluated the argument on its strength, as opposed to on whether or not they agreed with the assertions. Similarly, Neuman and Weizman (2003) found that students who were able to represent and recall the structure of an argument were more likely to identify the flaw and fallacies in the argument. Thus, there is some evidence to suggest that having participants draw out the explicit structure of an argument, clearly separating premises from conclusions, may increase the probability that they will analyze the argument on the basis of its strengths and weaknesses. Many psychotherapies, especially cognitive therapies (e.g., Dobson, 2001) and metacognitive therapies (e.g., A. Wells, 2000), address belief biases directly and with effectiveness.

INTEGRATIVE SUMMARY:
CAUSAL REASONING

The goal of this final section is to integrate and review the major themes that we have discussed in the last two chapters. To do this, we will apply the basic principles from these chapters to a central issue in cognitive functioning: causal reasoning, or deciding what we consider causes a given action or event. Causal reasoning involves two kinds of reasoning. The first is causal induction, which refers to the processes by which we learn that two classes of events are causally related. This includes information that applies to personal experience as well as to more general causal relationships (e.g., when I eat shrimp, I get hives; if I don't sleep, I can't concentrate well; if I leave the car out in the cold, it won't start; if a person works hard, they succeed; if children are disciplined, they learn respect; if plants are watered, then they grow, etc.). The second process is causal explanation, and involves applying the acquired knowledge to a particular context (e.g., I'm getting hives, there must have been shrimp in that sauce; My kids aren't respecting me, so I will have to increase discipline).

Theories and Similarity in Causal Reasoning

In chapter 8, we described the means by which our theories about how the world works determine our view of similarity between two objects or concepts, and by extension, whether or not they belong in the same category. That is, we understand what links "children, pets, wallet, photographs" as members of the category "things to take out of the house in case of fire," even though these elements appear to have little in common. Thus, our conceptual knowledge determines which dimensions are important in determining similarity and category membership.

Similarly, causal theories, both general and specific, guide our attention and select likely causal candidates from a potentially overwhelming number of options. As an example, suppose that I am trying to figure out what produced the nasty rash that has developed on my feet. I search for a cause that will be restricted to a relatively small number of candidates, and potentially irrelevant candidates such as the political situation in Afghanistan or the book I read before bed last night are unlikely to be considered. By the same token, however, potentially important alternatives may be eliminated early on because they are not a good fit with my usual causal models. Many individuals and families seeking therapy are looking for the cause or explanation for their distress and difficulties and hope that the therapist can assist with a causal explanation that will inform a reasonable and effective solution. This idea is intermittently controversial in psychotherapy with some approaches seeking causal explanations from the past (e.g., dynamic therapies), present circumstances (e.g., cognitive behavioral approaches), or the meaning individuals place on experience (e.g., constructivist and narrative approaches). Some therapies attempt to circumvent the process altogether by focusing on exceptions and building new concepts based on goals (e.g., brief and solution-focused approaches). Both client and therapist limit the causal candidates for consideration, the clients by life experience, and the therapist by life experience and formal clinical training. There is always the potential in therapy to eliminate important alternatives and thus decrease the effectiveness of the therapy (see chapter 2 for a discussion on limiting the problem space).

Some of the theories used to narrow the search for a likely cause will be general (see Einhorn & Hogarth, 1986, for a review). For example, causes precede their effects; thus, to understand my foot rash, my search will likely be restricted to things that happened before the rash occurred. Causes and effects tend to be contiguous (occur at similar times); thus, the longer the delay between cause and effect, the less likely the cause is to be implicated in producing the outcome (see Buehner & May, 2002; Hagmayer & Waldmann, 2000, for recent discussions). Thus, it is most likely I will search for something that has recently changed. There also needs to be a means or a mechanism by which the cause transmits its effect; thus, I might consider substances or objects (such as socks and shoes) that have come in contact with my feet as potential candidates (e.g., P. A. White, 1989). Causes and effects also tend to resemble each other and be similar in magnitudes (see Rozin & Nemeroff, 2002, for a review). Thus, in the case of a mild rash, I am more likely to consider allergens in the laundry detergent than a new strain of plague. Finally, causes tend to covary with their effects: The stronger the correlation, the more likely it is that a causal attribution will be made (see, e.g., Cheng, 1997; Fugelsang & Thompson, 2000, 2003; Wasserman, Chatlosh, & Neunaber, 1983).

In many cases, these causal principles are useful. Without some way to triage the input to our cognitive system, we would be overwhelmed by a large amount of irrelevant information. They can, however, sometimes lead us astray and give rise to beliefs in superstitions and other spurious causal relationships. Rozin and Nemeroff (2002) provide a number of compelling examples of this. For example, the principle that causes resemble their effects (the "like causes like" principle) may underlie certain myths about the AIDS virus. Specifically, because the disease is lethal and highly resistant to attempts at curing it, it is assumed that the cause of the disease is likewise potent. In contrast, however, the virus is relatively fragile outside of a suitable host; moreover, a substantial dose of the virus is required to produce a high probability of infection. However, as these two properties violate the similarity principle of causation, false beliefs about the transmission of the virus may be difficult to dispel.

Similarly, potentially relevant causes may be overlooked because they do not fit well with our pre-existing causal theories. A famous example is that of Louis Pasteur who argued that germs were the underlying cause of many serious illnesses. Although this is a causal relationship that we now take for granted, at the time, Pasteur experienced resistance to this idea. The resistance was likely attributable to the fact that the germ–illness relationship violates many causal principles. Specifically, germs do not resemble their effects, either physically or in terms of the magnitude of their impact. It must have been difficult for Pasteur's contemporaries to imagine that something so small as to be invisible could produce such a devastating and even deadly effect. Add to that the fact that the causal event and the outcome are often delayed by several days, that there is often no direct transmission between the source and the target (because many bacteria are airborne), it is little wonder that many doubted Pasteur's theory.

As in biological processes, therapists often attempt to help clients move beyond the usual views of cause and effect. There are some notable exceptions to the concepts of causes preceding effects and contiguity in a variety of therapies. For example, in systemic therapies, the therapist often attempts to alter the family system by helping the clients to appreciate and work with the concept of reciprocal causality. This is the idea that events do not cause each other in a linear or sequential fashion but affect one another in a circular or recursive manner (e.g., Hecker, Mims, & Boughner, 2003). Because families and couples often enter therapy with a sense of linear causality, with causes preceding effects, the therapists' reframing this into mutually affecting well-intentioned processes is a common intervention. For example, a very common interactional pattern in couples is that of pursuer–distancer. One member of the couple will ask the other to share something that triggers their partner's withdrawal or shutting down. This shutting down in turn triggers some anxiety/uncertainty in the first person who then pursues more, resulting in each of their behaviors triggering the other's reaction in an escalating feedback loop. In addition to helping the clients understand this concept, therapists help reframe the intentions of each partner in a positive manner. One partner's pursuit may be redefined as a sign of love and affection rather than nagging, whereas the other's withdrawal is defined as an attempt to keep conflict out of the relationship.

An exception to contiguity occurs in dynamic therapies where the causes of current patterns and events may be sought in the distant past. This is not just the result of the therapists' training and focus. Frequently clients enter therapy with the belief that their own or their family member's problematic behavior or state has been caused by childhood events. For example, one couple entered therapy to resolve parenting issues. The wife clearly stated within the first five minutes of the session that the cause of her husband's loss of temper with their son was the brutal beatings he received at the hands of his father as a young boy. The father unreservedly agreed with her. This and other similar beliefs about contiguity and causality must be attended to in therapy when directly raised by our clients or when needed to resolve problems.

Belief-Based Effects

In addition to general causal theories, causal reasoning is also mediated by more specific theories, that is, beliefs about how specific domains, situations, or events are likely to unfold (e.g., theories about what causes allergies, behaviors, illnesses, etc.). Causal beliefs concern the mechanism that underlies a causal relationship and the means by which a cause transmits its effect. Causal beliefs affect how many aspects of the causal environment are interpreted, including the assignment of causal roles (e.g., R. M. J. Byrne, 2002; Hilton, 2002; Hilton & Erb, 1996; Waldmann & Hagmayer, 2001; P. A. White, 1995, 2000, 2004), as well as how the general characteristics of causality, such as temporal delay and the co-variation of cause and effect, are interpreted (Ahn, Kalish, Medin, & Gelman, 1995; Buehner & May, 2002; Fugelsang & Thompson, 2000, 2003; Hagmayer & Waldmann, 2000).

To understand how causal roles are assigned, consider the problem of explaining why an airplane has crashed. Pilot error, rather than gravity, is likely to be identified as the cause of the crash, even though both may have contributed (Seelau, Seelau, Wells, & Windschitl, 1995). In any causal situation, there are multiple necessary conditions that must be in place to enable the outcome to occur (e.g., Einhorn & Hogarth, 1986; Hilton, 2002; Hilton & Erb, 1996; P. A. White, 1989, 1995). Identifying a cause usually involves identifying something unusual or different in this background, and will depend on the underlying causal model, context, and beliefs. For example, one might normally consider a hammer to be the cause of a broken watch-face; however, if one is thinking about a quality-control measure in a factory, one might instead attribute the break to a defect in the crystal.

Causal beliefs may also be used to limit the potential set of candidates that are considered as causes for a particular effect (Ahn et al., 1995; Koslowski & Masnick, 2002), and can be used to determine how information in the environment is interpreted. For example, long delays between the cause and an effect interfere with learning about the relationship. However, if one has a causal belief about a situation that suggests longer delays might be possible, then causal attributions can still be made even though the cause and effect are not contiguous (Buehner & May, 2002; Hagmayer & Waldmann, 2000). To illustrate, in the case of the foot rash described previously, I might consider two possible sources of allergic reactions. The first is a contact reaction, in which case I will look for items that have recently been in contact with my feet. The other is a reaction to a substance that has been ingested or inhaled, in which case the exposure may have occurred some time previously. In a more clinical vein, the previous example of parenting differences uncovered strong beliefs in both mother and father that past experiences caused present events. This attribution that past traumas result in the "damaged goods" view of people who are then incapable of performing in some way in the present is very common in the belief systems of both clients and therapists. It is beyond the scope of this book to comment on the accuracy of these views, but in any case these beliefs must be attended to as part of the resolution of problems. If the therapy does not allow for this by legislating out of existence or disrespecting a strong belief of the client, therapy is likely to be less effective. The literature on finding the right therapy for each client or family attempts to address this goodness of fit between clients and therapists (e.g., Lambert & Barley, 2002).

Causal beliefs may also determine how covariation information is interpreted. Covariation is the extent to which a change in one thing is accompanied by a corresponding change in another. Causes necessarily covary with their effects, so covariation is a primary clue to causality. In order to distinguish spurious from causal correlations, however, we need to have a causal model that gives selective priority to some correlations (Fugelsang & Thompson, 2000, 2003). Thus, in the case of the foot rash, I am more likely to look to the new laundry detergent than a new book that I am reading, even though both events may be coincident with the onset of the rash.

The corollary to this is that evidence that contradicts our beliefs may be overlooked or downplayed (Fugelsang & Thompson, 2000, 2003). Fugelsang and Thompson found that when judging probable cause, participants weighed evidence about the correlation between two events more heavily when they were considering a causal candidate that was believable than one that was unbelievable. Thus, strong evidence for a believable candidate was given more weight than strong evidence for an unbelievable candidate. These effects are reminiscent of the other belief-based effects that we discussed in this chapter and in chapter 9. That is, pre-existing beliefs determine how evidence is weighed, such that evidence that is inconsistent with prior beliefs may be overlooked or downplayed.

For example, a client entered therapy to address his increasing sense of panic and anxiety in public situations. In the assessment phase, he revealed an astounding array of stressors in his life. His only child had been killed two years previously, and his marriage had failed the following year. He was suffering some health problems and the financial outcome of his divorce and failing markets had seriously affected his plan to retire in two years ("I'll have to work at least another ten years"). In spite of all of these and other stressors, he had never considered that his symptoms could be stress-related rather than a personal lack of strength. Simply listing and exploring the correlative factors of stressful events and symptoms resulted in a change of view in this client. His original intention (influenced by his belief that his symptoms were a result of a personal weakness) to become stronger quickly shifted to taking better care of himself physically and psychologically. This client's belief that he had to have the strength to manage everything in life with serenity resulted in him considering a stress-related causal hypothesis as unbelievable (i.e., never considered). He stated several times how surprised he was to discover the correlation between his anxiety and stress in his life ("This is amazing, I never thought of this before, . . . I'm a smart guy, why have I never thought about it this way?").

Like belief effects, there is little evidence that we are able to introspect on the source of our causal attributions. Fugelsang and Thompson (2003), for example, observed that participants were quite accurate in explaining how they weighed objective evidence (such as the correlation between cause and effect) in their causal judgments, but had very poor metacognitions about the contribution that their beliefs made to their judgments. Also, the degree to which belief-based and evidence-based information contributes to causal judgment is a matter of individual difference, with some people drawing more from beliefs and others drawing more from evidence (Amsel, Langer, & Loutzenhiser, 1991; Fugelsang & Thompson, 2000).

Explanation-Based Reasoning

Earlier in this chapter, we reported that creating an explanation for a conclusion is often sufficient grounds for accepting that conclusion. It is not
surprising, therefore, that explanatory coherence is a strong, mediating
factor in causal inference as well. For example, when considering evidence that one event caused another, explanations of the mechanism underlying the relationship are often perceived as more convincing than evidence supporting a correlation between cause and effect (Ahn et al., 1995,
Slusher & Anderson, 1996). Similarly, when asked what type of information they would need to find out whether one event caused another to occur, participants sought information that clarified the underlying causal
mechanism (Ahn et al., 1995).

We also reported that generating an explanation for an event increases
the perceived probability that the event will occur. A similar phenomenon is
associated with causal reasoning. Ahn and her colleagues (Ahn, Novick, &
Kim, 2003) found that people, including therapists with many years experience, are more likely to perceive behavior as normal if they can understand
and explain it. In this study, participants were provided with brief sketches
of individuals that consisted of lists of symptoms or behaviors drawn from
the *DSM-IV-TR*. When the behaviors were linked by a plausible explanation, or when the behavior could be explained by a traumatic life event, the
people in the sketches were perceived to be more normal than when an explanation was lacking. Producing a viable explanation for an event, in this
case a person's behavior, can thus have a profound effect on how we view
and understand that event. For example, a common technique in many therapies is to assist clients by normalizing their experiences. This is often done
by providing an explanation about how something has occurred rather than
why something has occurred. While generally helpful to reframe in this
way, therapists must also be wary that their clients do not assume that they
are receiving a causal explanation for their experience.

Feature Positive Effects in Causal Reasoning

In the preceding chapter, we gave several examples of how reasoning tends
to be constrained by information that is immediately accessible, either in the
environment or in working memory. To wrap up, we will provide examples
of how feature positive thinking influences causal judgments.

Recall that the covariation or correlation between two events is a key cue to causality: The more strongly two events are associated, the more likely people are to consider them causally related. Normatively speaking, two types of information should contribute equally to the judgment of covariation: the probability that the effect is observed when the cause is present and the probability that the effect occurs when the cause is absent. The former should increase the perceived probability of a causal relationship, whereas the latter should decrease it. In the foot-rash example, for instance, suppose that I decide that a new laundry detergent is responsible for the rash. My confidence in this hypothesis should be increased if wearing socks washed in the new detergent frequently is followed by a rash. In contrast, my confidence in the hypothesis should be decreased if the rash occurs, regardless of the type of laundry detergent that is used.

A large number of studies, however, indicate that these two sources of information do not weigh equally in our judgments (e.g., Mandel & Lehman, 1998; Over & Green, 2001; P. A. White, 2003). Situations where the presumed cause is present are weighed more heavily that situations where the cause is absent. In the preceding example, we consider the joint occurrence of the laundry detergent and the rash to be the most compelling evidence, and weigh this evidence most heavily. Less weight is given to cases where the laundry detergent is used without the rash occurring, and still less to cases where the rash occurs without the detergent having been used. In clinical situations, therapists often attempt to help clients look at both sources of information. For example, a client sought therapy to decide whether to leave her intermittently violent husband. One of her hypotheses for a solution was that if he would just stop drinking then he would not be violent. The therapist simply asked, "Has he ever been violent to you when he was sober?" She responded, "Yes, but I'm sure he was hung-over." The therapist then asked, "Has there ever been a time when he hasn't been drinking for more than two days when he was violent?" Again there were many examples. This systematic exploration of situations where the believed cause was absent was very helpful in assisting the client to deal with the issue of violence. On the other hand, if the exploration had confirmed the association between alcohol and violence, it would have led to a consideration of a somewhat different issue, such as the effect of her husband's alcoholism on her.

Several explanations can be offered for this cause-present effect. One is a sufficiency bias, that is, a bias to establish the sufficiency, as opposed to the necessity, of a cause (Mandel & Lehman, 1998). In other words, we appear more concerned with establishing that a possible cause is capable of bringing about an effect than we are with ruling out possible competing explanations. The explanation effects that we described earlier undoubtedly play a role in this as well: Explanations are geared toward demonstrating how a cause can realize an effect, and they tend to focus attention away from alternative explanations that might also mediate the effect (Sanbonmatsu, Akimoto, & Biggs, 1993). In human interaction, it seems that once we have a plausible explanation for something, we have a tendency to stop there rather than continuing to search for the accurate explanation. For example, the view that "My kid is going through a phase" when she may be using drugs is often a sufficient rather than accurate causal attribution when avoidance is in play. The opposite view, "My kid is acting strange, she must be on drugs" when she is simply going through a developmental shift is the sufficient strategy for anxious or overprotective parents. In both cases, the therapist will need to help parents look at the accuracy rather than the sufficiency of their belief-biased judgments.

A second explanation for cause-present effects is a more generic positive test strategy (Mandel & Lehman, 1998), similar to that described in the previous chapter. Recall that a positive test strategy leads us to look for instances that would be true if the hypothesis were true. The consequence in causal reasoning is that attention is focused on instances where the hypothesized causal relationship holds, namely, when both the cause and effect are present. For example, with the hypothesis that a new laundry detergent caused the foot rash, we may be more inclined to seek out and attend to evidence that is consistent with the hypothesis (i.e., the joint occurrence of detergent and rash) than to evidence that would refute the hypothesis (i.e., the rash does not occur with the new detergent, or it occurs with another type of detergent).

In the previous chapter, we argued that a positive test strategy is most likely to produce suboptimal results when the initial hypothesis is too narrow and needs to be made more inclusive. That is, a strategy that is focused on an overly narrow hypothesis cannot uncover evidence to suggest that the hypothesis needs to be broadened. Sanbonmatsu et al. (1993) warn that causal hypotheses are often of this sort. Causal relationships often involve multiple causes or interactive causes. Thus, the conclusion that an outcome is mainly due to a particular cause is often overly specific. However, provided that the cause is sufficient to produce the effect, the evidence that is generated via a positive test is likely to support the hypothesis. This may result in the neglect of viable alternatives.

Sanbonmatsu et al. (1993) gave the example of an administrator who operates under the hypothesis that success in graduate school can be attributed to intelligence. A positive test strategy is likely to confirm this hypothesis, as nearly all of the students admitted to a graduate program will be smart. In turn, the accumulation of evidence in favor of the hypothesis might diminish consideration of viable alternatives, such as motivation, effort, and creativity.

Finally, it is possible that we have difficulty noticing and interpreting null information such as the absence of a cause or an effect (Einhorn & Hogarth, 1986; Hearst, 1991). That is, situations where something happened are easier to notice and remember than situations where nothing happened. The occurrence of the effect is likely to be more memorable than its absence, and the occurrence of the cause is likely to be more memorable than its absence (see also chapters 4 and 7). Therapists systematically exploring the problem space will help clients explore exceptions and absence. For example, in a marital therapy session, a couple briefly explained they had not had any fights in the last week and then began to discuss a conflict from several weeks ago. The therapist's intervention was a simple exploration of exception. He stated, "Wow, in all our sessions you have never gone that long without fighting. How did you do that?"

D. T. Miller and Taylor (1995) suggest that this kind of selective memory underlies superstitious beliefs, such as the widely held view that switching lines generally leads to longer delays than staying put: The occasions on which one switches lines and experiences an extended delay are more memorable than the occasions on which one does not switch lines and experiences delay. Thus, a relationship is likely to be detected between switching and delays, even if the evidence suggests that these are independent factors.

Indeed, in psychotherapy, a primary strategy of most therapies is to have clients consider broader or additional hypotheses in the search for truth, growth, and resolution. This expansion of the problem space is often a key to assisting clients in considering alternative solutions for their issues rather than doing "more of the same." However, feature-present and belief-based biases in causal reasoning can result in therapists focusing too heavily on the types of events that are considered important causes in their therapeutic model, sometimes to the detriment of other sources of a client's difficulties. In exploring and solving therapeutic problems, both clients and therapists routinely make decisions about likely causes and evaluate conclusions about both symptoms and treatment possibilities, so an understanding of the strengths and limitations of our reasoning abilities can be of considerable benefit to the therapy process.

KEY POINTS

- Reasoning and decision-making processes are biased by information that is present in the environment or easily available in memory, known as feature-positive effects. Available features can include concrete examples, plausible explanations, the wording of a question, or even knowledge about the actual outcome of an event (hindsight bias). With respect to clients' decisions, this means that a current situation can unduly influence their judgment, such as when women decide not to leave abusive relationships because their partners are not currently violent.

- Existing beliefs can also bias reasoning. Conclusions and arguments that are consistent with beliefs are more likely to be judged accurate and persuasive than those that are inconsistent with our beliefs. Clients' beliefs are often evident in their judgments and decisions, such as the case of the father who believed that his daughter needed to be more protected than his son, because he believed that girls are more easily damaged by their experiences than are boys.

- When generating arguments or providing reasons for our judgments, we find it easier to generate examples for our own position than for the opposite opinion. This is known as "my-side bias," a tendency that is often encountered in couples and family therapy. This tendency can make it difficult for clients to understand another's point of view or to seriously consider a novel solution to their difficulties.

- Causal reasoning involves determining what causes an effect and involves two processes: one that allows us to learn about a causal relationship between two things (e.g., reminders of my mother cause me to feel sad) and a second that enables us to apply our knowledge of such causal relationships to a particular situation (e.g., I'm feeling sad right now because that woman's voice sounds like my mother's).

- We use our world knowledge to select likely causes of an event, often using simple heuristics to generate possibilities. For example, causes must precede effects, and therefore we more often consider possibilities that both precede and occur at a similar time to a given effect. Similarly, our attention is often drawn to things that are similar to the effect we are interested in, such as considering social causes for emotional experiences, even though emotions can sometimes be caused by biological factors such as our diet. Both clients and therapists seek to explain a client's experience, so these processes are often evident in therapeutic conversations and thinking.

• Feature-present and belief-based effects are also observed in causal reasoning, leading us to suspect events that are salient to our attention or believable to us as causes more often. One particular example of this is our tendency to notice times when a cause is present more than we notice when an effect occurs in the absence of the supposed cause. For therapists, this can lead to an undue focus on causal theories described by our chosen therapeutic model, leading us to overlook other factors that may be sources of a client's difficulty.

11

Counterfactual Thinking: If Only and What If

> So, we have the paradox of a man shamed to death because he is only
> the second pugilist or the second oarsman in the world. That he is
> able to beat the whole population of the globe minus one is nothing;
> he has "pitted" himself to beat that one; and as long as he doesn't do
> that nothing else counts.
>
> —William James (1892, p. 186)

Thinking about events that might have happened, but didn't, is known as counterfactual thinking (thinking contrary to the facts) and is a common feature of human thought (Hofstadter, 1979). Counterfactual thinking is a form of hypothetical thinking that focuses on alternative realities. It is integral to considering alternative solutions (e.g., If I were to start an exercise program, would I be able to stick to it?), ascribing blame (e.g., If only he had more control of his temper, we might still be together), and making causal attributions (e.g., If I had only turned right at the corner, I wouldn't have had this accident). Such thinking is also a central feature in a variety of emotional experiences including regret (e.g., If I were less depressed, he wouldn't have left me), grief (e.g., If only we'd consulted a doctor sooner, she'd still be alive), and shame (e.g., If I weren't such a loser, they wouldn't laugh at me).

Counterfactual thinking influences many therapeutically relevant psychological processes including emotion, attitudes, expectancies, suspicion, and self-inference (Roese, 1997). Such thinking can be very useful in preventing adverse occurrences from recurring and in planning for the future, but it can also lead to difficulties such as rumination and ineffective decision making. Many important therapeutic conversations involve counterfactual thinking, so understanding what we know about this process can benefit therapists' effectiveness in helping clients to make use of and manage their counterfactual thoughts.

We think counterfactually both about the past (e.g., "If only I had spoken to her sooner . . ."), the present (e.g., "If I were back in school . . .") and the future (e.g., "If I change jobs rather than trying for that promotion . . ."). When an event doesn't happen as we wanted it to, such as when we fail to get a job promotion we expected, we spontaneously imagine how the event might have turned out differently (i.e., we imagine that we did get the promotion). Similarly, as we are anticipating future decisions, we frequently imagine alternatives, such as imagining during an election how local or national conditions would change if we voted for one political candidate or another. Counterfactual thinking is one of the fundamental ways that humans process their experiences (Hofstadter, 1979; Revlin, Cate, & Rouss, 2001; Sternberg & Gastel, 1989).

Because counterfactual thinking involves comparing circumstances with alternatives, it is also a powerful determinant of satisfaction and regret (Medvec, Madey, & Gilovich, 1995), as the opening quotation to this chapter suggests. As Medvec et al. point out, a 5% raise may be thrilling, until you learn that the person down the hall got an 8% raise; a 3% return on an investment may be quite disappointing unless one is reminded of the alternative that was almost chosen, and lost money. Thus, the intensity of one's reactions to events is in proportion to the ease with which better or worse outcomes come to mind.

Medvec et al. (1995) provide an interesting illustration of how counterfactual comparisons can render a better outcome less satisfying than a worse one. After examining the behavior, public comments, and self-reports of Olympic medal winners, they observed that silver medal winners were less satisfied with their performance than were bronze medal winners. The authors hypothesized that the two situations evoked different counterfactual comparisons leading to different levels of satisfaction: Silver medalists focused on the fact that they didn't win the gold medal, resulting in negative feelings, whereas the bronze medalists focused on how they almost didn't receive a medal, evoking more positive feelings. Thus, despite the fact that silver medalists were objectively more successful than bronze medalists, the feelings of satisfaction were in the opposite direction.

Just as it is a frequent element of everyday thought, counterfactual thinking is also an essential part of therapeutic conversations. Clients who enter therapy to deal with unfortunate events, such as job loss or the death of a loved one, almost always entertain counterfactual thoughts about how things would be different if the event hadn't occurred, and part of therapy is helping them to deal with such thoughts. Similarly, clients who are facing a decision often engage therapists in counterfactual discussions of what might happen if they had chosen one or another of their alternatives (see chapters 9 & 10). Thus, the literature on the characteristics, consequences, and purposes of counterfactual thinking can greatly help therapists to understand and manage this aspect of client thinking.

CHARACTERISTICS OF COUNTERFACTUAL THOUGHTS

Antecedents and Consequents

Counterfactual thoughts are conditional propositions, taking the form of "if . . . then" statements. As such, these thoughts have both an antecedent (the "if" or preceding condition of the statement) and a consequent (the "then" or outcome of the preceding condition). Like ordinary conditional statements, counterfactuals invite hypothetical or suppositional thinking (Evans & Over, 2004). For example, ordinary conditionals can invite us to consider positive (e.g., If I insist that my husband go to the doctor, maybe he will go) and negative (e.g., If you continue to overwater that plant, its roots will drown) outcomes to events. Unlike ordinary conditionals, however, counterfactual thoughts are often used to "undo" an adverse event, imagining a different world than the current reality. For example, when someone thinks, "If only I had insisted that my husband go to the doctor, he might not have had the stroke," she is thinking about ways in which the stroke could have been prevented. Counterfactuals are therefore understood on two distinct levels (R. M. J. Byrne, 2002; Thompson & Byrne, 2002). On one level, they are about events that actually happened (i.e., I did not insist that my husband go to the doctor and he had a stroke); on the other, they are about an alternative reality (i.e., the stroke was prevented). Thus, counterfactuals are interpreted by simultaneously representing both the real and imagined events, and this representation informs the interpretations people make and the inferences they are willing to draw (Thompson & Byrne, 2002).

In thinking about the past, the better consequence that is imagined is usually the motivation for the counterfactual thought, whereas the antecedent is the alternative that is considered that might have led to the better outcome. In thinking about future possibilities, however, different antecedents are used to estimate probable outcomes that may follow from them, such as when we consider what might happen if a Democrat or Republican wins an American presidential race.

Upward and Downward Comparisons

When imagining alternatives to reality, we can imagine either better or worse outcomes than our actual situation. *Upward* counterfactuals involve imagining better outcomes and tend to be the most frequently occurring type (Roese & Olson, 1997), at least with respect to thoughts of the past. *Downward* counterfactuals entail consideration of how things might have been worse (e.g., if the truck had come two inches closer, I would have been killed). Because counterfactual thoughts create alternatives that can be contrasted with our current situation, they can intensify our reaction to our present circumstances, either increasing or decreasing our affective response (Landman, 1995; D. T. Miller & Taylor, 2002). Thinking of better possible alternatives (upward comparisons) has the effect of increasing our negative affect, such as grief, regret, or guilt (Davis, Lehman, Wortman, Silver, & Thompson, 1995). Conversely, downward counterfactuals can provide comfort (Medvec et al., 1995) and can thus moderate negative affect (e.g., when victims of an accident console themselves that the outcome could have been worse).

In addition to being more common, upward counterfactuals have greater impact on our feelings and behavior than downward comparisons (Heath, Larrick, & Wu, 1999). Salient upward counterfactuals often result in negative evaluations of our decisions (Mellers, Schwartz, Ho, & Ritov, 1997). For example, a young woman was describing her perceived inability to develop a relationship and related the following story: "I was at a bar and this really cute guy came up and asked me to dance. . . . I was so nervous I giggled, and he thought I was making fun of him and left. . . . God, I am such a loser. . . . If only I hadn't laughed. . . . I could tell I would have liked him and I think he would have liked me if I actually got to dance with him . . . if only I could control myself and not do stupid things. . . . I don't know why I even try."

Case Illustration:

> *Megan was in her late forties, unmarried, and currently unable to work due to the effects of a depressive illness. She was referred by her doctor for assistance in managing the psychological effects of her illness. During the last four to five years, she had been diagnosed with depression, obsessive-compulsive disorder, and generalized anxiety disorder. She was greatly distressed by the reduced sense of stability in her life as she worried about her security financially and whether she would be able to return to work. Just prior to referral for psychotherapy, she had attempted a graduated return to work that had failed after just one week. In addition to the work and psychological issues, she was living with a brother who had suffered a work injury and was unemployed and dependent on her financially.*

> *She grew up in a small farming community. Her father was alcoholic and emotionally and verbally abusive to her mother. There was a great deal of conflict among the extended family members. Megan described herself as a quiet and shy young girl who was upset by all the turmoil in her extended family as she "liked everyone and couldn't understand why they didn't like each other."*

> *As Megan's current life and history were explored, it became clear that she perceived all of her problems as stemming from one tragic incident in her early teens. While doing dishes, she accidentally stepped on a kitten that was playing in the kitchen and injured it so badly it had to be put down. She felt guilt and shame for her actions, accusing herself of being unable to care for anything.*

ACTIVATION OF COUNTERFACTUAL THINKING

Exceptional and Surprising Events

People are more likely to generate counterfactuals in response to surprising or exceptional events than to ordinary or expected events. Kahneman and Miller (2002) hypothesize that a normal event evokes representation that resembles itself (i.e., is ordinary). Abnormal events, in contrast, evoke highly available alternatives such as the contrasting "normal" state. Consequently, the consideration of alternative outcomes tends to be triggered by events that are out of the ordinary, especially if those events have negative consequences (Davis & Lehman, 1995; Klauer & Migulla, 1995; Sanna & Turley, 1996).

Several years ago, one of the authors broke her ankle. It happened on a rainy day in early summer, and she and her family were packing up to return home from their cabin at the lake, hurrying to avoid getting too wet in the rain. On one of the trips to the car, loaded with several packages, she slipped on a slippery section of the wooden walkway, fell awkwardly, and broke her ankle. Because of this accident, she was immobilized for most of the summer and missed an international conference she was scheduled to attend. At the time, and many times since then, she has thought about how things might have happened differently that day, so that her ankle wouldn't have broken. These thoughts have primarily focused around prevention: imagining either that she had installed a gritty surface on the wooden walkway or that she had been wearing shoes with better grip.

This incident illustrates the common circumstances under which counterfactual thinking typically arises—after an aversive event, especially a surprising event that results in negative emotion. In general, negative events tend to be unexpected, and thoughts about how the past could have been different seem to arise spontaneously (Roese, 1997). This even extends to our reactions to stories about others that have negative outcomes (e.g., Crawford & McCrea, 2004; Kahneman & Tversky, 1984; Mandel, 2003). Counterfactual thinking does occur in other circumstances, of course, but negative affect seems to be its primary natural trigger. As discussed in the section on functions of counterfactual thinking, it can be beneficial in these circumstances.

Near Misses and Close Calls

Adverse events that were almost avoided, or near misses of a positive outcome, seem to encourage more counterfactual thoughts than events that would have been difficult to avoid (Meyers-Levy & Maheswaran, 1992; Roese, 1997; Roese & Olson, 1996). For example, someone who is in a traffic accident when they are almost at the end of their journey is likely to generate more counterfactual thoughts than someone who is in an accident far from their destination. Experimentally, Meyers-Levy and Maheswaran (1992) had participants read a story about a man who forgot to submit an insurance payment (thus canceling his insurance) either three weeks or six months before a serious fire, and then list what thoughts they imagined this man would have about his circumstances. Participants who read the three-week scenario listed more counterfactual thoughts than those who received the six-month scenario, even though the man's actual circumstances were the same regardless of when he forgot the insurance payment. This triggering of counterfactual thinking for near misses, although understandable, may not be particularly functional, as the closeness of an event to a more-desired outcome does not influence how useful it is to prevent or plan to avoid such failures in the future.

As another example, prior to the 2004 Olympic games, one of the Canadian athletes was widely publicized as a gold medal hopeful in the women's hurdles. This athlete did exceptionally well in all the preliminary matches, and hopes were high at the beginning of the final race. However, the athlete stumbled and fell over the first hurdle in that race, dashing her hopes for a medal. Media interviews with both this athlete and others immediately after this event suggested that people were considering many counterfactual possibilities, thinking of several ways the fall could have been avoided. If such an incident had occurred early in the competition, such as during one of the qualifying races, although the athlete and her fans would naturally be very disappointed, the adverse event wouldn't have been as close to her goal as when it happened during the final race. Thus, on the basis of perceived nearness to achieving a goal (the closeness of the adverse event to the hoped-for outcome), the research suggests that less frequent and intense counterfactual thinking would occur if she had failed a competition earlier in the games than when the event happened during the final race.

Availability

Near misses as a trigger for counterfactual thoughts are likely attributable to memory factors. Specifically, the closer we are to achieving a goal, whether that goal is related to achievement (e.g., winning a race) or safety (e.g., arriving home after a journey), the more likely it is that we have envisioned the successful completion of the goal. Thus, the counterfactual successful completion is easily available in our memory, encouraging contrast with the less successful actual outcome.

Common examples in psychotherapy arise in grief work. For instance, a middle-aged man sought therapy for assistance in dealing with the recent death of his father. He was informed about his father's impending death while on vacation. He chose to drive home (a trip of about two days) and his father died about one hour before he arrived at the hospital. A theme of the early sessions was his heightened sorrow, disappointment, and guilt that he was just an hour late and never had a chance to say good-bye to his

father. In addition, his list of "if only" scenarios included several alternatives for travel, which would have allowed him to arrive prior to his father's death ("If only I had taken a plane, train, or bus, I would have been
on time"). Tucked away in his memory, but not discussed until the therapist asked about it, was the doctor's reassurance that his father would
likely live for several weeks and there was plenty of time to see him. Once
this factor became explicit, he then also used that in his counterfactual
thinking ("If only I had had accurate information, I would have acted differently").

   This factor, outcome closeness, also seems to encourage the generation
of downward counterfactuals, although the generation of worse outcomes
occurs only rarely in natural circumstances. However, positive outcomes
for events that could easily have resulted in adverse events, such as missing a plane that subsequently crashed or surviving a risky surgery, does
evoke downward counterfactual thinking (McMullen, 1997), likely
through the memory mechanisms described previously.

CONTENT OF COUNTERFACTUAL THINKING:
SELECTION OF ANTECEDENTS
FOR MENTAL REVISION

Given the desire to "replay" reality, which factors does one focus on?
Events tend to have multiple possible antecedents, yet counterfactual thinking typically focuses on only a small subset of those possibilities. For example, the author who broke her ankle considered the effects of putting in a
walkway with a better surface, but did not imagine what might have happened if it had not rained. In this section, we review a number of factors that
have been shown to influence the choice of antecedent event for "undoing."

Causal Chains

When events are linked together in a causal chain (e.g., event A leads to
event B, leading to C, etc.), people are most likely to focus on the first
event in the sequence to undo (e.g., Segura, Fernandez-Berrocal, & Byrne,
2002; G. L. Wells, Taylor, & Turtle, 1987). For example, suppose you are
setting out to buy one of a limited number of DVDs that are on sale at a
store across town. On the way, you run over some glass, causing a flat tire;
you are then caught in rush hour traffic. Because you are late, you drive

too quickly, earning a speeding ticket, and finally have to wait for a group of senior citizens at a crosswalk. You arrive to find that the last DVD had been sold a few minutes earlier.

When you think about how you might have made it on time, which event do you focus on? In the Segura et al. and Wells et al. studies, people focused on the first event in the chain, perhaps because removing the first cause is enough to undo all the subsequent events (G. L. Wells et al., 1987). It is also possible that it is easier to imagine that a later event did not happen, given that the first one did not (G. L. Wells et al., 1987). That is, there may be a sense of inevitability associated with a causal chain, given that one event leads to the next. For example, you were speeding *because* you were late from the flat tire; thus, it may be difficult to imagine not getting a speeding ticket without first undoing the flat tire. In contrast, after undoing the first event, it is relatively easy to imagine that subsequent events will be different, because the causal chain has been broken.

Controllability

Another factor that influences the selection of antecedents in both natural and hypothetical situations is the controllability (or mutability) of the element (Davis & Lehman, 1995; Mandel, 2003; Mandel & Lehman, 1996; McCloy & Byrne, 2000; McMullen, Markman, & Gavanski, 1995). People tend to focus on antecedents of the situation that are under their (or others') control. For example, when the author who broke her ankle was engaging in counterfactual thoughts about how the accident could have been prevented, she didn't consider turning off gravity or stopping the rain. Although these elements were causally related to the broken ankle, such aspects are seldom the focus of counterfactual thinking (Mandel, 2003; Seelau, Seelau, Wells, & Windschitl, 1995; Wells et al., 1987). We are obviously able to mentally revise such factors, as the popularity of science fiction novels and movies attests, but we seldom do so in counterfactual situations. Rather, the author considered antecedents such as changing her footwear or the texture of the wooden walkway, events that were under her control prior to the event.

Similarly, Davis et al. (1995) interviewed bereaved participants who had lost either a spouse or a child under circumstances in which they had no causal role in the death. The majority of participants reported counterfactual thoughts undoing their loss, both soon after the incident and several years later. Most of these thoughts involved routine decisions and actions, especially those for which the participants had direct control, such as a decision not to take a child to the doctor for a minor cold or failure to check on a child in the middle of the night. Participants did not mention mentally altering antecedents, such as suspending the laws of motion (for accidents) or their child's biological need for oxygen (for SIDS deaths). Only actions that were possible, especially those under the direct control of the participants themselves, were considered for mental revision.

This constraint on counterfactual thinking in adverse circumstances is likely attributable to the function of such thinking (see discussion of function in the next section). We counterfactually consider alternatives that can actually be enacted in the future, rather than unrealistic or impossible options, even those that would have changed the outcome of the event.

This limitation on the selection of controllable antecedents also manifests in a general tendency to change case-specific antecedents rather than general ones (Revlin et al., 2001). In other words, we are unlikely to select antecedents related to general principles, such as category membership or laws of biology, chemistry, or physics, for revision (Seelau, Seelau, Wells, & Windschitl, 1995; Wells et al., 1987). This is universally true in the cases of natural laws (such as gravity), but is also observed with respect to category generalizations (Revlin et al., 2001). For example, if a client is thinking counterfactually about how an accident resulting in the death of her husband could have been avoided, she is more likely to consider faulty brakes in the cars involved in the accident (case-specific) than the design of vehicle brakes in general (general category).

Attitudes and Beliefs

Our selection of antecedents for counterfactual consideration is also influenced by factors discussed in chapters 9 and 10, such as information-present and belief-bias effects. In other words, we focus on those factors that are currently present or easily attended to and that conform with our existing beliefs. One consequence of this is that, although imaginary, counterfactuals tend to create alternatives that are very similar to the actual event. As Kahneman (1995) stated, "There are more possible worlds than our minds can construct, and those we do construct tend to be quite similar to the real story in which they are anchored" (p. 381). This occurs for reasons discussed in the previous chapters: Salient factors capture our limited attention and tend to be more accessible in our long-term memory. Thus, availability forms a second robust constraint on antecedent selection (Seelau, Seelau, Wells, & Windschitl, 1995). Specifically, we can only consider revising alternatives that are available to our thinking, and thus the salience of alternatives influences their selection for counterfactual revision (Gleicher et al., 1990).

The salience of alternatives may also depend on pre-existing attitudes (Crawford & McCrea, 2004). For example, a client whose fiancée had just ended their relationship because she found him with another woman said, "If only I hadn't been drinking that night, she never would have caught me." This was more salient and available to him than the more important (in the therapist's opinion) issues of alcohol abuse and a general disrespect for women. Similarly, attitudes about gun control influenced the counterfactual thoughts participants generated in response to a story about a woman who applies to buy a gun because she is being stalked by a coworker, and who was attacked either before or after the waiting period for obtaining the gun had expired (Crawford & McCrea, 2004). Those in favor of gun control generated more counterfactuals about how the woman could have responded differently, whereas those opposed to gun control generated more counterfactuals about changing the law requiring a waiting period. Political ideology can also play into counterfactual thinking. Counterfactual statements about history, such as the collapse of the Berlin wall at various times in the history of the world (e.g., earlier or later than when it actually came down), are judged more or less plausible based on a participant's political ideology (Tetlock, 1998; Tetlock & Visser, 2000). Finally, actions that are perceived to be inappropriate or immoral are more likely to be "undone" than behaviors that do not violate social norms (McCloy & Byrne, 2000; N'gbala & Branscombe, 1995). In sum, we tend to select antecedents and mentally revise them in ways that are consistent with our attitudes.

Case Illustration:

Megan quickly developed elaborate "if only" and "what if" thinking as a way to manage her feelings. Not only did she do the obvious "If only I hadn't stepped on the cat" but developed elaborate counterfactuals going right back to her birth and early childhood (e.g., "If only I hadn't been born," "If school had started two days sooner, I wouldn't have been there," "If I had a spidey sense like Spiderman, I would have sensed her"). She developed these elaborate scenarios but had never let her parents or anyone know that she was doing this and consequently this self-storytelling style developed unchecked for many years. She made a deliberate decision to never marry nor have children as she would be a harmful wife and parent. Her thinking style extended into the future with similar "what if" thinking of a catastrophizing nature (e.g., "If I was mar-

ried, had a child, and if I hurt them or something happened to them I couldn't bear it"). Her brother's accident and the declining health of her elderly mother further triggered this thinking and the emotional consequences. She described her life as filled with regret. When asked, she could not describe experiencing any grief as a result of the original tragedy nor in relation to her subsequent choices. On further exploration, it seemed her main experience of shame and regret as a result of her thinking overwhelmed all other emotions. In addition, regular and harsh criticism at the hands of both parents had already resulted in Megan developing a belief that if something was wrong in life, it was her fault.

OUTCOMES AND FUNCTIONS
OF COUNTERFACTUAL THINKING

Positive Versus Negative Emotions

The selection of particular antecedents for contrast with our current situation influences the emotions that we feel as a result. Many negative emotions can result from the consideration of upward counterfactuals, including disappointment, frustration, guilt, shame, and regret. Shame seems to occur in connection to revising antecedents associated with personal characteristics, such as honesty or intelligence (Niedenthal, Tangney, & Gavanski, 1994), whereas regret is associated with revising antecedents associated with personal actions (Kahneman, 1995). Indeed, regret has been shown to be uniquely associated with counterfactual thinking (Zeelenberg & Beattie, 1997; Zeelenberg et al., 1998). Specifically, regret about a previous decision or action seems to require contrasting thoughts that specify a more favorable outcome associated with a different action.

Understanding the generation of emotions in response to specific types of counterfactual thoughts can greatly benefit therapists in helping clients to counteract their habitual beliefs and habits when dealing with adverse events in their lives. For example, a woman in her mid-thirties sought therapy as a result of her distress surrounding her relationship. As she related her story, it was clear that she had regretted her decision to marry her current husband ever since they became engaged. The regret was connected to a love affair prior to meeting her husband. Not only did she continue to have strong feelings for the first man, but he had appeared the day before her wedding, pleading with her to run away with him. She refused, married her current husband, and began married life. As the years passed, she felt disappointed in her relationship and a great deal of regret about her decision twelve years earlier. To complicate matters, as her disappointment mounted, she contacted her early love and they had developed an "Internet affair." Not only were her counterfactual thoughts connected to regret for an action not taken, but they had resulted in the current problematic action of beginning an illicit relationship. She actually spoke of her current actions as being a way to undo her prior action which she regretted. An understanding of how this client's counterfactual thinking contributed to her inappropriate actions with respect to her current marital problems can greatly benefit therapeutic problem solving in such a situation.

Learning From Experience

Given that counterfactual thinking most commonly results in negative emotions, why do we do it? Several researchers propose that such thinking plays a role in the ways we learn from and manage the events of our lives (e.g., Mandel, 2003; Roese, 1997). For example, counterfactual thinking may distance us from the consequences of an adverse event for a time and allow us to learn from the event so as to prevent its future occurrence (Landman, 1993). Because of its hypothetical nature, counterfactual thought can be functional if it leads to insights about more appropriate behavior that could correct the problem. "Although the past cannot be changed, to the extent that similar circumstances may occur in the future, counterfactual reconstructions of the past pave the way for future improvement" (Roese, 1997, p. 135).

Upward counterfactuals highlight possible improvements in our circumstances and influence our intentions to perform success-facilitating behaviors in the future. For example, when students recalled a recent exam in which they performed poorly, and then generated upward or downward counterfactuals in response to experimental instructions, students who generated upward contrasts gave higher intention ratings about their performance on future exams than those who generated downward or no counterfactuals. Furthermore, they followed through on those intentions later in the study (Roese, 1994; see also Landman, 1995). Similarly, Morris and Moore (1998) observed that student pilots improved in computer-simulated landings after generating upward counterfactuals about their past performance. Counterfactuals also influence perceived personal control, an important factor in one's experience of stress. McMullen and her colleagues (1995) observed that participants induced to generate upward counterfactuals about a past event reported higher confidence and perceived control over the event than those who generated downward counterfactuals.

Causal Attribution

Many authors have suggested that we use counterfactual thinking to assist our identification of cause–effect relationships (e.g., R. M. J. Byrne, 2002; P. L. Harris, German, & Mills, 1996; McGill, 2000; Roese & Olson, 1995; Roese, 1999). If we mentally run a counterfactual experiment changing a particular antecedent and undoing the outcome, we are more likely to attribute causality to that antecedent (Kahneman, 1995; S. J. Sherman & McConnell, 1995). Thus, causal attribution depends, at least to some extent, on the counterfactual alternative that is selected for comparison. McGill (2000) illustrates this point in the context of a product failure. If one makes comparisons to other situations in which the product performed well, one is likely to attribute failure to something about the current situation; in contrast, if the comparison is made to other products that perform well under comparable circumstances, the product itself is more likely to be blamed.

In addition, counterfactual relations often express cause and effect relations (Roese & Olson, 1995). For example, the statement "If the sidewalk had been cleared of snow, the old lady would not have fallen" clearly implies that the icy sidewalk was the cause of the fall; the statement "If I had spent more time with my children, they would not have grown so distant" also clearly attributes causality. Conversely, people are more likely to give counterfactual interpretations to causal conditional situations than other types of conditionals (Thompson & Byrne, 2002).

However, although counterfactual and causal thinking are intimately related, they are not identical processes, and people often generate counterfactuals for purposes other than making causal attributions. Counterfactuals may be purely hypothetical (e.g., If Oswald hadn't shot Kennedy, someone else would have). Moreover, whereas causal thinking is geared toward identifying factors sufficient to bring about an event (see chapter 10), counterfactual thinking is often motivated by the need to identify factors that can prevent an event (Mandel & Lehman, 1996; Mandel, 2003; N'gbala & Branscombe, 1995). In some cases, these factors are linked in a straightforward way. For example, exposure to sunlight causes sunburns; preventing such exposure in the form of sunscreen can prevent them. In other cases, the relationship is less straightforward, such as when the actions that might have prevented an outcome are not directly linked to the cause (e.g., wishing school had started earlier to prevent Megan from stepping on the kitten).

This divergence between causality and prevention has to do with the fact that some antecedents are perceived as more mutable than others. For example, events that are under the control of the individual are more likely to be "undone" than uncontrollable events, even if those events are not considered to be causes of the outcome. Branscombe and her colleagues (Branscombe, Wohl, Owen, Allison, & N'gbala, 2003) observed such a divergence in rape victims. Women who had experienced sexual assault clearly placed the blame for the assault on their attacker; nonetheless, when asked to generate counterfactual thoughts about the episode, they focused on their own behavior (e.g., I should have resisted more strongly, I should not have drunk so much that night, etc.).

Prevention

Thus, although causal attribution results from counterfactual thinking under some circumstances, it may not be a primary function of such thinking. In testing this use of counterfactuals, Mandel (2003) observed a dissociation between selected counterfactual antecedents and causal attributions. Specifically, participants read a story about a man who was attacked by two different assassins, one of whom administered a lethal dose of slow-acting poison and the other who shot the man. When participants were asked to identify the cause of the death of the protagonist and list their counterfactual thoughts about the death, they reported different elements of the story. Causal attribution was related to the most immediate cause of death (i.e., the gunshot), whereas counterfactuals were related to a factor that could have prevented the entire situation (e.g., avoiding the behavior that drew the attention of both assassins). Thus, Mandel concluded that counterfactual reasoning is used primarily to enable us to learn how to prevent untoward outcomes (or plan for positive outcomes), rather than to support our causal judgment. Similarly, naturalistic studies of counterfactual thinking, such as Davis and colleagues' studies of bereaved parents (Davis et al., 1995) and spinal cord injury patients (Davis, Lehman, Silver, Wortman, & Ellard, 1996), found that victims' perceptions of the cause of their trauma differed from the content of their counterfactual thoughts. Specifically, although victims did not think that they had caused the accident or death, they did engage in counterfactual thinking about things they could have done to prevent the event.

Despite the negative affect associated with such thinking (S. J. Sherman & McConnell, 1995), such thoughts can serve to strengthen learning that might prevent future traumas, or at least strengthen the victims' sense of control and efficacy in the world. Even when such learning cannot prevent the trauma that gave rise to the counterfactual thinking, such as an accident that caused a spinal cord injury, it can usefully serve the goal of prevention, as is evident when such victims respond to their tragedy by speaking publicly about their experience to others who are potentially at risk. Many cases of personal tragedy spurring a person to become socially active as an educator attempting to persuade others to avoid injury are evident in most communities and in the media, such as bereaved mothers of children killed or injured in traffic accidents participating in Mothers Against Drunk Driving, or the recent case of a woman who developed lung cancer as a result of her extensive exposure to secondhand smoke in restaurants and who appeared in many antismoking ads in Canada.

To return to the example of the author's broken ankle, although footwear did not cause the ankle-breaking fall, shoes with better traction might have prevented it, highlighting the tendency for counterfactual thoughts to focus on prevention rather than causality. Learning based on such thoughts may occur without our awareness, simply as a consequence of engaging in counterfactual thinking. For example, although she didn't explicitly notice it until writing this, the author who broke her ankle is much more attentive to her footwear since that accident, especially on rainy or icy days.

However, such thinking can also occur consciously and is often the source of productive goal setting and planning in therapy. Thus, despite the increased negative affect that results from upward counterfactual thinking in response to a negative event, discussing such thoughts can be a productive technique in therapy, assisting the client to develop functional intentions that may decrease the likelihood of such adverse events in the future and giving them a stronger sense of self-efficacy and control. Furthermore, such counterfactual thinking in response to adverse events can increase a person's hope for the future, enabling them to move on from this particular difficult event. For example, a client was considering her relationship options after ending her second relationship (both with alcoholics). Although exploring and focusing on her many counterfactual thoughts was quite painful to her, it did lead to a complete list of warning signs she had observed but had not acted on (e.g., If only I had acted when I noticed him hiding the liquor, If only I had read the book on codependency my mom gave me, etc.). Consciously armed with this information, she felt more equipped to consider another relationship rather than giving up on future intimacy. Some therapists can be too quick to intervene and block counterfactual thinking, as they are afraid it is the path to self-blame. Although this is possible and needs to be guarded against, counterfactual thinking can be useful.

DYSFUNCTIONS OF COUNTERFACTUAL REASONING

Despite the benefits associated with counterfactual thinking, however, it can lead to psychological dysfunctions, particularly chronic negative affect and bias in judgment. One of the consequences of counterfactual thinking is negative affect, especially when we consider how an adverse event might have been avoided (upward counterfactual comparison). Such negative emotion occurs because we contrast our current situation (negative) with what it might have been in our counterfactual scenario (positive). This intensifies feelings of regret, shame, grief, disappointment, or frustration.

Victimization and Well-Being

Branscombe et al. (2003), for example, observed that measures of counterfactual thinking were negatively associated with self-blame, and in turn, with a number of measures of psychological well-being. That is, women who engaged in more counterfactual thinking after a sexual assault were more likely to blame themselves for how events turned out; these women scored high on measures of depression and low on measures of self-esteem and feelings of control. Branscombe et al. suggest helping victims with downward counterfactuals (e.g., how the victim's actions prevented worse outcomes), but note that there is little available evidence to show how best to address this issue.

Perseveration

Some individuals, in addition, seem to have difficulty moving on from counterfactual reasoning, becoming stuck in rumination and the negative emotions associated with contrast comparison (see chapters 13 & 14). For these individuals, therapists can provide a valuable service by helping them to suppress their unproductive counterfactual thoughts. For example, Goulding and Goulding (1979) challenged grieving clients who persistently reviewed the causes of a loved one's death, dwelling on how the death could have been prevented. Their approach was to show them that the cause of death doesn't matter (because we can't change the past) and to redirect clients' attention to their own lives and how they would carry on in the absence of this person.

So, how do people normally put counterfactuals behind them (Davis & Lehman, 1995)? The tendency to think counterfactually is a relatively stable trait, but one that is not related to other personality characteristics (Kasimatis & Wells, 1995). Taking advantage of the benefits of counterfactual thinking (i.e., preventing future misfortune) undoubtedly plays some role in moving on from counterfactual thinking; there also may be individual differences in such functional use of counterfactuals (Davis et al., 1995; Landman, 1995). It is also likely that one's social network plays a role, in that others can contribute to the frequency and direction of counterfactual thinking. For example, other people might suggest that another is to blame in a litigation situation, or offer downward counterfactuals as a means to console someone. Cultural norms regarding appropriate grief rituals and durations provide another example of such social influence on the tendency to engage in or move on from counterfactual thinking.

Different schools of therapy also likely differ in their willingness to assist clients with counterfactual thinking. Although all models, when skillfully applied, enable exploration of counterfactual thinking to gain benefits and encourage the client to avoid potential rumination and obsessive thinking, therapists need to avoid overzealous application of their principles in this case. For example, a cognitive behavioral therapist may too quickly label a counterfactual an erroneous belief and dispute it. A psychodynamic therapist may attribute motivation to a naturally occurring thinking process. A solution-focused therapist may move too quickly away from the upward comparisons, whereas a constructivist may allow for too much rumination as they follow clients in their construction of their reality, and so on. In summary, dealing with counterfactual thinking requires a combination of allowing for exploration and its benefits while knowing when and how to assist clients in moving beyond this type of thinking.

Errors in Judgment and Attributions

People tend to focus on certain events when "undoing" reality. Unfortunately, this focus may result in counterproductive attributions. For example, accidents are not more likely to occur on unusual than usual routes, although the former are more likely to be "undone" than the latter in counterfactual thoughts (Mandel & Lehman, 1996). This belief that an outcome may have been avoided had the usual route been followed may produce false attributions of cause and preventability. Antecedents that are the subject of counterfactual thought receive more attention than other antecedents, potentially resulting in skewed memory for the adverse event and its consequences. These problems are similar to the biases associated with other types of decision making and reasoning (discussed in depth in chapters 9 & 10) in that perceptions and inferences will be influenced by the presence of some factors and the absence of others. For example, a truck driver referred to therapy after an accident was terrified to drive again and was experiencing symptoms of acute stress. He experienced intrusive images and memories of the accident in which he helplessly observed the accident take place; due to the weight and size of his vehicle, he could not take evasive action. Interestingly, one of his counterfactual thoughts was "If only I had been driving a vehicle that was more maneuverable, this wouldn't have happened." Consistent with this thought, graduated exposure treatment beginning with driving his car worked very well in having him return to driving in all sorts of situations until the treatment required him to drive a semi-trailer truck. At this point, this specific counterfactual had to be explored and dealt with before treatment could proceed.

Counterfactual thinking can also cause errors in attribution by causing people to "undo" good decisions (Roese, 1999). That is, the original decision may have been appropriate, despite the negative outcome (i.e., bad outcomes can result from good decisions). In the driving example, the client had actually made the right decision by not overcorrecting his vehicle and as a result, no lives were lost. However, the persistent counterfactual that he should have done something different to avoid the accident made his usual calm and precise decision making in driving situations more erratic. This difficulty is more likely to occur if our counterfactual presents a strong contrast to our actual situation, thus increasing our affective response to our circumstances.

Superstitious Thinking

D. T. Miller and Taylor (1995, 2002) argue that counterfactual thinking may play a role in the development of superstitions. They point out that "if only" thinking is more likely to be triggered by negative outcomes than positive outcomes, and that this increased availability in memory may make the events seem objectively more probable (see chapters 9 & 10 for a discussion). For example, it is a widely held belief that switching lines in a busy store results in a net loss, because the old line speeds up and the new one slows down. Miller and Taylor argue that superstitious beliefs such as these occur because negative events preceded by an act of commission (switching lines) are more likely to give rise to counterfactual thoughts than negative outcomes preceded by an act of omission (staying put). The regret and recrimination that accompany the counterfactual thoughts make them highly available in memory, and this, in turn, leads people to overestimate their probability. When coupled with anticipatory regret that accompanies contemplation of an action that might initiate a negative outcome, the net result is a superstitious avoidance of certain behaviors.

Overconfidence

Finally, because counterfactual thinking increases our sense of control and self-efficacy, it can result in overconfidence (Kahneman, 1995; Roese & Olson, 1996; Roese, 1999), which, in turn, can lead to suboptimal decisions (see chapters 5, 10, & 12). To counteract these potential biases, Roese suggests that we generate several counterfactuals for any given situation, so that a single counterfactual thought does not unduly contrast with our current situation (Hirt & Markman, 1995). This is similar to the advice given in chapters 9 and 10 to consider several alternatives in reasoning and decision-making situations.

In therapy, we could also potentially minimize negative effects that result from contrasting a counterfactual with our current situation by focusing attention on the counterfactual itself (McMullen, 1997), reducing the tendency to directly compare such thought scenarios with our actual experience. Again, in reference to the truck accident, the client was encouraged to consider several additional counterfactual scenarios (e.g., What if the driver of the car had given some indication that he was going to swerve into the path of the truck?). In addition, by taking him through a counterfactual scenario in which he drove a vehicle with more responsiveness and control, he realized he was more, rather than less likely to be injured in the alternative reality. This realization, along with the knowledge that the other driver was recovering, seemed to allow the truck driver to move on from counterfactual thinking.

FUTURE COUNTERFACTUALS:
PLANNING AND PROBLEM SOLVING

Most of the previous discussion in this chapter relates to counterfactual thinking about past events because almost all counterfactual research has examined this situation. However, people also use counterfactual thinking extensively when thinking about and planning for the future. For instance, goal setting is essentially an example of an upward conditional, in which individuals consider how their life would be better with a particular accomplishment and plan ways to attain that. If several possible paths to the goal (or *operators*, see chapter 2) are considered, choosing among the alternatives also involves counterfactual thought. Although there has been less research conducted with future counterfactuals, in this section, we extrapolate from what we know about counterfactuals in the therapeutic context.

Encouraging counterfactual thinking (What would happen if you talked to him? Have you kept records about when this happens?) is itself a widely used technique in most therapies. Similarly, encouraging change in a client's counterfactuals is also widely used. For example, with a client who needs to address the potential dangers in an abusive relationship, a therapist will encourage downward counterfactuals ("You could get seriously hurt") to oppose the client's upward counterfactuals ("He'll change").

Counterfactual thinking is an essential element in the beginning of therapy, given that most begin with an explicit discussion of the potential benefits and risk of treatment. Discussion of benefits entails upward counterfactuals, encouraging clients to imagine how their lives would improve as a result of therapy. Considering risks, conversely, requires clients to consider untoward consequences that could occur, such as making a problem worse. Therapists must sensitively balance such discussions, so that clients can envision the value of therapeutic treatment when that is indicated, but be aware of potential difficulties that could arise, allowing clients to make their own decisions about the appropriate action for them (following the value of "informed consent" that is part of professional codes of ethics). Too much emphasis in either direction could result in a client failing to consider treatment that could improve her life (in the case of excessive downward comparison), or increased negative affect about her current situation (in the case of excessive upward comparison).

This balancing can potentially be improved by careful attention to the effects of counterfactual thinking. For example, it is common in relationship therapy for one member of a couple to enter therapy with a belief that talking about problems make them worse, whereas the other has the belief that talking problems through is helpful. One member will attend reluctantly, expecting negative results, whereas the other is hopeful and enthusiastic. Addressing these beliefs in a future-oriented counterfactual manner is often helpful in assisting reluctant attenders of psychotherapy to become more committed to the process. A therapist might ask, "So, what could happen here that would lead you to believe that talking about problems could be a positive experience?" and then incorporate the client's answers into the therapeutic goal.

It is important to note, however, that there are limits to how much we can extrapolate from past to future counterfactuals. For instance, future conditionals are known to differ from counterfactuals in at least one important respect (R. M. J. Byrne & Egan, 2004). Recall that counterfactuals are understood on two levels: They imply both a factual and a counterfactual reality (R. M. J. Byrne, 2002; Thompson & Byrne, 2002). For example, the counterfactual statement "If you had left him sooner, you would not have ended up in hospital" clearly suggests a factual reality in which the person did not leave and ended up in hospital. Future counterfactuals, in contrast, do not imply a factual reality (R. M. J. Byrne & Egan, 2004); thus, they more closely resemble ordinary conditionals and deal with hypothetical, rather than factual, possibilities (Thompson & Byrne, 2002). The ability to engage in this type of "mental experiment" may be one of the cornerstone abilities of our cognitive apparatus (Evans & Over, 2004).

CONCLUSION: USE OF COUNTERFACTUAL THINKING IN THERAPY

The evidence suggests that counterfactual thinking occurs spontaneously, especially in the types of situations that bring people to therapy, such as the experience of negative emotions or traumatic events. Thus, it behooves therapists to make the most of this natural phenomenon for the benefit of our clients. Counterfactual thinking is one method of problem solving and thus can support clients' exploration of their circumstances and reactions to their experiences. For example, the specific antecedents that a client chooses to "undo" in response to a misfortune can be indicative of his beliefs about his own limitations or his attitude to significant others. If such beliefs and attitudes are an aspect of the client's difficulties, changing them could then be targeted as a goal of therapy. The consideration of prefactuals or future possibilities can also be a valuable therapeutic practice, especially if therapist and client are alert to client beliefs or attitudes that unnecessarily limit her choices. There are many examples of the use of counterfactuals in a variety of therapies. The "miracle question" and emphasis on goal setting of solution-focused and brief therapies (e.g., Hoyt, 2003) are examples of future-oriented, prefactual thinking. Cognitive therapists help clients to dispute maladaptive "what ifs" and encourage the use of hypotheticals to introduce potential solutions to client problems (e.g., Newman, 2002). Narrative and other constructivist therapies regularly assist clients to develop future-based stories and narratives to promote more positive outcomes (e.g., M. White & Epston, 1990).

Counterfactual thoughts can also be problematic, especially if clients become mired in rumination and negative affect. For these individuals, therapists can help short-circuit such thoughts. Understanding the functions and characteristics of counterfactual thinking can thus enable therapists to sensitively assess whether a specific case of counterfactual thinking is likely to benefit or harm a client, thereby providing a firm foundation for intervention.

Case Illustration:

Megan had already received extensive therapy with both a cognitive behavioral and a solution-focused therapist. After consultation with her previous therapists and learning that Megan's previous therapy had been thorough, her current therapist decided to focus on the counterfactual thinking itself. He embarked on a "more of the same" strategy, somewhat in the tradition of prescribing the symptom techniques of some strategic and paradoxical schools of therapy. This additional thinking was quite structured and carried out in the presence of the therapist rather than given as homework. The scope of the "what ifs" was broadened to include factors outside Megan's perceived control and hypotheses less consistent with her attitudes and beliefs. For example, she was encouraged to develop stories about a scenario where the cat had not been born or the veterinarian could heal anything. Additionally, she developed stories about the same scenario except she was living with different parents. As therapy proceeded in this manner, Megan experienced strong bouts of anger and then sadness. Some of the anger was directed at the therapist (e.g., "Why are you making me make up things?"), but most related to the frustration of her experience of impotence at the life she had led. The therapist encouraged her to experience the feelings and introduced self-regulation techniques of self-soothing and self-comforting. As Megan began to experience grief and sadness, she was able to articulate that her sense of regret and personal responsibility likely protected (distanced) her from the intense feelings of loss at the time and from critical family reactions (e.g., her mom was away and said on her return, "Can't you just manage when I'm away?" and her father was angry, "See what you've done, you have to watch what you do"). She and the therapist then reframed her problems as a "complicated and delayed grief reaction" and embarked on relatively long-term treatment to assist her in coming to terms with the profound effects of one moment in time and defining a new structure for the future.

KEY POINTS

- Counterfactual thinking is thinking about events contrary to how they happened.

- Counterfactual thinking about the past is often used to "undo" an adverse outcome, by imagining how events that preceded it might have happened differently.

- We can imagine either better consequences (upward counterfactuals) or worse consequences (downward counterfactuals). The former generally evokes negative feelings such as regret or shame, whereas the latter evokes positive feelings such as relief or gratitude.

- Counterfactual thinking is often evoked by adverse events that are unexpected, especially when a more positive outcome seems to have been very close to happening instead.

- Elements that are chosen for counterfactual alteration are generally mutable, under our control, and consistent with our attitudes and beliefs.

- Counterfactual thinking functions to help us prevent adverse events from reoccurring (i.e., learning from our mistakes) and to plan for the future.

- Too much attention to counterfactual thoughts can result in prolonged or intensified negative affect and biased judgment, both of which interfere with recovery following an adverse event.

Metacognition: What You Know About How You Think

In a nutshell, metacognition refers to our knowledge and beliefs about our mental processes or, to put it more colloquially, thinking about thinking. Such thinking can be either specific, such as our awareness of current efforts to retrieve a memory, or general, such as beliefs about our own cognitive skills and abilities (e.g., "I have a good memory") or our theory about how human cognition operates (e.g., "Memory is an accurate record of previous experiences"). The reason such thinking is called "meta" is because its focus is thought itself, whereas the majority of our thinking focuses on thoughts about the physical and social world. For example, a client's thoughts about her family interactions are about the social world, whereas her awareness that she has a tendency to mistakenly interpret her family's actions and comments as insults is metacognition. A strategy common to many psycho-therapists is to increase our clients' metacognition with respect to their issues (i.e., to increase their psychological awareness).

Understanding metacognition can benefit therapists in a number of ways. First, a primary goal of therapy is often to increase a client's metacognitive awareness. For clients, metacognitive awareness can also lead to better self-management, improving the benefit of therapy they receive. Second, metacognitive knowledge can allow therapists to make the most efficient use of our and our clients' mental abilities, including avoiding failures caused by poor understanding of how our minds work, better understanding the cognitive mechanisms underlying poor mental health, and informing and directing decisions about interventions.

Simons (1996) discriminated among three components of metacognition: knowledge, skills, and beliefs. Metacognitive knowledge is largely the subject of this book, that is, understanding how cognitive processes, such as those involved in memory or problem solving, operate. This component also includes personal knowledge, such as knowledge about the efficiency of our own memory. Many clients identify these components through expressions such as "My memory is good, but short," "I'm having a senior moment," "My memory is like a sieve," and many others. Unfortunately, many such statements are both inaccurate and deprecating and often need to be addressed as a part of therapy. Metacognitive skills include predicting, planning, monitoring, and evaluating our own performance relative to a particular task. Metacognitive beliefs include general ideas we have about cognitive processes or our personal ability, such as beliefs about the effect of aging on memory and attention. Changes in any of these components can influence behavior and cognitive performance.

Research in several areas indicates that such thoughts and beliefs influence our cognitive behavior, especially the effort we put into a particular problem. In the area of aging cognition, for example, researchers have observed that elderly participants who believe that cognitive ability necessarily declines with age show poorer memory performance than elders who have no such beliefs (Dweck, 1999; Hertzog, 2002; Hertzog & Dixon, 1994). One clear way that such beliefs likely influence performance is by determining how much effort we apply to learning and retrieving information (Strack & Bless, 1994). If we believe that no amount of studying will enable us to remember information, we are much less likely to expend effort on studying than if we believe that our learning is related to our effort (e.g., self-efficacy beliefs; Bandura, 1997). Another example where belief affects effort can occur in psychotherapy with adolescents or children diagnosed with attention deficit disorder (ADD) or attention deficit hyperactivity disorder (ADHD). If they are not properly educated and supported, they can end up with beliefs such as "I can't concentrate," "No use trying to work unless there are no distractions," "I can only concentrate when I take my medication," and so on. These beliefs then seriously affect the level of effort many of these young people demonstrate in therapy and in their lives. One young client stated after ten minutes of a session, "My ADD is kicking in. . . . I can't think. . . . We might as well stop the meeting."

Similarly, our personal and intuitive theories about thinking influence how we interpret our thoughts and memories, so inaccurate theories result in erroneous conclusions. For example, when we are unable to retrieve information about an event, we use our beliefs about the memorability of such an event to judge whether our memory failure is diagnostic of our previous experience (Ghetti, 2003). If we think that we would surely remember an event if it has occurred, such as bedwetting until middle childhood, we take failure to retrieve any memories as evidence that we've had no such experience (i.e., that we were not bedwetters). However, if we think that forgetting such an event is possible, then we interpret the absence of memories otherwise, such as one of our clients who was erroneously convinced by his older brother that he had wet the bed until middle childhood, but that he had forgotten since it always occurred when he was asleep. Throughout this book, we have attempted to enrich the general cognitive theories held by psychotherapists in order to improve the conclusions they draw from their observations of their clients. However, the other two aspects of metacognition—awareness of current thinking and beliefs about our metacognitive skills and abilities—are perhaps more directly important to therapists because both are targets of therapeutic intervention.

One of the central strategies of psychotherapy is to alter clients' metacognitive beliefs and awareness in order to increase the range or functionality of activities they will consider to solve their problems. Cognitive behavioral therapists explicitly recognize the importance of dysfunctional beliefs and either challenge the content of these beliefs directly (e.g., A. Ellis, 2002) or assist clients to shift the metacognitive beliefs underlying them (e.g., A. Wells, 2000). Therapists of different theoretical orientations also engage in this strategy. Often metacognition is addressed in other therapies as an aspect of self-concept or self-awareness of which our thinking is a part. Psychodynamic therapists educate self-awareness through insight and interpretations, paradoxical therapists provide clients with real and imagined experiences that are contradictory to their problematic beliefs, postmodern therapists examine and shift their clients' central constructs and their meanings, and family therapists encourage clients to become aware of their contributions to a family dynamic. Cognitive research in the area of metacognition can contribute to the success of these interventions in two ways: (a) by increasing our understanding of how cognitive processes operate to create both valid and invalid conclusions and beliefs, and (b) by examining the conditions under which metacognitive instruction leads to improved performance and conditions under which it does not. The current chapter reviews research relevant to both of these areas.

With regard to understanding cognitive processes, research provides considerable support for therapists' intuition that clients' self-reflective beliefs are important to their functioning and well-being. Both clinical and educational research clearly demonstrate that people's metacognitive beliefs influence their mood and their behavior. Clinically, self-reports of metacognitive beliefs discriminate between groups with different psychological issues: Obsessive-compulsive patients show a greater tendency to engage in metacognition by monitoring themselves and their thoughts (Janeck, Calamari, Riemann, & Heffelfinger, 2002), schizophrenic patients think that their thoughts should be consistent with each other more than other people do (Lobban, Haddock, Kinderman, & Wells, 2002), and narcissistic patients may have deficits in their ability to self-reflect and take the perspective of others (Dimaggio et al., 2002). Furthermore, studies indicate that a particular pattern of beliefs about the potential benefits of thinking about one's problems and the controllability of ruminative thought characterize patients with mood disorders and related problems (depression, anxiety, and anger management; Papagiorgiou & Wells, 2003; Simpson & Papagiorgiou, 2003). These beliefs lead to a tendency to ruminate or dwell on mood-related issues, increasing the severity of the negative mood and preventing engagement in other behaviors more useful to changing the person's mood. Consistent with this, recovery from depression is associated with increased metacognitive control over such unproductive thoughts (Sheppard & Teasdale, 2004).

More generally, our beliefs about our ability in a particular area influence our metacognitive experience while we engage in activities associated with that area (e.g., feelings of difficulty and confidence) and self-regulation of our efforts in that area. This has been shown in relation to several academic skills such as mathematics (Desoete, Roeyers, & De Clerq, 2003; Efklides & Tsiora, 2002), reading comprehension (Glenberg, Sanocki, Epstein, & Morris, 1987; McNamara & O'Reilly, 2003), and academic learning (T. O. Nelson & Dunlosky, 1991; Thiede, Anderson, & Therriault, 2003). Thus, addressing clients' self-concepts and metacognitive thoughts is an important focus for potential change work.

Case Illustration:

Wayne was referred for therapy by his mother because of his distress at the end of a three-year relationship. He was twenty-five and attending university. He was a pleasant and cooperative young man who believed that although he was distressed about the breakup, it was "really for the best." He described a general sense of dissatisfaction and malaise with his life, great difficulty with making decisions ("I should have ended it much sooner, so I was also relieved when she did"), and a tendency to question and doubt himself. It was clear from the beginning that his distress at the breakup was not his major concern. Rather it had been his recognition of a repeating pattern in the ending that he wished to address. He described the pattern as follows: "I'm lost, I can't figure out what I want or need. Anytime I take a step, I question everything and can't enjoy anything; my head is so full I don't experience anything except worry and fear. I want to get out of my head and experience things." He gave many examples of feeling unable to make a decision, spending virtually all of his time considering every possible permutation and combination of all possible options. He was particularly distressed about his seeming lack of ability to make even very small decisions (e.g., "I want to go away for a few days and can't even get myself to do that," "I can't even accept an invitation for Friday on Wednesday just in case something else comes up"). He described his mind as frequently "gridlocked" and "frozen."

Given that his goal was "to get out of my head and experience life," the therapist began with an experiential approach to broaden Wayne's experiences, especially in his awareness of himself physically and emotionally. In addition to therapy sessions, Wayne agreed to begin taking tai chi lessons. While these interventions interested Wayne and did help him experience more of life, he still experienced difficulty in decision making and simply incorporated his new experiences into his tendency to "overthink." He became preoccupied with the new physical sensations, worrying that these sensations he was noticing might be indicative of an impending illness, and he was constantly internally visualizing and then evaluating his progress in his class. It quickly became apparent that the dysfunctional thinking patterns would have to be addressed directly.

Wayne was very naïve about his cognitive processes. The sense of ease with which he slipped into worrying, combined with his early learning to think everything through, led him to believe that his way of thinking was natural, normal, and effective. He felt like a victim of his thinking and was unaware that he could have any influence over what or how he thought.

At this point, the therapist gathered more history especially in relation to attitudes and behavior related to thinking in his home. His mother and father had divorced when he was five, and their caring but anxious mother raised him and his two younger sisters. His mother encouraged the children to be cautious and to think about everything thoroughly. During times spent with his father, he was often teased about being raised in a "girly" household and that he was becoming effeminate and a "sissy." He described developing a rule about thinking in early adolescence just after learning about fractions and percentages in mathematics classes (which was interesting in light of his feeling that he had no control over thinking). He called it the "1% rule." If there was as little as a 1% chance that something could happen, then he needed to think about it and be prepared for its eventuality. The theme underlying this rule, which was encouraged by his mother, was that worrying was helpful. As this rule was discussed in therapy, it became apparent that the rule had been developed and generalized into "If it can be conceived in the human imagination, it should be worried about." Whenever Wayne read about a physical or psychological issue he worried that he might have that, and when he was exposed to ideas of the spiritual world such as concepts of evil or of possession, he would worry for days that he would be possessed or succumb to evil and hurt someone.

The therapist began by developing a plan for Wayne to monitor the content of his thoughts in relation to one area of concern (career). He identified several constraints to reaching his goal state in the content of his beliefs (e.g., "Once I decide I'm committed for life, I'll miss out on my true calling if my attention is elsewhere," "Others will think I'm frivolous if I change my mind"). While identifying and countering these self-statements helped him feel better in the moment, there was no progress in making decisions or in the amount of worrying. Underlying the content of his thinking was a belief that constant thinking and worrying was the way to make good decisions ("I know if I think about it long enough I'll figure it out"). Consequently, he deliberately and constantly attended to thoughts of career. Even after he learned to interrupt and counter the dysfunctional beliefs, he simply incorporated the new techniques into further material for thinking about career ("It's okay to change, so now I have to figure out several careers rather than one"). Addressing his metacognition was the key to addressing his issues.

The therapist assisted Wayne to develop a metaphor to describe the thinking aspect of his personality and had him dialogue (in gestalt two-chair fashion) with the thinking part. Although Wayne did not seem to have confidence in the content of his worries, he certainly was confident in the rule that worrying was helpful ("That's just the way you solve problems") and the corollary that if he was not yet confident then thinking more would resolve his uncertainty (in spite of a decade of unsuccessful attempts). Again, the ease with which he could engage in worrying had given him confidence that this was the way in which problems were to be addressed. He easily recognized and acknowledged that these were rules he lived by but had been unaware of, and he was rather shocked to have them pointed out. The therapist had Wayne dispute the rule rather than the multiple examples by challenging the thinking part to produce evidence of efficacy (e.g., see A. Wells, 2000). In addition, the therapist set a specific homework task for Wayne to monitor the content of his thoughts for indications that the metacognitive rule was in action and then dispute the rule in the same way he had in therapy sessions.

During these gestalt dialogues, Wayne also began to experience and express a great deal of anger, in particular with the realization that as a result of his father's teasing, he had tried to think his way into understanding maleness to please his father. As he grew up in a largely female environment, and his father embarrassed him rather than providing him with a male role model, he had no one to teach or mentor him about maleness and manhood. This had become another content area for him to apply his metacognitive rules.

As Wayne became more adept at recognizing his belief that worrying was helpful and challenging it both in session and with intersession assignments, the therapist added the additional component that after successfully challenging himself, he was to take some direct action rather than thinking more. For example, when he met a young woman who was interested in him, he began with observing thought content ("What does she think of me? What if she says no? What if she says yes and then I meet someone else?"). He then moved to challenging "the part that worries" as he had been taught in sessions (an internal dialogue in which he assertively pointed out to the worrying self that there has only been distress and no benefit to worry). After this, he was to take some action in relation to his original interest in the young woman (e.g., ask her for coffee after class). Wayne found this shift very useful and relieving in multiple situations but also found it very effortful. He required a lot of support and coaching in therapy sessions. Adding the action component seemed to give him feedback that he could use to support his change.

The successful altering of his metacognitive beliefs (from "Worrying is helpful" to "Thinking briefly and then acting gives me the information I need to make decisions") was the key to change for Wayne. He also had to address other issues including his relationships with both parents and his sense of what it meant to be male. These issues were much easier to address once he had reached his goal ("I want to get out of my head and experience life").

Evidence is also beginning to mount about the dissociation between metacognitive beliefs and objective experience. Not only are our judgments about the truth of event memories relatively easily tricked (see next paragraphs and chapter 5), but our overall belief about our memory competence is often not accurate (e.g., Dunning, Johnson, Ehrlinger, & Kruger, 2003).

When comparing subjective reports and objective memory performance across client groups, several studies have shown that patients are significantly less confident in their abilities, although their objective performance is equal to that of control groups. For example, patients with obsessive-compulsive disorder (OCD) report less confidence in their memory ability than do controls (MacDonald, Antony, MacLeod, & Richter, 1997), including the ability to discriminate between their thoughts and actions (e.g., "Did I lock the door, or only think of doing so?"), leading to the characteristic OCD checking behavior. However, in an objective test of reality monitoring, the performance of participants with OCD is equal to that of nonpatient controls (Hermans, Martens, De Cort, Pieters, & Eelen, 2002). Similarly, dissociative participants show greater arousal and dissociation during the viewing of an aversive film and subjectively report that their memory for the experience is more fragmentary than that of control participants, but actually demonstrate performance in a test of sequential memory for the film that is equal to that of nondissociative control groups (Kindt & van den Hout, 2003). Elderly participants also show dissociation between their self-reported memory ability and their objective performance, reporting greater difficulty than younger participants, but equal performance in an objective memory test (Dweck, 1999; Hertzog, 2002; Larrabee, West, & Crook, 1991; Ponds, Boxtel, & Jolles, 2000). These findings indicate our metacognitive impressions about our memory behavior may not reflect actual performance; this validates therapists' efforts to have clients change their negative beliefs about their abilities. (It is not known whether such beliefs cause negative mood or vice versa, as most data are correlational. However, there is evidence that changing such negative beliefs leads to mood change [e.g., Sheppard & Teasdale, 2004], perhaps through the greater awareness of successful performance that such changes afford.)

In situations in which participants can self-regulate their effort at completing tasks, such beliefs do influence the effort and persistence participants show (Dweck, 1999; Hertzog, 2002; Hertzog & Dixon, 1994; Strack & Bless, 1994), undoubtedly influencing their experience of success in a given domain. For example, students who believe that they are skilled at mathematical problem solving expend greater effort in solving a problem than those who believe they are poor at math (Dermitzaki & Efklides, 2003; Efklides & Tsiora, 2002), and when we believe that we have the answer to a question in our memory (feeling-of-knowing), we persist in retrieval efforts longer than when we have a sense that we don't know the information (e.g., Miner & Reder, 1994). Thus, even though our beliefs about our cognitive abilities aren't always well-founded, we use such beliefs to govern our cognitive behavior, often giving ourselves "confirming" evidence about our beliefs.

In addition to the evidence that there are between-group differences in metacognitive beliefs that are subject to error, there is also evidence that we all make erroneous metacognitive judgments of certain types. For example, we apparently use our feelings of how easy it is to bring a topic to mind or the familiarity of the question itself to assess our knowledge or our confidence in the accuracy of our memories. In many cases, these heuristics or rules of thumb lead to a fairly accurate assessment of our memory performance, but there are also situations in which our judgments can be tricked using these factors, leading to false conclusions about our memory. Research on memory confidence indicates that although confidence and other metacognitive ratings are generally calibrated with actual memory performance (Arbuckle & Cuddy, 1996; Hart, 1965; Underwood, 1966), the relationship is not perfect (Blake, 1973; Metcalfe & Shimamura, 1994; T. O. Nelson & Dunlosky, 1991; B. K. Payne et al., 2004; Son & Schwartz, 2002).

One common metacognitive error is overconfidence in our memories (see chapter 5). Both children and adults show overconfidence in their judgments of event recall relative to their actual recall performance (Roebers, 2002), with younger children showing the greatest discrepancy between their metacognition and their performance. This is especially true when misleading information is given between the event and its recall. Misleading suggestions are particularly detrimental to children's metacognitive judgments about their recollection (Roebers, 2002). Furthermore, we sometimes use beliefs (such as what types of events are memorable) to guide our judgments (Ghetti, 2003). Recent work in the area of false memory indicates that therapy and other medical treatments can be a potent source of influence on such beliefs, which in turn influence judgments of memory accuracy (Mazzoni & Kirsch, 2002; see chapter 5). The accuracy of our own and clients' intuitive theories of memory are thus of central importance to psychotherapy. For example, as a couple argued about the occurrence of an event in a therapy session, the wife stated she had seen her husband kissing a woman at an office party and the husband vehemently denied the event. A central part of the argument was the wife's belief that she had a more accurate memory than her husband ("You know I remember details much better than you, and besides, you were drinking"). Her confidence had her husband doubting his own memory, leading to a minor crisis in therapy as each person acknowledged that if their memory were inaccurate, it would be equivalent to "being crazy." These arguments at the level of defining reality are common in couple and family therapy sessions and are difficult issues to address. Most therapists attempt to challenge their clients' beliefs without injuring their self-confidence or trust in the therapeutic relationship, and also to avoid triangulating. Knowledge of metacognition will help to address these issues without anyone "being crazy."

Another common metacognitive error is overconfidence in our understanding of complex phenomena (C. M. Mills & Keil, 2004; Rosenblit & Keil, 2002). When asked to rate how completely we understand how a mechanism (such as a motor) or theoretical system (such as planetary rotation) works, we tend to be overconfident relative to the quality of our actual explanations (as judged by others). If we are asked to provide an explanation prior to rating our understanding, our ratings are much more accurate, indicating that we are sensitive to the depth of our knowledge, but only in response to direct feedback. In contrast, ratings of our procedural knowledge, such as how to operate a motor, are very accurate whether we judge such knowledge before or after providing a description. For example, we are likely to be less accurate in judging how strategies such as organization work to improve our memory than we are in judging how well we can describe how to use such an organizational strategy. One implication of this finding is that we will tend to show overconfidence in our intuitive cognitive theories, perhaps leading to some of the erroneous judgments of memory described in chapter 5. Furthermore, problems can arise if we base our actions on such mistaken beliefs. For example, if we mistakenly believe that we understand how something works better than we do, we may volunteer to tutor someone or fix a broken device, only to add to the original problem. More commonly, in therapy, our clients are faced with an array of advice on relationships, parenting, careers, and many more, and this not only leads to confusion but can also lead to relationship disruptions when advice is not followed.

METACOGNITIVE PROCESSES

Two distinct but interacting metacognitive processes involve awareness of our current thinking (referred to in cognitive research as *monitoring*) and the use of such information to direct or control our thinking efforts (T. O. Nelson & Narens, 1994). The focus of monitoring is our thinking about the world or a particular problem, whereas the focus of control processes is to alter our thinking. Cognitive behavioral therapists have, since their inception, recommended that clients monitor their unwanted behavior, with the ultimate goal of preventing such behavior through intentional control (Burns, 1980; McMullin, 2000). For example, the cognitive behavioral technique of thought-countering requires a client to monitor himself for a particular type of thought (e.g., "I can't do this"), and then to control such thinking by countering it with an opposing thought (e.g., "Not true!") or action (e.g., relaxation technique). Or, in the mindfulness awareness techniques taught in many therapies (e.g., Bishop et al., 2004), clients are taught to simply observe a thought that compels action and do nothing in response.

   The other element that strongly influences the control processes we choose to employ is our understanding of what causes the symptoms and thinking we observe through monitoring. The client's understanding or model of her situation makes a great difference to her treatment in that models afford certain actions, leading to different control strategies. For example, a person who models his sadness as grief will consider actions such as honoring his connection to the lost person or object and finding new attachments, whereas a person modeling the same sadness as depression will consider actions such as medication. Finding a model or explanation that leads to useful actions (i.e., problem solving) is one of the roles of the therapist, and monitoring the resulting change in the client's situation is important feedback for the utility of a given model. If the client's situation changes for the better, this is taken as validation for the model, but if it doesn't, the search for a more useful model continues. The following section reviews evidence about the two processes of monitoring and control, as well as evidence about the importance of our beliefs.

Monitoring

Most research on cognitive monitoring applies to the areas of learning and memory and has been studied using people's judgments of such things as ease of learning, probability of recall, feeling of knowing, and confidence in an answer. The evidence indicates that we are aware of the state of our knowledge from mid-childhood until we are elderly (Hertzog, 2002; Hertzog & Dixon, 1994; Perner, 2000; W. Schneider & Lockl, 2002; Son & Schwartz, 2002).[1] Our judgments are fairly accurate, showing positive correlations with memory performance on the order of $r = .5$ for judgments given immediately after learning (B. K. Payne et al., 2004; Son & Schwartz, 2002). This imperfect correlation suggests that we are unaware of some of the consistent factors that influence our memory. This is especially true for memory performance that has not received accuracy feedback, such as the recognition of unfamiliar faces in an eyewitness situation (Perfect, 2002; see also Rosenblit & Keil, 2002).

One of the reasons for such imperfect predictions of memory appears to be that we are too sensitive to the subjective sense of familiarity or retrieval fluency in judging our memory performance (Benjamin, Bjork, & Schwartz, 1998; Jacoby & Kelley, 1987; Metcalfe, 2000; Metcalfe, Schwartz, & Joaquim, 1993; Reder, 1988; Schwartz & Metcalfe, 1992), neglecting to monitor for other diagnostic information such as contextual factors involved in the specific retrieval. In other words, we are more likely to predict that our memory performance will be good when the question seems familiar or it is easy to bring the questioned situation to mind. For example, conditions that influence the presence of a target memory at learning, such as priming (see chapter 3), increase people's ratings of their likelihood of recalling that information later when no such environmental assistance will be available (Benjamin et al., 1998). The later recall performance, which is not assisted by associative cues is, of course, worse than we expect. (As discussed in chapter 3, a cue will easily bring to mind items with which it is associated but without such an associative cue, retrieval of any item is much more effortful because we must create an appropriate cue with which to probe memory.) Anecdotally, most of us have had this experience: We think that we do not need to make a special effort to remember something such as a new friend's birthday because it is so obvious, only to forget that information when the time comes. Another unfortunately common example of this is when we hide an important document or object in a location that we believe we will easily recall when we need the object, only to forget where it is even though we remember taking special care in hiding it (Winograd & Soloway, 1986). With respect to psychotherapy, this means that what we learn in a particular session, which is immediately present in working memory, may not be remembered in a client's day-to-day life due to the change in environmental context and the passage of time. However, both client and therapist assume that they will be and thus may not engage in the relatively simple strategies that will help the client recall the new ideas and behavior when they are needed. For example, identifying an associative cue to trigger the new behavior (see chapter 6) or preparing an audiotape of the session which the client can review are often effective in increasing attention to therapeutic issues between sessions.

Furthermore, research indicates that we are less aware of environmental conditions that influence memory than we are of subjective factors like fluency or memory strength. Contextual factors, such as the influence of time since learning, practice, and the necessity of retrieval cues have less influence on our memory judgments than they should have (Koriat, 2002). In research settings, this results in poor correlations between memory predictions and performance when factors such as high versus low frequency words (e.g., *tree* vs. *oscillate*; Guttentag & Carroll, 1998), massed versus distributed practice (e.g., cramming vs. regular review; Bjork, 1999), and intrinsic versus extrinsic variables (e.g., organization vs. intensity of stimuli; Koriat, Sheffer, & Ma'ayan, 2002) influence performance. In other words, we are relatively unaware of contextual factors that systematically influence our memory, attending instead to internal factors such as familiarity or the ease with which a certain memory is brought to mind. Thus, when these factors influence performance, people tend to be overconfident in their predictions about their future memory. Simply teaching clients this may assist with their cooperation in constructing and carrying out effective homework assignments and developing ways to remember the therapeutic shift in the context of personal and social environments.

One interesting finding is that we are better at predicting the accuracy of our knowledge about general information than about eyewitness information (Perfect, 2002). Perfect hypothesized that this was because we are given considerable feedback about the accuracy of our informational knowledge in schools, but we seldom get feedback about eyewitness information. Consistent with this proposal, participants who are given practice and feedback in eyewitness identification show predictive judgments that are more consistent with their performance (Lindsay, Read, & Sharma, 1998; Read, Lindsay, & Nicholls, 1998). Such evidence indicates that we are able to use feedback to improve monitoring of our knowledge. The implications of this finding for psychotherapy relate to memory accuracy for autobiographical memory, including memory for the psychotherapy itself. Most of us receive some feedback about the accuracy of our autobiographical recollections during reminiscence with family members and friends, and so the accuracy of important autobiographical information is likely to be greater than that for random eyewitness situations. Similarly, therapists regularly receive feedback from their clients on their recall of conversational material such as that from previous therapy sessions. However, most clients do not receive much feedback on their recall of thoughts or conversational material, such as that important for psychotherapeutic change. Thus, without checking, a therapist cannot likely rely on the accuracy of a client's memory for moments of therapeutic progress. One possibility is to build memory rehearsal of therapeutic material into the therapy itself, such as by beginning each session with a question about the client's memory of the last session. An interesting development in therapy practice focuses on collecting and using outcome data on a session-by-session basis (S. D. Miller, Duncan, & Hubble, 2004). Information is collected at each session related to the client's experience of both the session and life outside the therapy room, and that information is used as feedback to guide the therapy process. The effect on therapeutic efficacy when such simple tools are incorporated is quite remarkable.

Beliefs About What Causes Cognitive Phenomena

Our theory about how memory and other cognitive processes operate is known as our intuitive theory, and we use this theory to judge the meaning of particular experiences, such as what the absence of a clear memory about a particular class of experiences means. For example, most people know that we can recall few memories from early childhood and infancy, and so the absence of clear memories from this period in our life is not interpreted as strong evidence that a given event did not happen. In this case, we are inclined to rely on the memories of someone who was older during the event, such as a parent or older sibling. As a result, misleading information from a purportedly authoritative source can have strong effects on people's beliefs that they must have experienced something in early childhood (Malinowski & Lynn, 1999; Mazzoni & Kirsch, 2002; Roebers, 2002). Conversely, the absence of clear memories of a distinctive event, such as a trip to a foreign country while one was an adult, is more likely taken as evidence that such an event did not happen, since we expect to recall vivid and distinctive experiences (Ghetti, 2003). For example, on a popular TV show, one of the main characters was accused by a woman of ignoring her even though they had previously had an affair. He did not recall ever meeting her previously, since she had substantially changed her appearance in the interim, but reasoned that he certainly would have remembered such an incident. He thus concluded, erroneously, that he had not previously met her. These intuitive theories thus also influence our judgments about our memory experiences, as well as the effort we expend on learning and recalling information. Research indicates that some of our incorrect beliefs about how memory works can result in "illusions of knowing" (Bjork, 1999; Jacoby & Kelley, 1987; D. A. Simon & Bjork, 2001), in which we believe that we know something due to our familiarity with the cue or question, when in fact we do not know the target information. For example, doctors' self-confidence in their ability to resuscitate patients suffering from cardiac arrest is influenced by the number of such patients they have encountered, but their actual resuscitation skills are not correlated with experience, at least for junior doctors (Martineau, Wynne, Kaye, & Evans, 1990). Similarly, when people rate their comprehension of an unfamiliar text, the ratings are uncorrelated with their performance to questions based on that text (Glenberg & Epstein, 1987; Glenberg, Sanocki, Epstein, & Morris, 1987). Most students recognize this situation: They think that they understand the information that is presented in a textbook but then are unable to use that information accurately to answer test questions (e.g., McNamara & O'Reilly, 2003). In particular, our intuitive theories of memory often don't include information about the influence of contextual factors such as the difference in memory for familiar versus unfamiliar words or the effect of effortful retrieval on subsequent memory (D. A. Simon & Bjork, 2001), often leading to the observed overconfidence in our memory predictions. Therapists of all modalities, particularly relationship and family therapists, have to frequently contend with the consequences of someone overconfidently predicting that his personal opinion is fact. This is also likely a factor in either a medical patient or a therapy client confidently self-diagnosing after seeing the latest commercial or reading the newest self-help book.

Memory judgment is influenced by both our memory experiences (e.g., sensory phenomenology) and our autobiographical beliefs (Conway, 1997a; chapter 4). As Mazzoni and Kirsch (2002) asserted, both factors are influenced by metacognitive criteria, or by our intuitive memory theories. What we make of the vividness of memory phenomenology is influenced by our theory about how such phenomenology is caused (i.e., its diagnosticity). Most typically, people believe that phenomenal clarity and vividness can only be caused by having experienced an event (Arbuthnott et al., 2004), although research indicates that repeatedly imagining an event in detail can also result in vivid sensory detail (Arbuthnott, in press). Most of us believe that for actual memories, our mental contents are vivid, clear, fluent, easy to recall, and richer in perceptual, contextual, semantic, and affective information (Arbuthnott et al., 2002; M. K. Johnson et al., 1988; Sheen et al., 2002; chapters 5 & 13). However, these same elements can sometimes arise in other ways, resulting in erroneous judgments about our past. Experimental manipulations that increase the ease with which target information comes to mind (Kelley & Jacoby, 1996), or instructions to rehearse an imagined event (Hyman & Pentland, 1996), increase erroneous reports that a given event is an actual memory. Autobiographical beliefs are also influenced by our theories about the plausibility of certain events and the diagnosticity of memory absence. Mazzoni and Kirsch (2002) demonstrated how autobiographical beliefs can be influenced by others expressing opinions about the plausibility or frequency of certain types of events, resulting in memory errors even though no memory phenomenology was present. Thus, experimental manipulations that increase our belief about the plausibility or frequency of a given event increase our judgment that such an event occurred to us, even though we have no specific memory (Pezdek et al., 1997; Mazzoni et al., 2001). This is obviously relevant to psychotherapy. Therapists are influential people in the lives of their clients, so their comments about possible underlying causes of a client's difficulty or about the frequency of certain social and psychological issues such as depression or childhood abuse can increase clients' beliefs about their own history, even in the absence of memories for such events (see chapter 5 for more detailed discussion of these issues).

Control

The second process discussed by metacognitive researchers involves the use of information that arises from monitoring to control our thinking (T. O. Nelson & Narens, 1994). For example, do people use their judgments about how likely they are to recall certain types of information to regulate the amount of time they spend studying various items? Presumably, we would allot more study time to material that is judged harder to learn or less likely to be recalled. In general, while we do use such information to regulate our behavior (Dunlosky & Hertzog, 1998; Son & Metcalfe, 2000; Thiede et al., 2003), we don't always use the metacognitive information we have to maximum advantage unless we are explicitly instructed to do so (e.g., instructed to study the most difficult items longer). Research indicates that our decisions to use the information available through our monitoring of cognitive processes is strongly influenced by the demands of the context. For example, when instructions emphasize the accuracy of responses, we are more likely to withhold answers we are not confident of than when instructions emphasize speed (Barnes et al., 1999; Koriat & Goldsmith, 1996). Similarly, we use judgments about which items are easy to learn to allocate study time to more difficult items when time is unlimited, but not when we are under time pressure (Son & Schwartz, 2002). For example, in the context of studying biographical essays of famous people for later recall, Son and Metcalfe (2000) allowed participants to return to any essay for review, but controlled the total study time allowed. When study time was constrained so that all the essays could not be studied, participants spent more time on the essays they judged to be easier, presumably because they hoped they would learn more from these essays than allocating their scarce time to more difficult material.

Because our decisions to use information made available through monitoring is strongly influenced by context, it is important that therapists take this into account when giving instructions to clients. For example, many cognitive therapy techniques require a client to monitor and collect information about her thoughts (e.g., thought content and frequency diaries). The therapist then usually wants the client to use the information gathered to make a change (e.g., countering an irrational thought with a rational one). The therapist will need to give the countering instructions explicitly and to take into account contextual factors (e.g., the effects of self-disputing in the middle of a conflict with a spouse) to maximize the likelihood of success (e.g., informing the spouse of the plan and gaining his co-operation).

However, we are not always aware of information that is relevant to our cognitive performance, resulting in failure to control processes due to a lack of monitoring accuracy. B. K. Payne et al. (2004) noted that we are not aware of the degree we use the automatic retrieval of stereotypic information in our judgments, resulting in a higher rate of errors that are consistent with our stereotype (e.g., mistakenly judging that "Don" was a doctor rather than a nurse) than the reverse (e.g., mistakenly judging that "Don" was a nurse rather than a doctor; Spaniol & Bayen, 2002; Stangor & McMillan, 1992). Direct recollection of a particular memory influences the confidence we have in our answer, but our easier access to information that is consistent with our expectations does not influence our confidence, although it clearly influences the type of errors we make. Thus, at an item-specific level, we cannot control errors due to our stereotypes because we are not aware of their influence. However, knowing this general pattern, we can be alert to situations of uncertainty and monitor for the influence of stereotypes in such circumstances. For example in a therapy session, one of the authors was discussing a workplace issue with a mid-level manager of aboriginal descent. As the client discussed an issue she had with her supervisor, the therapist became aware of categorizing the supervisor as both male and white (both inaccurate). As discussed in chapter 8, stereotypes are categorical information stored in long-term memory and are functional because they are often based on actual correlations. For example, it is a stereotype that women are smaller and weaker than men. This is clearly not always true in individual cases, but it is true on the average. So this stereotype is useful in making predictions about women and men that we have no information about. Similarly, although someone with a particular *DSM-IV-TR* diagnosis such as posttraumatic stress disorder (PTSD) may not have all characteristics of the disorder (e.g., someone who reports the requisite re-experiencing, avoidance, and arousal symptoms to be diagnosed with PTSD, but does not report much psychological distress in their current life due to the condition), the listing of such characteristics means that such symptoms are positively correlated with the disorder overall, justifying them as part of the stereotype of someone with PTSD.

Similarly, evidence of judgments based on multiple cues indicates that we have good knowledge of which cues we attend to, but poorer knowledge about how much we use those cues (i.e., their relative weighting) to make our judgment (Harries et al., 2000). For example, Harries et al. had doctors judge whether or not to prescribe a lipid-lowering medication to patients, giving them information about each patient's cholesterol level, blood pressure, age, family history, and so forth. The doctors showed good self-knowledge of which information they attended to, but poorer knowledge of the degree to which each selected cue influenced their prescription decision (as measured by regression analyses of their decisions). Other studies show that such cue information influences both implicit learning, based on associative memory links between cues and outcomes (see chapter 3), and explicit knowledge, such as the accepted criteria for a certain decision (Evans et al., 2003). We are able to monitor explicit but not implicit learning, resulting in our less-than-perfect awareness of the information that we use to make decisions. In therapy, clients often present reasons to justify current actions that do not take into account all the factors in their decisions, let alone the relative weight of each factor. For example, an adolescent client stated adamantly that his reason for not writing his final exams was that they were "crap and a way to control me." It was only after considerable exploration of his experiences around exams and the pressure he experienced that he was able to articulate that there were not only emotional factors (fear and anger) present but that they were stronger factors in his refusal than was his desire to resist being controlled.

METACOGNITIVE INSTRUCTION

Therapists of various theoretical orientations spend considerable time attempting to increase clients' self-monitoring and discussing their metacognitive beliefs. What is the evidence that such metacognitive instruction actually improves cognitive performance?

Work in the areas of developmental and educational psychology demonstrates that the explicit use of metacognition improves performance across a wide range of academic skills. Furthermore, this work amply demonstrates that metacognition can be taught. Within the area of cognitive psychology, the accuracy of young children's memory reports have been improved by accuracy instructions and incentives (Koriat, Goldsmith, Schneider, & Nakash-Dura, 2001; Roebers, Moga, & Schneider, 2001), suggesting that metacognitive attention does improve performance even in children as young as six years old (see also Rodriguez, Mischel, & Shoda, 1989). For example, three weeks after watching a video, Roebers et al. (2001) had children and adults answer questions about the video in one of three conditions which varied in accuracy motivation. The low accuracy group were forced to answer each question, whereas the high accuracy group were instructed to withhold answers they weren't sure of and were rewarded for each correct answer. Performance was best in the high accuracy condition, and there were no age differences in recall between children (six and eight years old) and adults. Furthermore, the development of mnemonic organizational strategies is associated with improved memory performance in children (Schlagmuller & Schneider, 2002). Thus, despite the sparcity of research evidence on this question, it seems likely that improved metacognition, including general knowledge about cognitive processes, will improve behavioral efficacy.

Research with very young children indicates that parents' metacognitive discussion while solving problems with their child influences both the child's problem-solving behavior and their later adjustment to a classroom learning environment (Neitzel & Stright, 2003). Neitzel and Stright observed mothers while they helped their preschool children solve four difficult problems, recording the mothers' use of metacognitive comments (e.g., "This puzzle is too hard to do all at once, so let's think of what we should do first"), efforts to break the problems into manageable steps for their child (e.g., "Maybe we could sort the pieces by color or find all the edge pieces"), emotional support of the child's ability to solve the problem ("You're so patient and good at puzzles, even when they're hard"), and their ability to provide help while leaving responsibility for solving the problem with the child (a process known as *scaffolding*; e.g., "Which colors do you notice?"). Several weeks later, they observed the children in their kindergarten classroom and recorded the children's metacognitive comments, task persistence, behavioral self-control, and other relevant behaviors. They observed that the mothers' metacognitive comments were associated with the children's self-regulatory behaviors and metacognitive management of problem solving, while mothers' emotional support and transfer of responsibility was related to the children's effort and behavioral control in the classroom. Thus, metacognitive ability is clearly learned through contact with others who have such ability. Some processes in therapy mirror these parental problem-solving teachings, with therapists helping clients to break problems into manageable steps, teaching them metacognitive strategies with which to approach issues, and providing emotional support for clients' problem-solving efforts. For example, the "mindfulness" strategy (Bishop et al., 2004) of teaching clients to simply observe and accept their own thoughts and experiences is largely a metacognitive strategy, whether applied to the cognitive behavioral treatment of borderline personality disorder (e.g., Linehan, Cochran, & Kehrer, 2001), as one of several meditative techniques regularly taught in postmodern and constructivist approaches (e.g., Mahoney, 2003), or taught to couples in relationship therapy (e.g., Jacobson & Christensen, 1998).

Metacognitive strategies are often specific to the cognitive activity they are designed to assist, such as reading comprehension or mathematical problem solving (Efklides & Tsiora, 2002; Glenberg & Epstein, 1987; Glenberg et al., 1987; Thiede et al., 2003). Direct evidence that meta-cognitive knowledge improves our decisions and behavior has only been tested in the fields of education and developmental psychology. In those areas, specific programs designed to increase children's use of meta-cognitive strategies have been used to improve children's use of study time and particular memory techniques (W. Schneider & Lockl, 2002). In general, these programs show improvement in school performance (Palin-scar & Brown, 1984; Moely, Santulli, & Obach, 1995; Pressley, 1995). Specific instruction in the use of metacognitive strategies has also been shown to improve reading (Kjeldsen, Niemi, & Oloffson, 2003; Thiede et al., 2003), spelling (Lazo, Pumfrey, & Peers, 1997; Kjeldsen et al., 2003), and mathematics (Desoete et al., 2003) performance in elementary school children. To the degree that metacognition requires attentional control, there is also evidence that populations that have difficulty with such con-trol, including those with brain injury or ADHD, benefit from programs designed to strengthen voluntary attentional control (Kerns, Esso, & Thompson, 1999; Klingberg, Forssberg, & Westerberg, 2002; Semrud-Clikeman, Nielson, & Clinton, 1999; Sohlberg, McLaughlin, Pavese, Heidrich, & Posner, 2000).

However, this research indicates that learning to use such strategies is also highly specific—the strategies must not only be described but amply demonstrated and practiced for children to begin to use them effectively (Moely et al., 1995; Palinscar & Brown, 1984; Pressley, 1995). These pro-grams demonstrate that the use of metacognitive knowledge must be prac-ticed in the specific situations for which the knowledge is useful. For exam-ple, Palinscar and Brown (1984) developed a program for teaching reading strategies to elementary school children through dialogue with their teach-ers. In this program, the reading strategies are explicitly named and their use in specific situations is both modeled and practiced by the students (e.g., strategies such as discerning meaning of unfamiliar words from context). Other programs used in educational settings (Moely et al., 1995; Pressley, 1995) have shown that explicit instruction in effective metacognitive strate-gies must be accompanied by modeling of where those strategies are useful, as well as ample opportunity for practice (Joyner & Kurtz-Costes, 1997). Similarly, a program designed to improve learning from scientific texts in a university setting also show that, although strategies such as explaining con-cepts to oneself as one is reading are successful in improving performance, the use of metacognitive knowledge must be explicitly considered and practiced (McNamara & O'Reilly, 2003).

Similar studies with elderly participants indicate that elders need to make an explicit link between a metacognitive strategy and its effect on performance (Larrabee et al., 1991; M. D. Murphy, Schmitt, Caruso, & Sanders, 1987; Rabinowitz, 1989). Programs designed to improve the everyday memory abilities of patients with memory difficulties similarly show that instruction in metacognitive strategies must be very specific to improve performance (e.g., the use of imagery to learn names of new individuals); such programs reliably show performance improvement even for patients who experience considerable difficulty (B. A. Wilson, 1987; B. A. Wilson & Moffat, 1984).

There is a long history of attention to metacognitive factors in psychotherapy, such as the focus on self-efficacy beliefs by social learning theorists (Bandura, 1997). In general, these techniques have focused more on monitoring content of thoughts (i.e., beliefs about cognition) than on cognitive control. More recently, psychotherapy specifically aimed at clients' metacognitive processes, rather than the content of their beliefs, has also been devised (A. Wells, 2000). As reviewed earlier in this chapter, there are consistent metacognitive beliefs and styles associated with several psychological disorders, so intervention targeting metacognition seems appropriate. For example, Wells advocates teaching clients to monitor their metacognitive plans that underlie beliefs and feelings associated with problematic situations. He then directly challenges the usefulness of those plans, such as having an anxious client who believes that worrying helps to alleviate anxiety write out the content of their worrying and then compare that with what actually occurs when they enter a feared situation. Similarly, clients with OCD, who believe that having bad thoughts makes bad things happen, are asked to detail the mechanism by which thoughts influence reality in this way or to run a behavioral experiment by trying to cause a negative event (such as having his car break down) by thinking of it. Such patients are then helped to formulate alternate metacognitive plans with which to respond to their difficulties (anxiety or obsessive-compulsive thoughts), and to practice a state of "detached mindfulness." Although such treatment strategies are logical, given evidence of the importance of beliefs and metacognitive monitoring to some disorders, there are as yet few studies examining the efficacy of these treatments (see Sheppard & Teasdale, 2004, for an exception).

In summary, the most obvious way that metacognitive knowledge is important is to improve thinking itself, an intervention strategy well known to psychotherapists. For example, research shows that our attention is not drawn to base-rate or contextual information (see chapter 9), including the context of our own recent thoughts (see chapter 3), thus causing errors in reasoning. Knowing this, we can deliberately consider such factors when we are making important decisions. For example, cognitive behavioral therapists often have clients keep records of the frequency of their problematic behaviors as well as the situations under which such behaviors occur (Rokke & Rehm, 2001). Similarly, knowing that we tend to judge the reality of a memory on the basis of phenomenological vividness, as well as consistency with other autobiographical memories (see chapter 5), and that such factors can be tricked by repeatedly imagining or discussing a plausible scenario, therapists can deliberately consider whether clients have engaged in such activities when judging the source of a given memory. Evidence also indicates that we are overconfident in our ability to remember something immediately after it has been presented. That is, we predict that our memory for the information will be higher immediately after we have learned it than it is shown to be after a delay of any duration. In the context of psychotherapy, this would influence clients' confidence in their ability to remember homework assignments given during a session. They and the therapist are likely to predict that the client will remember to do the assigned task, whereas the likelihood of forgetting the task is reasonably great. Knowing the likelihood of cognitive failure (rather than resistance, see chapter 6) despite the subjective feeling of confidence, would allow therapists and clients to plan strategies to increase recall at appropriate times.

We cannot, however, protect ourselves from all such errors caused by cognitive processes, as we are not aware of all such processes. As discussed earlier, memory errors attributable to stereotypes are partly caused by the memory accessibility of categorical information, a factor that we are not subjectively aware of (B. K. Payne et al., 2004). Even in this case, however, metacognitive knowledge can be useful to us in interpreting the meaning of judgments or decisions, taking into account such propensities. For example, knowing that we are much more likely to attribute events to persons even though contextual factors and situations are often important, we can consider our judgments of personality or causal attribution for unfortunate events with more circumspection. If, for example, we considered strong patriotic feelings as indicative of the natural primate tendency to form emotional ties to social groups and territory, rather than as indications of spiritual correctness, we might be less likely to go to war against other groups who also claim sovereignty over land we consider ours. As the business cliché claims, knowledge is power, and knowledge about our own cognitive processes, including the errors resulting from such processes, can enable us to make better decisions based on those thoughts.

KEY POINTS

- *Metacognition* is the knowledge that we have about our own mental processes. This includes the judgments that we make about the outcome of those processes (e.g., Have I remembered that correctly?), the confidence that we have in those outcomes (e.g., How confident am I that I understand this person's situation?), the attributions that we make about those processes (Does the fact that I can't remember an event imply that it didn't happen?), as well as our ability to monitor and regulate our thoughts and forecast the success of our thinking (e.g., If I take this approach, will I be able to solve that problem?).

- Many decisions to take or refrain from action are based on our metacognitive intuitions that we have correctly remembered something or reasoned something out.

- Many psychiatric disorders (e.g., OCD, schizophrenia) are associated with failures of metacognition, and many therapeutic techniques are designed to remedy faulty metacognitive beliefs (e.g., self-efficacy; assessment of the rates of problematic behaviors).

- Metacognition processes involve both monitoring current thoughts and using what we notice to control our subsequent thoughts and actions.

- Metacognition can be improved through instruction, but that instruction must be targeted to a specific task, the connection between metacognition and task performance must be explicitly drawn, and learners must be given ample opportunity to practice the metacognitive strategies.

NOTE

1. We may lose this metacognitive ability in extreme old age, such as with elders who unexpectedly fail written driving tests, thinking that they know the information when they do not.

13

Emotion and Cognition: Mutual Influences

One of psychotherapists' greatest skills is recognizing, understanding, and working with emotion: Psychotherapists are, in effect, applied affective scientists. With their training and experience, therapists become experts in the expression, action tendencies, and consequences of emotional experience. This is usually necessary, as dysphoric emotion is one of the main complaints that leads people to seek therapy, and a positive shift in emotional experience is one indicator for therapy termination. Although emotion has not always maintained a primary place in the theories of change and psychotherapy, it has been central to practicing therapists who must assist clients in managing their emotional states. Humanistic and experiential therapies attend to and use clients' emotional experiences as a key component in understanding their clients and as a means of facilitating change. The advent of process-based therapies and process research has begun to provide empirically validated evidence for the use of emotionally focused approaches with individuals (e.g., L. S. Greenberg & Paivio, 1997) and with couples (e.g., S. M. Johnson, 2002; S. M. Johnson & Denton, 2002).

Formal affective science has lagged behind practice, but it is now engaged in increasing scientific knowledge of the nature and operation of emotional processing. This is a very broad area examining a wide range of issues, such as the physiological, expressive, and contextual nature of emotions, whether a set of emotions is basic to humans across all cultures, and the like. Most of these issues are relevant to psychotherapy, but a review of the entire domain is not possible even within an entire volume (see Forgas, 2000, for an example). Instead, in this chapter we present an overview of the research examining mutual interactions between cognition and emotion to introduce several relevant areas of inquiry to the psychotherapeutic community. The interplay of thinking, feeling, and behavior is at the heart of most therapeutic systems, and thus understanding the interaction of these systems is very important to therapists of all schools. The work we discuss in this chapter is not solely that of cognitive scientists; we also draw on research in the areas of affective science and social cognition. We begin with a short discussion of the nature of emotion as it is conceived in these research programs. Then we review evidence of the influence of emotion on cognitive processes, and we end with a consideration of the influence of cognition on emotional experience.

THE NATURE OF EMOTION

Terminology is still evolving in this field, but *mood* is generally distinguished from *emotion*, and *affect* is used as the superordinate category encompassing both. Emotions are acute reactions to specific targets and involve well-defined action tendencies. Moods, on the other hand, are more diffuse, describing longer-term and usually less intense dispositions. However, both are considered to be outcomes of affective processing systems, and both interact with cognitive processes in the ways described in this chapter. Furthermore, both emotions and underlying moods are focal issues in therapy. Thus, for this chapter, the terms *mood* and *emotion* will be used somewhat interchangeably.

Similar to cognitive processes discussed in previous chapters, emotion is conceptualized as a multi-component collection of processes. Emotions include organized physiological responses involving facial, skeletomuscular, autonomic, and endocrine systems; subjective feeling states; and action tendencies (Niedenthal & Halberstadt, 2000; C. A. Smith & Kirby, 2000). Current affective theorists generally agree that emotion is adaptive (e.g., Tooby & Cosmides, 1990), providing rapid and flexible response to stimuli and situations (e.g., Zajonc, 2000). Emotions arise in response to conditions of potential benefit or harm to the individual, and they serve both self-regulatory and communicative functions (C. A. Smith & Kirby, 2000; C. A. Smith & Lazarus, 1993). Socially, emotional expressions alert us to others' behavioral intentions (Fridlund, 1991) and facilitate our social learning about the nature of stimuli (Walden, 1991). As with cognitive processes, emotional processes can occur either consciously or unconsciously.

Most affective theorists agree that emotional experience is fundamentally related to an individual's goals, including but not exclusive to the goals of survival and health (Blascovich & Mendes, 2000; Bower & Cohen, 1982; R. S. Lazarus, 1991; Oatley & Johnson-Laird, 1996). Many also agree that the eliciting conditions for the various emotions are organized prototypically (Hogan, 2003; Kovecses, 2000): Positive emotions such as happiness or love are felt when we advance toward or maintain a desired goal, and negative emotions such as sadness, fear, or anger are felt when progress is thwarted in some manner. The specific situation, or our understanding of it, determines which emotion is elicited. The prototypical context for sadness is loss, for fear it is danger, for happiness it is interpersonal union or success, and so forth. Emotions provide feedback on our progress in achieving current goals and generate physiological preparation for a response to the situation (known as "action tendencies").

Although it is a relatively rare subset within psychotherapy, bodywork therapies make explicit use of the physiological and muscular action tendencies associated with different emotions. Bioenergetics (Lowen, 1975), for example, encourages the direct expression of such action within a safe, contained therapeutic environment. Angry clients are encouraged to hit and kick soft materials such as pillows and mattresses, sad clients are encouraged to sob deeply, and so forth. Therapies that include bodywork as the main focus of therapy include Reichian (Reich, 1990), bioenergetics (Lowen, 1975), integrative body psychotherapy (Latorre, 2000), and Hakomi (Kurtz, 1990) models. Others, however, encourage the integration of body-based techniques into more traditional psychotherapies (e.g., Mahoney, 2003) or simply promote the use of good exercise and activities such as yoga or martial arts as an adjunct to psychotherapy treatments for a variety of diagnoses (e.g., Morgan & Goldston, 1987). Although seen as outside the mainstream of current psychotherapeutic practice and ethically troubling due to the physical contact that is usually central to such techniques, these therapies and methods offer an encouraging set of techniques to assist clients to experience, express, and contain emotion (e.g., see Totton, 2002).

There is some debate about whether emotion is best conceptualized in dimensional or categorical terms (Niedenthal & Halberstadt, 2000). The dimensional view is that emotion is the interaction of two dimensions: valence and intensity (M. M. Bradley, 1994; J. A. Russell, 1980). *Valence* refers to positive or negative affective tone, whereas *intensity* refers to the strength of the felt emotion, or the associated physiological arousal. Research suggests that the two dimensions may have somewhat different effects on cognitive processes. Categorical models of emotion, alternatively, propose that emotional experience and representation is specific to several basic emotions, such as happiness, sadness, fear, anger, and disgust (Ekman, 1984; Izard, 1977; Oatley & Johnson-Laird, 1996). Each emotion is associated with various types of information, including eliciting conditions, facial and postural expression, action tendencies, themes, and relevant memories (Bower, 1981). Perhaps the most well-developed categorical model is Bower's (1981, 1991) affect network model. Bower theorizes that emotions are mentally represented as nodes in an associative network (similar to the memory system described in chapter 3). Each node is linked with relevant indicators, including physiological and autonomic reactions, facial and postural expressions, verbal labels, action tendencies, prototypical situations in which the emotion is felt, and memories of life events featuring that emotion. As for any associative network, activation of any aspect of this network primes associates through the mechanism of spreading activation. In the exploration or problem space definition phase of therapy, most clinicians assist their clients in developing as complete a picture as possible of any emotional state relevant to their problem and in making any unconscious aspects of the emotion experience explicit. For example, a client seeking therapy for anger management may not be aware that the prototypical eliciting conditions for his rage are related to situations in which he feels embarrassed by others.

The categorical model is much more similar to emotional conceptions in psychotherapeutic theories (e.g., Goulding & Goulding, 1979; L. S. Greenberg & Paivio, 1997) than is the dimensional model. It is also the model used by many authors to explain emotional processes (e.g., emotional intelligence, Goleman, 1995; emotional literacy, Ladd, 2003; Steiner, 1996) and therefore the model most clients and therapists have been exposed to in popular literature. It is also more therapeutically useful in that understanding specific emotions is often necessary to adequately conceptualize a client's problem, whereas conceptualizing issues in terms of valence or intensity alone would be less helpful. Evidence more consistent with categorical than dimensional models has also been recently observed (e.g., C. A. Smith & Kirby, 2000). For example, Niedenthal and her colleagues (Niedenthal & Halberstadt, 2000; Niedenthal, Halberstadt, & Setterlund, 1997) observed priming of words that were associated with specifically induced mood states (i.e., happy or sad), but no priming for associates of similarly valenced states (i.e., other positive or negative moods). Furthermore, neuropsychological evidence suggests that there may be different patterns of autonomic activity for the various emotions (Levinson, 1992).

Although cognition and emotion are most likely independent processing streams (Zajonc, 2000), they influence each other in multiple ways. This interactivity is supported by anatomical observations of bidirectional excitatory and inhibitory connections between brain areas active in emotional (e.g., limbic regions) and cognitive processing (e.g., cortical regions, including the prefrontal cortex that is important in cognitive control; LeDoux, 1996; Mega & Cummings, 1994).

The Effect of Emotion on Cognition: Attention, Memory, Judgment, and Cognitive Style

Emotional experience influences many components of cognition, including perception (e.g., Niedenthal et al., 1994), attention (e.g., Derryberry & Tucker, 1994), memory (e.g., Bower, 1981), problem solving (Isen, Daubman, & Nowicki, 1987), and attitudinal judgments (e.g., Clore, Schwarz, & Conway, 1994; Fiedler, Asbeck, & Nickel, 1991). More recently, evidence of affective influences on the types of cognitive processes people employ has also been observed (Bless, 2000; Fiedler, 2000). In this section, we briefly review evidence of emotional influence in attention, memory, judgment, and cognitive style. Generally, emotion biases these processes in a mood-congruent manner, although these effects are observed only in specific contexts.

Attention

There is no doubt that emotional stimuli draw attention (Halberstadt & Niedenthal, 1997; Riemann & McNally, 1995), especially when we are in an emotional state (Dalgliesh & Watts, 1990; Derryberry & Tucker, 1994). There is also evidence that stimuli consistent with our current mood are particularly salient, leading us to pay greater attention to mood-congruent items and events (Bower & Forgas, 2000). For example, participants that have been inducted into a happy mood spend more time encoding positive information about fictional characters or viewing pleasant scenes than those in a sad mood, who spend relatively more time on negative information and unpleasant scenes (Forgas, 1992; Forgas & Bower, 1987). The same effects have also been observed in clients with affective disorders, especially depression (B. Bradley & Mathews, 1983; Watkins, Mathews, Williamson, & Fuller, 1992).

The consequence of such attentional capture depends on the specific emotion. For pleasant items such as a smiling face, initial attentional capture is likely to be sustained, at least to some degree, resulting in improved memory for that item, which in turn can potentially bias current judgments. For example, having a client describe a pleasant holiday or social encounter will both divert her attention from problematic issues and influence her subsequent memory and evaluation of the session. This may be why therapists who routinely laugh with their clients over amusing human tendencies or other matters are often considered effective by their clients. In the case of grief or depression, the presence of items related to a client's loss or sad mood will similarly draw and maintain attention. However, in the case of fear or anxiety, although material related to the feared event will initially capture attention, that attentional focus is generally short-lived (because we avoid danger), resulting in less overall attention to the feared items than to other things in the context (Mathews & MacLeod, 1994; Watts, McKenna, Sharrock, & Tzezise, 1986; J. M. G. Williams & Broadbent, 1986).

This also has memory consequences, with less subsequent memory for threat-related material, which may provide a basis for denial. Treatments for phobia and other anxiety disorders tend to alter this tendency, requiring clients to focus on feared stimuli for longer intervals, thus allowing habituation and logical inference processes to operate to counteract the fear reaction. This differential treatment of the different emotions in therapy can also extend to thought, as in the case of treatments where therapists encourage grieving clients to stop ruminating after expressing loss (e.g., Say good-bye and let it go) and encourage fearful clients to think more about scary situations (e.g., What is the worst that could happen?) as a way to manage these issues. In colloquial terms, it seems that fear can lead us to abort our thinking to our detriment, whereas sadness can lead us to bury ourselves in thinking to our detriment.

Intense emotional experience may also influence what we pay attention to during an event, including therapy sessions, increasing our attention to central or thematic details but decreasing attention to details peripheral to the event (Easterbrook, 1959). This has substantive consequences for memory of emotional events.

In social situations, including therapy sessions, emotion seems to draw and capture the attention of all participants, including therapists, until the emotion dissipates. This has serious implications both for the management of emotion in therapy and for assisting clients and their families to manage emotional states in their day-to-day lives. It is common in couple or family therapy to hear one participant accuse another of using emotion to manipulate or "hijack" the session or to "emotionally blackmail" the other(s). Gottman and colleagues (see Gottman, Driver, & Tabares, 2002, for a summary) named this capturing process as "flooding" and the results of flooding as "cascading" and have begun to introduce techniques such as self-regulation (see the regulation section later in the chapter) or self-soothing. For example, couples therapists may have their clients periodically take their pulse during a conflict and when someone's pulse rate reaches a particular rate, a time-out is called and the clients briefly engage in an emotionally soothing activity. As clients learn to soothe themselves and/or each other, they become less dependent on the therapist to fill this role.

Memory

Emotion typically makes events more memorable and vivid, but it is the intensity of the emotion, rather than its valence, that underlies this effect (e.g., Bohannon, 1988; Christianson & Loftus, 1990; Reisberg, Heuer, McLean, & O'Shaughnessy, 1988; Rubin & Kozin, 1984; R. T. White, 1989). Furthermore, emotional arousal can impair memory performance immediately, but then improve it after a delay. Kleinsmith and Kaplan (1964) observed that participants' memory for high arousal words was worse on an immediate test but better after a longer delay, whereas the reverse pattern was observed for low arousal words. A few studies, however, also indicate that valence, specifically positive emotion, also influences recollection, as positive events are recalled better than negative events (Isen, 1985; Robinson, Rosen, Revil, David, & Rus, 1980; see also chapter 4).

Two different memory effects are observed: mood congruence and mood dependence. Mood-congruent memory refers to the tendency to more easily learn material and recollect memories that are consistent with one's current mood. Individuals who are currently happy more efficiently learn positive aspects of a situation and more readily recall previous memories that are pleasant than someone who is currently sad. There is considerable evidence supporting mood congruence (Blaney, 1986). For example, depressive patients were less likely to recall a pleasant personal event and rated a given event as less happy during the saddest phase in their diurnal cycle than when they were in a more neutral mood (D. M. Clark & Teasdale, 1982). Some researchers, however, observe asymmetric congruency, with happy memories being more dependent on mood than sad memories (Dunbar & Lishman, 1984; Isen, Shalker, Clark, & Karp, 1978; Teasdale & Russell, 1983). Therapeutic techniques, such as having clients discuss a current example of their problem in detail (thus evoking and intensifying the relevant feeling) before asking them to describe earlier instances when they felt this way (e.g., Goulding & Goulding, 1979), directly use mood-congruent retrieval. According to Bower's (1981) associative model of affect priming, such events would be more accessible due to the activation of the particular emotion. Sometimes in therapy, simply educating clients about the idea of mood congruence is helpful. For example, a client who was feeling significantly depressed was assigned the task of finding positive life stories (in memory, in talking to family, etc.). His cooperation was significantly enhanced by an explanation that this was partially to counter the common human tendency to "remember more of the same" (see discussion of mood repair later in the chapter).

Mood congruence is not always observed, and researchers have isolated the relevant factors that account for this variability (Eich & Schooler, 2000). Mood is much more likely to influence learning and retrieval when an individual is aware of the relationship between the memory and the current mood (Rothkopf & Blaney, 1991), when the current mood is relatively strong (Rinck, Glowalia, & Schneider, 1992), and when the to-be-learned material is self-referential (Nasby, 1994). Each of these conditions is likely to be present very often in therapy, especially when clients are discussing autobiographical memories related to their issues. For example, practitioners of most psychodynamic therapies explicitly ask their clients when and under what circumstances they have experienced similar emotions in the past; often the use of interpretations implicitly suggests a relationship between mood and memory.

Thus, in contrast to the increased memorability of emotional events, which is due to arousal, mood congruence is dependent on the valence of the emotion, with the positive or negative tone of one's mood influencing retrieval of memories that are consistent with that valence.

In contrast to mood congruence, mood-dependent memory posits that memories formed while one is in a specific mood (e.g., sad), are recalled better when one is once again in that mood (sad), regardless of the emotional valence of the learned material. However, research evidence has shown that this is not typically the case (Blaney, 1986; Bower & Forgas, 2000). Rather, memory is not mood dependent, except under very particular conditions (R. C. Beck & McBee, 1995; Bower & Forgas, 2000; Eich, 1995; Eich & Schooler, 2000). The relevant conditions are when there is a causal relation between the target stimulus and one's mood, the retrieval situation provides no other cues (Eich, 1980), and the mood in question is intense (Eich & Schooler, 2000). State-dependent memory, which is similar to mood dependence, is reliably observed for drug-induced states (Eich, 1980; R. Peters & McGee, 1982), so therapists of all theoretical perspectives working with addicted individuals need to be aware of this fact. Other than this exception, mood dependence is not generally relevant to therapeutic situations and so will not be discussed further.

As described, the research on affective influences on memory tends to use a dimensional model of memory, focusing on emotion intensity and valence rather than effects associated with specific emotions. However, some research indicates that the memorial effects of emotional material is influenced by the particular emotion. Sadness, for instance, apparently impairs memory more than other moods. Leight and Ellis (1981) observed that participants induced into a sad mood performed worse on a list learning task than all others, primarily because they did not benefit from the usual effects of repetition. Sadness and depression apparently interfere with elaborative encoding of material, especially difficult material (H. C. Ellis, Thomas, & Rodriguez, 1984; Weingartner, Cohen, Murphy, Martello, & Gerdt, 1981). Although the observation of mild memory disturbance with depression is quite reliable (e.g., Watts, 1988), there is speculation that this is not due to emotional effects on memory itself, but on other factors that influence memory. Cognitive behavioral theorists claim, for instance, that emotional states such as depression and anxiety interfere with the organizational processes of memory (Leight & Ellis, 1981; P. N. Russell & Beekhuis, 1976), such as increasing intrusive thoughts that interfere with attention to the to-be-learned material. In support of this contention, research findings show the number of distracting thoughts reported by participants is negatively correlated with their recall of to-be-learned material (H. C. Ellis, Moore, Varner, Ottaway, & Becker, 1997; Siebert & Ellis, 1991). Another hypothesis is that depression reduces a person's willingness to process information actively (M. H. Johnson & Magaro, 1987; Watts, Morris, & MacLeod, 1987; Watts & Sharrock, 1987), thereby reducing elaborative encoding, which involves integrating new material with existing memories by such activities as categorizing new information or making the new material distinctive by techniques such as imagining the information in a bizarre context. At the very least, depressed individuals clearly have trouble retrieving specific, detailed autobiographical memories and instead report generic memories (Moore, Watts, & Williams, 1988; J. M. G. Williams & Broadbent, 1986; see chapter 4).

Anxiety has different effects on memory than sadness, further indicating the superiority of the categorical model of emotion, as both are negatively valenced moods. Some authors claim that anxiety has a greater impact on attention than on memory (Mogg, Mathews, & Weinman, 1987; Watts, 1986): Anxiety increases alertness to the feared stimuli, but this is in the service of avoiding such stimulation, resulting in reduced analysis of such material and consequent impoverished memory. Furthermore, although anxiety disrupts performance in some circumstances (Darke, 1988), the effect is not consistent, perhaps because fear increases both worry and arousal. Worry impairs performance due to the distracting thoughts. For example, public speaking anxiety has been observed to decrease digit span and verbal fluency (Idzikowski & Baddeley, 1983), perceptual fluency (Simoniv, Frolov, Evtushenko, & Svirodov, 1977), and tasks that involve complex motor control, such as aiming (Molander & Backman, 1989). Anxiety may also impair some aspects of reasoning (Tohill & Holyoak, 2000; but see Idzikowski & Baddeley, 1983). Conversely, increased arousal may facilitate effort, thereby counteracting the effect of distraction.

Considerable effort has been expended lately examining autobiographical memory for fearful events such as assassinations of political figures, witnessed crimes, or personal trauma. As for mood dependence, this evidence paints a complex picture of the effect of intense fear on memory reliability. In some contexts, intense emotion improves recall, but in others, it impairs recall, depending on the conditions of encoding and retrieval (Eich & Schooler, 2000). One factor that influences the direction of the effect seems to be how much the emotional event impacts one personally. For example, flashbulb memories, that is, recollections associated with surprising news events, are more detailed and accurate than memories for less emotional news events (Conway, 1995; Conway et al., 1994), whereas memories of personal trauma can sometimes be entirely forgotten (P. J. Taylor & Kopelman, 1984; Widom & Morris, 1997; L. M. Williams, 1994, 1995). This suggests that intensely fearful events are less likely to benefit memory the more they impact the person himself.

Flashbulb memories are unusually clear, detailed, and recalled with great confidence (R. Brown & Kulik, 1977; Weaver, 1993; Winograd & Neisser, 1993). However, research indicates that such memories are seldom completely accurate, especially after long delays (Neisser & Harsch, 1992; Wagenaar & Groenweg, 1990). In other words, although subjectively we are very confident in the accuracy of flashbulb memories, our recollections are not entirely accurate. People do, however, recall a great deal about such events (McClosky, Wible, & Cohen, 1988), especially when the event is important to them (Conway et al., 1994; Neisser, Winograd, & Weldon, 1991; Palmer, Schreiber, & Fox, 1991).

Intense emotion has been observed to narrow attention to the central details of an event, improving recall for those features but impairing memory for background events (Christianson, 1992). For instance, Burke, Heuer, and Reisberg (1992) showed participants an arousing or bland story. When tested two weeks later, participants who were shown the arousing story showed improved recall of the main characters but worse recall of other details than those who were shown the bland story. However, recall of the central details of emotional events is very good. Yuille and Cutshall (1986) interviewed thirteen eyewitnesses to a shooting crime five months after the event and observed 83% accuracy in event details, 76% accuracy in descriptions of the people, and 90% accuracy in object descriptions.

Clinicians who treat clients for posttraumatic stress disorder (PTSD) or other trauma-related disorders are no doubt aware of the intense debate over the quality of traumatic memories, which now appears to be evolving to a more moderate position by both sides (e.g., Lindsay & Briere, 1997; Schooler, Bendiksen, & Ambradar, 1997). In this context, researchers and clinicians are also divided about whether intensely emotional memories evoke a specialized memory mechanism, such as R. Brown and Kulik's (1977) "now print" device (flashbulb memories), or a repression/dissociation mechanism for intense personally threatening memories (e.g., J. L. Herman, 1992; Terr, 1991; van der Kolk & Fisler, 1995). Clinicians generally support special memory mechanism accounts, whereas cognitive scientists favor the explanation that the apparently unique memory effects are due to the normal operation of memory, augmented by the influence of emotional factors (Berntsen et al., 2003; Conway et al., 1994). Recent neurological evidence suggests that both may be correct. Intensely emotional stimulation does modify the operation of memory-relevant processes to some degree and in a manner that would fit clinical observations that traumatic memories are sensitive to retrieval in the presence of environmental cues but are not accessible to deliberate recall (Brewin, Dalgleish, & Joseph, 1996). Specifically, the learning of emotional details is enhanced by adrenergic hormones (Cahill, Prins, Weber, & McGaugh, 1994), such as those that would be present in one's body during emotionally intense events. Furthermore, emotional stimuli increase amygdala activation (Cahill, Babinsky, Markowitsch, & McGaugh, 1995; Cahill et al., 1996) and decrease hippocampal activation (McClelland, McNaughton, & O'Reilly, 1995). This may lead to enhanced encoding of perceptual memories (amygdala contribution) but decreased consolidation of those memories in the autobiographical knowledge base (hippocampal contribution), resulting in the observed pattern of enhanced sensitivity to recall of the memory in the presence of relevant environmental cues but impaired deliberate recall of the event (Krystal, Southwick, & Charney, 1995). If further research supports this model, this would reflect standard memory processes but atypical operation of those processes in response to intense emotion, which could be considered a special mechanism.

Emotion also apparently slows forgetting (Cahill, Prins, Weber, & McGaugh, 1994; Pillemar, 1984; Yuille & Tollestrup, 1992). This may be due to more frequent rehearsal of emotional memories or other differences in the way people think about emotional events (Christianson & Loftus, 1991; Heuer & Reisberg, 1990). For example, when recalling a neutral story, participants make errors in their recall of the plot, whereas for an arousing story, errors are more likely related to presumed motives or reactions of the story's protagonists (Burke et al., 1992).

In summary, the effect of emotion on memory is consistent but complex. Emotion itself improves memory for the central details of an event, and current mood influences what previous memories are recalled (mood congruence). Furthermore, more long-lasting emotional states, such as depression or anxiety, influence memory performance in idiosyncratic ways. Therapists who understand the relationship between emotion and memory can better help their clients navigate change without attributing normal memory processes to some flaw in their personality. For example, a client who understands mood congruence is less likely to see himself as a "negative person" and more likely to attribute his recall of primarily negative memories to his current state.

Judgment

Considerable research also indicates that emotion influences people's judgments about themselves, other people, objects, and abstract concepts such as life satisfaction or health status. Unlike the case for memory, these effects appear to be strongest when we are not paying attention to our emotions (Bower & Forgas, 2000). In general, affective influence on judgment is mood congruent, but, as for memory, the effects are observed only under certain conditions. We first review evidence of emotional effects on judgments and then outline the conditions under which such effects are likely to occur.

Self-judgments have been studied with respect to (a) attributions of success or failure (Forgas, Bower, & Moylan, 1990), (b) personal judgments such as health status and life satisfaction (Forgas & Moylan, 1987; Salovey & Birnbaum, 1989), and (c) expectations or predictions of future activities (Gilbert & Wilson, 2000). As cognitive behavioral therapists note, individuals who are currently sad are self-depreciating in that they are more likely to attribute failures to personal factors, such as their ability or effort, and successes to external factors, such as good luck or the kindness of others. When we're in a happy mood, these attribution patterns are reversed: We take credit for successes but think that failures are due to situational factors (Forgas et al., 1990). This attributional pattern is also observed in our acceptance or rejection of personal feedback from others. When we are happy, we accept positive and reject negative feedback, whereas when we are sad, we accept negative but reject positive feedback (Esses, 1989). This means that depressed clients are less likely to notice their successes or, if they do, they are more likely to attribute those successes to situational factors. Thus, techniques that challenge negative beliefs (e.g., McMullin, 2000; A. Wells, 2000) will be less efficacious with depressed clients, as such clients won't attribute the successes that are recalled to themselves to the same degree that they own their failures. We are also likely to judge ourselves as more prosocial when we are happy and more antisocial when we are sad, even in situations where objective observers can detect no difference in our behavior (Forgas, Bower, & Krantz, 1984). We predict more positive outcomes, both for ourselves (Kavenaugh & Bower, 1985) and for the world in general (W. F. Wright & Bower, 1992), when we are in a happy mood. These effects may be due to mood-congruent priming that influences the examples we think of to answer such judgment questions. Whatever the cause, it appears that hope for the future is stronger when we are happy and weaker when we need it most, that is, when we are sad or depressed. Thus, it appears that the neutrality and accuracy of feedback is compromised by mood and must be accounted for at times in therapy. For example, a client referred for interpersonal problems at work reports that generally he is a positive and happy person although he has received feedback from supervisors and coworkers that he is intruding inappropriately into others' personal space (e.g., standing too close for their comfort, asking personal questions about their sexual relationships, etc.). He rejected all feedback by asserting, "Once they get to know me better, they will understand I'm just being friendly, and things will be okay." He maintained this position even in the face of threats of disciplinary action by his supervisor. While there were serious underlying personality issues to address, a major part of the therapy was to assist this client to accept and act on the feedback he received, attributing it to himself, rather than to others or the situation.

Beyond ourselves, we also rate our satisfaction with many types of things higher when we are happy. When happy, we are more satisfied with our possessions (Isen et al., 1978), our lives (Forgas & Moylan, 1987), and our health status (Salovey & Birnbaum, 1989) than when we are in more neutral or negative moods. This mood-congruent satisfaction also extends to our memories of other people. Lewinsohn and Rosenbaum (1987) studied depressed clients over three years, noting that they recalled their parents as rejecting and unloving during depressive episodes but as more loving and nurturant when they were not depressed.

Our judgments of other people, including attributions we make about them, are also influenced by our mood. In the study of Forgas et al. (1984), for instance, happy participants judged other people's behavior, as well as their own, as more prosocial. We are apt to judge strangers more critically when we are in a sad (relative to happy) mood (R. Baron, 1987; Forgas & Bower, 1987), especially when their descriptions present a complex profile (e.g., they are described as "warm and moody"; Erber, 1991), or they appear atypical in some way (e.g., Forgas & Moylan, 1991). For example, sad mood induction increases the negativity of ethnic and other social stereotypes (Esses, Haddock, & Zanna, 1993; Forgas & Fiedler, 1996; see chapter 8), whereas mood intensity (both happy and sad) increases our ratings of our own social group (e.g., we are more likely to rate our own group as smarter or more socially skilled). These effects on person attribution, however, are not observed when there are clear social consequences of such assessment, such as when we are selecting classmates as potential task partners (e.g., Forgas, 1991b; Weary, Marsh, & McCormick, 1994). The careful choice of words to focus on the positive in solution-focused therapies and the more recent description of a "possibility approach" to therapy (e.g., O'Hanlon & Beadle, 1999) are helpful in avoiding priming negative emotion and the subsequent influence of emotion on judgments about self and others.

Our mood also influences how we interact with others. For instance, we most readily accept information that is congruent with our current mood. We are more disposed to accept persuasive messages (Bless, 2000; Razran, 1940) and more inclined to be helpful (Isen & Levin, 1972; Lay, Waters, & Park, 1989) when we are happy. Mood also influences how we word requests for assistance (Forgas, 1999a, 1999b), framing our utterances more directly when we are happy and more cautiously and politely when we are sad. Mood influences our response to requests from others in a similar manner (Forgas, 1998a). It also alters the negotiation strategies we plan and use, with more cooperative and integrative strategies predominating when we are happy and more competitive strategies used when we are sad (R. Baron, 1990; Berkowitz, 1993; Carnevale & Isen, 1986; Forgas, 1998b). Of particular relevance for family therapists is evidence that moods also influence naturalistic judgments of interpersonal relationships (e.g., how friendly or helpful your bank teller is) and the attributions people make about conflicts with intimate others (Forgas, Levinger, & Moylan, 1994). These findings of the influence of mood on negotiation plans and behavior should be of particular interest to therapists involved in mediation. For instance, clients involved in such processes are likely to be in a negative mood because most situations requiring mediation are negative (e.g., divorce, workplace conflicts). Thus, clients' negotiation strategies may be more competitive than they would be if the clients were in a more positive mood. In cases where this is problematic, mediation therapists could consider using techniques to improve their clients' moods prior to beginning a negotiation, such as meeting in beautiful locations, providing food, and the like (Thayer, 1996; see mood regulation section later in this chapter). This evidence also supports the use of mood induction strategies in therapy sessions (e.g., starting sessions with stories of success or positiveness, using a sense of humor to induce laughter). Humor as a factor in psychotherapy has begun to receive some attention for its potential psychological and physical benefits (e.g., Association for Applied and Therapeutic Humor, www.aath.org; Fry & Salameh, 1993; Salovey, Rothman, Detweiller, & Steward, 2000; but see R. A. Martin, 2001, for a critique).

Emotion does not always bias our judgments, however. Forgas (1995a) observed that moods influence our judgments most strongly in two contrasting situations: (a) when the judgment is not personally important and is performed quickly, and (b) when considerable processing and reasoning are necessary. He developed the affect infusion model to provide an integrative explanation of these observations. According to this model, emotion and thoughts combine to influence reasoning either when judgments are performed heuristically or when considerable effort and retrieval of information from memory is required. For heuristic judgment, our current mood serves as a readily accessible type of information, and is used, sometimes mistakenly, as an indication of our opinion about the judgment in question (Schwarz & Clore, 1983, 1988). As discussed in chapters 5 and 12, when information is accessed easily, it can inflate our confidence in our own reasoning or judgment. For more substantive processing, conversely, retrieval of information is susceptible to affect infusion via mood-congruent retrieval, and this information is then used in the reasoning process, biasing the result. The latter suggests that the detailed processing involved in therapy may increase clients' mood-congruent judgments of both themselves and others, which could possibly exacerbate clients' issues. Therapists with knowledge of these processes can mitigate potential negative effects by balancing this effect with another intervention or technique. For example, a client told several negative stories about her mother and ended by calling her "a bitch." The therapist asked about positive experiences the client had had with her mother and then assisted the client to redefine the problem space to some aspects of her relationship with her mother rather than the whole relationship. This assisted the client to see the relationship issues as specific and situational rather than global and overwhelming. This fits with the teachings of many brief therapies (e.g., see Hoyt, 2003), that is, to develop objectives and goals that are clear and achievable.

According to the affect infusion model, affect will have no influence on judgments when the judgment is a familiar one and can be directly retrieved from memory, or when the problem-solving process and the types of relevant information are well defined. Consistent with this conception, mood influences our interpretation of ambiguous stimuli (e.g., an unfamiliar person), for which we would have little prior information (Eysenck, MacLeod, & Mathews, 1987; Isen et al., 1978), but it has no effect on unambiguous stimuli (e.g., a friend), for which the judgment would be easily retrieved from memory. In other words, the influence of mood is subtle and can only be observed when stronger processes such as perception or memory do not influence judgment.

Cognitive Style

Affect apparently influences both what we think (i.e., content of thoughts) and how we think (i.e., our cognitive style, the types of processes and strategies we use; Bower & Forgas, 2000). Specifically, people in positive moods show more heuristic, superficial, and integrative processing strategies, leading to more creative, flexible, and inclusive solutions in problem-solving situations. People in negative moods, conversely, use more analytic and vigilant processing strategies, producing more conservative and predictable solutions (e.g., Bless & Fiedler, 1995; H. C. Ellis & Ashbrook, 1988; Isen, Means, Partick, & Nowicki, 1982; Tucker, Vannatta, & Rothlind, 1990). One characterization of this difference is that happiness promotes knowledge-driven thinking (based on memory of previous experiences), whereas negative moods promote data-driven thinking (based on current input; Bless, 2000; Fiedler, 2000). For example, when in a happy mood, people are more influenced by stereotypes and heuristic influences such as group category membership in making judgments, whereas when they are in a sad mood, they are influenced more by individuating information (Bless, Schwarz, & Wieland, 1996; Bodenhausen, Kramer, & Susser, 1994; J. A. Edwards & Weary, 1993; Forgas & Fiedler, 1996). These effects also extend to social influence, in that people in a sad mood are influenced more by the quality of persuasive arguments, whereas those in a happy mood are more influenced by heuristics such as consensus information (Bohner, Crow, Erb, & Schwarz, 1993) or their own prior judgments (Sinclair & Mark, 1992).

There are several alternative explanations for this pattern, including lateralized neurological specializations (Tucker et al., 1990), the functional relevance of previous knowledge in benign versus problematic situations (Bless, 2000), or strategic effort deployment to maintain the current mood (Isen, 1987). In a model similar to that of Bless (2000), Fiedler (2000) asserts that these effects, as well as mood-congruent memory, are observed because positive mood biases exploratory processing/behavior, whereas negative mood promotes avoidance processing/behavior (see Shah & Higgins, 2001, for a parallel dispositional model). Exploratory behavior, which is observed in appetitive situations, is curiosity-driven and weights novel information seeking more highly than error avoidance. Avoidance behavior, observed in aversive situations, aims instead for error avoidance and optimal performance. Fiedler (2000) has successfully tested these assumptions with a computational model that simulates both the memory congruence and cognitive style effects that are observed in human performance. These processes may partially explain the puzzle of the difference between clients' feelings, actions, and thoughts in the therapy setting and the way they experience and express their moods in their home environments. Therapists often notice that in the therapy office a client can demonstrate exploratory and novel behaviors, whereas they fall back into the error avoidance of familiar but dysfunctional patterns in other environments.

Although evidence of affective influence on cognitive style is reliable, as with the other effects, the influence can be overcome by other demands of a task (Forgas, 1995b), such as when a task is preceded by strong accuracy instructions. It can also be overshadowed by individual differences such as our need for approval or Type A behavior (Rusting, 1998; S. M. Smith & Petty, 1995), which biases the types of information we would routinely seek.

The evidence that moods can influence our judgments and our manner of processing should be part of therapists' metacognitive knowledge (see chapter 12). Given that emotion affects judgment mainly in mood-congruent ways, especially when we are not aware of our emotions, it is useful for the therapist to employ skills of empathy and probing to bring a level of awareness to emotional processes and a level of consciousness to judgments clients may make. These findings apply to both therapist and client and suggest that therapists' judgments of their clients and their work will be biased by their own mood, especially when their attention is focused outside themselves, as it would typically be during sessions. This could be particularly problematic for assessment or treatment planning judgments. This is an important rationale for the admonition against working with clients whom therapists don't respect or like in some manner: Interaction with such individuals will likely influence the therapists' mood, and therefore their judgments of the client, negatively. At the very least, awareness of such mood-biasing effects can protect against undue consequences, at least to some degree (see Berkowitz, Jaffee, Jo, & Troccoli, 2000, for evidence that such processes often result in overcompensation). Similarly, therapists' moods can influence the types of interventions they consider, focusing on creative solutions to a client's issues when they are happy versus focusing on avoiding risks to themselves or their client when their mood is more negative.

THE EFFECT OF COGNITION ON EMOTION: APPRAISAL AND REGULATION

In the previous section, we examined the influence of emotional experience on cognitive processes and outcomes. In this section, we examine the reverse: the role of thoughts on emotional experiences. This issue has been studied with respect to two issues: (a) the role of cognitive appraisals on the valence and intensity of emotional experience, and (b) the use of metacognition to regulate emotional experience. The interest in the mediating role of thought on emotion has been a direct focus for cognitive behavioral therapy (CBT) from its inception, and is the primary basis of CBT treatments for affective disorders (e.g., A. Wells, 2000). However, this is also an implicit assumption of emotion-focused therapies, such as that of

Greenberg and his colleagues (L. S. Greenberg & Paivio, 1997; L. S. Greenberg, Rice, & Elliot, 1993) and gestalt therapy (Perls, 1969; Polster & Polster, 1973). For example, after identifying and intensifying a client's emotional experience, these therapies explore associated thoughts via techniques such as two-chair dialogue or psychodrama, in order to alter the emotional experience by reformulating the problem space (see chapter 2).

Appraisal

Although emotion and cognition are largely independent processing systems (Zajonc, 2000), they interact in most situations. For example, many affective scientists are convinced that one's emotional reaction and its intensity are mediated by cognitive appraisals of a situation, such as how an event impacts on one's goals (Blascovich & Mendes, 2000; Forgas, 1998b). Appraisal theorists conceptualize emotions as responses to one's evaluation of the implications a current situation has for one's goals or well-being. The goal of appraisal theory is to comprehensively model how emotions are generated, and several precise theories of appraisal–affect pairings have been tested (C. A. Smith & Kirby, 2000), using retrospective recall (e.g., Fridja, Kuipers, & ter Schure, 1989), participants' response to hypothetical vignettes (e.g., C. A. Smith & Lazarus, 1993), and ongoing experiences (e.g., C. A. Smith & Kirby, 2000). Much of the content of CBT focuses on clients observing, managing, challenging, and changing their appraisal systems or schemas with the goal of altering emotions in the process, hopefully without having to address them directly.

Appraisal theorists (and many other observers) have noted that emotions are not generated in a strict stimulus–response fashion, as different individuals react to the same situation differently, and the same individual will respond to similar situations differently at different times. Emotional responses, rather, seem to be simultaneously sensitive to both environmental circumstances and the current state of an individual, including her goals, desires, abilities, and beliefs (R. S. Lazarus, 1991; C. A. Smith & Kirby, 2000) or, as appraisal theorists frame it, to the appraisal of what the circumstances imply for the individual's well-being. The identification of very specific stimulus–affect pairings means that a mood or emotion can communicate very rich information about how an environmental stimulus has been interpreted. Although the details of these appraisal–affect pairings differ across appraisal models (e.g., Frijda, 1986; Roseman, 1984; Scherer, 1984; C. A. Smith & Ellsworth, 1985; C. A. Smith & Lazarus,

1990), all involve evaluation of two types of factors: the consistency of the situation with one's goals, and evaluation of one's own and others' involvement in the situation, including one's ability to cope with the circumstances. The evaluation of whether a situation is conducive to achieving or maintaining one's goals distinguishes between positive and negative emotions, whereas the latter evaluation determines the precise emotion that is experienced and the intensity of that emotion. For example, if a person judges that a situation is inconsistent with his goals, he will experience a negative emotion (e.g., sadness, fear, anger). If he further judges that his resources for coping with the situation are inadequate, he will experience fear. Whether the intensity of that fear is high (panic) or low (anxiety) depends on the precise evaluation of the magnitude of the danger, and the person's assessed ability to respond to it. Similar precise equations have been developed for most of the emotions that are relevant to psychotherapists (see the specific models for more details; e.g., Frijda, 1986; Roseman, 1984; Scherer, 1984; C. A. Smith & Ellsworth, 1985; C. A. Smith & Lazarus, 1990). For example, a client referred for treatment of anxiety described that, since he was a small child, he had been unable to watch scenes on television shows or movies in which someone was embarrassed or humiliated. He stated, "I know logically that I'm not immediately at risk, but I can't help thinking after I see something that it could happen to me and then I start to worry." His tendency to appraise these scenes as possible and his assessment that "I couldn't handle it" meant that viewing embarrassment happening to others had a personal impact on him and resulted in high levels of anxiety. Theoretically, appraisal theory integrates both the dimensional and categorical model of emotions.

The description in the previous paragraph implies that appraisals involve effortful conscious deliberations, but this is not necessarily the case. It is clear that emotions can be evoked very quickly, often without awareness of the stimulus that elicited it, and thus such evaluations must occur more automatically (Izard, 1993; Zajonc, 1980), at least some of the time. Most appraisal theorists assume that such evaluations can be accomplished rapidly and automatically (e.g., Arnold, 1960; Leventhal & Scherer, 1987). For example, therapists working with couples and families frequently have to attend to these seemingly automatic and ritualized appraisals that lead to intense distress and conflict. These self-reinforcing, repetitive patterns are often described as part of a recursive cybernetic feedback loop or as "circular causality" (L. L. Hecker, Mims, & Boughner, 2003), in which the actions, words, or expressions of both partners set off a reciprocal reaction in the other. A client who appraised her husband's insecurity as control deliberately set out to do more of the behaviors that distressed him; this led to rageful conflicts. The therapist began by deconstructing the feedback loop and assisted the clients in determining the accuracy of their appraisals prior to developing an action plan for change.

At this level, appraisal theory is not strongly related to cognitive science, except in the global sense that such evaluations are thoughts, generated by the processes discussed in previous chapters (e.g., attention, memory, reasoning, or categorization). However, a recent process model of appraisal (C. A. Smith & Kirby, 2000) integrates these theories more closely with cognitive processes. Smith et al. posit the existence of "appraisal detectors" that are attuned to information that is relevant to one's well-being, much as visual neurons are sensitive to specific patterns of light activation from the retina. These detectors monitor perceptual input (external input from sense organs and internal sensations such as pain), memory representations that have been associatively activated, and the output of more effortful reasoning processes. We will not describe the details of this model other than to note that it incorporates and integrates both associative memory processes (see chapter 3) and reasoning processes (see chapters 9 & 10) to account for both automatic and conscious appraisal effects. One feature of this model that is particularly relevant for psychotherapy is the hypothesis that appraisals that have previously been made or modified using reasoning are stored in long-term memory as associates of the relevant experience. Thus, if similar circumstances are subsequently encountered, such complex appraisals can be associatively activated, leading to automatic emotional arousal that initially required complex appraisal reasoning. Thus, fewer situational cues are necessary to evoke a specific, even complex, emotion. This process could underlie the value of historical interpretations such as those of psychodynamic or humanistic therapies. The similarity between a current and historical situation may not be immediately evident, because the emotion is automatically evoked through associative processes, so it could have arisen through input of sensory or conceptual information that had not reached the level of awareness. In this case, therapeutic reframing or interpretation could be very useful, especially in allowing reassessment of the differences between current and historical situations.

These theories model emotional experience as dependent on cognitive judgments and indicate that feelings thus contain rich information, due to the specific appraisal–affect pairings. For example, if a client feels angry, this means that she has assessed a situation as not conducive to her goals in some way and has further judged that someone else is responsible for the situation being as it is (e.g., Berkowitz, 1993). Many therapeutic techniques make use of this informational value of emotion, integrating the expression of advanced empathy with probes about the appraisals, in order to bring such processing into the focus of attention (e.g., L. S. Greenberg & Paivio, 1997).

The appraisal models of emotion generation bear a family resemblance to prototype theories of emotion (Hogan, 2003; Oatley & Johnson-Laird, 1996). These theories describe prototypical narrative structures for each category of emotion. For example, the prototypical scenario for sadness is the loss of a loved one. Prototype theories similarly ascribe emotion generation to cognitive processes, in this case, the recognition and retrieval of relevant schemas from memory. At this stage of research, the similarities and differences between prototype and appraisal theories have not been explored, but it is likely that the two are mutually consistent, and their integration will provide greater understanding of the mental representation of emotion-evoking scenarios and how these representations operate to cause the wide range of human emotional experience.

These theories of the cognitive influence on emotion generation, especially models that suggest the contribution of associative memory retrieval, provide a rich source of possible therapeutic interventions for emotion control. Specifically, if primed material in memory influences emotion appraisal, then memories associated with particular emotions can be either strategically avoided or encouraged. For example, clients with anxiety disorders could be encouraged to avoid fearful stimuli such as horror movies or murder mystery novels, in favor of recreational fictional experiences more related to happiness or contentment. Or, a client with violent, jealous, and angry outbursts could be encouraged to avoid violent and conspiracy-driven movies. Since the 1970s, there have been numerous recommendations for the use of bibliotherapy and other self-help resources to assist clients in either learning about the issues they present or learning alternative behaviors or interpretations relevant to their problems (e.g., Campbell & Smith, 2003; Gregory, Canning, Lee, & Wise, 2004; Joshua & DiMenna, 2000; Norcross et al., 2000; but for a critique see Rosen & Glascow, 2003).

Regulation

Humans are not simply passive recipients of their emotional reactions, but rather active participants seeking to regulate their mood: maximizing the duration and frequency of positive moods and emotions while minimizing negative emotions (Gilbert & Wilson, 2000; Larsen & Prizmic, 2004). Because affect regulation is often a goal (or at least a subgoal) of therapy, psychotherapists are experts in such management techniques.

Affect regulation refers to the processes by which a person influences what moods and emotions they experience or express. Such strategies are a natural component of human processing and begin to develop early in infancy (e.g., Campos, Campos, & Barrett, 1989; Gaensbauer, 1982). All cultures have social norms regarding constraints on emotional expression (and implicitly, emotional experience), and most of us therefore learn affect management strategies over the course of childhood (Bower & Forgas, 2000). Affect regulation processes include both controlled/conscious strategies, such as changing a conversational topic to defuse emotion, and automatic/unconscious processes, such as diverting one's attention from an upsetting scene (Mayer & Salovey, 1995; Parrott, 1993). It can therefore occur either in or out of awareness. In either case, it relies on cognitive processing to manipulate our internal or external environment. Conscious affect regulation is essentially problem solving, with emotion regulation as the goal state and the various strategies as potential operators (see chapter 2). Defense mechanisms, as discussed by psychoanalytic theorists, are examples of affect regulation strategies that usually operate out of our awareness.

One source of evidence for mood regulation is the observation of mood-incongruent effects for negative mood conditions in mood-congruent memory and judgment studies (Erber & Erber, 1994; Forgas, 1991a; Parrott, 1993; Sedikides, 1995), in which participants induced into negative moods report positive memories or judgments. This has been widely attributed to mood repair: Participants notice their bad mood and actively take steps to move their mood in a more positive direction (e.g., S. M. Smith & Petty, 1995). Spontaneous efforts in this regard include attentional direction (such as focusing on external rather than internal stimuli; Nolan-Hoeksema & Morrow, 1993), memory retrieval (deliberately retrieving positive memories; Boden & Baumeister, 1997; Josephson, Singer, & Salovey, 1996; Parrott & Sabini, 1990), or voluntary stimulus selection (exposing oneself to enjoyable stimuli; Aspinwall & Taylor, 1997). Furthermore, the mood-congruent nature of our attributional style also tends to defend positive affect, in that we more often attribute failure to external factors and success to personal factors, thereby reducing ego-threat (Achee, Tesser, & Pilkington, 1994; Baumgardner & Arkin, 1988).

Gross (1998) outlined five general strategies used to regulate emotions (see also Larsen & Prizmic, 2004): situation selection, situation modification, attention deployment, cognitive change (or reinterpretation), and response modulation. Each of these is very familiar to psychotherapists, as all are used as specific therapeutic techniques. All are examples of using thought processes, especially attention and problem solving, to influence our emotional experience.

Situation selection refers to avoiding or seeking out particular locations, people, or events, such as avoiding a work colleague that we find upsetting or seeking out a friend for support (Aspinwall & Taylor, 1997). This strategy is actively used by CBT therapists who coach their clients about situations or stimuli they should seek or avoid (Kanfer & Gaelick, 1986; Lewinsohn, Munoz, Youngren, & Zeiss, 1986). Either avoiding or seeking out situations can, of course, be effective or dysfunctional strategies. Therapists working with clients with PTSD attend closely to symptoms of avoidance (e.g., J. G. Allen, 2001), and couples therapists help couples adjust to the dance of avoidance and pursuit that is so common in relationships (e.g., Gottman, 1994). Situation modification is similar, except that one attempts to change a given situation in order to reduce its emotional impact, rather than avoid it completely. For instance, when someone is unable to travel to the location of an important meeting, the meeting could be conducted by telephone, thereby avoiding the negative consequences of missing the meeting. Examples of this strategy are common in the literature on problem-focused coping (e.g., R. S. Lazarus & Folkman, 1984).

Attention deployment involves selecting which aspect of a situation one focuses on (Mischel & Ayduk, 2004). It is the first affect-regulation strategy that appears in infancy (Rothbart, Ziaie, & O'Boyle, 1992), and most parents readily use this method, especially distraction, to modify the moods of their infants. By age six, children are able to use this strategy themselves (Rodriguez et al., 1989). To modify emotional experience, our attention can be directed away from an undesired emotional stimulus and toward a desired one (distraction & concentration) or toward the feeling itself (rumination). To distract ourselves, we can focus on a nonemotional aspect of the situation (Nix, Watson, Pyszczynski, & Greenberg, 1995) or on a different situation entirely (Derryberry & Rothbart, 1988). Furthermore, we can also use this method to change our internal focus, shifting attention away from unsolvable goals to solvable ones (McIntosh, 1996), or halting undesirable trains of thought ("Don't go there") and seeking preferable ones (Boden & Baumeister, 1997; Josephson et al., 1996). The latter techniques are particularly familiar in psychotherapy: Shifting attention to solvable goals is the main strategy of solution-focused therapies (de Shazer, 1988; O'Hanlon & Weiner-Davis, 1989), and controlling one's thoughts to accomplish mood goals is one of the primary techniques of CBT (e.g., thought stopping; Meichenbaum, 1985; thought countering techniques; McMullin, 2000; challenging one's negative assumptions; A. Ellis, 2002). Concentration is very similar to this, except that one's attention is maintained on a single activity, either a desired one such as a hobby (to shift mood; Erber & Tesser, 1992) or on emotional triggers to evoke a particular emotion (as in method acting; Wegner & Bargh, 1998). Directing one's attention to feelings themselves is often called rumination, and this increases the intensity of emotional experience (Borkovec, Roemer, & Kinyon, 1995; Just & Alloy, 1997). Rumination can be either problematic or beneficial, because sometimes the way out of a distressing feeling is to get more into it, as illustrated by mindfulness techniques of postmodern and constructivist therapies (Bishop et al., 2004; Mahoney, 2003) and person-centered strategies and techniques of focusing (Gendlin, 1996).

Gross (1998) terms his next strategy *cognitive change*, but we consider that all of these strategies involve cognition, and so we will discuss it as reinterpretation. This strategy, also a common one in psychotherapy, involves changing the meaning attached to a situation by modifying one's evaluation or appraisal of it. For example, when Langer, Janis, and Wolfer (1975) had patients think of their postsurgical hospital stay as a vacation away from the stress of daily life, the patients showed better recovery than patients who did not reframe their situation this way. Therapeutic techniques such as reframing (Carver, Lawrence, & Scheier, 1996) or redecision (Goulding & Goulding, 1979) are direct examples of reinterpretation. Automatic mood-regulation processes, such as the psychodynamic defense mechanisms of denial and intellectualization or the tendency to interpret events more positively than they deserve (S. E. Taylor & Armor, 1996), are also examples of reinterpretation. Reappraisal of a situation, mentally altering it to reduce its emotional impact (Dandoy & Goldstein, 1990), is more successful with complex situations than with events that automatically trigger emotional arousal (Stemmler, 1997); this is consistent with the assertions of Forgas' (1995a) affect infusion model.

The final strategy, response modulation, is used after an emotion has already been evoked. This involves modifying one's expression of the response tendencies associated with that emotion (Gross & Levinson, 1997). Anger management strategies often involve response modulation, as the person chronically experiences anger and his difficulty arises through its inappropriate expression (e.g., McKay & Rogers, 2000). Recent research suggests that there may be cognitive costs for using this regulation strategy relative to the others (Richards & Gross, 2000; Wegner, 1994; see chapter 14). Specifically, people who actively suppress facial, verbal, and musculoskeletal emotional behaviors show memory impairment for stimuli experienced during that time, perhaps due to the attentional demand associated with withholding prepotent behavior.

Thayer (1996) similarly outlined several strategies for regulating our mood, including social interaction with friends and family; distracting ourselves from the issue, using such things as music, hobbies, and exercise; controlling our thoughts about the issue; and engaging in problem solving to address the cause of our bad mood. Participants in Thayer's studies also reported using less desirable options such as consuming mood-modifying drugs (e.g., caffeine, alcohol) and food (e.g., sugar). Although moods and emotions differ in several respects (e.g., Gross, 1998), the methods we use to regulate them are quite similar.

CONCLUSION

This chapter provided a brief review of several streams of research investigating the mutual interactions between cognitive and emotional processes and outcomes. Emotion biases most cognitive processes in mood-congruent ways. However, these effects are subtle and often rely on specific conditions such as intense emotions that are either the focus of attention (memory congruence) or not in awareness (judgment congruence). Emotion also apparently biases the type of cognitive processing we are likely to use, with positive moods supporting creative, knowledge-based processing and negative moods evoking more conservative, stimulus-based processing. Cognition also influences emotional experience, especially through the processes of appraisal and affect regulation.

All of these findings are potentially useful to psychotherapeutic practice. Mood-congruent findings, for example, can increase our understanding of how clients' reports of and judgments about their issues can be influenced by their current emotional state (or can minimize our misattribution of such effects when the specific conditions are absent). This understanding can then be used both to avoid erroneous attributions about causes or contributors to the clients' problems and to design interventions that alter the clients' thoughts about their situation. The findings of emotional influence on problem-solving style and solutions can similarly increase therapists' awareness of potential mood-based strategies to shift clients' processing toward either greater creativity or more careful attention to detail, whichever is necessary. Affect regulation strategies are already used widely in therapeutic interventions, but a firmer understanding of how specific cognitive processes, such as attention, reasoning, and cognitive control, operate can increase the effective use of such techniques.

Each of these integrative cognitive-affective processes also influences therapists' own processing. Thus, therapists should remain alert to the possible biasing effects of their own mood state on their learning, recollection, and judgment of their clients. Furthermore, therapists could also make creative use of mood-influencing effects on problem-solving style to improve their own range of therapeutic reasoning, by manipulating their own moods using affect-regulation processes in a manner similar to the way they would with clients. As we have argued in previous chapters, knowledge provides power, and firmer understanding of the ways that thoughts and emotions influence each other is potentially one of the most important bases of power for therapeutic change.

KEY POINTS

- Emotion is a collection of processes including organized physiological, cognitive, and experiential systems. It functions to provide rapid and flexible response to situations, especially those related to one's goals.
- Emotion can be conceptualized as both dimensional (i.e., valence & arousal) and categorical (joy, fear, anger, etc.).
- Emotion influences many cognitive processes including attention, memory, and judgment, usually biasing processing in a mood-congruent manner.
- Appraisal theory posits that cognition also influences emotion, because our interpretation of a given situation will influence our belief about how that situation influences our goals.
- We regulate our emotions using cognitive processes including selective attention, reminiscence, and metacognition.

14

Catharsis or Containment: Inhibition and Health

Psychologists have a long history of interest in inhibition, the active suppression of a behavior, thought, or feeling. Whether, or under what conditions, inhibition is problematic or beneficial is not clear. In the clinical world, inhibition has often been considered a negative tendency, resulting in psychological problems due to nonexpression of the inhibited emotion, thought, or behavior (Pennebaker, 1997; Polivy, 1998).[1] For example, suppression of one's memory for a traumatic event in childhood has been associated with problems such as depression and addiction (D. Brown, Scheflin, & Hammond, 1998; L. M. Williams, 1994). On the positive side, cognitive researchers have documented how necessary inhibition is to human functioning, facilitating abilities such as selective attention, decisional action, and the like (Bjorklund & Harnishfeger, 1995). Similarly, clients frequently seek out or are referred to therapists for things they wish to inhibit, including behaviors (e.g., drinking, smoking, acting out behaviors, compulsive rituals, etc.), thoughts (e.g., general worries, ruminations, obsessive thinking patterns), and uncomfortable or debilitating emotional states (e.g., anger, anxiety, sadness, and depression).

So, which is it? Is inhibition a positive or a negative force in human lives? There is empirical evidence to support both positions: Suppression of emotion experience and expression is associated with poorer mental and physical health (e.g., Smyth, 1998), and deficiencies in inhibition are associated with serious social and psychological difficulties such as schizophrenia, attention deficit hyperactivity disorder (ADHD) and obsessive-compulsive disorder (OCD; e.g., Bannon, Gonsalvez, Croft, & Boyce, 2002; Barkley, 1997; E. R. Peters et al., 2000).

Since the time of Freud, we have considered inhibition to be one of the factors that make people ill, both mentally and physically. Freud (1915/ 1957) theorized that it is our unacknowledged goals and emotions, kept out of our awareness through defense mechanisms such as repression and dissociation, that lead to psychotic and neurotic symptoms. Thus, in therapeutic terms, inhibition is a negative force, one that leads to illness. As a consequence, therapists, especially those in psychodynamic and humanistic traditions have developed methods to bring such disavowed goals and emotions into awareness, with the aim of integrating them into the person's thought, action, and life. Techniques such as projective assessment (e.g., Rorschach, Thematic Apperception Test), dream interpretation, free association, and the like were all designed to allow inhibited material to enter an individual's consciousness. Once identified, it is thought that integrating such goals and expressing such emotions will lead to the cessation of symptoms of mental distress and illness. More recently, process-experiential theorists have asserted that it is the self-regulatory value in expressing emotion more than the cathartic value that is helpful in psychotherapy (L. S. Greenberg, Rice, & Elliott, 1993). For example, a client sought therapy for assistance with depression after both his parents died, and early in therapy it became apparent that the client was actively suppressing his sadness, especially its expression. As soon as the therapist noticed a moistening in his client's eyes and a slight shift in facial color, the client would begin looking around the room, breathe loudly through pursed lips, and say, "No, mustn't lose control." Part of the therapy process was to bring these behaviors into the client's awareness, teach him about the potential benefits of crying when sad, and help him cry through the use of breathing and bodywork techniques. As in most actual therapeutic settings, it was not possible to distinguish whether it was the cathartic expression of emotion or the improvement in self-regulatory function that was more beneficial. This client stated on termination that learning he did not have to fear his emotional state was of most benefit to him.

More recently, however, cognitive researchers have observed several inhibitory phenomena in the context of cognitive tasks (see Arbuthnott, 1995, for a review), and these inhibitory processes seem to operate for our benefit. Specifically, inhibition operates to prevent distracting sources of information from impairing performance on a current goal, essentially enabling selective attention and action (see chapter 7). These inhibitory processes are discernable by examining performance related to the distracting information itself, and it is observed that such distractors are generally acted on more slowly and less accurately than are normal stimuli.

For example, when we pay attention to a client's body language, we often inhibit our perception of their words, and if our memory for the specific words that the client spoke while we were not attending to them were tested, we would likely show poorer performance than if those words had not been spoken at all (except when we are able to infer what was most likely said through extension from previously attended comments). Similarly, a process known as self-inhibition operates to reduce the activation of recently processed information, information that could result in incorrect perseveration. Essentially, once a stimulus has been processed, the representation of that stimulus is inhibited, preventing its re-processing and allowing access to later stimuli in the sequence (Arbuthnott, 1996; Arbuthnott & Campbell, 2003; Houghton, 1990; MacKay, 1986). In speech production this prevents stuttering, and in sequential memory tasks it prevents people from getting stuck on the first answer they give. So, in this tradition, inhibition is a valuable process, one that enables selective attention and efficient action to one among many possible goals. More importantly, deficient inhibition is associated with serious psychological disorders, such as schizophrenia, ADHD, and OCD.

These two contradictory views of inhibition involve suppression of the same material, such as thoughts that are kept out of awareness in order to pursue other goals effectively. So what is the actual story? Is it helpful to bring inhibited material to light and encourage its expression, or is it better to support such inhibition, allowing clients to pursue their chosen goals more effectively? Is it better to support expression or containment? How can we best help our clients to both pursue their goals and become emotionally mature, integrated individuals?

Although both of these types of research are evident in clinical publications (e.g., *Journal of Consulting and Clinical Psychology*; *Abnormal Psychology*), the two are seldom considered together. Given the somewhat contradictory evidence, it is not clear under what conditions therapists should encourage their clients to avoid inhibition or foster it. The purpose of this chapter is to review the evidence of inhibition from both perspectives and to offer some mediating considerations to guide therapists' actions with respect to inhibition.

DEFINITIONS AND DISTINCTIONS

Inhibition is the suppression of thoughts, feelings, or behaviors, and can occur either in or out of awareness. Its function is self-control to enable effective pursuit of goals, whether those goals involve a perceptual task such as selective attention or self-improvement such as controlling an addiction. Although inhibition can occur either deliberately or automatically (Consedine, Magai, & Bonanno, 2002), it is always related to our intentions in that we inhibit representations and actions that would interfere with the pursuit of a current goal. Even in the case of repression, we inhibit the troublesome emotions and thoughts so that we can function better in our current context. Inhibition can be automatic, such as inhibiting the perception of distractors to enable selective attention (e.g., focusing on one conversation in a noisy environment), or voluntary, such as when we withhold our negative reaction to a friend's new haircut, but it always serves to limit the processing or expression of material that is unrelated or contrary to one's current goals (e.g., attending to a conversation or maintaining good relations with the friend in the previous examples).

One other distinction is useful to the consideration of whether inhibition is helpful or harmful. Cognitive researchers distinguish between cognitive inhibition, the suppression of a mental representation, and behavioral inhibition, the suppression of an action (Harnishfeger, 1995). Cognitive inhibition involves suppression or reduced access to a mental representation, such as a thought or feeling.[2] One indicator of cognitive inhibition (including emotion) is verbal–autonomic dissociation (e.g., Bonanno, Znoj, Siddeque, & Horowitz, 1999), in which there is a discrepancy between an individual's report of their emotional state and physiological measures of their arousal, such as heart rate or skin conductivity. Behavioral inhibition, conversely, involves withholding or modulating (Gross, 1998) a motor action that has been prepared in the motor centers of our brain. In this case, reports and physiology would match, although neither would be indicated by the individual's observable behavior. These two types of inhibition are influenced by different personal and environmental variables, and thus are likely enabled by different cognitive mechanisms. For example, behavioral inhibition develops earlier in life than does cognitive inhibition: Infants and toddlers show behavioral inhibition such as withholding overlearned behavior when it is not rewarded (e.g., Diamond, 1991), whereas cognitive inhibition, such as being able to switch attention between tasks, does not develop until later childhood or adolescence (Pearson & Lane, 1991).

In therapeutic terms, this difference amounts to a distinction between experience and expression. With behavioral inhibition, the individual may be aware of a goal, desire, or other such information, but choose not to act on it (either voluntarily or involuntarily, as in cases where clients feel unable to act against their habitual patterns). Thus, the client would be aware of the disavowed feelings or goals, but choose to contain expressions and actions related to them. Conversely, cognitive inhibition is involved in clinically defined processes such as denial, repression, or dissociation, in which some feeling or thought is denied or not experienced. Most therapists have experienced clients who verbally report the absence of a feeling (e.g., "I'm not scared") while nonverbally demonstrating the presence of that feeling (e.g., shaky, higher pitched voice, perspiring) or clients who show neither verbal nor nonverbal indicators of an emotion when it would be expected (e.g., describing a recent sexual assault in a casual manner).

The case of traumatic memories, which individuals often react to with some form of inhibition such as dissociation or repression, is an example of cognitive rather than behavioral inhibition in that it is the thoughts of such memories or impulses that are suppressed. Cognitive evidence suggests that these processes do operate for unwelcome thoughts and feelings (M. C. Anderson & Green, 2001; chapter 15). Furthermore, when we consider the events of our lives in unconstrained circumstances, it seems that most of us have better recollection of the pleasant events of our lives than the negative occurrences (Berntsen & Rubin, 2002), and the recalled intensity of negative emotion apparently fades faster than recalled positive emotion (Walker, Rodney, & Thompson, 1997), suggesting some type of repression.

As mentioned previously, cognitive and behavioral inhibition differ in their developmental schedule (i.e., when children are able to do each): Behavioral inhibition develops in infancy, whereas cognitive inhibition develops in later childhood or adolescence. Children who receive modeling from their caregivers are better able to inhibit their behaviors when the situation calls for it (Neitzel & Stright, 2003; Vygotsky, 1991; see chapter 13). Shifting attention facilitates cognitive inhibition of an undesired thought (e.g., distraction), and while children are externally distracted by attentionally arresting stimuli early in childhood, later in their development they are able to assume independent mental control of this process. Distraction facilitates inhibition through the processes of selective attention: When we are attending to a target, other stimuli are suppressed. Thus, distracting a child or ourselves to a desired focus is accompanied by inhibition of the previous focus (e.g., Wegner, 1989). However, such strategies are not without consequences since, ironically, suppressing our thoughts of a particular object can result in an increase in those thoughts when the prohibition is lifted or when our self-control resources are limited in some way (Wegner, 1994).

Therapeutically, the discussion of inhibition often refers to the inhibition of emotional experience and expression. Cognitive scientists seldom examine emotion as the inhibitory target of their research, but there is likely little difference in inhibitory mechanisms when emotion is the target of suppression. Furthermore, emotions involve both thoughts and actions (Wenzlaff & Wegner, 1998; see chapter 13). Thus, with respect to emotions, cognitive inhibition involves the suppression of experience, whereas behavioral inhibition involves withholding the expression of an emotion. Because the functions of emotional experience and expression serve different purposes, inhibition of each likely has different consequences. Within a functional view of emotion (e.g., Johnson-Laird & Oatley, 1992; Polivy, 1998), the function of emotional experience is to indicate a relevant action or goal for the individual in his current situation. In this case, emotion provides important information to the individual. For example, sadness is experienced in response to an unrecoverable loss, and it serves to conserve the individual's energy (L. A. Clark & Watson, 1994) and alter her relationship goals (Johnson-Laird & Oatley, 1992). Expression of an emotion, on the other hand, serves more social and communication functions, such as to elicit help from our friends when we are sad (Levine, 1996). For example, redecision therapy (Goulding & Goulding, 1979) posits that children adapt to environmental demands, especially to the reactions that important figures have to the child's expressed emotions. If the parental or environmental demand is that the child inhibit or suppress an emotion, the child may make a "decision" (based on their developmental stage, abilities, resources, etc.) about how to respond in the future (adapt his expression). If the demand for inhibition is strong enough, the child may learn to suppress the emotion totally (experience). Using the example of sadness, a child may learn that the expression of sadness leads to ridicule and may learn not to express sadness (inhibiting behavior), or if the environmental demand is extreme he may not experience sadness in the future (inhibition of cognitive experience or emotion).

In part then, whether inhibition is considered beneficial or problematic depends on our view of whether emotions (or other thoughts and behaviors) are functional or dysfunctional, either absolutely or in a given context. If we view emotions as a functional means of information processing, such as a way to orient an individual to how she is doing with her current goals (Johnson-Laird & Oatley, 1992; Tooby & Cosmides, 1990) and to motivate useful actions (Polivy, 1998), then inhibition of emotions would necessarily limit her effectiveness. However, if emotions are seen as irrelevant or dysfunctional responses in most situations, related more to an individual's biochemical state than his purposes, then their suppression would be helpful for effective problem solving or action. However, even if emotional experience is useful, inhibition of expression can be functional in that it prevents others from anticipating our likely behavior, which can be beneficial in competitive social situations (Tooby & Cosmides, 1992).

The question of whether inhibition is beneficial or detrimental can be seen to underlie some of the differences between psychodynamic therapies and cognitive behavioral therapies (CBT). The psychodynamic model is based on the central assumption that inhibition, and the various defense mechanisms that support it, are unhealthy for an individual, whereas CBT often makes use of distraction and other inhibitory techniques to divert a client's attention away from a to-be-extinguished desire and toward the preferred (therapeutically contracted) behavior. Our resolution of the question of whether to support or discourage inhibition influences how we let clients tell their stories or process their difficulties. For example, those who favor inhibition of the past are disinclined to let clients discuss the past, suggesting instead that they focus their attention on the present or their current goals. In contrast, those who consider inhibition a negative influence insist that clients discuss the past, even when they do not want to. In general, most therapists discourage cognitive inhibition of emotions, desires, and goals. Psychodynamic and humanistic-experiential therapists, however, also generally discourage behavioral inhibition of emotional expression and actions related to those goals, encouraging instead creative integration of those actions into a person's life. CBT therapists, on the other hand, encourage behavioral inhibition related to undesired behaviors.

Therapists of all modalities use skills to encourage and expand a client's expression of some portion of his experience and to inhibit others. For example, dynamically oriented therapists will use probing and evocative empathy skills to encourage clients to disclose and elaborate on their earlier experiences. Similarly a narrative therapist would encourage a client to develop a structured narrative that includes the history of the problem and to develop the narrative in such a way as to lead to solutions. Cognitive behavioral or reality therapists would likely give minimal responses to such disclosures and redirect the client to the present. A solution-focused therapist would use strong encouraging skills when clients reveal strengths or solutions from prior experiences and discourage or inhibit the desire of a client to focus on the painful aspects of her experiences. The point is that all therapists of all schools are actively encouraging expression or inhibition of particular aspects of a client's experience on a moment-by-moment basis in a therapy session. The major reason for this is likely to limit the problem space definition (see chapter 2); however, it needs to be done thoughtfully and carefully so the inhibiting tendencies of the therapist do not cause problems when they do not match the needs of the client.

INHIBITION AS PROBLEMATIC

One common view among therapists is that emotion inhibition is associated with poorer mental and physical health (Consedine, Magai, & Bonanno, 2002; M. A. Greenberg & Stone, 1992). The suppression of mental representations, such as uncomfortable emotions, memories, or thoughts, is known among psychodynamic therapists as *repression* and is theorized to be the root cause of many mental illnesses. Freud (1917/1959) emphasized the dangers of repressed emotions, hypothesizing that emotional repression leads to depression, obsessive thoughts, deviant behaviors, and hysterical symptoms. Consistent with this, research indicates that emotion suppression is associated with increased rates of negative thoughts (Becker, Rinck, Roth, & Margraf, 1998) and psychological distress (Joseph et al., 1997; Lynch, Robins, Morse, & Krause, 2001; Roemer, Litz, Orsillo, & Wagner, 2001), including depression, anxiety, posttraumatic stress disorder (PTSD), and other stress disorders (Harvey & Bryant, 1998; Steil & Ehlers, 2000; Wenzlaff & Bates, 1998).[3] For example, Joseph et al. (1997) found that, among the survivors of a disastrous ferry accident, those who reported less willingness to experience emotion thirty months following the accident showed greater PTSD symptomatology five years later.

More specifically, cognitive inhibition (i.e., the suppression of mental representations or experiences) is associated with increased rumination (Janoff-Bulman, 1992), or persistently dwelling on negative feelings or thoughts. Rumination is consistently associated with poorer mental health (Nolen-Hoeksema, 1998), especially for individuals suffering from dysphoric mood (Lyubomirsky, Caldwell, & Nolen-Hoeksema, 1998; Lyubomirsky & Nolen-Hoeksema, 1995). One consequence of deliberate suppression of unwanted thoughts appears to be a rebound effect, or greater intrusion of the suppressed thought once the prohibition is removed or the control processes are compromised in some fashion, such as with fatigue or greater attentional demand (Baumeister, Bratslavsky, Muraven, & Tice, 1998; Wegner, 1994; Wenzlaff & Wegner, 1998). Furthermore, this rebound effect seems to be greater for depressed patients (Wenzlaff, Wegner, & Roper, 1988) and for those who are under stress (Wegner, Broome, & Blumberg, 1997). Wegner refers to this rebound as the ironic process of mental control, in which having the goal of avoiding certain thoughts requires a monitoring process targeted to the to-be-avoided material. For example, if I wish to avoid stressful thoughts, this monitoring process must identify potentially stressful thoughts in order to suppress them. Thus, the contents of the monitoring process are the very thoughts I wish to avoid. When mental control resources are taxed in some way, the contents of this monitor are likely to come to awareness, resulting in the observed rebound effect for suppressed material. If I wish to avoid thoughts about an impending surgery, the monitoring process must identify such thoughts. When my attentional control is taxed, such as when I am fatigued or engaged in a complex activity, the contents of this monitor will more likely come to awareness, releasing the very thoughts I wish to avoid.

Many therapies have recognized this rebound effect and have developed techniques that include attending to alternative and generally more positive thoughts and experiences rather than simply attempting to inhibit or stop attending to negative thoughts and memories and the distressing experiences that accompany them. For example, children who need to stop anxiety-triggering fantasies are encouraged to imagine their minds as televisions (radio tuners for older folks) and to "change channels" rather than "turning off the television." Therapists spend a good deal of time helping children develop a set of channels and having them practice. Also the techniques of mindfulness and meditation help clients to neutrally observe the contents of their thoughts rather than attempting to banish them. Some of the techniques of stress inoculation training (e.g., Meichenbaum, 1985) help clients to develop a sense of self-efficacy by exposing them to mild versions of very stressful possibilities so they can partially inhibit the overwhelming thoughts of catastrophe and "change the channel" to a more functional sense of self-control and self-efficacy in handling a difficult situation.

With respect to cognitive inhibition, many of our therapeutic interventions are designed to bring awareness to unrecognized (or inhibited) thoughts and feelings. For example, skills such as empathy and what used to be known as concreteness[4] are used to encourage clients to explore themselves more deeply, often with the goal of unearthing unacknowledged aspects of a situation (Egan, 1994; Rogers, 1980). Therapists of all theoretical orientations generally consider such exploration to be valuable, and so cognitive inhibition is generally considered problematic in most situations.

There is also research evidence that behavioral inhibition, especially restriction of emotional expression, is detrimental to our health (Pennebaker, 1997; Polivy, 1998), resulting in anxiety and greater vulnerability to stress-related ailments such as hypertension or respiratory difficulty (e.g., Buck, 1993). For example, restricting our behavior to eliminate un-

wanted habits such as smoking increases our emotionality and distracti-
bility (C. P. Herman & Polivy, 1988; Laessle, Platte, Schweiger, & Pirke,
1996). Self-reported expressiveness often correlates with fewer physical
symptoms (Malatesta, Jonas, & Izard, 1987), fewer visits to medical clin-
ics (Pennebaker, 1993; Pennebaker & Francis, 1996), and fewer major illnesses such as cancer (Bonanno & Singer, 1990; Gross, 1989). Similarly,
people who suppress thoughts of grief and loss have worse physical and
psychological health over time than those who do not (Folkman, Chesney,
Collette, Boccellari, & Cooke, 1996). One hypothesis is that the suppression of emotional expression is effortful (Ochsner & Gross, 2004; Polivy,
1998) and stressful (Buck, 1984), leading to greater physiological "wear
and tear" and selectively inhibiting components of the immune response
(Petrie, Booth, & Davidson, 1995), resulting in more illness over the long
term (Francis & Pennebaker, 1992; Pennebaker, 1993). Consistent with
this proposal, inhibition and rumination scores are observed to be correlated with physiological symptoms of stress, including delayed heart-rate
recovery (Roger & Jamieson, 1988), cortisol elevations (Roger & Najarian, 1998), and delayed muscle tension recovery (Kaiser, Hinton,
Krohne, Stewart, & Burton, 1995). These researchers also posit that emotions evolved for the purposes of guiding behavior and communicating
with others, so ignoring emotions is also likely to be associated with negative consequences (Polivy, 1998; Richards & Gross, 2000). From this perspective, catharsis or the intense expression of emotions is viewed as beneficial to our mental and physical health (Freud, 1923/1961). Although
research on catharsis is not unequivocal, it appears that expressing emotion reduces physiological and psychological arousal when the action is
performed in a context that includes a cognitive working-through component (L. S. Greenberg & Safran, 1987). For example, encouraging the expression of sadness and anger in relation to grief should likely include a
component of explaining or helping the client make sense of the process
and purpose of a grief reaction in addition to simply supporting emotional
expression.

Behavioral inhibition, on the other hand, is handled differently by therapists of different orientations. Techniques such as gestalt two-chair dialogues (e.g., L. S. Greenberg & Paivio, 1997), bioenergetic exercises
(Lowen, 1975), and psychodrama (Moreno, 1972) are designed to encourage expression, breaking down the barriers of behavioral inhibition. For
example, a therapist with a client whose goal is to increase assertiveness
may develop dialogues with increasingly difficult characters in gestalt
two-chair fashion or, in a psychodrama group setting, may develop a com-

plete drama of a situation, including a list of protagonists and supporting characters, so that the client can practice. But behavioral and cognitive behavioral therapies generally adopt a more conservative approach to inhibition and expression: Some action is encouraged as part of problem solving, but both cognitive (e.g., thought-countering techniques; McMullin, 2000) and behavioral inhibition (e.g., reward contingencies for abstaining from unwanted habits) are used as central parts of treatment. For example, prevention of ritual responses in OCD (Franklin & Foa, 2002) involves a client waiting until an impulse recedes.

The benefits of emotion experience and expression rather than inhibition are evidenced in the work of Pennebaker and his colleagues, who showed that expressive writing of undisclosed trauma experiences result in better physical health relative to writing about a neutral topic such as one's weekly schedule. The medical benefits of such disclosure include fewer visits to a doctor, less minor illness such as colds and flu, and less major illness such as cancer or hypertension (Pennebaker, 1997; Pennebaker & Seagal, 1999; Smyth, 1998).

INHIBITION AS BENEFICIAL

On the other side of the issue, there is evidence that cognitive, emotional, and behavioral inhibition plays a central role in mental and social health. A substantial portion of referrals for psychotherapy are for problems with impulse control, addictions, criminal and acting-out behaviors, self-harm behavior, pain management, and other areas where clients' inability or unwillingness to inhibit their behavior or cognitive experience is a major factor in their dysfunction. Some therapists argue that excessive emotional displays may be disruptive or unhealthy (Consedine, Magai, & Bonanno, 2002), because too much disclosure can result in increasing negative emotion (Afifi & Guerrero, 2000; Bushman, 2002; Larsen & Prizmic, 2004) or negative social consequences (Bonanno & Kaltman, 1999; Roloff & Ifert, 2000). The chronic experience of negative affect such as anger or sadness may cause health problems (Bonanno et al., 1999; Friedman & Booth-Kewley, 1987; Kennedy-Moore & Watson, 1999; Mayne, 1999), so if expression intensifies a person's arousal, inhibition might be preferable from a health perspective (Bonanno & Keltner, 1997; Bonanno et al., 1999; T. W. Smith, 1992). Consistent with this view, verbal–autonomic dissociation, defined as discrepancy between one's expressed affect and physiological measures of arousal, are not related to one's number of doctor visits (Consedine, Magai, & Bonanno, 2002). Similarly, people who avoid thoughts of grief and loss sometimes show lower levels of physical and distress symptoms than those who don't inhibit their grief (Bonanno & Keltner, 1997).

More generally, inhibition of culturally or situationally inappropriate behaviors is considered a mark of maturity, and children's increasing ability to withhold behaviors in response to requests is considered important to their development (e.g., adaptation to school; Neitzel & Stright, 2003). Our capacity for self-regulation, which involves at least behavioral inhibition, is undoubtedly important for adaptive success (Heatherton & Vohs, 1998; Richards & Gross, 2000) and maturity (Muraven, Tice, & Baumeister, 1998). Furthermore, some have argued that the failure to suppress impulses is central to many societal problems, including family violence, excessive debt, addiction, or road rage (Tice & Ciarocco, 1998; Vohs & Baumeister, 2004). Thus, inhibitory processes are vitally important to our social functioning.

In therapy, many of the difficulties associated with impulsivity and lack of ability or willingness to inhibit are treated in settings in which environmental controls and cues can be used to assist with the learning of self-regulatory processes. The use of self-help groups, residential treatment for addictive and eating disorders, programs for fetal alcohol syndrome, rehabilitation for brain-injured patients, and relapse prevention models are examples of treatments that include social and environmental controls to assist clients to establish, develop, and maintain stronger internal inhibitory abilities.

One example of the therapeutic use of inhibition is the process of pulse-taking during conversation between spouses in marital therapy. Specifically, clients are encouraged to take their pulse, stop conversation when a specific level is reached, and wait until their heart rate returns to normal (Gottman, 1994). Other examples of directly inhibiting emotional expression are commonly used anger management strategies such as time-out techniques (e.g., a short walk or counting to ten when feeling angry).

Perhaps most significant for the view that inhibition is beneficial, deficient inhibition is implicated in several psychiatric disorders, including schizophrenia (E. R. Peters et al., 2000; Woodward et al., 2005), ADHD (Barkley, 1997; Nigg, Butler, Huang-Pollack, & Henderson, 2002; Nyberg, Bohlin, Berlin, & Janois, 2003; Stevens, Quittner, Zuckerman, & Moore, 2002), OCD (Bannon et al., 2002; McNally, Wilhelm, Buhlmann, & Shin, 2001), anxiety (Fox, 1994), and dissociative identity disorder

(DID; Dorahy, 2001; Dorahy, Irwin, & Middleton, 2002). Some of these deficits reflect behavioral inhibition or the inability to withhold overt behavior (e.g., ADHD), whereas some reflect cognitive inhibition or the inability to control cognitive contents (e.g., schizophrenia). Some disorders, such as OCD, seem to reflect deficiencies in both types of inhibition. Some authors (e.g., Skodol & Oldham, 1996) describe symptoms of impulsivity and compulsivity as a spectrum of difficulties with inhibitory processes. At one end is extreme disinhibition where impulsivity becomes problematic, and at the other end are high levels of inhibitory processes where compulsive thoughts and behaviors keep clients trapped in a repeating loop. Prototypically, *DSM-IV-TR* diagnoses of Borderline Personality or Impulse Control Disorders Not Elsewhere Classified are at one end of the spectrum and Obsessive-Compulsive Disorders at the other end.

For these studies, cognitive inhibition is examined using a selective attention task such as the Stroop task, in which participants must ignore one aspect of a stimulus in order to respond to another aspect. The standard version of the Stroop task is to use color words (e.g., *blue, red, green*) printed in different colors of ink, and the participant is to name the ink color. For example, if the word BLUE is printed in red ink, the participant would say "red." Deficient inhibition in this task is observed as poorer performance when the word name is different than the color, shown either as more color-naming errors or slower speed in naming the correct ink color. Even more indicative of inhibition is a negative priming version of the task, in which, after suppressing BLUE, as in the previous example, the next word (e.g., GREEN) is printed in blue ink, requiring "blue" as a correct response. For most people, this situation results in poorer performance to name the color blue than when the previous word labeled some other color.

On Stroop and negative priming tasks, schizophrenics and those high in schizotypy are observed to have impaired cognitive inhibition relative to control participants (Beech & Claridge, 1987; Fox, 1994; Moritz, Mass, & Junk, 1998; E. R. Peters et al., 2000; Watson & Tipper, 1997). In the case of negative priming, this means that schizophrenics, unlike normal controls, do NOT show worse performance when naming an ink color after suppressing it on the previous trial, but this is accompanied by worse general performance when dealing with interference stimuli (i.e., worse Stroop performance) because they are less able to selectively attend to the relevant features of the task. This deficit is associated with the positive psychotic symptoms of schizophrenia, such as hallucinations, delusions, and irrelevant speech (Salo, Robertson, Nordahl, & Kraft, 1997). Similarly, patients with dissociative identity disorder (DID) show impaired inhibition in negative priming tasks, consistent with their psychotic symptoms. Within normal populations, individuals high in trait anxiety also show reduced negative priming relative to low trait-anxious participants (Fox, 1994), suggesting that anxiety is associated with impaired inhibition. OCD patients also show reduced negative priming relative to normal controls and those with other diagnoses such as panic disorder (Bannon et al., 2002; Enright & Beech, 1993; McNally et al., 2001). This reduction in cognitive inhibition is apparently related to the presence of obsessive thoughts. OCD patients, especially those showing compulsive behaviors such as handwashing, also have deficiencies in behavioral inhibition (Bannon et al., 2002).

Behavioral inhibition is measured by tasks such as the anti-saccade task. In this task, participants fixate their gaze in the middle of a screen and then move their eyes to a target (e.g., a dot) that appears to the left or right of the screen. On pro-saccade trials, the eyes are to move to the target, whereas on anti-saccade trials, the eyes are to move to the opposite side of the screen from the target. The latter involves inhibition of the habitual orienting response to changes in our visual field, and thus participants' success (measured as speed and accuracy) in this anti-saccade situation is a mark of the efficiency of their ability to withhold actions. Using this task, researchers observe worse performance for adults and children with ADHD (Castellanos et al., 2000; Nigg et al., 2002; Rosenberg et al., 1997). Another way to assess behavioral inhibition is with a stop-signal or no-go task. In these tasks, participants make a simple speeded response to a stimulus, such as pressing a button whenever a letter appears, but on some portion of trials (usually < 20%), the participants are to withhold their response, either because a no-go stimulus appears (e.g., a digit), or because a second signal such as a tone indicates that the participants are to inhibit their response on that trial (stop-signal). Using this method, ADHD clients consistently show poorer inhibition than control participants (Barkley, 1997; Nigg et al., 2002; Pliszka, Liotti, & Woldorff, 2000), as do those with OCD (Bannon et al., 2002).

Thus, deficits in the ability to inhibit either cognition or behavior is associated with severe psychological pathologies. These inhibitory deficits appear to be selective, in that ADHD children and adults do not show reduced negative priming (cognitive inhibition; Nigg et al., 2002), whereas schizophrenic patients do not show reduced behavioral inhibition. Only some groups, such as those with OCD, show deficits in both cognitive and behavioral inhibition (Bannon et al., 2002).

RESOLUTION: CONTEXTUALIZED
INHIBITORY REGULATION

Both the presence and absence of inhibition have been associated with poor mental and physical health. The inability to inhibit seems to result in several serious types of psychopathology, but chronic inhibition also seems to result in negative health consequences over the long term. Mixed evidence is present for several diverse areas, including grief and HIV/ AIDS (Consedine, Magai, & Bonanno, 2002). With respect to grief, people who suppress their grief and loss are observed to show either better (Folkman et al., 1996) or worse (Bonanno & Keltner, 1997) recovery over the long term. Similarly, children with HIV/AIDS who disclosed their situation to their friends showed increased immune function over the course of a study manipulating disclosure, but disclosers did not differ from nondisclosers at the beginning of the study, suggesting that the general tendency to disclose did not affect immune function (Sherman, Bonanno, Wiener, & Battles, 2000). These researchers suggest that this pattern indicates that, although disclosure is beneficial to immune functioning, nondisclosure may not be especially harmful.

A simple prescription to either inhibit or avoid inhibiting emotional experience and expression is thus not supported. Rather, personal and contextual factors seem to determine whether inhibition will be beneficial or problematic (Consedine, Magai, & Bonanno, 2002). Researchers are beginning to examine this more complex view of inhibition, and several factors are hypothesized to influence the consequences of inhibition, including the developmental and social characteristics of the individual, cultural views on emotion expression, and characteristics of the experience being inhibited. That is, negative health consequences as a result of inhibition may depend on our reasons for, and reactions to, inhibiting a particular experience or behavior (Gross, 1998; Kennedy-Moore & Watson, 1999). With respect to emotion inhibition, both personal and cultural factors have impact on the meaning of particular emotion expressions. This includes personally developed, familial, and culturally supported metacognitive beliefs about expressiveness and containment (see chapter 12).

A relatively early example of this more contextualized view of the relationship between inhibition and illness was articulated by Buck (1993). Buck distinguished between control exerted over our emotions for social reasons and chronic emotional suppression. The former is an essential aspect of human social interactions and is not generally harmful to health as long as expression is possible in some contexts and with some people

(Buck, 1984). Buck emphasized the importance of self-regulation, which requires emotional competence, that is, the ability to respond in an appropriate and satisfactory way with our feelings and desires. Such competence is accomplished initially through communication of, and education about, emotions in childhood. A child's communication of her emotional experiences is perceived by her caregivers and, if education proceeds appropriately, the caregiver teaches the child to understand her emotions, both correctly labeling the sensations and choosing actions that appropriately satisfy the needs signaled by her emotions. This emotional communication then forms the basis for emotional competence throughout life, with contact with others providing both the impetus for inhibition of expression when socially appropriate and expression when the situation is available.

However, if emotional education is deficient, resulting in either a mislabeling of felt emotions or learning to withhold emotions under all conditions, emotional arousal will result in stress. Stress causes changes to our autonomic, endocrine, and immune systems, contributing to cardiovascular disease (Dembrowski, MacDougall, Williams, Haney, & Blumenthal, 1985), cancer (Grossarth-Matticek, Bastiaans, & Kanzin, 1985; Pettigale, 1985), and other stress-related illnesses (C. D. Anderson, 1981), and simultaneously impairing our ability to cope with such illnesses. Buck's (1993) view is that both too much and too little expression is detrimental to effective emotional communication, and thus he advises the judicious use of both inhibition and expression. Although Buck's discussion most centrally applies to behavior inhibition, in some circumstances the best means to accomplish such containment of urges is to practice cognitive inhibition as well, such as when we distract ourselves from grief by concentrating on a work project. These and related ideas about the inhibition and expression of emotion have been presented in the popular literature as emotional intelligence (e.g., Goleman, 1995), emotional literacy (e.g., Ladd, 2003; Steiner, 1996), and the like.

Given that inhibition is an essential aspect of social interaction, Consedine, Magai, and Bonanno (2002) further specify the important conditions for determining whether inhibition will be harmful or helpful to an individual. Individual characteristics, such as personal preferences and ethnicity, are proposed to play a role in the relationship between inhibition and health. Consistent with Buck's (1993) view, individuals who are chronically inhibited in their expression seem to benefit more from disclosure than less inhibited individuals (Derryberry & Rothbart, 1997). However, both a person's comfort with his level of expressivity and the meaning a particular act of expression or inhibition has for him seem to influence stress reactivity (Kennedy-Moore & Watson, 1999; Roloff & Ifert, 2000). The evidence suggests that the match between the level of expression and one's preferred expressivity is important, in that physiological arousal is observed to be greatest for expression that does not match one's preference by being either too constrained or too intense (Engebretson, Matthews, & Scheier, 1989). Consequently, if the demands of a situation or our own goals do not match our own usual style of expressivity or containment, we will experience ambivalence and stress. In other words, stress results more from ambivalence about suppressing or expressing a given experience than from the thought or action itself (King & Emmonds, 1990; Pennebaker, 1998). If we are ambivalent—perhaps because previous expression of a behavior was sometimes rewarded and sometimes punished—suppression requires much more effort than if we unequivocally desire to suppress the behavior. A simple example is that individuals who are trying to break a habit that was enjoyable, such as smoking, will be more ambivalent about avoiding smoking than those who had never smoked (i.e., never enjoyed cigarettes). Therapists are often privy to the strong ambivalence clients have toward expressing thoughts or feelings. For example, a client referred for therapy for depression began to tell stories about his mistreatment at the hands of his father. He voiced his ambivalence by directly saying, "I want to talk about this, I think I need to . . . but every time I start I feel like I'm betraying my family and I remember my dad saying, 'Don't air your dirty linen in public.' " The strong ambivalence can also be demonstrated nonverbally with clients' struggling to say anything or showing symptoms of a stress response. This greater effort to accomplish suppression is hypothesized to result in greater physical and mental ill health than inhibiting behaviors about which we are less ambivalent.

Our early training is an important influence on whether inhibition or expression is valued. Such training is strongly influenced by the cultural mores of our parents. Parental response to a child's emotion largely determines whether that child learns to habitually express or suppress emotional expression or experience (Buck, 1993; Krause, Mendelson, & Lynch, 2003). Evidence indicates that our ability to regulate emotional arousal appears relatively early in life (Cicchetti, 1996) and remains relatively stable over our life span (Magai, 2001). The culture in which we are raised has a strong impact on valuation of expression (e.g., Matsumoto, 1993; McConatha, Lightner, & Deaner, 1994), as different cultures ascribe to different beliefs about emotions and their inhibition (Kennedy-Moore & Watson, 1999; Mesquita, 2001). Consistent with this proposal, cultural variation is observed in whether or not emotional inhibition results in ill health (Consedine, Magai, Cohen, & Gillespie, 2002; Roger, de la Banda, Lee, & Olason, 2001). For example, Eastern Europeans, who show a greater degree of emotional intensity in self-report measures, show fewer health difficulties associated with inhibition than do European Americans (Consedine, Magai, Cohen, et al., 2002). Psychodynamically oriented and constructivist therapists assist clients to understand these early training influences and use this understanding to make changes in their current lives.

Furthermore, although emotion inhibition is consistently observed to result in physiological arousal (e.g., Gross, 1998; Gross & Levinson, 1997), whether such arousal is associated with ill health depends on whether our bodies are able to deal with that arousal or not (Leventhal, Patrick-Miller, Leventhal, & Burns, 1998). For example, healthy individuals may be more able to accommodate the arousal associated with suppressing their emotions than those who are ill. One characteristic that influences our physical flexibility to deal with arousal is age. Presumably this ability is compromised for older adults, suggesting that emotion inhibition, which requires energetic resources, would be particularly problematic for them (Panksepp & Miller, 1995), but instead there is evidence that expression may result in worse health for older adults (Stroebe & Stroebe, 1991). Whether this is due to increased arousal associated with inhibition or expression, older adults seem to regulate their emotion experience and expression differently than do younger adults (Gross et al., 1997; Labouvie-Vief & Diehl, 2000; Lawton, Kleban, & Dean, 1993; McConatha, Leone, & Armstrong, 1997). Specifically, they report less negative emotion than do younger adults (Magai, 2001; Mroczek & Kolarz, 1998; Pennebaker & Stone, 2003).

The third factor that Consedine, Magai, and Bonanno (2002) suggest as important moderators of the inhibition–health relationship is the characteristics of the inhibited experience itself. Emotion is a multidimensional phenomenon, including experience, physiology, and expression, so for any specific situation it is important to determine exactly which aspects of emotion should or should not be inhibited. Furthermore, different emotions signal different needs and serve different purposes (Consedine, 2001; see chapter 13), and so the consequences of inhibition will likely differ for the different emotions. For example, emotions that extend over longer periods of time, such as grief, may require more resources to inhibit than emotions of shorter duration, such as anger. This is reflected in treatment for anger management and grief: Many anger management techniques are "quick and dirty," whereas grief management techniques are gentler, slower, and take longer to complete. Similarly, intense emotions may require more resources to inhibit than milder experiences. Furthermore, if one is practiced in suppressing a given emotion, inhibition of that experience or expression may be less effortful than less frequently suppressed emotions.

Several researchers propose that self-regulation is a limited resource, so that suppression that requires greater effort is more likely to deplete that resource, potentially resulting in ill health (Baumeister & Heatherton, 1996; Heatherton & Vohs, 1998; Tice & Ciarocco, 1998). Consistent with the view that self-regulation is a limited resource, when participants are required to inhibit behavior, such as in delay of gratification tasks, their performance on subsequent efforts to control their behavior, even on very different tasks, is poorer (Baumeister et al., 1998; Muraven, Tice, & Baumeister, 1998). For example, if a dieter succeeds at resisting tempting food, he may later be unsuccessful with a different type of self-control, such as containing his anger with his children. Clinicians working with clients with chronic or acute pain are very aware of the limiting effect that managing pain has on their clients' abilities to attend to other parts of their lives or to regulate their own emotional state. Much of the treatment for chronic pain focuses on a skillful combination of expression and inhibition of, or distraction from (see chapter 7), the pain experience (e.g., D. W. Arbuthnott, Church, Lasiuk, & Arbuthnott, 1994; Caudill, 2002). Relapse prevention (Gorski & Miller, 1982) and developmental models of addiction recovery (e.g., S. Brown, 1995) that recommend leaving some aspects of treatment (such as family of origin issues) for later in the recovery process recognize that self-regulation is a limited resource. On the other hand, self-regulatory capacity can increase through exercise or practice such that with continued inhibition of the same behavior, attention becomes automatized and less effort is needed to control that impulse (Muraven, Baumeister, & Tice, 1998). This suggests that when a person successfully breaks a bad habit, the effort needed to control her behavior related to that habit decreases over the years.

Tice and Ciarocco (1998) further distinguish between desires that get stronger if they are inhibited, such as hunger, and desires that dissipate naturally if they are inhibited, such as behavioral urges associated with transient moods (e.g., anger). With the former urges, self-regulatory effort becomes greater over time, potentially resulting in negative health consequences for suppressing such urges. For desires that dissipate over time, however, the costs of suppression may be outweighed by the benefits associated with reduced arousal. Thus, Tice and Ciarocco argue, catharsis may work to reduce emotional arousal only under some circumstances. If cathartic expression serves to focus attention on an issue associated with the latter type of urge, it can increase arousal, distress, and illness, relative to ignoring the impulse until it dissipates (Baumeister, Heatherton, & Tice, 1994; M. H. L. Hecker, Chesney, Black, & Frautschi, 1988). For example, if the experience of anger is bad for our health (Hull et al., 2003), then cathartic expression may result in more illness than would suppression of that emotion (Ecton & Feindler, 1990).

So, given this evidence, when should we encourage our clients to express a behavior or actively think about an issue, and when should we encourage inhibition of such actions and thoughts? The evidence suggests that both too much and too little inhibition can lead to psychological and physical health problems. Too little inhibition seems to arise from a disability in inhibitory mechanisms and is a characteristic of serious psychiatric disorders, such as schizophrenia, ADHD, and OCD. Even if an individual does not show these deficiencies, too little inhibition can also strain relationships and cause difficulty for the individual in social situations. Too much inhibition can result in stress-related illnesses or affective disorders. Thus, therapists must be alert to both of these extremes, assisting clients to make informed decisions about when and where to inhibit, and developing plans to assist with inhibition of specific behaviors when clients are unable to self-regulate in this way.

When individuals either cannot or choose not to inhibit either thoughts and actions, they are often seen as acting out and judged as socially deviant or problematic because they don't suppress behavior that is socially unacceptable. In many cultures, this is seen as a serious problem, and can result in a psychiatric diagnosis depending on the specific nature of the inhibitory "transgression." Impaired cognitive inhibition, defined as being unable to suppress mental representations such as thoughts and perceptions, seems to underlie the psychotic symptoms of schizophrenia and obsessive thoughts in OCD. Impaired behavioral inhibition, on the other hand, is associated with impulsive or compulsive behaviors, as in ADHD or OCD. Therapists treating such clients must recognize these as limitations in self-regulation and must help their clients to organize or restructure their environments to minimize the socially undesirable behaviors. For example, ADHD clients can be encouraged to arrange environments that do not cue their inappropriate urges, such as eliminating sources of unwanted habits from their homes (e.g., cigarettes, alcohol, or fatty foods). Children with acting-out difficulties, impulsive tendencies, and/or diagnosed with disruptive behavior disorders are often taught social and self-regulatory skills in individual or group settings (e.g., Friedberg & Mc-

Clure, 2002), and their parents are trained to adjust their own responses and arrange their children's environment to assist with the learning of self-soothing and other self-regulatory skills (e.g., Frick, 1998).

Too much inhibition seems to be more voluntary or willful, although there are likely temperamental or cultural factors that lead an individual to prefer a less expressive style. Problems associated with this extreme are more socially acceptable, such as being shy or restrained, but the evidence suggests that there may be negative health consequences for people with this style (Pennebaker, 1997; Polivy, 1998). As discussed previously, there are many therapeutic techniques aimed at increasing expression. Given the social value of inhibition and the evidence that a match between expressive style and preference is important, therapists should be attentive to these factors and aim to match clients' preferences and minimize the possible negative consequences they might experience from expressing issues. For example, a client who sought therapy for assistance with "blurting" frequently found herself in situations with family and friends where she would blurt out a piece of information or an opinion, and then feel "mortified." In exploring examples, it did not seem that she was revealing damaging information; rather, she preferred to have a style in which she thoughtfully considered information (at least briefly) prior to revealing it. In addition, her habit of unthinkingly disclosing had led to a reputation of being a gossip among family and friends, and she was worried that this might result in less trusting relationships. The solution for this client was to insert a time delay between her urge to speak and speaking, allowing her time to consider the question, "Do I want/need to say this now?"

In summary, whether inhibition is problematic or beneficial to mental health depends on many factors: the type of inhibition (cognitive or behavior), what is being inhibited (a perceptual distractor or an emotion), individual characteristics (age and temperament), context (cultural mores, social situation), and individual choice (e.g., voluntary vs. habitual). Given this complexity, theories of the relationship between inhibition and health must be specific and comprehensive, defining both the inhibitory target, the characteristics of the person, and the situation before useful prescriptions about catharsis or containment can be given (Consedine, Magai, & Bonanno, 2002). Therapists are familiar with such contextualized decisions regarding expression or suppression because they personally either express or contain their reactions to a client based on their judgment about which is in the client's best interest. We can be most useful by assisting our clients to have a similar degree of flexibility, as well as to develop principles on which to make such decisions.

There is also evidence that we can minimize the possible negative consequences of inhibition by using the techniques of reframing and distraction. Some of the negative consequences of cognitive inhibition, such as rumination, can be attributed to Wegner's (1994) ironic processes of mental control. Specifically, to avoid certain types of thoughts or stimuli, a monitoring process must be attuned to such information and must operate to keep its contents out of awareness. As Wegner described it, any reduction in concentration or mental control enables the contents of the monitoring system to become conscious, accounting for increased rumination that accompany attempts to suppress thoughts (Wenzlaff & Wegner, 1998). In other words, whenever self-control becomes more difficult or effortful, we are more likely to become aware of the material that we have been keeping out of our mind. When the goal of suppression is framed as a to-be-avoided target, such as avoiding stressful thoughts, the contents of the monitoring process would be exactly the material that is to be avoided, that is, stressful thoughts. However, if we reframe our mental goals in a positive way, such as to think peaceful and relaxing thoughts, then the contents of the monitoring process would be anything that wasn't peaceful, including both stressful and neutral thoughts (Wegner et al., 1997). Thus, a breakdown in concentration would be less harmful to clients' well-being if they frame their goals positively because they would become aware of a mixture of negative and neutral thoughts when their concentration falters. (See chapter 2 for other reasons to frame goals positively rather than negatively.)

Similarly, providing positive distractions (e.g., "changing the channel") for a client to focus on rather than instructing her to suppress negative thoughts is both more effective (Nolen-Hoeksema, 1998; Wenzlaff et al., 1988) and reduces problems resulting from a rebound increase in the avoided material. For example, it is much easier to remind ourselves of pleasant events whenever we notice ourselves considering a negative moment than it is to simply stop the negative thought (Wegner, 1989). This is especially important for therapeutic clients, as dysphoric individuals who are induced to ruminate (which is a consequence of cognitive inhibition) show poorer problem-solving performance, recall more negative memories, make more self-depreciating attributions and evaluations of current events, and predict more negative outcomes for the future than do dysphorics who are induced to distract themselves (Lyubomirsky et al., 1998; Lyubomirsky & Nolen-Hoeksema, 1995).

In summary, both containment (or distraction) and catharsis (or expression) are useful under different circumstances. To change bad habits, reduce our attention to unwanted thoughts and behaviors, or deal with circumstances that are beyond our control, inhibition may be a valuable tool. Similarly, evidence seems to support the use of inhibition for the emotions of anger and sadness under some conditions. Cathartic expression of anger or grief can decrease well-being rather than increase it (Bonanno et al., 1999; Bushman, 2002; T. W. Smith, 1992) unless very specific elements enable working through the emotion (L. S. Greenberg & Safran, 1987). However, for reasonable goals that are denied for social reasons (Krause et al., 2003), bringing such desires into awareness and expressing them in both emotional and decisional action seem most useful. In this case, some degree of anti-inhibition practice seems useful.

An important part of many therapies is to assist clients to appropriately express and withhold emotion (a process often referred to as *self-regulation*). On the other hand, therapists who teach self-regulatory skills to acting-out clients (whose ambivalence is about inhibiting rather than expressing) realize that the goal is often to help clients understand that the large effort required to inhibit previously expressed emotions or actions is worthwhile. In fact, psychotherapy is in large part the intricate dance and balance between inhibition and action in various aspects of human experience.

Thus, we conclude that inhibition neither makes us sick nor makes us well. Rather, it is a cognitive tool that humans can use as they pursue the goals of their lives. All therapies aid clients in developing and maintaining skills in the appropriate inhibition or expression of thoughts, emotions, and actions. Therapists should be aware that the tools are dependent on the theoretical underpinnings of the therapy and may not always match the needs and style of the client. For example, clients who are relieved by disinhibiting their emotional expressiveness may not be a good match for a strictly cognitive behavioral approach, and clients who become ruminative and distressed after experiencing deep emotion may not be a good match for expressive therapies. This illustrates the need to get feedback concerning the effects of our approach and techniques with each client (e.g., see S. D. Miller et al., 2004) and for therapists to be able to shift approaches when the feedback dictates a need to do so.

KEY POINTS

- Inhibition is the suppression of thoughts, feelings, or behaviors.
- Inhibition is considered detrimental to health in some literatures and beneficial to efficiency and social adjustment in others.

- We can distinguish between cognitive inhibition (suppression of experience) and behavioral inhibition (suppression of action).

- Cognitive inhibition has been associated with greater rumination, whereas behavioral inhibition of emotion expression has been associated with stress-related disorders.

- Deficient inhibition, both cognitive and behavioral, is implicated in several psychiatric disorders, including schizophrenia, OCD, ADHD, and DID.

- Inhibition or self-regulation is a limited resource.

- Whether inhibition is beneficial or detrimental to health and psychological function depends on several factors, including the target of inhibition (e.g., cognitive or behavioral), the context, cultural attitudes, and personal characteristics such as habitual expressive style, age, and ethnicity.

- Appropriate levels of inhibition for each individual are influenced by three factors: (a) the match between level of expression and preferred style and resulting ambivalence, (b) early training and culture, and (c) characteristics of the inhibited experience.

NOTES

1. This is not to suggest that therapists encourage unstructured or random expressions. Rather, inhibition of important thoughts, acts, or emotions, is considered problematic.

2. Emotions are considered to be mental representations in the same way that thoughts are (see chapter 13).

3. These studies show that the clinical populations perform differently than normal individuals, but they do not indicate the direction of causality. Thus, it is not entirely clear whether deficiencies in inhibition lead to psychiatric symptoms or whether psychiatric illness leads to impairment of inhibitory mechanisms. In the case of schizophrenia, relatives of patients also indicate impaired inhibition (Beech & Claridge, 1987), so this likely indicates a genetic contribution, suggesting that deficient inhibition leads to the psychiatric problems. Similarly, Barkley (1997) suggests that children with ADHD have deficiencies in inhibition, and this leads to their later symptomatic behavior.

4. The skill of concreteness is more recently discussed as effective inquiry or questioning, but the original term is more appropriate in this context, because it emphasizes the exploration of the facts of an issue in detail, whereas effective inquiry can refer to either abstract (thematic) or detailed discussion of an issue and thus may either encourage or discourage cognitive inhibition.

15

Psychodynamic Principles as Cognitive Mechanisms

As we have emphasized throughout this book, knowledge of cognitive processes is beneficial to the theory and practice of all therapeutic modalities. However, it seems that cognitive theory has been of special benefit to psychodynamic theory. Various researchers have separated Freudian observations from his psychosexual drive theory, which is not amenable to empirical verification, and recast them as special cases of cognitive mechanisms, which can be tested empirically. This recasting covers fundamental psychodynamic principles such as the ubiquity of unconscious processing, interpersonal processes such as transference, and intrapersonal processes such as repression. In the process of this recasting, psychodynamic mechanisms have been determined to apply to healthy human functioning as well as to pathology. Researchers in this new tradition argue that these processes represent human functioning in the relevant domains and only sometimes result in psychological difficulty and suffering.

Several researchers have noted the fundamental compatibilities of the psychodynamic and cognitive enterprises. Conway (1997a), for example, commented that his cognitive model of autobiographical memory is very similar to the speculations of Freud. The current psychodynamic model, however, operates without a coherent theoretical framework because the psychosexual drive theory proposed by Freud has been discounted, and this theory was not amenable to empirical verification, which is the standard for scientific proposals (Bucci, 1997, 2000; Fisher & Greenberg, 1985). The goal of cognitive science is to formulate models of human mental functioning (Newell, 1990), and thus cognitive science is compatible with psychodynamic goals. Cognitive science seeks to understand all mental processes, both healthy and disordered, whereas psychodynamic models focus primarily on disordered or problematic mental activity; the latter goal is clearly within the global context of cognitive science. Thus, cognitive models could provide a theoretical alternative to the discredited "hydraulic energy" model proposed by Freud. Moreover, some authors note that the field of cognitive science would also be improved by consideration of psychodynamic concepts, especially with respect to emotional processing (Bucci, 1997, 2000; Westen, 1998). In this chapter, we review work examining psychodynamic principles and processes from the viewpoint of cognitive mechanisms.

PRINCIPLES: UNCONSCIOUS PROCESSING

One of the foundational principles of psychodynamic theory is the existence and importance of unconscious mental processes as determinants of human thought, affect, and behavior. Freud (1915/1957) postulated that although unpleasant thoughts, feelings, and behavioral impulses are actively dismissed from awareness, they continue to influence behavior unconsciously. More recently, cognitive science has convincingly demonstrated that much of mental processing occurs unconsciously. The evidence for this ranges from observations of implicit memory (evidence of memory influencing performance without the person's knowledge that memory is being used; Schacter, 1992; Squire, 1987) to observations that people's decisions are strongly influenced by factors outside their awareness (Nisbett & Wilson, 1977). For example, T. Wilson and Nisbett (1978) showed that people's judgment of consumer goods was strongly influenced by the position of the samples, with the rightmost sample receiving greatest favor even when the items were identical. No participant in this study, however, mentioned position as a factor in their judgment. Similarly, participants were inaccurate in their assessments of both the influence of previously studied words on subsequent free association tests and the effect of prose passages on their emotional response (Wilson & Nisbett, 1978). There is considerable debate about the operation and relative contributions of conscious and unconscious processing in implicit memory performance (e.g., Graf & Komatsu, 1994; Jacoby, 1991; Jacoby, Begg, & Toth, 1997; Jacoby, Toth, Yonelinas, & Debner, 1994; Joordens & Merikle, 1993; Toth, Reingold, Eyal, & Jacoby, 1995), but there is agreement among cognitive researchers that all processing has both conscious and unconscious components. Thus, according to cognitive scientists, Freud was correct about the existence of unconscious mental processes.

However, is the unconscious described by Freud the same as the cognitive unconscious? Some researchers highlight the similarity of the cognitive and psychodynamic conceptions of unconscious processing (Westen, 1998), whereas others claim that the two are very different (Reisberg, 1997). Reisberg, for example, argued that Freud's conception is related to instinctual and emotional processes rather than procedures that are unconscious due to the structure of mental architecture, as is held with respect to the cognitive unconscious. According to this interpretation, anxiety and pain do not selectively influence what is unconscious, as Freud contended. One of the distinctions to be made in this regard is the distinction between unconscious process and the contents of unconscious thought. Both models specify that processing occurring outside awareness interacts with conscious processing to determine behavior at any given moment. Furthermore, the mechanisms of such processing are hypothesized as similar to mechanisms of conscious processing, including associative memory activation in response to internal or external cues (see chapter 3). However, the contents of unconscious thought discussed by cognitive researchers and psychodynamic theorists differ greatly. Psychodynamic unconscious contents are hypothesized to be unpleasant or anxiety-provoking thoughts and motivations, whereas cognitive researchers focus on neutral knowledge contents, such as previously encountered words or activities. As Westen (1998) commented, there is no reason to presume that affective and motivational information is processed differently than semantic information, so this distinction with respect to unconscious content may not be as divisive as it appears (see also Bucci, 1997). In fact, neuropsychological evidence about implicit affective learning, such as that evident in amnesic patients, suggests that emotional information is processed in ways very similar to factual information (Bechara et al., 1995; Milner, Corkin, & Teuber, 1968). Thus, while there would be reason to suspect that unconscious processing of unpleasant thoughts is more motivationally relevant than unconscious processing of neutral thoughts, the architecture and mechanisms underlying the two types of information may not differ. Pain and anxiety do not selectively influence what is unconscious, but neither are painful thoughts and memories excluded from being unconscious. In other words, painful and anxiety-provoking thoughts and memories may be excluded from consciousness, but such exclusions are likely to be conscious, at least initially (see section on repression).

In general, whether they speak directly about unconscious processes or memory, awareness or the lack thereof, most therapists implicitly attend to the unconscious in the sense that clients are unaware of certain aspects of their experience. For example, simply expanding the problem space by the application of exploration skills and uncovering previously unknown or unconsidered aspects of clients' experiences assumes that there are unconscious elements to all issues. This new information is examined, discussed, and incorporated into problem-solving actions in order to reach a goal or expand repertoires of skills.

Another difference that has been noted is whether unconscious and conscious processes are presumed to cooperate or conflict in human functioning (Reisberg, 1997). Cognitive researchers presume cooperation between the two types of processing results in efficient performance (e.g., Jacoby, 1991), whereas Freud emphasized the conflicts between conscious and unconscious goals. This difference is most likely related to the context of performance that is under consideration. Cognitive researchers primarily examine intellectual performance, such as that involved in recalling words. In this case, parallel processing would likely converge on the same lexical or verbal entries in associative memory (i.e., activation would spread to the same items in verbal memory), thus resulting in joint facilitation of the same target by conscious and unconscious influences (i.e., cooperation). In interpersonal situations, however, parallel processing seems more likely to result in activation of potentially conflicting goals or action possibilities, such as conflicts between motives for independence and communality. Thus, the presence of cooperation or conflict may not be a property of the unconscious and conscious systems themselves, but rather a function of the particular task and context to which processing is directed. The absence of investigation of emotional targets by cognitive researchers may thus contribute to this apparent discrepancy (Westen, 1998; see also Baars, Cohen, Bower, & Berry, 1992, for an example of conflict related to speech production).

Evidence clearly indicates that information processed unconsciously influences behavior and decisions. For example, H.M., the man who was rendered amnesic through removal of his hippocampus (Milner et al., 1968), showed improvement of procedural skills despite his lack of awareness that he had performed such skills previously (Warrington & Weiskrantz, 1970). Similarly, the mere exposure effect, by which preference for an object is increased by having viewed it previously even though the object is not consciously recognized (Zajonc, 1980), indicates that affective behavior is similarly influenced unconsciously. More strikingly, measures of physiological response are observed despite lack of conscious awareness of affect, both for subliminal affective conditioning (Ohman, 1994; Wong, Shevrin, & Williams, 1994) and for situations in which expression of emotion is suppressed (Rachman, 1978; Wegner, Shortt, Blake, & Page, 1990). This can lead to behavioral contradictions, such as the lack of correlation between implicit and explicit measures of racial or gender bias (Banaji & Hardin, 1996; Fazio, Jackson, Dunton, & Williams, 1995). In sum, the existence and influence of unconscious processes is well supported in cognitive research.

PROCESSES: TRANSFERENCE

Some central psychodynamic processes are accounted for by the associative, cue-sensitive nature of memory (see chapter 3). This explains the observed importance of childhood experiences to adult processing and behavior (Westen, 1998) and the process of transference (Andersen & Berk, 1998). Freud's conception of transference was that early parental relationships form a template that strongly influences expectations and interactions in subsequent relationships. In other words, people react to new individuals as if they were similar to the known others from their past. When the term is applied therapeutically, *transference* refers to the client's responses to the therapist and *countertransference* refers to the therapist's reactions to the client. In Freud's model, this process then forms the basis of repetition compulsion, in which an individual continually re-enacts the interpersonal patterns of their early relationships, even troublesome dynamics that are not consciously desired. Susan Andersen and her colleagues (e.g., Andersen & Berk, 1998; Andersen & Chen, 2002; Andersen & Cole, 1990) tested the hypothesis that significant others, and our patterns of relationship with them, are mentally represented and influence our interactions with new people. Significant others and relational patterns are important to satisfy basic biological and social needs, and thus they are important objects of learning throughout life. According to this view, knowledge of significant others is represented in associative memory in the same manner as other semantic knowledge and thus functions in the same manner as other concepts, facilitating recognition, categorization, and selection of actions based on previous experience. Andersen measures individuals' representations of their significant others by having them fill in sentence completion questionnaires about the others, usually two weeks prior to experimental testing. Over many experiments using this methodology, Andersen has observed that significant other representations influence evaluation, inferences, and expectations of novel individuals, and behavioral and affective responses to them. As with other memory constructs (see chapters 3 & 4), representations of significant others can be activated in a variety of ways: by presenting similar features between the new and represented people (providing retrieval cues), through priming (reviewing representation prior to meeting a new person), or through chronic activation (Andersen & Berk, 1998; Andersen & Cole, 1990). Andersen thus characterizes transference as a basic mechanism of social information processing, one that is not necessarily associated with error or suffering.

The processes of associative memory also explain the importance of childhood experiences to adult functioning. Memory structures and schemas are created in childhood and then influence the perception and interpretation of subsequent stimuli and experiences. Mental representations of significant others are especially important for humans, given the social nature of our species (e.g., Cosmides & Tooby, 1992). Freud emphasized the central role of parental representations and relationships for all subsequent relations; this is the central basis for psychodynamic interpretation. However, the modern psychodynamic-cognitive theorists such as Andersen consider that all significant relationships, no matter when they occur in the life span, influence our conceptions of and interactions with other people. Our first significant others may play a unique representational role because they provide the first templates, but the process of significant other representation is not limited to parents or to the early important figures in our lives.

MOTIVATIONS AND STRATEGIES: REPRESSION

A third psychodynamic element to receive cognitive reframing is that of human pleasure/pain motivation (Moretti & Higgins, 1999) and the accompanying strategy of repression to achieve the goals of maximizing pleasure and minimizing pain. Researchers examining the role of chronic motivations in human behavior have reaffirmed the centrality of seeking pleasant experiences and avoiding unpleasant ones (Walker, Skowronski, & Thompson, 2003). The motive that is most influential at a given moment influences cognitive processing, such as self-appraisal and appraisal of environmental objects (Shah & Higgins, 2001). Furthermore, several mechanisms by which these motives are accomplished have received support (e.g., S. E. Taylor, 1991).

One means by which we regulate our thoughts and emotions in a manner consistent with the bias to discourage unpleasant experiences is to not think about such thoughts and experiences: the process of repression. It is widely believed that Freud specified that repression is an unconscious, involuntary process, but Erdelyi (1990, 2001) pointed out that this designation of repression as unconscious was a revision made by Anna Freud, rather than the original conception of Sigmund Freud. Erdelyi argued that there is no mechanistic distinction between conscious suppression and unconscious repression (Erdelyi, 1990). He further argued that the mechanism can be used for either defensive (e.g., suppression of unpleasant thoughts and feelings) or nondefensive purposes. From this viewpoint, Ebbinghaus (1885) provided the first experimental evidence of the amnesic consequences of repression. In his classic experiments, after Ebbinghaus had committed his lists of nonsense syllables to memory, he deliberately avoided thinking of them in the retention interval in order to eliminate uncontrolled repetition effects. Erdelyi argued that this amounts to repression of the material from thought. More recently, Michael Anderson and his colleagues (M. C. Anderson & Green, 2001; Anderson & Levy, 2002; Levy & Anderson, 2002) demonstrated that this effect is due to active inhibition of the item that was excluded from thought. Using a think/no-think task, in which participants are instructed not to think about some learned words for a specific time, Anderson observed that such effort results in poorer retrieval of the no-think words relative to both words that were reviewed and words that were not reviewed, even when the no-think prohibition is lifted. Thus, deliberately keeping verbal material from our thoughts does seem to result in a greater difficulty retrieving that specific material from memory. Erdelyi (2001) further speculated that an exclusion process that begins consciously can become automated with practice, thus rendering it unconscious (see also Baars et al., 1992; Melchert, 1996; Power & Dalgleish, 1997). It is likely that the more often we dismiss a particular thought from consideration, the easier that dismissal will become. Along these lines, M. C. Anderson and Green (2001) observed that the frequency of occasions the undesired thought needs to be excluded from memory increases the strength of the inhibitory effect. They speculated, similar to Erdelyi, that this is the mechanism underlying repression.

Although inhibition of excluded material is observed, the suppression is not permanent. When repression is lifted, such as when Ebbinghaus decided to recall his lists, the material can be at least partially recovered. Furthermore, when greater effort is expended on recovery of the material, as with reminiscence or repeated recall attempts, more of the repressed material can be retrieved (hypermnesia; Bluck, Levine, & Laulhere, 1999; Erdelyi & Kleinbard, 1978). This is consistent with the theories of Freud, in that the goal of psychoanalysis is to render repressed material conscious, through the combined efforts of the analyst and the patient. Erdelyi's conception of repression differs from Freud's, however, in his emphasis on repression as a normal cognitive mechanism that is sometimes helpful and sometimes harmful, depending on the content and context of the suppressed material (see also chapter 14).

Many of the specific defense mechanisms discussed in psychodynamic theory are elaborations of the general mechanism of repression. For example, projection involves individuals avoiding thinking about unpleasant personal aspects and feelings. However, to continuously exclude aspects of ourselves from awareness requires consistent vigilance (Erdelyi, 1990), and thus those traits will be chronically activated, resulting in increased sensitivity to such traits in others (L. S. Newman, Duff, & Baumeister, 1997; Wegner, 1992, 1994). Furthermore, this selective attention to repressed features apparently results in poorer social cognition generally (Heilbrun & Cassidy, 1985).

Psychodynamic theory explains the phenomena of childhood amnesia on the basis of the assumed anxiety-provoking contents of thought in early childhood, leading to repression of childhood experiences and impulses. However, a much more likely explanation rests on the cue-dependent nature of memory retrieval. Once infants acquire language, it serves as a powerful organizing strategy and cue to memory. Thus, it is likely that young children's memories are organized in a manner quite different from that of older children and adults. Access to memories requires a cue by which to access the associative network. It is likely that cues similar enough to the context in which very early memories are encoded will not be available after the advent of language or self-concept representation. This can account for childhood amnesia using known principles of human memory (Howe et al., 2003; Reisberg, 1997). More concretely, the theory that childhood amnesia results from the absence of a coherent self-concept in early life (Howe et al., 2003) specifies a representation of the self as the central retrieval cue for autobiographical memories (see chapter 4).

ARCHITECTURAL PHENOMENA:
FREUDIAN SLIPS

Cognitive researchers have also examined the phenomenon of goal-consistent speech errors, or Freudian slips (Baars et al., 1992; Birnbaum & Collins, 1992). According to Freud, slips of the tongue and other action errors are meaningful acts expressing suppressed intentions. Freud viewed slips of the tongue as evidence of the existence and ubiquitous influence of the unconscious, but some cognitive researchers argue, rather, that such errors are an inevitable characteristic of an architecture directed by an opportunistic goal-satisfaction planning system. It is evidence that goals, once formed, can influence behavior despite intervening decisions to suppress them. Baars and his colleagues (1992) argued that these goals need not reflect instinctual or anxiety-provoking motives (i.e., repressed content), but that such errors can occur with any suppressed goals.

The argument is this: Intelligent, goal-directed behavior requires the ability to recognize and capitalize on opportunities to satisfy goals, even when an opportunity arises unexpectedly. For example, while engaged in conversation about personal matters with a close friend (affiliative goal), if the friend mentions an attractive job opening in his company, I could redirect my attention to finding out about the job (career goal). In order for this to occur, the features of the unexpected opportunity would need to cue the relevant goal either directly or through inference; once cued, the new goal could then direct thought and behavior. In the present example, mention of a job could cue employment aspirations, and this goal would then supersede the previously active affiliation goal, at least temporarily.

Many theorists have commented on the necessity of serial processing of goal pursuit, given the limitations of human resources (e.g., attention, working memory, muscle control; J. R. Anderson, 1983; Shallice, 1982, 1988; see chapter 7). This leads to the necessity to choose one or two goals at any one time toward which to direct behavior. Thus, although we always have multiple goals, some of these goals need to be suppressed (or "paused") in order to pursue a single goal successfully. However, an opportunistic action planner would need to be able to override the suppression of the relevant goal if the situation changes. Thus, although we make momentary decisions to forgo pursuit of a given goal, the goal will not be entirely suppressed unless it is completed and eliminated from our set of goal representations (see the discussion of intention superiority in chapter 6). For biological and social goals, such as those of obtaining food and social contact, completion is never completely accomplished, and thus such goals are always available to be activated by situational cues (i.e., opportunities).

This is clearly functional when there is no social or personal reason to exclude pursuit of a given goal in the context. But Freudian slips are embarrassing expressions of goals that are socially inappropriate in a given context. For example, if the conversation (mentioned previously) had been with a grieving friend, and my goal was to indicate my commitment and attention to the friend, shifting the conversation to gain information about an available job would have been less acceptable. However, the career goal is not absolutely suppressed; it is just not chosen in the current context. Thus, exclusion of career goal pursuit would require conscious editorial control of my expressions. If control processes are not optimal, an opportunistic planner can select expression of that goal. In a minor way, linguistic errors such as Freudian slips are evidence of such opportunistic action because of the time constraint operating in online lexical (word) selection while speaking. For example, a young therapist who noticed how attractive his new client was used self-talk to "stop it" and redirected his attention to the client's issues, which centered around several abortive attempts to launch a much wanted career. In paraphrasing some aspect of his client's experience, the therapist said, "So, you haven't yet been **sex**cessful in your efforts" (a classic Freudian slip).

This speculation about the underlying source of such slips was tested using a method developed by Baars (Baars et al., 1992) to encourage the production of speech errors. Participants were asked to read two-word phrases aloud as quickly as they could, and Spoonerism errors were encouraged by priming certain phonological features. For example, after reading several phrases such as "bark dog" and "bean deck," "dart board" was read as "bart doard." To assess whether motivations can increase the rate of Freudian slips, Baars and his colleagues primed universal human motives (sexual attraction and fear of shock) situationally, and observed increased rates of motive-consistent Freudian slips ("lice legs" → "nice legs" or "shad bok" → "bad shock"; Baars et al., 1992). To assess the psychodynamic interpretation of slips being caused by a chronic inner conflict, they then selected participants on the basis of high sexual guilt (assessed using a standardized questionnaire), and observed more sex-related slips than for participants rated as showing low sex guilt (Baars et al., 1992). Thus, they observed an increase in Freudian slips both when the situation cued a motivation and when assessment indicated individual differences in the intention to suppress a particular motive. However, their model suggests that the Freudian competition between alternative goals reflected by such speech errors is a special case of general competition between goals for access to a limited capacity system, rather than a specialized pathological mechanism.

CONCLUSION

In summary, there are now several programs of research investigating psychodynamic principles and processes as special cases of general cognitive mechanisms. These special cases involve motivations, emotions, and interpersonal components of human mental life and are thus special only in the sense that cognitive research has tended to avoid such contents. These researchers have all divorced themselves from Freud's theoretical interpretations of his observations (i.e., psychosexual drive theory) and have moved toward social-cognitive models. Furthermore, all emphasize that the processes they investigate are general features of human cognition rather than features specific to pathological functioning. These processes, like all human cognitive processes, can result in good or ill mental health, and thus the processes should not be confused with their contents. This move to render the insightful observations of Freud amenable to empirical verification is to be lauded, and highlights the value of considering therapeutic issues in the light of cognitive science discoveries.

KEY POINTS

- Psychodynamic principles and processes have been divorced from Freud's drive theory and are evaluated as special cases of basic cognitive mechanisms.
- Cognitive research has revealed several examples of processes that are not available to conscious awareness, supporting the general psychodynamic principle of the importance of unconscious processes.
- Transference, the influence of previous relationships on current ones, is viewed as an example of priming in associative memory extended to the social sphere.
- Repression of undesired thoughts and memories is examined as an example of the inhibition associated with selective attention applied to memory retrieval.
- Freudian slips are evidence of goal-consistent speech errors that occur when goals are quickly changed or their expression is contained. Such errors represent the competition between goals for access to a limited capacity system (i.e., speech production).
- Most of this recasting indicates that psychodynamic principles and processes are normal aspects of human cognitive functioning, as they operate under conditions of intense emotion or motivation rather than by pathological mechanisms.

16

Prospect and Review: Cognition Throughout the Process of Therapy

So how might cognitive science influence the practice of psychotherapy? As we have seen, many cognitive processes are involved in the thoughts, emotions, and conversations that emerge in psychotherapy. Information about these processes could potentially overwhelm a therapist. So how are therapists to proceed? Choose topics one at a time and integrate the lessons associated with that knowledge into practice until it becomes automatic? This is one way to proceed, but it is neither the most efficient, nor does it honor the integrity of human functioning. Although human cognition is studied componentially, we think holistically, with all of these processes operating simultaneously. Furthermore, the process of psychotherapy requires attention to entire persons. Thus, it would be more efficient to consider how the cognitive processes that we have reviewed in this book interact, and when such processes become important in the psychotherapeutic process. This chapter puts the pieces together, to enable psychotherapists to recognize the relevance of cognitive processes (and knowledge thereof) in their interactions with clients.

The chapter is organized according to the general flow of therapy, from initial session, to diagnosis and goal setting, and then to treatment. Within each of these categories, the relevant cognitive processes are highlighted. We discuss their relevance to therapists' thinking, the therapeutic conversation, the client's thinking and experience in that stage, and refer readers back to the relevant previous chapters throughout. Our generalizations about the importance of cognitive processes in each stage are usually necessarily speculative, as relatively little integrative work has been done.

However, we hope not only to encourage therapists to integrate knowledge about cognitive processes into their practice, but to inspire clinical researchers to test some of our assertions.

INITIAL SESSION

The initial meeting with a client is key for both the therapist and the client. The initial sessions constitute a period in which to gather the evidence for problem solving and decision making, while developing a good working relationship. During early sessions, the therapist will begin to categorize the client and his issues (chapter 8), which will strongly influence the therapist's attentional focus (chapter 7) and the treatment plans that occur to her. As discussed in chapter 4, first experiences are important for memory, so the initial encounter will provide a foundation for the later relationship. It is at this point that many of the reasoning and decision-making biases (chapters 9 & 10) come into play. The range of factors that the therapist will consider prior to diagnosis or categorization will be influenced by priming (chapter 3), attentional focus (chapter 7), and surface similarity of features with other clients and clinical examples (chapters 2 & 8). Similarly, the client will begin to categorize what type of experience this is, which will influence their metacognitive beliefs about whether help is available for him or not. Social categorization such as judgments about others' temperament, role, or race occurs automatically, serves as the basis of our predictions about others' behavior and motivations, and thus guides our actions with them (see chapter 8). Given the limitations on future information processing often imposed by our initial assessments, we recommend that therapists form their early opinions tentatively, remaining open to both confirming and disconfirming feedback from the client.

What is primed in each initial session depends on what the therapist has recently been thinking of. Thus, things such as the day's previous sessions, the therapist's current reading, current personal issues, and wider factors such as current news events can all influence what easily comes to mind. This influences the therapist's initial impressions of the client through directing her attention, influencing the questions that she asks the client, and focusing her attention on various aspects of the client's answers over others. The information that is elicited from the client, and the manner in which that information is elaborated is influenced by what is currently on the therapist's mind (i.e., primed). Similar processes will also influence the client during this meeting. In addition to the local influences that also influence the therapist, such as current news events, current reading, and previous conversations from that day, the client's expectations will also be influenced by their previous experiences with other therapists or other professionals. Cues provided by the therapist's office, attire, and the formal routines, such as registration with a receptionist or sitting in a waiting room, will cue clients' previous encounters in similar professional settings, and thus prime them for the meeting based on their experiences in the previous settings. Thus, therapists should be attentive to the cues their setting initially presents to clients, including telephone contact to set appointments, bureaucratic procedures, and office arrangement. For example, if a therapist does not want clients to assume a passive role in therapy, looking to the therapist as the expert who will diagnose and treat their problem with the only effort required on their part being compliance with the therapist's prescriptions, then the therapist should not set her office up as a medical clinic. Cultural scripts for medical encounters generally include an active doctor/compliant patient role assignment that is usually not effective for successful therapy. Arrangements that prime more equal and active participation by the client, such as educational or community settings, might be preferred (e.g., see Oakley, 2004). Within the therapeutic conversation, skills such as empathy, respect, or active inquiry are designed to prime certain topics for the client, such as emotion, self-esteem thoughts, or facts, respectively.

Attention will be both captured and directed during this session. For the therapist, attention will be captured by the client's unusual characteristics, both physical and social, and by features that are expected or primed. In addition to current thinking, features will be primed both by a therapist's habitual practice and by comments and questions in a referral report. In addition, attention will be directed to aspects of the client's reported experiences that are theoretically important in the therapist's therapeutic model. It is somewhat important for therapists to metacognitively monitor their thoughts during this session (chapter 12), because these features are what will be used to categorize the client and his issues, both socially (implicitly) and diagnostically. For example, actively considering two alternative hypotheses about a client's issue will increase the range of features noticed (discussed in chapter 9). Metacognitive research suggests that attention will need to be explicitly directed to contextual factors, such as the client's home or work environment, as such factors are frequently overlooked. Obtaining such contextual information is one purpose for formal interviews at the beginning of therapy, as they frequently include questions about the client's context.

The client will also notice any unusual features of the therapist or the therapist's setting, particularly features that do not correspond with prototypes developed from previous experiences. For example, most doctors' or lawyers' offices do not have sand boxes or other toys in them, so these elements of a child or family therapist's office will automatically attract a client's attention. Similarly, if a therapist dresses in a way that is not typical of other professionals, clients will notice this. Whether such attention leads clients to positive or negative expectations depends on their previous experiences: For example, one of the authors had a client who had very negative interactions with professionals in her childhood, who typically dressed in suits, so when the therapist dressed more casually, the client felt more at ease and sessions were often more productive.

If a therapist routinely takes a history from clients during the initial sessions, autobiographical memory will also be important. As discussed in chapters 3 and 4, the therapist should attend to how the client is cued to probe his memory, such as whether questions cue lifetime period, general event, or event-specific detail knowledge. For the purposes of a history, lifetime period knowledge is most relevant, but this is a more difficult way to access autobiographical memory than general events, and so may be more difficult for clients. Priming will also occur during a history taking, and thus therapists should be attentive to the wording and sequencing of questions. The topics that are raised during this history will have attentional importance for both the therapist and the client, as they will form the first issues to be discussed in the beginning relationship. Furthermore, if either the client or the therapist engage in subtle selection of memories, the therapy could come to be based on incomplete or false impressions of the client's life. Common selection biases involve memories of early adulthood, distinctive memories, and mood-congruent memories. Care must be taken not to overinterpret such biases, as that could result in forming incorrect schemas of the client and his issues, which would then influence treatment plans and later sessions. More positively, if the client shows evidence of overgeneral memories, such as being unable to describe examples of problematic situations in detail, this could be taken as an indication of depression, and evidence suggests that helping the client to review his memories in more detail can be of assistance in itself (see chapter 13).

Therapists should also be aware of the influence of their own mood on early judgment of clients because negative moods lead to less favorable opinions of others than do positive moods (chapter 13). Although we cannot control our moods at all times, we can be alert to the influence of mood on our assessments of others. Similarly, our mood can influence the type of problem solving we do; for example, we are more creative when happy and more risk-avoidant when feeling more negatively. If such moods are long-lasting, this may influence the types of treatment plans therapists consider, or may create a mismatch between the therapist's preferred strategies and those of the client.

DIAGNOSIS AND GOAL SETTING

The diagnosis of the client's difficulty is a classification task, as discussed in chapter 8. For such a task, therapists generally focus on information that is diagnostic of differences between categories, such as auditory hallucination being a characteristic of schizophrenia but not of obsessive-compulsive disorder (OCD). The consequences of this categorization for therapists is that a diagnosis influences their attentional focus and the information they access from memory to understand and work with the client's issues. Once a diagnosis has been given, we use the assumed category to predict unknown features. For example, if a client comes to us who has been diagnosed as OCD by another clinician or physician, we would predict that they would engage in excessive rumination, relative to other clients. The use of category labels (or diagnoses) to predict symptoms and characteristics can be useful to therapists in building the trust of a client; if the client has not mentioned his difficulty with persistent negative thoughts but the therapist accurately predicts that he has such trouble, this increases the sense that the therapist understands his problem and thus increases the client's willingness to follow therapeutic suggestions for treatment. Although we have used diagnostic labels from the *DSM-IV-TR*, we would point out that all comprehensive therapeutic systems have categories related to describing client experiences and the potential etiological reasons for those experiences or symptoms.

At some point during assessment, it is probably useful to assess clients' inhibitory/expressive style, their beliefs about such, and their cultural context (chapter 14). In addition to helping increase the therapist's understanding of the client, this will help to determine whether treatment should focus on suppression of problematic thoughts and behavior or attention to avoided thoughts and expression of avoided behavior.

We suggest that the content of early sessions be devoted, at least in part, to clarifying the four elements of problem solving related to the client's presenting problem and desired change: the client's current state, goal state, the resources and abilities that he has to reach the goal, and the limitations and constraints that will pose difficulty for him in the journey from current to goal states. As discussed throughout the book, conceptualization of these elements is strongly influenced by attention, memory, and metacognition. Thus, therapists can be very useful in this process by monitoring the attentional, categorization, and metacognitive processes clients are using and discuss the memory associations that are evoked from these processes.

The end of this phase is that (a) the therapist has tentatively decided on a categorization of the client and his problem, and (b) decided on a contract or goal state to pursue (even if the initial goal is simply to work together and develop a working relationship). The results of this categorization will also reflect the assessment of the client's emotional style (chapter 13) and whether he needs help inhibiting or expressing thoughts and emotions (chapter 14). The therapeutic relationship that is developed will be influenced by the type of relationship that therapist and client prime in each other (transference; chapter 15), which partly reflects the roles and categories that each assigns to the other.

TREATMENT

The specifics of the therapeutic treatment will depend on the therapist's therapeutic orientation and the specifics of the diagnosis and treatment plan, but monitoring such work will use the processes of attention, priming, autobiographic memory, and reasoning. During this phase, therapist and client flesh out and act on problem-solving plans and strategies developed in the earlier phases of therapy. Specifically, therapists help clients to develop their resources and operators relating to the current problem, adding necessary knowledge and skills to clients' repertoires and limiting their habitual but dysfunctional strategies. The focus of this treatment will vary according to therapists' orientations, but all of these techniques involve cognitive processes in some fashion.

For example, all forms of therapy aim to alter some aspects of clients' cognitive processes, such as clients' self-concepts and emotions. Regardless of the therapist's orientation or the client's goals, almost all therapies include emotion regulation. This regulation may be necessary as clients undertake change in their lives, to contain the inevitable uncertainty or anxiety that accompanies such change. Or, emotion regulation may be a weak area for the client generally, as in the case of posttraumatic stress disorder (PTSD) sufferers, in which development of such skills becomes part of the therapeutic plan. The five general strategies of mood regulation outlined by Gross (1998)—situation selection, situation modification, attention deployment, reinterpretation, and response modulation—are the basis of various therapeutic techniques (see chapter 13). Reframing or shifting meaning is also used in most therapy orientations: Psychodynamic therapists attempt to reframe the meaning of feelings or behaviors using interpretation, redecision therapists attempt to link an issue to a developmental or lifetime theme, and reframing is a central goal for both solution-focused and narrative therapists. Reframing essentially results in reassigning the category of an issue or event, which results in refocusing attention, eliciting different memory associations and different metacognitive beliefs. This technique, when it works, essentially restructures the problem space, revealing more functional operators and possibly side-stepping constraints.

Cognitive processes can also provide the basis for direct treatment interventions. Processes used in this way include attention, categorization, metacognition, and issues of emotional experience and expression (chapters 13 & 14). Although cognitive behavioral therapies (CBT) acknowledge cognitive processes as a focus of their treatment, all therapies do so to some extent. However, different therapies take different cognitive objects and processes as the target of treatment. Several modalities, for example, focus on autobiographical memory, either in order to change the client's interpretations or construction of the past (e.g., constructivist and narrative therapists) or to analyze the client's reactions to past occurrences and the effect these reactions have had on current experience (e.g., psychodynamic and gestalt therapists). In both cases, the goal is to establish autobiographical themes that will lead to more productive future options for the client. In contrast, family therapists focus more of their treatment on issues of categorization and mental models, attempting to develop more functional models of family relationships and dynamics in their clients, and assisting them to clarify their prototypes of each other, hopefully leading to more benign and productive images of family members. CBT therapists focus their treatment strategies on attention and metacognition. Some CBT therapists focus directly on altering attentional and metacognitive processes of clients (e.g., A. Wells, 2000), whereas others challenge clients' reasoning and beliefs (e.g., A. Ellis, 2002). In particular, CBT therapists remain alert to indications of clients' beliefs that support or exacerbate their difficulties, such as the belief that rumination (about negative mood or obsessive thoughts) is useful. CBT therapists also make extensive use of therapeutic homework, although they are often unaware of the contribution of prospective memory processes to the success of such techniques (chapter 6), preventing them from using simple strategies such as designing salient cues to signal the homework situation at the appropriate moment.

During this phase, therapists also need to take the clients' habitual mood into account in designing treatment, as emotion often influences judgment and memory. For instance, mood influences the degree to which individuals notice or take credit for success experiences: Sad mood is associated with greater weight given to failure experiences, whereas happy individuals are more likely to notice successes and attribute them to their own abilities and efforts. Thus, techniques that are designed to give clients positive feedback about themselves will have less effect with depressed individuals. Given the influence of emotion on attention, judgment, and memory, some therapeutic interventions (such as reframing the motives of significant others or challenging a client's overly negative self-concept) would appear to be most effective when clients are in a happy mood. Thus, therapists may want to design methods to temporarily lift a client's mood as they engage in such techniques, such as sharing a laugh with the client or encouraging happiness in some other way (see the research of Isen et al., 1987, and Thayer, 1996, for examples).

Knowledge of emotional processes developed by appraisal or emotion prototype theorists is also useful for emotion-focused processing. The use of advanced empathy can elicit a client's deep emotional response to a situation, and the specific emotion will give clues as to the client's assessment of how the situation interferes with his goals, as discussed during the initial sessions. Therapists could then reframe or challenge the client's assessments, or help the client develop strategies to continue pursuing his goals, despite the presence of interfering elements in his life.

Although there is much more to the treatment phase of therapy than a focus on cognitive processes, being aware of and appropriately integrating such processes can make treatment more effective and prevent serious errors in judgment and misattribution of clients' symptoms, behaviors, and described experiences.

TERMINATION

In addition to meeting several other goals, the rituals involved in ending of therapy provide a chance to consolidate and conclude the therapy narrative in autobiographical memory. Termination conversations enable therapists to reinforce important elements of change that have occurred throughout the therapy, strengthening and highlighting these elements in the client's memory. This facilitates the use of these elements in the client's future thinking, in part through the mechanism of priming.

CONCLUSION

Throughout the history of psychotherapy, there has been considerable discussion of the factors that are common to all therapeutic orientations. The importance of such common factors is highlighted by research that indicates no differences in effectiveness as a result of therapeutic orientation (Chambliss & Ollendick, 2001; Saunders, 2004). The focus is usually on factors such as the therapeutic relationship, but this book draws attention to even more fundamental common factors—the minds of clients and therapists. Cognitive processes are the common ground of all therapy, as they are the basic mechanisms by which we operate. As we have argued, knowledge of cognitive processes and its judicious deployment can greatly strengthen therapeutic effectiveness, regardless of the theoretical orientation of the therapist.

Cognitive science encompasses a large, growing, and ever more technical field of research. Generally, each specific area has evolved its own methods and theoretical models, making general knowledge of the entire field extremely difficult. Furthermore, the methods and models are often inaccessible to lay readers, even those with advanced education. The purpose of this book has been to explain to therapists cognitive findings that are most relevant to the activities of psychotherapy, to enhance understanding and use of this common factor for the benefits of clients and psychotherapeutic practice.

References

Aarts, H., & Dijksterhuis, A. (2003). The silence of the library: Environment, situational norms and social behavior. *Journal of Personality and Social Psychology, 78*, 53–63.

Achee, J., Tesser, A., & Pilkington, C. (1994). Social perception: A test of the role of arousal in self-evaluation maintenance processes. *European Journal of Social Psychology, 24*, 147–160.

Adams, J. (2003). Milan systemic therapy. In L. H. Hecker & J. L. Wetchler (Eds.), *An introduction to marriage and family therapy* (pp. 123–148). New York: Haworth Clinical Practice Press.

Adelson, B. (1981). Problem solving and the development of abstract categories in programming languages. *Memory and Cognition, 9*, 422–433.

Adler, R. B., Towne, N., & Rolls, J. A. (2001). *Looking out looking in* (1st Canadian ed.). Orlando, FL: Harcourt College.

Afifi, W. A., & Guerrero, L. K. (2000). Motivations underlying topic avoidance in close relationships. In S. Petronio (Ed.), *Balancing the secrets of private disclosures* (pp. 165–179). Mahwah, NJ: Lawrence Erlbaum Associates.

Ahn, W., Kalish, C. W., Medin, D. L., & Gelman, S. A. (1995). The role of covariation versus mechanism information in causal attribution. *Cognition, 54*, 299–352.

Ahn, W., Kalish, C., Gelman, S. A., Medin, D. L., Luhmann, C., Atran, S., et al. (2001). Why essences are essential in the psychology of concepts. *Cognition, 82*, 59–69.

Ahn, W., Novick, L. R., & Kim, N. S. (2003). Understanding behavior makes it normal. *Psychonomic Bulletin and Review, 10*, 746–752.

Allen, J. G. (2001). *Traumatic relationships and serious mental disorders*. New York: Chichester, UK: Wiley.

Allen, S. W., & Brooks, L. R. (1991). Specializing the operation of an explicit rule. *Journal of Experimental Psychology: General, 120*, 3–19.

Alloy, L. B., & Tabachnik, N. (1984). Assessment of covariation by humans and animals: The joint influence of prior expectation and current situational information. *Psychological Review, 91*, 112–148.

Allport, A. (1989). Visual attention. In M. Posner (Ed.), *Foundations of cognitive science* (pp. 631–682). Cambridge, MA: MIT Press.

Allport, A., Styles, E., & Hsieh, D. (1994). Shifting intentional set: Exploring the dynamic control of tasks. In C. Umilta & M. Moscovitch (Eds.), *Attention and performance XV* (pp. 421–452). Cambridge, MA: MIT Press.

American Association for Marriage and Family Therapy. (2000). *Readings in family therapy supervision*. Washington, DC: AAMFT Press.

American Psychiatric Association. (2000). *Diagnostic and Statistical Manual of Mental Disorders* (4th ed., text rev.). Washington, DC: Author.

Amsel, E., Langer, R., & Loutzenhiser, L. (1991). Do lawyers reason differently from psychologists? A comparative design for studying expertise. In R. J. Sternberg & P. A. Frensch (Eds.), *Complex problem solving: Principles and mechanisms* (pp. 223–250). Hillsdale, NJ: Lawrence Erlbaum Associates.

Andersen, S. M., & Berk, M. S. (1998). Transference in everyday experience: Implications of experimental research for relevant clinical phenomena. *Review of General Psychology, 2,* 81–120.

Andersen, S. M., & Chen, S. (2002). The relational self: An interpersonal social-cognitive theory. *Psychological Review, 109,* 619–645.

Andersen, S. M., & Cole, S. W. (1990). "Do I know you?" The role of significant others in social perception. *Journal of Personality and Social Psychology, 59,* 384–399.

Anderson, C. A., & Sechler, E. S. (1986). Effects of explanation and counterexplanation on the development and use of social theories. *Journal of Personality and Social Psychology, 50,* 24–34.

Anderson, C. D. (1981). Expression of affect and physiological response in psychosomatic patients. *Journal of Psychosomatic Research, 25,* 143–149.

Anderson, J. R. (1983). *The architecture of cognition*. Cambridge, MA: Harvard University Press.

Anderson, M. C., & Green, C. (2001, March). Suppressing unwanted memories by executive control. *Nature, 410,* 366–369.

Anderson, M. C., & Levy, B. (2002). Repression can (and should) be studied empirically. *Trends in Cognitive Sciences, 6,* 502–503.

Anderson, S. A., & Conway, M. A. (1993). Investigating the structure of autobiographical memories. *Journal of Experimental Psychology: Learning, Memory, and Cognition, 19,* 1178–1196.

Andrzejewski, S. J., Moore, C. M., Corvetter, M., & Herrmann, D. (1991). Prospective memory skill. *Bulletin of the Psychonomic Society, 29,* 304–306.

Arbuckle, T. Y., & Cuddy, L. L. (1969). Discrimination of item strength at time of presentation. *Journal of Experimental Psychology, 81,* 126–131.

Arbuthnott, D. W., Church, S., Lasiuk, G., & Arbuthnott, K. D. (1994). Emotional and behavioral management of chronic pain. *The Pain Clinic, 7,* 39–43.

Arbuthnott, K. D. (1995). Inhibitory mechanisms in cognition: Phenomena and models. *Current Psychology of Cognition, 14,* 30–45.

Arbuthnott, K. D. (1996). To repeat or not to repeat: Repetition facilitation and inhibition in sequential retrieval. *Journal of Experimental Psychology: General, 125,* 261–283.

Arbuthnott, K. D. (in press). The effect of repeated imagery on memory. *Applied Cognitive Psychology.*

Arbuthnott, K. D., & Arbuthnott, D. W. (1999). The best intentions: Prospective remembering in psychotherapy. *Psychotherapy, 36,* 247–256.

Arbuthnott, K. D., & Arbuthnott, D. W. (2004). *Non-completion of psychotherapeutic homework: Non-compliance or prospective memory?* Unpublished manuscript.

Arbuthnott, K. D., Arbuthnott, D. W., & Rossiter, L. (2001). Guided imagery and memory: Implications for psychotherapists. *Journal of Counseling Psychology, 48*, 123–132.

Arbuthnott, K. D., Arbuthnott, D. W., & Ylioja, S. (2003). Memory errors for everyday events: Forensic implications. *Canadian Journal of Police and Security Studies, 1*, 323–336.

Arbuthnott, K. D., & Campbell, J. I. D. (2003). The locus of self-inhibition in sequential retrieval. *European Journal of Cognitive Psychology, 15*, 177–194.

Arbuthnott, K. D., & Frank, J. (2000). Executive control in set switching: Residual switch cost and task-set inhibition. *Canadian Journal of Experimental Psychology, 54*, 33–41.

Arbuthnott, K. D., Geelen, C. B., & Kealy, K. L. K. (2002). Phenomenal characteristics of guided imagery, natural imagery, and autobiographical memory. *Memory and Cognition, 30*, 519–528.

Arbuthnott, K. D., Ylioja, S., & Topp, L. (2004). *The basis of confidence in childhood memories: Think-aloud protocols and reasoning probes.* Unpublished manuscript.

Arnold, M. B. (1960). *Emotion and personality.* New York: Columbia University Press.

Ashcraft, M. H. (2002). *Cognition* (3rd ed.). Upper Saddle River, NJ: Prentice Hall.

Aspinwall, L. G., & Taylor, S. E. (1997). A stitch in time: Self-regulation and proactive coping. *Psychological Bulletin, 121*, 417–436.

Atkins, D. C., Dimidjian, S., & Christensen, A. (2002). Behavioral couple therapy: Past, present, and future. In T. L. Sexton, G. R. Weeks, & M. S. Robbins (Eds.), *Handbook of family therapy: The science and practice of working with families and couples.* New York: Brunner-Routledge.

Ayers, M. S., & Reder, L. M. (1998). A theoretical review of the misinformation effect: Predictions from an activation-based memory model. *Psychonomic Bulletin and Review, 5*, 10–21.

Baars, B. J., Cohen, J., Bower, G. H., & Berry, J. W. (1992). Some caveats on testing the Freudian slip hypothesis: Problems in systematic replication. In B. J. Baars (Ed.), *Experimental slips and human error: Exploring the architecture of volition* (pp. 289–313). New York: Plenum.

Baddeley, A. D. (1986). *Working memory.* Oxford, UK: Clarendon Press.

Banaji, M., & Hardin, C. (1996). Automatic stereotyping. *Psychological Science, 7*, 136–141.

Banbury, S., & Berry, D. C. (1997). Habituation and dishabituation to speech and office noise. *Journal of Experimental Psychology: Applied, 3*, 181–195.

Bandler, R., & Grinder, J. (1975). *The structure of magic I.* Palo Alto, CA: Science and Behavior Books.

Bandura, A. (1997). *Self-efficacy: The exercise of control.* New York: Freeman.

Bannon, S., Gonsalvez, C. J., Croft, R. J., & Boyce, P. M. (2002). Response inhibition deficits in obsessive-compulsive disorder. *Psychiatry Research, 110*, 165–174.

Barclay, C. R. (1988). Truth and accuracy in autobiographical memory. In M. M. Greenberg, P. E. Morris, & R. N. Sykes (Eds.), *Practical aspects of memory. Current research and issues: Volume 1. Memory in everyday life* (pp. 289–294). Chichester: Wiley.

Barkley, R. A. (1997). Behavioral inhibition, sustained attention, and executive functions: Constructing a unifying theory of ADHD. *Psychological Bulletin, 121*, 65–94.

Barnes, A. E., Nelson, T. O., Dunlosky, J., Mazzoni, G., & Narens, L. (1999). An integrative system of metamemory components involved in retrieval. In D. Gopher & A. Koriat (Eds.), *Attention and performance XVII—Cognitive regulation of performance: Interaction of theory and application* (pp. 287–313). Cambridge, MA: MIT Press.

Baron, J. (1995). Myside bias in thinking about abortion. *Thinking and Reasoning, 1*, 221–235.

Baron, J. (1998). *Judgment misguided: Intuition and error in public decision making.* Oxford: Oxford University Press.

Baron, J. (2000). *Thinking and deciding* (3rd ed.). Cambridge: Cambridge University Press.

Baron, R. (1987). Interviewers' moods and reactions to job applicants: The influence of affective states on applied social judgments. *Journal of Applied Social Psychology, 16,* 16–28.

Baron, R. (1990). Environmentally induced positive affect: Its impact on self-efficacy, task performance, negotiation, and conflict. *Journal of Applied Social Psychology, 20,* 368–384.

Barsalou, L. W. (1987). The instability of graded structure: Implications for the nature of concepts. In U. Neisser (Ed.), *Concepts and conceptual development: Ecological and intellectual factors in categorization* (pp. 101–140). Cambridge, UK: Cambridge University Press.

Barsalou, L. W. (1988). The content and organization of autobiographical memories. In U. Neisser & E. Winograd (Eds.), *Remembering reconsidered: Ecological and traditional approaches to the study of memory* (pp. 193–243). Cambridge, UK: Cambridge University Press.

Barsalou, L. W. (1989). Intraconcept similarity and its implications for interconcept similarity. In S. Vosniadou & A. Ortony (Eds.), *Similarity and analogical reasoning* (pp. 76–121). New York: Cambridge University Press.

Bartlett, F. C. (1932). *Remembering: A study in experimental and social psychology.* Cambridge, UK: Cambridge University Press.

Battino, R. S. (2002). *Metaphoria: Metaphor and guided metaphor for psychotherapy and healing.* Williston, VT: Crown House.

Baucom, D. H., Epstein, N., & LaTaillade, J. J. (2002). Cognitive-behavioral couples therapy. In A. S. Gurman & N. S. Jacobson (Eds.), *Clinical handbook of couple therapy* (3rd ed., pp. 26–58). New York: Guilford.

Bauer, P. J. (1996). What do infants recall of their lives? Memory for specific events by one- and two-year olds. *American Psychologist, 51,* 29–41.

Baumeister, R. F., Bratslavsky, E., Muraven, M., & Tice, D. M. (1998). Ego depletion: Is the active self a limited resource? *Journal of Personality and Social Psychology, 74,* 1252–1265.

Baumeister, R. F., & Heatherton, T. F. (1996). Self-regulation failure: An overview. *Psychological Inquiry, 7,* 1–15.

Baumeister, R. F., Heatherton, T. F., & Tice, D. M. (1994). *Losing control: How and why some people fail at self regulation.* San Diego, CA: Academic Press.

Baumgardner, A. H., & Arkin, R. M. (1988). Affective state mediates causal attributions for success and failure. *Motivation and Emotion, 12,* 99–111.

Bechara, A., Tranel, D., Damasio, H., Adolphs, R., Rockland, C., & Damasio, A. (1995). Double dissociation of conditioning and declarative knowledge relative to the amygdala and hippocampus in humans. *Science, 29,* 1115–1118.

Beck, A. T., Rush, A. J., Shaw, B. F., & Emery, G. (1979). *Cognitive therapy of depression.* New York: Guilford.

Beck, R. C., & McBee, W. (1995). Mood-dependent memory for generated and repeated words: Replication and extension. *Cognition and Emotion, 9,* 99–111.

Becker, F. S., Rinck, M., Roth, W. T., & Margraf, J. (1998). Don't worry and beware of white bears: Thought suppression in anxiety patients. *Journal of Anxiety Disorders, 12,* 39–55.

Beech, A., & Claridge, G. (1987). Individual differences in negative priming: Relations with schizotypal personality traits. *British Journal of Psychology, 78,* 349–356.

Benjamin, A. S., Bjork, R. A., & Schwartz, B. L. (1998). The mismeasure of memory: When retrieval fluency is misleading as a metamnemonic index. *Journal of Experimental Psychology: General, 127,* 55–68.

Berk, L. E., & Landau, S. (1993). Private speech of learning disabled and normally achieving children in classroom academic and laboratory contexts. *Child Development, 64*, 556–571.

Berkowitz, L. (1993). Towards a general theory of anger and emotional aggression. In T. K. Srull & R. S. Wyer (Eds.), *Advances in social cognition* (Vol. 6, pp. 1–46). Hillsdale, NJ: Lawrence Erlbaum Associates.

Berkowitz, L., Jaffee, S., Jo, E., & Troccoli, B. T. (2000). On the correction of feeling-induced judgmental biases. In J. P. Forgas (Ed.), *Feeling and thinking: The role of affect in social cognition* (pp. 131–152). Cambridge, UK: Cambridge University Press.

Berman, J. S., & Norton, N. C. (1985). Does professional training make a therapist more effective? *Psychological Bulletin, 98*, 401–407.

Berne, E. (1972). *What do you say after you say hello?* New York: Bantam.

Berntsen, D. (1996). Involuntary autobiographical memories. *Applied Cognitive Psychology, 10*, 435–454.

Berntsen, D. (1998). Voluntary and involuntary access to autobiographical memory. *Memory, 6*, 113–141.

Berntsen, D., & Rubin, D. C. (2002). Emotionally charged autobiographical memories across the life span: The recall of happy, sad, traumatic, and involuntary memories. *Psychology and Aging, 17*, 636–652.

Berntsen, D., Willert, M., & Rubin, D. C. (2003). Splintered memories or vivid landmarks? Reliving and coherence of traumatic memories in PTSD. *Applied Cognitive Psychology, 17*, 675–693.

Beutler, L. E., Alomohamed, S., Moleiro, C., & Romanelli, R. (2002). Systematic treatment selection and prescriptive therapy. In J. Lebow (Ed.), *Comprehensive handbook of psychotherapy: Vol. 4. Integrative-eclectic* (pp. 255–272). New York: Guilford.

Beyebach, M., Morejon, A. R., Palenzuela, D. L., & Rodriguez-Arias, J. L. (1996). Research on the process of solution-focused therapy. In S. D. Miller, M. A. Hubble, & B. L. Duncan (Eds.), *Handbook of solution-focused brief therapy* (pp. 299–334). San Francisco: Jossey-Bass.

Birnbaum, L., & Collins, G. (1992). Opportunistic planning and Freudian slips. In B. J. Baars (Ed.), *Experimental slips and human error: Exploring the architecture of volition* (pp. 121–125). New York: Plenum.

Bishop, S. R., Lau, M., Shapiro, S., Carlson, L., Anderson, N. D., Carmody, J., et al. (2004). Mindfulness: A proposed operational definition. *Clinical Psychology: Science and Practice, 11*, 230–241.

Bjork, R. A. (1999). Assessing our own competence: Heuristics and illusions. In D. Gopher & A. Koriat (Eds.), *Attention and performance XVII: Cognitive regulation of performance: Interaction of theory and application* (pp. 435–459). Cambridge, MA: MIT Press.

Bjorklund, D. F., & Harnishfeger, K. K. (1995). The evolution of inhibition mechanisms and their role in human cognition and behavior. In F. N. Dempster & C. J. Brainerd (Eds.), *Interference and inhibition in cognition* (pp. 141–173). San Diego: Academic Press.

Blake, M. (1973). Prediction of recognition when recall fails: Exploring the feeling-of-knowing phenomenon. *Journal of Verbal Learning and Verbal Behavior, 12*, 311–319.

Blaney, P. H. (1986). Affect and memory: A review. *Psychological Bulletin, 99*, 229–249.

Blankstein, K. R., & Segal, Z. V. (2001). Cognitive assessment: Issues and methods. In K. S. Dobson (Ed.), *Handbook of cognitive behavioral therapies* (2nd ed., pp. 40–85). New York: Guilford.

Blascovich, J., & Mendes, W. B. (2000). Challenge and threat appraisals: The role of affective cues. In J. P. Forgas (Ed.), *Feeling and thinking: The role of affect in social cognition* (pp. 59–82). Cambridge, UK: Cambridge University Press.

Bless, H. (2000). The interplay of affect and cognition: The mediating role of general knowledge structures. In J. P. Forgas (Ed.), *Thinking and feeling: The role of affect in social cognition* (pp. 201–222). Cambridge, UK: Cambridge University Press.

Bless, H., & Fiedler, K. (1995). Affective states and the influence of activated general knowledge. *Personality and Social Psychology Bulletin, 21,* 766–778.

Bless, H., Schwarz, N., & Wieland, R. (1996). Mood and the impact of category membership and individuating information. *European Journal of Social Psychology, 26,* 935–959.

Bluck, S., & Habermas, T. (2000). The life story schema. *Motivation and Emotion, 24,* 121–145.

Bluck, S., Levine, L. J., & Laulhere, T. M. (1999). Autobiographical remembering and hypermnesia: A comparison of older and younger adults. *Psychology and Aging, 14,* 671–682.

Boden, J. M., & Baumeister, R. F. (1997). Repressive coping: Distraction using pleasant thoughts and memories. *Journal of Personality and Social Psychology, 73,* 45–62.

Bodenhausen, G. V., Kramer, G. P., & Susser, K. (1994). Happiness and stereotypic thinking in social judgement. *Journal of Personality and Social Psychology, 66,* 621–632.

Bohannon, J. N. (1988). Flashbulb memories of the space shuttle disaster: A tale of two theories. *Cognition, 29,* 179–196.

Bohannon, J. N., & Symons, V. L. (1992). Flashbulb memories: Confidence, consistency, and quantity. In E. Winograd & U. Neisser (Eds.), *Affect and accuracy in recall: Studies of "flashbulb memories"* (pp. 65–91). New York: Cambridge University Press.

Bohart, A. C. (2003). Person-centered psychotherapy and related experiential approaches. In A. S. Gurman & S. B. Messer (Eds.), *Essential psychotherapies: Theory and practice* (pp. 107–148). New York: Guilford.

Bohner, G., Crow, K., Erb, H.-P., & Schwarz, N. (1993). Affect and persuasion: Mood effects on the processing of message content and context cues. *European Journal of Social Psychology, 22,* 511–530.

Bonanno, G. A., & Kaltman, S. (1999). Toward an integrative perspective on bereavement. *Psychological Bulletin, 125,* 760–776.

Bonanno, G. A., & Keltner, D. (1997). Facial expressions of emotion and the course of conjugal bereavement. *Journal of Abnormal Psychology, 106,* 126–137.

Bonanno, G. A., & Singer, J. L. (1990). Repressor personality style: Theoretical and methodological implications for health and pathology. In J. L. Singer (Ed.), *Repression and dissociation* (pp. 435–470). Chicago: University of Chicago Press.

Bonanno, G. A., Znoj, H., Siddique, H. I., & Horowitz, J. J. (1999). Verbal-autonomic dissociation and adaptation to midlife conjugal loss: A follow-up at 25 months. *Cognitive Therapy and Research, 23,* 605–624.

Borkovec, T. D., Roemer, L., & Kinyon, J. (1995). Disclosure and worry: Opposite sides of the emotional processing coin. In J. W. Pennebaker (Ed.), *Emotion, disclosure, and health* (pp. 47–70). Washington, DC: American Psychological Association.

Bourne, E. J. (2000). *The anxiety and phobia workbook* (3rd ed.). Oakland, CA: New Harbinger.

Bousfield, W. A. (1953). The occurrence of clustering in the recall of randomly arranged associates. *Journal of General Psychology, 49,* 229–240.

Bousfield, W. A., & Sedgewick, C. H. W. (1944). An analysis of sequences of restricted associative responses. *Journal of General Psychology, 30,* 149–165.

Bower, G. H. (1981). Mood and memory. *American Psychologist, 36,* 129–148.

Bower, G. H. (1991). Mood congruity of social judgments. In J. P. Forgas (Ed.), *Emotion and social judgments* (pp. 31–53). Oxford, UK: Pergamon Press.

Bower, G. H., & Cohen, P. R. (1982). Emotional influences in memory and thinking: Data and theory. In M. S. Clark & S. T. Fiske (Eds.), *Affect and cognition* (pp. 291–331). Hillsdale, NJ: Lawrence Erlbaum Associates.

Bower, G. H., & Forgas, J. P. (2000). Affect, memory, and social cognition. In E. Eich, J. F. Kihlstrom, G. H. Bower, J. P. Forgas, & P. M. Niedenthal (Eds.), *Cognition and emotion* (pp. 87–168). Oxford, UK: Oxford University Press.

Bradley, B., & Mathews, A. (1983). Negative self-schemata in clinical depression. *British Journal of Clinical Psychology, 22*, 173–181.

Bradley, M. M. (1994). Emotional memory: A dimensional analysis. In S. H. M. van Goozen, N. E. Van de Poll, & J. A. Sergeant (Eds.), *Emotions: Essays on emotion theory* (pp. 97–134). Hillsdale, NJ: Lawrence Erlbaum Associates.

Branscombe, N. R., Wohl, M. J. A., Owen, S., Allison, J. A., & N'gbala, A. (2003). Counterfactual thinking, blame assignment, and well-being in rape victims. *Basic and Applied Social Psychology, 25*, 265–273.

Brandimonte, M., Einstein, G. O., & McDaniel, M. A. (1996). *Prospective memory: Theory and applications*. Mahwah, NJ: Lawrence Erlbaum Associates.

Brandimonte, M. A., & Passolunghi, M. C. (1994). The effect of cue-familiarity, cue-distinctiveness, and retention interval of prospective remembering. *The Quarterly Journal of Experimental Psychology, 47A*, 565–587.

Bransford, J. D., & Stein, B. S. (1984). *The ideal problem solver: A guide for improving thinking, learning, and creativity*. New York: Freeman.

Brem, S. K., & Rips, L. J. (2000). Explanation and evidence in informal argument. *Cognitive Science, 24*, 573–604.

Brenner, L. A., Koehler, D. J., & Tversky, A. (1996). On the evaluation of one-sided arguments. *Journal of Behavioral Decision Making, 9*, 59–70.

Brewer, N., & Burke, A. (2002). Effects of testimonial inconsistencies and eyewitness confidence on mock-juror judgments. *Law and Human Behavior, 26*, 353–364.

Brewer, W. F. (1988a). Memory for randomly sampled autobiographical events. In U. Neisser & E. Winograd (Eds.), *Remembering reconsidered: Ecological and traditional approaches to the study of memory* (pp. 21–90). Cambridge, UK: Cambridge University Press.

Brewer, W. F. (1988b). Qualitative analysis of the recalls of randomly sampled autobiographical events. In M. M. Gruneberg, P. E. Morris, & R. N. Sykes (Eds.), *Practical aspects of memory: Current research and issues, Volume 1: Memory in everyday life* (pp. 263–268). New York: Wiley.

Brewer, W. F. (1996). What is recollective memory? In D. C. Rubin (Ed.), *Remembering our past: Studies in autobiographical memory* (pp. 19–66). Cambridge, UK: Cambridge University Press.

Brewin, C. R., Dalgleish, T., & Joseph, S. (1996). A dual representation theory of Posttraumatic Stress Disorder. *Psychological Review, 103*, 670–686.

Broadbent, D. (1958). *Perception & communication*. New York: Pergamon Press.

Brooks, L. (1968). Spatial and verbal components of the act of recall. *Canadian Journal of Psychology, 22*, 349–368.

Brooks, L. R., Norman, G. R., & Allen, S. W. (1991). The role of specific similarity in a medical diagnostic task. *Journal of Experimental Psychology: General, 120*, 278–287.

Brown, D., Scheflin, A. W., & Hammond, D. C. (1998). *Memory, trauma treatment, and the law*. New York: Norton.

Brown, R., & Kulik, J. (1977). Flashbulb memories. *Cognition, 5*, 73–99.

Brown, S. (1995). A developmental model of alcoholism and recovery. In S. Brown (Ed.), *Treating alcoholism* (pp. 27–53). San Francisco: Jossey-Bass.

Brunfaut, E., Vanoverberghe, V., & d'Ydewalle, G. (2000). Prospective remembering of Korsakoffs and alcoholics as a function of the prospective-memory and ongoing tasks. *Neuropsychologia, 38*, 975–984.

Bucci, W. (1997). *Psychoanalysis and cognitive science: A multiple code theory*. New York: Guilford.

Bucci, W. (2000). The need for a "psychoanalytic psychology" in the cognitive science field. *Psychoanalytic Psychology, 17*, 203–224.

Buck, R. (1984). *The communication of emotion*. New York: Guilford.

Buck, R. (1993). Emotional communication, emotional competence, and physical illness: A developmental-interactionist view. In H. C. Traue & J. W. Pennebaker (Eds.), *Emotion inhibition and health* (pp. 32–56). Seattle: Hogrefe & Huber.

Buehner, M. J., & May, J. (2002). Knowledge mediates the timeframe of covariation assessment in human causal induction. *Thinking and Reasoning, 8*, 269–295.

Burke, A., Heuer, F., & Reisberg, D. (1992). Remembering emotional events. *Memory and Cognition, 20*, 277–290.

Burns, D. D. (1980). *Feeling good: The new mood therapy*. New York: Signet.

Burns, D. D., & Auerback, A. H. (1992). Does homework compliance enhance recovery from depression? *Psychiatric-Annals, 22*, 464–469.

Burns, D. D., & Nolen-Hoeksema, S. (1992). Coping styles, homework compliance, and the effectiveness of cognitive-behavioral therapy. *Journal of Consulting and Clinical Psychology, 59*, 305–311.

Burns, D. D., & Spangler, D. L. (2000). Does psychotherapy homework lead to improvements in depression in cognitive-behavioral therapy or does improvement lead to increased homework compliance? *Journal of Consulting and Clinical Psychology, 68*, 46–56.

Burt, C. D. B., Kemp, S., & Conway, M. A. (2003). Themes, events, and episodes in autobiographical memory. *Memory and Cognition, 31*, 317–325.

Bushman, B. J. (2002). Does venting anger feed or extinguish the flame? Catharsis, rumination, distraction, anger, and aggressive responding. *Personality and Social Psychology Bulletin, 28*, 724–731.

Byrne, M. D., & Bovair, S. (1997). A working memory model of a common procedural error. *Cognitive Science, 21*, 31–61.

Byrne, R. M. J. (2002). Mental models and counterfactual thoughts about what might have been. *Trends in Cognitive Sciences, 6*, 426–431.

Byrne, R. M. J., & Egan, S. M. (2004). Counterfactual and prefactual conditionals. *Canadian Journal of Experimental Psychology, 58*, 113–120.

Cahill, L., Babinsky, R., Markowitsch, H., & McGaugh, J. L. (1995). The amygdala and emotional memory. *Nature, 377*, 295–296.

Cahill, L., Haier, R., Fallon, J., Alkire, M., Tang, C., Keator, D., Wu, J., & McGaugh, J. L. (1996). Amygdala activity at encoding correlated with long-term free recall of emotional information. *Proceedings of the National Academy of Sciences, 93*, 8016–8021.

Cahill, L., Prins, B., Weber, M., & McGaugh, J. L. (1994). Beta-adrenergic activation and memory for emotional events. *Nature, 371*, 702–704.

Campbell, L. F., & Smith, T. P. (2003). Integrating self-help books into psychotherapy. *Journal of Clinical Psychology/In Session: Psychotherapy in Practice, 59*, 177–186.

Campos, J. J., Campos, R. G., & Barrett, K. C. (1989). Emergent themes in the study of emotional development and emotion regulation. *Developmental Psychology, 25*, 394–402.

Cantor, N., Smith, E. E., French, R., & Mezzich, J. (1980). Psychiatric diagnosis as prototype categorization. *Journal of Abnormal Psychology, 89*, 181–193.

Carey, S. (1985). *Conceptual change in childhood*. Cambridge, MA: Plenum.

Carkhuff, R. R. (1987). *The art of helping* (6th ed.). Amherst, MA: Human Resource Development Press.

Carlson, M. B. (1988). *Meaning-making: Therapeutic processes in adult development*. New York: Norton.

Carnevale, P. J. D., & Isen, A. M. (1986). The influence of positive affect and visual access on the discovery of integrative solutions in bilateral negotiation. *Organizational Behavior and Human Decision Processes, 37*, 1–13.

Carr, A. (1997). Positive practice in family therapy. *Journal of Marital and Family Therapy, 23*, 271–293.

Carver, C. S., Lawrence, J. W., & Scheier, M. F. (1996). A control-process perspective on the origins of affect. In L. L. Martin & A. Tesser (Eds.), *Striving and feeling: Interactions among goals, affect, and self-regulation* (pp. 11–52). Mahwah, NJ: Lawrence Erlbaum Associates.

Cassells, W., Schoenberger, A., & Grayboys, T. B. (1978). Interpretation by physicians of clinical laboratory results. *New England Journal of Medicine, 299*, 999.

Castellanos, F. X., Marvasti, F. F., Ducharme, J. L., Walter, J. M., Israel, M. E., Drain, A., et al. (2000). Executive function oculomotor tasks in girls with ADHD. *Journal of the American Academy of Child and Adolescent Psychiatry, 39*, 644–650.

Caudill, M. A. (2002). *Managing pain before it manages you*. New York: Guilford.

Caverni, J. P., & Pris, J. L. (1990). The anchoring-adjustment heuristic in an "information rich, real world setting": Knowledge assessment by experts. In J. P. Caverni, J. M. Fabre, & M. Gonzalez (Eds.), *Cognitive biases*. Oxford, UK: North-Holland.

Cervone, D., & Peake, P. K. (1986). Anchoring, efficacy and action: The influence of judgmental heuristics on self-efficacy judgments and behavior. *Journal of Personality and Social Psychology, 50*, 492–501.

Chambliss, D. L., & Ollendick, T. H. (2001). Empirically supported psychological interventions: Controversies and evidence. *Annual Review of Psychology, 52*, 685–716.

Chan, C. S. (1997). Mental image and internal representation. *Journal of Architectural and Planning Research, 14*, 52–77.

Chandler, C. (1994). Studying related pictures can reduce accuracy, but increase confidence, in a modified recognition test. *Memory and Cognition, 22*, 273–280.

Chapman, G. B., & Bornstein, B. H. (1996). The more you ask for, the more you get: Anchoring in personal injury verdicts. *Applied Cognitive Psychology, 10*, 519–540.

Chapman, G. B., & Johnson, E. J. (2002). Incorporating the irrelevant: Anchors in judgment of belief and value. In T. Gilovich & D. Griffin (Eds.), *Heuristics and biases: The psychology of intuitive judgment* (pp. 120–138). Cambridge, UK: Cambridge University Press.

Chapman, L. J., & Chapman, J. P. (1967). Genesis of popular but erroneous psychodiagnostic observations. *Journal of Abnormal Psychology, 72*, 193–204.

Chapman, L. J., & Chapman, J. P. (1969). Illusory correlation as an obstacle to the use of valid psychodiagnostic signs. *Journal of Abnormal Psychology, 74*, 271–280.

Chapman, L. J., & Chapman, J. P. (1971). Test results are what you think they are. *Psychology Today, 5*, 18–22.

Cheng, P. W. (1997). From covariation to causation: A causal power theory. *Psychological Review, 104*, 367–405.

Chernev, A. (1997). The effect of common features on brand choice: Moderating the effect of attribute importance. *Journal of Consumer Research, 23*, 304–311.

Cherry, E. C. (1953). Some experiments on the recognition of speech, with one and with two ears. *The Journal of the Acoustical Society of America, 25*, 975–979.

Cherry, K. E., & LeCompte, D. C. (1999). Age and individual differences influence prospective memory. *Psychology and Aging, 14*, 60–76.

Chi, M. T., Bassok, M., Lewis, M. W., Reinman, P., & Glaser, R. (1989). Self-explanations: How students study and use examples in learning to solve problems. *Cognitive Science, 13*, 145–182.

Chi, M. T., de Leeuw, N., Chiu, M.-H., & LaVancher, C. (1994). Eliciting self-explanations improves understanding. *Cognitive Science, 18*, 439–477.

Chi, M. T. H., Feltovich, P. J., & Glaser, R. (1981). Categorization and representation of physics problems by experts and novices. *Cognitive Science, 5*, 121–152.

Chi, M. T. H., Glaser, R., & Rees, E. (1982). Expertise in problem solving. In R. S. Sternberg (Ed.), *Advances in the psychology of human intelligence* (Vol. 1, pp. 1–75). Hillsdale, NJ: Lawrence Erlbaum Associates.

Christianson, S.-A. (1992). Emotional stress and eyewitness memory: A critical review. *Psychological Bulletin, 112*, 284–309.

Christianson, S.-A., & Loftus, E. (1990). Some characteristics of people's traumatic memories. *Bulletin of the Psychonomic Society, 28*, 195–198.

Christianson, S.-A., & Loftus, E. F. (1991). Remembering emotional events: The fate of detail information. *Cognition and Emotion, 5*, 81–108.

Chu, S., & Downes, J. J. (2002). Proust nose best: Odors are better cues of autobiographical memory. *Memory and Cognition, 30*, 511–518.

Cicchetti, D. (Ed.). (1996). Regulatory processes [Special issue]. *Development and Psychopathology, Regulatory Processes, 8*.

Cicogna, P. C., & Nigro, G. (1998). Influence of importance of intention on prospective memory performance. *Perceptual and Motor Skills, 87*, 1387–1392.

Clark, D. M., & Teasdale, J. D. (1982). Diurnal variation in clinical depression and accessibility of memories of positive and negative experiences. *Journal of Abnormal Psychology, 91*, 87–95.

Clark, L. A., & Watson, D. (1994). Distinguishing functional from dysfunctional affective bursts. In P. Ekman & R. J. Davidson (Eds.), *The nature of emotion: Fundamental questions* (pp. 131–136). Oxford, UK: Oxford University Press.

Clark, M. S., & Isen, A. M. (1982). Toward understanding the relationship between affect and social behavior. In A. Hastorf & A. M. Isen (Eds.), *Cognitive social psychology* (pp. 73–108). New York: Elsevier.

Clore, G. L., Schwarz, N., & Conway, M. (1994). Affective causes and consequences of social information processing. In R. S. Wyer & T. K. Srull (Eds.), *Handbook of social cognition* (Vol. 2, 2nd ed., pp. 323–417). Hillsdale, NJ: Lawrence Erlbaum Associates.

Close, H. T. (1998). *Metaphor in psychotherapy*. San Luis Obispo, CA: Impact.

Cockburn, J. (1996). Failure of prospective memory after acquired brain damage: Preliminary investigation and suggestions for future directions. *Journal of Clinical and Experimental Neuropsychology, 18*, 304–309.

Cohen, A.-L., Dixon, R. A., Lindsay, D. S., & Masson, M. E. J. (2003). The effect of perceptual distinctiveness on prospective and retrospective components of prospective memory in young and old adults. *Canadian Journal of Experimental Psychology, 57*, 274–289.

Cohen, A.-L., West, R., & Craik, F. I. M. (2001). Modulation of the prospective and retrospective components of prospective remembering in younger and older adults. *Aging, Neuropsychology, and Cognition, 8*, 1–13.

Cohen, G. (1989). *Memory in the real world*. Hillsdale, NJ: Lawrence Erlbaum Associates.

Cohen, G., & Faulkner, D. (1988). Life span changes in autobiographical memory. In M. M. Gruenberg, P. E. Morris, & R. N. Sykes (Eds.), *Practical aspects of memory: Current research and issues. Vol. 1: Memory in everyday life* (pp. 277–282). New York: Wiley.

Collins, A. M., & Quillian, M. R. (1969). Retrieval time from semantic memory. *Journal of Verbal Learning and Verbal Behavior, 8*, 240–247.

Consedine, N. S. (2001). *On being clear about function in the study of emotions: A four level framework for organizing functional analysis* (Vol. 2). London: International Society for Research on Emotions Press.

Consedine, N. S., Magai, C., & Bonanno, G. A. (2002). Moderators of the emotion inhibition-health relationship: A review and research agenda. *Review of General Psychology, 6*, 204–228.

Consedine, N. S., Magai, C., Cohen, C. I., & Gillespie, M. (2002). Ethnic variation in the impact of negative affect and emotion inhibition on the health of older adults. *Journal of Gerontology: Psychological Sciences, 57B*, P396–P408.

Conway, M. A. (1993). Impairments of autobiographical memory. In F. Boller & J. Grafman (Eds.), *Handbook of neuropsychology* (Vol. 8, pp. 175–191). Amsterdam: Elsevier.

Conway, M. A. (1995). *Flashbulb memories*. Hillsdale, NJ: Lawrence Erlbaum Associates.

Conway, M. A. (1997a). Past and present: Recovered memories and false memories. In M. A. Conway (Ed.), *Recovered memories and false memories* (pp. 150–191). Oxford, UK: Oxford University Press.

Conway, M. A. (1997b). What are memories? In M. A. Conway (Ed.), *Recovered memories and false memories* (pp. 1–22). Oxford, UK: Oxford University Press.

Conway, M. A., Anderson, S. J., Larsen, S. F., Donnelly, C. M., McDaniel, M. A., McClelland, A. G. R., et al. (1994). The formation of flashbulb memories. *Memory & Cognition, 22*, 326–343.

Conway, M. A., & Bekerian, D. A. (1987). Organisation in autobiographical memory. *Memory and Cognition, 15*, 119–132.

Conway, M. A., Collins, A. F., Gathercole, S. E., & Anderson, S. J. (1996). Recollections of true and false autobiographical memories. *Journal of Experimental Psychology: General, 125*, 69–95.

Conway, M. A., & Pleydell-Pearce, C. W. (2000). The construction of autobiographical memories in the self-memory system. *Psychological Review, 107*, 261–288.

Conway, M. A., Pleydell-Pearce, C. W., Whitcross, S. E., & Sharpe, H. (2002). Neurophysiological correlates of memory for experienced and imagined events. *Neuropsychologica, 41*, 334–340.

Conway, M. A., & Rubin, D. C. (1993). The structure of autobiographical memory. In A. F. Collins, S. E. Gathercole, M. A. Conway, & P. E. Morris (Eds.), *Theories of memory* (pp. 103–137). Hillsdale, NJ: Lawrence Erlbaum Associates.

Coon, D. W., & Gallagher-Thompson, D. (2002). Encouraging homework completion among older adults in therapy. *Journal of Clinical Psychology, 58*, 549–563.

Corteen, R. S., & Dunn, D. (1974). Shock-associated words in a nonattended message: A test for momentary awareness. *Journal of Experimental Psychology, 102*, 1143–1144.

Corteen, R. S., & Wood, B. (1972). Autonomic responses to shock-associated words in an unattended channel. *Journal of Experimental Psychology, 94*, 308–313.

Cosmides, L., & Tooby, J. (1992). Cognitive adaptations for social exchange. In J. H. Barkow, L. Cosmides, & J. Tooby (Eds.), *The adapted mind: Evolutionary psychology and the generation of culture* (pp. 163–228). Oxford, UK: Oxford University Press.

Cosmides, L., & Tooby, J. (1996). Are humans good intuitive statisticians after all? Rethinking some conclusions from the literature on judgment under uncertainty. *Cognition, 58*, 1–73.

Cowan, N. (1988). Evolving conceptions of memory storage, selective attention, and their mutual constraints within the human information processing system. *Psychological Bulletin, 104*, 163–191.

Cowan, N. (1995). *Attention and memory: An integrated framework.* Oxford, UK: Oxford University Press.

Cowan, N., Lichty, W., & Grove, T. R. (1990). Properties of memory for unattended spoken syllables. *Journal of Experimental Psychology: Learning, Memory, and Cognition, 16,* 258–269.

Cozolino, L. J. (2002). *The neuroscience of psychotherapy: Building and rebuilding the human brain.* New York: Norton.

Crawford, M. T., & McCrea, S. M. (2004). When mutations meet motivations: Attitude biases in counterfactual thought. *Journal of Experimental Social Psychology, 40,* 65–74.

Cummins, D. D., Lubart, T., Alksnis, O., & Rist, R. (1991). Conditional reasoning and causation. *Memory and Cognition, 10,* 274–282.

Czaczkes, B., & Ganzach, Y. (1996). The natural selection of prediction heuristics: Anchoring and adjustment versus representativeness. *Journal of Behavioral Decision Making, 9,* 125–139.

Dalgliesh, T., & Watts, F. N. (1990). Biases of attention and memory disorders of anxiety and depression. *Clinical Psychology Review, 10,* 589–604.

Dandoy, A. C., & Goldstein, A. G. (1990). The use of cognitive appraisal to reduce stress reactions: A replication. *Journal of Social Behavior and Personality, 5,* 275–285.

Darke, S. (1988). Anxiety and working memory capacity. *Cognition and Emotion, 2,* 145–154.

Dattilio, F. M. (2002). Homework assignments in couple and family therapy. *Journal of Clinical Psychology, 58,* 535–547.

Davies, D. R., & Parasuraman, R. (1982). *The psychology of vigilance.* New York: Academic Press.

Davis, C. G., & Lehman, D. R. (1995). Counterfactual thinking and coping with traumatic life events. In N. J. Roese & J. M. Olson (Eds.), *What might have been: The social psychology of counterfactual thinking* (pp. 353–374). Hillsdale, NJ: Lawrence Erlbaum Associates.

Davis, C. G., Lehman, D. R., Silver, R. C., Wortman, C. M., & Ellard, J. H. (1996). Self-blame following a traumatic event: The role of perceived avoidability. *Personality and Social Psychology Bulletin, 22,* 557–567.

Davis, C. G., Lehman, D. R., Wortman, C. M., Silver, R. C., & Thompson, S. C. (1995). The undoing of traumatic life events. *Personality and Social Psychology Bulletin, 21,* 109–124.

Dawes, R. M. (1994). *House of cards: Psychology and psychotherapy built on myth.* New York: Free Press.

DeJong, P., & Berg, I. K. (1998). *Learner's workbook for interviewing for solutions.* Pacific Grove, CA: Brooks/Cole.

DeLoach, J. S., Cassidy, D. J., & Brown, A. L. (1985). Precursors of mnemonic strategies in very young children's memory. *Child Development, 56,* 125–137.

Dembrowski, T. M., MacDougall, J. M., Williams, R. B., Haney, T. L., & Blumenthal, J. A. (1985). Components of Type A, hostility, and anger in relationships to angiographic findings. *Psychosomatic Medicine, 47,* 219–233.

De Neys, W., Schaeken, W., & d'Ydewalle, G. (2003). Inference suppression and semantic memory retrieval: Every counterexample counts. *Memory and Cognition, 13,* 581–595.

Dermitzaki, I., & Efklides, A. (2003). Goal orientations and their effect on self-concept and metacognition in adolescence. *The Journal of the Hellenic Psychological Society, 10,* 214–227.

Derryberry, D., & Rothbart, M. K. (1988). Arousal, affect, and attention as components of temperament. *Journal of Personality and Social Psychology, 55,* 958–966.

Derryberry, D., & Rothbart, M. K. (1997). Reactive and effortful processes in the organization of temperament. *Development and Psychopathology, 9,* 633–652.

Derryberry, D., & Tucker, D. M. (1994). Motivating the focus of attention. In P. M. Niedenthal & S. Kitayama (Eds.), *The heart's eye: Emotional influences in perception and attention* (pp. 167–196). San Diego, CA: Academic Press.

DeRubeis, R. J., Tang, T. Z., & Beck, A. T. (2001). Cognitive therapy. In K. S. Dobson (Ed.), *Handbook of cognitive behavioral therapies* (2nd ed., pp. 349–392). New York: Guilford.

de Shazer, S. (1988). *Clues: Investigating solutions in brief therapy*. New York: Norton.

Desjarlais, M. D. (2002). *Self-generated versus assigned intentions in everyday prospective memory of students*. Unpublished honours thesis, Psychology Department, University of Regina.

Desoete, A., Roeyers, H., & De Clerq, A. (2003). Can offline metacognition enhance mathematical problem solving? *Journal of Educational Psychology, 95*, 188–200.

Diamond, A. (1991). Frontal lobe involvement in cognitive changes during the first year of life. In K. R. Gibson & A. C. Petersen (Eds.), *Brain maturation and cognitive development: Comparative and cross-cultural perspectives* (pp. 127–180). New York: De Gruyter.

Diesendruck, G., & Gelman, S. A. (1999). Domain differences in absolute judgments of category membership: Evidence for an essentialist account of categorization. *Psychonomic Bulletin and Review, 6*, 338–346.

Dimaggio, G., Semerari, A., Falcone, M., Nicolo, G., Carcione, A., & Procacci, M. (2002). Metacognition, states of mind, cognitive biases, and interpersonal cycles: Proposal for an integrated narcissism model. *Journal of Psychotherapy Integration, 12*, 421–451.

Ditto, P. H., & Lopez, D. F. (1992). Motivated scepticism: Use of differential decision criteria for preferred and nonpreferred conclusions. *Journal of Personality and Social Psychology, 63*, 568–584.

Dixon, R. A., de Frias, C. M., & Backman, L. (2001). Characteristics of self-reported memory compensation in older adults. *Journal of Clinical and Experimental Neuropsychology, 23*, 650–661.

Dobson, K. S. (Ed.). (2001). *Handbook of cognitive behavioral therapies* (2nd ed.). New York: Guilford.

Doherty, M. E., Mynatt, C. R., Tweeney, R. D., & Schiavo, M. D. (1979). Pseudodiagnosticity. *Acta Psychologica, 43*, 111–121.

Dorahy, M. J. (2001). Dissociative identity disorder and memory dysfunction: The current state of experimental research and future directions. *Clinical Psychology Review, 21*, 771–795.

Dorahy, M. J., Irwin, H. J., & Middleton, W. (2002). Cognitive inhibition in dissociative identity disorder (DID): Developing an understanding of working memory function in DID. *Journal of Trauma and Dissociation, 3*, 111–132.

Dryden, W., & Ellis, A. (2001). Rational emotive behavior therapy. In K. S. Dobson (Ed.), *Handbook of cognitive-behavioral therapies* (2nd ed., pp. 295–348). New York: Guilford.

Dunbar, D. C., & Lishman, W. A. (1984). Depression, recognition memory and hedonic tone: A signal detection analysis. *British Journal of Psychiatry, 144*, 376–382.

Duncan, J. (1994). Attention, intelligence, and the frontal lobes. In M. Gazzaniga (Ed.), *The cognitive neurosciences* (pp. 721–723). Cambridge, MA: MIT Press.

Dunlosky, J., & Hertzog, C. (1998). Training programs to improve learning in later adulthood: Helping older adults educate themselves. In D. J. Hacker, J. Dunlosky, & A. C. Graesser (Eds.), *Metacognition in educational theory and practice* (pp. 249–275). Mahwah, NJ: Lawrence Erlbaum Associates.

Dunning, D., Johnson, K., Ehrlinger, J., & Kruger, J. (2003). Why people fail to recognize their own incompetence. *Current Directions in Psychological Science, 12*, 83–87.

Dweck, C. S. (1999). *Self-theories: Their role in motivation, personality, and development*. Philadelphia: Psychology Press.

D'Zurillo, T. J., & Nezu, A. M. (1999). *Problem-solving therapy: A social competence approach to clinical intervention* (2nd ed.). New York: Springer.

D'Zurillo, T. J., & Nezu, A. M. (2001). Problem-solving therapies. In K. S. Dobson (Ed.), *Handbook of cognitive-behavioral therapies* (2nd ed., pp. 211–245). New York: Guilford.

Easterbrook, J. A. (1959). The effect of emotion on cue utilization and the organization of behavior. *Psychological Review, 66*, 183–201.

Ebbinghaus, H. (1964). *Memory* (H. A. Ruger & C. E. Bussenius, Trans.). New York: Dover. (Original work published 1885)

Ecton, R. B., & Feindler, E. L. (1990). Anger control training for temper control disorders. In E. L. Feindler & G. R. Kalfur (Eds.), *Adolescent behavior therapy handbook* (pp. 351–371). New York: Springer.

Edelman, R. E., & Chambless, D. L. (1995). Adherence during sessions and homework in cognitive-behavioral group treatment of social phobia. *Behavior Research and Therapy, 33*, 573–577.

Edwards, D. (1990). Cognitive therapy and the restructuring of early memories through guided imagery. *Journal of Cognitive Psychotherapy: An International Quarterly, 4*, 33–50.

Edwards, J. A., & Weary, G. (1993). Depression and the impression-formation continuum: Piecemeal processing despite the availability of category information. *Journal of Personality and Social Psychology, 64*, 636–645.

Edwards, K., & Smith, E. E. (1996). A disconfirmation bias in the evaluation of arguments. *Journal of Personality and Social Psychology, 71*, 5–24.

Efklides, A., & Tsiora, A. (2002). Metacognitive experiences, self-concept, and self-regulation. *Psychologia: An International Journal of Psychology in the Orient, 45*, 222–236.

Egan, G. (1994). *The skilled helper: A problem-management approach to helping* (5th ed.). Pacific Grove, CA: Brooks/Cole.

Eich, E. (1995). Theoretical issues in state dependent memory. In H. L. Roediger & F. I. M. Craik (Eds.), *Varieties of memory and consciousness: Essays in honor of Endel Tulving* (pp. 331–354). Hillsdale, NJ: Lawrence Erlbaum Associates.

Eich, E., & Schooler, J. W. (2000). Cognition/emotion interactions. In E. Eich, J. F. Kihlstrom, G. H. Bower, J. P. Forgas, & P. M. Niedenthal (Eds.), *Cognition and emotion* (pp. 3–29). Oxford, UK: Oxford University Press.

Eich, J. E. (1980). The cue-dependent nature of state-dependent retention. *Memory and Cognition, 8*, 157–173.

Einhorn, H. J., & Hogarth, R. M. (1986). Judging probable cause. *Psychological Bulletin, 99*, 3–19.

Einstein, G. O., Holland, L. J., McDaniel, M. A., & Guynn, M. J. (1992). Age related deficits in prospective memory: The influence of task complexity. *Psychology and Aging, 7*, 471–478.

Einstein, G. O., & McDaniel, M. A. (1990). Normal aging and prospective memory. *Journal of Experimental Psychology: Learning, Memory, and Cognition, 16*, 717–726.

Einstein, G. O., & McDaniel, M. A. (1996). Retrieval processes in prospective memory: Theoretical approaches and some new empirical findings. In M. Brandimonte, G. O. Einstein, & M. A. McDaniel (Eds.), *Prospective memory: Theory and applications* (pp. 115–142). Mahwah, NJ: Lawrence Erlbaum Associates.

Einstein, G. O., McDaniel, M. A., Manzi, M., Cochran, B., & Baker, M. (2000). Prospective memory and aging: Forgetting intentions over short delays. *Psychology and Aging, 15*, 671–683.

Eisen, M. L., Morgan, D. Y., & Mickes, L. (2002). Individual differences in eyewitness memory and suggestibility: Examining relations between acquiescence, dissociation, and resistance to misleading information. *Personality and Individual Differences, 33*, 553–571.

Ekman, P. (1984). Expression and the nature of emotion. In K. Scherer & P. Ekman (Eds.), *Approaches to emotion* (pp. 319–343). Hillsdale, NJ: Lawrence Erlbaum Associates.

Ekman, P. (1994). All emotions are basic. In P. Ekman & R. J. Davidson (Eds.), *The nature of emotion: Fundamental questions* (pp. 15–19). Oxford, UK: Oxford University Press.

Elkind, I. (1994). The NIMH treatment of depression collaborative research program: Where we began and where we are. In A. E. Bergin & S. L. Garfield (Eds.), *Handbook of psychotherapy and behavior change* (4th ed., pp. 114–142). New York: Wiley.

Ellis, A. (1970). A weekend of rational encounter. *Rational Living, 4,* 1–8.

Ellis, A. (2002). *Overcoming resistance: A rational emotive behavior therapy integrated approach* (2nd ed.). New York: Springer.

Ellis, H. C., & Ashbrook, P. W. (1988). Resource allocation model of the effects of depressed mood states on memory. In K. Fiedler & J. Forgas (Eds.), *Affect, cognition, and social behavior* (pp. 25–43). Toronto: Hogrefe.

Ellis, H. C., Moore, B. A., Varner, L. J., Ottaway, S. A., & Becker, A. S. (1997). Depressed mood, task organization, cognitive interference, and memory: Irrelevant thoughts predict recall performance. *Journal of Social Behavior and Personality, 12,* 453–470.

Ellis, H. C., Thomas, R. L., & Rodriguez, I. A. (1984). Emotional mood states and memory: Elaborative encoding, semantic processing, and cognitive effort. *Journal of Experimental Psychology: Learning, Memory, and Cognition, 10,* 470–482.

Ellis, S., & Siegler, R. S. (1994). Development of problem solving. In R. J. Sternberg (Ed.), *Thinking and problem solving* (pp. 334–367). San Diego, CA: Academic Press.

Emery, G. (2000). *Overcoming depression: A cognitive-behavior protocol for the treatment of depression.* Oakland, CA: New Harbinger.

Engebretson, T. O., Matthews, K. A., & Scheier, M. F. (1989). Relations between anger expression and cardiovascular reactivity: Reconciling inconsistent findings through a matching hypothesis. *Journal of Personality and Social Psychology, 57,* 513–521.

Enright, S. J., & Beech, A. R. (1993). Reduced cognitive inhibition in obsessive-compulsive disorder. *British Journal of Clinical Psychology, 32,* 67–74.

Epley, N., & Gilovich, T. (2004). Are adjustments insufficient? *Personality and Social Psychology Bulletin, 30,* 447–460.

Erber, R. (1991). Affective and semantic priming: Effects of mood on category accessibility and inference. *Journal of Experimental Social Psychology, 27,* 480–498.

Erber, R., & Erber, M. W. (1994). Beyond mood and social judgment: Mood incongruent recall and mood regulation. *European Journal of Social Psychology, 24,* 79–88.

Erber, R., & Tesser, A. (1992). Task effort and the regulation of mood: The absorption hypothesis. *Journal of Experimental Social Psychology, 28,* 339–359.

Erdelyi, M. H. (1990). Repression, reconstructions, and defense: History and integration of the psychoanalytic and experimental frameworks. In J. L. Singer (Ed.), *Repression and dissociation: Implications for personality theory, psychopathology, and health* (pp. 1–31). Chicago: University of Chicago Press.

Erdelyi, M. H. (2001). Defense processes can be conscious or unconscious. *American Psychologist, 56,* 761–762.

Erdelyi, M. H., & Kleinbard, J. (1978). Has Ebbinghaus decayed with time? The growth of recall (hypermnesia) over days. *Journal of Experimental Psychology: Human Learning and Memory, 4,* 275–289.

Erickson, M. H., Rossi, E. L., & Rossi, S. I. (1976). *Hypnotic realities: The induction of clinical hypnosis and forms of indirect suggestion.* New York: Irvington.

Ericsson, K. A., & Charness, N. (1994). Expert performance: Its structure and acquisition. *American Psychologist, 49,* 725–747.

Esses, V. M. (1989). Mood as a moderator of acceptance of interpersonal feedback. *Journal of Personality and Social Psychology, 57*, 769–781.

Esses, V. M., Haddock, G., & Zanna, M. P. (1993). Values, stereotypes, and emotions as determinants of intergroup attitudes. In D. M. Mackie & D. L. Hamilton (Eds.), *Affect, cognition, and stereotyping: Interactive processes in group perception* (pp. 137–166). San Diego, CA: Academic Press.

Estes, Z. (2003). Domain differences in the structure of artifactual and natural categories. *Memory and Cognition, 31*, 199–214.

Evans, J. St. B. T. (1996). Deciding before you think: Relevance and reasoning in the selection task. *British Journal of Psychology, 87*, 223–240.

Evans, J. St. B. T. (1998). Matching bias in conditional reasoning: Do we understand it after 25 years? *Thinking and Reasoning, 4*, 45–82.

Evans, J. St. B. T. (2002). Logic and human reasoning: An assessment of the deduction paradigm. *Psychological Bulletin, 128*, 978–996.

Evans, J. St. B. T. (2003). In two minds: Dual processing accounts of reasoning. *Trends in Cognitive Sciences, 7*, 454–459.

Evans, J. St. B. T., Clibbens, J., Cattani, A., Harris, A., & Dennis, I. (2003). Explicit and implicit processes in multicue judgment. *Memory and Cognition, 31*, 608–618.

Evans, J. St. B. T., Handley, S. J., Perham, N., Over, D. E., & Thompson, V. A. (2000). Frequency versus probability formats in statistical word problems. *Cognition, 77*, 197–213.

Evans, J. St. B. T., Legrenzi, P., & Girotto, V. (1999). The influence of linguistic form on reasoning. *Quarterly Journal of Experimental Psychology: Human Experimental Psychology, 52A*, 185–216.

Evans, J. St. B. T., Newstead, S. E., Allen, J. L., & Pollard, P. (1994). Debiasing by instruction: The case of belief bias. *European Journal of Cognitive Psychology, 61*, 263–285.

Evans, J. St. B. T., & Over, D. E. (1996). Rationality in the selection task: Epistemic utility versus uncertainty reduction. *Psychological Review, 103*, 356–363.

Evans, J. St. B. T., & Over, D. E. (2004). *If.* Oxford, UK: Oxford University Press.

Evans, J. St. B. T., Venn, S., & Feeney, A. (2002). Implicit and explicit processes in a hypothesis testing task. *British Journal of Psychology, 93*, 31–46.

Eysenck, M. W., & Keane, M. T. (1995). *Cognitive psychology: A student's handbook* (3rd ed.). East Sussex, UK: Psychology Press.

Eysenck, M. W., MacLeod, C., & Mathews, A. (1987). Cognitive functioning in anxiety. *Psychological Research, 49*, 189–195.

Fazio, R., Jackson, J. R., Dunton, B., & Williams, C. J. (1995). Variability in automatic activation as an unobtrusive measure of racial attitudes: A bona fide pipeline? *Journal of Personality and Social Psychology, 69*, 1013–1027.

Feltovich, P. J., Johnson, P. E., Moller, J. H., & Swanson, D. B. (1984). Acquiring expertise. In J. R. Anderson (Ed.), *Tutorials in learning and memory* (pp. 31–60). San Francisco: Freeman.

Feltovich, P. J., Spiro, R. J., & Coulson, R. L. (1997). Issues in expert flexibility in contexts characterized by complexity and change. In P. J. Feltovich, K. M. Ford, & R. R. Hoffman (Eds.), *Expertise in context* (pp. 126–146). Cambridge, MA: MIT Press.

Fennel, M. J. V., Teasdale, J. D., Jones, S., & Damle, A. (1987). Distraction in neurotic and endogenous depression: An investigation of negative thinking in major depressive disorder. *Psychological Medicine, 17*, 441–452.

Fiedler, K. (2000). Toward an integrative account of affect and cognition phenomena using the BIAS computer algorithm. In J. P. Forgas (Ed.), *Thinking and feeling: The role of affect in social cognition* (pp. 223–252). Cambridge, UK: Cambridge University Press.

Fiedler, K., Asbeck, J., & Nickel, S. (1991). Mood and constructive memory effects on social judgment. *Cognition and Emotion, 5*, 363–378.

Fieldler, K. (2000). Beware of samples! A cognitive-ecological sampling approach to judgment biases. *Psychological Review, 107*, 659–676.

Fischhoff, B. (1996). The real world: What good is it? *Organizational Behavior and Human Decision Processes, 65*, 232–248.

Fisher, S., & Greenberg, R. P. (1985). *The scientific credibility of Freud's theories and therapy.* New York: Columbia University Press.

Fitzsimons, G. M., & Bargh, J. A. (2004). Automatic self-regulation. In R. F. Baumeister & K. D. Vohs (Eds.), *Handbook of self-regulation: Research, theory, and applications* (pp. 151–170). New York: Guilford.

Fivush, R., & Haden, C. A. (Eds.). (2003). *Autobiographical memory and the construction of a narrative self.* Mahwah, NJ: Lawrence Erlbaum Associates.

Foa, E. B. (1997). Psychological processes related to recovery from a trauma and effective treatment for PTSD. In R. Yehuda & A. C. McFarlane (Eds.), *Psychobiology of posttraumatic stress disorder* (Vol. 823, pp. 410–424). New York: New York Academy of Sciences.

Folkman, S., Chesney, M., Collette, L., Boccellari, A., & Cooke, M. (1996). Postbereavement depressive mood and its prebereavement predictors in HIV+ and HIV– gay men. *Journal of Personality and Social Psychology, 70*, 336–348.

Foote, W. W. (1996). Guided imagery therapy. In B. N. Scotton, A. B. Chicen, & J. R. Battista (Eds.), *Textbook of transpersonal psychiatry and psychology* (pp. 355–365). New York: Basic Books.

Forgas, J. P. (1991a). Affect and cognition in close relationships. In G. Fletcher & F. Fincham (Eds.), *Cognition in close relationships* (pp. 151–174). Hillsdale, NJ: Lawrence Erlbaum Associates.

Forgas, J. P. (1991b). Mood effects on partner choice: Role of affect in social decisions. *Journal of Personality and Social Psychology, 61*, 708–720.

Forgas, J. P. (1992). Mood and the perception of unusual people: Affective asymmetry in memory and social judgments. *European Journal of Social Psychology, 22*, 531–547.

Forgas, J. P. (1995a). Mood and judgment: The Affect Infusion Model (AIM). *Psychological Bulletin, 117*, 39–66.

Forgas, J. P. (1995b). Strange couples: Mood effects on judgments and memory about prototypical and atypical targets. *Personality and Social Psychology Bulletin, 21*, 747–765.

Forgas, J. P. (1998a). Asking nicely? The effects of mood on responding to more or less polite requests. *Personality and Social Psychology Bulletin, 24*, 173–185.

Forgas, J. P. (1998b). On feeling good and getting your way: Mood effects on negotiator cognition and bargaining strategies. *Journal of Personality and Social Psychology, 74*, 565–577.

Forgas, J. P. (1999a). Feeling and speaking: Mood effects on verbal communication strategies. *Personality and Social Psychology Bulletin, 25*, 850–863.

Forgas, J. P. (1999b). On feeling good and being rude: Affective influences on use and request formulations. *Journal of Personality and Social Psychology, 76*, 928–939.

Forgas, J. P. (2000). *Thinking and feeling: The role of affect in social cognition.* Cambridge, UK: Cambridge University Press.

Forgas, J. P., & Bower, G. H. (1987). Mood effects on person perception judgements. *Journal of Personality and Social Psychology, 53*, 53–60.

Forgas, J. P., Bower, G. H., & Krantz, S. (1984). The influence of mood on perceptions of social interactions. *Journal of Experimental Social Psychology, 20*, 497–513.

Forgas, J. P., Bower, G. H., & Moylan, S. J. (1990). Praise or blame? Affective influences on attributions for achievement. *Journal of Personality and Social Psychology, 59*, 809–818.

Forgas, J. P., & Fiedler, K. (1996). Us and them: Mood effects on intergroup discrimination. *Journal of Personality and Social Psychology, 20*, 497–513.

Forgas, J. P., Levinger, G., & Moylan, S. (1994). Feeling good and feeling close: Mood effects on the perception of intimate relationships. *Personal Relationships, 2*, 165–184.

Forgas, J. P., & Moylan, S. (1991). Affective influences on stereotype judgments. *Cognition and Emotion, 5*, 379–397.

Forgas, J. P., & Moylan, S. J. (1987). After the movies: The effects of transient mood states on social judgments. *Personality and Social Psychology Bulletin, 13*, 478–489.

Fox, E. (1994). Attentional bias in anxiety: A defective inhibition hypothesis. *Cognition and Emotion, 8*, 165–195.

Francis, M. E., & Pennebaker, J. W. (1992). Putting stress into words: The impact of writing on physiological, absentee, and self-reported emotional well-being measures. *American Journal of Health Promotion, 6*, 280–287.

Franklin, M. E., & Foa, E. B. (2002). Cognitive behavioral treatments for obsessive compulsive disorder. In P. E. Nathan & J. M. Gordon (Eds.), *A guide to treatments that work* (2nd ed., pp. 367–386). London: Oxford University Press.

Freedman, E. G., & Smith, L. D. (1996). The role of data and theory in covariation assessment: Implications for the theory-ladenness of observations. *Journal of Mind and Behavior, 17*, 321–343.

Freeman, M. (1993). *Rewriting the self: History, memory, and narrative.* London: Routledge.

Freud, S. (1957). The unconscious. In J. Strachey (Ed. & Trans.), *The standard edition of the complete psychological works of Sigmund Freud* (Vol. 14, pp. 159–215). London: Hogarth Press. (Original work published 1915)

Freud, S. (1959). Inhibition, symptoms, and anxiety. In J. Strachey (Ed. & Trans.), *The standard edition of the complete psychological works of Sigmund Freud* (Vol. 20, pp. 167–172). London: Hogarth Press. (Original work published 1917)

Freud, S. (1961). *The ego and the id* (J. Strachey, Trans.). New York: Norton. (Original work published 1923)

Frick, P. J. (1998). *Conduct disorders and severe antisocial behavior.* New York: Plenum.

Friedberg, R. D., & McClure, J. M. (2002). *Clinical practice of cognitive therapy with children and adolescents.* New York: Guilford.

Friedman, H. S., & Booth-Kewley, S. (1987). The "disease-prone personality": A meta-analytic view of the construct. *American Psychologist, 42*, 539–555.

Fridja, N. J. (1986). *The emotions.* Cambridge, UK: Cambridge University Press.

Fridja, N. J., Kuipers, P., & ter Schure, E. (1989). Relations among emotion, appraisal, and emotional action readiness. *Journal of Personality and Social Psychology, 57*, 212–228.

Fridlund, A. J. (1991). Evolution and facial action in reflex, social motive, and paralanguage. *Biological Psychology, 32*, 3–100.

Fry, W. F. Jr., & Salameh, W. A. (Eds.). (1993). *Advances in humor and psychotherapy.* Sarasota, FL: Professional Resource Press/Professional Resource Exchange.

Fugelsang, J. A., Stein, C. B., Green, A. E., & Dunbar, K. N. (2004). Theory and data interactions of the scientific mind: Evidence from the molecular and the cognitive laboratory. *Canadian Journal of Experimental Psychology, 58*, 86–95.

Fugelsang, J. A., & Thompson, V. A. (2000). Strategy selection in causal reasoning: When beliefs and covariation collide. *Canadian Journal of Experimental Psychology, 54*, 15–32.

Fugelsang, J. A., & Thompson, V. A. (2003). A dual-process model of belief and evidence interactions in causal reasoning. *Memory and Cognition, 31*, 800–815.

Gaensbauer, T. J. (1982). Regulation of emotional expression in infants from two contrasting caretaking environments. *Journal of the American Academy of Child Psychiatry, 21*, 163–170.

Gallo, D. A., Roberts, M. J., & Seamon, J. G. (1997). Remembering words not presented in lists: Can we avoid creating false memories? *Psychonomic Bulletin and Review, 4*, 271–276.

Galton, F. (1880). Statistics of mental imagery. *Mind, 5*, 301–318.

Garb, H. N. (1996). Taxometrics and the revision of diagnostic criteria. *American Psychologist, 51*, 553–554.

Garb, H. N. (1998). *Studying the clinician: Judgment research and psychological assessment.* Washington, DC: American Psychological Association.

Gawronski, B., Ehrenberg, K., Banse, R., Zukova, J., & Klauer, K. C. (2003). It's in the mind of the beholder: The impact of stereotypical associations on category-based and individuating impression formation. *Journal of Experimental Social Psychology, 39*, 16–30.

Gelman, S. A. (2000). The role of essentialism in children's concepts. In H. W. Reese (Ed.), *Advances in child development and behavior* (pp. 55–98). San Diego, CA: Academic Press.

Gendlin, E. T. (1996). *Focusing-oriented psychotherapy: A manual of the experiential method.* New York: Guilford.

Gentner, D., Ratterman, M. J., & Forbus, K. D. (1993). The roles of similarity in transfer: Separating retrievability from inferential soundness. *Cognitive Psychology, 25*, 524–575.

Ghetti, S. (2003). Memory for nonoccurrences: The role of metacognition. *Journal of Memory and Language, 48*, 722–739.

Gick, M. L., & Holyoak, K. J. (1980). Analogical problem solving. *Cognitive Psychology, 12*, 306–355.

Gick, M. L., & Holyoak, K. J. (1983). Schema induction and analogical transfer. *Cognitive Psychology, 15*, 1–38.

Gigerenzer, G. (1998). Ecological intelligence: An adaptation for frequencies. In D. Cummins & C. Allen (Eds.), *The evolution of mind* (pp. 9–29). Oxford, UK: Oxford University Press.

Gilbert, D. T. (2002). Inferential correction. In T. Gilcovich & D. Griffin (Eds.), *Heuristics and biases: The psychology of intuitive judgment* (pp. 167–184). Cambridge, UK: Cambridge University Press.

Gilbert, D. T., & Wilson, T. D. (2000). Miswanting: Some problems in the forecasting of future affective states. In J. P. Forgas (Ed.), *Thinking and feeling: The role of affect in social cognition* (pp. 178–197). Cambridge, UK: Cambridge University Press.

Giles, J. W. (2003). Children's essentialist beliefs about aggression. *Developmental Review, 23*, 413–443.

Girotto, V., & Gonzalez, M. (2001). Solving probabilistic and statistical problems: A matter of information structure and question form. *Cognition, 78*, 247–276.

Glaser, R. (1996). Changing the agency for learning: Acquiring expert performance. In K. A. Ericsson (Ed.), *The road to excellence: The acquisition of expert performance in the arts and sciences, sports, and games.* Mahwah, NJ: Lawrence Erlbaum Associates.

Gleicher, F., Kost, K. A., Baker, S. M., Strathman, A. J., Richman, S. A., & Sherman, S. J. (1990). The role of counterfactual thinking in judgments of affect. *Personality and Social Psychology Bulletin, 16*, 284–293.

Glenberg, A. M., & Epstein, W. (1987). Inexpert calibration of comprehension. *Memory & Cognition, 15*, 84–93.

Glenberg, A. M., Sanocki, T., Epstein, W., & Morris, C. (1987). Enhancing calibration of comprehension. *Journal of Experimental Psychology: General, 116*, 119–136.

Goddard, L., Dritschel, B., & Burton, A. (1996). Role of autobiographical memory in social problem solving and depression. *Journal of Abnormal Psychology, 105*, 609–616.

Goleman, D. (1995). *Emotional intelligence.* New York: Bantam.

Gollwitzer, P. M. (1999). Implementation intentions: Strong effects of simple plans. *American Psychologist, 54*, 493–503.

Gollwitzer, P. M., Fujita, K., & Oettingen, G. (2004). Planning and the implementation of goals. In R. F. Baumeister & K. D. Vohs (Eds.), *Handbook of self-regulation: Research, theory, and applications* (pp. 211–228). New York: Guilford.

Gonsalves, B., & Paller, K. A. (2000). Neural events that underlie remembering something that never happened. *Nature Neuroscience, 3,* 1316–1321.

Goodie, A. S., & Fantino, E. (1995). An experientially derived base-rate error in humans. *Psychological Science, 6,* 101–106.

Goodie, A. S., & Fantino, E. (1996). Learning to avoid the base-rate error. *Nature, 380,* 247–249.

Gordon, L. H., & Durana, C. (1999). The PAIRS program. In R. Berger & M. T. Hannah (Eds.), *Prevention approaches in couples therapy* (pp. 219–236). Philadelphia: Brunner/Mazel.

Gorman, M. E., & Gorman, M. E. (1984). A comparison of disconfirmatory, confirmatory, and control strategies on Wason's 2-4-6 task. *Quarterly Journal of Experimental Psychology: Human Experimental Psychology, 36,* 629–648.

Gorski, T. T., & Miller, M. (1982). *Counseling for relapse prevention.* Independence, MO: Independence Press.

Goschke, T., & Kuhl, J. (1993). Representation of intentions: Persisting activation in memory. *Journal of Experimental Psychology: Learning, Memory, and Cognition, 19,* 1211–1226.

Gottman, J. M. (1994). *What predicts divorce: The relationship between marital processes and marital outcomes.* Hillsdale, NJ: Lawrence Erlbaum Associates.

Gottman, J. M., Driver, J., & Tabares, A. (2002). Building the sound marital house: An empirically derived couple therapy. In A. Gurman & N. Jacobson (Eds.), *Clinical handbook of couple therapy* (3rd ed., pp. 373–399). New York: Guilford.

Goulding, M. M., & Goulding, R. L. (1979). *Changing lives through redecision therapy.* New York: Brunner/Mazel.

Gouvier, W. D., Pinkston, J. B., Santa-Maria, M. P., & Cherry, K. E. (2002). Base rate analysis in cross-cultural clinical psychology—diagnostic accuracy in the balance. In F. R. Ferraro (Ed.), *Minority and cross-cultural aspects of neuropsychological assessment. Studies on neuropsychology, development, and cognition* (pp. 375–386). Lisse, Netherlands: Swets & Zeitlinger.

Graf, P., & Komatsu, S. (1994). Process dissociation procedure: Handle with caution. *European Journal of Cognitive Psychology, 6,* 113–129.

Graf, P., & Uttl, B. (2001). Prospective memory: A new focus for research. *Consciousness and Cognition, 18,* 437–450.

Greenberg, L. S., & Paivio, S. C. (1997). *Working with emotions in psychotherapy.* New York: Guilford.

Greenberg, L. S., Rice, L. N., & Elliott, R. (1993). *Facilitating emotional change: The moment-by-moment process.* New York: Guilford.

Greenberg, L. S., & Safran, J. D. (1987). *Emotion in psychotherapy: Affect, cognition, and the process of change.* New York: Guilford.

Greenberg, M. A., & Stone, A. A. (1992). Emotional disclosures about traumas and its relation to health: Effects of previous disclosure and trauma severity. *Journal of Personality and Social Psychology, 71,* 588–602.

Greenspan, S. I. (1997). *Developmentally based psychotherapy.* Madison, CT: International Universities Press.

Gregory, R. J., Canning, S. S., Lee, T. W., & Wise, J. C. (2004). Cognitive bibliotherapy for depression: A meta-analysis. *Professional Psychology: Research and Practice, 35,* 275–280.

Grice, H. P. (1975). Logic and conversation. In P. Cole & J. L. Morgan (Eds.), *Syntax and semantics 3: Speech acts* (pp. 41–58). New York: Academic Press.

Gross, J. J. (1989). Emotional expression in cancer onset and progression. *Social Science and Medicine, 28*, 1239–1248.

Gross, J. J. (1998). The emerging field of emotion regulation: An integrative review. *Review of General Psychology, 2*, 271–299.

Gross, J. J., Carstensen, L. L., Pasupathi, M., Tsai, J., Goetestam Skorpen, C., & Tsu, A. Y. C. (1997). Emotion and aging: Experience, expression, and control. *Psychology and Aging, 12*, 590–599.

Gross, J. J., & Levinson, R. W. (1997). Hiding feelings: The acute effects of inhibiting positive and negative emotions. *Journal of Abnormal Psychology, 106*, 95–103.

Grossarth-Matticek, R., Bastiaans, J., & Kanzin, D. T. (1985). Psychosocial factors as strong predictors of mortality from cancer, ischaemic heart disease and stroke: The Yugoslav prospective study. *Journal of Psychosomatic Research, 29*, 168–176.

Gudykunst, W. H., Ting-Toomy, S., Sudweeks, S., & Stewart, L. P. (1995). *Building bridges: Interpersonal skills for a changing world.* Boston: Houghton Mifflin.

Guttentag, R., & Carroll, D. (1998). Memorability judgments for high- and low-frequency words. *Memory and Cognition, 26*, 951–958.

Guynn, M. J., McDaniel, M. A., & Einstein, G. O. (1998). Prospective memory: When reminders fail. *Memory and Cognition, 26*, 287–298.

Habermas, T., & Bluck, S. (2000). Getting a life: The emergence of the life story in adolescence. *Psychological Bulletin, 91*, 435–460.

Hadjichristidis, C., Sloman, S., Stevenson, R., & Over, D. (2004). Feature centrality and property induction. *Cognitive Science, 28*, 45–74.

Hagmayer, Y., & Waldmann, M. R. (2000). Simulating causal models: The way to structural sensitivity. In L. R. Gleitman & A. K. Joshi (Eds.), *Proceedings of the Twenty-Second Annual Conference of the Cognitive Science Society* (pp. 214–219). Mahwah, NJ: Lawrence Erlbaum Associates.

Halberstadt, J. B., & Niedenthal, P. M. (1997). Emotional state and the use of stimulus dimensions in judgment. *Journal of Personality and Social Psychology, 72*, 1018–1034.

Hanna, F. J. (2002). *Therapy with difficult clients: Using the precursors model to awaken change.* Washington, DC: American Psychological Association.

Hannah, E., & Meltzoff, A. N. (1993). Peer imitation by toddlers in laboratory, home, and daycare contexts: Implications for social learning and memory. *Developmental Psychology, 29*, 701–710.

Harley, K., & Reese, E. (1999). Origins of autobiographical memory. *Developmental Psychology, 35*, 1338–1348.

Harnishfeger, K. K. (1995). The development of cognitive inhibition: Theories, definitions, and research evidence. In F. N. Dempster & C. J. Brainerd (Eds.), *Interference and inhibition in cognition* (pp. 175–204). San Diego, CA: Academic Press.

Harries, C., Evans, J. St. B. T., & Dennis, I. (2000). Measuring doctors' self-insight into their treatment decisions. *Applied Cognitive Psychology, 14*, 455–477.

Harries, C., Evans, J. St. B. T., Dennis, I., & Dean, J. (1996). A clinical judgment analysis of prescription decisions in general practice. *Travail Humain, 59*, 87–111.

Harris, J. E. (1982). External memory aids. In U. Neisser (Ed.), *Memory observed: Remembering in natural contexts* (pp. 337–342). San Francisco: Freeman.

Harris, P. L., German, T., & Mills, P. (1996). Children's use of counterfactual thinking in causal reasoning. *Cognition, 61*, 233–259.

Hart, J. T. (1965). Memory and the feeling-of-knowing experience. *Journal of Educational Psychology, 56*, 208–216.

Harvey, A. G., & Bryant, R. A. (1998). The effect of thought suppression in acute stress disorder. *Behavior Research and Therapy, 36*, 983–990.

Haslam, N., & Ernst, D. (2002). Essentialist beliefs about mental disorders. *Journal of Social and Clinical Psychology, 21*, 628–644.

Haslam, N., Rothschild, L., & Ernst, D. (2000). Essentialist beliefs about social categories. *British Journal of Social Psychology, 39*, 113–127.

Haslam, N., Rothschild, L., & Ernst, D. (2002). Are essentialist beliefs associated with prejudice? *British Journal of Social Psychology, 41*, 87–100.

Hastie, R., & Dawes, R. M. (2001). *Rational choice in an uncertain world: The psychology of judgment and decision making.* Thousand Oaks, CA: Sage.

Hatala, R., Norman, G. R., & Brooks, L. R. (1999). Influence of a single example on subsequent electrocardiogram interpretation. *Teaching and Learning in Medicine, 11*, 110–117.

Haverkamp, B. E. (1993). Confirmatory bias in hypothesis testing for client-identified and counsellor self-generated hypotheses. *Journal of Counseling Psychology, 40*, 303–315.

Hawkins, S. A., & Hastie, R. (1990). Hindsight biased judgments of past events after the outcomes are known. *Psychological Bulletin, 107*, 311–327.

Hayes, J. R. (1981). *The complete problem solver.* Philadelphia: Franklin Institute Press.

Heaps, C., & Nash, M. (2001). Comparing recollective experience in true and false autobiographical memories. *Journal of Experimental Psychology: Learning, Memory and Cognition, 27*, 920–930.

Hearst, E. (1991). Psychology and nothing. *American Scientist, 79*, 432–443.

Heath, C., Larrick, R. P., & Wu, G. (1999). Goals as reference points. *Cognitive Psychology, 38*, 79–109.

Heatherton, T. F., & Vohs, K. D. (1998). Why is it so difficult to inhibit behavior? *Psychological Inquiry, 9*, 212–216.

Hecker, L. L., Mims, G. A., & Boughner, S. R. (2003). General systems theory, cybernetics, and family therapy. In L. Hecker & J. Wetchler (Eds.), *An introduction to marriage and family therapy.* New York: Haworth Clinical Practice Press.

Hecker, M. H. L., Chesney, M. A., Black, G. W., & Frautschi, N. (1988). Coronary prone behaviors in the Western Collaborative Group Study. *Psychosomatic Medicine, 50*, 153–164.

Heilbrun, A. B., & Cassidy, J. C. (1985). Toward an explanation of defensive projection in normals: The role of social cognition. *Journal of Social & Clinical Psychology, 3*, 190–200.

Henkel, L. A., & Franklin, N. (1998). Reality monitoring of physically similar and conceptually related objects. *Memory and Cognition, 26*, 678–680.

Henkel, L. A., Franklin, N., & Johnson, M. K. (2000). Cross-modal source monitoring confusions between perceived and imagined events. *Journal of Experimental Psychology: Learning, Memory, and Cognition, 26*, 321–335.

Henkel, L. A., Johnson, M. K., & De Leonardis, D. M. (1998). Aging and source monitoring: Cognitive processes and neuropsychological correlates. *Journal of Experimental Psychology: General, 127*, 251–268.

Herman, C. P., & Polivy, J. (1988). Studies of eating in normal dieters. In B. T. Walsh (Ed.), *Eating behavior in eating disorders* (pp. 95–112). Washington, DC: American Psychiatric Association Press.

Herman, J. L. (1992). *Trauma and recovery.* New York: Basic Books.

Hermans, D., Martens, K., De Cort, K., Pieters, G., & Eelen, P. (2002). Reality monitoring and metacognitive beliefs related to cognitive confidence in obsessive-compulsive disorder. *Behavior Research and Therapy, 41*, 383–401.

Henry, W. P. (1998). Science, politics, and the politics of science: The use and misuses of empirically validated treatments. *Psychotherapy Research, 8*, 126–140.

Hertzog, C. (2002). Metacognition in older adults: Implications for application. In T. J. Perfect & B. L. Schwartz (Eds.), *Applied metacognition* (pp. 169–196). Cambridge, UK: Cambridge University Press.

Hertzog, C., & Dixon, R. A. (1994). Metacognitive development in adulthood and old age. In J. Metcalfe & A. P. Shimamura (Eds.), *Metacognition: Knowing about knowing* (pp. 227–251). Cambridge, MA: MIT Press.

Heuer, F., & Reisberg, D. (1990). Vivid memories of emotional events: The accuracy of remembered minutiae. *Memory & Cognition, 18*, 496–506.

Heyman, G. D., & Gelman, S. A. (2000). Beliefs about the origins of human psychological traits. *Developmental Psychology, 36*, 665–678.

Heyman, G. D., & Giles, J. W. (2004). Valence effects in reasoning about evaluative traits. *Merrill-Palmer Quarterly, 50*, 86–109.

Hilton, D. (2002). Thinking about causality: Pragmatic, social, and scientific rationality. In P. Carruthers, S. Stich, et al. (Eds.), *The cognitive basis of science* (pp. 211–231). New York: Cambridge University Press.

Hilton, D., & Erb, H. (1996). Mental models and causal explanation: Judgements of probable cause and explanatory relevance. *Thinking and Reasoning, 2*, 273–308.

Hirshman, E., & Durante, R. (1992). Prime identification and semantic priming. *Journal of Experimental Psychology: Learning, Memory, and Cognition, 18*, 255–265.

Hirst, W. (1986). The psychology of attention. In J. E. LeDoux & W. Hirst (Eds.), *Mind and brain* (pp. 105–141). Cambridge, UK: Cambridge University Press.

Hirt, E. R., & Markman, K. D. (1995). Multiple explanation: A consider-an-alternative strategy for debiasing judgments. *Journal of Personality and Social Psychology, 69*, 1069–1086.

Hofstadter, D. R. (1979). *Godel, Escher, Bach: An eternal golden braid.* New York: Vintage Books.

Hogan, P. C. (2003). *The mind and its stories: Narrative universals and human emotion.* Cambridge, UK: Cambridge University Press.

Holmes, D. S. (1970). Differential change in affective intensity and the forgetting of unpleasant personal experiences. *Journal of Personality and Social Psychology, 3*, 234–239.

Holyoak, K. J. (1995). Problem solving. In E. E. Smith & D. N. Osherson (Eds.), *An invitation to cognitive science: Thinking* (pp. 267–296). Cambridge, MA: MIT Press.

Holyoak, K. J., & Koh, K. (1987). Surface and structural similarity in analogical transfer. *Memory and Cognition, 15*, 332–340.

Holyoak, K. J., & Thagard, P. (1997). The analogical mind. *American Psychologist, 52*, 35–44.

Houghton, G. (1990). The problem of serial order: A neural network model of sequence learning and recall. In R. Dale, C. Mellish, & M. Zock (Eds.), *Current research in natural language generation* (pp. 287–319). London: Academic Press.

Howe, M. L., Courage, M. L., & Edison, S. C. (2003). When autobiographical memory begins. *Developmental Review, 23*, 471–494.

Hoyt, M. F. (2003). Interviews with brief therapy experts. *American Journal of Psychotherapy, 57*, 149–150.

Hudson, J. L., & Kendall, P. C. (2002). Showing you can do it: Homework in therapy for children and adolescents with anxiety disorders. *Journal of Clinical Psychology, 58*, 525–534.

Hull, L., Farrin, L., Unwin, C., Everitt, B., Wykes, T., & David, A. S. (2003). Anger, psychopathology, and cognitive inhibition: A study of UK servicemen. *Personality and Individual Differences, 35*, 1211–1226.

Hunt, E. (1994). Problem solving. In R. J. Sternberg (Ed.), *Thinking and problem solving* (pp. 215–232). San Diego, CA: Academic Press.

Hyman, I. E. Jr., Husband, T. H., & Billings, J. F. (1995). False memories of childhood experiences. *Applied Cognitive Psychology, 9*, 181–197.

Hyman, I. E. Jr., & Pentland, J. (1996). The role of mental imagery in the creation of false childhood memories. *Journal of Memory and Language, 35*, 101–117.

Idzikowski, C., & Baddeley, A. D. (1983). Fear and dangerous environments. In G. R. J. Hockey (Ed.), *Stress and fatigue in human performance* (pp. 123–144). Chichester, UK: Wiley.

Ingram, R. E., & Kendall, P. L. (1986). Cognitive clinical psychotherapy: Implications of an information processing perspective. In R. E. Ingram (Ed.), *Information processing approaches to clinical psychology* (pp. 3–21). Orlando, FL: Academic Press.

Isen, A. (1985). The asymmetry of happiness and sadness in effects on memory in normal college students. *Journal of Experimental Psychology: General, 114*, 388–391.

Isen, A. M. (1987). Positive affect, cognitive processes, and social behavior. In L. Berkowitz (Ed.), *Advances in experimental social psychology* (Vol. 20, pp. 203–253). San Diego, CA: Academic Press.

Isen, A. M., Daubman, K. A., & Nowicki, G. P. (1987). Positive affect facilitates creative problem solving. *Journal of Personality and Social Psychology, 52*, 1122–1131.

Isen, A. M., & Levin, P. F. (1972). The effect of feeling good on helping: Cookies and kindness. *Journal of Personality and Social Psychology, 15*, 294–301.

Isen, A. M., Means, B., Partick, R., & Nowicki, G. (1982). Some factors influencing decision-making strategy and risk-taking. In M. S. Clark & S. T. Fiske (Eds.), *Affect and cognition: The 17th Annual Carnegie symposium on cognition* (pp. 243–261). Hillsdale, NJ: Lawrence Erlbaum Associates.

Isen, A. M., Shalker, T. E., Clark, M., & Karp, L. (1978). Affect, accessibility of material and memory, and behavior: A cognitive loop? *Journal of Personality and Social Psychology, 36*, 1–12.

Ito, T. A., & Urland, G. R. (2003). Race and gender on the brain: Electrocortical measures of attention to the race and gender of multiply categorizable individuals. *Journal of Personality and Social Psychology, 85*, 616–626.

Ivey, A. E., & Ivey, M. B. (1999). *Intentional interviewing and counseling: Facilitating development in a multicultural society* (4th ed.). Pacific Grove, CA: Brooks/Cole.

Izard, C. E. (1977). *Human emotions*. New York: Plenum.

Izard, C. E. (1993). Four systems for emotion activation: Cognitive and noncognitive processes. *Psychological Review, 100*, 68–90.

Jacobson, N. S., & Christensen, A. (1998). *Acceptance and change in couple therapy: A therapist's guide to transforming relationship*. New York: Norton.

Jacoby, L. L. (1991). A process dissociation framework: Separating automatic from intentional uses of memory. *Journal of Memory and Language, 30*, 513–541.

Jacoby, L. L., Begg, I. M., & Toth, J. P. (1997). In defense of functional independence: Violations of assumptions underlying the process-dissociation procedure? *Journal of Experimental Psychology: Learning, Memory, & Cognition, 23*, 484–495.

Jacoby, L. L., & Kelley, C. M. (1987). Unconscious influences of memory for a prior event. *Personality and Social Psychology Bulletin, 13*, 314–336.

Jacoby, L. L., Toth, J. P., Yonelinas, A. P., & Debner, J. A. (1994). The relationship between conscious and unconscious influences: Independence or redundancy? *Journal of Experimental Psychology: General, 123*, 216–219.

James, W. (1890). *The principles of psychology*. New York: Dover.

James, W. (1892). *Psychology*. New York: Holt.

Janeck, A. S., Calamari, J. E., Riemann, B. C., & Heffelfinger, S. K. (2002). Too much thinking about thinking?: Metacognitive differences in obsessive-compulsive disorder. *Journal of Anxiety Disorders, 17*, 181–195.

Janoff-Bulman, R. (1992). *Shattered assumptions: Toward a new psychology of trauma*. New York: Free Press.

Jobe, J. B., Tourangeau, R., & Smith, A. F. (1993). Contributions of survey research to the understanding of memory. *Applied Cognitive Psychology, 7*, 567–584.

Johnson, M. H., & Magaro, P. A. (1987). Effects of mood and severity on memory processes in depression and mania. *Psychological Bulletin, 101*, 28–40.

Johnson, M. K., Foley, M. A., Suengas, A. G., & Raye, C. L. (1988). Phenomenal characteristics of memories for perceived and imagined autobiographical events. *Journal of Experimental Psychology: General, 117*, 371–376.

Johnson, M. K., Hashtroudi, S., & Lindsay, D. S. (1993). Source monitoring. *Psychological Bulletin, 114*, 3–28.

Johnson, M. K., Nolde, S. F., & De Leonardis, D. M. (1996). Emotional focus and source monitoring. *Psychological Bulletin, 114*, 3–28.

Johnson, S. M. (2002). *Emotionally focused couple therapy with trauma survivors: Strengthening the attachment bond*. New York: Guilford.

Johnson, S. M., & Denton, W. (2002). Emotionally focused couple therapy: Creativity connection. In A. S. Gurman & N. S. Jacobson (Eds.), *Clinical handbook of couple therapy* (3rd ed., pp. 221–250). New York: Guilford.

Johnson, W. A., & Dark, V. J. (1986). Selective attention. *Annual Review of Psychology, 37*, 43–75.

Johnson, W. A., & Heinz, S. P. (1978). Flexibility and capacity demands of attention. *Journal of Experimental Psychology: General, 107*, 420–435.

Johnson-Laird, P. N., & Byrne, R. M. J. (1991). *Deduction*. Hillsdale, NJ: Lawrence Erlbaum Associates.

Johnson-Laird, P. N., & Byrne, R. M. J. (2002). Conditionals: A theory of meaning, pragmatics, and inference. *Psychological Review, 109*, 646–678.

Johnson-Laird, P. N., & Oatley, K. (1992). Basic emotions, rationality and folk theory. *Cognition and Emotion, 6*, 201–223.

Jones, G. (2003). Testing two cognitive theories of insight. *Journal of Experimental Psychology: Learning, Memory, and Cognition, 29*, 1017–1027.

Joordens, S., & Merikle, P. M. (1993). Independence or redundancy? Two models of conscious and unconscious influences. *Journal of Experimental Psychology: General, 122*, 462–467.

Joseph, S. A., Dalgleish, T., Williams, R., Thrasher, S., Yule, W., & Hodgkinson, P. (1997). Attitudes toward emotional expression and post-traumatic stress at 5 years following the Herald of Free Enterprise disaster. *British Journal of Clinical Psychology, 36*, 133–138.

Josephson, B. R., Singer, J. A., & Salovey, P. (1996). Mood regulation from memory: Repairing sad moods with happy memories. *Cognition and Emotion, 10*, 437–444.

Joshua, J. M., & DiMenna, D. (2000). *Read two books and let's talk next week: Using bibliotherapy in clinical practice*. New York: Wiley.

Joyner, M. H., & Kurtz-Costes, B. (1997). Metamemory development. In N. Cowan (Ed.), *The development of memory in childhood* (pp. 275–300). Hove, UK: Psychology Press.

Juola, J. F. (1986). Cognitive psychology and information processing: Content and process analysis for a psychology of mind. In R. E. Ingram (Ed.), *Information processing approaches to clinical psychology* (pp. 51–74). San Diego, CA: Academic Press.

Just, N., & Alloy, L. B. (1997). The response styles theory of depression: Tests and an extension of the theory. *Journal of Abnormal Psychology, 106*, 221–229.

Kahneman, D. (1995). Varieties of counterfactual thinking. In N. J. Roese & J. M. Olson (Eds.), *What might have been: The social psychology of counterfactual thinking* (pp. 375–396). Hillsdale, NJ: Lawrence Erlbaum Associates.

Kahneman, D., & Frederick, S. (2002). Representativeness revisited: Attribute substitution in intuitive judgment. In. T. Gilovich, D. Griffin, & D. Kahneman (Eds.), *Heuristics and biases: The psychology of intuitive judgment*. Cambridge, UK: Cambridge University Press.

Kahneman, D., & Henik, A. (1981). Perceptual organisation and attention. In M. Kubovy & J. R. Pomerantz (Eds.), *Perceptual organisation*. Hillsdale, NJ: Lawrence Erlbaum Associates.

Kahneman, D., & Miller, D. T. (2002). Norm theory: Comparing reality to its alternatives. In T. Gilovich, D. Griffin, & D. Kahneman (Eds.), *Heuristics and biases: The psychology of intuitive judgment*. Cambridge, UK: Cambridge University Press.

Kahneman, D., & Tversky, A. (1982). On the psychology of prediction. In D. Kahneman, P. Slovic, & A. Tversky (Eds.), *Judgment under uncertainty: Heuristics and biases*. Cambridge, UK: Cambridge University Press.

Kahneman, D., & Tversky, A. (1984). Choices, values, and frames. *American Psychologist, 39*, 341–350.

Kahney, H. (1986). *Problem solving: A cognitive approach*. Milton Keynes, UK: Open University Press.

Kaiser, J., Hinton, J. W., Krohne, H. W., Stewart, R., & Burton, R. (1995). Coping dispositions and physiological recovery from a speech preparation stressor. *Personality and Individual Differences, 19*, 1–11.

Kalish, C. W. (2002). Essentialist to some degree: Beliefs about the structure of natural kinds categories. *Memory and Cognition, 30*, 340–352.

Kamphuis, J. H., & Finn, S. E. (2002). Incorporating base rate information in daily clinical decision making. In J. N. Butcher (Ed.), *Clinical personality assessment: Practical approaches* (2nd ed., pp. 256–268). Oxford, UK: Oxford University Press.

Kanfer, F. H., & Gaelick, L. (1986). Self-management methods. In K. H. Kanfer & A. P. Goldstein (Eds.), *Helping people change: A textbook of methods* (3rd ed., pp. 283–345). Elmsford, NY: Pergamon Press.

Kaplan, A. S., & Murphy, G. L. (2000). Category learning with minimal prior knowledge. *Journal of Experimental Psychology: Learning, Memory, and Cognition, 26*, 829–846.

Kaplan, C. A., & Simon, H. A. (1990). In search of insight. *Cognitive Psychology, 22*, 374–419.

Kareev, Y., & Halberstadt, N. (1993). Evaluating negative tests and refutations in a rule discovery task. *Quarterly Journal of Experimental Psychology: Human Experimental Psychology, 46*, 715–727.

Kasimatis, M., & Wells, G. L. (1995). Individual differences in counterfactual thinking. In N. J. Roese & J. M. Olson (Eds.), *What might have been: The social psychology of counterfactual thinking* (pp. 81–101). Hillsdale, NJ: Lawrence Erlbaum Associates.

Kavenaugh, D. L., & Bower, G. H. (1985). Mood and self-efficacy: Impact of joy and sadness on perceived capabilities. *Cognitive Therapy and Research, 9*, 507–525.

Kazantzis, N. (2000). Power to detect homework effects in psychotherapy outcome research. *Journal of Consulting and Clinical Psychology, 68*, 166–170.

Kazantzis, N., & Deane, F. P. (1999). Psychologists' use of homework assignments in clinical practice. *Professional Psychology: Research and Practice, 30*, 581–585.

Kazantzis, N., Deane, F. P., & Ronan, K. R. (2000). Homework assignments in cognitive and behavioral therapy: A meta-analysis. *Clinical Psychology: Science and Practice, 7*, 189–202.

Kazantzis, N., & Lampropoulos, G. K. (2002). Reflecting on homework in psychotherapy: What can we conclude from research and experience. *Journal of Clinical Psychology, 58*, 577–585.

Kealy, K. L., & Arbuthnott, K. D. (2003). Phenomenal characteristics of guided imagery and autobiographical memories: Effects of conversational encoding and delay. *Applied Cognitive Psychology, 17*, 801–818.

Keane, M. (1989). Modelling problem solving in Gestalt "insight" problems. *Irish Journal of Psychology, 10*, 201–215.

Kegan, R. (1982). *The evolving self.* Cambridge, MA: Harvard University Press.

Kegan, R. (1994). *In over our heads.* Cambridge, MA: Harvard University Press.

Keil, F. C. (1989). *Concepts, kinds, and cognitive development.* Cambridge, MA: MIT Press.

Kelley, C. M., & Jacoby, L. L. (1996). Memory attributions: Remembering, knowing, and feeling of knowing. In L. M. Reder (Ed.), *Implicit memory and metacognition* (pp. 287–307). Mahwah, NJ: Lawrence Erlbaum Associates.

Kelley, C. M., & Lindsay, D. S. (1993). Remembering mistaken for knowing: Ease of retrieval as a basis for confidence in answers to general knowledge questions. *Journal of Memory and Language, 32,* 1–24.

Kennedy, M. C., Willis, W. G., & Faust, D. (1997). The base-rate fallacy in school psychology. *Journal of Psychoeducational Assessment, 15,* 292–307.

Kennedy-Moore, E., & Watson, J. C. (1999). *Expressing emotion: Myths, realties and therapeutic strategies.* New York: Guilford.

Kerns, K. A., Esso, K., & Thompson, J. (1999). Investigation of a direct intervention for improving attention in young children with ADHD. *Developmental Neuropsychology, 16,* 273–295.

Kershaw, T. C., & Ohlsson, S. (2004). Multiple causes of difficulty in insight: The case of the nine-dot problem. *Journal of Experimental Psychology: Learning, Memory, and Cognition, 30,* 3–15.

Kim, N. S., & Ahn, W. (2002). Clinical psychologists' theory-based representations of mental disorders predict their diagnostic reasoning and memory. *Journal of Experimental Psychology: General, 131,* 451–476.

Kindt, M., & van den Hout, M. (2003). Dissociation and memory fragmentation: Experimental effects on meta-memory but not on actual memory performance. *Behavior Research and Theory, 41,* 167–178.

King, L. A., & Emmonds, R. A. (1990). Conflict over emotional expression: Psychological and physical correlates. *Journal of Personality and Social Psychology, 58,* 864–877.

Kintsch, W., Healy, A. F., Regarty, M., Pennington, B. F., & Salthouse, T. A. (1999). Models of working memory: Eight questions and some general issues. In A. Miyake & P. Shah (Eds.), *Models of working memory: Mechanisms of active maintenance and executive control* (pp. 412–441). Cambridge, UK: Cambridge University Press.

Kjeldsen, A.-C., Niemi, P., & Oloffson, A. (2003). Training phonological awareness in kindergarten level children: Consistency is more important than quantity. *Learning and Instruction, 13,* 349–365.

Klaczynski, P. A. (1997). Bias in adolescents' everyday reasoning and its relationship with intellectual ability, personal theories, and self-serving motivation. *Developmental Psychology, 33,* 273–283.

Klaczynski, P. A., & Gordon, D. H. (1996). Everyday statistical reasoning during adolescence and young adulthood: Motivational, general ability, and developmental influences. *Child Development, 67,* 2873–2891.

Klaczynski, P. A., & Robinson, B. (2000). Personal theories, intellectual ability, and epistemological beliefs: Adult age differences in everyday reasoning biases. *Psychology and Aging, 15,* 400–416.

Klahr, D., Fay, A., & Dunbar, K. (1993). Heuristics for scientific experimentation: A developmental study. *Cognitive Psychology, 5,* 111–146.

Klauer, K. C., & Migulla, G. (1995). Spontaneous counterfactual processing. *Zeitschrift fur Sozialpsychologie, 26,* 34–42.

Klauer, K. C., Munsch, J., & Naumer, B. (2000). On belief bias in syllogistic reasoning. *Psychological Review, 107,* 852–884.

Klayman, J., & Ha, Y. (1987). Confirmation, disconfirmation, and information in hypothesis testing. *Psychological Review, 94*, 211–228.

Kleinsmith, L. J., & Kaplan, S. (1964). Interaction of arousal and recall interval in nonsense syllable paired associate learning. *Journal of Experimental Psychology, 67*, 124–126.

Kliegel, M., Martin, M., McDaniel, M. A., & Einstein, G. O. (2001). Varying the importance of a prospective memory task: Differential effects across time- and event-based prospective memory. *Memory, 9*, 1–11.

Klingberg, T., Forssberg, H., & Westerberg, H. (2002). Training on working memory in children with ADHD. *Journal of Clinical and Experimental Neuropsychology, 24*, 781–791.

Knauff, M., & Johnson-Laird, P. N. (2002). Visual imagery can impede reasoning. *Memory and Cognition, 30*, 363–371.

Knoblach, G., Ohlsson, S., & Rainey, G. E. (2001). An eye movement study of insight problem solving. *Memory and Cognition, 29*, 1000–1009.

Koehler, D. J. (1991). Explanation, imagination, and confidence in judgment. *Psychological Bulletin, 110*, 499–519.

Koehler, D. J. (1994). Hypothesis generation and confidence in judgment. *Journal of Experimental Psychology: Learning, Memory, and Cognition, 20*, 461–469.

Koehler, J. J. (1996). The base rate fallacy reconsidered: Descriptive, normative, and methodological challenges. *Behavioral and Brain Sciences, 9*, 1053.

Korb, M. P., Gorrell, J., & Van DeRiet, V. (1989). *Gestalt therapy: Practice and theory* (2nd ed.). Elmsford, NY: Pergamon.

Koriat, A. (2002). Metacognitive research: An interim report. In T. J. Perfect & B. L. Schwartz (Eds.), *Applied metacognition* (pp. 261–286). Cambridge, UK: Cambridge University Press.

Koriat, A., & Goldsmith, M. (1996). Monitoring and control processes in the strategic regulation of memory accuracy. *Psychological Review, 103*, 490–517.

Koriat, A., Goldsmith, M., Schneider, W., & Nakash-Dura, M. (2001). The credibility of children's testimony: Can children control the accuracy of their memory reports? *Journal of Experimental Child Psychology, 79*, 405–437.

Koriat, A., Lichtenstein, S., & Fischhoff, B. (1980). Reasons for confidence. *Journal of Experimental Psychology: Human Learning and Memory, 6*, 107–118.

Koriat, A., Sheffer, L., & Ma'ayan, H. (2002). Comparing objective and subjective learning curves: Judgments of learning exhibit decreased underconfidence with practice. *Journal of Experimental Psychology: General, 131*, 147–162.

Korte, J. (1995). *White gloves: How we create ourselves through memory*. New York: The Free Press.

Koslowski, B., & Masnick, A. (2002). The development of causal reasoning. In U. Goswami (Ed.), *Blackwell handbook of childhood cognitive development* (pp. 257–281). Oxford, UK: Blackwell.

Kovecses, Z. (2000). *Metaphor and emotion: Language, culture, and body in human feeling*. Cambridge, UK: Cambridge University Press.

Krause, E. D., Mendelson, T., & Lynch, T. R. (2003). Childhood emotional invalidation and adult psychological distress: The mediating role of emotional inhibition. *Child Abuse and Neglect, 27*, 199–213.

Kraut, A. G., & Smothergill, D. W. (1978). A two-factor theory of stimulus-repetition effects. *Journal of Experimental Psychology: Human Perception and Performance, 4*, 191–197.

Kreutzer, M. A., Leonard, C., & Flavell, J. H. (1982). Prospective remembering in children. In U. Neisser (Ed.), *Memory observed: Remembering in natural contexts* (pp. 343–348). San Francisco: Freeman.

Krystal, J. H., Southwick, S. M., & Charney, D. (1995). Post traumatic stress disorder: Psychobiological mechanisms of traumatic remembrance. In D. L. Schacter (Ed.), *Memory distortion: How minds, brains, and societies reconstruct the past* (pp. 150–172). Cambridge, MA: Harvard University Press.

Kuhn, D. (1989). Children and adults as intuitive scientists. *Psychological Review, 96*, 674–689.

Kuhn, D. (1991a). *The skills of argument.* New York: Cambridge University Press.

Kuhn, D. (1991b). Thinking as argument. *Howard Educational Review, 62*, 155–178.

Kunda, Z. (1999). *Social cognition: Making sense of people.* Cambridge, MA: MIT Press.

Kurtz, R. (1990). *Body-centered psychotherapy: The Hakomi method.* Mendocino, CA: Life Rhythm.

Kvavilashvili, L. (1987). Remembering intention as a distinct form of memory. *British Journal of Psychology, 78*, 507–518.

Kvavilashvili, L., & Ellis, J. A. (1996). Varieties of intention: Some distinctions and classifications. In M. Brandimonte, G. O. Einstein, & M. A. McDaniel (Eds.), *Prospective memory: Theory and applications* (pp. 23–52). Mahwah, NJ: Lawrence Erlbaum Associates.

Labarge, A. S., McCaffrey, R. T., & Brown, T. A. (2003). Neuropsychologists' abilities to determine the predictive value of diagnostic tests. *Archives of Clinical Neuropsychology, 15*, 1165–1175.

Labouvie-Vief, G., & Diehl, M. (2000). Cognitive complexity and cognitive-affective integration: Related or separate domains of adult development. *Psychology and Aging, 15*, 490–504.

Ladd, A. (2003). Emotional literacy and healthy relationships. In R. DeMaria & M. T. Hannah (Eds.), *Building intimate relationships: Bridging treatment, education, and enrichment through the PAIRS program* (pp. 131–148). New York: Brunner-Routledge.

Laessle, R. G., Platte, P., Schweiger, U., & Pirke, K. M. (1996). Biological and psychological correlates of intermittent dieting behavior in young women: A model for bulimia nervosa. *Physiology and Behavior, 60*, 1–5.

Lafferty, P., Beutler, L. E., & Crago, M. (1989). Differences between more and less effective psychotherapists: A study of select therapist variables. *Journal of Consulting and Clinical Psychology, 57*, 76–80.

Lakoff, G. (1987). *Women, fire, and dangerous things: What categories reveal about the mind.* Chicago: University of Chicago Press.

Lambert, J. J., & Barley, D. E. (2002). Research summary on the therapeutic relationship and psychotherapy outcome. In J. C. Norcross (Ed.), *Psychotherapy relationships that work: Therapist contributions and responsiveness to patients* (pp. 17–32). Oxford, UK: Oxford University Press.

Lampinen, J. M., Odegard, T. N., & Bullington, J. L. (2003). Qualities of memories for performed and imagined actions. *Applied Cognitive Psychology, 17*, 881–893.

Landman, J. (1993). *Regret: The persistence of the possible.* Oxford, UK: Oxford University Press.

Landman, J. (1995). Through a glass darkly: Worldviews, counterfactual thought, and emotion. In N. J. Roese & J. M. Olson (Eds.), *What might have been: The social psychology of counterfactual thinking* (pp. 233–258). Hillsdale, NJ: Lawrence Erlbaum Associates.

Landman, J. T., & Dawes, R. M. (1982). Psychotherapy outcome: Smith and Glass' conclusions stand up to scrutiny. *American Psychologist, 37*, 504–516.

Langer, E. J., Janis, I. L., & Wolfer, J. A. (1975). Reduction of psychological stress in surgical patients. *Journal of Experimental Social Psychology, 11*, 155–165.

Lankton, S. (1980). *Practical magic: A translation of basic neuro-linguistic programming into clinical psychotherapy.* Cupertino, CA: Meta.

Lankton, S. R., & Lankton, C. H. (1986). *Enchantment and intervention in family therapy: Training in Eriksonian approaches*. New York: Brunner/Mazel.

Larkin, J. H., McDermott, J., Simon, D. P., & Simon, H. A. (1980). Expert and novice performance in solving physics problems. *Science, 208*, 1335–1342.

Larrabee, G. J., West, R. L., & Crook, T. H. (1991). The association of memory complaint with computer-simulated everyday memory performance. *Journal of Clinical and Experimental Neuropsychology, 13*, 466–478.

Larsen, R. J., & Prizmic, Z. (2004). Affect regulation. In R. F. Baumeister & K. D. Vohs (Eds.), *Handbook of self-regulation: Research, theory, and applications* (pp. 40–61). New York: Guilford.

Latorre, M. A. (2000). A holistic view of psychotherapy: Connecting mind, body, and spirit. *Perspectives in Psychiatric Care, 36*, 67–68.

Lawton, M. P., Kleban, M. H., & Dean, J. (1993). Affect and age: Cross-sectional comparisons of structure and prevalence. *Psychology and Aging, 8*, 165–175.

Lay, K. L., Waters, E., & Park, K. A. (1989). Maternal responsiveness and child compliance: The role of mood as a mediator. *Child Development, 60*, 1405–1411.

Lazarus, A. A. (1992). Multimodel therapy: Technical eclecticism with minimal integration. In J. C. Norcross & M. R. Goldfried (Eds.), *Handbook of psychotherapy integration* (pp. 231–263). New York: Basic Books.

Lazarus, R. S. (1991). *Emotion and adaptation*. Oxford, UK: Oxford University Press.

Lazarus, R. S., & Folkman, S. (1984). *Stress, appraisal, and coping*. New York: Springer.

Lazo, M. G., Pumfrey, P. D., & Peers, I. (1997). Metalinguistic awareness, reading, and spelling: Roots and branches of literacy. *Journal of Research in Reading, 20*, 85–104.

Leahy, R. L. (2002). Improving homework compliance in the treatment of generalized anxiety disorder. *Journal of Clinical Psychology, 58*, 499–511.

Leblanc, V. R., Brooks, L. R., & Norman, G. R. (2002). Believing is seeing: The influence of a diagnostic hypothesis on the interpretation of clinical features. *Academic Medicine, 77*, S67–S69.

LeDoux, J. E. (1996). *The emotional brain*. New York: Simon & Schuster.

Leight, K. A., & Ellis, H. C. (1981). Emotional mood states, strategies, and state-dependency in memory. *Journal of Verbal Learning and Verbal Behavior, 20*, 251–266.

Lesgold, A., Rubinson, H., Feltovich, P., Glaser, R., Klopfer, D., & Wang, Y. (1988). Expertise in a complex skill: Diagnosing X-ray pictures. In M. T. H. Chi, R. Glaser, & M. J. Farr (Eds.), *The nature of expertise* (pp. 311–342). Hillsdale, NJ: Lawrence Erlbaum Associates.

Leung, A. W., & Heimberg, R. G. (1996). Homework compliance, perceptions of control, and outcome of cognitive-behavioral treatment of social phobia. *Behavior Research and Therapy, 34*, 423–432.

Leventhal, H., Patrick-Miller, L., Leventhal, E. A., & Burns, E. A. (1998). Does stress-emotion cause illness in elderly people? *Annual Review of Gerontology and Geriatrics, 17*, 138–184.

Leventhal, H., & Scherer, K. R. (1987). The relationship of emotion to cognition: A functional approach to a semantic controversy. *Cognition and Emotion, 1*, 3–28.

Levine, L. J. (1996). The anatomy of disappointment: A naturalistic test of appraisal models of sadness, anger, and hope. *Cognition and Emotion, 10*, 337–359.

Levinson, R. W. (1992). Autonomic nervous system differences among emotions. *Psychological Science, 3*, 23–27.

Levy, B., & Anderson, M. C. (2002). Inhibitory processes and the control of memory retrieval. *Trends in Cognitive Sciences, 6*, 299–305.

Lewinsohn, P. M., Munoz, R. F., Youngren, M. A., & Zeiss, A. M. (1986). *Control your depression* (Rev. ed.). New York: Prentice-Hall.

Lewinsohn, P. M., & Rosenbaum, M. (1987). Recall of parental behavior by acute depressives, remitted depressives, and nondepressives. *Journal of Personality and Social Psychology, 52,* 611–619.

Leynes, P. A., Marsh, R. L., Hicks, J. L., Allen, J. D., & Mayhorn, C. B. (2002). Investigating the encoding and retrieval of intentions with event-related potentials. *Consciousness and Cognition, 12,* 1–18.

Lindsay, D. S., & Briere, J. (1997). The controversy regarding recovered memories of childhood sexual abuse: Pitfalls, bridges, and future directions. *Journal of Interpersonal Violence, 12,* 631–647.

Lindsay, D. S., & Johnson, M. K. (1989). The eyewitness suggestibility effect and memory for source. *Memory and Cognition, 17,* 349–358.

Lindsay, D. S., Johnson, M. K., & Kwon, P. (1991). Developmental changes in memory source monitoring. *Journal of Experimental Child Psychology, 52,* 297–318.

Lindsay, D. S., Nilsen, E., & Read, J. D. (2000). Witnessing-condition heterogeneity and witnesses' versus investigators' confidence in the accuracy of witnesses' identification decisions. *Law and Human Behavior, 24,* 685–697.

Lindsay, D. S., Read, D. J., & Sharma, K. (1998). Accuracy and confidence in person identification: The relationship is strong when witnessing conditions vary widely. *Psychological Science, 9,* 215–218.

Linehan, M. M., Cochran, B. N., & Kehrer, C. A. (2001). Dialectical behavior therapy for borderline personality disorder. In D. H. Barlow (Ed.), *Clinical handbook of psychological disorders* (3rd ed., pp. 470–522). New York: Guilford.

Lobban, F., Haddock, G., Kinderman, P., & Wells, A. (2002). The role of metacognitive beliefs in auditory hallucinations. *Personality and Individual Differences, 32,* 1351–1363.

Loftus, E. F., & Palmer, J. C. (1974). Reconstruction of automobile destruction: An example of the interaction between language and memory. *Journal of Verbal Learning and Verbal Behavior, 13,* 585–589.

Lowen, A. (1975). *Bioenergetics.* London: Penguin Books.

Luchins, A. S., & Luchins, E. H. (1959). *Rigidity of behavior.* Eugene, OR: University of Oregon Press.

Lynch, T. R., Robins, C. J., Morse, J. Q., & Krause, E. D. (2001). A mediational model relating affect intensity, emotion inhibition, and psychological distress. *Behavior Therapy, 32,* 519–536.

Lyubomirsky, S., Caldwell, N. D., & Nolen-Hoeksema, S. (1998). Effects of ruminative and distracting responses to depressed mood on retrieval of autobiographical memories. *Journal of Personality and Social Psychology, 75,* 166–177.

Lyubomirsky, S., & Nolen-Hoeksema, S. (1995). Effects of self-focused rumination on negative thinking and interpersonal problem-solving. *Journal of Personality and Social Psychology, 69,* 176–190.

MacCoon, D. G., Wallace, J. F., & Newman, J. P. (2004). Self-regulation: Context-appropriate balanced attention. In R. F. Baumeister & K. D. Vohs (Eds.), *Handbook of self-regulation: Research, theory, and applications* (pp. 422–444). New York: Guilford.

MacDonald, P. A., Antony, M. M., MacLeod, C. M., & Richter, M. A. (1997). Memory and confidence in memory judgments among individuals with obsessive compulsive disorder and non-clinical controls. *Behavior Research and Therapy, 35,* 497–505.

MacGregor, J. N., Omerod, T. C., & Chronicle, E. P. (2001). Information processing and insight: A process model of performance on the nine-dot and related problems. *Journal of Experimental Psychology: Learning, Memory, and Cognition, 27,* 176–201.

MacKay, D. G. (1986). *Self-inhibition and the disruptive effects of internal and external feedback in skilled behavior* (Experimental Brain Research Series 15). Berlin: Springer-Verlag.

MacLeod, C. M., & Dunbar, K. (1988). Training and Stroop-like interference: Evidence for a continuum of automaticity. *Journal of Experimental Psychology: Learning, Memory, and Cognition, 14*, 126–135.

Magai, C. (2001). Emotion over the lifecourse. In J. Birren & K. W. Schaie (Eds.), *Handbook of the physiology of aging* (pp. 299–426). San Diego, CA: Academic Press.

Mahoney, M. J. (1979). *Self-change: Strategies for solving personal problems.* New York: Norton.

Mahoney, M. J. (1991). *Human change processes: The scientific foundations of psychotherapy.* New York: Basic Books.

Mahoney, M. J. (2003). *Constructive psychotherapy: A practical guide.* New York: Guilford.

Maier, N. R. F. (1931). Reasoning in humans: II. The solution of a problem and its appearance in consciousness. *Psychological Bulletin, 109*, 163–203.

Malatesta, C. Z., Jonas, R., & Izard, C. E. (1987). The relation between low facial expressivity during emotional arousal and somatic symptoms. *British Journal of Medical Psychology, 60*, 169–180.

Malinowski, P. T., & Lynn, S. J. (1999). The plasticity of very early memory reports: Social pressure, hypnotizability, compliance, and interrogative suggestibility. *International Journal of Clinical and Experimental Hypnosis, 47*, 320–343.

Malt, B. C. (1994). Water is not H-sub-2O. *Cognitive Psychology, 27*, 41–70.

Mandel, D. R. (2003). Judgment dissociation theory: An analysis of differences in causal, counterfactual, and covariational reasoning. *Journal of Experimental Psychology: General, 132*, 419–434.

Mandel, D. R., & Lehman, D. R. (1996). Counterfactual thinking and ascriptions of cause preventability. *Journal of Personality and Social Psychology, 71*, 450–463.

Mandel, D. R., & Lehman, D. R. (1998). Integration of contingency information in judgments of cause, covariation, and probability. *Journal of Experimental Psychology: General, 3*, 269–285.

Mandler, G. (1967). Organization and memory. In K. W. Spence & J. T. Spence (Eds.), *The psychology of learning and motivation* (Vol. 1, pp. 327–372). New York: Academic Press.

Marcell, A. J. (1980). Conscious and preconscious recognition of polysemous words: Locating the selective effects of prior verbal context. In R. S. Nickerson (Ed.), *Attention and performance VII* (pp. 435–457). Hillsdale, NJ: Lawrence Erlbaum Associates.

Markman, A. B., & Gentner, D. (1997). Structure mapping in analogy and similarity. *American Psychologist, 52*, 45–56.

Markman, A. B., & Ross, B. H. (2003). Category use and category learning. *Psychological Bulletin, 129*, 592–613.

Markovits, H. (1984). Awareness of the possible as a mediator of formal thinking in conditional reasoning problems. *British Journal of Psychology, 75*, 367–376.

Markovits, H. (1986). Familiarity effects in conditional reasoning. *Journal of Educational Psychology, 78*, 492–494.

Marsh, R. L., Hancock, T. W., & Hicks, J. L. (2002). The demands of an ongoing activity influence the success of event-based prospective memory. *Psychonomic Bulletin and Review, 9*, 604–610.

Marsh, R. L., & Hicks, J. L. (1998). Event-based prospective memory and executive control of working memory. *Journal of Experimental Psychology: Learning, Memory, and Cognition, 24*, 336–349.

Marsh, R. L., Hicks, J. L., & Bink, M. L. (1998). The activation of completed, uncompleted, and partially completed intentions. *Journal of Experimental Psychology: Learning, Memory, and Cognition, 24*, 350–361.

Marsh, R. L., Hicks, J. L., & Bryan, E. S. (1999). The activation of unrelated and canceled intentions. *Memory and Cognition, 27*, 320–327.

Marsh, R. L., Hicks, J. L., Cook, G. I., Hansen, J. S., & Pallos, A. L. (2003). Interference to ongoing activities covaries with the characteristics of an event-based intention. *Journal of Experimental Psychology: Learning, Memory, and Cognition, 29*, 861–870.

Marsh, R. L., Hicks, J. L., & Hancock, T. W. (2000). On the interaction of ongoing cognitive activity and the nature of an event-based intention. *Applied Cognitive Psychology, 14*, S29–S42.

Marsh, R. L., Hicks, J. L., & Landau, J. D. (1998). An investigation of everyday prospective memory. *Memory & Cognition, 26*, 633–643.

Marsh, R. L., Hicks, J. L., & Watson, V. (2002). The dynamics of intention retrieval and coordination of action in event-based prospective memory. *Journal of Experimental Psychology: Learning, Memory, and Cognition, 28*, 652–659.

Marsh, R. L., Landau, J. D., & Hicks, J. L. (1997). Contributions of inadequate source monitoring to unconscious plagiarism during idea generation. *Journal of Experimental Psychology: Learning, Memory, and Cognition, 23*, 886–897.

Martin, M., & Williams, R. (1990). Imagery and emotion: Clinical and experimental approaches. In P. J. Hampson, D. F. Marks, & J. T. E. Richardson (Eds.), *Imagery: Current developments* (pp. 268–306). London: Routledge.

Martin, R. A. (2001). Humor, laughter and physical health: Methodological issues and research findings. *Psychological Bulletin, 127*, 504–519.

Martineau, T. M., Wynne, G., Kaye, W., & Evans, T. R. (1990). Resuscitation: Experience without feedback increases confidence but not skill. *British Medical Journal, 300*, 849–850.

Mather, M., Henkel, L. A., & Johnson, M. K. (1997). Evaluating characteristics of false memories: Remember/know judgments and memory characteristics questionnaire compared. *Memory & Cognition, 25*, 826–837.

Mathews, A. M., & MacLeod, C. (1994). Cognitive approaches to emotion and emotional disorders. *Annual Review of Psychology, 45*, 25–50.

Matsumoto, D. (1993). Ethnic differences in affect intensity, emotion judgments, display rule attitudes, and self-reported emotional expression in an American sample. *Motivation and Emotion, 17*, 107–123.

Mayer, J. D., & Salovey, P. (1995). Emotional intelligence and the construction and regulation of feelings. *Applied and Preventive Psychology, 4*, 197–208.

Maylor, E. A. (1996). Age-related impairment in an event-based prospective-memory task. *Psychology and Aging, 11*, 74–78.

Maylor, E. A. (1998). Changes in event-based prospective memory across adulthood. *Aging, Neuropsychology, and Cognition, 5*, 107–128.

Maylor, E. A., Darby, R. J., & Della Sala, S. (2000). Retrieval of performed versus to-be-performed tasks: A naturalistic study of the intention superiority effect in normal aging and dementia. *Applied Cognitive Psychology, 14*, S83–S98.

Mayne, T. J. (1999). Negative affect and health: The importance of being earnest. *Cognition and Emotion, 13*, 601–635.

Mayr, U., & Keele, S. (2000). Changing internal constraints on action: The role of backward inhibition. *Journal of Experimental Psychology: General, 129*, 4–26.

Mazzoni, G., & Kirsch, I. (2002). Autobiographical memories and beliefs: A preliminary metacognitive model. In T. J. Perfect & B. L. Schwartz (Eds.), *Applied metacognition* (pp. 121–145). Cambridge, UK: Cambridge University Press.

Mazzoni, G., Loftus, E. F., & Kirsch, I. (2001). Changing beliefs about implausible autobiographical events: A little plausibility goes a long way. *Journal of Experimental Psychology: Applied, 7,* 51–59.

McCann, R., & Johnson, J. (1992). Locus of the single-channel bottleneck in dual-task interference. *Journal of Experimental Psychology: Human Perception and Performance, 18,* 471–484.

McClelland, J. L., McNaughton, B. L., & O'Reilly, R. C. (1995). Why there are complementary learning systems in the hippocampus and neocortex: Insights from the successes and failures of connectionist models of learning and memory. *Psychological Review, 3,* 419–457.

McClosky, M., Wible, C. G., & Cohen, N. J. (1988). Is there a special flashbulb-memory mechanism? *Journal of Experimental Psychology: General, 117,* 171–181.

McCloy, R., & Byrne, R. M. J. (2000). Counterfactual thinking about controllable actions. *Memory and Cognition, 28,* 87–109.

McConatha, J. T., Leone, F. M., & Armstrong, J. M. (1997). Emotional control in adulthood. *Psychological Reports, 80,* 499–507.

McConatha, J. T., Lightner, E., & Deaner, S. L. (1994). Culture, age, and gender as variables in the expression of emotions. *Journal of Social Behavior and Personality, 9,* 481–488.

McDaniel, M. A., & Einstein, G. O. (2000). Strategic and automatic processes in prospective memory retrieval. *Applied Cognitive Psychology, 14,* 127–144.

McDaniel, M. A., Guynn, M. J., Einstein, G. O., & Breneiser, J. (2004). Cue-focused and reflexive-associative processes in prospective memory retrieval. *Journal of Experimental Psychology: Learning, Memory, and Cognition, 30,* 605–614.

McDaniel, M. A., Robinson-Riegler, B., & Einstein, G. O. (1998). Prospective remembering: Perceptually driven or conceptually driven processes? *Memory and Cognition, 26,* 121–134.

McGill, A. L. (2000). Counterfactual reasoning in causal judgments: Implications for marketing. *Psychology and Marketing, 17,* 323–343.

McGinnis, D., & Roberts, P. (1996). Qualitative characteristics of vivid memories attributed to real and imagined experiences. *American Journal of Psychology, 109,* 59–77.

McIntosh, W. D. (1996). When does goal nonattainment lead to negative emotional reactions, and when doesn't it? The role of linking and rumination. In L. L. Martin & A. Tesser (Eds.), *Striving and feeling: Interactions among goals, affect, and self-regulation* (pp. 53–77). Mahwah, NJ: Lawrence Erlbaum Associates.

McKay, P., & Rogers, P. (2000). *The anger control workbook.* Oakland, CA: New Harbinger.

McKenzie, C. R. M. (1998). Taking into account the strength of an alternative hypothesis. *Journal of Experimental Psychology: Learning, Memory, and Cognition, 24,* 771–792.

McMullen, M. N. (1997). Affective contrast and assimilation in counterfactual thinking. *Journal of Experimental Social Psychology, 33,* 77–100.

McMullen, M. N., Markman, K. D., & Gavanski, I. (1995). Living in neither the best nor the worst of all possible worlds: Antecedents and consequences of upward and downward counterfactual thinking. In N. J. Roese & J. M. Olson (Eds.), *What might have been: The social psychology of counterfactual thinking* (pp. 133–167). Mahwah, NJ: Lawrence Erlbaum Associates.

McMullin, R. E. (2000). *The new handbook of cognitive therapy techniques.* New York: Norton.

McNally, R. J., Wilhelm, S., Buhlmann, U., & Shin, L. M. (2001). Cognitive inhibition in obsessive-compulsive disorder: Application of a valence-based negative priming paradigm. *Behavioral and Cognitive Psychotherapy, 29,* 103–106.

McNamara, D. S., & O'Reilly, T. (2003). *Self-explanation and reading strategy training: Overcoming knowledge deficits.* Paper presented at the 44th annual meeting of the Psychonomic Society, Vancouver, BC.

McRae, K., & Boisvert, S. (1998). Automatic semantic similarity priming. *Journal of Experimental Psychology: Learning, Memory, and Cognition, 24*, 558–572.

Medin, D. L. (1989). Concepts and conceptual structure. *American Psychologist, 44*, 1469–1481.

Medin, D. L. (1998). *The psychology of learning and motivation: Advances in research and theory* (Vol. 38). San Diego, CA: Academic Press.

Medin, D. L., Coley, J. D., Storms, G., & Hayes, B. K. (2003). A relevance theory of induction. *Psychonomic Bulletin and Review, 10*, 517–532.

Medin, D. L., & Ortony, A. (1989). Psychological essentialism. In S. Vosniadou & A. Ortony (Eds.), *Similarity and analogical reasoning* (pp. 179–195). Cambridge, UK: Cambridge University Press.

Medin, D. L., & Ross, B. H. (1989). The specific character of abstract thought: Categorization, problem solving, and induction. In R. J. Sternberg (Ed.), *Advances in the psychology of human intelligence* (Vol. 5, pp. 189–223). Hillsdale, NJ: Lawrence Erlbaum Associates.

Medvec, V. H., Madey, S. F., & Gilovich, T. (1995). When less is more: Counterfactual thinking and satisfaction among Olympic athletes. *Journal of Personality and Social Psychology, 69*, 603–610.

Mega, M. S., & Cummings, J. L. (1994). Frontal-subcortical circuits and neuropsychiatric disorders. *Journal of Neuropsychiatry and Clinical Neurosciences, 6*, 358–370.

Meichenbaum, D. A. (1985). *Stress innoculation training.* New York: Pergamon Press.

Meier, B., & Graf, P. (2000). Transfer appropriate processing for prospective memory tests. *Applied Cognitive Psychology, 14*, 511–527.

Meiran, N. (2000). Reconfiguration of stimulus task sets and response task sets during task switching. In S. Monsell & J. Driver (Eds.), *Control of cognitive processes: Attention and performance XVIII* (pp. 377–399). Cambridge, MA: MIT Press.

Melchert, T. P. (1996). Childhood memory and a history of different forms of abuse. *Professional Psychology: Research and Practice, 27*, 438–446.

Mellers, B. A., Schwartz, A., Ho, K., & Ritov, I. (1997). Decision affect theory: Emotional reactions to the outcomes of risky options. *Psychological Science, 8*, 423–429.

Meltzoff, A. N. (1995). What infant memory tells us about infantile amnesia: Long-term recall and deferred imitation. *Journal of Experimental Child Psychology, 59*, 497–515.

Mesqita, B. (2001). Emotions in collectivist and individualist contexts. *Journal of Personality and Social Research, 80*, 68–74.

Metcalfe, J. (1986). Feeling of knowing in memory and problem solving. *Journal of Experimental Psychology: Learning, Memory, and Cognition, 12*, 288–294.

Metcalfe, J. (2000). Metamemory: Theory and data. In E. Tulving & F. I. M. Craik (Eds.), *The Oxford handbook of memory* (pp. 197–211). Oxford, UK: Oxford University Press.

Metcalfe, J., Schwartz, B. L., & Joaquim, S. G. (1993). The cue familiarity heuristic in metacognition. *Journal of Experimental Psychology: Learning, Memory, and Cognition, 19*, 851–861.

Metcalfe, J., & Shimamura, A. P. (Eds.). (1994). *Metacognition: Knowing about knowing.* Cambridge, MA: MIT Press.

Meyers-Levy, J., & Maheswaran, D. (1992). When timing matters: The influence of temporal distance on consumers' affective and persuasive responses. *Journal of Consumer Research, 19*, 424–433.

Miller, D. T., & Taylor, B. R. (1995). Counterfactual thought, regret, and superstition: How to avoid kicking yourself. In N. J. Roese & J. M. Olson (Eds.), *What might have been: The social psychology of counterfactual thinking* (pp. 305–331). Hillsdale, NJ: Lawrence Erlbaum Associates.

Miller, D. T., & Taylor, B. R. (2002). Counterfactual thought, regret, and superstition: How to avoid kicking yourself. In T. Gilovich, D. Griffin, & D. Kahneman (Eds.), *Heuristics and biases: The psychology of intuitive judgment* (pp. 367–378). Cambridge, UK: Cambridge University Press.

Miller, G. A. (1956). The magical number seven, plus or minus two: Some limits on our capacity for processing information. *Psychological Review, 63*, 81–97.

Miller, S. D., Duncan, B. L., & Hubble, M. A. (1997). *Escape from Babel: Toward a unifying language for psychotherapy practice.* New York: Norton.

Miller, S. D., Duncan, B. L., & Hubble, M. A. (2004). Beyond integration: The triumph of outcome over process in clinical practice. *Psychotherapy in Australia, 10*(2), 2–19.

Miller, S. D., & Sherrard, P. (1999). Couple communication: A system for equipping partners to talk, listen, and resolve conflicts effectively. In R. Berger & M. T. Hannah (Eds.), *Prevention approaches in couples therapy* (pp. 125–148). Philadelphia: Brunner/Mazel.

Mills, C. M., & Keil, F. C. (2004). Knowing the limits of one's understanding: The development of an awareness of an illusion of explanatory depth. *Journal of Experimental Child Psychology, 87*, 1–32.

Mills, J. C., & Crowley, R. J. (1986). *Therapeutic metaphors for children and the child within.* New York: Brunner/Mazel.

Milner, B., Corkin, S., & Teuber, H. L. (1968). Further analysis of the hippocampal amnesic syndrome: Fourteen year follow-up study of H.M. *Neuropsychologia, 6*, 215–234.

Miner, A. C., & Reder, L. M. (1994). A new look at feeling of knowing: Its metacognitive role in regulating question answering. In J. Metcalfe & A. P. Shimamura (Eds.), *Metacognition: Knowing about knowing* (pp. 47–70). Cambridge, MA: MIT Press.

Mischel, W., & Ayduk, O. (2004). Willpower in a cognitive-affective processing system: The dynamics of delay of gratification. In R. F. Baumeister & K. D. Vohs (Eds.), *Handbook of self-regulation: Research, theory, and applications* (pp. 99–129). New York: Guilford.

Mitchell, K. J., & Johnson, M. K. (2000). Source monitoring: Attributing mental experiences. In E. Tulving & F. Craik (Eds.), *The Oxford handbook of memory* (pp. 179–195). Oxford, UK: Oxford University Press.

Miyake, A., & Shah, P. (Eds.). (1999). *Models of working memory: Mechanisms of active maintenance and executive control.* Cambridge, UK: Cambridge University Press.

Moely, B. E., Santulli, K. A., & Obach, M. S. (1995). Strategy instruction, metacognition, and motivation in the elementary school classroom. In F. E. Weinert & W. Schneider (Eds.), *Memory performance and competencies: Issues in growth and development* (pp. 301–321). Hillsdale, NJ: Lawrence Erlbaum Associates.

Mogg, K., Mathews, A., & Weinman, J. (1987). Memory bias in clinical anxiety. *Journal of Abnormal Psychology, 96*, 94–98.

Molander, B., & Backman, L. (1989). Adult age differences in heart rate patterns during concentration in a precision sport: Implications for attentional functioning. *Journal of Gerontology, 44*, 80–87.

Moore, R. G., Watts, F. N., & Williams, J. M. G. (1988). The specificity of personal memories in depression. *British Journal of Clinical Psychology, 27*, 275–276.

Moray, N. (1959). Attention in dichotic listening: Affective cues and the influence of instructions. *Quarterly Journal of Experimental Psychology, 11*, 56–60.

Moreno, J. L. (1972). *Psychodrama.* New York: Beacon House.

Moretti, M. M., & Higgins, E. T. (1999). Own versus other standpoints in self-regulation: Developmental antecedents and functional consequences. *Review of General Psychology, 3*, 188–233.

Morgan, W. P., & Goldston, S. E. (Eds.). (1987). *Exercise and mental health*. Washington, DC: Hemisphere Publishing.

Moritz, S., Mass, R., & Junk, U. (1998). Further evidence of reduced negative priming in positive schizotypy. *Personality and Individual Differences, 24*, 521–530.

Morris, M. W., & Moore, P. (1998). *Learning from a brush with danger: Evidence that pilot learning from dangerous incidents is enabled by counterfactual thinking and hindered by organizational accountability* (Working Paper No. 1492). Palo Alto, CA: Stanford University, Graduate School of Business.

Moscovitch, M. (1982). A neuropsychological approach to memory and perception in normal and pathological aging. In F. I. M. Craik & S. Trehub (Eds.), *Aging and cognitive processes* (pp. 57–78). New York: Plenum.

Mroczek, D. K., & Kolarz, C. M. (1998). The effect of age on positive and negative affect: A developmental perspective on happiness. *Journal of Personality and Social Psychology, 75*, 1333–1349.

Muraven, M., Baumeister, R. F., & Tice, D. M. (1998). Longitudinal improvement of self-regulation through practice: Building self-control through repeated exercise. *Journal of Social Psychology, 74*, 774–789.

Muraven, M., Tice, D. M., & Baumeister, R. F. (1998). Self-control as limited resource: Regulatory depletion patterns. *Journal of Personality and Social Psychology, 74*, 774–789.

Murphy, G. L., & Medin, D. L. (1985). The role of theories in conceptual coherence. *Psychological Review, 92*, 289–316.

Murphy, M. D., Schmitt, R. A., Caruso, M. J., & Sanders, R. E. (1987). Metamemory in older adults: The role of monitoring in serial recall. *Psychology and Aging, 2*, 331–339.

Mynatt, C. R., Doherty, M. E., & Dragan, W. (1993). Information relevance, working memory, and the consideration of alternatives. *Quarterly Journal of Experimental Psychology: Human Experimental Psychology, 46A*, 759–778.

Nasby, W. (1994). Moderators of mood congruent encoding: Self-/other-reference and affirmative/non-affirmative judgment. *Cognition and Emotion, 8*, 259–278.

Nasby, W., & Kihlstrom, J. F. (1986). Cognitive assessment of personality and psychopathology. In R. E. Ingram (Ed.), *Information processing approaches to clinical psychology* (pp. 217–239). San Diego, CA: Academic Press.

Neely, J. H. (1977). Semantic priming and retrieval from lexical memory: Role of inhibitionless spreading activation and limited capacity attention. *Journal of Experimental Psychology: General, 106*, 226–254.

Neimeyer, R. A., & Bridges, S. K. (2003). Postmodern approaches to psychotherapy. In A. S. Gurman & S. B. Messer (Eds.), *Essential psychotherapies: Theory and practice* (2nd ed., pp. 272–316). New York: Guilford.

Neimeyer, R. A., & Feixas, G. (1990). The role of homework and skill acquisition in the outcome of group cognitive therapy for depression. *Behavior Therapy, 21*, 281–292.

Neisser, U., & Harsch, N. (1992). Phantom flashbulbs: False recollections of hearing the news about Challenger. In E. Winograd & U. Neisser (Eds.), *Affect and accuracy in recall: Studies of "flashbulb" memories* (pp. 9–31). Cambridge, UK: Cambridge University Press.

Neisser, U., Winograd, E., & Weldon, M. S. (1991, November). *Remembering the earthquake: "What I experienced" vs "How I heard the news."* Paper presented at the annual meeting of the Psychonomic Society, San Francisco.

Neitzel, C., & Stright, A. D. (2003). Mothers' scaffolding of children's problem solving: Establishing a foundation of academic self-regulatory competence. *Journal of Family Psychology, 17*, 147–159.

Nelson, K. (2003). Narrative and self, myth, and memory: Emergence of the cultural self. In R. Fivush & C. A. Haden (Eds.), *Autobiographical memory and the construction of a narrative self* (pp. 3–28). Mahwah, NJ: Lawrence Erlbaum Associates.

Nelson, T. O., & Dunlosky, J. (1991). When people's judgments of learning (JOL) are extremely accurate at predicting subsequent recall: The delayed JOL effect. *Psychological Science, 3,* 317–318.

Nelson, T. O., & Narens, L. (1994). Why investigate metacognition? In J. Metcalfe & A. P. Shimamura (Eds.), *Metacognition: Knowing about knowing* (pp. 1–25). Cambridge, MA: MIT Press.

Neuman, Y., & Weizman, E. (2003). The role of text representation in students' ability to identify fallacious arguments. *Quarterly Journal of Experimental Psychology. Section A: Human Experimental Psychology, 56A,* 849–864.

Newell, A. (1990). *Unified theories of cognition.* Cambridge, MA: Harvard University Press.

Newell, A., & Simon, H. A. (1972). *Human problem solving.* Englewood Cliffs, NJ: Prentice-Hall.

Newman, C. F. (2002). Hypotheticals in cognitive psychotherapy: Creative questions, novel answers, and therapeutic change. In R. L. Leahy & E. T. Dowd (Eds.), *Clinical advances in cognitive psychotherapy: Theory and application* (pp. 311–324). New York: Springer.

Newman, L. S., Duff, K., & Baumeister, R. (1997). A new look at defensive projection: Thought suppression, accessibility, and biased person perception. *Journal of Personality and Social Psychology, 72,* 980–1001.

Newstead, S. E., Pollard, P., & Evans, J. St. B. T. (1992). The source of belief bias effects in syllogistic reasoning. *Cognition, 45,* 257–284.

Newstead, S. E., Thompson, V. A., & Handley, S. J. (2002). Generating alternatives: A key component in human reasoning? *Memory and Cognition, 30,* 129–137.

N'gbala, A., & Branscombe, N. R. (1995). Mental stimulation and causal attribution: When stimulating an event does not affect fault assignment. *Journal of Experimental Social Psychology, 31,* 139–162.

Nickerson, R. S. (1994). The teaching of thinking and problem solving. In R. J. Sternberg (Ed.), *Thinking and problem solving* (pp. 409–449). San Diego, CA: Academic Press.

Nickerson, R. S. (1998). Confirmation bias: A ubiquitous phenomenon in many guises. *Review of General Psychology, 2,* 175–230.

Niedenthal, P. M., & Halberstadt, J. B. (2000). Emotional response as conceptual coherence. In E. Eich, J. F. Kihlstrom, G. H. Bower, J. P. Forgas, & P. M. Niedenthal (Eds.), *Cognition and emotion* (pp. 169–203). Oxford, UK: Oxford University Press.

Niedenthal, P. M., Halberstadt, J. B., & Setterlund, M. B. (1997). Being happy and seeing 'happy': Emotional state mediates visual word recognition. *Cognition and Emotion, 11,* 403–432.

Niedenthal, P. M., Setterlund, M. B., & Jones, D. E. (1994). Emotional organization of perceptual memory. In P. M. Niedenthal & S. Kitayama (Eds.), *The heart's eye: Emotional influences in perception and attention* (pp. 87–113). San Diego, CA: Academic Press.

Niedenthal, P. M., Tangney, J. P., & Gavanski, I. (1994). "If only I weren't" versus "If only I hadn't": Distinguishing shame and guilt in counterfactual thinking. *Journal of Personality and Social Psychology, 67,* 585–593.

Niedzwienska, A. (2003). Distortion of autobiographical memories. *Applied Cognitive Psychology, 17,* 81–91.

Nigg, J. T., Butler, K. M., Huang-Pollack, C. L., & Henderson, J. M. (2002). Inhibitory processes in adults with persistent childhood onset ADHD. *Journal of Consulting and Clinical Psychology, 70,* 153–157.

Nigro, G., & Cicogna, P. C. (2000). Does delay affect prospective memory performance? *European Psychologist, 5*, 228–233.

Nijenhuis, E. R. S., & van der Hart, O. (1999). Forgetting and reexperiencing trauma. In J. Goodwin & R. Cittias (Eds.), *Splintered reflections: Images of the body in trauma* (pp. 39–65). New York: Basic Books.

Nisbett, R., & Wilson, T. (1977). Telling more than we can know: Verbal reports on mental processes. *Psychological Review, 84*, 231–259.

Nix, G., Watson, C., Pyszczynski, T., & Greenberg, J. (1995). Reducing depressive affect through external focus of attention. *Journal of Social and Clinical Psychology, 14*, 36–52.

Nolen-Hoeksema, S. (1998). The other end of the continuum: The costs of rumination. *Psychological Inquiry, 9*, 216–219.

Nolan-Hoeksema, S., & Morrow, J. (1993). Effects of rumination and distraction on naturally occurring depressed mood. *Cognition and Emotion, 7*, 561–570.

Norcross, J. C. (1997). Emerging breakthroughs in psychotherapy integration: Three predictions and one fantasy. *Psychotherapy, 34*, 86–90.

Norcross, J. C. (Ed.). (2002). *Psychotherapy relationships that work.* New York: Oxford University Press.

Norcross, J. C., & Goldfried, M. R. (Eds.). (1992). *Handbook of psychotherapy integration.* New York: Basic Books.

Norcross, J. C., & Newman, M. R. (1992). Psychotherapy integration: Setting the context. In J. C. Norcross & M. R. Newman (Eds.), *Handbook of psychotherapy integration* (pp. 3–45). New York: Basic Books.

Norcross, J. C., Santrock, J. W., Campbell, L. F., Smith, T. P., Sommer, R., & Zuckerman, E. L. (2000). *Authoritative guide to self-help resources in mental health.* New York: Guilford.

Norman, G. R., Brooks, L. R., Coblentz, C. L., & Babcock, C. J. (1992). The correlation of feature identification and category judgments in diagnostic radiology. *Memory and Cognition, 20*, 344–355.

Norman, K., & Schacter, D. L. (1998). False recognition in younger and older adults: Exploring the characteristics of illusory memories. *Memory and Cognition, 25*, 838–848.

Novick, L. R., & Holyoak, K. J. (1991). Mathematical problem solving by analogy. *Journal of Experimental Psychology: Learning, Memory, and Cognition, 17*, 398–415.

Nyberg, L., Bohlin, G., Berlin, L., & Janois, L.-O. (2003). Inhibition and executive functioning in Type A and ADHD boys. *Nordic Journal of Psychiatry, 57*, 438–445.

Oakhill, J., Johnson-Laird, P., & Garnham, A. (1989). Believability and syllogistic reasoning. *Cognition, 31*, 117–140.

Oakley, R. (2004). How the mind hurts and heals the body. *American Psychologist, 59*(1), 29–40.

Oaksford, M., Roberts, L., & Chater, N. (2002). Relative informativeness of quantifiers used in syllogistic reasoning. *Memory and Cognition, 30*, 138–149.

Oatley, K. (1992). *Best laid schemes: The psychology of emotions.* Cambridge, UK: Cambridge University Press.

Oatley, K., & Johnson-Laird, P. N. (1996). The communicative theory of emotions: Empirical tests, mental models, and implications for social interaction. In L. L. Martin & A. Tesser (Eds.), *Striving and feeling: Interactions among goals, affect, and self-regulation* (pp. 363–393). Mahwah, NJ: Lawrence Erlbaum Associates.

Ochsner, K. N., & Gross, J. J. (2004). Thinking makes it so: A social cognitive neuroscience approach to emotion regulation. In R. F. Baumeister & K. D. Vohs (Eds.), *Handbook of self-regulation: Research, theory, and applications* (pp. 229–255). New York: Guilford.

O'Hanlon, W. H. (1987). *Taproots: Underlying principles of Milton Erickson's therapy and hypnosis*. New York: Norton.

O'Hanlon, W. H., & Beadle, S. (1999). *A guide to possibility land: Fifty-one methods for doing brief, respectful therapy*. New York: Norton.

O'Hanlon, W. H., & Hexum, A. L. (1990). *An uncommon casebook: The complete clinical work of Milton H. Erickson, M.D.* New York: Norton.

O'Hanlon, W. H., & Weiner-Davis, M. (1989). *In search of solutions: A new direction in psychotherapy*. New York: Norton.

Ohlsson, S. (1992). Information processing explanations of insight and related phenomena. In M. T. Keane & K. J. Gilhooly (Eds.), *Advances in the psychology of thinking* (pp. 1–43). London: Harvester-Wheatsheaf.

Ohman, A. (1979). The orienting response, attention, and learning: An information-processing perspective. In H. K. Kimmel, E. H. Van Olst, & J. F. Orlebeke (Eds.), *The orienting reflex in humans* (pp. 443–471). Hillsdale, NJ: Lawrence Erlbaum Associates.

Ohman, A. (1994). "Unconscious anxiety": Phobic responses to masked stimuli. *Journal of Abnormal Psychology, 103*, 231–240.

Olsen, D., & Stephens, D. (2001). *The couples survival workbook: What you can do to reconnect with your partner and make your marriage work*. Oakland, CA: New Harbinger.

Olson, K. R., Lambert, A. J., & Zacks, J. M. (2003). Graded structure and the speed of category verification: On the moderating effects of anticipatory control for social vs. non-social categories. *Journal of Experimental Social Psychology, 40*, 239–246.

Openshaw, D. K. (1998). Increasing homework compliance: The SEA method. *Journal of Family Psychotherapy, 9*, 21–29.

Orne, M. T. (1962). On the social psychology of the psychology experiment: With particular reference to demand characteristics and their implications. *American Psychologist, 17*, 776–783.

Ornstein, R. (1991). *The evolution of consciousness: The origins of the way we think*. New York: Simon & Schuster.

Over, D. E., & Green, D. W. (2001). Contingency, causation, and adaptive inference. *Psychological Review, 108*, 682–684.

Palinscar, A. S., & Brown, A. L. (1984). Reciprocal teaching of comprehension-fostering and comprehension-monitoring activities. *Cognition and Instruction, 1*, 117–175.

Palmer, S., Schreiber, C., & Fox, C. (1991, November). *Remembering the earthquake: 'Flashbulb' memory for experienced vs. reported events*. Paper presented at the annual meeting of the Psychonomic Society, San Francisco.

Panksepp, J., & Miller, A. (1995). Emotions and the aging brain: Regrets and remedies. In C. Magai & S. H. McFadden (Eds.), *Handbook of emotion, adult development, and aging* (pp. 3–26). San Diego, CA: Academic Press.

Papagiorgiou, C., & Wells, A. (2003). An empirical test of a clinical metacognitive model of rumination and depression. *Cognitive Therapy and Research, 27*, 261–273.

Parrott, W. G. (1993). Beyond hedonism: Motives for inhibiting good moods and for managing bad moods. In D. M. Wegner & J. W. Pennebaker (Eds.), *Handbook of mental control* (pp. 278–308). Englewood Cliffs, NJ: Prentice Hall.

Parrott, W. G., & Sabini, J. (1990). Mood and memory under natural conditions: Evidence for mood incongruent recall. *Journal of Personality and Social Psychology, 59*, 321–336.

Pashler, H. (1992). Attentional limitations in doing two tasks at the same time. *Current Directions in Psychological Science, 1*, 44–47.

Payne, B. K., Jacoby, L. L., & Lambert, A. J. (2004). Memory monitoring and the control of stereotype distortion. *Journal of Experimental Social Psychology, 40*, 52–64.

Payne, D. G., & Weneger, M. J. (1998). *Cognitive psychology*. New York: Houghton Mifflin.

Pearson, D. A., & Lane, D. M. (1991). Auditory attention switching: A developmental study. *Journal of Experimental Child Psychology, 51*, 320–334.

Pennebaker, J. W. (1993). Overcoming inhibition: Rethinking the roles of personality, cognition, and social behavior. In H. C. Traue & J. W. Pennebaker (Eds.), *Emotion inhibition and health* (pp. 100–115). Seattle: Hogrefe & Huber.

Pennebaker, J. W. (1997). Writing about emotional experiences as a therapeutic process. *Psychological Science, 8*, 162–166.

Pennebaker, J. W. (1998). Conflict and canned meat. *Psychological Inquiry, 9*, 219–220.

Pennebaker, J. W., & Francis, M. E. (1996). Cognitive, emotional, and language processes in disclosure. *Cognition and Emotion, 10*, 601–626.

Pennebaker, J. W., & Seagal, J. D. (1999). Forming a story: The health benefits of a narrative. *Journal of Clinical Psychology, 55*, 1243–1254.

Pennebaker, J. W., & Stone, L. D. (2003). Words of wisdom: Language use over the life span. *Journal of Personality and Social Psychology, 85*, 291–301.

Pennington, N., & Hastie, R. (1988). Explanation-based decision making: Effects of memory structure on judgment. *Journal of Experimental Psychology: Learning, Memory, and Cognition, 14*, 521–533.

Pennington, N., & Hastie, R. (1991). A cognitive theory of juror decision making: The story model. *Cardozo Law Review, 13*, 519–557.

Pennington, N., & Hastie, R. (1992). Explaining the evidence: Tests of the story model for juror decision making. *Journal of Personality and Social Psychology, 62*, 189–206.

Pennington, N., & Hastie, R. (1993). The story model for juror decision making. In R. Hastie (Ed.), *Inside the juror: The psychology of juror decision making* (pp. 192–221). Cambridge, UK: Cambridge University Press.

Perfect, T. J. (2002). When does eyewitness confidence predict performance? In T. J. Perfect & B. L. Schwartz (Eds.), *Applied metacognition* (pp. 95–120). Cambridge, UK: Cambridge University Press.

Perls, F. (1969). *Gestalt therapy verbatim*. Lafayette, CA: Real People Press.

Perkins, D. N. (1985). Postprimary education has little impact on informal reasoning. *Journal of Educational Psychology, 77*, 562–571.

Perkins, D. N., Farady, M., & Bushey, B. (1991). Everyday reasoning and the roots of intelligence. In J. F. Voss, D. N. Perkins, & J. W. Segal (Eds.), *Informal reasoning and education*. Hillsdale, NJ: Lawrence Erlbaum Associates.

Perner, J. (2000). Memory and theory of mind. In E. Tulving & F. I. M. Craik (Eds.), *The Oxford handbook of memory* (pp. 297–312). Oxford, UK: Oxford University Press.

Persons, J. B., Burns, D. D., & Perloff, J. M. (1988). Predictors of dropout and outcome in cognitive therapy for depression in a private practice setting. *Cognitive Therapy and Research, 12*, 557–575.

Peters, E. R., Hemsley, D. R., Pickering, A. D., Glasper, A., Irani, M., Kent, A., et al. (2000). The relationship between cognitive inhibition and psychotic symptoms. *Journal of Abnormal Psychology, 109*, 386–395.

Peters, R., & McGee, R. (1982). Cigarette smoking and state-dependent memory. *Psychopharmacology, 76*, 232–235.

Petrie, K. J., Booth, R. J., & Davidson, K. P. (1995). Repression, disclosure, and immune function: Recent findings and methodological issues. In J. W. Pennebaker (Ed.), *Emotion, disclosure, and health* (pp. 223–237). Washington, DC: American Psychological Association.

Pettingale, K. W. (1985). Towards a psychobiological model of cancer: Biological considerations. *Social Science and Medicine, 20*, 779–787.

Pezdek, K., Finger, K., & Hodge, D. (1997). Planting false memories: The role of event plausibility. *Psychological Science, 8*, 437–441.

Pezdek, K., & Hodge, D. (1999). Planting false childhood memories in children: The role of
event plausibility. *Child Development, 70*, 887–895.

Pezdek, K., Whetstone, T., Reynolds, K., Askari, N., & Dougherty, T. (1989). Memory for real-
world scenes: The role of consistency with schema expectation. *Journal of Experimental
Psychology: Learning, Memory, and Cognition, 15*, 587–595.

Pfeiffer, A. M., Whelan, J. P., & Martin, J. M. (2000). Decision-making bias in psychotherapy:
Effects of hypothesis source and accountability. *Journal of Counseling Psychology, 47*,
429–436.

Philippot, P., Schaefer, A., & Herbette, G. (2003). Consequences of specific processing of emotional information: Impact of general versus specific autobiographical memory priming on
emotion elicitation. *Emotion, 3*, 270–283.

Pillemer, D. B. (1984). Flashbulb memories of the assassination attempt on President Reagan.
Cognition, 16, 63–80.

Pliszka, S. R., Liotti, M., & Woldorff, M. G. (2000). Inhibitory control in children with atten-
tion-deficit/hyperactivity disorder: Event-related potentials identify the processing component and timing of an impaired right-frontal response-inhibition mechanism. *Biological Psychiatry, 43*, 238–246.

Polivy, J. (1998). The effects of behavioral inhibition: Integrating internal cues, cognition, behavior, and affect. *Psychological Inquiry, 9*, 181–204.

Polk, T., & Newell, A. (1995). Deduction as verbal reasoning. *Psychological Review, 102*,
533–566.

Polster, E., & Polster, M. (1973). *Gestalt therapy integrated*. New York: Brunner/Mazel.

Ponds, R. W. H. M., Boxtel, M. P. J., & Jolles, J. (2000). Age-related changes in subjective cognitive functioning. *Educational Gerontology, 26*, 67–81.

Porter, S., Yuille, J. C., & Lehman, D. R. (1999). The nature of real, implanted, and fabricated
memories for emotional childhood events: Implications for the recovered memory debate.
Law and Human Behavior, 23, 517–537.

Posner, M., & Snyder, C. (1975). Facilitation and inhibition in the processing of signals. In P.
Rabbitt & S. Dornic (Eds.), *Attention and performance V* (pp. 669–682). New York: Academic Press.

Power, M. J., & Dalgleish, T. (1997). *Cognition and emotion: From order to disorder*. Hove,
UK: Psychology Press.

Pressley, M. (1995). What is intellectual development about in the 1990s? In F. E. Weinert & W.
Schneider (Eds.), *Memory performance and competencies: Issues in growth and development* (pp. 1–25). Hillsdale, NJ: Lawrence Erlbaum Associates.

Proust, M. (1960). *Swan's way* (C. K. Scott Moncrieff, Trans.). London: Chatto & Windus.
(Original work published 1922)

Quinn, S., & Markovits, H. (2002). Conditional reasoning with causal premises: Evidence for a
retrieval model. *Thinking and Reasoning, 8*, 179–191.

Rabinowitz, J. C. (1989). Age deficits in recall under optimal study conditions. *Psychology and
Aging, 4*, 378–380.

Rachman, S. J. (1978). *Fear and courage*. San Francisco: Freeman.

Raes, F., Hermans, D., de Decker, A., Eclen, P., & Williams, J. M. G. (2003). Autobiographical
memory specificity and affect regulation: An experimental approach. *Emotion, 3*, 201–206.

Razran, G. H. S. (1940). Conditioned response changes in rating and appraising socio-political
slogans. *Psychological Bulletin, 37*, 481–493.

Read, J. D., & Lindsay, D. S. (Eds.). (1997). *Recollections of trauma: Scientific evidence and clinical practice*. New York: Plenum.

Read, J. D., Lindsay, D. S., & Nicholls, T. (1998). The relationship between accuracy and confidence in eyewitness identification studies: Is the conclusion changing? In C. P. Thompson, D. J. Herrman, J. D. Read, D. Bruce, D. G. Payne, & M. P. Toglia (Eds.), *Eyewitness memory: Theoretical and applied aspects* (pp. 107–130). Mahwah, NJ: Lawrence Erlbaum Associates.

Reber, R., & Zupanek, N. (2002). Effects of processing fluency on estimates of probability and frequency. In P. Sedlmeier (Ed.), *Frequency processing and cognition* (pp. 175–188). Oxford, UK: Oxford University Press.

Reder, L. M. (1988). Strategic control of retrieval strategies. *The Psychology of Learning and Motivation, 22*, 227–259.

Rehder, B. (2003). A causal-model theory of conceptual representation and categorization. *Journal of Experimental Psychology: Learning, Memory, and Cognition, 29*, 1141–1159.

Reich, W. (1990). *Character analysis*. New York: Noonday Press. (Originally published in 1945)

Reisberg, D. (1983). General mental resources and perceptual judgments. *Journal of Experimental Psychology: Human Perception and Performance, 9*, 966–979.

Reisberg, D. (1997). *Cognition: Exploring the science of the mind*. New York: Norton.

Reisberg, D., Heuer, F., McLean, J., & O'Shaughnessy, M. (1988). The quantity, not the quality, of affect predicts memory vividness. *Bulletin of the Psychonomic Society, 26*, 100–103.

Rendell, P. G., & Thompson, D. M. (1999). Aging and prospective memory: Differences between naturalistic and laboratory tasks. *Journal of Gerontology: Psychological Sciences, 54*, P256–P269.

Revlin, R., Cate, C. L., & Rouss, T. S. (2001). Reasoning counterfactually: Combining and rending. *Memory and Cognition, 29*, 1196–1208.

Richards, J. M., & Gross, J. J. (2000). Emotion regulation and memory: The cognitive costs of keeping one's cool. *Journal of Personality and Social Psychology, 79*, 410–424.

Richardson, A. (1994). *Individual differences in imaging: Their measurement, origins, and consequences*. Amityville, NY: Baywood.

Riemann, B. C., & McNally, R. J. (1995). Cognitive processing of personally relevant information. *Cognition and Emotion, 9*, 325–340.

Rinck, M., Glowalia, U., & Schneider, K. (1992). Mood-congruent and mood-incongruent learning. *Memory and Cognition, 20*, 29–39.

Rips, L. J. (1989). Similarity, typicality, and categorization. In S. Vosniadou & A. Ortony (Eds.), *Similarity and analogical reasoning* (pp. 21–59). Cambridge, UK: Cambridge University Press.

Rips, L. J. (1998). Reasoning and conversation. *Psychological Review, 105*, 411–441.

Rips, L. J. (2000). The cognitive nature of instantiation. *Journal of Memory and Language, 43*, 20–43.

Ritov, I. (1996). Anchoring in simulated competitive market negotiation. *Organizational Behavior and Human Decision Processes, 1*, 16–25.

Robertson, S. I. (2001). *Problem solving*. Philadelphia: Psychology Press.

Robinson, J. O., Rosen, M., Revill, S. I., David, H., & Rus, G. A. D. (1980). Self-administered intravenous and intramuscular pethidine. *Anaesthesia, 35*, 763–595.

Rodriguez, M. L., Mischel, W., & Shoda, Y. (1989). Cognitive person variables in the delay of gratification of older children at-risk. *Journal of Personality and Social Psychology, 57*, 358–367.

Roebers, C. M. (2002). Confidence judgments in children's and adults' event recall and suggestibility. *Developmental Psychology, 38*, 1052–1067.

Roebers, C., Moga, N., & Schneider, W. (2001). The role of accuracy motivation on children's and adult's event recall. *Journal of Experimental Child Psychology, 78*, 313–329.

Roemer, L., Litz, B. T., Orsillo, S. M., & Wagner, A. W. (2001). A preliminary investigation of the role of strategic withholding of emotions in PTSD. *Journal of Traumatic Stress, 14*, 149–156.

Roese, N. J. (1994). The functional basis of counterfactual thinking. *Journal of Personality and Social Psychology, 66*, 805–818.

Roese, N. J. (1997). Counterfactual thinking. *Psychological Bulletin, 121*, 133–148.

Roese, N. (1999). Counterfactual thinking and decision making. *Psychonomic Bulletin and Review, 6*, 570–578.

Roese, N. J., & Olson, J. M. (Eds.). (1995). *What might have been: The social psychology of counterfactual thinking*. Mahwah, NJ: Lawrence Erlbaum Associates.

Roese, N. J., & Olson, J. M. (1996). Counterfactuals, causal attributions, and the hindsight bias: A conceptual integration. *Journal of Experimental Social Psychology, 32*, 197–227.

Roese, N. J., & Olson, J. M. (1997). Counterfactual thinking: The intersection of affect and function. In M. P. Zanna (Ed.), *Advances in experimental social psychology* (Vol. 29, pp. 1–59). San Diego, CA: Academic Press.

Roger, D., de la Banda, G. G., Lee, H. S., & Olason, D. T. (2001). A factor-analytic study of cross-cultural differences in emotional rumination and emotional inhibition. *Personality and Individual Differences, 31*, 227–238.

Roger, D., & Jamieson, J. (1988). Individual differences in delayed heart-rate recovery following stress: The role of extraversion, neuroticism, and emotional control. *Personality and Individual Differences, 9*, 721–726.

Roger, D., & Najarian, B. (1998). The relationship between emotional rumination and cortisol secretion under stress. *Personality and Individual Differences, 24*, 531–538.

Rogers, C. R. (1980). *A way of being*. Boston: Houghton Mifflin.

Rokke, P. D., & Rehm, L. P. (2001). Self-management therapies. In K. S. Dobson (Ed.), *Handbook of cognitive therapies* (2nd ed., pp. 173–210). New York: Guilford.

Roloff, M. E., & Ifert, D. E. (2000). Conflict management through avoidance: Withholding complaints, suppressing arguments, and declaring topics taboo. In S. Petronio (Ed.), *Balancing the secrets of private disclosures* (pp. 151–163). Mahwah, NJ: Lawrence Erlbaum Associates.

Rosch, E. (1978). Principles of categorization. In E. Rosch & B. B. Lloyd (Eds.), *Cognition and categorization* (pp. 27–48). Hillsdale, NJ: Lawrence Erlbaum Associates.

Roseman, I. J. (1984). Cognitive determinants of emotion: A structural theory. In P. Shaver (Ed.), *Review of personality and social psychology: Vol. 5. Emotions, relationships, and health* (pp. 11–36). Beverly Hills, CA: Sage.

Rosen, G. M., Glascow, R. E., & Moore, T. E. (2003). Self-help therapy: The science and business of giving psychology away. In S. O. Lilienfield, S. J. Lynn, & J. M. Lohr (Eds.), *Science and pseudoscience in clinical psychology* (pp. 399–425). New York: Guilford.

Rosenberg, D. R., Averbach, D. H., O'Hearn, K. M., Seymour, A. B., Birmaher, B., & Sweeney, J. A. (1997). Oculomotor response inhibition abnormalities in pediatric obsessive-compulsive disorder. *Archives of General Psychiatry, 54*, 831–838.

Rosenblit, L., & Keil, F. (2002). The misunderstood limits of folk science: An illusion of explanatory depth. *Cognitive Science, 26*, 521–562.

Rosenhan, D. L. (1973). On being sane in insane places. *Science, 179*, 250–258.

Ross, B. H. (1987). This is like that: The use of earlier problems and the separation of similarity effects. *Journal of Experimental Psychology: Learning, Memory, and Cognition, 13*, 629–639.

Ross, L., Lepper, M. R., & Hubbard, M. (1975). Perseverance in self perception and social perception: Biased attributional processes in the debriefing paradigm. *Journal of Personality and Social Psychology, 32*, 880–892.

Ross, L., Lepper, M. R., Strack, F., & Stienmetz, J. L. (1977). Social explanation and social expectation: The effects of real and hypothetical explanations upon subjective likelihood. *Journal of Personality and Social Psychology, 35*, 817–829.

Rothbart, M. K., Ziaie, H., & O'Boyle, C. G. (1992). Self-regulation and emotion in infancy. In N. Eisenberg & R. A. Fabes (Eds.), *Emotion and its regulation in early development* (pp. 7–23). San Francisco: Jossey-Bass.

Rothkopf, J. S., & Blaney, P. H. (1991). Mood-congruent memory: The role of affective focus and gender. *Cognition and Emotion, 5*, 53–64.

Rothman, A. J., & Schwarz, N. (1998). Constructing perceptions of vulnerability: Personal relevance and the use of experiential information in health judgments. *Personality and Social Psychology Bulletin, 24*, 1053–1064.

Rothschild, L., & Haslam, N. (2003). Thirsty for H_2O? Multiple essences and psychological essentialism. *New Ideas in Psychology, 21*, 31–41.

Rovee-Collier, C. (1987). Learning and memory in infancy. In J. Osofsky (Ed.), *Handbook of infant development* (pp. 98–148). New York: Wiley.

Rovee-Collier, C. K., & Shyi, G. C. W. (1992). A functional and cognitive analysis of infant long-term retention. In C. J. Brainerd, M. L. Howe, & V. F. Reyna (Eds.), *The development of long-term retention* (pp. 3–55). New York: Springer.

Rozin, P., & Nemeroff, C. (2002). Sympathetic magical thinking: The contagion and similarity "heuristics." In T. Gilovich, D. Griffin, & D. Kahneman (Eds.), *Heuristics and biases: The psychology of intuitive judgment* (pp. 201–216). Cambridge, UK: Cambridge University Press.

Rubin, D. C. (1995). Stories about stories. In R. S. Wyer, Jr. (Ed.), *Knowledge and memory: The real story* (pp. 153–164). Hillsdale, NJ: Lawrence Erlbaum Associates.

Rubin, D. C., & Berntsen, D. (2003). Life scripts help to maintain autobiographical memories of highly positive, but not highly negative, events. *Memory and Cognition, 31*, 1–14.

Rubin, D. C., Burt, C. D. B., & Fifield, S. J. (2003). Experimental manipulations of the phenomenology of memory. *Memory and Cognition, 31*, 877–886.

Rubin, D. C., & Greenberg, D. L. (1998). Visual memory-deficit amnesia: A distinct amnesic presentation and etiology. *Proceedings of the National Academy of Sciences, 95*, 5413–5416.

Rubin, D. C., & Greenberg, D. L. (2003). The role of narrative in recollection: A view from cognitive and neuropsychology. In G. Fireman, T. McVay, & O. Flanagan (Eds.), *Narrative and consciousness: Literature, psychology, and the brain* (pp. 53–85). Oxford, UK: Oxford University Press.

Rubin, D. C., & Kozin, M. (1984). Vivid memories. *Cognition, 16*, 81–95.

Rubin, D. C., Rahhal, T. A., & Poon, L. W. (1998). Things learned in early adulthood are remembered best. *Memory and Cognition, 26*, 3–19.

Rubin, D. C., Schrauf, R. W., & Greenberg, D. L. (2003). Belief and recollection of autobiographical memories. *Memory and Cognition, 31*, 887–901.

Russell, J. A. (1980). A circumplex model of affect. *Journal of Personality and Social Psychology, 39*, 1161–1178.

Russell, P. N., & Beekhuis, M. E. (1976). Organization in memory: A comparison of psychotics and normals. *Journal of Abnormal Psychology, 85*, 527–534.

Rusting, C. L. (1998). Personality, mood, and cognitive processing of emotional information: Three conceptual frameworks. *Psychological Bulletin, 124,* 165–196.

Salo, R., Robertson, L. C., Nordahl, T. E., & Kraft, L. W. (1997). The effects of antipsychotic medication on sequential inhibitory processes. *Journal of Abnormal Psychology, 106,* 639–643.

Salovey, P., & Birnbaum, D. (1989). Influence of mood on health-related cognitions. *Journal of Personality and Social Psychology, 57,* 539–551.

Salovey, P., Rothman, A. J., Detweiler, J. B., & Steward, W. T. (2000). Emotional states and physical health. *American Psychologist, 55,* 110–121.

Saltzman, N., & Norcross, J. (Eds.). (1990). *Therapy wars: Contention and convergence in differing clinical approaches.* San Francisco: Jossey-Bass.

Sanbonmatsu, D. M., Akimoto, S. A., & Biggs, E. (1993). Overestimating causality: Attributional effects of confirmatory processing. *Journal of Personality and Social Psychology, 65,* 892–903.

Sanbonmatsu, D. M., Posavac, S. S., Kardes, F. R., & Mantel, S. P. (1998). Selective hypothesis testing. *Psychonomic Bulletin & Review, 5,* 197–220.

Sanna, L. J., Schwarz, N., & Stocker, S. L. (2002). When debiasing backfires: Accessible content and accessibility experiences in debiasing hindsight. *Journal of Experimental Psychology: Learning, Memory, and Cognition, 28,* 497–502.

Sanna, L. J., & Turley, K. J. (1996). Antecedents to spontaneous counterfactual thinking: Effects of expectancy violation and outcome valence. *Personality and Social Psychology Bulletin, 22,* 906–919.

Sartory, G., Rachman, S., & Grey, S. J. (1982). Return of fear: The role of rehearsal. *Behavior Research and Therapy, 20,* 123–134.

Saunders, D. (2004). Evaluating ESTs: Nothing more than psychotherapy's power in technique's clothing. *Psynopsis, 26*(2), 13.

Schacter, D. L. (1992). Understanding implicit memory: A cognitive neuroscience approach. *American Psychologist, 47,* 559–569.

Schacter, D. L. (1996). *Searching for memory: The brain, the mind, and the past.* New York: Basic Books.

Schacter, D. L., Norman, K. A., & Koutstaal, W. (1997). The recovered memory debate: A cognitive neuroscience perspective. In M. A. Conway (Ed.), *Recovered memories and false memories* (pp. 63–99). Oxford, UK: Oxford University Press.

Schaefer, E. G., Kozak, M. V., & Sagness, K. (1998). The role of enactment in prospective remembering. *Memory and Cognition, 26,* 644–650.

Schaeken, W., Johnson-Laird, P. N., & d'Ydewalle, G. (1996). Mental models and temporal reasoning. *Cognition, 60,* 205–234.

Scherer, K. R. (1984). On the nature and function of emotion: A component process approach. In K. R. Scherer & P. Ekman (Eds.), *Approaches to emotion* (pp. 293–317). Hillsdale, NJ: Lawrence Erlbaum Associates.

Scherer, K. R. (1994). Toward a concept of "modal emotions". In P. Ekman & R. J. Davidson (Eds.), *The nature of emotion: Fundamental questions* (pp. 25–31). Oxford, UK: Oxford University Press.

Schiraldi, G. R. (2000). *The post-traumatic stress disorder sourcebook: A guide to healing, recovery, and growth.* Los Angeles, CA: Lowell House.

Schlagmuller, M., & Schneider, W. (2002). The development of organizational strategies in children: Evidence from a microgenetic study. *Journal of Experimental Child Psychology, 81,* 298–319.

Schmeichel, B. J., & Baumeister, R. F. (2004). Self-regulatory strength. In R. F. Baumeister & K. D. Vohs (Eds.), *Handbook of self-regulation: Research, theory, and applications* (pp. 84–98). New York: Guilford.

Schmeichel, B. J., Vohs, K. D., & Baumeister, R. F. (2003). Intellectual performance and ego depletion: Role of the self in logical reasoning and other information processing. *Journal of Personality and Social Psychology, 85*, 33–46.

Schneider, K. J. (2003). Existential-humanistic psychotherapies. In A. S. Gurman & S. B. Messer (Eds.), *Essential psychotherapies: Theory and practice* (pp. 149–181). New York: Guilford.

Schneider, W., & Lockl, K. (2002). The development of metacognitive knowledge in children and adolescents. In T. J. Perfect & B. L. Schwartz (Eds.), *Applied metacognition* (pp. 224–257). Cambridge, UK: Cambridge University Press.

Schneider, W., & Shiffrin, R. (1977). Controlled and automatic human information processing: I. Detection, search, and attention. *Psychological Review, 84*, 1–66.

Schooler, J. W., Bendiksen, M. A., & Ambradar, Z. (1997). Taking the middle line: Can we accommodate both fabricated and recovered memories of sexual abuse? In M. Conway (Ed.), *False and recovered memories* (pp. 251–292). Oxford, UK: Oxford University Press.

Schuman, H., & Rieger, C. (1992). Collective memory and collective memories. In M. A. Conway, D. C. Rubin, H. Spinnler, & W. A. Wagenaar (Eds.), *Theoretical perspectives on autobiographical memory* (pp. 323–336). Dordrecht, Netherlands: Kluwer.

Schwartz, B. L., & Metcalfe, J. (1992). Cue familiarity but not target retrievability enhances feeling-of-knowing judgments. *Journal of Experimental Psychology: Learning, Memory, and Cognition, 18*, 1074–1083.

Schwarz, N., Bless, H., Strack, F., Klumpp, G., Rittenauer-Schatka, H., & Simons, A. (1991). Ease of retrieval as information: Another look at the availability heuristic. *Journal of Personality and Social Psychology, 61*, 195–202.

Schwarz, N., & Clore, G. L. (1983). Mood, misattribution, and judgments of well-being: Informative and directive functions of affective states. *Journal of Personality and Social Psychology, 45*, 513–523.

Schwarz, N., & Clore, G. L. (1988). How do I feel about it? Informative functions of affective states. In K. Fiedler & J. P. Forgas (Eds.), *Affect, cognition, and social behavior* (pp. 44–62). Toronto, Canada: Hogrefe International.

Schwarz, N., & Vaughn, L. A. (2002). The availability heuristic revisited: Ease of recall and content of recall as distinct sources of information. In T. Gilovich, D. Griffin, & D. Kahneman (Eds.), *Heuristics and biases* (pp. 103–119). Cambridge, UK: Cambridge University Press.

Sedikides, C. (1995). Central and peripheral self-conceptions are differentially influenced by mood: Tests of the differential sensitivity hypothesis. *Journal of Personality and Social Psychology, 69*, 759–777.

Seelau, E. P., Seelau, S. M., Wells, G. L., & Windschitl, P. D. (1995). Counterfactual constraints. In N. J. Roese & J. M. Olson (Eds.), *What might have been: The social psychology of counterfactual thinking* (pp. 57–79). Hillsdale, NJ: Lawrence Erlbaum Associates.

Segal, Z. V., Williams, J. M. G., & Teasdale, J. D. (2002). *Mindfulness-based cognitive therapy for depression: A new approach to preventing relapse.* New York: Guilford.

Segura, S., Fernandez-Berrocal, P., & Byrne, R. M. J. (2002). Temporal and causal order effects in thinking about what might have been. *The Quarterly Journal of Experimental Psychology, 55A*, 1295–1305.

Semrud-Clikeman, M., Nielsen, K. H., & Clinton, A. (1999). An intervention approach for children with teacher and parent-identified attentional difficulties. *Journal of Learning Disabilities, 32*, 581–589.

Serrano, J. P., Latorre, J. M., Gatz, M., & Montanes, J. (2004). Life review therapy using auto-biographical retrieval practice for older adults with depressive symptomatology. *Psychology and Aging, 19,* 272–277.

Setliff, A. E., & Marmurek, H. H. C. (2002). The mood regulatory function of autobiographical recall is moderated by self-esteem. *Personality and Individual Differences, 32,* 761–771.

Shafir, E. (1993). Choosing versus rejecting: Why some options are both better and worse than others. *Memory and Cognition, 21,* 546–556.

Shafir, E., Simonson, I., & Tversky, A. (1993). Reason-based choice. *Cognition, 49,* 11–36.

Shafto, P., & Coley, J. D. (2003). Development of categorization and reasoning in the natural world: Novices to experts, naïve similarity to ecological knowledge. *Journal of Experimental Psychology: Learning, Memory, and Cognition, 29,* 641–649.

Shah, J., & Higgins, E. T. (2001). Regulatory concerns and appraisal efficiency: The general impact of promotion and prevention. *Journal of Personality and Social Psychology, 80,* 693–705.

Shallice, T. (1982). Specific impairments of planning. *Philosophical Transactions of the Royal Society, London B298,* 199–209.

Shallice, T. (1988). *From neuropsychology to mental structure.* Cambridge, UK: Cambridge University Press.

Shapiro, F. (1995). *Eye movement desensitization and reprocessing: Basic principles, protocols, and procedures.* New York: Guilford.

Shaw, V. F. (1996). The cognitive processes in informal reasoning. *Thinking and Reasoning, 2,* 51–80.

Sheen, M., Kemp, S., & Rubin, D. (2002). Twins dispute memory ownership: A new false memory phenomenon. *Memory and Cognition, 29,* 779–788.

Sheppard, L. D., & Teasdale, J. D. (2004). How does dysfunctional thinking decrease during recovery from major depression? *Journal of Abnormal Psychology, 113,* 64–71.

Sherman, J. W., Lee, A. Y., Bessenoff, G. R., & Frost, L. A. (1998). Stereotype efficiency reconsidered: Encoding flexibility under cognitive load. *Journal of Personality and Social Psychology, 75,* 589–606.

Sherman, R., Bonanno, G. A., Wiener, L., & Battles, H. B. (2000). When children tell their friends they have AIDS: Possible consequences for psychological well-being and disease progression. *Psychosomatic Medicine, 62,* 238–247.

Sherman, S. J., Castelli, L., & Hamilton, D. L. (2003). The spontaneous use of a group typology as an organizing principle in memory. *Journal of Personality and Social Psychology, 82,* 328–342.

Sherman, S. J., Cialdini, R. B., Schwartzman, D. F., & Reynolds, K. D. (2002). Imagining can heighten or lower the perceived likelihood of contracting a disease: The mediating effect of ease of imagery. In T. Gilovich & D. Griffin (Eds.), *Heuristics and biases: The psychology of intuitive judgment* (pp. 98–102). Cambridge, UK: Cambridge University Press.

Sherman, S. J., & McConnell, A. R. (1995). Dysfunctional implications of counterfactual thinking: When alternatives to reality fail us. In N. J. Roese & J. M. Olson (Eds.), *What might have been: The social psychology of counterfactual thinking* (pp. 199–231). Hillsdale, NJ: Lawrence Erlbaum Associates.

Shum, M. S. (1998). The role of temporal landmarks in the autobiographical memory processes. *Psychological Bulletin, 124,* 423–442.

Sia, T. L., Lord, C. G., Belssum, K. A., Ratcliff, C. D., & Lepper, M. R. (1997). Is a rose always a rose? The role of social category exemplar change in attitude stability and attitude-behavior consistency. *Journal of Personality and Social Psychology, 72,* 501–514.

Siebert, P. S., & Ellis, H. C. (1991). Irrelevant thoughts, emotional mood states, and cognitive task performances. *Memory and Cognition, 19,* 507–513.

Silverman, W. H. (1996). Cookbooks, manuals, and paint-by-numbers: Psychotherapy in the 90s. *Psychotherapy, 33*, 207–215.

Simon, D. A., & Bjork, R. A. (2001). Metacognition in motor learning. *Journal of Experimental Psychology: Learning, Memory, and Cognition, 27*, 907–912.

Simon, H. A., & Chase, W. G. (1973). Skill in chess. *American Scientist, 61*, 394–403.

Simoniv, P. V., Frolov, M. V., Evtushenko, V. F., & Svirodov, E. (1977). Effect of emotional stress on recognition of visual patterns. *Aviation, Space, and Environmental Medicine*, 856–858.

Simons, P. R. J. (1996). Metacognition. In E. De Corte & F. E. Weinert (Eds.), *International encyclopedia of developmental and instructional psychology* (pp. 436–444). Oxford, UK: Elsevier.

Simpson, C., & Papagiorgiou, C. (2003). Metacognitive beliefs about rumination in anger. *Cognitive and Behavioral Practice, 10*, 91–94.

Sinclair, R. C., & Mark, M. M. (1992). The influence of mood state on judgment and action: Effects of persuasion, categorization, social justice, person perception, and judgmental accuracy. In L. L. Martin & A. Tesser (Eds.), *The construction of social judgment* (pp. 165–193). Hillsdale, NJ: Lawrence Erlbaum Associates.

Skodol, A. E., & Oldham, J. M. (1996). Phenomenology, differential diagnosis, and comorbidity of the impulsive-compulsive spectrum of disorders. In J. M. Oldham, E. Hollander, & A. E. Skodol (Eds.), *Impulsivity and compulsivity* (pp. 1–36). Washington, DC: American Psychiatric Press.

Sloman, S. A. (1994). When explanations compete: The role of explanatory coherence in judgments of likelihood. *Cognition, 52*, 1–21.

Sloman, S. A. (1996). The empirical case for two systems of reasoning. *Psychological Bulletin, 119*, 3–22.

Sloman, S. A. (2002). Two systems of reasoning. In T. Gilovich & D. Griffin (Eds.), *Heuristics and biases: The psychology of intuitive judgment* (pp. 379–396). Cambridge, UK: Cambridge University Press.

Sloman, S. A., Over, D., Slovak, L., & Stibel, J. M. (2003). Frequency illusions and other fallacies. *Organizational Behavior and Human Decision Processes, 91*, 296–309.

Slovic, P., & Fischhoff, B. (1977). On the psychology of experimental surprises. *Journal of Experimental Psychology, 3*, 544–551.

Slusher, M. P., & Anderson, C. A. (1996). Using causal persuasive arguments to change beliefs and teach new information: The mediating role of explanation availability and evaluation bias in the acceptance of knowledge. *Journal of Educational Psychology, 88*, 110–122.

Smith, C. A., & Ellsworth, P. C. (1985). Patterns of cognitive appraisal in emotion. *Journal of Personality and Social Psychology, 48*, 813–838.

Smith, C. A., & Kirby, L. D. (2000). Consequences require antecedents: Toward a process model of emotion elicitation. In J. P. Forgas (Ed.), *Thinking and feeling: The role of affect in social cognition* (pp. 83–106). Cambridge, UK: Cambridge University Press.

Smith, C. A., & Lazarus, R. S. (1990). Emotion and adaptation. In L. A. Pervin (Ed.), *Handbook of personality: Theory and research* (pp. 609–637). New York: Guilford.

Smith, C. A., & Lazarus, R. S. (1993). Appraisal components, core relational themes, and the emotions. *Cognition and Emotion, 7*, 233–269.

Smith, E. E., & Medin, D. L. (1981). *Categories and concepts*. Cambridge, MA: Harvard University Press.

Smith, J. D., & Minda, J. P. (2000). Thirty categorization results in search of a model. *Journal of Experimental Psychology: Learning, Memory, and Cognition, 26*, 3–27.

Smith, M. L., & Glass, G. V. (1977). Meta-analysis of psychotherapy outcome studies. *American Psychologist, 32*, 752–760.

Smith, S. M., & Petty, R. E. (1995). Personality moderators of mood congruence effects on cognition: The role of self-esteem and negative mood regulation. *Journal of Personality and Social Psychology, 68*, 1092–1107.

Smith, S. M., Ward, T. B., & Schumacher, J. S. (1993). Constraining effects of examples in a creative generation task. *Memory and Cognition, 21*, 837–845.

Smith, T. W. (1992). Hostility and health: Current status of a psychosomatic hypothesis. *Health Psychology, 11*, 139–150.

Smyth, J. M. (1998). Written emotional expression: Effect sizes, outcome types, and moderating variables. *Journal of Consulting and Clinical Psychology, 66*, 174–184.

Sohlberg, M. M., McLaughlin, K. A., Pavese, A., Heidrich, A., & Posner, M. I. (2000). Evaluation of attention process therapy training in persons with acquired brain injury. *Journal of Clinical and Experimental Neuropsychology, 22*, 656–676.

Sokolov, E. N. (1963). *Perception and the conditioned reflex.* New York: Pergamon Press.

Son, L. J., & Metcalfe, J. (2000). Metacognitive control and strategies in study-time allocation. *Journal of Experimental Psychology: Learning, Memory, and Cognition, 26*, 204–221.

Son, L. K., & Schwartz, B. L. (2002). The relation between metacognitive monitoring and control. In T. J. Perfect & B. L. Schwartz (Eds.), *Applied metacognition* (pp. 15–38). Cambridge, UK: Cambridge University Press.

Spaniol, J., & Bayen, U. J. (2002). When is schematic knowledge used in source monitoring? *Journal of Experimental Psychology: Learning, Memory, and Cognition, 28*, 631–651.

Spellman, B., & Holyoak, K. J. (1996). Pragmatics in analogical mapping. *Cognitive Psychology, 31*, 307–346.

Spellman, B. A., Lopez, A., & Smith, E. E. (1999). Hypothesis testing: Strategy selection for generalising versus limiting hypotheses. *Thinking and Reasoning, 5*, 67–91.

Squire, L. (1987). *Memory and brain.* Oxford, UK: Oxford University Press.

Stadnyk, B. (2003). *Posttraumatic stress disorder, psychiatric comorbidity and physical illness in corrections workers.* Unpublished master's thesis, Dept. of Psychology, University of Regina.

Stangor, C., & McMillan, D. (1992). Memory for expectancy-congruent and expectancy-incongruent information: A review of the social and social developmental literatures. *Psychological Bulletin, 111*, 42–61.

Stanovich, K. E. (1999). *Who is rational: Studies of individual differences in reasoning.* Mahwah, NJ: Lawrence Erlbaum Associates.

Stanovich, K. E. (2002). Rationality, intelligence, and levels of analysis in cognitive science: Is dysrationalia possible? In R. J. Sternberg (Ed.), *Why smart people can be so stupid* (pp. 124–158). New Haven, CT: Yale University Press.

Stanovich, K. E., & West, R. F. (1997). Reasoning independently of prior belief and individual differences in actively open-minded thinking. *Journal of Educational Psychology, 89*, 342–357.

Startup, M., & Edmonds, J. (1994). Compliance with homework assignments in cognitive-behavioral psychotherapy for depression: Relation to outcome and methods of enhancement. *Cognitive Therapy and Research, 18*, 567–579.

Steil, R., & Ehlers, A. (2000). Dysfunctional meaning of posttraumatic intrusions in chronic PTSD. *Behavior Research and Therapy, 38*, 537–558.

Stein, D. M., & Lambert, M. J. (1984). On the relationship between therapist experience and psychotherapy outcome. *Clinical Psychology Review, 4*, 127–142.

Steiner, C. M. (1996). Emotional literacy training: The application of transactional analysis to the study of emotions. *Transactional Analysis Journal, 26*, 31–39.

Stemmler, G. (1997). Selective activation of traits: Boundary conditions for the activation of anger. *Personality and Individual Differences, 22*, 213–233.

Sternberg, R. J., & Gastel, J. (1989). If dancers ate their shoes: Inductive reasoning with factual and counterfactual premises. *Memory and Cognition, 17*, 1–10.

Stevens, J., Quittner, A. L., Zuckerman, J. B., & Moore, S. (2002). Behavioral inhibition, self-regulation of motivation, and working memory in children with attention-deficit hyperactivity disorder. *Developmental Neuropsychology, 21*, 117–140.

Strack, F., & Bless, H. (1994). Memory for non-occurrence: Metacognitive and presuppositional strategies. *Journal of Memory and Language, 33*, 203–217.

Strayer, D. L., & Johnson, W. A. (2001). Driven to distraction: Dual-task studies of simulated driving and conversing on a cellular telephone. *Psychological Science, 12*, 462–466.

Strean, H. S. (1990). *Resolving resistances in psychotherapy.* New York: Brunner/Mazel.

Strevens, M. (2000). The essentialist aspect of naive theories. *Cognition, 74*, 149–175.

Stricker, G., & Gold, J. (2003). Integrative approaches to psychotherapy. In A. S. Gurman & S. B. Messer (Eds.), *Essential psychotherapies* (2nd ed., pp. 317–349). New York: Guilford.

Stroebe, M., & Stroebe, W. (1991). Does 'grief work' work? *Journal of Consulting and Clinical Psychology, 59*, 479–482.

Strohmer, D. C., Boas, G. J., & Abadie, M. N. (1996). The role of negative information in mental health counselor hypothesis testing. *Journal of Mental Health Counseling, 18*, 164–178.

Strohmer, D. C., & Shivy, V. A. (1994). Bias in counselor hypothesis testing: Testing the robustness of counselor confirmatory bias. *Journal of Counseling and Development, 75*, 191–197.

Strohmer, D. C., Shivy, V. A., & Chiodo, A. L. (1990). Information processing strategies in counselor hypothesis testing: The role of selective memory and expectancy. *Journal of Counseling Psychology, 37*, 465–472.

Strupp, H. H., & Binder, J. L. (1984). *Psychotherapy in a new key: A guide to time-limited psychodynamic psychotherapy.* New York: Basic Books.

Strupp, H. H., & Hadley, S. W. (1979). Specific versus non-specific factors in psychotherapy. *Archives of General Psychiatry, 36*, 1125–1136.

Stuss, D. T., & Benson, D. F. (1986). *The frontal lobes.* New York: Raven Press.

Suedfeld, P., & Eich, E. (1995). Autobiographical memory and affect under conditions of reduced environmental stimulation. *Journal of Environmental Psychology, 15*, 321–326.

Suengas, A. G., & Johnson, M. K. (1988). Qualitative effects of rehearsal on memories for perceived and imagined complex events. *Journal of Experimental Psychology: General, 117*, 377–389.

Takahashi, A. (1998). The relationship of the proportion correct in recognition and the confidence rating. *Japanese Journal of Psychology, 69*, 9–14.

Taylor, P. J., & Kopelman, M. D. (1984). Amnesia for criminal offenses. *Psychological Medicine, 14*, 581–588.

Taylor, R. S., Marsh, R. L., Hicks, J. L., & Hancock, T. W. (2004). The influence of partial-match cues on event-based prospective memory. *Memory, 12*, 203–213.

Taylor, S. E. (1991). Asymmetrical effects of positive and negative events: The mobilization-minimization hypothesis. *Psychological Bulletin, 110*, 67–85.

Taylor, S. E. (1996). Meta-analysis of cognitive behavioral treatment for social phobia. *Journal of Behavior Therapy and Experimental Psychiatry, 27*, 1–9.

Taylor, S. E., & Armor, D. A. (1996). Positive illusions and coping with adversity. *Journal of Personality, 64*, 873–898.

Teasdale, J. D., & Russell, M. L. (1983). Differential effects of induced mood on the recall of positive, negative, and neutral words. *British Journal of Clinical Psychology, 22*, 163–172.

Terr, L. C. (1991). Childhood traumas: An outline and overview. *American Journal of Psychiatry, 148*, 10–20.

Tetlock, P. E. (1998). Close-call counterfactuals and belief system defense: I was not almost wrong but I was almost right. *Journal of Personality and Social Psychology, 75*, 639–652.

Tetlock, P. E., & Visser, P. S. (2000). Thinking about Russia: Plausible past and plausible futures. *British Journal of Social Psychology, 39*, 173–196.

Thayer, R. E. (1996). *The origin of everyday moods: Managing energy, tension, and stress.* Oxford, UK: Oxford University Press.

Thiede, K. W., Anderson, M. C. M., & Therriault, D. (2003). Accuracy of metacognitive monitoring affects learning of texts. *Journal of Educational Psychology, 95*, 66–73.

Thompson, V. A. (1994). Interpretational factors in conditional reasoning. *Memory and Cognition, 22*, 742–758.

Thompson, V. A. (1995). Conditional reasoning: The necessary and sufficient conditions. *Canadian Journal of Experimental Psychology, 49*, 1–60.

Thompson, V. A. (2000). The task-specific nature of domain-general reasoning. *Cognition, 76*, 209–268.

Thompson, V. A., & Byrne, R. M. J. (2002). Reasoning counterfactually: Making inferences about things that didn't happen. *Journal of Experimental Psychology: Learning, Memory, and Cognition, 28*, 1154–1170.

Thompson, V. A., Streimer, C. L., Reikoff, R., Gunter, R. W., & Campbell, J. I. D. (2003). Syllogistic reasoning time: Disconfirmation disconfirmed. *Psychonomic Bulletin and Review, 10*, 184–189.

Tice, D. M., & Ciarocco, N. J. (1998). Inhibition and self-control. *Psychological Inquiry, 9*, 228–231.

Tipper, S. P. (1985). The negative priming effect: Inhibitory priming by ignored objects. *The Quarterly Journal of Experimental Psychology, 37A*, 571–590.

Tipper, S. P., MacQueen, G. M., & Brehaut, J. C. (1988). Negative priming between response modalities: Evidence for the central locus of inhibition in selective attention. *Perception and Psychophysics, 43*, 45–52.

Toglia, M. (1995). Repressed memories: The way we were? *Consciousness and Cognition, 4*, 111–115.

Tohill, J. M., & Holyoak, K. J. (2000). The impact of anxiety on analogical reasoning. *Thinking and Reasoning, 6*, 27–40.

Tompkins, M. A. (2002). Guidelines for enhancing homework compliance. *Journal of Clinical Psychology, 58*, 565–576.

Tooby, J., & Cosmides, L. (1990). The past explains the present: Emotional adaptations and the structure of ancestral environments. *Ethology and Sociobiology, 11*, 375–424.

Tooby, J., & Cosmides, L. (1992). Psychological foundations of culture. In J. H. Barkow, L. Cosmides, & J. Tooby (Eds.), *The adapted mind* (pp. 19–136). Oxford, UK: Oxford University Press.

Toplak, M. E., & Stanovich, K. E. (2003). Associations between myside bias on an informal reasoning task and amount of post-secondary education. *Applied Cognitive Psychology, 17*, 851–860.

Torrens, D., Thompson, V. A., & Cramer, K. M. (1999). Individual differences and the belief bias effect: Mental models, logical necessity, and abstract thinking. *Thinking and Reasoning, 5*, 1–28.

Toth, J. P., Reingold, E. M., Eyal, M., & Jacoby, L. L. (1995). A response to Graf and Komatsu's critique of the process dissociation procedure: When is caution necessary? *European Journal of Cognitive Psychology, 7*, 113–130.

Totton, N. (2002). The future for body psychotherapy. In T. Staunton (Ed.), *Body psychotherapy* (pp. 202–224). New York: Taylor & Francis.

Treisman, A. M. (1960). Contextual cues in selective listening. *The Quarterly Journal of Experimental Psychology, 12*, 242–248.

Treisman, A. M. (1964). Monitoring and storage of irrelevant messages in selective listening. *Journal of Verbal Learning and Verbal Behavior, 3*, 449–459.

Treisman, A. M. (1992). Spreading suppression or feature integration? A reply to Duncan and Humphries (1992). *Journal of Experimental Psychology: Human Perception and Performance, 18*, 589–593.

Treisman, A. M., & Gelade, G. (1980). A feature integration theory of attention. *Cognitive Psychology, 14*, 107–141.

Trick, L. M., & Pylyshyn, Z. W. (1993). What enumeration studies can show us about spatial attention: Evidence for limited capacity preattentive processing. *Journal of Experimental Psychology: Human Perception and Performance, 19*, 331–351.

Trolier, T. K., & Hamilton, D. L. (1986). Variables influencing judgments of correlational relatedness. *Journal of Personality and Social Psychology, 50*, 879–888.

Tronick, E. Z. (1989). Emotions and emotional communication in infants. *American Psychologist, 44*, 112–119.

Tucker, D. M., Vannatta, K., & Rothlind, J. (1990). Arousal and activation systems and primitive adaptive controls on cognitive priming. In N. L. Stein, B. Leventhal, & T. Trabasso (Eds.), *Psychological and biological approaches to emotion* (pp. 145–166). Hillsdale, NJ: Lawrence Erlbaum Associates.

Tulving, E. (1962). Subjective organization in free recall of 'unrelated' words. *Psychological Review, 69*, 344–354.

Turk, D. C., & Salovey, P. (1986). Clinical information processing: Bias innoculation. In R. E. Ingram (Ed.), *Information processing approaches to clinical psychology* (pp. 305–323). San Diego, CA: Academic Press.

Tversky, A., & Kahneman, D. (1973). Availability: A heuristic for judging frequency and probability. *Cognitive Psychology, 5*, 207–232.

Tversky, A., & Kahneman, D. (1974). Judgment under uncertainty: Heuristics and biases. *Science, 185*, 1124–1131.

Tversky, A., & Kahneman, D. (1986). Judgment under uncertainty: Heuristics and biases. In H. R. Arkas & K. R. Hammond (Eds.), *Judgment and decision making: An interdisciplinary reader* (pp. 38–55). Cambridge, UK: Cambridge University Press.

Tweney, R. D., Doherty, M. E., Worner, W. J., Pliske, D. B., & Mynatt, C. R. (1980). Strategies of rule discovery in an inference task. *Quarterly Journal of Experimental Psychology, 32*, 109–123.

Underwood, B. J. (1966). Individual and group predictions in item difficulty for free-recall learning. *Journal of Memory and Language, 24*, 363–376.

Uttl, B., & Graf, P. (2000, July). *Event-cued ProM proper differences in old age.* Presented at the 1st international conference on prospective memory, Hatfield, UK.

van der Kolk, B. A., & Fisler, R. (1995). Dissociation and the fragmentary nature of traumatic memories: Overview and exploratory study. *Journal of Traumatic Stress, 8*, 505–525.

Vohs, K. D., & Baumeister, R. F. (2004). Understanding self-regulation. In R. F. Baumeister & K. D. Vohs (Eds.), *Handbook of self-regulation: Research, theory, and applications* (pp. 1–9). New York: Guilford.

Voss, J. F., & Means, M. L. (1991). Learning to reason via instruction in argumentation. *Learning and Instruction, 1*, 337–350.

Vygotsky, L. S. (1991). Genesis of the higher mental functions. In P. Light, S. Sheldon, et al. (Eds.), *Learning to think: Child development in social context* (Vol. 2, pp. 32–41). Florence, KY: Taylor & Francis.

Wagenaar, W. A. (1986). My memory: A study of autobiographical memory over six years. *Cognitive Psychology, 18*, 225–252.

Wagenaar, W. A., & Groenweg, J. (1990). The memory of concentration camp survivors. *Applied Cognitive Psychology, 4*, 77–88.

Walden, T. A. (1991). Infant social referencing. In J. Garber & K. A. Dodge (Eds.), *The development of social regulation and dysregulation* (pp. 69–88). Cambridge, UK: Cambridge University Press.

Waldmann, M. R., & Haymayer, Y. (2001). Estimating causal strength: The role of structural knowledge and processing effort. *Cognition, 82*, 27–58.

Walker, W. R., Rodney, J. V., & Thompson, C. P. (1997). Autobiographical memory: Unpleasantness fades faster than pleasantness over time. *Applied Cognitive Psychology, 11*, 399–413.

Walker, W. R., Skowronski, J. J., Gibbons, J. A., Vogl, R. J., & Thompson, C. P. (2003). On the emotions that accompany autobiographical memories: Dysphoria disrupts the fading affect bias. *Cognition and Emotion, 17*, 703–723.

Walker, W. R., Skowronski, J. J., & Thompson, C. P. (2003). Life is pleasant—and memory helps to keep it that way! *Review of General Psychology, 7*, 203–210.

Walker, W. R., Vogl, R. J., & Thompson, C. P. (1997). Autobiographical memory: Unpleasantness fades faster than pleasantness over time. *Applied Cognitive Psychology, 11*, 399–413.

Wampold, B. E. (2001). *The great psychotherapy debate: Models, methods, and findings.* Mahwah, NJ: Lawrence Erlbaum Associates.

Warrington, E. K., & Weisenkrantz, L. (1970). The amnesic syndrome: Consolidation or retrieval? *Nature, 228*, 628–630.

Wason, P. C. (1960). On the failure to eliminate hypotheses in a conceptual task. *Quarterly Journal of Experimental Psychology, 12*, 129–140.

Wasserman, E. A., Chatlosh, D. L., & Neunaber, D. J. (1983). Perception of causal relations in humans: Factors affecting judgments of response-outcome contingencies under free-operant procedures. *Learning and Motivation, 14*, 406–432.

Waters, W. F., McDonald, D. G., & Koresko, R. L. (1977). Habituation of the orienting response: A gating mechanism subserving selective attention. *Psychophysiology, 14*, 228–236.

Watkins, T., Mathews, A. M., Williamson, D. A., & Fuller, R. (1992). Mood congruent memory in depression: Emotional priming or elaboration. *Journal of Abnormal Psychology, 101*, 581–586.

Watson, F. L., & Tipper, S. P. (1997). Reduced negative priming in schizotypal subjects does reflect reduced cognitive inhibition. *Cognitive Neuropsychology, 2*, 67–79.

Watts, F. N. (1986). Cognitive processing in phobias. *Behavioral Psychotherapy, 14*, 295–301.

Watts, F. N. (1988). Memory deficit in depression: The role of response style. In M. M. Gruneberg, P. E. Morris, & R. N. Sykes (Eds.), *Practical aspects of memory: Current research and issues: Vol. 2. Clinical and educational implications* (pp. 255–260). Chichester, UK: Wiley.

Watts, F. N., McKenna, F. P., Sharrock, R., & Tzezise, L. (1986). Colour naming of phobia related words. *British Journal of Psychology, 77*, 97–108.

Watts, F. N., Morris, L., & MacLeod, A. (1987). Recognition memory in depression. *Journal of Abnormal Psychology, 96*, 273–275.

Watts, F. N., & Sharrock, R. (1987). Cued recall in depression. *British Journal of Clinical Psychology, 26,* 149–150.

Watzlawick, P., Weakland, J., & Fisch, R. (1974). *Change: Principles of problem formulation and problem resolution.* New York: Norton.

Weary, G., Marsh, K. L., & McCormick, L. (1994). Depression and social comparison motives. *European Journal of Social Psychology, 24,* 117–130.

Weaver, C. (1993). Do you need a 'flash' to form a flashbulb memory? *Journal of Experimental Psychology: General, 122,* 39–46.

Wegner, D. M. (1989). *White bears and other unwanted thoughts.* New York: Viking/Penguin.

Wegner, D. M. (1992). You can't always think what you want: Problems in the suppression of unwanted thoughts. *Advances in Experimental Social Psychology, 25,* 193–225.

Wegner, D. M. (1994). Ironic processes of mental control. *Psychological Review, 101,* 34–52.

Wegner, D. M., & Bargh, J. A. (1998). Control and automaticity in social life. In D. Gilbert, S. T. Fiske, & G. Lindzey (Eds.), *Handbook of social psychology* (4th ed., pp. 446–496). New York: McGraw-Hill.

Wegner, D. M., Broome, A., & Blumberg, S. J. (1997). Ironic effects of trying to relax under stress. *Behavior Research and Therapy, 35,* 11–21.

Wegner, D., Shortt, J., Blake, A. W., & Page, M. S. (1990). The suppression of exciting thoughts. *Journal of Personality and Social Psychology, 58,* 409–418.

Weingartner, H., Cohen, R. M., Murphy, D. L., Martello, J., & Gerdt, C. (1981). Cognitive processes in depression. *Archives of General Psychiatry, 38,* 42–47.

Wells, A. (1990). Panic disorder in association with relaxation-induced-anxiety: An attentional training approach to treatment. *Behavior Therapy, 21,* 273–280.

Wells, A. (2000). *Emotional disorders and metacognition: Innovative cognitive therapy.* Chichester, UK: Wiley.

Wells, A., White, J., & Carter, K. (1997). Attentional training: Effects on anxiety and beliefs in panic and social phobia. *Clinical Psychology and Psychotherapy, 4,* 226–232.

Wells, G. L., Ferguson, T. J., & Lindsay, R. C. (1981). The tractability of eyewitness confidence and its implications for triers of fact. *Journal of Applied Psychology, 66,* 688–696.

Wells, G. L., Lindsay, R. C. L., & Ferguson, T. J. (1979). Accuracy, confidence, and juror perceptions in eyewitness identification. *Journal of Applied Psychology, 64,* 440–448.

Wells, G. L., Luus, C. A. E., & Windschitl, P. (1994). Maximizing the utility of eyewitness identification evidence. *Current Directions in Psychological Science, 3,* 194–197.

Wells, G. L., & Murray, D. M. (1984). Eyewitness confidence. In G. L. Wells & E. F. Loftus (Eds.), *Eyewitness testimony* (pp. 155–170). Cambridge, UK: Cambridge University Press.

Wells, G. L., Olson, E. A., & Charman, S. D. (2002). The confidence of eyewitnesses in their identifications from lineups. *Current Directions in Psychological Science, 11,* 151–154.

Wells, G. L., Taylor, B. R., & Turtle, J. W. (1987). The undoing of scenarios. *Journal of Personality and Social Psychology, 53,* 421–430.

Wenzlaff, R. M., & Bates, D. E. (1998). Unmasking a cognitive vulnerability to depression: How lapses in mental control reveal depressive thinking. *Journal of Personality and Social Psychology, 75,* 1559–1571.

Wenzlaff, R. M., & Wegner, D. M. (1998). The role of mental processes in the failure of inhibition. *Psychological Inquiry, 9,* 231–233.

Wenzlaff, R. M., Wegner, D. M., & Roper, D. W. (1988). Depression and mental control: The resurgence of unwanted negative thoughts. *Journal of Personality and Social Psychology, 55,* 882–892.

West, R., & Craik, F. I. M. (2001). Influences on the efficiency of prospective memory in younger and older adults. *Psychology and Aging, 16,* 682–696.

West, R., Herndon, R. W., & Crewdson, S. (2001). Neural activity associated with the realization of a delayed intention. *Cognitive Brain Research, 12,* 1–16.

Westen, D. (1998). The scientific legacy of Sigmund Freud: Toward a psychodynamically informed psychological science. *Psychological Bulletin, 124,* 333–371.

White, M., & Epston, D. (1990). *Narrative means to therapeutic ends.* New York: Norton.

White, P. A. (1989). A theory of causal processing. *British Journal of Psychology, 80,* 431–454.

White, P. A. (1995). Use of prior beliefs in the assignment of causal roles: Causal powers versus regularity-based accounts. *Memory and Cognition, 23,* 243–254.

White, P. A. (2000). Causal judgment from contingency information: The interpretation of factors common to all instances. *Journal of Experimental Psychology: Learning, Memory, and Cognition, 26,* 1083–1102.

White, P. A. (2003). Causal judgement as the evaluation of evidence: The use of confirmatory and disconfirmatory information. *Quarterly Journal of Experimental Psychology, 56A,* 491–513.

White, P. A. (2004). Judgement of two causal candidates from contingency information: Effects of relative prevalence of the two causes. *Quarterly Journal of Experimental Psychology, 57A,* 961–991.

White, R. T. (1982). Memory for personal events. *Human Learning, 1,* 171–183.

White, R. T. (1989). Recall of autobiographical events. *Applied Cognitive Psychology, 3,* 127–136.

Whitely, B. E., & Greenberg, M. S. (1986). The role of eyewitness confidence in juror perceptions of credibility. *Journal of Applied Social Psychology, 16,* 387–409.

Widom, C. S., & Morris, S. (1997). Accuracy of adult recollections of childhood victimization: Part 2. Childhood sexual abuse. *Psychological Assessment, 9,* 34–46.

Wilkins, A. J., & Baddeley, A. D. (1988). Remembering to recall in everyday life: An approach to absentmindedness. In M. M. Gruneberg, P. E. Morris, & R. N. Sykes (Eds.), *Practical aspects of memory* (pp. 349–353). London: Academic Press.

Willats, P. (1990). Development of problem solving in infancy. In D. Bjorklund (Ed.), *Children's strategies: Contemporary views of cognitive development* (pp. 23–66). Hillsdale, NJ: Lawrence Erlbaum Associates.

Williams, J. M. G. (1995). Depression and the specificity of autobiographical memories. In D. C. Rubin (Ed.), *Remembering our past: Studies in autobiographical memory* (pp. 244–270). Cambridge, UK: Cambridge University Press.

Williams, J. M. G., & Broadbent, J. (1986). Distraction by emotional stimuli: Use of a Stroop task with suicide attempters. *British Journal of Clinical Psychology, 25,* 101–110.

Williams, J. M. G., Ellis, N. C., Tyers, C., Healy, H., Rose, G., & MacLeod, A. K. (1996). The specificity of autobiographical memory and imageability of the future. *Memory and Cognition, 24,* 116–125.

Williams, J. M. G., Teasdale, J. D., Segal, Z. V., & Soulsby, J. (2000). Mindfulness-based cognitive therapy reduces overgeneral autobiographical memory in depressed patients. *Journal of Abnormal Psychology, 109,* 150–155.

Williams, L. M. (1994). Recall of childhood trauma: A prospective study of women's memories of child sexual abuse. *Journal of Consulting and Clinical Psychology, 62,* 1167–1176.

Williams, L. M. (1995). Recovered memories of abuse in women with documented child sexual victimization histories. *Journal of Traumatic Stress, 8,* 649–673.

Wilson, B. A. (1987). *Rehabilitation of memory.* New York: Guilford.

Wilson, B. A., & Moffat, N. (1984). *Clinical management of memory problems.* London: Croom Helm.

Wilson, T., & Nisbett, R. (1978). The accuracy of verbal reports about the effects of stimuli on evaluations and behavior. *Social Psychology, 41*, 118–131.

Winfrey, L. P. L., & Goldfried, M. R. (1986). Information processing and the human change process. In R. E. Ingram (Ed.), *Information processing approaches to clinical psychology* (pp. 241–258). San Diego, CA: Academic Press.

Winograd, E., & Neisser, U. (Eds.). (1993). *Affect and accuracy in recall: Studies of 'flashbulb' memories*. New York: Cambridge University Press.

Winograd, E., & Soloway, R. M. (1986). On forgetting the locations of things stored in special places. *Journal of Experimental Psychology: General, 115*, 366–372.

Wise, E. H., & Hayes, S. N. (1983). Cognitive treatment of test anxiety: Rational restructuring versus attentional training. *Cognitive Therapy and Research, 7*, 69–78.

Wolpe, J. (1997). Thirty years of behavior therapy. *Behavior Therapy, 28*, 633–635.

Wong, P., Shevrin, H., & Williams, W. J. (1994). Conscious and nonconscious processes: An ERP index of an anticipatory response in a conditioning paradigm using visually masked stimuli. *Psychophysiology, 31*, 87–101.

Woodward, T. S., Whitman, J. C., Arbuthnott, K., Kragelj, T. L., Lyons, J., & Stip, E. (2005). Visual search irregularities in schizophrenia depend on display size switching. *Cognitive Neuropsychiatry, 10*, 137–152.

Worthington, E. L. (1986). Client compliance with homework directives during counseling. *Journal of Counseling Psychotherapy, 33*, 124–130.

Wright, J. H., & Davis, D. (1994). The therapeutic relationship in cognitive-behavioral therapy: Patient perceptions and therapist responses. *Cognitive and Behavioral Practice, 1*, 25–45.

Wright, W. F., & Bower, G. J. (1992). Mood effects on subjective probability assessment. *Organizational Behavior and Human Decision Processes, 52*, 276–291.

Yalom, V., & Bugental, J. F. T. (1997). Support in existential-humanistic psychotherapy. *Journal of Psychotherapy Integration, 7*, 119–128.

Yamagishi, K. (1994). Consistencies and biases in risk perception: I. Anchoring process and response-range effect. *Perceptual and Motor Skills, 79*, 651–656.

Yuille, J., & Cutshall, J. L. (1986). A case study of eyewitness memory of a crime. *Journal of Applied Psychology, 71*, 291–301.

Yuille, J., & Tollestrup, P. (1992). A model of the diverse effects of emotion on eyewitness memory, In S.-A. Christianson (Ed.), *The handbook of emotion and memory: Research and theory* (pp. 201–215). Hillsdale, NJ: Lawrence Erlbaum Associates.

Zajonc, R. B. (1980). Feeling and thinking: Preferences need no inferences. *American Psychologist, 35*, 151–175.

Zajonc, R. B. (2000). Feeling and thinking: Closing the debate over the independence of affect. In J. P. Forgas (Ed.), *Thinking and feeling: The role of affect in social cognition* (pp. 31–58). Cambridge, UK: Cambridge University Press.

Zaragoza, M. S., & Mitchell, K. J. (1996). Repeated exposure to suggestion and the creation of false memories. *Psychological Science, 7*, 294–300.

Zeelenberg, M., & Beattie, J. (1997). Consequences of regret aversion 2: Additional evidence for effects of feedback on decision making. *Organizational Behavior and Human Decision Processes, 72*, 63–78.

Zeelenberg, M., van Dijk, W. W., van der Pligt, J., Manstead, A. S. R., van Empelen, P., & Reinderman, D. (1998). Emotional reactions to outcomes of decisions: The role of counterfactual thinking in the experience of regret and disappointment. *Organizational Behavior and Human Decision Processes, 75*, 117–141.

Zeitz, C. M. (1997). Some concrete advantages of abstraction: How experts' representations facilitate reasoning. In P. J. Feltovich & K. M. Ford (Eds.), *Expertise in context: Human and
machine* (pp. 43–65). Cambridge, MA: MIT Press.
Zuckerman, M., Knee, C. R., Hodgins, H. S., & Miyake, K. (1995). Hypothesis confirmation:
The joint effect of positive test strategy and acquiescence response set. *Journal of Personality and Social Psychology, 68*, 52–60.

Author Index

A

Aarts, H., 41
Abadie, M. N., 186
Achee, J., 298
Adams, J., 149
Adelson, B., 8, 12
Adler, R. B., 152
Adolphs, R., 329
Afifi, W. A., 313
Ahn, W., 143, 145, 146, 220, 221, 223
Akimoto, S. A., 225
Alkire, M., 286
Alksnis, O., 211
Allen, J. D., 100, 102
Allen, J. G., 59, 60, 299
Allen, J. L., 210, 216
Allen, S. W., 142, 149, 151
Allison, J. A., 243, 285
Alloy, L. B., 187, 300
Alomohamed, S., 4
Allport, A., 118, 127
Ambradar, Z., 286
Amsel, E., 222
Andersen, S. M., 331, 332
Anderson, C. A., 201, 223
Anderson, C. D., 318
Anderson, M. C., 307, 333
Anderson, M. C. M., 256, 268, 272
Anderson, J. R., 335
Anderson, N. D., 262, 271, 300

Anderson, S. A., 58
Andrzejewski, S. J., 92, 110, 285, 286
Antony, M. M., 259
Arbuckle, T. Y., 261
Arbuthnott, D. W., 71, 84, 85, 87, 88, 90, 92, 93, 96, 113, 321
Arbuthnott, K. D., 45, 65, 68, 71, 72, 77, 84, 85, 86, 87, 88, 90, 92, 93, 96, 113, 127, 267, 304, 305, 314, 321
Arkin, R. M., 298
Armor, D. A., 300
Armstrong, J. M., 320
Arnold, M. B., 295
Asbeck, J., 280
Ashbrook, P. W., 291
Ashcraft, M. H., 39
Askari, N., 80
Aspinwall, L. G., 298, 299
Atkins, D. C., 80
Atran, S., 145
Auerback, A. H., 112, 114
Averbach, D. H., 316
Ayduk, O., 299
Ayers, M. S., 90

B

Baars, B. J., 330, 333, 334, 335, 336
Babcock, C. J., 149, 153
Babinsky, R., 286

405

H

Subject Index